JAMES P. CHAPLIN
St. Michael's College

T. S. KRAWIEC

Systems and Theories of Psychology

FOURTH EDITION

x

HOLT, RINEHART and WINSTON
New York   Chicago   San Francisco   Dallas
Montreal   Toronto   London   Sydney

Library of Congress Cataloging in Publication Data

Chaplin, James Patrick, 1919-
  Systems and theories of psychology.

  Bibliography: p. 615
  Includes index.
  1. Psychology — History. I. Krawiec, Theophile Stanley, 1913-   joint author.
II. Title. [DNLM: 1. Psychology — History. 2. Psychological theory — History. BF81
C464s]   BF81.C43 1979   150'.19   78-21930
ISBN 0-03-020271-X

Preface

In preparing the fourth edition of this text for the centennial of psychology as an experimental science, the aim of the previous editions has been followed, that is, to treat contemporary systems and theories of psychology as evolutionary developments from their historical roots.

The two introductory chapters from the third edition have been expanded to three in order to incorporate new material on humanistic psychology, the experimental method, pseudoscience and psychology, as well as a survey of major developments in the various fields of psychology over the past century.

Material on sensation and perception has been updated to reflect new research, with emphasis on information processing points of view.

Developmental psychology is presented in a separate chapter for the first time, and consistent with the treatment of other processes, is a historical survey of theoretical points of view and supporting empirical findings.

The chapters on learning have been updated with the elimination of the derivative systems of Rotter and Mowrer and with the incorporation of Spence's and Miller's theories into the section on Hull in the chapter on miniature systems.

Thinking and language, motivation and emotion have been updated with new material added on aggressive behavior and on the cognitive and situational determinants of emotional behavior.

The chapter on physiological theories has been expanded to include recent work on split-brain experiments, the physiological basis of learning, and on food and wate regulation.

In the discussion of intelligence, Guilford's theory has been included for the first time, the discussion of heredity-environment controversy has been modified to reflect recent writings, as has the material on artificial intelligence.

There are two major changes in the treatment of personality. The discussion of Sheldon's constitutional theory has been eliminated while behavioristic theory has been expanded.

In the chapter on social psychology nearly all of the material on recent developments has been rewritten to clarify theoretical positions and supporting experiments.

The final chapter, an epilogue, has been rewritten as an evaluative summary of psychology as a field during its first century as an experimental science and to permit a discussion of enduring problems.

Appreciation is once again due colleagues past and present and other psychologists who have assisted in the preparation of this edition. Among colleagues are H. L. Ansbacher of the University of Vermont and Robert Lavallee and Barry Krikstone of St. Michael's College. Special thanks are also due to Madeline W. Chaplin for typing the manuscript and to Aline Demers for proofreading the galleys.

J. P. Chaplin
Burlington, Vermont

iii

Contents

Chapter 10
LEARNING III: SELECTED THEORETICAL ISSUES
IN VERBAL LEARNING   303

Chapter 11
THINKING AND LANGUAGE   335

Chapter 12
MOTIVATION   378

Chapter 13
FEELING AND EMOTION   422

Chapter 14
PHYSIOLOGICAL THEORIES OF BEHAVIOR   446

Chapter 15
QUANTITATIVE PSYCHOLOGY   494

Chapter 16
PERSONALITY   528

Chapter 17
SYSTEMS AND THEORIES IN
SOCIAL PSYCHOLOGY   570

Chapter 18
EPILOGUE   607

The Evolution of the Scientific Method in Psychology

1

The history of science is the story of men and women of science, their ideas, their contributions, and the records they left behind. For every great scientist there are hundreds who remain obscure. The immortality of Newton, Marie Curie, Darwin, and Freud is assured. But some who were famous in their own time have been harshly treated by history and are forgotten, while others who were relatively unknown during their lives became famous as the perspective of time lent new significance to their work. Few people today have heard of Henry Bastian, although he was a famous British scientist of the last century who believed he had witnessed the spontaneous generation of living organisms out of nonliving matter under his microscope. Most people, however, have heard of Gregor Mendel, the father of modern genetics, even though he was an obscure Austrian monk whose work had little impact on his contemporaries. The history of science, therefore, needs to be rewritten from generation to generation, since contemporary discoveries make necessary the reevaluation of older discoveries and the scientists who made them.

It has been said that psychology has a short history but a long past. This remark, made by a pioneer German psychologist, Hermann Ebbinghaus, over half a century ago is still true. If we reckon the beginning of experimental psychology from its formal founding as a separate academic discipline in 1879 by another German pioneer, Wilhelm Wundt, psychology is only a century old. But psychology goes back far beyond Wundt and his little laboratory in Leipzig to the philosophers of ancient Greece, many of whom thought and wrote about human nature.

In this book our task will be to tell the story of psychology from its origins in philosophy, the predecessor of all of the sciences, through its formative years as a young experimental science up to the recent past. We shall be telling of famous psychologists, of not so famous psychologists, of great experiments and bold ideas, and of failures, for science is not always a record of successes. Indeed, failures, like successes, are instructive, and one of the values of studying history is to avoid repeating them.

Since the pioneers began utilizing the scientific method in psychology about a century ago, psychologists have developed powerful tools for studying the behavior of humans and animals. An impressive number of theories about behavior have also been formulated and tested by observation and experimentation. There are literally thousands of books and research reports that contain the factual and theoretical foundation of the first hundred years of psychology. It has been an exciting century for psychology, a century of great ideas, techniques, and discoveries. Freud's impact has been felt in every department of thought. The IQ test, the public opinion poll, the brain implant—all uniquely psychological contributions—are totally entwined in the fabric of our culture. Even as we turn to the fate of humanity in the future, the dreams of a Utopia must be written in the language of contemporary psychology for, as Plato observed over two thousand years ago, the governance of people and the viability of a society require a knowledge of human nature.

Because methods are the foundation of any science, we shall begin our survey of psychology by examining the scientific method as it is used by psychologists. We shall then look backward briefly to the origins of psychology in philosophy to see how psychologists adapted the scientific method for the study of human behavior. The rest of the story is an account of how psychology in its various branches has evolved from those beginnings to the near present.

THE SCIENCE OF PSYCHOLOGY

Psychologists have not always agreed as to how they ought to proceed with their investigations and theoretical formulations. Some, as we shall see, believe that psychology should ally itself with the natural sciences, whereas others hold that it belongs with the social sciences. Among the early psychologists were those who thought it best to develop a science of psychology through the formulation of elaborate theoretical or systematic frameworks to achieve a synthesis of the facts that were rapidly emerging from the experimental laboratories. These systematic-minded psychologists were convinced that a thoroughly worked-out point of view would shed new light on old problems, direct research into fruitful channels, and provide a theoretical schema within which the results of such research could be interpreted. There was considerable precedent in the natural sciences for this chain of reasoning. Darwin's theory of evolution had revolutionized biology. Newton's conceptualizations of physical laws had made possible several centuries of rapid advance in physics and provided a working theory of celestial mechanics. Even the more restricted or miniature systems among the other sciences, such as Mendeleev's Periodic Table of the Elements, provided ample evidence for the great scientific value of an orderly and systematic orientation in the pursuit of knowledge.

It would be wrong to give the impression that theoretical viewpoints are merely remnants from the past of the natural sciences or little more than growing pains in the formative stages of a new science such as psychology. Nothing is further from the truth, for a mere accumulation of facts without some frame of reference for their interpretation would be meaningless at any stage of scientific development. Every science grows through the development of theory as well as through the accumulation of factual information. Indeed, the gathering and systematic interpretation of facts are really complementary processes, since the absence of either leads to confusion and wasted effort. Theory without a factual foundation is a structure founded on sand, and fact without theory is a meaningless jumble of information, useless for building an orderly scientific structure. Therefore, psychology and contemporary science in general are an admixture of fact and theory; and since theory attempts to bridge gaps in factual knowledge or to go beyond what is known, it is necessarily someone's point of view.

Because systematists and theoreticians must take into account not only facts when erecting their conceptual structures but also any existing theories that may be relevant, it follows that theoretical viewpoints rarely spring into existence full-blown; rather, they are the result of an evolutionary process. Each new theory or system is partly new and partly old; and the past, present, and future in science are a continuum.

It should be noted that not all historians are in agreement that science grows through an evolutionary process. Thomas Kuhn in his widely discussed *The Structure of Scientific Revolutions* (1970)[1] argues that important advances in science occur through revolutions. In other words, outworn scientific models—called paradigms by Kuhn—collapse and new models take their place. When a new paradigm appears, it becomes the model on which scientists conduct the everyday business of science—until it proves inadequate and is in turn overthrown. In Kuhn's words:

> The transition from a paradigm in crisis to a new one from which a new tradition of normal science can emerge is far from a cumulative process, one achieved by an articulation or extension of the old paradigm. Rather it is a reconstruction of the field from new fundamentals, a reconstruction that changes some of the field's most elementary theoretical generalizations as well as many of its paradigm methods and applications. During the transition period there will be a large but never complete overlap between the problems that can be solved by the old and by the new paradigm. But there will also be a decisive difference in the modes of solution. When the transition is complete, the profession will have changed its view of the field, its methods, and its goals. (1970, pp. 84–85)

By way of illustrating Kuhn's argument, one may cite the revolution brought about by Copernicus' heliocentric view of the universe, which completely overthrew the Ptolemaic system in which the earth was the fixed center of the universe. Similar revolutions were caused by Newton's theory of celestial mechanics and Einstein's theory of relativity.

---

[1]Dates in parentheses refer to references listed at the end of this volume.

In the final analysis, the evolutionary and revolutionary points of view are not necessarily incompatible. The revolutionist must have something to revolt against and, in this sense, utilizes the past to move into the future. Even though the past is discarded, it nevertheless stimulates new models, if in no other way than by its inadequacy.

SCIENCE AND METHODOLOGY

It has become a truism to say that not only does science begin with a method but that its very essence is its methodology. More specifically, we are saying that science is a set of rules that must be followed by anyone who aspires to be a scientist. Contrary to a widespread popular view, this statement implies that any science—such as chemistry, biology, geology, or psychology—is not so much a compilation of facts or a collection of impressive apparatus as it is an attitude or willingness on the part of the scientist to follow the rules of the scientific game. Facts have an annoying way of changing, and what is considered truth today may be held in error tomorrow. Therefore, facts alone are the transient characteristics and not the enduring stuff of science.

Apparatus, too, however imposing it may appear, is not science but only the tool of the scientist—a tool whose application may or may not be scientific. Anyone can purchase a white coat and a laboratory full of "scientific" paraphernalia, but the possession of such equipment does not qualify such a person as a scientist. Rather, the scientific status of the individual and the value of the information being collected are evaluated according to the manner in which investigations are planned, the kind of procedures employed in collecting data, and the way in which the findings are interpreted. So crucial is the methodology followed in any scientific investigation that no reputable scientist will accept a fellow scientist's results as valid until he knows precisely what procedures were employed in arriving at those results. This conservative attitude has been dignified by the name *operationism* and has been elevated into a basic working principle of the natural sciences. In formal terms we may define operationism as follows: *The validity of any scientific finding or concept depends on the validity of the procedures employed in arriving at that finding or concept.* This means that both the results of an experiment and the conclusions the investigator derives from it can never transcend the methodology employed.

The fundamental characteristic that distinguishes the scientific method from other approaches to knowledge is its *objectivity,* which can be defined as the scientist's endeavor to perceive and to record all the facts in an investigation—not only those that correspond to his or her expectations. By carefully formulating hypotheses and clearly identifying and controlling the variables in investigations, the scientist ensures that his or her work can be replicated by other scientists. Replication is a critical test of objectivity. It is also at the heart of the scientific method for another fundamental reason, namely, that what the scientist is ultimately seeking is uniformity or well-established generalizations about natural phenomena; for example, that the pressure of a gas kept at constant temperatures varies inversely with the volume. Generalizations such as this become scientific laws only when they are repeatedly verified by empirical observations. A body of related scientific laws is a science. For instance, chemistry is the science that seeks to establish the laws of the relationships among elements, compounds, and the atomic and subatomic particles that make up all matter.

The scientist may utilize both deduction and induction. Deduction is the process that starts with certain premises or propositions and attempts to draw valid conclusions from them. In developing new systems or branches of mathematics, the mathematician utilizes deductive reasoning. That is, he or she begins with certain fundamental propositions or axiomatic statements and from them attempts to construct a logically defensible system. The geometry of Euclid is an example familiar to everyone.

Induction is the process by which the scientist concludes that what is true of certain individual cases is true of all cases, or what is true at certain times will be true under the same circumstances at all times. The astronomer observing that a number of heavenly bodies are round concludes that it is probable that all heavenly bodies are round. Note that this conclusion is formulated in the language of probability, since no astronomer can possibly observe all heavenly bodies—some are beyond the reach of the most powerful telescopes. The importance of the probable nature of scientific findings cannot be overemphasized. To the layman, science is synonymous with certainty; to the scientist, science is a set of probabilities based on samplings of observables. The care with which the scientist chooses samples and the objectivity with which investigations are carried out determine the validity of the conclusions.

Bearing in mind this brief analysis of the importance of methodology, we should realize that in order to understand systems, schools, and theoretical points of view in psychology, we must first have some appreciation of the methodology that lies at their foundation. In the last analysis the exposition of a systematic point of view is a statement of its *aims, methods,* and *findings*. From what has already been said, the value of the findings is contingent upon the validity of the methods used in the investigation. Aims tend to be inextricably interwoven with methods. For example, it is obvious that if the scientist's goal is to investigate the nature of the solar system, the methodology will be quite different from that to be employed in a study of Australian mammals. As a consequence of this interdependent relationship between aims and methods, it is apparent that although it is correct to speak of the scientific method, each science has, in addition, its own specialized methodology. It is largely this specialization in aims and procedures that distinguishes each science from every other.

To summarize, it seems logical to begin our survey of systematic psychology with a study of the aims and methods that were instrumental in establishing the various systems, for this approach alone makes possible an operationistic frame of reference. However, because psychology and the methods employed in psychological investigations have evolved slowly over the centuries, we shall begin by relating the evolution of the scientific method in psychology to the development of science in general. With this broader perspective as a background, we shall see that the problems and methods involved in the understanding of human behavior are not new, but represent the evolution of generations of thought, research, and debate.

PSYCHOLOGY WITHIN THE FRAMEWORK OF SCIENCE

In attempting to relate psychology to the other sciences as they evolved from their common ancestor, philosophy, we are immediately faced with a dilemma. Is psychology a natural science or a social science? Would it be best to look for the roots of psychology in the history of chemistry, physics, and zoology? Or should our search begin with those intellectual movements that led to the development of sociology, anthropology, economics, and political science? If we turn to the history of psychology for the solution to our problem, we find that psychology evolved out of a coalescence of natural science and the branch of philosophy known as *epistemology,* or the theory of knowledge.

To put it another way, great thinkers have always been interested in the problems associated with the validity of human knowledge; and, as a result, an entire branch of philosophy, epistemology, came to be devoted almost exclusively to the study of such problems. But when the question is raised as to how we obtain knowledge of our environment, it quickly becomes involved with such corollary questions as: What are the avenues of knowledge? What organ is the repository of knowledge? How well does our mental picture of the physical world correspond to reality? These are legitimate philosophical questions, but their answers require an understanding of the sense organs, which are the avenues of knowledge, and the brain as the interpreter of sensations and the repository and integrator of experiences. Moreover, we need to know something of the physics of light, sound, and of the stimuli for the sense of smell as well as of the other sense modalities. We also need to know how nerves and neurons work and how faithfully the brain can produce representations of physical objects from nervous impulses generated in the sense organs by the stimuli from those objects. Obviously what we have here is the beginning of a hybrid science that must concern itself with problems of how the physical, physiological, and psychological all relate to each other. And, in its beginnings, psychology was such a three-way synthesis of physics, physiology, and mental philosophy.

As the new science grew out of its infancy, many psychologists became impatient with restricting psychological research to the threefold problem of mind-body-physical relationships and insisted on broadening the young science to include the social, cultural, and interpersonal problems of human behavior that make up such a large segment of psychology today. As a consequence of this division of interests within the field, it is impossible to be black and white in categorizing psychology as a natural or a social science. It is allied to both of these broad areas of knowledge, and, according to their own interests and theoretical leanings, psychologists tend to divide themselves along similar lines. Some, notably the physiological psychologists with their strong interest in the workings of the nervous system, resemble physiologists more than they do psychologists. On the other hand, some psychologists, at least in the kind of work they do, are more appropriately described as social rather than natural scientists, and at a dinner party they would find it easier to keep up a conversation with a social anthropologist than with a physiological psychologist. In the face of such a dilemma, it seems wise to beat a strategic retreat and let the future decide whether psychology will ultimately become a pure natural science, go over into the camp of the social sciences, or simply remain as it is. In any case, we can resolve the issue for our purposes by examining both sides of the question, first considering the working assumptions of the psychologist as a natural scientist and then examining those assumptions he or she must embrace as a social scientist.

PSYCHOLOGY AS A NATURAL SCIENCE

With the rise of the natural sciences to a position of preeminence during the latter part of the nineteenth century and the early twentieth century, scientists developed a credo of fundamental assumptions about the processes of nature and their investigation. The early experimental psychologists, particularly those of the physiological and behavioristic orientation, adopted these working principles for psychology in the hope of allying it with the natural sciences. These assumptions, each of which will be discussed in turn, are (1) *natural monism,* (2) *mechanism,* (3) *operationism,* and (4) *determinism.*

Natural Monism

Natural monism holds that the natural sciences form a family tree, with physics, chemistry, and the other physical sciences at the roots and with biology, physiology, and psychology branching off at the top. Stated somewhat differently, physics and chemistry deal with matter in its simplest and most fundamental forms, whereas biology and psychology study nature's most complex organic compounds. If all sciences lie along a single continuum, then according to this point of view, psychology can theoretically be reduced to physiology, and physiology in turn can be reduced to the physics and chemistry of organic compounds. Of course, no one has demonstrated that mental processes are literally reducible to the physics and chemistry of brain matter, but such a hypothesis has led to many interesting discoveries in the area of psychoneural relationships.

While natural monism continues to be a working assumption on the part of many physiological psychologists, the increasingly popular approach among even the most natural-science–minded psychologists is to study behavior *at the level of behavior,* seeking to establish valid predictive principles without necessarily attempting to discover their counterparts in underlying glandular or nervous processes. By analogy, many people make good automobile drivers and could learn a great deal of predictive value about a new model's performance characteristics without knowing much about the engine. By contrast, the earlier psychologists who were interested in developing psychology as a natural science felt that a close kinship existed between psychology and the biological sciences; and many of them, as will be demonstrated later, made some attempt to relate psychological theory to underlying physiological processes. This point of view, it might be noted, has often been called "reductionism."

Mechanism

Mechanism has many shades of meaning, some of which have acquired an undesirable connotation. As applied in its most literal sense, mechanism means that the scientist looks upon the universe as a vast machine peopled by machines. Human behavior, from this point of view, is no more than the functioning of the bodily machine. According to some of the more extreme proponents of this point of view, living forms will ultimately be created in the laboratory out of inorganic compounds. Mechanism enjoyed considerable popularity in the early 1900s, as a result of the teachings of Jacques Loeb (1859–1924), a prominent physiologist of the day, who vigorously championed the mechanistic viewpoint in biology. He was dedicated to the goal of demonstrating that all living things are elaborate chemical machines and are consequently understandable solely in physiochemical terms. Loeb and his associates were fully confident that they were on the track to creating living organisms in the laboratory by combining inert chemicals. Such radical views generated considerable opposition during the first two decades of the present century. Today, such a position seems far less extreme in the wake of recent scientific advances.

Psychologists are not concerned with the validity of mechanism in its original sense. Rather, from the point of view of contemporary psychology, mechanism is the attitude that human behavior, or the functioning of any other subject of scientific inquiry, can best be understood *without an appeal to explanations external to the system under investigation*. In short, it denies the validity of the *deus ex machina* as an explanatory concept. As a result of the general acceptance of this point of view, contemporary psychologists do not postulate that evil spirits account for bad dreams or that demoniac possession explains abnormal behavior. Rather, just as the astronomer seeks to understand the universe in terms of natural law, the psychologist attempts to account for human behavior without going outside the laws of the natural sciences.

Operationism

Operationism has already been defined as asserting that the validity of a scientific finding or theoretical construct is contingent upon the validity of the operations involved in arriving at that finding or construct. Operationism came into modern science in 1927 and was championed by Percy W. Bridgman (1882–1961), a well-known physicist and mathematician.

Bridgman (1927) developed the concept of operationism after a careful analysis of the Newtonian concepts of time, space, length, and so on, following the publication of Einstein's special theory of relativity, which also called into question Newton's physics. Finding that some of Newton's concepts contained meanings that had not been justified by physical experimentation, Bridgman proposed the much more stringent criterion that all concepts be defined operationally, hoping thereby to free physical constructs of unwarranted meanings.

Operationism was quickly accepted by many psychologists[2] who believed that the concepts of their field—particularly the mentalistic concepts—carried meanings far in excess of what could be demonstrated empirically. It seemed that if the exact science of physics could benefit from a conceptual housecleaning, psychology—a budding science with many loosely defined terms—could profitably emulate its example.

Slowly, but with increasing insistence, Bridgman's operationism came under criticism by physicists and psychologists as well as by philosophers who were developing what is now a specialization within philosophy, the philosophy of science. S. S. Stevens (1906–1973), an American psychologist noted for his work in scaling and psychological measurements, pointed out in a key article (1939) that there are fundamental differences between psychology and physics and that many psychologists believe that certain concepts can be useful even though not immediately specifiable in operational terms. Indeed, Bridgman himself came to reexamine the concept of operationism (1954), pointing out that he had not intended it to be a panacea or even a normative concept. Rather, it was and still is intended only to remind scientists constantly that at *some* stage in the evolution of a concept they must specify the procedures utilized in its development.

It should be noted that many contemporary theoretical physicists and philosophers of science no longer adhere to the idea that there is one method that when discovered will yield "truth." As long as half a century ago, in announcing his principle of uncertainty, Werner Heisenberg pointed out that the very act of observation (the operation) disturbs the system and thus casts doubt on the validity of the results. Heisenberg went on to argue that we can never know anything for certain in science. At best we can arrive only at statistical probabilities. Some contemporary physicists would go even further and suggest that in many instances theory may take precedence over so-called fact where methods of measurement do not exist to confirm theory (Toulmin, 1960, chap. 4).

During the same decade that Bridgman published his *Logic of Modern Physics* (1927), a group of European scholars initiated a movement in philosophy known as "logical positivism," which has come to dominate American philosophy. The logical positivists proposed that philosophy complement science by performing rigid, logical analyses of the language employed by scientists in expressing the relationships between the variables studied in their experimental programs. Thus the positivists would probe the meanings of scientific concepts, sentences, and symbols, substituting wherever possible the language and symbols of mathematics for ordinary language. In this endeavor Ludwig Wittenstein, Bertrand Russell, and Rudolph Carnap became world famous as leaders of this new branch of philosophy. Obviously, an analytical analysis of the meaning of scientific terms is closely related

---

[2]For the identities of prominent psychologists of the 1930s who adopted operationism, see Stevens (1939).

to operationism. The philosopher, however, is not concerned with the experimental or empirical verification of terms, but only with the language of science, its coherence, logicality, and freedom from spurious meanings.[3]

Finally, it is also worth pointing out that the operationistic attitude is in part a reflection of the more general spirit of self-criticism and self-correction so characteristic of science. Each facet of human endeavor has its critics. There are art critics, literary critics, drama critics, and so on. But science is unique in being self-critical and therefore self-correcting. The scientist expects—and indeed invites—criticism of hypotheses, methods, and findings from fellow scientists, since only peers are capable of relevant and intelligent criticism. Naturally, this does not imply that scientists never make mistakes or that science alone holds the final answer to every question. Rather, it means that scientists open their work to criticism, that they are willing to change their minds, and that science is not likely to perpetuate error for very long. All of this may seem rather obvious, but a moment's reflection on how different the case has been in recent decades for political, economic, or philosophical systems (and "science") under totalitarian regimes will reiterate its importance.

Determinism

Determinism is the assumption that everything that happens in the universe can be accounted for by definite laws of causation. As applied to human behavior, the principle holds that all actions are subject to natural laws and must therefore be explained in terms of causative factors lying in the individual's heredity and environment. Consequently, from the deterministic point of view, freedom of action is an illusion. All choices, great and small, are determined by the chain of causes and effects that reach back over the individual's entire life history and even beyond into the genetic determiners inherited from his or her parents.

Largely because of its antithetical position to free will, determinism is sometimes confused with predestination, a theological concept in which it is held that, irrespective of what an individual does, his or her ultimate fate after death is already determined. Psychological determinism implies no such fatalistic view of one's postmortem destiny, since scientific determinism deals only with earthly matters and does not concern itself with spiritual or theological issues. Neither should determinism be used to rationalize a philosophy of irresponsibility by those who argue that if one's behavior is determined by the past, he or she is not a free agent and consequently is not responsible.

Such a notion is embodied in the story of the slave who was caught stealing by the philosopher Zeno. When Zeno got out the whip, the slave protested, "Master,

---

[3]Further elaboration of the implications of operationism and logical positivism for psychology is beyond the scope of this book. The interested reader will find Shapere's introduction (1965) to the philosophy of science valuable for an easy-to-understand integrated discussion of positivism and operationism. Kaplan's survey (1963) of modern philosophy has a highly readable chapter on analytic philosophy. Marx (1963), a psychologist, provided a compilation of papers by leading psychologists on the special problems of theory and system construction in psychology. For general introductions to the philosophy of science, see Hempel (1966) and Toulmin (1960).

according to thy teachings it was determined that I would steal from thee and thou shouldst not beat me for that for which I am not responsible.''

Zeno replied, ''It is also determined that I will beat thee.''

The answer to these difficulties lies in appreciating that determinism is a point of view or a working principle in science that has led to fruitful research but is not to be construed as a guide for individual conduct. In fact, the ethical tradition of Western civilization is one of self-determinism in conduct. This within its own sphere is a useful point of view; however, if carried over into the sciences, it would become ridiculous. For example, any astronomer who ''explained'' the earth's rotation around the sun as caused by the earth's desire to go around the sun would be expelled from the fellowship of scientists.

In summary, psychology as a natural science subscribes to four broad scientific principles: monism, mechanism, operationism, and determinism. Their function is to provide the psychologist with working hypotheses for guidance in the conduct of research and in the interpretation of research results. Each, as we have seen, is useful within its own frame of reference, but none is to be construed as an established fact or as an ethical principle for the guidance of individual behavior.

PSYCHOLOGY AS A SOCIAL SCIENCE

For the most part the social scientist, like the natural scientist, makes use of studies or experiments, is careful to observe all precautions of scientific observation and control, and interprets the results with the aid of quantitative or statistical techniques. However, there is no commonly accepted set of scientific assumptions to which social scientists adhere; and, as a result, the individual scientist has considerable latitude in formulating aims, in designing studies or experiments, and in interpreting results.

The greater flexibility that is characteristic of the social sciences derives in part from the fact that, as established and recognized areas of knowledge, most of the social sciences are relatively young compared to the natural sciences. Moreover, the social sciences deal with highly complex economic, political, sociological, and psychological processes in which there is greater room for divergent views on just how investigations should be conducted. In a sense this means that each investigation must stand on its own merits, often without the advantage of an evaluation based on prior experience or on broad theoretical principles.

Perhaps the most striking differences, at least in psychology, between the psychologist as a natural scientist and the psychologist as a social scientist lie in the philosophical orientation and in the nature of the theoretical constructs that each employs. In general, one who views psychology as a social science fails to see the necessity for grounding psychology in physiology and is therefore not a physiological reductionist in his or her explanations of behavior.[4] Moreover, he or she is less interested in tracing the antecedents of present behavior back to earlier periods in the

---

[4]Many ''natural-science'' psychologists also fail to see the necessity for grounding psychology in physiology. However, many do favor physiological reductionism—in contrast to social psychologists, for example, who never do.

individual's development. Instead, there is a tendency to emphasize the contemporary nature of causative factors in behavior. For this reason, the genetic point of view is rarely stressed. Finally, research interests are likely to lie in such areas as social psychology, personality, or group dynamics rather than in the traditional fields of experimental or physiological psychology.

It has often been said that all generalizations are intrinsically invalid, and we would have to admit that exceptions could readily be found for any of the above characterizations of either the naturalistic or social science points of view in psychology. It is impossible to establish absolute categories into which scientists can be neatly fitted, just as it is impossible to type people into extroverts and introverts or some similar dichotomy. Still, such broad generalizations have their value as aids in thinking, provided that we recognize that they may not fit individual cases.

NOMOTHETIC AND IDIOGRAPHIC PSYCHOLOGY

Another useful way to describe the aims, procedures, and theoretical orientation of psychologists is in terms of nomothetic and idiographic points of view. Nomothetic psychologists seek to establish the general laws and principles governing mental and behavioral processes. This is the traditional manner in which psychologists have investigated the processes of development, sensation, perception, learning, thinking, motivation, and emotion. In striving to formulate laws of general applicability that pertain to psychological processes, the psychologist must necessarily ignore the individual. Indeed, every effort will be made to overcome any effects of individual differences among research subjects that might obscure the validity and general applicability of the findings. This is accomplished primarily by utilizing a large number of subjects who are carefully selected as being a representative sample of the population as a whole. When the data have been collected and are undergoing analysis, elaborate statistical safeguards are employed to ensure that the inferences or generalizations drawn from the experiment are warranted by the data on hand.

The idiographic point of view stresses the understanding of a particular individual or event. Here the psychologist's emphasis is on the discovery of the laws of the individual case; consequently, the investigation is focused on the person. Many clinical psychologists who favor the idiographic point of view emphasize that each individual is unique and therefore must be understood in terms of his or her own set of laws. They argue that to study generalized mental or behavioral processes is to force the individual into a mold or a type and to overlook the very differences that, in the final analysis, make that person unique.

Of course, the study of large numbers of individuals from the idiographic point of view will reveal many similarities as well as differences among them. Thus the clinician who attempts to account for behavioral disorders is likely to formulate general laws of personality development and deviation, thus becoming something of a nomothetic psychologist. This is particularly true of clinicians who are strongly research oriented. Similarly, the differential psychologist who studies intellectual and personality differences in terms of standardized tests will generalize his or her findings, sometimes stressing likenesses as well as differences among individuals. For this reason the two approaches, nomothetic and idiographic, often complement each other.[5]

Closely related to the division of the field in nomothetic and idiographic psychology is the type of laws the psychologist seeks to establish. Most nomothetic or general psychologists strive to formulate laws of the type $R = f(S)$, or, more simply, S-R laws. That is, given certain observable responses (R), they seek to establish the functional (f) relationships between those responses and the antecedent stimulating conditions (S). If the psychologist can accomplish this, a major objective of science has been achieved, since given the antecedent conditions, it will then be possible to predict the response and—if this were considered desirable—to control it.

Other psychologists search for R-R laws, or laws that govern the relationships among response variables. As an example, a research psychologist may wish to establish a functional relationship between conflict and anxiety, operating on the hypothesis that conflicts lead to anxiety states. Because the environmental conditions that promote the development of conflicts in people cannot be directly controlled, the relationship between the variables chosen must be investigated by administering tests or measuring such variables and then correlating the results. For example, the psychologist might assess the presence of conflicts by means of a clinical test or projective technique, quantify the results, and then measure anxiety in the same group of subjects by means of an appropriate anxiety scale. Finally, the coefficient of correlation between the two variables would be calculated. A significant correlation between two sets of responses would not guarantee that a causal relationship exists, but it would enable the psychologist to predict from one variable to another and to contribute to the prediction, understanding, and control of behavior.

Some psychologists have objected to a strict S-R formula as a model for psychology. They regard any system predicated on such a basis as dealing with an "empty organism." Instead, they advocate the S-O-R formula, in which S represents stimuli, O the organism, and R the responses. From this point of view psychology is the study of intervening variables within the organism that mediate between stimuli and responses. For example, the process of memory is an intervening variable whose investigation must be undertaken by utilizing various stimuli (word lists, nonsense syllables, and the like), and then measuring the subject's responses under various conditions of memorizing. Therefore, the psychologist never investigates memory directly, but only indirectly through the subject's responses. He or she *infers* information about the memory process by studying the subject's responses.

The investigation of intervening variables is not limited to psychology. Physicists and chemists often study intervening variables in much the same manner.

---

[5]For a strongly antithetical point of view that denies the validity of the nomothetic-idiographic distinction, see Cronbach (1957) and Holt (1962).

Resistance, for example, is an inferred variable that is measured by the flow of current through electric circuits; gravity is inferred from the behavior of celestial bodies.

Each of these points of view is useful in psychology. We have already pointed out how the important work of the clinical psychologist is furthered by an *R-R* orientation. Strongly behavioristic and operationistic psychologists tend to favor an *S-R* approach, arguing that little is gained by adding hypothetical intervening variables to the formula. They emphasize that responses are all we can *measure* and what cannot be measured cannot be dealt with scientifically. Others, particularly those who take a more organismic or humanistic point of view, believe that psychologists should keep the individual or the organism in the picture even though general or behavioral processes are under study.

BEHAVIORISTIC AND PHENOMENOLOGICAL PSYCHOLOGY

Another widely discussed set of contrasting viewpoints in psychology that we shall present here can be broadly characterized as *behavioristic* and *phenomenological*. As Table 1-1 shows, these points of view differ on four important variables as-

TABLE 1-1   A Comparison between Behavioristic and Phenomenological Psychology

Variable	Behavioristic Psychology	Phenomenological Psychology
Subject matter	Behavior	Mental events or direct experience
Method of study	Experimental analysis	Phenomenal description
Unit of analysis	Molecular (parts)	Molar (wholes)
Areas of specialization	Learning, comparative, physiological, developmental	Perceptual, cognitive, psychodynamics, personality

sociated with the development of psychology as a science. In general, behaviorists insist that the proper subject matter of psychology is behavior, not mental events or conscious processes. They argue strongly that mental events are private and subjective and therefore cannot meet the criterion of scientific objectivity.

According to the behavioristic point of view, behavior is to be studied by objective experimental methods and is to be analyzed into its constituent processes in the same way that chemical and physical events are studied and analyzed. For this reason behavioral analyses are sometimes characterized as "molecular" in contrast to the molar units favored by the phenomenologists, who advocate the study of whole acts or mental activities without reductionistic analyses. Clearly, the analogy is derived from chemists' studies of gases, which may be conducted at either the molecular level (the investigation of the behavior of molecules) or at the larger molar level (the investigation of the gas as a whole in terms of pressure, volume, and so on). The analogy is not a fortunate one, however. Behaviorists study acts, not their molecular substrates. Nor does the behaviorist study fragmented or meaninglessly small units of behavior.

What is really implied by the molar-molecular continuum is that behaviorists are more likely to interest themselves in smaller units of analysis and in trying to understand behavior by reducing it to its simplest levels. The phenomenologist, on the other hand, is more likely to insist that behavior or mental events be studied or described as naturally given without reductionistic analysis in the spirit of the original meaning of the term *phenomenon,* that is, to appear or show.

Since we have already commented extensively on the types of laws subsumed under *S-R* and *S-O-R* formulas, we need only reemphasize that the behaviorist typically objects to "hidden" variables, which are neither directly observable nor measurable. If a behaviorist utilizes intervening variables or *O* factors in theoretical formulations, as some have, they must be firmly anchored on both the *S* and the *R* sides of the equation. Finally, the table shows typical areas of interest pursued by behavioristically oriented as opposed to phenomenologically oriented psychologists.

It must be admitted that exceptions can be found for each of these categories. There have been psychologists (structuralists) who were interested in mental events and, as we shall find, were highly analytic and objective in their studies of those events. Similarly, there have been some behaviorists who have studied what they insist is molar behavior. In spite of such exceptions, these categories, as is true in all categories, remain useful, for they reveal the broad divisions of opinion as to methodological procedures and aims that are characteristic of psychology.[6]

HUMANISTIC PSYCHOLOGY

Although the final point of view that we are about to summarize is not associated with traditional scientific psychology (in fact, it often stands in opposition to science in general), it has evolved into a widespread movement both within and outside the field of psychology that cannot be ignored. We refer to the humanistic viewpoint and the programs that are associated with it.

Humanism is any system of thought that places primary emphasis on human interests, values, and the dignity and freedom of the individual. The human being is held to be a free agent, capable of choosing whatever line of conduct he or she wills. As a consequence of this freedom, the individual must assume responsibility for all of his or her actions. Clearly, because of its position on freedom, humanism is opposed to determinism. It is also opposed to natural monism and reductionistic mechanism. Deterministic and mechanistic psychologies (and science in general) are seen as dealing with abstract and artificial "essences" while at the same time ignoring those characteristics that distinguish humans from the lower forms. In fact, the more extreme humanists not only reject science as being a totally invalid approach to understanding human nature, but also believe that many of the problems of twentieth-century society are the result of generations of scientific and tech-

------

[6]For an extended discussion of these contrasting points of view, see Wann (1964).

nocratic growth run rampant. Such a viewpoint is characteristic of existential philosophers, much of whose thinking on social issues has found its way into humanistic psychology.

There is general agreement among humanistic psychologists that humans have an inherent potential for growth and self-actualization. However, except for a few self-actualizers, most individuals' development is blocked or hampered by social and environmental obstacles, particularly by huge, technocratic, or bureaucratic institutions that are said to dehumanize the individual.

The humanistic psychologist seeks to establish a psychology of subjective experience whose purpose is to explore the problems of existence, freedom of will, values, and human potential, not in an analytic, scientific sense, but as directed toward freeing the individual from those cultural contingencies that are hampering his or her development. It is no surprise that this point of view has found support among individuals and groups concerned with human perfectability, such as encounter groups, advocates of meditation and consciousness expansion, and to some extent among mystics and occultists.

As will be brought out more fully in Chapter 17, the humanistic movement has made an important contribution to personality and psychotherapy in reminding psychologists in those areas that their analyses and procedures must be relevant to human beings and their problems. However, humanism remains fundamentally a position or point of view closely allied with existential philosophy and as such remains outside the scope of experimental psychology.

THE EXPERIMENTAL METHOD IN PSYCHOLOGY

When the pioneer psychologists began to apply the experimental method to the investigation of human behavior, they modeled their work on that of physicists and physiologists. The ideal experiment as conceived by early experimenters involved the selection of an *independent or experimental variable,* which is applied to the organism or subject under *controlled conditions,* and the measurement of a *dependent variable,* which is the subject's reaction to the independent variable. Diagrammatically the schema of an experiment parallels the *S-O-R* formula which we described earlier in this chapter (see Figure 1-1). In the schema, *S* stands for the independent or experimental variable, *O* for the organism or subject, and *R* for the dependent variable or subject's reaction. $C_1, C_2, C_3, \ldots, C_n$ represent constants or controlled conditions. The constants or controls are either environmental or organismic factors, which must not be allowed to vary during the experiment so that they will not influence the dependent variable. If this were allowed to happen, the experimenter would not know which factor—the independent variable or one of the uncontrolled conditions—was responsible for the organism's reaction. If only the independent variable is allowed to vary, then it must be the one responsible for the dependent variable or subject's reaction. This experimental design or paradigm, commonly known as "the rule of one variable," is still a fundamental experimental design technique in psychology.

By way of illustration we shall describe a once popular experiment from the

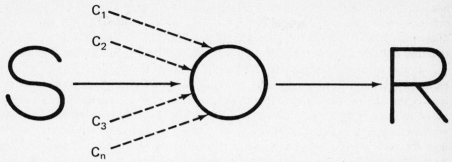

Figure 1-1.   The scheme of an experiment. S stands for the independent or experimental variable, O for the organism, and R for the dependent variable or subject's response. C_1, C_2, C_3, C_n represent variables to be controlled. The dotted lines indicate they have been prevented from influencing the organism or subject.

early psychology laboratories involving reaction time. The organism, a human subject, sat in front of a panel upon which was mounted a small lamp. The subject's forefinger was pressed down on a switch completing an electric circuit. The lamp and switch were connected through a clock in such a way that when the lamp came on the clock would begin to run and would continue to run until the subject lifted his or her finger, breaking the contact. The intervening time between the onset of the signal lamp and the lifting of the finger was the subject's reaction time. Because of variations in reaction time from trial to trial, many trials were conducted and the results averaged.

In terms of our experimental schema, the lamp was the independent variable, and the time for lifting the finger after the lamp came on the dependent variable. The experimenter attempted to control various external distractions by conducting the experiment in an isolated room. He or she also tried to control any extraneous factors within the subject by means of special instructions that urged the subject to attend carefully to the signal and to respond as quickly as possible. In practice all sorts of independent variables could be designed into the basic reaction time experiment in order to assess their effects. Complications might be introduced on the stimulus side, such as having the subject respond to one color of light and not to another (discrimination reaction). Or the subject's set or readiness could be manipulated by special instructions directing him or her to attend to either the motor side of the process or to the stimulus side. The influence of drugs could be readily tested by administering these to the subject as the independent variable.

To account for the processes going on in the organism when stimulated by an independent variable, experimenters postulated *intervening variables,* or *O*-factors, that could explain the observed behavior. These intervening variables were not directly observable. Rather, they were inferred from the organism's reaction to the experimental variable. In a simple reaction time experiment, for example, a strong mental set or readiness to respond might be postulated to account for a subject's extremely short reaction time. In a learning experiment, the subject's ability to remember the material over a period of time was accounted for by assuming the intervening variable of retention. From one point of view psychology could be defined as the study of the relationships among intervening variables. However, many psychologists objected (and still do) to the use of intervening variables, pointing out that they are not directly observable and are therefore not verifiable.

It also became clear early in the history of experimental psychology that it is extremely difficult, if not impossible, to control *all* conditions that may be impinging on the subject during an experiment. Sometimes the experiment has simply failed to identify an extraneous variable that should have been controlled but was not. Therefore, in many instances the investigation of a behavioral process involves an entire series of experiments designed to test the possible effect of variables that were not controlled in prior experiments. Human behavior is highly complex, and the subject is not comparable to a chemical compound that reacts only if manipulated by the experimenter. Rather, human subjects are highly reactive; they make all sorts of assumptions about the nature of the experiment that may influence the results (J. Jung, 1971). They may strive to excel; they may sit back and try to frustrate the experimenter. They may attempt to outguess the ''real'' purpose of the experiment; or, like ''ideal'' subjects, they may try to be as docile as possible.

The experimenter, too, is involved in an interpersonal relationship with the subject that is never free from possible bias and extraneous factors. He or she may inadvertently convey to the subjects what results are expected or may behave in such a manner as to bring about subtly the very conclusions that are expected—a self-fulfilling prophecy. Problems such as these have become the focus of intensive research in recent years, particularly by social psychologists. We shall examine them in more detail in Chapter 18.

Experimenters must also be on guard against two types of error which may creep into their designs and either bias or nullify the results. The first of these, *random errors,* are extraneous variables, such as minor events that occur during experiments, and subject variables, such as momentary inattention, changing sets, and differences in confidence. These errors are impossible to control directly, and therefore the experimenter utilizes a large number of subjects and repeats the experimental trials in order to cancel out their effects. Random errors tend to be distributed around the mean according to the normal probability curve. For this reason experimenters typically report not only a mean or average result but a standard deviation in order to show the range of random errors that can be expected if the experiment is repeated.

Much more insidious is the *systematic error,* which influences the dependent variable in only one direction. An error of this type is exemplified in an experiment on extrasensory perception where the experimenter utilizes only volunteers who strongly believe in the existence of ESP. Strong belief accompanied by strong motivation to find results supporting the existence of ESP can lead to errors in observation, recording, or experimenter interactions that collectively could show spurious statistically significant results favoring the operation of ESP. Although it is not possible to predict the distribution of such errors around the mean, they can be eliminated by careful experimental designs.

As experimental methodology evolved during the first century of psychology, sophisticated statistical methods were developed to study the interaction among two or more variables that were allowed to vary concomitantly. The analysis of variance provided a highly useful tool for studying variance in the dependent variable under differing experimental conditions and evaluating whether such differences could be attributed to chance or to the independent variable. In fact, it is correct to say that quantitative methods for the design and evaluation of experiments evolved hand in hand with the evolution of experimental psychology. Each is necessary to the other.

Also available to psychologists is the *method of naturalistic observation* for use in those cases where the imposition of experimental controls might influence the process under study. Naturalistic observation means an objective, scientific description of events or behavior in their natural setting. The oldest method in science, naturalistic observation, was the only method available to astronomers until space travel made experimental astronomy possible. In psychology, naturalistic observation is employed primarily when the experimenter is studying children or animals. It has become very popular with comparative psychologists and biologists (ethologists) who specialize in the study of animal behavior in its natural environment. The great disadvantage of the method is the lack of control.

As nineteenth-century psychology evolved into twentieth-century psychology, the *testing method* became the primary tool of psychologists working in the area of intelligence and personality. The test as a standardized sample of behavior not only allows the psychologist to make comparisons among individuals, but may also be utilized in highly sophisticated mathematical designs for investigating the basic nature of aptitudes and personality traits. We shall consider these techniques in detail in Chapters 15 and 16.

A variety of other techniques were either borrowed from other disciplines or were invented by psychologists for studying special problems. Prominent among these are various types of interview utilized by the clinical psychologist, the case history (borrowed from medicine) also used by clinicians, and the public opinion poll and field study which make up an important segment of social psychology.

Each of the methods used by psychologists has undergone considerable evolution during the past century as psychology has grown more and more sophisticated in the design of investigations. Many of these changes came about as a result of criticism that pointed out the inadequacy of traditional methods. In this we have an example of the application of operationism as experimenters called into question the validity of concepts based on relatively simple, unsophisticated methodology.

SCIENCE AND PSEUDOSCIENCE

The history of science as the story of man's attempt to understand the natural world in terms of rational laws is paralleled by the history of pseudoscience, magic, and superstition whose aims are the same—that is, understanding natural phenomena—but whose methods and assumptions are unacceptable to scientists and to educated and critically minded persons in general. Although all sciences have had their parallel pseudosciences, psychology has been especially vulnerable to pseudoscientific attempts to account for human behavior. Perhaps the earliest of the major pseudosciences is astrology whose proponents claim to make all kinds of predictions about human behavior on the basis of planetary, solar, and lunar influences. Among other early pseudoscientists were the phrenologists and palmists who asserted they could "read" personality traits from examining bumps on the head or lines on the palms of the hands. Similarly, graphologists made extravagant claims about the degree of relationship presumed to exist between handwriting and personality. Among other systems that pretend to explain, predict, or control human behavior by pseudoscientific or magic means are numerology, cartomancy (the prediction of the future by reading patterns of ordinary playing cards or special packs such as the Tarot), the I Ching, an ancient Chinese method of divination using patterns of thrown sticks, witchcraft, and demonology.

In the areas of psychotherapy and psychosomatic disorders, pseudoscientists and cultists have always enjoyed a rich field for exploitation, since the victim of a serious behavior disorder or an illness is particularly vulnerable to pseudoscientific claims, quackery, or fraud. In the early stages of the development of most religions, faith healing played a significant part in attracting followers, and continues to do so today among certain evangelical sects. Hypnotists, such as Franz Anton Mesmer (1734–1815), exploited the vulnerability of hysterical individuals in pretending to achieve cures through the use of "animal magnetism," in reality hypnotic suggestions. Modern practitioners of dianetics claim to treat behavior disorders by utilizing techniques considered totally unscientific by psychiatrists and clinical psychologists.

In addition to the pseudoscientists who back their claims with elaborate and often ancient systems of philosophy in combination with the superficial trappings of science, there appear in each generation individuals who seemingly possess "psychic" powers and who claim to be able to contradict the ordinary laws of physics and biology. Uri Geller is a contemporary example. Most of the practitioners of spiritualism made similar claims. Spiritualism was once a popular belief that some persons (mediums) possess special powers for "astral projection," clairvoyance, communication with the dead, or transporting or otherwise influencing material objects by psychic means. Its adherents at one time numbered Sir Arthur Conan Doyle, author of the famous Sherlock Holmes stories, and Sir James Jeans, an eminent physicist, both of whom had tragically lost their only sons in World War I and so were particularly vulnerable to such claims.

The claims of pseudoscientists and those who pretend to have psychic powers of healing, clairvoyance, magic, and the like, have enormous popular appeal as revealed by their durability and the large investment of money that they attract. Because their advocates pretend to have answers to highly complex problems and situations beyond the current scope of science, they sometimes seem to put science and scientists in an unfavorable light. Indeed, the recent wave of interest in the occult amounting to a fad appears to be a distinct reaction against modern science and technology, presumably because of the inability of science and technology to cope adequately with complex problems of modern life—most of which are political rather than scientific problems. Since science needs popular support and is dependent upon federal and private funding, many prominent scientists have expressed serious concern for the future of science in a society in which a large proportion of people harbor anti-scientific attitudes or beliefs.

Scientists rarely have the time or means to investigate the claims of pseudo-scientists or psychics, although there have been exceptions to this generalization. Many of the claims are so general, are formulated in such imprecise form, or are emotionally held by desperate people (for example, belief in cancer cures by people who are terminally ill), that science has had surprisingly little impact on pseudo-science. The will to believe, as William James put it, is strong, particularly in ambiguous or critical times, or where the trappings of science are cleverly and deceptively employed to support exaggerated or misleading claims.

It is beyond the scope of a book devoted to the exposition of scientific psychol-ogy to trace the long and complex history of pseudoscience and allied beliefs.[7] However, it is important to recognize the influence of pseudoscience and such beliefs for social legislation and for the welfare of individuals and to emphasize how the same guiding principles of science described in this chapter can be critically applied by educated people to assess the claims of pseudoscientists, cultists, and the like. It is, in fact, one of the important achievements of science that whenever this has been done such claims are revealed to be without merit or are explainable on a scientific basis. Of course, those who reject science will assert that its rules and principles do not apply in certain cases. However, few truly educated people are willing to accept the irrationalism of the pseudoscientist, the superstitious, and the fraud. The entire history of science stands as eloquent testimony to the value of rationalism in astronomy, chemistry, biology, and psychology and cannot be dis-missed so lightly.

SUMMARY AND CONCLUSIONS

We have adopted the position that science is a specialized point of view held by a group of investigators who are in general agreement that all processes in the uni-verse follow natural law. Scientific laws, however, are far from self-evident and only upon careful, objective observation and experimentation can the necessary data be discovered upon which to build the generalizations that underlie such laws.

Traditional experimental psychology accepted the viewpoint of the natural sciences as it sought to establish itself as an independent scientific discipline. However, within the broad framework of experimental psychology there are differ-ences in approach and points of view, with some psychologists stressing the study of behavior from the frame of reference of psychology as a natural science and others taking the point of view that psychology is a social science. Similarly, some favor highly objective, behavioral methods; others advocate more phenomenological techniques. And some who class themselves as humanistic psychologists would go so far as to reject the scientific method altogether in favor of an approach concerned with human freedom, dignity, and development. In the course of its first century of evolution, modern psychology has proved that it is broad enough to tolerate many viewpoints, finding something of value and significance in each.

---

[7]See Garner (1957), Evans (1958), Chaplin (1976) for extensive treatments of the subject.

The Origins of
Scientific
Psychology:
The
Preexperimental
Period

2

The dawn of science was far from a dramatic and sudden burst of illumination that forever dispelled the darkness of ignorance and superstition. In fact, the point of view to be presented here envisages modern science as a relatively recent system of thought that gradually evolved partly out of and partly parallel to two antecedent systems—animism and religion. This, of course, does not imply that science has supplanted religion and that religion in turn has displaced animism, for both religion and animism still remain fundamental modes of thought throughout the world. Rather, it suggests that as social orders began to take shape among primitive prehistoric tribes, animism was the first organized and more or less universal system of thought. Religion evolved much later, and science is an even more recent product of human civilization. Each earlier system has remained in force, however, even though its explanatory power has diminished. Let us trace these developments by considering briefly how each system of thought is related to the others in terms of their historical antecedents.

ANIMISM, RELIGION, AND SCIENCE

Animism is the primitive belief system characteristic of early totemic social orders and is still widespread among preliterate peoples today. As people began to form social groups, they organized into clans whose guiding spirit and supreme authority was a totem. The totem might be a bear, rain, a river, or whatever natural phenomenon appeared to have potential power over the weal and woe of the clan. The totem was consulted as an oracle, was offered sacrifices to propitiate its wrath, and was worshiped as a kind of primitive god. Animism also meant attributing spirits to clouds, plants, or to anything that moved or seemed potentially powerful. This naive conception of causality is sometimes found in children's explanations of why clouds move or why the winds blow (Piaget, 1930).

However erroneous in its conception of cause and effect, animism was the first faltering step on the road to science, since it involved an attempt to understand, predict, and control natural phenomena. These are the aims of contemporary science, but the methodology and interpretations of scientists are, to be sure, totally lacking in animism.

As is true of animism, the origins of the ancient religions are obscured by the mists of antiquity. There is good reason, however, to believe that religion evolved as a natural outgrowth of animism (Freud, 1938b). When specialization of function began to take place in the clan society, some members became warriors, others hunters, and still others assumed the role of shaman or medicine man. These primitive priests took over the office of dealing with the totem. Theirs was the job of interpreting the wishes of the clan to the totem and the totem to the clan. Gradually a body of ritual, symbolism, and dogma accrued to the priestly office, and in this manner primitive religion took form. Still later, new religions came into existence largely through revelation to individuals who then became the prophets and promulgators of the new creeds.

Primarily because of their origins, most of the major religious systems are characteristically authoritarian, dogmatic, and founded on revelation rather than on rationalistic speculation or experimentation. As a consequence, religion and science are said to have developed along antagonistic lines. On the positive side, however, many great theologians have attempted to rationalize religious beliefs and in the process have made searching inquiries into human nature and its relationship to the deity. This technique for seeking knowledge is the rational method so familiar to the philosopher.

Rationalism in religious (and secular) philosophy has carried over into science, and every scientific deduction or hypothesis is an inquiry that must be put to nature for an answer. Thus, religion is not necessarily antagonistic to the spirit of inquiry, since this selfsame spirit in a different frame of reference becomes the quest for scientific knowledge.

Unlike animism and organized religion, science is primarily a Western system of thought. Science, especially as a venerated system, in no sense occupies such a prominent place in the Orient as it does in Western culture. This geographical dissimilarity in attitudes extends into other areas such as politics, economics, and agricultural systems. In part, this is a reflection of the fact that our Western heritage in its various manifestations stems from a common intellectual ancestor, ancient Greece. Moreover, the Oriental thinker puts more emphasis on intuitive knowledge, paradoxical thinking, and mystical approaches to ultimate reality. However valuable these modes of thought may be in other spheres, they tend to stifle scientific progress.

Finally, in attempting to interrelate animism, religion, and science, we may borrow from the philosopher Hans Vaihinger (1924), who suggested that in the evolution of thought an ideational shift takes place in the direction of myth → dogma → hypothesis → myth. Thus, what at first is animistic myth becomes religious dogma, but with increasing knowledge such dogma is challenged successfully and retreats into hypothesis. Dogmas unable to stand the test of time finally return once again to myths. Such, certainly, has been the fate of the old Greek and Roman religions. But in a sense scientific concepts are no more than a set of fictions or myths that work in practice. The physicist, chemist, or psychologist constructs elaborate theoretical or "fictional" systems that "explain" only in the sense that they hang together logically and can be used to account for scientific observations. This is why what was once considered truth in science has now been discarded and has reverted to the status of myth.

Insofar as we have any records of its early beginnings, science as we know it appears to have originated among the ancient civilizations of both the Old and New Worlds. We find evidence of scientific accomplishments, often striking in their intellectual sophistication, among the Sumerians, Egyptians, Aztecs, and Greeks. Each of these ancient peoples realized the relatively high degree of civilization that is prerequisite for the emergence of science. Here, however, we shall be concerned only with the development of science among the Greeks, since it is to them that the origins of European thought, and consequently of modern experimental psychology, can be traced.

SCIENCE AMONG THE GREEKS[1]

Two branches of Greek thought were significant for the development of modern science. These were cosmology and rationalism. Cosmology is the study of the cosmos—how it originated, its structure, and its evolution. This school of thought was typified by the teachings of the philosopher Democritus (circa 460–370 B.C.), one of the later cosmologists, who postulated an atomic theory of the universe. He also believed that sensations arise when atoms emanate from the surface of objects and come into contact with the sense organs. His interest in sensation led him to develop a theory of color vision, in which he postulated four primaries: black, white, red, and green, all other colors being mixtures of these.

In general, the cosmologists were reductionists who sought to resolve the physical universe into the irreducible elements of which they believed it to be fashioned. Some of Democritus' predecessors, however, were enlightened enough and broad enough in their interests to give a correct explanation of eclipses, to formulate a nebular or gas condensation theory of the origin of the universe, to argue that the stars are balls of fire, and finally, to antedate Darwin's theory of the origin of species by assuming a process of natural selection to account for the diversity of living forms. To maintain a proper perspective, however, it must be admitted that much Greek science was also childish and unworthy of a modern high school student.

---

[1]The account of Greek science and philosophy has been drawn from Boring (1929), Brett (1953), Durant (1933), and Murphy (1949).

In keeping with their attempts to formulate mechanistic models of the universe, the speculations of the cosmologists were generally materialistic. This empirical trend in philosophy never disappeared from Greek thought. For a time, however, it was obscured by the rationalists, typified by Plato (427–347 B.C.), and by the Sophists, noted for their love of argument and their devotion to trick reasoning.

However, the empirical spirit reemerged in Aristotle (384–322 B.C.), who has often been called the world's greatest thinker. Whether or not he deserves such an exalted title, it is true that in his writings he tried to span the scope of knowledge as it existed in his time. He was a logician, esthetician, biologist, ethical theorist, and the administrator of an educational institution. He wrote dozens of works not only in philosophy but also in physics, biology, meteorology, psychology, and politics.

For our purposes it is noteworthy that he authored a psychological treatise in which he systematically dealt with the various mental processes of sensation, perception, and memory. He was the first scholar to list the five senses of vision, audition, olfaction, taste, and touch. Perception is aroused by events in the environment by way of the senses, and memory is the persistence of sense impressions. Associations between memories are held together by similarity, contrast, and contiguity. The modern historian Will Durant, in his *Story of Philosophy* (1933), calls Aristotle "the *Encyclopaedia Britannica* of ancient Greece." So powerful was the domination of Aristotle's intellect that he is generally acknowledged to be the father of modern science, and, among scholars, his opinion was accepted as the final word on scientific questions up to the time of the Renaissance.

The rationalists sought enlightenment on philosophical problems by exercising the kind of thinking that we today call deductive as opposed to inductive. To put it another way, pure rationalists are convinced that they can get at the truth by the use of reason; and they believe that knowledge derived from reason is just as valid as—and often superior to—knowledge originating from sense perceptions. Such a view was the basis for Plato's philosophy, which because of its subjective orientation is something of a mixture of poetry, science, and art.

Plato is most widely known for his *Republic* and for his interest in an ideal state—or *Utopia,* to use the name made famous by Sir Thomas More in 1516. It was Plato's desire to found a perfect society that led him into psychological speculation, for in order to create the utopian conditions necessary for bringing about the betterment of humanity, a prior knowledge of human nature is demanded. In the course of his speculation on human nature, Plato concluded that behavior stems from three sources: *desire,* primarily sexual in nature; *emotion,* which arises from the heat of the blood; and *knowledge,* which stems from the head. In a utopian society the "man of desire" would be assigned the job of running business enterprises; the "man of emotion" would be trained as a soldier; the "man of reason" would become a philosopher; and, understandably enough, philosophers would govern Utopia. It is noteworthy that Plato anticipated Freud by centuries in characterizing much of human behavior as irrational, stemming from conflicts between reason and desire.

Plato also posed a psychological problem that has persisted down through the ages to contemporary psychology. This is the question of the nature of mind and body and their relation to each other. Plato took a dualistic position, separating the two and asserting that they were different entities. Of course, he failed to resolve the dilemma by separating mind and body, but he was clearly more interested in the nature of mind than of body. The material body, he pointed out, perishes all too soon, but mind is permanent in the sense that ideas may live on for generations after the body has turned to dust. For this reason, in Plato's Utopia the mind is to be cultivated by education so that ideals and worthwhile generalizations might bring order and reason into man's often chaotic society.

By way of summarizing the contributions of classical Greek society to the development of the scientific method, we may credit the cosmologists with originating both naturalistic observation and the principle of understanding the unknown by reducing it to its constituent elements. Both of these methodological approaches are fundamental first stages in every science, whether ancient or modern. From Aristotle we have the idea of organizing the phenomena of nature into broad descriptive categories, which is the second stage in scientific endeavor, since before we can explain natural phenomena we must describe them and put them into some kind of order.

Plato and the rationalists were less scientists than philosophers; yet their rationalistic approach has its counterpart in modern science in the hypotheticodeductive method, by means of which the scientist attempts to postulate a rational set of assumptions to be tested by experiment. Similarly, psychologists who develop elaborate theories and systems of psychology draw heavily upon the deductive method to fill gaps in empirical knowledge. However, most are in agreement that although the deductive method makes a valuable contribution to the field, only experimental or empirical techniques offer a valid test of the probable truth or falsity of assumptions about behavior.

Finally, we ought to mention that one school among the ancient philosophers recognized the value of quantitative, or mathematical, methods. Mention of this group was omitted in the previous discussion since its members belonged to neither the cosmologists nor the rationalists, but constituted a school unto themselves. Euclid and Pythagorus, two prominent Greeks who interested themselves in mathematical methods, are universally known, at least by hard-pressed high school students who must learn their theorems. Today quantitative methods play such a crucial role in both the natural and the social sciences that mathematics is often called "the tool of the sciences."

In summary, then, the Greeks in essence recognized the significance of what we believe to be four important stages in the scientific method: (1) naturalistic observation, (2) analysis and classification of natural phenomena into meaningful descriptive categories, (3) formulation of hypotheses of cause and effect on the basis of such analyses, and (4) value of quantitative methods. All that remains is the testing of hypotheses by experiment or by critical observations. In this last step the Greeks were quite limited, although they did carry out a few crude experiments. The experimental attack on nature had to wait for many centuries before coming into its own. However, to their great credit, these ancient people were able to develop what amounts to a sophisticated scientific methodology more than 2000 years ago.

Science in the Middle Ages and Renaissance

With the death of Aristotle and the collapse of the Greek city-states, Greek science and philosophy suffered a decline. Barbarian invasions swarmed over Europe, and at the same time Christianity began to catch fire and spread from the Middle East. These political and religious upheavals led to an intellectual darkness in the West that is popularly characterized as the Dark Ages. The intellectual atmosphere was dominated by authoritarianism, both political and theological; and consequently, scientific progress came to a virtual halt. The science of Aristotle was considered universally binding in its sphere, and the Church actively discouraged independent scientific inquiries, which might embarrass or challenge the teachings of canon law.

Toward the end of the Middle Ages, a few thinkers and scholars were willing to challenge dogmatism and to risk the wrath of the Church. Those who stand out in the history of science during the 1400s and 1500s will be mentioned briefly. First there was Leonardo da Vinci (1452–1519)—artist, engineer, geologist—in fact, all-around genius. Copernicus (1473–1543) also belongs to this period. He postulated a heliocentric theory of the solar system in opposition to the ancient Ptolemaic view that had erroneously placed the earth at the center of the solar family. Copernicus' theories paved the way for Galileo's telescopic observations, Kepler's laws of motion, and Newton's celestial mechanics and theories of gravitation. Galileo (1564–1642) is, of course, famous for his experiments with falling objects at the Leaning Tower of Pisa, but his astronomical observations in support of Copernicus were even more significant. In a very real sense, Galileo may be said to be the father of modern science, since he broke with the Aristotelian mode of thought, which was based on authority and dogma and relied too heavily on anthropomorphic concepts in the absence of precise empirical observations and measurements. Instead of looking up the behavior of planets and stars in Aristotle's works or in the writings of theologians, Galileo turned his telescope on the heavens. Instead of debating the laws of falling bodies in the time-honored manner of philosophers, he made measurements of falling objects and so pioneered in the utilization of empirical methods as scientific yardsticks.[2]

Finally, the British scholar Francis Bacon (1561–1626) ought to be mentioned, since he successfully challenged the notion that classical science had already discovered everything of importance. He pleaded for the recognition of modern science and championed the inductive method of collecting facts and drawing conclusions from them.

None of the intellectual giants that we have been discussing is directly related to the evolution of psychology, but indirectly they and men of similar caliber created an atmosphere in which scientific inquiry could once again flourish. Thus, they are important in the general evolution of modern science.

One Renaissance scholar stands in a direct relationship to the history of modern

---

[2]For a further elaboration of the differences between Aristotelian and Galilean modes of thought and their significance for modern psychology, see Lewin (1935).

psychology. This was the French philosopher and mathematician, René Descartes (1596–1650). In many ways Descartes symbolizes a transition in human thought from the Renaissance to the modern period. Torn as he was between the safe, dogmatic beliefs of the medieval Church and the disturbing, revolutionary ideas that were taking shape in his own mind, he took the crucial step and became a man of enlightenment. His philosophical method, which consisted of doubting every philosophical proposition in order to reach the bedrock of truth, carried him even to the brink of disbelief in God, but he retreated from that extreme position. However, he could not doubt that he thought, and hence he was able to assert the primacy of existence *(cogito, ergo sum)*.

His reasoning led him to distinguish clearly between mind, or consciousness, and body, or material substance, thus reaffirming Plato's dualism. But he was a special kind of dualist who believed that although mind and body are separate, they interact with each other. For this reason Descartes is called an interactionist. He decided that the site of interchange between mind and body is the pineal gland, located at the base of the cerebrum. We still are not certain just what this gland's function is, but no modern psychologist believes it is a two-way gate between body and mind. In other respects Descartes more accurately anticipated modern psychology. Not trusting entirely in deduction, he advocated the mechanistic position that animals lacked souls and were therefore essentially machines. He urged physiologists to use the empirical method of dissection to discover the machinery of the animal body. Dissection of the human body was then forbidden by an edict of the Church. To some extent he must have engaged in the forbidden practice of human dissection, since he left amazingly accurate descriptions of the nervous system. While he reaffirmed the old Greek notion of the nerves as conductors of "animal spirits," he did anticipate modern discoveries by arguing that the nervous impulses that travel out over nerves originate in the brain.

Descartes is also considered the father of modern philosophy, particularly by the existentialists. His distinction between existence and material essence led to the dichotomy between scientific abstractionism and humanistic existentialism which has become a focal conflict in modern philosophy, literature, and art. The study of abstractions and essences culminated in the development of modern mathematics and the physical sciences. Descartes, himself, was one of the leaders in the development of mathematics. He laid the foundation for analytic geometry and also made a number of contributions to modern algebra.

Following Descartes, the great systems of philosophy and science concerned themselves almost exclusively with building the abstract and symbolic edifices that have changed the face of Western civilization and have given rise to our dominantly scientific and technocratic society. But doubt in the wisdom of the primacy of essence over existence remained a kind of dormant filament in philosophy, which at last found responsive soil in the philosophy of Soren Kierkegaard (1813–1855) and Friedrich Nietzsche (1844–1900) and their followers. And in the decades immediately following World War II, existentialism, which asserts the primacy of the individual, his or her consciousness, and his or her freedom of will, became the dominant European philosophy and profoundly influenced American philosophy and theology.[3]

As we have pointed out, from Descartes onward the development of modern science was both rapid and prolific. It would not be feasible to trace its further progress in a general way; rather, we shall narrow our perspective to encompass only those intellectual developments that are directly related to the emergence of psychology. Indeed, for a while we shall turn away from science altogether in favor of pursuing certain developments in British philosophy that, as was pointed out earlier in this chapter, coalesced with physiology, ultimately to produce psychology. When we have completed our survey of British philosophy, we shall return briefly to the further developments in natural science relevant for psychology.

British Empiricism[4]

The ancient Greek modes of thought—empiricism and rationalism—echoed in British and Continental philosophy in the seventeenth and eighteenth centuries. Descartes, as we have shown, was in part mechanistic in his thinking and leaned toward empirical observation in studying nature. Yet he also had a rationalistic side, since he believed in the value of deduction and a priori axioms in philosophical speculation. In general, the British philosophers associated themselves with the empirical tradition, whereas on the continent of Europe both points of view had their adherents. Several of the British empirical philosophers' contributions will be considered in some detail, since they deal with psychological problems that have a bearing on both the methodology and the systematic structure of modern psychology.

We may begin with Thomas Hobbes (1588–1679), who opposed Descartes' notion of innate ideas and instead held that sensations are the source of all knowledge. He explained memory and imagination as decaying sense impressions held together by association. These teachings enabled British philosophy to break completely with the rationalism of the Middle Ages and initiated the philosophical school of empiricism, which paved the way for the psychological school of associationism. Empiricism places the origin of mind in sensation and explains the higher mental processes such as memory, thinking, and imagination as complexes of persistent impressions held together by associations. The associations in turn are said to arise because of certain conditions that existed at the time of impression, such as repetition and contiguity. For example, "grass" brings to mind "green" because throughout our lives we repeatedly experience visual and auditory sense impressions of the two ideas in close temporal contiguity. We shall return to the problem of association of ideas in the chapters on learning, where associationism as

---

[3]For a more detailed account of the development of existentialism and its place in philosophy, literature, and psychology, see Barrett (1958). See also Chapter 15 of this volume.

[4]For a more detailed account of the British empiricists, see Boring (1950), Murphy (1949), or R. I. Watson (1978).

such is treated more fully. Meanwhile, we may reiterate that Hobbes' importance lies in the fact that he provided a foundation for the empirical and associationistic movements in British philosophy, which ultimately carried over into psychology.

John Locke (1632–1704) extended Hobbes' principle of the empirical sources of human knowledge. In his *Essay Concerning Human Understanding,* Locke put the essence of his doctrine in the now famous comparison of the infant's mind to a *tabula rasa,* or blank paper, upon which experience writes. By teaching that the infantile mind is a blank, Locke was denying the existence of innate ideas and asserting instead that all knowledge derives from experience and is therefore empirical in origin. Simple, uncompounded ideas originate directly in sense experience. By combining these simple ideas, mind forms complex ideas. Part of Locke's doctrine had to do with another problem of interest to psychology, and this was a distinction that he drew between "primary" and "secondary" qualities. The primary qualities are characteristics such as solidity, extension, mobility, and number. Primary qualities are inherent in external objects, whereas secondary qualities such as color or odor are dependent on mind. Thus, the size of a house is a primary quality inherent in the physical structure of that house. The perception of the color of the house or the recognition of the architectural period to which it belongs is dependent on the experiencing person.

The problem with which Locke was struggling is often stated in another setting in an old folk puzzle: If a tree falls in the woods and nobody is around to hear the crash, does it make any noise? The answer depends on the frame of reference one assumes. Physically, sound waves are present in that the tree creates a molecular disturbance in the atmosphere, but psychologically there is no "sound" if there is no one there to hear it. Locke's position has reappeared as a distinction in modern psychology between the physical situation and the psychological field. All people listening to the same radio or viewing a beautiful landscape are experiencing identical physical stimulation. This is the physical situation, but each perceives the situation differently according to his or her interests, past experience, and intelligence. Individual perception is a psychological field unique for each perceiver.

The importance of Locke's contribution lies in the fact that he developed the first completely worked-out empirical theory of knowledge. Many of the issues first raised by him are still current in philosophy.

George Berkeley (1685–1753), Locke's successor in British empirical philosophy, carried the problem of inherent versus secondary qualities to its logical extreme by denying the validity of Locke's distinction. He asserted that there are no primary qualities but that *all* knowledge is dependent on the experiencing person. This means that even those seemingly well-entrenched physical qualities of shape, size, and position are in reality man-made constructs that we attribute to the environment. Therefore, the only "reality" is mind. Berkeley's extremist position never gained popular support either in his own field of philosophy or in science. This is understandable in view of the fact that such a position essentially precludes the possibility of any kind of systematic and collective philosophy or science, since there would be no constants upon which to base these disciplines. One could not be certain that anything exists except individual ideas.

In addition to this philosophical tour de force, Berkeley also contributed the first book primarily devoted to the analysis of a psychological process. This was his treatise entitled *A New Theory of Vision*. In it he dealt with the problem of how we perceive depth in space in spite of the two-dimensional nature of our retinas. His solution anticipated a widely accepted explanation of depth perception among contemporary psychologists, since he included what we today call the physiological cues of convergence and accommodation and the psychological cues of interposition, shadows, and aerial perspective. In Chapters 6 and 7 we shall discuss the problem of space perception in detail.

Finally, it is worth mentioning that Berkeley accepted the principle of associationism in accounting for the more complex processes involved in the relation between experiences and ideas. Thus, he continued the associationistic tradition originated by his predecessors Hobbes and Locke.

David Hume (1711–1776) not only agreed with Berkeley about the unreality of matter apart from the experiencing mind but went a step further. He abolished "mind" entirely as a true entity or substance. Mind, Hume argued, is only a name we give to the flow of ideas, memories, imagination, and feelings. Moreover, mind, like matter, is a "secondary quality" observable only through perception. When we think we are perceiving mind, we are, in fact, perceiving separate ideas or internal sensations.

Not satisfied with applying the coup de grace to mind, Hume proceeded to abolish any notion of lawfulness in nature. Scientific laws, he argued, are in no sense the children of nature, but fictional constructs in the minds of men. Even general ideas, such as the idea of triangularity, are only concepts that designate collections of similar particular experiences that we have repeatedly had in the past. Thus, he arrived at the position where nature, mind, and natural law are no more than ideational phenomena. In Hume's time such ideas were considered shocking and dangerously radical, for they destroyed the very foundations of rational thought, science, and psychology. The dogmas of religion and the principles of science were no longer seen as the eternal truths that people had traditionally believed them to be.

Even though Hume had done away with mind, there remained the problem of differentiating among the processes of ideation, memory, and imagination. It seems one cannot do away with "mind" completely! Hume distinguished between "ideas of memory" and "ideas of imagination." Ideas of imagination were less distinct than ideas of memory, since the imaginative processes are less closely related to the original source of stimulation. He went on to discuss simple and complex ideas, the latter of course posing the problem of what causes ideas to cohere into complex cognitive structures.

In agreement with his philosophical predecessors, Hume invoked the doctrine of associationism to account for the connectedness of complex ideas. Associational attraction could in turn be reduced to the "laws" of association, which for Hume were ultimately reducible to the principles of resemblance and contiguity. We shall deal with this aspect of Hume's psychology more fully in the chapters on learning. For the present it is sufficient to reiterate the strong affinity that exists between the philosophical position of empiricism and the psychological doctrine of associationism. In a sense each demands the other, for both views are reductionistic and highly analytic in their approach to both epistemological and psychological problems, and these same trends were carried over into psychology when it came of age.

Hume's *Treatise on Human Nature* proved to be a rich source of inspiration for succeeding generations of philosophers. His strongly empirical philosophy not only supported the established empirical tradition but also contributed to contemporary systems of logical positivism and linguistic analysis. His extreme skepticism about the nature of reality has had an impact on both contemporary philosophers and theologians. His psychological analyses influenced both the pragmatists and the instrumentalists, such as James and Dewey. Many philosophers regard the *Treatise* as the most profound work written in the English language.

In this same tradition we may briefly mention David Hartley (1705–1757), who is considered by Boring (1950) to be the founder of associationism as a distinct school within philosophy and psychology. Hartley was one of the first philosophers to suggest that motor processes form chains of associated movements, one leading to the next, from the simple to the complex. He also suggested that psychologists should look in underlying physiological processes for the physical basis of association of ideas and motor movements. Boring rates Hartley as an ''important'' but not a ''great'' man. This characterization our historian justifies on the grounds that while Hartley systematized and organized the various threads of thought from Hobbes to Berkeley and formulated them into the formal doctrine of associationism, he did not originate new ideas or insights into the nature of mind. For this reason we need only mention that Hartley's laws of association were contiguity and repetition, and then we can pass on to James Mill and his son John Stuart Mill, the last of the philosophers in our survey of the empirical-associationistic tradition.

James Mill (1773–1836) was the greatest associationist of them all, and he carried the doctrine to its local extreme in a kind of reductio ad absurdum. He began by accepting the principle made famous by his empirical predecessors that sensations and ideas are the primary material of mind. Knowledge begins with sensation, whereas perceptions or ideas are derived processes or complexes. Thus once again we have the familiar argument that mind is developed from elements and can therefore be reduced to elements by analysis. Perhaps no better illustration of this kind of thinking occurs than in the following often-quoted passage from James Mill's *Analysis of the Phenomena of the Human Mind:*

> Brick is one complex idea, mortar is another complex idea; these ideas, with ideas of position and quantity, compose my idea of a wall. My idea of a plank is a complex idea, my idea of a rafter is a complex idea, my idea of a nail is a complex idea.
>
> These, united with the same ideas of position and quantity, compose my duplex idea of a floor. In the same manner my complex ideas of glass, wood, and others, compose my duplex idea of a window; and these duplex ideas, united together, compose my idea of a house, which is made up of various duplex ideas. How many complex, or duplex ideas, are all united in the idea of furniture? How many more in the idea of merchandise? How many more in the idea called Every Thing? (1869, vol. I, p. 115)

So extreme were James Mill's doctrines that his son John Stuart Mill (1806–1873) took issue with them on a very fundamental point. This was to argue that elements may *generate* complex ideas, but the ideas thus generated are *not* merely the sum of the individual parts. James Mill had previously argued that simple ideas *combine* into complex ideas. But in John Stuart Mill's way of viewing the matter, a new quality emerges, which may be unrecognizable as a mere conglomeration of elements. If, for example, we combine blue, green, and red lights in proper proportions, we get white. But the naive observer would never predict such an outcome, and even the sophisticated observer cannot see the separate colors in the final product. Nor does one perceive a chair as a bundle of sticks. John Mill's critique of his father's doctrine anticipated an important principle of Gestalt psychology, which is often quoted in the catch phrase, "The whole is different from the sum of its parts."

Before we leave the empiricists and associationists, it would be well to recapitulate the various lines of thought that came to psychology from this philosophical tradition by the third quarter of the nineteenth century. To begin with, the problem of the nature of mind first formulated by the Greeks had already undergone considerable evolution from its inception to the time of the Mills. The Greeks provided general questions that generated fresh problems. To recognize that mind and body differ in nature, to suggest that analysis into elements solves the problem of combinations of the many into one unitary whole, and to pursue two opposed methodological approaches—empirical and rational—in many ways raise more questions than they answer. We might say that the Greeks posed the problems for the future to solve.

When philosophy freed itself from dogmatism and subservience to the rationalistic approach, the same old problems presented themselves anew: What is mind? How does it develop its complex cognitive structures? What are the laws of memory? The empirical-associationistic tradition found the answers in elementalism and associationism. Mind is built from sense experiences. These experiences provide elemental ideas or memories, which coalesce into complex ideas by virtue of associations, which in turn arise through contiguity, repetition, similarity, and so on. In understanding mind, then, the most promising approach was held to be the empirical. In short, philosophy was becoming "scientific" and was turning away from its traditional rationalism. What was needed was an *experimental* or *observational* approach to these problems and issues to create a psychology. Philosophy had done all it could. The stage was set for the introduction of the methods of the natural sciences to provide an experimental attack on the problems of mind.

The Physiological Influence

We left the evolution of natural sciences at the Renaissance when we began our excursion into philosophy. During the period that saw the rise of British empiricism, there were also developments in physiology that had a profound influence on the fate of the new psychology. In focusing on these developments, we shall span three-quarters of a century, from 1800 to the 1870s—the period when the physiological foundations of modern medicine were being laid. Great strides were being made in the understanding of the nervous system, that most complex of all physiological problems.

At the same time, because of their research interests, physiologists were moving more and more into the bailiwick of psychology. This was the beginning of an interdisciplinary approach or the development of a physiological psychology devoted to discovering the nervous mechanisms underlying mental processes. Such an approach seemed promising for an emerging psychology on purely logical grounds. After all, the philosopher can speculate on the nature of mind indefinitely, but this does not convince the natural scientist that the answers offered are correct. A direct attack on the sense organs to discover the nature of sensation and the study of the brain to uncover the neural equivalents of mental processes are more valid from a scientific point of view. This is the task of physiology.

EXPERIMENTAL PHYSIOLOGY

Physiology became an experimental discipline in the 1830s. Major responsibility for this development is assigned to two outstanding men of the period, Johannes Müller (1801–1858) and Claude Bernard (1815–1878). Both were strong advocates of the experimental method in physiology, and each made significant and lasting contributions to his chosen field. Müller is noted for two contributions. First, he wrote a *Handbook of Physiology* (which was published in several volumes between 1833 and 1840), in which he summarized the physiological research of the period, thus presenting an impressive body of knowledge in support of the new standing of physiology as an independent science.

Second, he is also famous both in physiology and psychology for his doctrine of the specific energies of nerves. In his statement of the doctrine, Müller pointed out that we are only indirectly aware of our world through environmental stimuli, which in turn generate nervous impulses in our sense organs and nerves. But even more important was the principle contained in the doctrine that each sensory nerve has its specific energy, so the arousal of a given nerve always gives rise to a characteristic sensation. The optic nerve when stimulated generates a sensation of light, and stimulation of the auditory nerve gives rise only to auditory sensations. Even if nerves are stimulated by inappropriate stimuli, they respond with their characteristic sensation, if they respond at all. William James, the famous philosopher-psychologist, restated Müller's doctrine in this way: If a master surgeon were to cross the optic and auditory nerves, we would see the thunder and hear the lightning.

The principle of Müller's doctrine that is most important, since it stimulated a good deal of research, was the assumption of a functional localization within the nervous system and a corresponding specificity of sensory organs on the periphery of the body. As it turns out, it is not that nerves are specific in their energies but that the brain centers where they terminate are specialized in their functions. We shall return to this problem again in connection with our study of sensory processes in Chapter 5.

Claude Bernard was an early French physiologist who experimented in an area that in recent years has had considerable significance for psychology. Broadly speaking, we refer to his work on the endocrine processes, which along with the nervous system are important integrating mechanisms in the body. Bernard correctly identified the sugar-storing function of the liver and related it and other physiological effects to what he called the ''constant internal environment.'' He saw the bloodstream with its relatively stable thermal, carbohydrate, and saline levels as an internal environment that maintains a steady state for the cells. A great deal of subsequent work on the physiological mechanisms of constancy was done by the Harvard physiologist Walter B. Cannon (1871–1945), who called the overall process *homeostasis*. The study of steady states is a lively area of research in contemporary psychology, especially in the study of food selection and thirst, both of which are believed to be influenced by homeostatic processes.

BRAIN FUNCTIONS AND METHODS

Several men contributed to the experimental study of brain functions. They not only discovered functionally specialized areas but also introduced what were to become widely used research methods in physiological psychology.

A Scots physician, Marshall Hall (1790–1857), pioneered in the investigation of reflex behavior. He observed decapitated animals, noting that they continue to move for some time if appropriately stimulated. From such observations he concluded there are several levels of behavior dependent on certain broadly localized brain areas: (1) voluntary movement, a function of the cerebrum, or large brain; (2) reflex movement, dependent on the spinal cord; (3) involuntary movement, dependent on direct muscular stimulation; and (4) respiratory movement, dependent on the medulla.

Pierre Flourens (1794–1867) extended Hall's experiments to include systematic destruction of the cerebrum, midbrain, medulla, cerebellum, and spinal cord in animals. He concluded, on the basis of alterations in the animals' behavior following such destructions, that the higher mental processes are mediated by the cerebrum. The midbrain in turn contains centers for the visual and auditory reflexes, whereas the cerebellum governs coordination. The medulla is a center for the control of respiration, heartbeat, and other vital functions.

Hall's and Flourens' conclusions, though very broad, are still accepted as valid. But more important than the conclusions themselves is the fact that these men attacked the functions of the brain experimentally, in opposition to the unscientific procedures of the phrenologists, whose doctrines were popular at the time.[5] Hall and Flourens are also important because they introduced into psychology the method of extirpation of parts, which essentially consists of studying a part's function by removing it and then observing consequent changes in the animal's behavior.

---

[5]For a more extended discussion of the relationship between the phrenologists and the work of Hall and Flourens, see Chapter 14.

The midpart of the nineteenth century saw the introduction of two new approaches to the understanding of the brain. One of these was the clinical method used by Paul Broca (1824–1880) in 1861, and the other was the method of electrical stimulation developed by Fritsch and Hitzig in 1870. Broca discovered the speech center, and for this reason it is often called "Broca's area." Quite by chance, Broca was given the care of a patient who for many years had been hospitalized because of an inability to speak intelligibly. Shortly before the patient died, Broca examined him carefully and after the man's death performed an autopsy. He found a lesion in the third frontal convolution of his former patient's cerebral cortex and called this the speech center. This marked the introduction of a new method, the clinical method, as well as the discovery of a new brain center. The clinical method has proved a valuable supplement to the method of extirpation. Because it is not possible to perform extirpations on human beings, psychologists are forced to accept the next best thing from nature in the way of lesions caused by tumors or injuries.

G. Fritsch (1838–1927) and E. Hitzig (1838–1907) worked jointly to explore the cerebral cortex with weak electric currents. Contrary to the prevailing opinion of the day, which held the brain to be unresponsive to stimulation, they found that stimulation of certain frontal areas gives rise to motor responses. Because stimulation of the rear portion of the brain behind the central fissure failed to result in muscular responses, they concluded that motor processes are located in the frontal lobes just ahead of the central fissure. The usefulness of the electrical method has been greatly extended since its introduction by Fritsch and Hitzig; and with the invention of precise electronic equipment in recent years, this method has become the single most important technique for studying brain functions.

The work of Fritsch and Hitzig was confirmed and extended by David Ferrier (1843–1928), who utilized the methods of electrical stimulation and extirpation to discover localized sensory areas, particularly those for vision and audition in the occipital and temporal lobes, respectively.

SUMMARY AND CONCLUSIONS

The emergence of the scientific attitude during the Golden Age of Greece marked the beginning of psychology as one of the disciplines concerned with understanding human behavior. The heritage of the Greeks developed along two fundamental lines, the empirical and the rational. The empiricists, whose greatest representative was Aristotle, contributed the doctrine of elementalism or reductionism, which is the principle that the complex can best be understood through reducing it to its elements. In psychology this took the form of analyzing mind by reducing it to sensation and associations, the latter being derived from the former. The sensory-associationistic school reemerged in British philosophy and remained a dominant theme in modern experimental psychology.

The Greeks typified by Plato also developed a rival school of thought—that rationalism, not empiricism, is the road to true knowledge. The senses, they argued, give us only imperfect and unreliable copies of true reality, which can be discovered only by reflection, meditation, and deduction. The rationalistic method remained a fundamental method in medieval, Renaissance, and modern philosophy. It is both an adjunct to the experimental method in contemporary psychology where it evolved into the hypotheticodeductive method and a primary technique for discovering knowledge about the self among the subjective schools of psychology, such as the existentialist.

The emergence of physiology as an experimental science during the nineteenth century strongly influenced psychologists to turn their attention to searching for the neural mechanisms underlying behavior. In pursuit of this goal they had available the fundamental methods of extirpation and electrical stimulation as well as the clinical method that had been contributed by physiologists and neurologists. Pioneer work on the localization of function in the brain has remained a dominant theme in contemporary physiological psychology. The new experimental psychology of the mid–nineteenth century originated in the work of those early physiologists who broadened their horizons to explore psychological problems. It is to these scientists that we turn our attention in the following chapter.

The First Century of Experimental Psychology

3

PSYCHOLOGY COMES OF AGE

Four nineteenth-century scientists were intimately associated with the debut of psychology as an experimental science. They were Ernst Weber (1795–1878), Gustav Fechner (1801–1887), Hermann von Helmholtz (1821–1894), and Wilhelm Wundt (1832–1920). All were Germans and therefore were fully aware of the impressive developments that were taking place in European physiology in the middle decades of the nineteenth century. Indeed, each had considerable training in this discipline in the course of his professional education, and it was through research in physiology that each became interested in psychological problems. In addition to this common core of interest in physiology, each made a unique contribution to the development of psychology.

Weber, a physiologist, demonstrated the feasibility of applying experimental methods to the investigation of psychological processes. Fechner was a complex mixture of physicist, mathematician, and philosopher, who extended Weber's work and in doing so developed a number of fundamental experimental designs in psychology. Helmholtz, though primarily a physicist, was an all-around genius who, like Weber, had a passion for exact knowledge derived from experimentation. When his great intellect was brought to bear on sensory problems in optics and acoustics, the result was a significant advance in the understanding of the structure and functions of the eye and ear. Wundt's special talent was that of an organizer and systematizer. He brought together the various lines of research and theoretical speculation of his day in the first systematic textbook of psychology, published in 1873 to 1874, which, significantly, he entitled *Physiological Psychology*. Wundt also founded the first experimental laboratory of psychology in Leipzig in 1879.[1]

---

[1]William James had a small demonstration laboratory at Harvard as early as 1871, which he used as an adjunct to teaching, but Wundt's laboratory was the first of any significance. Wundt is credited with the "founding" partly because of his intent to establish a laboratory and partly because of the official administrative recognition accorded to the laboratory by the University of Leipzig.

Because of the critical and timely importance of these pioneers, we shall examine the contributions of each in some detail.

Weber

We may point to two specific contributions made by Weber to the embryonic science of psychology. First, as we have already pointed out, he applied the experimental methods of physiology into the investigation of psychological processes. This great step forward occurred in connection with his systematic investigation of the sense of touch and the kinesthetic sense. The details of his work need not concern us here, but it should be noted that these experiments marked a fundamental shift in the status of psychology. The new science had at last severed its ties with mental philosophy, and the court of last resort for the resolution of psychological issues was no longer philosophical debate but an appeal to empirical investigation. Weber thus allied psychology with the natural sciences and blazed the way for the *experimental* investigation of human behavior.

His second contribution was a discovery that ultimately led to the first truly quantitative law in psychology and indirectly to the development of the psychophysical methods which we shall take up in the following section. Weber's discovery developed out of an investigation of the muscle sense by means of weight-lifting experiments. He found that the just noticeable difference between two weights is a certain constant ratio (1:40) of the standard stimulus. Thus, a weight of 41 grams would be just noticeably different from a standard weight of 40 grams, and an 82-gram weight just perceptibly different from a standard weight of 80 grams. Weber extended his investigation of difference thresholds into the area of visual brightness discrimination and the two-point threshold on the surface of the skin, but he never formulated the results into a general law. However, his discoveries stimulated considerable interest in sensory processes among contemporary physiologists and psychologists. In fact, Weber's fame is primarily the result of Gustav Fechner's further development of his basic discoveries. In the following section we shall trace the evolution of Weber's concepts in his successor's work.

Fechner

Fechner repeated and extended Weber's careful work on sensory discriminations. In addition, he carried out a large number of experimental tests of what he called "Weber's Law," namely, that *the j.n.d., or just noticeable difference, between two stimulus magnitudes, is a certain constant ratio of the total magnitude.* In the symbolic language of mathematics the law reads, $\Delta R/R = K$, where ΔR is a stimulus increment, K a constant, and R the standard stimulus magnitude.

At the same time that he was formulating and testing Weber's law, Fechner was also puzzling over the age-old enigma of the relationship between mind and body. His interest in this problem stemmed partly from his unusual background and partly from an obsessive and somewhat mystical preoccupation with the problem of the relationship between the material and the immaterial. He began his academic career as a physician, but turned to physics and mathematics, accepting an appointment as a professor of physics at Leipzig. But along with his materialistic and scientific interests, he had a humanistic, philosophical bent, which he exercised by writing satires on the science of his day and by publishing serious philosophical works, many of which dealt with the place of mind in the material world. Indeed, for Fechner the *nature* of the relationship between the spiritual and the material was a consuming passion. One morning, following a long incubation of the problem, he had an insightful experience in which he found the long-sought answer. This was the simple and forthright solution that mind and body are identical. This view has since been known as Fechner's *identity hypothesis*.

Fechner attempted to establish the validity of his hypothesis through the mathematical manipulation of Weber's law. He reasoned that because we can measure stimuli directly, such as the physical intensity of sounds or of lights, *physical* measurement is possible. What was lacking was psychological measurement. Fechner reasoned further that *if it can be assumed that j.n.d.'s are equal* along the range of sensations measured by Weber's law, then j.n.d.'s can be used to measure sensation *indirectly* by a process of summation and scaling. After manipulating Weber's Law mathematically,[2] he arrived at the equation $S = K \log R$, where S = sensation, K = a constant, and R = stimulus intensity (*Reiz* is German for stimulus). Sensation is thus measured and—because an equation of equality can be written for sensation and physical stimuli—the identity hypothesis is proved!

Fechner's tour de force of measuring the seemingly unmeasurable stirred up a controversy that lasted for years. Most of the arguments centered on his assumptions about j.n.d.'s being equal and therefore logically additive.[3] However, Fechner's place in psychology does not rise or fall with the validity of his formula, but with his psychophysical methods, which became milestones in mental measurement, and with his direction of the new science into a large-scale study of sensory and perceptual processes. Since we are concerned in this chapter with the evolution of methodology, it is appropriate that these methods be discussed in detail.

The Method of Average Error

Because it is employed in virtually every type of psychological experiment, the most basic of Fechner's methods is the method of average error. It assumes that in a sense every measurement in psychology is an error for the simple reason that we can never measure the true value of anything. Our instruments and sense organs are subject to trial-to-trial variability, which prevents us from obtaining a single "true" measure of any quantity. Instead, we obtain a large number of approximate measures that are distributed on either side of a mean in the form of a normal probability curve. The mean of these measures represents the best single approximation that we can make to the true value. From this point of view, the mean is the average of the individual "errors," or measurements, and for this reason the method is aptly called

---

[2] The mathematical processes involved are complex. Consequently, we shall not attempt to go into them here. Those interested in the derivation of Fechner's formula may find it in Boring (1950, pp. 287–289).

[3] For an account of the controversy, see Boring (1950, pp. 289–295).

the "method of average error." The standard deviation of the measurements gives us an estimate of how reliable the obtained mean is.

Moreover, techniques are also available for calculating any constant errors or tendencies for the measurements to fall more on one side of the mean than on the other. This technique is especially useful in measuring reaction time, visual or auditory discriminations, extent of illusions, and the like. More generally, every time we calculate an average or mean we are employing the method of average error.

The Method of Limits

The second of Fechner's original methods, known as the method of limits, is a more specialized technique chiefly useful in the determination of sensory thresholds. For example, when we are testing the range of pitches a child can hear on the audiometer, we are using the method of limits. As we approach the upper limit, which is around 20,000 hertz (Hz) or cycles per second, the stimuli presented are higher and higher in frequency until they can no longer be heard. Similarly, on the lower end of the scale we present tones in a descending series until they are no longer heard. We have now established the upper and lower limits for auditory frequency. However, one determination is not sufficient to establish a threshold. Many ascending and descending series are run, and the threshold is taken as that point at which the subject can discriminate correctly 50 percent of the time. With slight modifications, the same method is also useful for the determination of difference thresholds.

The Method of Constant Stimuli

Fechner's method of constant stimuli, with the many variations worked out by subsequent investigators, is also broadly useful. It is applicable whenever we have a situation in which a response can be treated according to a dichotomy, such as *right* or *wrong, heavier* or *lighter, more* or *less*. For example, in determining the two-point threshold, we stimulate the skin by applying two points simultaneously, with the points sometimes a few millimeters apart and sometimes widely separated, perhaps 10 or 12 millimeters apart. The problem is to find the minimal separation that the subject reliably recognizes as "two." In such an experiment, five to seven *constant* settings are employed. These are presented in random order a large number of times; hence the name "constant method." When sufficient data have been collected, the stimulus separation is calculated for that point at which the subject correctly discriminates "twoness" 75 percent of the time. Several methods are available for performing the necessary calculations.[4] The 75 percent level is chosen because the subject could guess correctly 50 percent of the time. Therefore, the 75 percent level is actually halfway between chance and a perfect discrimination. There are many variations of the basic procedure outlined above, and these have been found useful in the wide range of measurement problems encountered in the determination of sensory thresholds and the measurement of aptitudes and attitudes.

---

[4]For an account of the various statistical procedures available, see Guilford (1936) or Woodworth and Schlosberg (1954).

The Method of Paired Comparisons

The method of paired comparisons grew out of Fechner's esthetic interests. Seeking a technique for expressing subjective, esthetic preferences in as quantitative and objective a manner as possible, Fechner developed the *method of choice*. In his first application of this rudimentary method, he prepared cardboard rectangles of various proportions, from squares to long, narrow oblongs. These were distributed haphazardly on a table, and his subjects were asked to select the most and least pleasing shapes among the stimuli presented. It is interesting to note that most choices fell in the middle of the range, around Aristotle's Golden Mean.

More sophisticated versions of Fechner's method involve detailed comparisons of each stimulus with every other; hence the method is now called the "method of comparisons." For example, if one wished to determine subjects' preferences for composers, the names of the latter could be presented on sheets so that all subjects could compare and decide preferentially between each composer and every other one on the list. These preferential choices could then be converted into a scale with the composers finally ranked in the order of preference.[5]

Although the method is a laborious one, often involving hundreds of individual comparisons, it has been widely used in research on color, taste, and odor preferences, and in ranking composers, scientists, and works of art, where subjective judgments or ratings are involved.

It is but a step from the method of paired comparisons to various types of scaling methods. Although Fechner did not develop rating scales, it seems appropriate to mention that the essential techniques are not dissimilar from those involved in the method of choice or paired comparisons. The importance of rating scales in modern psychology is evident from even a superficial survey of the area of social psychology, where such techniques are widely employed in attitude scaling, in public opinion polling, and in the assessment of personality traits and aptitudes in small groups.

The complete story of the psychophysical methods is long and involved. Many variations of the basic methods were developed by Fechner and others, and a definitive description of these variations may be found in Guilford (1954). It is only necessary to point out here that the methods have stood the test of time to become fundamental procedures in psychophysical measurements, mental testing, and attitude scaling to assure Fechner a permanent niche in the psychological hall of fame.

Helmholtz

Helmholtz was not a psychologist, and psychological problems were not his main interest. Nevertheless, he is important in the annals of psychology for measuring the rate of conduction of the nervous impulse and for his famous theories of color vision and hearing. His contributions to the psychology of vision and

---

[5]For an actual ranking of composers by the Philadelphia, Boston, Minneapolis, and New York Philharmonic orchestras, see Woodworth and Schlosberg (1954).

audition will be taken up in Chapter 5. Meanwhile, we may note that his research in sensory physiology and his measurement of the rate of the nervous impulse not only provided worthwhile knowledge of these processes for their own sake, but also lent impetus to the embryonic psychology of the day by demonstrating that the old problems of how we sense and how we know are amenable to experimental investigation.

In his writings on perception (a psychological process in which he became interested through his work in acoustics and optics) he allied himself with the empirical tradition by adopting the association theory of meaning, which held that sensations become meaningful only when associated with previous experiences. Thus, meaningful sensations are percepts derived from empirical sources. In this alliance he broke with German tradition, which held the opposite view of nativism, or the doctrine that the meaning of percepts may be inherent. For example, ideas of space and time were held to be inherent by the nativists, meaning that the capacity to perceive space and time is inborn and can function without having to be developed through experience.

In summary, then, this great physicist contributed an important body of knowledge to sensory psychology, helped strengthen the budding experimental approach to the investigation of psychological problems, and, finally, contributed indirectly to systematic psychology by espousing the empirical tradition and thus helping it to gain momentum on the European continent.

Wundt

It has already been said that Wundt was the founder of psychology as a formal academic discipline and that this event took place in 1879 in Leipzig, Germany, where he established the first experimental laboratory. Aside from this important achievement, Wundt's place in the evolution of psychology may be considered from two points of view. First, he may be evaluated in terms of the nature of his system—what he believed psychology to be and what its aims and methods are. On the other hand, his contribution may be considered from the point of view of his influence as a leader in the new scientific discipline that he founded. For this aspect of the man, the reader is referred to the histories (Boring, 1950; Murphy, 1949). Here we shall confine our analysis to Wundt the systematist.

Wundt believed that the subject matter of psychology is experience—immediate experience—to be studied by self-observation, or, more technically, by *introspection,* an objective, analytic observation of one's own conscious processes. The primary aim or problem of psychology is the analysis of conscious experience into its elements. Thus, Wundt associated himself with mental chemistry and the empirical-associationistic tradition. Once this systematic analysis into elements had been accomplished, the manner in which the elements are interrelated or compounded could be determined. Consequently, Wundt set a twofold task for himself and for psychology: first, the *analysis* of consciousness and, second, discovering the laws of *synthesis*.

A system such as Wundt's, which seeks to analyze the contents of consciousness, is known as *content psychology*—as opposed to *act psychologies,* which take as their unit of study mental acts or processes. This distinction will be developed further in Chapter 5.

It is unnecessary to go into a fuller summary of Wundt's system at this point, since we shall shortly consider it in considerable detail as it was developed and expounded by his pupil, Titchener. It would be well, however, to point out that Wundt's general definition of psychology and his analytic approach show the culmination of the various trends we have emphasized in the preceding chapter. First, the concept that mind is reducible to elements and that these elements cohere in some lawful way is obviously a heritage from the empirical-associationistic tradi-

Wilhelm Wundt, father of experimental psychology and founder of structuralism, was born in Neckarau, Baden, a village near Heidelberg, on August 16, 1832. He attended the universities of Tübigen and Heidelberg and received the M.D. degree from the latter in 1856. The following year he accepted an appointment as an instructor at Heidelberg, where he remained until 1874. There Wundt began his career as a physiologist, but soon became interested in the more complex mental processes and was convinced that the objective, experimental methods of the physiologist could be applied to research on consciousness. He began offering a course in psychology in 1867, entitled *Physiological Psychology,* and in

Photo courtesy of The Bettmann Archive.

1873–1874 published his most important work, *Outline of Physiological Psychology.*

Most of Wundt's professional career was spent at the University of Leipzig, where he founded the first laboratory of experimental psychology and became the leader of the new school of structuralism, which approached the study of consciousness by means of the special technique of introspection or objective self-observation. Wundt's most significant contributions were in the descriptive psychology of the sensory processes, although during the latter part of his career he became interested in social psychology and published a number of volumes in that area between 1900 and 1920. Among his most famous doctoral students were Edward Bradford Titchener (1867–1927) of Cornell University, who brought the psychology of structuralism to the United States, and James McKeen Cattell (1860–1944) of Columbia University, who became famous for his work in the psychology of individual differences. Wundt died on August 31, 1920, having lived to see psychology established as an independent science with laboratories in all major nations of the world.

tion. Second, the use of experimental observation and analysis for understanding mental phenomena is the culmination of the trend begun by Weber and Fechner utilizing physiological and physical methods in psychological investigations. Finally, Wundt's choice of introspection as the method of psychology places him in the category of those psychologists who favor highly objective techniques for the study of mental and behavioral processes.

One of the immediate reactions to the new laboratory was a migration to Leipzig of young students interested in this promising new approach to the study of the human mind. There Wundt became a leader of a school of psychologists whose common purpose was mental analysis by means of introspection, with the ultimate aim of discovering the laws of mind.

The term "school" as it is used in psychology refers to the groups of psychologists who associated themselves both geographically and systematically with the early leaders in the new science. For the most part, the psychologists who made up a school worked on common problems and shared a common systematic orientation. For these reasons it is proper to speak of a "Leipzig school" in the sense that Wundt and his associates at Leipzig shared the aims and methods of structuralism. Freud and his associates founded a school of psychoanalysis in Vienna in the first decade of the present century, which became the focal point of the psychoanalytic movement. Similarly, the psychologists who were attracted to the "Chicago school" of functionalism were typically in agreement in their aims and research programs.

As psychology began to spread, either as an offshoot of the Leipzig laboratory or by indigenous growth outside of Germany, other schools were formed, composed of psychologists with common systematic interests. For several decades, from 1900 to 1930 approximately, this was the most conspicuous characteristic of the new psychology, and it was through these schools that contemporary psychology took shape. Because of their central importance in the evolution of modern psychology, we shall examine five of these schools in some detail: structuralism, functionalism, behaviorism, Gestalt psychology, and psychoanalysis. We do not mean to imply that these are the only schools of psychology that developed in the early twentieth century. Rather, those we have selected for presentation have been, in our opinion, the most influential in shaping the course of contemporary psychology. Moreover, most of the others are variations or offshoots of those we are about to consider, and the interested reader can readily find detailed accounts of any variants in which he or she may be interested by consulting Boring (1950), Heidbreder (1933), Keller (1937), and Woodworth (1948).

THE SCHOOLS OF PSYCHOLOGY

Wundt's psychology was transplanted to the United States by his most outstanding student, Edward Bradford Titchener (1867–1927). In Titchener's hands the master's conception of psychology underwent its fullest development. Thus, for most purposes, a study of Titchener's psychology provides a reasonably accurate view of Wundt's system. This does not mean the two systems are identical. There were differences of opinion between the two men, but in a general way it is fair to say that Titchener's system is Wundtian in spirit, in method, and in the types of problems investigated.

Titchener's Structuralism

Our primary concern in this chapter is with Titchener's aims and methods. Other aspects of his psychology will be dealt with from time to time as we take up sensation, emotion, thinking, and other mental processes in chapters to follow. Therefore, what we hope to do here is make clear his definition of psychology and its place among the sciences.[6] Let us start, logically enough, with his definition of psychology.

Titchener begins by relating psychology to science in general. He espouses a monistic view, arguing that in the last analysis all sciences have the same subject matter: "some aspect or phase of the world of human experience." The biologist deals with living forms; the physicist studies nonliving forms. In the study of nonliving forms the physicist specializes in those facets of experience concerned with energy changes, electricity, magnetism, and the like. The chemist, on the other hand, investigates the elements and their compounds. In the realm of living forms the botanist specializes in the study of plants, while the zoologist concentrates on animals. What, then, of psychology? The subject matter of psychology is human experience from the special point of view of *experience as dependent on the experiencing person*. Thus, both the physicist and psychologist may be investigating light and sound; but the physicist is concerned with these phenomena from the viewpoint of the physical processes involved, whereas the psychologist is interested in how they are experienced by the observer.

Conscious experience, then, is the subject matter of psychology. But conscious experience is a private affair and can be observed only by the experiencing person; consequently, a special technique is needed for psychological observation. The method is *introspection,* which, of course, Titchener took over from Wundt.

Introspection, as Titchener employed the process, is a highly specialized form of self-observation in which the psychologist studies his or her own consciousness scientifically. The aim is to observe the *contents* of consciousness—not in the dreamy, informal manner of everyday reflection, but in a detached, objective, and systematic manner. Because of the difficulties inherent in a situation where the observed and the observer are, in a sense, one and the same, the introspectionists required considerable laboratory training in this special method of observation before their results could be considered valid. As we take up Titchener's system in detail, some of the special problems confronting the introspectionist will be brought out more fully.

Titchener next deals with the broad problem of the aim of psychology which,

---

[6]Our exposition of Titchener's psychology is based on his *Textbook of Psychology* (1910), first published in 1896.

he believes, is to answer the tripartite question of the "what," "how," and "why" of experience. The question of *what* is to be answered by systematic introspective analyses of the mental processes. The question of *how* is the problem of synthesis: How are mental processes interrelated or combined? In other words, when the various elements of consciousness have been discovered through introspective analyses, the next step is to find out how they are combined into compounds. And so Titchener's psychology, like Wundt's, was mental chemistry.

Titchener then considers the problem of *why* by first arguing that the answer is *not* to be sought in the mental processes themselves. One mental process, he points out, cannot be regarded as the cause of another. If, for example, one runs afoul of some painful or noxious stimulus, the consciousness of pain is not due to past consciousnesses but to present stimuli. This line of reasoning would seem to suggest that stimuli must be the cause of consciousness, but this, too, is a false conclusion. Stimuli belong to the physical world; pain, to the mental; and a science that must go outside its own boundaries for explanations is committing the error of accounting for its phenomena by invoking a *deus ex machina*.

Perhaps, Titchener suggests, we ought to look into the nervous system for the cause of consciousness. Is it not logical to assume that activities in the brain cause corresponding changes in consciousness? To this commonsensible question, Titchener answers with a resounding no! Brain is part of body; consequently, both are aspects of the same physical world. Consciousness *parallels* nervous processes in the brain, but one is not the cause of the other. Therefore Titchener embraces a dualistic position on the mind-body problem that takes the form of *psychophysical parallelism*. This seems to leave psychology bereft of those cause-effect relationships so dear to the heart of the scientist. But Titchener gets around the difficulty this way:

> Physical science, then, explains by assigning a cause; *mental science explains by reference to those nervous processes which correspond with the mental processes that are under observation.* We may bring these two modes of explanation together, if we define explanation itself as the statement of the proximate circumstances or conditions under which the described phenomenon occurs. Dew is formed under the condition of a difference of temperature between the air and the ground; ideas are formed under the condition of certain processes in the nervous system. Fundamentally, the object and the manner of explanation, in the two cases, are one and the same. (1910, p. 41; italics added)

To recapitulate Titchener's position up to this point, psychology is the study of consciousness by the method of introspection for the purpose of answering three questions about mental phenomena: What? How? Why? The overall program for psychology is essentially similar to that of the other natural sciences. When the scientist has decided what aspect of nature to study, he or she then proceeds to discover its elements, shows how these are compounded into more complex processes, and finally formulates the laws that govern the behavior of the phenomena under study.

Titchener then addresses himself to certain problems resulting from the special method of introspection. He admits that, upon first impression, introspection as a method smacks of subjectivity. How can there be an objective, "scientific" psychology if the very process under observation is also doing the observing? The answer, Titchener believes, is to be found partly in training and partly in the observer's attitude. The introspectionist needs considerable laboratory experience under supervision before qualifying as a psychologist. One must learn to take on an objective attitude while in the laboratory—to step outside oneself, so to speak, and to look back within. In addition, one must be on guard to avoid the "stimulus error" (an insidious trap for introspectionists), that is, the description of a stimulus object in terms of everyday language instead of a report on the conscious content to which the stimulus gives rise. For example, to see and report an apple as an apple is to fall victim to the stimulus error. To describe the hue, brightness, and spatial characteristics in one's consciousness when an apple or other object is under observation is valid introspection.

Another vexing problem arises when the psychologist is attempting to observe an emotional consciousness. In this case the calm, scientific attitude which is necessary for laboratory work destroys the very process under observation. Titchener readily admits the difficulty and suggests that in such instances introspection must become *retrospection*. To put it another way, the psychologist allows the emotional experience to go on uninterrupted by introspection and then describes his conscious memory of the experience when it is completed. Clearly, this is a second-best procedure which is subject to distortions of memory, but it is the only one possible in such instances.

The question also arises of how the psychologist can study the conscious processes of children, animals, and mentally disturbed individuals. Obviously, subjects such as these cannot be trained in introspection. In these and similar cases Titchener's answer is "introspection by analogy." After carefully observing the behavior of the subject, the psychologist must put himself or herself in the subject's place and try to interpret what the individual is experiencing. It might be noted parenthetically that in reading Titchener on this point, one gets the impression that he was aware that this method was roundabout and unsatisfactory. Such an impression is suggested by the amount of space he devotes to arguments in support of the validity of introspection by analogy. This weak spot became a prime target for attack by Watson, the behaviorist (see "The Behavioristic Revolt" below).

It is beyond the scope of this chapter to attempt any extended discussion of what Titchener and his associates discovered in their pursuit of introspective psychology. Their contributions were many and varied; some we shall meet in subsequent chapters on sensation, perception, and thinking. Here we shall be content with a brief summary of the findings in order to convey some notion of how structuralism worked in practice.

True to his aim, Titchener and his associates proceeded to analyze consciousness into its elements. These were found to be three in number: *sensations, images,* and *affective states*. Each of these is an element, with attributes such as quality, intensity, and duration. From these three building blocks all the complex and varied higher mental processes are derived. As this research was progressing, it became clear to Titchener that in spite of their differences, the several elements were nevertheless all related to a "common mental ancestor." In view of Titchener's intellectual heritage, it is not surprising that this ancestor appeared to be sensation—the basic "element" of mind in the empirical-associationistic tradition.

After devoting approximately half of his text to the sensory processes, Titchener takes up the affective states: attention, perception, memory, and thought. In each case the exposition is centered on the data derived from the introspective work of psychologists who associated themselves with Titchener's point of view. The discussions on memory and retention, for example, bear only faint resemblance to the treatment typical of a modern textbook in general psychology. There are no behavioristic reports of animal learning; there is nothing on conditioning; memory and retention are treated as manifestations of the mental image.

Generally speaking, Titchener's structuralism was the most consistent and tightly knit of all the early systems. In fact it has often been said that it remained too narrow because of Titchener's refusal to change with the times. American psychologists were not content with restricting psychology to the introspective analysis of consciousness. Consequently, structuralism weakened and finally collapsed. Structuralism as a movement, however, had brought science to psychology and established psychology as a science. This alone was a great contribution, and the fact that its method and scope proved too narrow to contain psychology cannot detract from its accomplishments.

Functionalism

Functionalism is the name given to a system of psychology promulgated by a number of prominent American psychologists whose primary interest was the study of mind as it functions in adapting the organism to its environment. The roots of this point of view extend back to the evolutionary biology of Charles Darwin (1809–1882) and the pragmatic philosophy of William James (1842–1910). When the functionalistic point of view came into psychology, it developed into a movement that took on the attributes of a school whose center was the psychology department at the University of Chicago. Here the school came under the leadership of John Dewey (1859–1952) and James Rowland Angell (1869–1949) in the early days of the 1900s and later, in the 1920s, under Harvey Carr (1873–1954), who was Angell's successor.

Functionalism, then, ranges over a long period from the mid-1850s to contemporary times. Indeed it can be said that, broadly speaking, American psychology today *is* functionalistic because of its emphasis on learning, intelligence, testing, perception, and other such "functional" processes. Moreover, functionalism, unlike structuralism, developed under the influence of a number of leaders with varied interests and backgrounds. It was partly this flexibility in leadership that kept the movement from ultimately becoming stultified and from suffering the same fate as structuralism. At the same time, and for the same reason, it is a less sharply defined system than structuralism. Because of this it is difficult and perhaps unfair to select any one psychologist's work as a definitive statement of functionalism, yet the risk must be run for the sake of presenting the system in a coherent form. Harvey A. Carr's 1925 exposition has been chosen, since it represents functionalism at its maturity and in its most definitive form. However, in order to provide a perspective for appreciating Carr's system, we shall first outline briefly the chief contributions of his predecessors, James, Dewey, and Angell.

William James' academic career in psychology at Harvard University spanned the years from 1872 to 1907. Something of the man's versatile intellect and personality is indicated by the fact that during this period he was in turn a physiologist,

John Dewey, philosopher, educator, and psychologist, was born in Burlington, Vermont, October 25, 1859. Dewey's interest in philosophy developed during his undergraduate career at the University of Vermont, and after a three-year period of secondary school teaching he entered Johns Hopkins University to continue his studies in that field. There an interest in psychology developed out of his doctoral work on the psychology of Immanuel Kant. This interest continued to strengthen at the University of Michigan, where he held his first academic appointment. It was at Michigan, where he taught psychology as well as philosophy, that he wrote the first functionalistically oriented textbook of psychology *(Psychology,*

Photo courtesy of The Bettmann Archive.

1886)*, which proved to be highly popular with undergraduate students. However, it was at the University of Chicago, where he held an appointment from 1894–1929, that he exerted a profound influence on James Rowland Angell, who subsequently developed functionalism as a formal school of psychology. There he also published his famous 1896 paper, "The Reflex Arc Concept in Psychology," in which he argued against elementalism in psychology and insisted that reflex and other behavior be treated as acts and functions that adapt the organism to its environment.

In keeping with his functional point of view in psychology, Dewey's philosophy—which saw social change as inevitable but capable of being directed for man's benefit—was based on an evolutionary point of view. He treated ideas as plans for action that help the individual solve problems of living and adjustment. In 1904 Dewey accepted an appointment at Teachers College, Columbia University, where he became world famous as an exponent of the pragmatic point of view in philosophy and for his advocacy of progressive education. He died in New York City on June 1, 1952.

psychologist, and philosopher. His outstanding contribution in psychology was his brilliant *Principles of Psychology,* published in 1890, in which he analyzed and criticized the structuralistic psychology originating in Germany. James made it clear that his was a *functional* psychology, whose aim was not to reduce mind to elements but to study consciousness as an ongoing process or stream. Mind, as it is revealed in habits, knowledge, and perception, is constantly engaged in active give-and-take relations with the environment. Mind, therefore, is useful or functional in adjustment; it is anything but a collection of static conscious states. Moreover, since mind is highly personal, it cannot be subjected to the objective and reductionistic analyses favored by structuralists without destroying this personal flavor.

James' position put him in fundamental opposition to the highly objectified German psychology of the day. As a result, he performed the service of clarifying issues that arose between structuralism and its opponents. In addition, his remarkable insights into human nature stirred up a great deal of interest in psychology and also left a heritage of hypotheses for the coming generation of experimental psychologists to test in their laboratories.

Dewey, who succeeded James as the dean of American philosophers, was also his spiritual successor in psychology. In fact, Dewey is credited with sparking functionalism as a definite movement in psychology. This occurred with the publication of an article in 1896 on the reflex-arc concept, in which he attacked psychological molecularism and reductionism. In his article Dewey argued that the behavioral act involved in a reflex response cannot be reduced to its sensorimotor elements and still remain a meaningful act. All that is left after such a dissection are abstractions of its sensory and motor phases existing solely in the minds of psychologists. He went on to argue that reflexes and other forms of behavior ought to be interpreted in terms of their significance for adaptation and not treated as artificial scientific constructs. In short, Dewey believed that the study of the *organism as a whole functioning in its environment* was the proper subject matter for psychology.

The torch of functionalism lighted by James and Dewey was passed on to James Rowland Angell at the University of Chicago. He molded the functionalistic movement into a working school, and, incidentally, made the psychology department at Chicago the most influential of his day. This scholarly heritage was taken over by Harvey A. Carr, Angell's successor as chairman of the psychology department and the new leader of functionalism. From the time that Dewey gave the "keynote address" in his 1896 article to Carr's administration during the 1920s and 1930s, functionalism had become a well-established and recognized school of psychology.

Carr and Functionalism

In his 1925 text, Carr defines psychology as the "study of mental activity." Mental activity, in turn, "is concerned with the acquisition, fixation, retention, organization, and evaluation of experiences, and their subsequent utilization in the guidance of conduct" (p. 1). Here is a functional point of view indeed! Not only is there heavy emphasis on learning (a highly functional process) in the wording of the definition, but Carr also specifically states that the functionalist is interested in how the mental processes are utilized in conduct. If this were not sufficiently functional, he points out in a subsequent paragraph that mind is concerned with "attaining a more effective adjustment to the world." Clearly, in functionalism we have an *is for* psychology as compared to Titchener's *is* psychology.

Carr then considers the various traditional problems confronting systematists, beginning with the mind-body problem. He admits that these two aspects of the individual must be taken into account in any analysis of behavior and that all mental activity is psychophysical in the sense that both mind and body are involved in any given act of adjustment. He feels, however, that any ultimate resolution of the problem is a task for philosophy rather than for psychology.

In discussing the problem of methodology, Carr recognizes the necessity for introspection (to get at the conscious side of mind) but gives more emphasis to objective observation. And in the research programs at Chicago, fewer and fewer problems were attacked by introspective techniques as time went on. The inevitable result was that objective methods became the favored techniques of the functionalists.

With regard to scope, Carr's psychology is much broader than Titchener's—at least as far as Titchener's program worked out in practice. Functional psychology, Carr believes, is closely allied with physiology, since both disciplines study the animal organism; but, in addition, psychology should feel free to call on sociology, neurology, education, anthropology, and related sciences for facts and methodological contributions that might add in any significant way to psychology. He also makes clear that, whenever possible, psychology in turn ought to contribute freely to other disciplines. In this way he opens the door to the possibility of an applied psychology.

Turning from aims and methods, Carr presents a survey of the nervous system and sense organs as a basis for understanding the higher mental processes. To this extent, at least, his exposition follows the traditional pattern of approaching the complex by way of the elementary. It is in the fourth chapter of his 1925 text, however, that Carr's functionalistic position is most clearly developed. In that chapter, entitled "Principles of Organic Behavior," Carr discusses the nature of an adaptive act. Such an act results from motivating conditions arising either in the individual as drives or in the environment as stimuli. The stimulation from such conditions persists until the individual responds in such a way as to achieve satisfaction. Consequently, behavior is adaptive in the sense that the individual's responses result in a better adjustment to the environment.

Carr goes on to deal with learning, which, as pointed out earlier, he considers a central problem in psychology and which he treats as a "perceptual-motor" process. When confronted with a problem for which it has no habitual or immediate solution, the organism engages in a persistent and varied attack on the situation. This problem-solving behavior is neither blind nor random, but utilizes previous experience and thus demonstrates that the learner perceives the relevant relationships in the elements making up the problem. When a solution is found, it is fixated and becomes a part of the organism's repertoire of responses.

The strongly functionalistic nature of Carr's psychology is revealed in two additional ways. First, he argues that adaptive acts involve two stages: a *preparatory stage* of attentive adjustment, making for more efficient perception by excluding irrelevant and distracting stimuli, and a *response stage,* which is the adaptive act itself. Therefore, attention in Carr's system is considered in terms of its functional utility in dealing with the environment. Second, his functionalistic bias is revealed by his interest in perception. Not only do the perceptual processes occupy a central position in the 1925 text from which we are drawing this summary of functionalism, but it is also significant that Carr wrote an advanced textbook on perception (1935). For Carr, perception is a basic process in adjustment, since how we perceive our environment and its challenges largely determines how we respond to it.

Surely a functionalistic psychology ought to emphasize those aspects of mind, such as learning, attention, perception, and intelligence, that are useful and aid us in adaptive behavior. In this respect Carr's psychology, along with the functional movement as a whole, lives up to expectation. In "classical" functionalism it is precisely these processes that received the major emphasis in both theory and research. Today a large segment of contemporary functionalists are pursuing research in human learning. The popularity of learning and mental testing as research areas among psychologists in the United States is ample testimony to the functionalistic flavor of American psychology. As a systematic point of view, functionalism was an overwhelming success, but largely because of this success it is no longer a distinct school of psychology. It was absorbed into mainstream psychology. No happier fate could await any psychological point of view.

The Behavioristic Revolt

While structuralism was at its zenith and during the two decades that functionalism was developing into a mature system, a revolution directed against both of these systems was brewing in the work of a young American psychologist, John B. Watson (1878–1958). Watson began his career in psychology as a graduate student at the University of Chicago during the formative years of the functionalistic movement. He became interested in animal research, founded an animal laboratory at the University of Chicago, and carried his interests with him to Johns Hopkins University, where he accepted an appointment in 1908.

Watson's strong bias in favor of animal psychology weaned him from the functionalism on which he had been nurtured and led him to embrace the position of a strict behaviorist. So completely was he converted to this new point of view, that he strongly opposed the analysis of consciousness by introspection as a suitable aim for a scientific psychology, and in its place emphasized the study of behavior by objective experimental procedures.

Watson's stand on these issues had all the earmarks of a revolt as opposed to mere disagreement on matters of principle. His youthful optimism and strong personality, coupled with a trenchant style of writing, admitted no compromise with existing systems of psychology, which, from his point of view, were totally unsatisfactory. His stand was formally published for the first time in 1913 as an article in the *Psychological Review* entitled, "Psychology as the Behaviorist Views It." In addition, he developed his systematic position in lectures at Columbia and Johns Hopkins, in various journals, and in several books. His two most important books are *Behavior: An Introduction to Comparative Psychology* (1914) and *Psychology from the Standpoint of a Behaviorist* (1919). A third, semipopular exposition of the behavioristic position was published in 1925 and was entitled, simply, *Behaviorism*. The following summary of Watson's systematic program is drawn primarily from the first two books mentioned.

In the introductory chapter in his comparative text (1914), Watson sounds the tocsin for the coming of a millennium in psychology. The state of psychology in 1914 he found "unsatisfactory" for several reasons. To begin with, a psychology whose method is introspection excludes, for all practical purposes, contributions from the animal laboratory. It is, Watson states, no answer to argue that data from comparative studies can be collected by analogous introspection. Such an alternative he dismisses as "absurd." Second, he believes that mentalistic concepts such as "mind," "consciousness," and "image" have no place in a *scientific, objective* science; they are a carry-over from the days of mental philosophy. Moreover, Watson points out that the introspective study of conscious processes such as sensations, affective states, and imagery had resulted in disagreement and confusion even in the stronghold of the inner camp of the structuralists. Indeed, Watson charges the structuralists with an inability to resolve such a fundamental problem as how many independent attributes are associated with the elements of consciousness—sensation, images, and affective states. Again, where introspectionists failed to obtain reliable results, the blame, Watson argues, was *mis*placed on the observer. He refuses to accept the validity of such excuses as "faulty training" or "poor introspection," which were offered by the structuralists to account for these difficulties. In reality, Watson asserts, the fault was with the *method*. If introspection were abolished in favor of objective experimental observation, such difficulties could not occur.

Watson makes it clear that he is no more satisfied with functionalism than with structuralism. The functionalists, too, employ terms that are "elusive," such as "emotion," "volition," and "process" and, of course, are guilty of using introspection—an already discredited method from Watson's frame of reference.

Turning to the constructive side, Watson states what he believes to be a proper definition of psychology. It is "the science of behavior," and behavioral acts are to be described objectively in "terms of stimulus and response, in terms of habit formation, habit integration, and the like" (1914, p. 9). Psychologists need never go back to such mentalistic concepts as consciousness, mind, imagery, and affective states.

The aim of behaviorism, as stated by Watson, is characteristically forthright and objective: *given the stimulus, to be able to predict the response, and given the response, to be able to predict the antecedent stimulus*. To take a simple example, every fundamental reflex in the body has a specific and appropriate stimulus. The knee jerk, elicited by tapping just below the patella with a small rubber hammer, is familiar to everyone. Now there is very little psychology involved in predicting kick from tap or tap from kick in an experiment on the knee jerk. Nevertheless, it illustrates in minuscule form the essence of the behavioristic program. More complex forms of behavior may involve a complex of stimuli rather than a single stimulus. Similarly, most responses studied by psychologists are far more complex than simple reflexes. Nevertheless, the principle is the same, and putting Watson's argument in a formula, psychology is the science of S-R, where S represents the stimulus and R the response.

The methods proposed by Watson (1919, p. 24) for the behaviorists' research programs are four in number:

1. observation, with and without instrumental control
2. the conditioned reflex method
3. the verbal report method
4. testing methods

Although Watson's methods are largely self-explanatory, items 2 and 3 require further comment. The conditioned response was taken over from the Russian physiologist, Pavlov. In a limited way, conditioning was already in use in psychology before the advent of behaviorism; however, Watson was largely responsible for its subsequent widespread usage in American psychological research. As we shall find in Chapters 7 and 8, conditioning has also played a prominent role in a great deal of subsequent theory construction (Hilgard & Bower, 1966). However, of all the psychologists who have sought the explanation of human learning in conditioning theory, Watson went to extremes in his enthusiasm:

> Give me a dozen healthy infants, well-formed, and my own specified world to bring them up in and I'll guarantee to take any one at random and train him to become any type of specialist I might select—doctor, lawyer, artist, merchant-chief and, yes, even beggarman and thief, regardless of his talents, penchants, tendencies, abilities, vocations, and race of his ancestors. (1930, p. 82)

This stand reveals not only Watson's extreme behaviorism but also his environmentalism, leaving as it does very little room for heredity as an explanatory concept in human behavior.

The verbal report method is also of special interest, since by admitting the validity of such reports, Watson was letting a kind of introspection in the back door after having thrown it out the front. But Watson looked upon the verbal report as an ''inexact'' method at best and a poor substitute for objective observation. The only reason given for allowing verbal reports in the laboratory is expediency. After all, it would be cumbersome and inefficient to go through an elaborate conditioning process in order to determine whether a human subject could discriminate between two stimuli. How much simpler to ask him or her. Furthermore, Watson promises to treat verbal reports purely as objective data in no way fundamentally different from any other response or reaction given by the subject. He also makes it clear that the verbal report is entirely different from introspection. In introspection the psychologist and the subject are one and the same. In the use of the verbal report method, the psychologist does not report on his or her own behavior or mental processes but utilizes subjects whose reports become data for the psychologist.

John Broadus Watson, founder of behaviorism, was born in Greenville, South Carolina, January 9, 1878. Following elementary and secondary schooling in Greenville, he entered Furnam University, where he was granted the master's degree in 1899. His doctoral work was carried out at the University of Chicago under the functionalist, James Rowland Angell. While at Chicago, Watson also came under the influence of John Dewey. He remained at Chicago until 1908 as an instructor doing research in the field of comparative psychology. Upon accepting an appointment at Johns Hopkins University in 1908, Watson entered upon the most important part of his career. Rejecting both functionalism and structuralism in a 1913

Photo courtesy of James B. Watson.

article, "Psychology as the Behaviorist Views It," he became the leader of the new school of behaviorism, which was destined to become a dominant point of view in the United States.

In 1914 his *Behavior: An Introduction to Comparative Psychology* was published, a book in which he advocated the study of animal behavior without recourse to mentalistic concepts. In 1919 his *Psychology from the Standpoint of a Behaviorist* showed how the objective, analytic methods of the animal laboratory could be applied to human subjects, particularly through the use of the conditioned response. One other book, *The Psychological Care of the Infant and Child* (1929), reflected Watson's deep interest in the use of infants and children as subjects for psychological investigation. As a result of a divorce scandal, he left the field of academic psychology in 1920 to become associated with advertising. He died in New York City on September 25, 1958.

Here, then, is the new psychology—a real *science,* free from mentalistic concepts and subjective methods. It is a psychology capable of ultimate reduction to the stimulus-response level and just as objective as chemistry or physics. In keeping with its new status as a natural science, it is forever free and independent of its philosophical ancestry.

Like all systematists before and since, Watson develops his behaviorism in line with his fundamental theses. Emotions and feelings—knotty problems for the introspectionist—he treats as behavior patterns or reactions, predominantly visceral and largely acquired through conditioning during childhood. Even thought, which might appear to be the last stronghold of the psychology of consciousness, is reduced to "laryngeal habits." In support of this conception he suggests observing a deaf-mute's fingers or attaching a suitable recording device to a normal person's larynx. In either subject, while "thinking" is taking place, muscle movements can be seen and recorded. This, for Watson, is thinking. While admitting that such experiments are not always successful, he believes failures can be eliminated by more delicate instruments that will detect faint, "implicit" forms of behavior and make them explicit. Assuming the validity of these arguments, man's complex thought system is reducible to laryngeal habits, which are no more mysterious than a rat's maze habits and acquired in essentially the same manner—through conditioning.

Finally, in this brief survey of the program of the behaviorists, it should be pointed out that Watson was favorably inclined toward applied psychology. One aspect of this broad field is concerned with the practical problem of handling children. Watson contributed a great deal of fundamental research in the area of child psychology, as well as in publishing a guide for parents on the psychological care of infants and children (1928). But in addition, Watson suggested that a behavioristic psychology had much to offer such professions as advertising, law, industry, and education. He reasoned that such professions would be ideal testing grounds for a psychology interested in discovering the principles involved in prediction and control of behavior. On this practical and hopeful note we shall leave behaviorism as a system. However, we shall meet with some of Watson's specific contributions throughout this volume. Meanwhile, it seems worthwhile to cast a backward glance by way of summary and interpretation.

Behaviorism, as Watson formulated it, represents the end point in the evolution of certain concepts and issues that we have been tracing in both this and the preceding chapter. We have seen how the dilemma of the relationship between mind and body returned again and again—always demanding but never reaching a satisfactory solution. Watson solved the problem by disposing of mind altogether. Moreover, with his deterministic, mechanistic, and strongly scientific attitude toward the study of human behavior, Watson was reflecting what Boring (1950) has called the *Zeitgeist,* or spirit of the times. The early twentieth century was a time for the ascendance of a mechanistic determinism not only in psychology but in science in general. The preceding century had witnessed incredible scientific successes in every branch of knowledge, and science either seemed to have found—or given enough time, would be able to find—the answer to everything.

In keeping with this ascendance of science, literature, art, and philosophy also turned to realistic, material themes. It was the beginning of an era in which idealism was giving way to realism. There are those who are convinced that Watson went too far. But most observers agree that his crusade for an objective behaviorism did American psychology a service *at that time* by shifting the emphasis from an overconcern with consciousness to the broader horizons of the behavioral studies. Finally, although Watson's ambitious program remained primarily a *program* and never realized all that he claimed for it, the behavioristic point of view has remained a strong force in contemporary psychology. We shall meet it again.

Gestalt Psychology[7]

To trace the development of the next school of psychology, we must return to the continent of Europe after our long excursion into developments in psychology in the United States. At about the time that Watson was closing in on his battle with both structuralism and functionalism in the United States, a new movement was

Max Wertheimer, founder of Gestalt psychology, was born April 15, 1880, in Prague, Czechoslovakia. After early studies in law and philosophy he turned to psychology, obtaining the Ph.D. degree at the University of Würzburg in 1904. He held academic appointments at the University of Frankfurt and the University of Berlin, and beginning in 1933, at the New School for Social Research in New York City. It was in 1910 that Wertheimer made his famous discovery that if two identical visual stimuli are presented successively a short distance apart with an appropriate time interval between them, they appear not as two objects, one following the other, but as a single moving object. He embarked on a research program

Photo courtesy of UPI.

relating this finding to perceptual phenomena using as subjects Wolfgang Köhler and Kurt Koffka. He became convinced that structuralism with its reductionistic point of view could not explain apparent movement as well as a number of other important perceptual phenomena that are only experienced as wholes or Gestalts.

His scientific papers on these findings launched the Gestalt school as a new movement opposed to both structuralism and behaviorism. In 1923 a key publication of Wertheimer's outlined the school's position on the fundamental laws of perception all subsumed under the general law of Prägnanz, or the tendency for perceived fields to be as good Gestalts as circumstances permit. Wertheimer's later work at the New School for Social Research was on the psychology of thinking, culminating in his well-known *Productive Thinking* (1945), in which he attacked the traditional view of associationism and rote learning as the foundations of the thought processes. He died in New Rochelle, New York, October 12, 1943.

---

[7]For Gestalt psychology there is no single textbook that serves as a standard reference, such as those we have drawn upon for definitive statements of the preceding schools. Our sources will be found in Boring (1950), Heidbreder (1933), F. S. Keller (1937), Koffka (1935), Köhler (1929), Murphy (1949), Max Wertheimer (1959), and Woodworth (1948).

getting under way in Germany. It began as a revolt against Wundtian structuralism; but once it gained momentum, it also took up arms against behaviorism. In essence, the new school was against reductionistic *analysis,* regardless of whether such analysis was structuralistic or behavioristic in origin.

This antianalytic school was Gestalt psychology, and its founder was Max Wertheimer (1880–1943). Closely associated with Wertheimer at that time were two other Germans, Wolfgang Köhler (1887–1967) and Kurt Koffka (1886–1941), who contributed a great deal to the new program—so much, in fact, that it has become conventional to think of all three as founders. The new movement had its inception as a result of Wertheimer's interest in the stroboscopic motion, an illusion of movement. This occurs when two lines such as

are exposed in rapid succession. The effect on the observer is not

but   followed by ———

or the apparent movement of the vertical line through an arc. A similar phenomenon occurs in moving pictures, for what is shown physically is a rapidly exposed series of still pictures with short blank intervals between them. The perceptual effect, however, is smooth movement—illusory, it is true, but just as "good" as real movement.

Here, Wertheimer believed, was a phenomenon for which structuralism had no adequate explanation. Introspection of the test figure ought to give two successive lines and nothing more. But, instead, the illusion of a single line in motion persists no matter how hard one tries to introspect the separate exposures. Here was a case where analysis failed—where, indeed, a fundamental Gestalt principle was strikingly illustrated, namely, *that the whole is different from the sum of its parts.* In fact, in the eyes of its discoverers, this relatively simple finding seemed to challenge the entire traditional empirical-associationistic-structuralistic psychology that had dominated the field for so many years.

The Gestalt psychologists were quick to seize upon other perceptual phenomena in support of their thesis that analysis often fails to explain experiences, and they found ample grist for their mill in the perceptual constancies. In object constancy, for example, the table remains a table in appearance in spite of wide variations in viewing conditions. Look at it edge-on from one corner; it forms an oblique rectangular image on the retina, but perceptually it remains a conventionally rectilinear table. Such object constancy is scarcely explicable in terms of structuralism, for if the elements of perception change, the perception ought to change with them. Similarly, in brightness and size constancy, the sensory elements may change radically under different viewing conditions, yet the percept keeps its quality of unique wholeness. Other examples abound in everyday experience. Transpose a tune into another key, and it is still the same tune even though the elements are all different. Dismantle a chair, and you no longer have a chair but a mere bundle of sticks.

Hence, the Gestalt psychologists could argue that experiences carry with them a quality of wholeness that cannot be found in the parts. For this reason, the German noun "Gestalt" is appropriate to characterize their system, since it denotes form, figure, or configuration and carries with it the connotation that reductional analysis destroys a figure, or "Gestalt." The Gestalt psychologists quickly extended their observations and theoretical interpretations to other areas: to learning, thinking, problem solving—in fact, to the whole of psychology.

As the new movement grew in strength, Wertheimer and his associates proposed nothing short of the complete overthrow of the traditional psychology represented by structuralism and also found themselves just as strongly opposed to behaviorism. Specifically, they deplored the "brick and mortar" psychology of Wundt—and were equally dissatisfied with the reductionism of the behaviorists. In either case, they argued, the psychologist is dealing only with artifacts and abstractions as the end products of analysis. It makes little difference whether the analysis is in terms of introspection, on the one hand, or in terms of the reduction of behavior to conditioned or natural reflexes, on the other. Perhaps the best summary of this fundamental aspect of Gestalt psychology is that it represents a *molar* as opposed to *molecular* point of view.

Equally objectionable to the Gestalt psychologists were attempts to seek the physiological foundations of behavior in a machinelike nervous system in which a point-for-point correspondence is assumed to exist between the environmental stimulus and sensory excitation in the cortex. This so-called machine view of the nervous system arose in connection with behavioristic explanations of learning that likened the brain to a telephone switchboard, where each new habit is represented by a neural connection between two cortical centers, just as a telephone operator establishes a connection by plugging in circuits. Experimental evidence opposed to this theory was to be found in Gestalt studies of transposability. For example, an animal can learn to discriminate in favor of the darker of two shades of gray, A and B, where A is light and B dark. If a new shade, C, which is darker than B, is introduced, and the animal then is tested for the ability to discriminate between B and C, it readily makes the discrimination in favor of the darker C—despite the fact that the animal had been previously responding to B as "darker."

Finally, on the negative side of the ledger, the Gestaltists took issue with the behaviorists' denial of the validity of introspection as a psychological method. This is not to say that the Gestalt school approved the kind of introspection employed by Wundt and Titchener—far from it. But the Gestaltists did favor the study of conscious experience in a phenomenological sense and frequently made use of critical demonstrations that appealed to direct experience for their validity.[8]

---

[8]Numerous examples of such demonstrations can be found in any Gestalt source book.

On the positive side, it has already been pointed out that the Gestalt psychologists utilized phenomenological analysis and favored the study of molar behavior. In addition, it should be noted that they took a "dynamic" or "field" view of the nervous system in place of the behavioristic machine view. Although they did not deny a correspondence between cortical processes and outside stimulation, they saw the relationship as "isomorphic" instead of the point-by-point correspondence implied by the S-R formula. The situation here would be similar to the way a road map corresponds to the countryside. The map differs in many respects from the actual landscape, but the essential correspondence is valid or the map would be useless as a guide. This problem will be dealt with more fully in Chapter 5, on perception. Meanwhile, we turn our attention from these methodological considerations in order to outline some of the more important findings in support of the principles we have been considering.

In the area of perception the Gestalt program provided many valuable and original contributions which at the same time lent support to the molar viewpoint. Specifically, we refer to the principles of organization of perceptual fields. Among these are the familiar principles of figure ground so fundamental in all perceptual experiences and the organizing factors of proximity, continuity, similarity, and closure. (See Figure 4-2 in Chapter 4.)

Although these principles of organization are most obvious in visual perception, they are equally important in other sensory fields and in the "higher" mental processes of learning and thinking. Indeed, among the classical experiments of the Gestalt school is Köhler's work (1927) on insight learning in apes (Woodworth & Schlosberg, 1954, p. 820). The ape's insightful solution of a box-and-banana problem[9] can be interpreted as "closure" of the gap in the animal's psychological field. Similarly, Wertheimer brought the Gestalt techniques to the field of education, where he demonstrated with considerable success that when the teacher arranged problems to organize the elements of classroom exercises into meaningful wholes, insight would occur. This he contrasted sharply with the usual educational practices of drill and rote learning. Moreover, he was able to demonstrate that once it had been grasped, the principle of a problem would carry over or transfer to other situations (Max Wertheimer, 1959).

Since these earlier, more or less classic experiments were carried out, Gestalt psychology made its influence felt in ever-widening circles. There were extensions of the Gestalt point of view into personality, child psychology, and motivation (especially by Lewin, 1935, 1936, 1938, 1946), and into social psychology (Asch, 1946, 1951, 1956; Krech & Crutchfield, 1948; Lewin, 1939a, 1939b, 1947, 1948). Meanwhile, research in the area of perceptual phenomena has continued to occupy the attention of the group (F. H. Allport, 1955, pp. 131–134), and the primary influence of the Gestalt school on contemporary psychology has been in the fields of perception and thinking, especially perception. Indeed, it is impossible today to find

---

[9]The problem confronting the animal is to reach a banana suspended from the ceiling by stacking boxes until the fruit can be reached.

a chapter on perception in any general or experimental textbook of psychology that does not show the influence of this school.

Psychoanalysis[10]

The last of the schools that we shall consider in this chapter is known as *psychoanalysis*. However, psychoanalysis was never a school or a systematic theory of psychology comparable to those we have been considering thus far. This is true largely because the psychoanalytic movement developed outside academic circles and never attempted to take a systematic position on all of the mental processes. For example, the psychoanalysts have shown little interest in sensation, attention, depth perception, learning, and a variety of other processes that have been the traditional areas of concern for other schools. The psychoanalysts neglected these academic fields primarily because their aim was the very practical one of providing therapeutic aid for neurotic patients. As a consequence, psychoanalysis *as a theory* is primarily centered on the etiology, development, and treatment of mental disorders. Psychoanalysis *as a therapy* is a nonexperimental clinical technique for treating patients suffering from disorders that are psychogenic in origin.

However, despite the restricted theoretical position of psychoanalysis with its nonexperimental and nonacademic background, modern psychology has been profoundly influenced by this school. Moreover, the social sciences, philosophy, ethics, and the arts have also felt the impact of psychoanalytic theory. In fact, of all the schools of psychology, psychoanalysis has captured the imagination of the general public to the extent that many laymen erroneously equate psychology with psychoanalysis.

This highly influential movement got under way in Vienna near the end of the last century under the leadership of Sigmund Freud (1856–1939). Freud began his career as a practicing physician who specialized in diseases of the nervous system. He became aware that many of his patients were in reality suffering from mental conflicts and neurotic states that were manifested as physical disorders or as complaints of extreme fatigue, "nervousness," insomnia, and the like.

At that time an honest recognition of this problem left the physician in a dilemma. Treating the patient's physical symptoms failed to get at the root of the problem, yet there was no real alternative. Clearly, what the patient needed was psychotherapy rather than physical therapy, but psychotherapy had not yet been developed as a recognized branch of clinical medicine. While Freud was puzzling over these difficulties, he learned that a French practitioner, Jean Martin Charcot (1825–1893), and a German, Joseph Breuer (1842–1925), had achieved considerable success with the hypnotic treatment of hysterics who were suffering from paralyses, anesthesias, and mental confusion—all caused by psychogenic factors. The therapeutic technique consisted of hypnotizing the patient and then encouraging

---

[10]For those interested in pursuing this system further, *A General Introduction to Psychoanalysis* (1920) and *New Introductory Lectures on Psychoanalysis* (1933) make an excellent introduction to the system and have the advantage of being written by Freud himself. For additional references, see Munroe (1955). Our account has been drawn from a number of primary and secondary sources.

Sigmund Freud, founder of psychoanalysis, was born in Freiberg, Moravia, on May 6, 1856, and died in London, England, on September 23, 1939. At the age of four his parents moved to Vienna, which became his home until he fled to England to escape the Nazis in 1938. Freud's academic training at the University of Vienna culminated in a degree in medicine with a specialization in neurology. His interest in mental disorders began in 1884 when he became associated with Joseph Breuer (1842–1925), a neurologist who had been utilizing hypnosis in the treatment of hysteric patients. Freud's keen interest in hypnotherapy led him to spend a year in Paris studying with Jean Charcot (1825–1893), a famous French

Photo courtesy of Sigmund Freud Copyrights Ltd.

neurologist. There he not only learned the technique of hypnosis but also became convinced that sexual malfunctions underlie hysteria and other neurotic disorders.

Returning to Vienna, Freud abandoned hypnotism in favor of free association and dream analysis and began to lay the groundwork for the theory and practice of psychoanalysis. During the early years three landmark publications, *The Interpretation of Dreams* (1900), *The Psychopathology of Everyday Life* (1904) (see Freud, 1938a), and *Three Essays on the Theory of Sexuality* (1905), established psychoanalysis as an internationally recognized movement and also developed the foundation for a dynamic psychology of personality and psychosexual development. During the latter phase of his career, Freud's views broadened to encompass the application of psychoanalytic theory to religion and social problems as reflected in such books as *Beyond the Pleasure Principle* (1920), *The Future of an Illusion* (1928), and *Civilization and Its Discontents* (1930). His collected works over the span of his professional career fill twenty-four volumes. Freud lived to see his views on infantile sexuality, the Oedipus complex, the division of the personality into the id, ego, and superego, and his emphasis on the importance of the unconscious in mental life profoundly influence every department of twentieth-century thought.

him or her to "talk out" his or her difficulties. This reliving of the troublesome experiences that appeared to be at the root of the symptoms frequently resulted in considerable improvement in the patient.

Freud studied the technique of hypnotherapy and for a time collaborated with Breuer in treating patients with this new clinical weapon. However, he discovered that some patients could not be hypnotized deeply enough to enable the therapist to take them back to the source of their emotional difficulties. Even more discouraging was the discovery that in many cases where the therapy had been initially successful and the patient's symptoms relieved, the illness subsequently broke out in another form with a different set of symptoms. Evidently the "cure" had been superficial—nothing more than a temporary alleviation of symptoms.

Freud eventually recognized that the real value in hypnotic treatments lay in the psychic analysis involved and had nothing to do with the hypnotic trance as such. The problem then became one of discovering a therapeutic technique that would render hypnosis unnecessary while at the same time making possible a deeper and more complete analysis of the patient's psyche. This end was achieved by having the patient relax on a couch and freely tell whatever came into his or her mind. This is the method of *free association*. The psychoanalyst listens to and observes the patient as unobtrusively as possible for emotional reactions, signs of distress, and resistance to the treatment. During such a session, the therapist will discuss with the patient interpretations of the material brought to light during the analytic hour.

Out of his clinical experience Freud developed a number of important concepts such as those that he used to describe the structure of personality—the ego, id, and superego—and those he employed in elaborating the various stages of psychosexual development—the oral, anal, and genital stages, the Oedipus complex, and so forth. These more technical aspects of Freudian theory will be considered in detail in Chapters 12 and 17.

In the course of his practice Freud also became convinced that dreams were of special significance for the new therapy, since, if properly analyzed, they reveal hidden wishes. Indeed, he considered the dream a main route into unconscious mental processes. For this reason, dream interpretation became an important part of both the therapeutic process and theory of psychoanalysis. Again, we shall have more to say about dream interpretation in Chapter 12.

When Freud published accounts of his revolutionary technique and the discoveries he was making in his clinical chambers, a number of young medical men were attracted to Vienna to become students of the new therapy. As might be expected, an association for the development of psychoanalysis was soon formed (1902). Most of the original leaders in the school became famous either by virtue of their efforts in behalf of Freud's theories or because they dissented from their leader's doctrines and promulgated psychotherapeutic systems of their own. Of those who broke away from the master, the most important were Alfred Adler (1870–1937), founder of individual psychology, and Carl Jung (1875–1961), founder of analytical psychology. Of the two, Jung remained much closer to Freud's original position in both theory and practice, whereas in most respects Adler's views came to be diametrically opposed to Freud's.[11]

To return to Freud, our main concern in this chapter is with his contribution to the methodology and aims of psychology. Clearly, both psychoanalytic aims and methods are highly specialized for clinical work and as a consequence are not

---

[11]For recent and exhaustive comparative treatments of the various schools of psychoanalysis, the reader is referred to Ellenberger (1970), Ford and Urban (1963), or Munroe (1955).

directly comparable to those of the academic schools. Perhaps the simplest and most valid generalization that can be offered is that neither Freud's methods nor his aims have appreciably influenced the evolution of *experimental* psychology. They created, it is true, a revolution in the treatment of mental disorders, but this occurred in psychiatry rather than in academic psychology. On the other hand, Freud's systematic theories did profoundly influence *academic* psychology in several ways.

To begin with, before the advent of psychoanalysis, academicians had devoted relatively little attention to the psychology of motivation, particularly unconscious motivation. The stimulation from Freud's writings did much to remedy this deficiency, since his system heavily emphasized this aspect of mental life. Freud did not, as some people think, "discover" the unconscious;[12] nor was he the first to struggle with the problems of human motivation. However, it was Freud who emphasized these processes and who recognized that, traditionally, the rational side had been overemphasized in accounting for human behavior. Perhaps, as some of his critics believe, Freud went too far in the opposite direction of explaining behavior almost entirely in terms of irrational processes. No final evaluation can be given at this time, since his hypotheses have proved difficult or impossible to test. They were formulated on the basis of clinical practice from a highly selected sample of the population (neurotics) and are frequently cast in such a form as to make experimental verification impossible.

Freud is also indirectly responsible for a great deal of the contemporary interest in child psychology and child development. His conclusions that neurotic disturbances originate in early childhood have made virtually everyone who has anything to do with the care or training of children extremely child-centered. Before Freud's influence was so widely felt, the child was thought of as a miniature adult who had to be indoctrinated and trained according to adult standards. Today, interest centers more on the child's own nature, needs, and potentialities, and in discovering how these may be developed at the least cost to his or her individualism and with the least risk of doing psychological harm.

Freud and his followers are also largely held responsible for the radical change that has taken place in sexual mores since the end of the Victorian era. The change, needless to say, has been in the direction of increased freedom in sexual behavior. To some extent Freudian psychology is used as a rationalization instead of a true reason for the new sexual ethic. As has been true of other scientific theories as they percolate down to the grass roots, Freudian psychoanalysis has become greatly oversimplified in the public mind. Just as the whole of Darwinian evolution was reduced to the popular catch phrase, "Man is descended from apes," so Freud's position on the sexual basis of the neuroses is oversimplified, "It is psychologically harmful to repress sex."

As we shall see in Chapter 12, Freud actually considered sexual repression necessary if civilization and culture were to survive. But rightly or wrongly, the notion of sexual freedom is attributed to Freud, and the end result has been a general

---

[12]For a history of the unconscious before Freud, see Ellenberger (1970).

loosening of sexual restraint in literature, art, the media of entertainment, and behavior in general.

Finally, there can be little doubt that psychoanalysis has played an important part in creating the strong interest exhibited by a large number of psychologists in the relatively new field of clinical psychology. This branch of psychology has grown rapidly in recent years, primarily as a result of the impetus provided by World War II. Thousands of soldiers returning from battle zones were suffering from combat fatigue or more serious mental disturbances. Because of the shortage of psychiatrists, it was necessary to train hundreds of psychologists to help provide skilled therapists for work in government hospitals. Moreover, the keener awareness on the part of the general public of the desirability of obtaining psychological assistance for adjustment problems has resulted in a great increase in counseling agencies, both public and private, whose personnel, in part, are clinical psychologists.

The clinical psychologist is rarely a psychoanalyst and seldom is committed exclusively to Freudian theory. His or her academic training is typically grounded in experimental psychology, with specialization in psychometrics, abnormal psychology, and psychotherapy. We do not mean to imply any indoctrination *against* Freudian theory but, rather, that the clinical psychologist is imbued with an eclectic point of view that recognizes the worth of various approaches and whose guiding principle is to test the value of any clinical principle or method by experimental techniques whenever feasible.

To summarize, we have taken the position that Freudian free association, dream analysis, and psychoanalytic theory and technique in general have largely developed outside the scope of traditional academic and systematic psychology. Psychoanalytic methodology is specialized and thus far appears to be irrelevant to experimental psychology. On the other hand, Freud's theories of human motivation and psychogenic development have profoundly influenced academic psychology and, in addition, have generated a great deal of research, debate, and interest in the areas of personality and adjustment.

THE SECOND HALF-CENTURY

The Collapse of the Schools

The heyday of the schools passed with the end of the third decade of the twentieth century. The reason was simple: Psychology had outgrown schools. With the great increase in research results pouring into the general fund of knowledge from all sides, it became increasingly difficult not to recognize that *all schools* and systematic positions were making valuable contributions. Moreover, it became virtually impossible for any one psychologist to attempt to encompass the entire science in a single comprehensive system. The inevitable result was specialization, which, in turn, led to the development of miniature systems, theories, and models.

Because miniature systems, theories, and models occupy a central position in contemporary psychology, we shall discuss and compare each of these conceptual tools for the organization of factual and theoretical material before outlining recent trends in systematic psychology. In this way we shall be in a better position to illustrate how the older, more programmatic systems have been replaced by miniature systems, complex theories, and models.

Miniature Systems

A miniature system attempts to provide a framework for a particular area within the broad field of psychology, such as learning, motivation, or perception. These miniature systems differ from the older global systems that were associated with the schools of psychology in being restricted to a single behavioral process or more often to some aspects of a behavioral process. For example, a miniature system that attempts to organize the factual and theoretical information in the field of learning concerns itself only with learning or with a particular type of learning, such as verbal learning, conditioning, or maze learning. Similarly, a miniature system in personality is likely to be organized around factual information and theory that represent a particular approach to personality, perhaps through factor analysis, traits, or constitutional types.

The miniature system begins with a definition of the process under consideration, states the postulates it is undertaking to verify, specifies the nature of its data and the units of description and measurement to be employed, the finally, organizes the data around the postulated theoretical framework. The essential steps in developing a miniature system are the same as those employed in developing a global system. The difference is one of range or scope. The global systems associated with the schools attempted to organize the field as a whole; whereas, as has been pointed out, the miniature system deals only with a single behavioral process. It might also be noted that the originators of miniature systems are specialists in their areas; consequently, the systems that they construct are typically formulated around large bodies of empirical data from their own laboratories.

Theories

A theory is an integrated set of propositions that serves as an explanation for a class of phenomena. In general, theories are introduced into a science only after a class of phenomena has already revealed a systematic set of uniformities. There remain, however, areas of conjecture—of incomplete knowledge of underlying entities or processes. Propositions are formulated to fill in these gaps and to afford a better understanding of the observed phenomena. Theories, therefore, are based on limited empirical evidence, and so in their initial stages are constructed on a foundation of inductive reasoning. Uniformities are observed in nature, but certain aspects are poorly understood or cannot be related to known facts. Using deductive reasoning, the scientist formulates propositions or statements that will coherently and systematically relate all observed phenomena. Theoretical constructs require careful definition, preferably in terms of already established facts or entities if they are to be clear, precise, scientifically useful, and, ultimately, testable or verifiable.

The popular, somewhat derogatory, connotation of "theoretical" as "impractical" or "useless" is not shared by scientists. Theories not only serve to fill in areas of uncertainty; they also provide propositions for testing that may subsequently, if verified, become new scientific laws. In the history of science many important hypotheses were developed directly from theories. For example, cells sensitive to red, green, and blue light were found in the human eye after having been predicted a century earlier by Helmholtz. The planet Pluto was discovered in 1930 after years of search carried out on the basis of theoretical calculations by Percival Lowell and observers at the Flagstaff Observatory. Similarly, scientists from the time of Mendel and Morgan postulated that certain biological entities must underlie the transmission of observed genetic characteristics. For many decades, these were called genes and the classic laws of Mendelian inheritance were developed on the basis of their assumed behavior. Research in recent decades has shown that genes, in fact, are DNA and RNA molecules that are responsible for the genetic code and its transmission from generation to generation. Many hypotheses, experimental tests, alternative theories, and models had to be formulated, worked through, and either discarded or modified before our knowledge of how the eye sees color or how genetic characteristics are transmitted reached its present stage of development.

Models

The term *model* is employed in two ways in psychology. First, a model may be a mechanical copy of a physiological or anatomical entity designed in a way to show how the various parts function and relate to the whole. For example, models of the neuron, eye, ear, and brain have been developed in various degrees of complexity as aids to our understanding of how these organs work. Second, models are sometimes a particular subclass of theory. Used in this way, a model, in contrast to a theory, is purely abstract and makes no pretense of being a copy of nature. For example, a statistical model of learning utilizes abstract mathematical symbols that represent the learning process but do not pretend to be an exact representation of that process. The model is chosen in such a manner as to stimulate research and to provide a better understanding of the learning process. It must be emphasized, however, that the model does not attempt to explain the processes underlying learning, but only to represent them. Theories, on the other hand, do strive to explain psychological processes and so may be said to have truth value.

In summary, the early psychologists favored broad programmatic systems of psychology. These were useful in defining aims and methods and in initiating research programs. As psychologists became more sophisticated in their research during the second half-century of experimental psychology, the older programmatic systems gave way to more limited theories and to models that were closely related to ongoing research. We may expect that as psychology becomes even more mature and more sophisticated, psychologists will make increasing use of complex theoretical formulations and models, just as when physics and chemistry matured they became, in a sense, more theoretical and less empirical.

RECENT TRENDS: THE SECOND HALF-CENTURY

In subsequent chapters in this book many examples of miniature systems, theories, and models will be presented. However, to lend perspective to both our past treatment of the traditional schools and our subsequent discussion of the evolution of contemporary concepts and limited systems and theories, we shall briefly summarize the main trends in systematic theory of the second half-century. These will be outlined under eleven headings: (1) sensation; (2) perception; (3) developmental psychology; (4) learning; (5) thinking; (6) motivation; (7) feeling and emotion; (8) physiological theories of behavior; (9) intelligence and quantitative theories; (10) personality; and (11) social psychology.

Sensation

During the first half-century of experimental psychology the descriptive analysis of the sensory consciousness dominated the field. This emphasis reflected the preeminence of the structuralistic influence in research on sensory processes. However, developments in physiology provided strong impetus for research on the underlying neural mechanisms of sensation, and this influence eventually proved to be the most significant. From the beginning, theorists had predicted that for each sensory quality a specialized neural system would someday be discovered, but not until the development of high-fidelity stimulation and recording equipment was the eventual realization of this goal made possible.

Through use of such electronic equipment, enormous progress has been made during the second half-century of experimental psychology in our understanding of neural processes in the major sense organs, particularly the eye and the ear. However, much remains to be done. We are still lacking precise knowledge of the neurology of olfaction and the cutaneous senses. Our knowledge of how touch, temperature, and pain are mediated remains incomplete in the case of touch and fragmentary in the case of pain and temperature. Nevertheless, the great advances made in sensory physiology since World War II contribute an exciting and significant chapter in the evolution of experimental psychology.

Perception

In perceptual research and theorizing during the first half-century of experimental psychology, emphasis was on S factors. By S factors we mean those stimulus conditions that are important in visual depth perception, in attention, and in auditory and cutaneous localization. We might also include under this category, research in psychophysics, since many of the problems brought under investigation by psychophysicists were perceptual in nature, involving an S-R orientation, while ignoring personality and motivational variables in the subject.

Shortly after World War II a strong movement developed in perceptual psychology, known as the "New Look," that emphasized the importance of O

factors. The role of learning, motivational, emotional, and personality factors as determinants of perception was thoroughly explored. The *S-R* orientation of the traditional psychophysicists became an *S-O-R* orientation, in which *O* factors were considered at least as important as *S* factors as determiners of the dependent variable.

A second major trend during the second half-century of experimental psychology has been an attempt to relate perceptual experience to underlying cortical processes in the brain. Early in the development of their program the Gestalt psychologists theorized that brain fields and perceptual fields mirror each other—not literally, of course, but in parallel patterns, similar to the way a map mirrors the earth's terrain. Gestalt research programs in part confirmed this assumption.

Independently of the Gestalt group, a Canadian psychologist, Donald Hebb, formulated a perceptual theory in 1949 that took as its point of departure the relationship between perceived experience and underlying cortical fields, emphasizing the role of learning in the establishment of cortical connections that mediate new experiences. His postulates, gave impetus to a large body of research designed to test various aspects of the theory.

The most recent trend in perceptual psychology was stimulated in the 1950s and 1960s by interest in the field of information processing by means of high-speed electronic computers. Many psychologists believe that information processing can be used as a model of the perceptual processes to aid in understanding the problems of attention, apprehension of information, recognition, search and retrieval of stored experiences, and related processes that have their counterparts in the machine processing of coded information.

Developmental Psychology

The traditional view of the child as a miniature adult to be trained according to a predetermined pattern dominated psychology, education, and the family from the time of Plato to the rise of the behavioristic school under Watson, who believed that through learning any infant could be molded into any kind of adult regardless of his or her hereditary potentialities or personal wishes. Something of the same philosophy has remained a theme in behavioristic programs advocated by B. F. Skinner, whose well-known utopian designs for society are built around the principles of operant conditioning.

The impact of Freudian psychoanalysis had a profound influence on the direction of developmental psychology. The child was no longer looked at as a miniature adult by most psychologists but as an individual with his or her own needs, potentials, and problems. The overall effect of this change was (1) a more permissive attitude on the part of parents, pediatricians and teachers and (2) a massive research program designed to determine the intellectual capacities, emotional, and motivational needs of the child. This line of research has had an enormous and somewhat controversial impact on child rearing practices and education in the United States.

While these dynamically oriented programs were in progress, experimental psychologists specializing in development turned to the child as a subject of basic research, particularly in the areas of perceptual and intellectual processes. We shall consider these findings in detail in Chapters 7 and 15.

Learning

One trend in the psychology of learning that has remained strong during the past century is associationism. Originating with the Greeks, it reemerged in British empirical philosophy and achieved experimental status in the work of Hermann Ebbinghaus (1850–1909) during the closing decades of the nineteenth century. For the next 50 years an enormous amount of research was directed toward exploring variables that are important in the acquisition, retention, and reproduction of verbal material. This effort continues among contemporary learning theorists, although the extent and intensity of the effort has diminished in recent years.

Beginning with the work of the Gestalt school during the first three decades of the twentieth century, a contrary view of learning arose, which emphasized more cognitive, insightful processes in learning and thinking. The Gestalt view never became a dominant one, but it has continued to offer a strong challenge for traditional associationism.

A second major trend in the psychology of learning has been the formulation of comprehensive theories known as miniature systems. These largely evolved around research in the animal laboratory, where psychologists believe that through highly controlled conditions they can more easily discover the fundamental nature of learning in less complex organisms. These programs, most of which reached their zeniths in the 1940s and 1950s, were primarily concerned with the way in which rewarded or reinforced trials are related to the relatively permanent change in the organism that we call learning. Although one of these programs, the operant analysis of behavior under B. F. Skinner of Harvard, continues to be a major contributor to the area of learning, the construction and testing of miniature systems is no longer a dominant area in psychology.

Thinking

The early experimental psychology of thinking was oriented around the descriptive psychology of the thought processes, as reflected in the work emanating from the structuralists' program. In their view the basis of thinking was mental imagery. Meaning was mediated by associations. But as the Gestalt school emerged, a new viewpoint emphasizing understanding and insight along with the immediate meaningfulness of some stimulus patterns offered an alternative account of thinking that was widely accepted by many psychologists. The basic assumptions of these rival schools—one emphasizing learning and association, the other a more holistic and phenomenological approach—still find their share of adherents.

In the past two decades, however, this traditional conflict of viewpoints has moved out of the foreground of research in thinking as a strong interest in language, and its relationship to the thought processes has captured the attention of psychologists. This new field of psycholinguistics, as it is known, had emphasized the search for deep, underlying structures of language that make possible its orderly development in the child regardless of his or her place of origin.

Motivation

Motivational processes were not a focus of research and theorizing among the leaders of the early academic schools. The psychology of motivation had to await several developments before taking its place as a major division of the field. One of these was the advent of psychoanalysis, which placed heavy emphasis on drives and motives as the causative factors in behavior. The second was studies made by social anthropologists that stressed the relativism of much human motivation. These scientists, while agreeing on the communality of the basic animal drives of hunger, thirst, and sex, emphasized the importance of learning and cultural factors in more characteristically human motives, such as security, the need for achievement, and gregariousness. The third factor that generated strong interest in motivation was the development of miniature systems of learning. Because one of the basic issues in learning has been the role of reward or reinforcement, drive became a central concept in most of these systems.

With the development of high-fidelity stimulation and amplification equipment in the past several decades, a rapid expansion of studies of the physiological motives—particularly of hunger, thirst, and sex—has taken place. An impressive body of research has revealed many of the basic neural mechanisms of these drives. We shall consider these exciting developments in detail in Chapter 12.

Feeling and Emotion

As was true of sensation and thinking, the early psychology of feeling and emotion concentrated on introspective analyses. The pitfalls of this approach when dealing with subjective processes such as feeling and emotion became a major source of controversy among the leaders of the early schools, and little real progress was made. However, the same advances in the techniques of neural stimulation and recording that brought about revolutionary developments in sensation have also made possible significant advances in our understanding of the emotions during the past half-century. Many important centers of emotional behavior have been identified through the use of implanted electrodes in the subcortical centers of the brain. We shall examine these discoveries in detail in Chapter 12.

Physiological Theories of Behavior

Beginning with the stimulation provided by nineteenth-century physiology, this branch of psychology has enjoyed a steady and impressive growth throughout the past century. In the area of sensory psychology, motivation, emotion, and the neural basis of learning and intelligence, progress in research has been spectacular.

The impressive results in this area include significant advances in our knowledge of the neural mechanisms of the eye, ear, and other sense organs, the motor processes, motivation and emotion, learning and intelligence. In these giant steps forward in understanding the basis for human behavior, we once again are provided with evidence of the importance of technical discoveries that make such progress possible in psychology, just as the telescope and space rocket were responsible for revolutionary periods of progress in astronomy.

Intelligence and Quantitative Psychology

The intelligence testing movement, which gained so much momentum from the mass testing programs of World War I and from the introduction of the Binet test into the United States in 1916, inevitably gave rise to the question: What do intelligence tests measure? Indeed, it seemed possible that much could be learned about the nature of intelligence from a searching analysis of the tests themselves. Some years later when personality tests came into wide use, the same type of question was asked in connection with these tests: can analysis of the tests reveal anything about personality?

As early as 1914, Charles Spearman (1863–1945), a British psychologist, began to attack the problem of the nature of intelligence with correlational techniques. If a large number of different intellectual tasks are given to a group and the scores on the various tasks are intercorrelated, then high correlations between tasks can be interpreted to mean that the successful completion of such tasks depends on the presence of a common intellectual factor. Spearman found moderately high correlations around $+0.70$ among *all* cognitive tests, and on the basis of these findings he formulated his G and s theory of intelligence, in which G stands for a general intellectual factor common to all tasks and s represents a specific factor required for any given task. Since s factors are independent or uncorrelated, each task requires its special s, or specific ability; consequently, there is one G but there are many s's.

From this beginning, interest in the quantitative approach to the understanding of aptitudes and personality increased rapidly. Newer and better mathematical tools were developed to analyze both intelligence and personality tests. In the United States, L. L. Thurstone, in the area of intelligence, and R. B. Cattell, in the area of personality, have been leaders in the development of factor analytic theories.

Model making on a grand scale is relatively new in psychology, yet this type of research stems from a long past. As early as 1885 Ebbinghaus began a program of systematic research in memory which led to his mathematical formula $R = 100K/[(\log t)^c + K]$—where R = percent retained, t = time, and c and K are constants—to account for his research findings in the retention of nonsense syllables. In a broad sense this formula is a model, for it attempts to provide a generalized working construct for the prediction of the course of memory over time.

From these early beginnings there have been rapid developments in model making, partly because of advances in electronics and partly as a result of the increase in data coming from psychological laboratories that serve as the foundation of such models. As a result, we have a number of recent mathematical models in learning theory.

Information theory is not a theory but an interdisciplinary area of research that draws upon mathematics, electronics engineering, psychophysics, and perceptual psychology for the solution of problems that involve the measurement, transmission, detection, and reception of messages or communications. Since World War II, scientists have been increasingly concerned with the problems involved in telemetry, data processing, encoding, decoding, and transmitting signals and messages. In our modern world machines—automatons—are doing human tasks. The machine, like the human perceiver, must selectively receive signals from its environment, transmit those signals to a central processing station, and, depending on the "decision" arrived at in that station, carry out some action affecting the environment.

Many broad analogies are possible between the human "machine" and electronic receivers and computers and the processes in which they engage. However, if information theory had not gone beyond drawing analogies, it would have remained no more significant for psychology than any other model. Information theory becomes of special interest to the psychologist when he or she is called upon to help the engineer design machines to perform human functions or to make them more efficient. To do this the psychologist must understand those functions. His or her knowledge of the sense organs and central nervous processes must be approached from new perspectives, and in the process his or her understanding is broadened and deepened. In recent years psychologists in the fields of learning, perception, psychophysics, and social psychology have shown considerable interest in information theory and have made significant contributions to its empirical and theoretical literature. In Chapter 15 we shall review some of these developments in more detail.

Personality Theory

As we pointed out earlier in this chapter, the development of personality theory was given great impetus by Freud. The past half-century has been characterized by a rapid proliferation of theories; some of these are offshoots of Freudian theory, whereas others have evolved within academic circles. Generally speaking, deviations and modifications of psychoanalytic theory have taken a socially oriented point of view as opposed to the original biological orientation of Freud. In other words, the post-Freudian theories have tended to minimize the importance of "instinct" or drives as important factors in psychogenic development while maximizing the importance of interpersonal relationships.

Among the academically nurtured personality theories there are widely divergent viewpoints that defy any simple classification. There are representatives of Gestalt or field theory, constitutional or body-type theories, factoral theories, learning theories, an eclectic theory, and several personalistic or individual-centered theories. In the past several decades behaviorists under the leadership of B. F. Skinner have applied the principles of operant conditioning to personality theory and psychotherapy. At the same time we have witnessed the rapid growth of a humanistically oriented theory of personality development that is in more or less direct opposition to behavioristic theory. Personality, in a sense, is a way of looking at the individual as a whole; and because molar points of view invite many possible approaches and interpretations, psychologists with different orientations have investigated personality along different lines. As a consequence of such diversity we have the complex picture just described.

Social Psychology

Social psychology began as social philosophy in the writings of the classical philosophers. Their analyses of human nature evolved out of attempts to formulate systems of ethics and programs for the improvement of social institutions. There was, of course, no attempt to verify assumptions about human nature by means of empirical measurements. The empirical movement in the social sciences began with the work of the French sociologists Gabriel Tarde (1843–1904) and Émile Durkheim (1858–1917), who initiated pioneer studies of social institutions.

However, early twentieth-century social psychology was dominated by instinct theories of group behavior, and it was not until the late 1920s and the 1930s that empirical studies of group norms, attitudes, and conformity got under way. From that point on, social psychology has enjoyed a rapid growth along with the rest of the field. In addition to research on the processes just mentioned, studies of decision making, attitudes, attitude change, cultural factors in psycholinguistics, social norms, social perception, impression formation, and altruistic behavior have received a major share of attention. During the past two decades a strong trend in social psychology has been concern with the special problems of applying the experimental method to the study of social behavior.

Sensation in Systematic Psychology

4

The evolution of method and theory in sensory psychology extends over the entire period of recorded history. In Chapter 2 we found that the empiricists, from Aristotle to Mill, sought in the analysis of sensory processes the key that would explain the complexities of mind. The basic premise of this school of philosophy was that mind was compounded of simple ideas originally derived from sense experience. For this reason, sensory psychology found favor among the empiricists and their descendants, the objective psychologists of the early scientific period.

We also noted that the empirical tradition allied itself with associationism, for to argue that mind was no more than an unrelated conglomeration of simple ideas was logically indefensible as well as a violation of common sense. Therefore, the principles of association were invoked by the empiricists to account for the complexities of mind. Consequently, in relating sensation to the empirical-associationistic tradition, we may consider all three to be inexorably interwoven, each lending meaning and support to the others. Considered from this point of view, empiricism demands sensationism, and both logically lead to associationism. This tripartite alliance is the philosophical antecedent of modern sensory psychology, an area that for many years was the dominant theoretical and research area within the field.

In contemporary research and theorizing the study of sensation is no longer preeminent, as it was throughout the prescientific period and during the heyday of structuralism. However, even as the field of sensation has become more restricted in recent years, it has enjoyed at the same time a rebirth of interest on the part of physiological psychologists. This is a result of the tremendous advances that have taken place in the design of electronic equipment over the past several decades. The availability of highly sensitive amplifiers and recording devices has made possible direct electrophysiological studies of the sense organs and their centers in the brain.

Before taking up these significant advances in the neurophysiology of sensation, we shall briefly consider its development over the first half-century of experimental psychology, emphasizing the contribution of the schools, since we have already considered the work of the pioneers in psychophysics, Weber and Fechner.

SENSATION AND THE SCHOOLS OF PSYCHOLOGY

Structuralism and Sensation[1]

It will be recalled that Titchener's psychology took as its aim the analysis of consciousness into elements by the method of introspection (see Chapter 3). We also pointed out that sensations were one of Titchener's three elements of consciousness, the other two being images and affective states. With this as a starting point, let us consider his position on sensation in more detail.

Titchener defines sensation as "an elementary mental process which is constituted of at least four attributes—*quality, intensity, clearness,* and *duration*" (1910, p. 52). Let us analyze both parts of this definition in turn. First, what does Titchener mean by an elementary process? As he uses the concept, it means *irreducible,* or incapable of analysis into anything simpler. His criterion for determining whether a conscious process is elemental is to subject that process to "rigorous and persistent" introspection. If under these conditions it remains unchanged—if it refuses, so to speak, to break down into something simpler—then it is a true element. Both Titchener's definition of elements and his test for their genuineness are analogous to chemists' criteria for establishing chemical elements. To cite a specific example, if the conscious experience aroused by a rose proves to be a compound of the elementary sensation of smell and a reaction of pleasantness, then the experience is not elementary but a complex of two or more elementary processes. Similarly, if the chemist can reduce common salt to something simpler (in this case, sodium and chlorine), then salt is not an element but a compound.

However, although elements are the primary, irreducible, stuff of consciousness, they can be classified or put into groups, just as the chemical elements can be organized into classes such as metals, heavy earths, rare gases, and halogens. In other words, in spite of their simplicity, elements possess *attributes* that enable us to make distinctions among them, and this brings us to a consideration of the second part of Titchener's definition of sensation.

Titchener puts *quality* at the head of his list of attributes. Quality is the most important attribute that permits us to distinguish one elementary process from another. Thus, we discriminate salt from cold, yellow from blue, or middle C from green, on the basis of quality differences. In simpler terms, quality is the attribute from which every sensation takes its particular name; and for this reason it is the most fundamental attribute of all sensations.

The second attribute, *intensity,* is familiar from everyday experience. This is the attribute responsible for the distinctions and comparisons of strength or degree that we make among sensations of both the same and different qualities. To exemplify, when we have several shades of blue paper, the attribute of quality is the same, namely, the quality of blueness. But the papers also differ in brightness or brilliance of color; hence we can distinguish between them on the basis of intensity differences. Similarly, we are able to make cross-comparisons between, say, a

---

[1]Our exposition is based on Titchener's *A Textbook of Psychology* (1910).

bright red and a *dark blue*. In this instance we are either ignoring quality or holding it constant, while concentrating on intensity. More generally, when we use terms like *brighter, duller, louder, softer, stronger, weaker* and the like, we are referring to the experienced attribute of intensity.

Turning to *clearness,* Titchener held that this attribute characterizes a sensation in terms of its place in consciousness. The clear sensation is dominant and in the foreground of consciousness; the less clear sensation is subordinate and in the background. To cite a simple example, if in the course of a laboratory investigation we are studying tones introspectively, our consciousness of those tones will be clear. However, the same tones coming over the radio while we are at home and absorbed in a book might go entirely unheard, or, if noticed at all, form part of the obscure background noise found in the best of homes. We shall have to return to the attribute of clearness, for it proved to be involved with the problem of attention, which is considered later in this section. But meanwhile we shall go on to describe Titchener's fourth attribute, duration.

Duration describes the temporal course of a sensation. In Titchener's words, it marks the sensation's ''rise, poise, and fall as a process in consciousness'' (1910, p. 53). Duration also makes the temporal course of one sensation characteristically different from the temporal course of another. Thus, a sustained tone or noise is characteristically different from a short click of the same pitch and intensity.

The attributes of quality, intensity, duration, and clearness are basic characteristics of *all* sensations. They are the essential four, always present to some degree in every sensory experience. However, Titchener points out that some sensations may also possess the attribute of extensity. The sensation aroused by a long strip of blue paper, for example, can be characterized by extensity in addition to the four fundamental attributes. Tones, on the other hand, do not possess extensity, but they, too, may have a special attribute, in this case, *volume.*[2] Volume is best exemplified by comparing the sound of an explosion to the tone of a piccolo. The explosion appears to fill all space, while the piccolo produces a highly circumscribed sound. Moreover, there is always the possibility that two or more attributes may join or concur in consciousness to produce what Titchener defines as a ''second-order'' attribute.

Before we conclude this summary of Titchener's treatment of sensation, a brief discussion of his position on the process of attention will be presented. Although attention is typically not included under sensation in contemporary texts, Titchener, as implied earlier in the chapter, held that attention is closely related to the sensory attribute of clearness. For this reason we have chosen to include his treatment of attention in this chapter.

Taking up the challenge of the complex problems of attention, Titchener reports that introspective studies distinguish between passive or involuntary attention and active or voluntary attention. The former type is most readily experienced as a

---

[2] Volume proved to be a troublesome attribute to isolate. For a detailed history of the problem, see Boring (1942), who also presents an extensive treatment of the methodology involved in separating and isolating attributes.

result of stimuli "that take consciousness by storm" (1910, p. 268). All intense stimuli, such as pistol shots, bright lights, or sudden pain, give rise to passive or involuntary attentiveness. In addition, anything that is novel or anything that fits into habits of attention gives rise to involuntary attentive states. In this way Titchener accounts for both the compelling effect of the strange or unusual and for the common observation that our individual habits predispose us to attend to certain aspects of our environment. Titchener summarizes all such instances under the category of "primitive attention."

Active or voluntary attention is characteristically experienced whenever we have to "force" ourselves to attend, as frequently occurs when we are tired, distracted, or engaged in some uninteresting task. At first reading it may appear that Titchener is falling into the commonsensical approach of describing secondary attention as a "power" or as dependent on an act of will. But in employing terms such as "active" or "force," he is deliberately reverting to everyday language in order to state the problem clearly for his readers. He hastens to explain that in such secondary attentive states the experience of strain or the necessity of forcing concentration is due to a "conflict of primary attentions" (1910, p. 272). Again we have a deterministic psychology; for, it will be recalled, primary or involuntary attention is aroused by strong, compelling stimuli or ideational impressions and not by acts of will. Therefore, what seems to be an active striving within is, in reality, the feeling or affective state associated with the conflict in our consciousness and its underlying parallel processes in the cerebral cortex. When the conflict has been resolved and the "strain" disappears, this does not imply that "we" have resolved the conflict, but that one of the excitatory processes has, to quote Titchener, "won the day" (1910, p. 273).

Fundamentally, the essence of Titchener's position is this: Attention *is* clearness and therefore is nothing more or less than a state of consciousness wherein some sensory experience or mental image is in the foreground, while all other processes are for the moment in the background. No new elements are involved, but what first appears to present a complex and difficult problem for introspection is analyzable into the familiar elementary processes of clear sensations or images!

Finally, Titchener undertakes an explanation of attention in terms of the nervous system. Here again we shall quote a particularly characteristic passage from the *Textbook*.

Now take a case that lies nearer home. Suppose that you are in your room, preparing for to-morrow's examination, and that you hear an alarm of fire in a neighbouring street. Both ideas, the idea of examination and the idea of fire, are imperative; there is a conflict. The cortex is set in one part for work: and this setting is reinforced by a large number of associated excitations,—the nervous processes corresponding to ideas of the examination mark, the consequences of failure, and so on. The cortex is set in another part for going to the fire: and this setting is similarly reinforced, by the processes corresponding to the ideas of a run in the fresh air, an exciting scene, a possible rescue, and so on. The struggle may last some little time, and its effects may persist for a while after you have made your choice. So long as there is any trace of it, your attention is secondary or "active" attention. (1910, pp. 272–273)

We can only add that this is *introspective* psychology at its best. Still, Titchener's parallelistic "explanation" in terms of cortical "sets" raises more questions for the modern reader than it resolves, since the neurological nature of these sets is not specified. Titchener, in a manner of speaking, is hiding behind the nervous system.

By way of summary, sensations for the structuralist are elements that possess the attributes of quality, intensity, clearness, and duration. The important classes of sensations are visual, auditory, olfactory, gustatory, cutaneous, and kinesthetic. In the structuralists' program each modality is analyzed introspectively to reveal its unique attributes, if any, and to describe and explain its important phenomena. Finally, the complex mental process of attention is reducible to the attribute of clearness. And as a parting comment, we might add that introspective psychology was most successful in the area of the sensory processes.

Functionalism and Sensation

In our discussion of the aims and methodology of functionalism in Chapter 3, it was pointed out that this system is characteristically an *is for* psychology in contrast to the *is* psychology of the structuralists. Moreover, functionalism represents a transition from the associationistic tradition of Wundt and Titchener to the biosocial orientation of an adjustmental psychology. Clearly, by embracing an adaptive or utilitarian frame of reference, the functionalist cannot afford to ignore the sensory processes completely. If mind functions to adapt the organism to its environment, then the senses are important adjuncts to mind, for they make possible awareness of the environment; and without awareness there can be no behavior, adaptive or otherwise. However, this is the extent of the functionalists' interest in sensation. It is to be investigated as the first stage in an act of interaction with the environment. The second stage is perception or the actual knowing of the environment. Unlike structuralistic psychology, where the emphasis is on sensory processes, functional psychology stresses the perceptual processes since it is through perception that the individual comes to adapt to his or her environment.

A second reason for the functionalists' lack of interest in sensation is their concern with *mental activities* as opposed to conscious contents. For functionalists, sensation smacks of statics, whereas perception is dynamic. Moreover, the functionalists' interest in learning and their description of learning as a "perceptual-motor" process again emphasize their concern with the behaving organism rather than with the organism's states of consciousness. With these general principles in mind, let us turn to Carr, who is our spokesman for the functionalistic point of view.[3]

In passing from Titchener to Carr, one is immediately struck by the brevity with which he treats the sensory processes. Carr (1925) devotes but a single short chapter to "Sensory and Motor Equipment," whereas, it will be recalled, Titchener re-

---

[3]The exposition follows Carr's *Psychology: A Study of Mental Activity* (1925).

quired ten chapters for his exposition of the same topic. Moreover, the flavor of Carr's approach is quite different. The emphasis is primarily on the basic anatomical details of the sense organs and only secondarily on the experiences to which they give rise, although the latter aspect of the sensory processes is not entirely neglected. Titchener, on the other hand, puts experience first, and physiology and structure are relegated to the background.

Carr treats the adaptive value of the sensory processes for living forms under the broad heading of *spatial ability,* which includes discriminative ability. In developing his theme, Carr first notes that, as we move up the phylogenetic scale, animals show an increasingly well-developed ability to localize objects in space. At the same time, capacity for form and size discrimination increases with the organism's phylogenetic status. And, finally, under spatial discrimination, he points to the fact that as we move from primitive to advanced forms we find increasing emphasis on distance receptors, such as the eye and ear, and decreasing emphasis on contact receptors, such as those found in the cutaneous senses. The animal with distance receptors is able to deal with space far more effectively by anticipating threats or sensing food supplies at long range than an organism with poorly developed distance receptors.

The relevance of these evolutionary modifications of spatial capacities for better adaptive reactions is undeniable. Because successful adaptation involves dealing with objects in space, the better the organism's equipment, the more successful it will be in adjustments involving both locomotor and manipulative acts. Indeed, in adapting to nature in the raw, one misperception might well prove fatal. For similar reasons, the finer the animal's discriminative ability, the more successful it is likely to be in selecting a balanced diet, detecting potential enemies, and identifying objects in general.

After summarizing his position on sensation in terms of these principles of adaptation, Carr turns from sensation to those psychological processes of greater interest to the functionalistic program. Clearly, as has been pointed out previously, the brevity of the treatment of sensation reflects the school's greater concern with other mental activities, notably perception and learning. Nevertheless, despite its brief treatment of sensation, the strong evolutionary point of view characteristic of this school is clearly developed. Functionalism is, in short, a Darwinian psychology whose orientation is the activity of the *whole organism* in its give-and-take relations with the environment. With this précis of Carr's position, we shall leave this school for the time being and turn to the behavioristic view of sensation.

Behaviorism and Sensation[4]

It may seem strange to discover that Watson devoted considerable space to the sensory processes in his first exposition of behaviorism. Six chapters of his com-

---

[4]Our account is drawn from Watson's *Behavior: An Introduction to Comparative Psychology* (1914) and *Psychology from the Standpoint of a Behaviorist* (1919).

parative text (1914) deal with problems of definition and methodology in the area of sensation, and in addition, he includes a summary of experimental results. In his later book, *Psychology from the Standpoint of a Behaviorist* (1919), only one chapter is given to sensory psychology; it is, however, several times longer than the equivalent chapter in Carr's text. On the surface, this much emphasis on the sensory processes seems more appropriate in a structuralist's text. If—as was brought out in discussing methods and aims of behaviorism—Watson was primarily interested in *behavior* as revealed by experimental observation, how can such aims and methods be reconciled with a heavy emphasis on sensory psychology?

The answer lies in two factors. First, it must be remembered that in his early work Watson was attempting to meet Titchener on his own grounds. If he could demonstrate that sensory processes, which at first impression seem open only to introspective methods, are in reality amenable to investigation by behavioristic techniques, he would weaken the structuralists' position and thereby strengthen his own. Second, the objective methods of the natural sciences that Watson favored were (and to a considerable degree still are) most useful in reductional analysis. Because sensation lends itself to this kind of treatment more readily than intelligence, personality, thinking, and such "higher" mental processes, it is natural that Watson found the study of sensation congenial to his overall aims and methods.

However, because of his affinity with animal research, Watson had to face certain methodological problems at the outset in his comparative text (1914). How is it possible to investigate an animal's sensory capacities? There is no way for the psychologist to question animals about what they see, hear, taste, or smell; and even if such were possible, this would be going over to the structuralists' camp by admitting that introspection is a legitimate technique of investigation. The answer, Watson believes, is to be found in studying the animal's *motor* responses. For example, if the psychologist is interested in determining whether a certain species of animal can discriminate red from blue, he must arrange experimental conditions in such a way that the animal can *respond differentially* to the two colors. The animal must be motivated to learn the discrimination either by rewards for correct responses or by punishment for incorrect responses or possibly by a combination of both.

In his earlier book (1914), Watson marshals an impressive collection of plans and descriptions for apparatus that both he and other psychologists had already employed in testing animals' reactions in sensory discrimination problems. Moreover, he devotes the last four chapters of the book to a summary of experimental results from comparative laboratories.

In the section on apparatus, Pavlov's conditioning technique is given prominence as a research method of great potential importance for psychology. Watson's forecast that conditioning would become a basic technique in psychology proved correct, since the method rapidly assumed a central position in the behaviorists' research programs and theoretical systems. Watson also describes discrimination boxes already in use by pioneers in animal work, such as Yerkes and Yoakum. Such techniques, he points out, proved successful even before the advent of behaviorism for studying every one of the major senses in animals. Problems such as the animal's range of both quality and intensity discriminations proved amenable to testing by conditioning in the visual, auditory, cutaneous, and kinesthetic modalities.

Watson, therefore, was able to demonstrate that insofar as sensory processes were concerned, behaviorism was more than a mere theoretical program; it could offer concrete results gathered by its methods, if not by its proponents. And these results were in the traditional bailiwick of the structuralists—the senses. Moreover, as we shall find in Chapter 5, Watson's methods also proved highly useful in the fields of learning and problem solving.

We may, therefore, credit Watson with broadening sensory psychology to include the study of animals and with contributing to the methodology of comparative psychology. However, Watson is not noted for any outstanding specific discoveries in sensation. As a contributor to the experimental literature of psychology, his work on infantile emotions and the conditioning of fears (see Chapter 13) is much more widely known than his earlier work in comparative psychology. This, in part, reflects a shift in his research interests from the area of animal to child psychology, a change of interest that occurred in the mature phase of his career. We may, therefore, leave Watson's treatment of the sensory processes with the conclusion that his chief contributions were in broadening the methodology and scope of sensory psychology to include work in the comparative area.

Gestalt Psychology and Psychoanalysis

Gestalt psychologists and psychoanalysts have shown little direct interest in the sensory processes. Their lack of interest can best be understood in terms of their aims and methods. The chief concern of Gestalt psychologists is the study of holistic units of behavior, whether mental or overt, employing a molar approach. Thus, molecular analyses at the level of sensation fall outside the scope of their program. The study of perception offers a more rewarding field; indeed, it becomes their major area of research. In the case of the psychoanalysts, sensory psychology proved irrelevant to their program. On the purely theoretical side, their main areas of interest lie in development, motivation, and personality—processes that have obvious significance in abnormal psychology and psychotherapy.

Because neither of these schools contributed in a significant way to the psychology of the sensory processes, we shall pass them by for the time being and turn instead to the contemporary trends in sensation. However, because we are concerned with the evolution of concepts and methods in this volume, it seems wise at this transition point to try to summarize in a general way the contribution of the traditional schools to the evolution of sensory psychology.

Clearly, the structuralists' outstanding contribution to sensory psychology was their *descriptive psychology* of the sensory consciousness. Within this frame of reference, Titchener and his associates mined the field of sensation thoroughly, and little or nothing was added by the subsequent schools to this aspect of the evolution of sensory psychology. In the realm of *methodology,* Watson's behavioristic approach offered the most significant contribution. This is not only true because of the healthy shift of emphasis he provided at a period when psychology had become overly mentalistic, but also because the heritage Watson and the comparative psychologists of his day left in the form of theoretical and methodological approaches has carried over into contemporary psychology. Today the study of the lower forms through the use of empirical techniques dominates the comparative field, for it is primarily on animals that direct neurophysiological studies favored by contemporary psychologists are most feasible.

Carr and the functionalists, having fitted sensation into the strong adaptive orientation of their system, contributed nothing new or original to the field. And, as has just been pointed out, the virtual exclusion of sensory psychology from the Gestalt and psychoanalytic programs precluded significant contributions from either of these schools. To conclude, then, the descriptive psychology of consciousness had fully answered the what and how of the sensory processes. The behaviorists provided a methodology for investigating the mysteries of the neurological correlates of sensory experience.

CONTEMPORARY TRENDS IN SENSORY PSYCHOLOGY

We have already taken the position that contemporary interest in sensation is primarily along neurophysiological lines. This, in part, reflects the rapid advances in recent years in the development of high-fidelity electronic amplifiers, microstimulators, and recording devices. For many decades the old method of extirpation, first developed over one hundred years ago, was the chief tool of the physiological psychologist. As applied to sensory problems, the method involves the establishment of a sensory discrimination habit in animal subjects, after which destructions are made in cortical or subcortical centers—sometimes in one center, sometimes in another in different animals—until the center mediating the habit is identified. This is evidenced by the animal's inability to perform the habit postoperatively once the critical center has been localized and destroyed.

But the method suffers from difficulties, some of which are methodological, some theoretical. For example, if the animal fails to perform a discrimination following a brain lesion, the question arises as to whether it no longer has the sensory capacity or whether its memory for the habit has suffered. Again, in many cases the limits of a cortical area responsible for mediating a sensory or discriminative process cannot be established with accuracy.

Microelectrode techniques, on the other hand, make possible precise recording from either individual sense cells or the afferent neurons that conduct impulses from the sense organs to the brain. So sophisticated have these techniques become that the effects of stimuli confined to a single receptor cell can be measured on an individual neuron leading away from that cell. It is also possible to apply microelectrodes to subcortical and cortical centers in the brain to evaluate the effects of stimulation of the peripheral sense mechanisms on these centers. By utilizing these techniques, researchers have been able to make enormous strides in discovering: (1) how sense cells respond to stimulation; (2) how the reaction of the sense cell to the stimulus is converted into a neural response; (3) how the neural response is further coded into a message directed toward an appropriate center in the brain; and (4) how patterns of excitation on the periphery are paralleled by patterns of excitation on the cerebral cortex. Considerable progress has been made on enabling the blind to see by fashioning artificial eyes in the form of miniature television cameras worn like spectacles whose electronic impulses are fed directly to electrodes implanted in the cerebral cortex in the visual area. This arrangement has enabled blind subjects to see simple geometric patterns of light.

Considered from a somewhat different point of view, two fundamental age-old problems in psychobiology have been brought under direct attack by microelectrode techniques: (1) the problem of transduction, or how the sense organs convert one form of energy (the stimulus energy) into another form (neural energy); (2) the mind-body problem or how processes in the physical body can give rise to conscious experience. We are still a long way from a complete understanding of how transduction is accomplished in the various sense organs and how physical events in the nervous system are correlated with experience. The technical problems involved are complex. During the past several decades we have had a surplus of empirical data from the research laboratories awaiting coordination with theory (Uttal, 1973; Carterette & Friedman, 1973).

Since this is not a handbook of experimental research, we shall confine ourselves primarily to examples of recent research in vision and audition as illustrative of the methodological and theoretical problems involved. In so doing we shall be able to give a fair sample of the experimental findings obtained with such techniques in the two most important areas of sensory research. We shall, however, set the stage for our dip into the contemporary literature with a brief historical summary of the field of sensory neurology.

The Historical Setting

One of the oldest theoretical principles in physiological psychology attributes *quality* to the sense organ stimulated and *intensity* to the number of sensory neurons aroused by the stimulus. For example, when the ear is stimulated appropriately, sounds of various qualities are experienced depending on the stimulus-object from which the sound emanates. For the sake of simplicity, let us assume that the stimulus-object is a tuning fork vibrating 256 times per second. The effect as experienced is a tonal quality of medium pitch. If another fork vibrating at 60 cycles per second is substituted, the resulting experience is a low-pitched tone. In either case the quality dimension is pitch, and our ability to sense pitch has traditionally been associated with the particular portion of the inner ear and auditory cortex aroused by the stimulus. In short, specific sense cells mediate specific qualities.

In the case of intensity, stronger stimuli (or in our example of the tuning forks, the greater amplitude sound waves) arouse more sense cells or cortical cells to activity and so give rise to more intense auditory experiences. These in turn are experienced as "louder" sounds.

The specific end-organ theory of sensory function was given strong support by Johannes Müller's doctrine of the specific energies of nerves, which, as we pointed out in Chapter 2, held to a strict specificity of qualitative experiences as dependent on the sense organ stimulated. Later Max von Frey (1852–1932), a physiologist who had done considerable work on the skin senses, announced a specific end-organ theory of cutaneous sensitivity in a series of papers published between 1894 and 1896. Such was von Frey's prestige that not only was the specific end-organ theory greatly reinforced, but a considerable amount of research during the next generation was devoted to the investigation of the skin in a search for the specialized sensory organs presumed to lie in the subcutaneous tissues.

With this summary of the traditional attitude toward the two most important dimensions of sensory experience—quality and intensity—to serve as a background, we may now turn to the development of systematic visual and auditory theories in modern psychology.

Contemporary Trends in Scotopic Vision

Visual theory and research divides itself along the lines of the *duplicity theory,* formulated by Johannes von Kries (1853–1928). The theory assumes that there are two types of receptors in the retina, rods and cones, each with separate properties and functions. The rods are presumed to function in scotopic, or twilight, vision or more generally at low levels of illumination. The cones function in photopic, or daylight, vision. Because the cones are more numerous in the fovea, or central portion, of the eye, this is the center of clearest daylight vision. Outside of the fovea toward the periphery, rods become increasingly numerous until they are the only receptors represented. Moreover, the cones are typically connected to the visual centers by single, point-to-point neuronal chains while many rods converge on a few ganglion cells. These neurological correlates suggest that the cones are more specialized for fine spatial discrimination and color vision, whereas the rods are for intensity vision and vision under conditions of very weak stimulation.

The discovery that many nocturnal animals possess only rod retinas and that many diurnal animals possess only cones led to the widespread acceptance of the duplicity theory as essentially true. For the past century psychological research has divided itself according to this theory, with some psychologists concerning themselves with the nature of scotopic vision and others with the mechanisms of photopic vision. Those who are primarily interested in scotopic vision have shown little interest in attempting to formulate comprehensive systematic theories of vision. Rather, their research has been concerned with the establishment of laws governing the tripartite relationships among the stimulus, psychological, and neurological variables in brightness vision. Similarly, those who are primarily interested in photopic vision have been almost exclusively preoccupied with color vision.

Although the duplicity theory represents a generally valid description of the dualistic nature of the visual processes, recent research has shown that there are exceptions to it, and we shall cite some of them in this chapter. However, accepting its broad outlines as essentially valid, we shall begin with a description of Selig Hecht's (1892–1947) photochemical theory (1929, 1938) as representative of systematic work in the area of scotopic vision, following which we shall consider more recent theoretical and empirical work in both scotopic and color vision.

Hecht began his long and fruitful series of researches on vision in 1919. His overall aim was to formulate precise quantitative laws for the prediction of visual phenomena. More specifically, he attempted to account for all the important phenomena of brightness vision, such as light adaptation, the threshold behavior of the retina in various organisms under various conditions, flicker-fusion phenomena, and the influence of metabolic factors on adaptation and threshold phenomena. Hecht assumed there were three basic chemical reactions taking place in the photo-receptors: first, a primary light reaction involving the breakdown of the photo-chemical substances by light; second, a primary dark reaction involving the regen-eration of the photochemical substances from the breakdown products in darkness; and third, a secondary dark reaction involving the generation of nervous impulses by the photochemical reactions.

Hecht's assumptions about the reversible photochemical reactions taking place in vision may be expressed in terms of the behavior of the photosensitive pigments that have since been discovered in the retina. Wald (1951, 1959) and his col-laborators have identified the various substances involved in photochemical reac-tions, the most important of which is rhodopsin, or visual purple.[5] When exposed to light it breaks down through a series of intermediate stages to opsin and retinene, or visual yellow. Retinene, however, is unstable and tends to combine with opsin to reform rhodopsin or to convert to vitamin A. Vitamin A and opsin can, in turn, convert back to retinene in darkness. Hence two parallel and reversible reactions are going on simultaneously. These may be diagrammed in simplified form as follows:

$$\text{(light)}$$
$$\text{Rhodopsin} \rightleftarrows \text{retinene} + \text{opsin}$$

$$\uparrow$$

$$\text{Retinene} + \text{opsin} \rightleftarrows \text{vitamin A} + \text{opsin}$$

Light and Dark Adaptation

Another way of demonstrating the relationships involved in Hecht's assump-tions is to express them graphically. Figure 4-1 shows threshold values for the dark-adapting eye plotted against time in darkness. It will be noted that the curve has two limbs, an upper branch for cones that show some ability to dark-adapt, and the lower branch for rods. The rods show very rapid dark adaptation during the first 15 minutes in darkness followed by slowly increasing sensitivity over the next 15

---

[5]In working with frog eyes in 1876, Franz Boll noted that the dark-adapted eye was purplish in color but upon exposure to light bleached out to a yellowish hue; hence the names "visual purple" and "visual yellow."

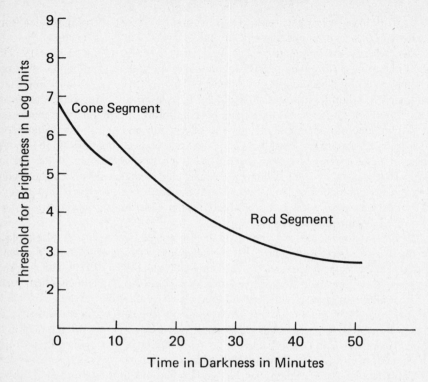

FIGURE 4-1.   A typical curve for dark adaptation. Note that the curve has two segments, one for the cones and one for the rods which take over from the cones after 7 or 8 minutes.

minutes. The sequence of temporal events involved in dark adaptation has led one psychologist (Buss, 1973) to suggest that since the natural transition from daylight to darkness takes about one-half hour, the evolutionary process favored eyes that could make the necessary adaptive shift in sensitivity. Obviously, the organism that is visually deficient under twilight and night conditions will easily fall prey to predators who have the ability to modify their sensitivity. The ability of the human eye to change sensitivity is truly remarkable, since within 30 minutes the eye can become 100,000 times more sensitive to light and, it has been calculated, one rod under conditions of complete dark adaptation can respond to one photon of light.

In light adaptation the reverse occurs, so that the eye becomes increasingly less sensitive to light with continued exposure. In other words, light adaptation is essentially a fatigue process, whereas dark adaptation is a recovery process. Hecht makes use of his basic equations in developing more complex equations with which he can predict the various thresholds and summative and discriminative retinal reactions. He then fits the hypothetical curves drawn from his equations to actual data collected from experimental studies on the eye of both human and animal subjects.

Flicker and Fusion

Flicker functions, Figure 4-2, are of particular interest to psychologists because they permit a breakdown of visual functions into rod and cone responses. Flicker functions refer to studies of the perception of stimuli that are alternately dimmed and brightened. At low rates of modulation the stimulus is perceived as flickering. As rate of flicker is increased, a critical point is reached where the light appears to be continuous. This is called the "critical flicker-fusion frequency." In pure rod eyes or pure cone eyes, flicker functions are continuous. But in mixed eyes a rod component appears at the lower limb of the sigmoid curve, indicating that rods are functioning only at low levels of illumination as demanded by the duplicity theory. At higher levels of illumination their functioning is evidently inhibited by the cones or by chemical bleaching.

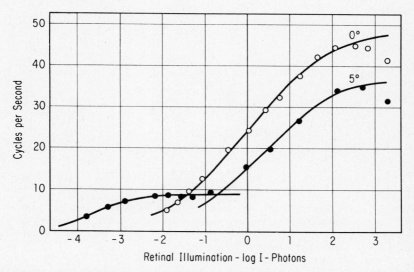

FIGURE 4-2.   Theoretical curves of flicker-fusion frequency as a function of illumination fitted to empirical data. The lower left-hand curve is for rods; the other curves are for cones in the fovea (0 degrees) and 5 degrees off center. (From Hecht, S. The nature of the photoreceptor process. In C. Murchison (ed.) Handbook of general experimental psychology. Worcester, Mass.: Clark University Press, 1934.)

Visual Acuity

Measures of the relationship of visual acuity to the intensity of illumination, Figure 4-3, also show the duplex function clearly. As illumination increases, the rod limb of the curve fails to increase, showing that there is little visual acuity contributed by the rods. Therefore, these curves also show that the two major variables in visual acuity are the portion of the retina stimulated and the intensity of the stimulating light. Because the fovea contains only cones, visual acuity is high in the fovea. As stimulus is moved toward the periphery, acuity falls off.

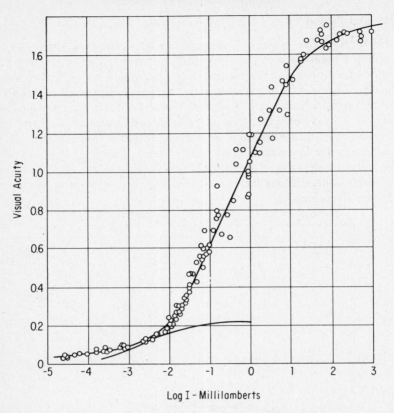

FIGURE 4-3. The relationship between visual acuity and illumination. The steep upper curve is for cones; the shallow curve at the bottom, for rods. (From Hecht, S. The nature of the photoreceptor process. In C. Murchison (ed.) Handbook of general experimental psychology. Worcester, Mass.: Clark University Press, 1934.)

Although Hecht's is a photochemical theory and as such tends to emphasize the chemical basis for scotopic vision, modern visual theory has also emphasized neural processes in the retina. To round out this account of scotopic vision, we shall briefly discuss interaction in the retinal neurons, a process that has important implications for visual theory.

Spatial Interaction

With its complex layers of cells (Figure 4-4) the retina is, in a functional sense, an extension of the brain. This view is justified on the grounds that retinal elements, like cortical elements, are capable of associative interaction. As may be seen in Figure 4-4, horizontal cells may connect spatially distant sense cells, and amacrine fibers may interconnect two or more bipolar cells. It is this neural arrangement that makes spatial interaction possible. One form of spatial interaction is *summation,* in which two or more separate responses must add, or summate, before reaching a

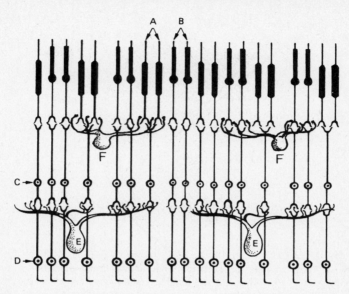

FIGURE 4-4. Schematic diagram of the retina. A, rods; B, cones; C, bipolar cells; D, optic neurons; E, amacrine cells; F, horizontal cell.

threshold level. Thus two weak or subthreshold patches of light may fall on the retina at separate points, neither of which alone could be seen but which by summating produce a visual sensation.

That spatial summation does in fact occur is demonstrated in everyday life when larger shapes are seen easier than smaller shapes in very dim light. In the laboratory, summation can be demonstrated when two adjacent patches of light produce a response, even though a single one of the same total area cannot (Riggs, 1971). It is also true that spatial *inhibition* may occur when an intense patch of light on one area of the retina inhibits adjacent areas. Direct stimulation of the retina by patches of light while ganglion cell responses are being recorded reveals that the area surrounding a central response area fires in the opposite way (Figure 4-5). Thus if a central area consistently fires with an ''on'' response,[6] the peripheral fibers will fire in the opposite way. These physiological facts may be related to intensity discrimination and to contrast effects, particularly along borders and edges (Riggs, 1971, p. 295).

A number of investigators have suggested that spatial inhibition in the retina may result in the enhancement of edges and contours in our perception of objects (contour coding). For example, Ratliff and Hartline (1959) in working with the giant neurons of the horseshoe crab, *limulus,* found that when firing was induced in

---

[6]Recordings made with the electroretinogram reveal that some fibers fire in response to the onset of a stimulus, some are ''off'' fibers, and some are ''on-off'' types that fire both upon the initiation and termination of stimulation.

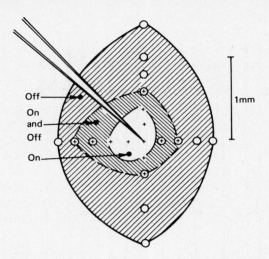

FIGURE 4-5.   Receptive fields in the retina. The micro-electrode placed on a ganglion cell records an impulse in + areas when a light is turned on and when turned off at O areas. (Redrawn from Küffler, S. W. Discharge patterns and functional organization of mammalian retina. J. Neurophysiol. 16: 37–68, 1953, Fig. 6.)

one neuron by stimulating its attached receptor cell with light, not only did its rate of firing increase but the rate of spontaneous firing in neighboring cells decreased. This effect they called *lateral inhibition.* Applying lateral inhibition to contours, we see that increased frequency of firing would correspond to edges and figures, whereas decreased firing rates would correspond to sides or backgrounds.

However, Cornsweet (1970) has pointed out that inhibitory effects in and of themselves cannot enhance information. Inhibitory effects can only suppress information, and if there were no inhibition in the retina, more rather than less information would become available to the brain. Enhancement, therefore, is not a positive process but, rather, a negative one in which less important characteristics are inhibited, thus making the more important characteristics of the stimulus object stand out.

A study of Figures 4-1, 4-2, and 4-3 will demonstrate that Hecht's assumptions and rational equations are generally accurate predictions of empirical findings. However, it must be admitted that there are other instances in which his equations do not fit the data with the high degree of accuracy demanded by a "perfect" theory. Riggs (1971, pp. 287–289) has summarized evidence to show that light and dark adaptation are not exclusively functions of the bleaching and regeneration of visual pigments but also depend on neural interaction effects, such as those we have been discussing. Moreover, a word of warning must be interjected that when hypothetical equations are employed in this way, some of the constants must be manipulated to fit the empirical data. Consequently, there is always a possibility that a different set of equations might fit equally well. What we are dealing with in the last analysis is a *model,* and all models have the defect of being representations rather than the real thing.

The merit of Hecht's theory for our purposes lies in the fact that it is our first example of a "miniature system," or elaborate theory, developed in a restricted area of psychology. Moreover, it is an excellent example of the combination of rational and empirical methods, or, in the more popular current phase, the *hypotheticodeductive method,* in which a complex theory can be systematically evaluated by developing hypotheses from it that are then subjected to experimental verification. We shall meet with additional examples of this method in subsequent chapters.

To return to the more general problem of the contemporary treatment of scotopic vision, theories of Hecht and others have served to stimulate investigations of light and dark adaptation, spatial and temporal summation, metabolic influences on visual phenomena, and the electrical correlates of various scotopic processes. In fact, it is fair to say that a great deal of research on the photochemistry of the retina has been stimulated by Hecht's theory. However, it is no longer demanded of a visual theory that it "explain" everything or fall by the wayside. Instead, any theory is considered useful so long as it leads to fruitful investigation of even limited aspects of visual phenomena. Psychologists who have devoted years of research to the task of uncovering the complex psychophysical and neurological relationships in brightness vision can point with pride to the impressive fund of information now available as the result of research designs based on limited or miniature theories.

Contemporary Trends in Color Vision

Contemporary research in color vision evolved from a number of classical theories, two of which are widely known: the Young-Helmholtz and the Hering. Before reviewing these theories, let us consider the basic phenomena of color vision, which any theory must explain if it is to be comprehensive. Briefly, the phenomena in question are as follows:

1. Color mixture. What are the primaries out of which all other colors can be made? Why are some colors antagonistic or complementary, yielding gray or white when mixed?
2. The psychological uniqueness of red, green, blue, and yellow. Why are these colors incapable of being subjectively resolved into other colors?
3. Color blindness, or the inability of some people to see certain colors or, in rare cases, all colors.
4. Color zones, or the finding that red and green are seen only near the center of the retina, whereas blue and yellow are seen farther out toward the periphery.
5. Adaptation and contrast phenomena. Why does the appearance of colors change under prolonged stimulation? Why do colors seem to persist in their original form or in complementary form following stimulation?
6. Transduction, or the process of converting a photochemical reaction in the retina into nervous impulses.
7. Neural transmission from retina to brain, or the process whereby nervous impulses are encoded and transmitted to the appropriate centers in the brain there to be decoded.

Since none of the classical theories attempts to account for transduction (item 6) or neural transmissions of retinal impulses to the brain via the optic nerve (item 7), we shall defer a discussion of these processes until later. Meanwhile, we may consider how the two most influential classical theories attempted to account for the first five basic phenomena.

To account for color mixing, primary colors, and complements, the Young-Helmholtz theory—formulated by Thomas Young (1773–1829) and modified by Hermann von Helmholtz (1821–1894)—postulates that there are three types of cones in the retina (red, green, and blue), which correspond to the physical primaries. Each type of cone is aroused by *all* wavelengths but is maximally excited by the wavelength to which it is most sensitive (see Figure 4-6). For this reason, primary experiences are the result of the excitation of the appropriate conal processes in the retina.

Complementary colors when mixed give a gray or whitish experience, since all three processes are stimulated simultaneously. Mixtures of wavelengths give rise to intermediate color experiences, since two or more wavelengths arouse two or more cone types simultaneously. The theory makes no attempt to explain the psychological uniqueness of yellow.

The chief limitation of the theory is its failure to explain red-green color blindness. In order to account for red-green blindness, the theory in its original form would have to assume the congenital absence of the red and green processes. This would explain the absence of both red and green experiences in red-green color-blind individuals. However, since yellow is presumably a mixture of red and green, such individuals should not see yellow, but they do. This difficulty can be overcome by assuming not an absence of cones but a weakness in the red-green processes, so that singly they may fail to give the appropriate response but when aroused simultaneously they are still capable of exciting the yellow experience. Color zones could be accounted for on the assumption of an appropriate zonal distribution of the cone processes. However, yellow is typically seen farther out on the retina than the outer

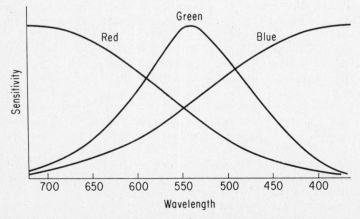

FIGURE 4-6.   Relative sensitivity of the primary retinal processes to different wavelengths.

limits of red and green; hence, the theory suffers from essentially the same limitation in explaining color zones as was true in the case of color blindness.

Adaptation and successive contrast (negative afterimages) are explicable in terms of fatigue. Adaptation is the result of fatigue in a given cone process, which in turn raises the threshold for that hue. Negative afterimages are associated with complete fatigue of one or two cone types, with the result that only the remaining processes can be aroused by white light. This, at the same time, accounts for the fact that the resultant experience is complementary to the original stimulus color. Finally, simultaneous contrast is only inadequately explained by the theory as an "unconscious inference," a process presumably dependent on higher-level neural centers.

The Young-Helmholtz theory has the advantage of parsimony in that it assumes only three cone types, corresponding to the physical primaries. The chief limitation of the theory as originally formulated is its failure to explain color blindness, color zones, and contrast. But despite these limitations, the theory has served as a reference point for most subsequent theories and in addition, has stimulated a great deal of research.

The theory formulated by Ewald Hering (1834–1918) postulates three processes in the form of paired opponent qualities: black-white; red-green; blue-yellow. Further, these are presumed to depend on the existence of three substances in the retina that are excitable in two opposite ways. Catabolic, or destructive, excitation gives rise to white, red, and yellow color sensations; whereas anabolic, or constructive, excitation gives rise to black, green, and blue. Mixtures resulting in the complementary phenomenon of gray are explained by the simultaneous arousal of any two antagonistic processes. Mixtures of noncomplements give rise to incomplete fusion colors (for example, orange) when nonantagonistic processes are aroused. Color zones are accounted for by assuming a zonal distribution of the three substances. Color blindness is explained by postulating anatomical defects involving the red-green or blue-yellow substances.

The chief weakness of the Hering theory is the assumptions involving anabolic-catabolic processes in the retina. The assumptions are complex and involve the postulation of events for which there is no physiological evidence. The theory also suffers from the limitation of having to account for certain aspects of brightness phenomena in color mixing in a highly complex manner. The problems involved are beyond the scope of this volume, but the interested reader will find a more detailed discussion of the theory in Boring (1942, pp. 208–209) or in Stevens (1951, pp. 831–843).

The Search for Underlying Neurological Mechanisms

Understandably, those interested in either substantiating or verifying the various theories began the search for "cone types" to correspond to the three or more primary colors postulated by the theorists. To represent this type of systematic approach to the psychophysiology of color vision, we may begin with the pioneer researches of Ragnar Granit, a Scandinavian physiologist, who investigated the

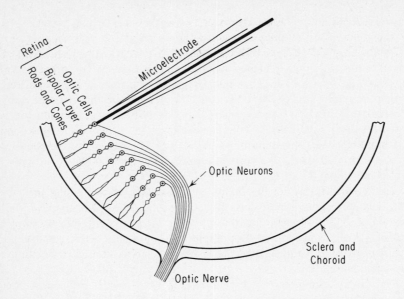

FIGURE 4-7.   A schematic cross section of the eye with the retina greatly enlarged with respect to the outer coats. Note that the microelectrode stimulates the optic neurons.

relationship between observed psychophysical functions and their underlying neurological correlates. (See Granit, 1955, especially chap. 4.)

Granit made use of the excised eyes of animals in which the anterior structures (cornea and lens) were removed to allow direct access to the retina by microelectrodes. Figure 4-7 shows a highly diagrammatic view of the posterior portion of an eye with a microelectrode in position for recording neural impulses from the retina. Microelectrodes are made of finely drawn hollow glass tubes in which a silver wire or another conductor for recording electrical activity has been incorporated. So fine is the tip (a few micrometers in diameter) that it can pick up impulses from single neurons.

Because the retina is "upside down," with the optic neurons leading to the brain forming the inner retinal layer while the actual sensory cells—rods and cones—form the outer layer, Granit's technique records third-order retinal responses rather than first-order rod or cone activity (see Figure 4-7). This must be borne in mind as a possible limiting factor in evaluating the results. However, "seeing" is ultimately dependent on the occipital cortex, and because this center receives its "messages" from the optic neurons, the underlying logic of the technique seems sound.

With eyes prepared in this fashion it is possible to study the comparative responses of pure rod retinas such as the guinea pig's, pure cone retinas such as the reptile's, and the mixed rod-and-cone retina of the cat. Whichever type is under investigation, the retina can be stimulated by various wavelengths, and the electrical response, if any, recorded. The results can be plotted on a graph with relative

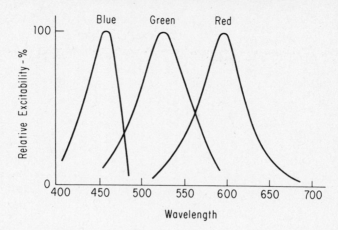

FIGURE 4-8.   Photopic components from the cat retina. (After Granit, 1955. Reproduced by permission from Physiological Psychology, by C. T. Morgan and E. Stellar. Copyright 1950. McGraw-Hill Book Co., Inc.)

excitability as a function of wavelength. See for example, Figure 4-8, which reproduces Granit's findings for the cat retina. Like the human retina, it is mixed. It will be noted that there are three peaks of excitability corresponding to blue, green, and red wavelengths. This corresponds remarkably well with the Young-Helmholtz theory. Granit called these response units *modulators*—in contrast with response units of broad sensitivity, which he called *dominators*. The latter serve scotopic sensitivity or rod vision.

Even more direct evidence in favor of the Young-Helmholtz theory at the receptor level has been provided by direct measurements of spectral sensitivity in single cones. E. F. MacNichol, Jr. (1964a, 1964b), at Johns Hopkins University and P. K. Brown and G. Wald (1964) at Harvard have independently made direct spectral-sensitivity tests involving single receptor cells in the retina.

MacNichol, whose work is representative of this type of investigation, utilized a microspectrophotometer. This device permits the casting of a tiny dot of light on a single receptor cell and records the relative light absorption for different wavelengths by means of an elaborate computer arrangement that prints out the absorption spectrum on a spectral sensitivity graph. Figure 4-9 shows the smoothed and combined curves taken from the original curves recorded directly by the microspectrophotometer. Note the peaks at 445, 535, and 570 nanometers, respectively. Although the "red" curve peaks at yellow, it extends far enough into red to sense adequately all wavelengths that give rise to the experience of red.

Nobel prize winner George Wald discovered three types of iodopsin, the photochemical mediating color vision, in the retina corresponding to red, green, and blue. These are known as erythrolabe, chlorolabe, and cynolabe.

As a result of experiments such as MacNichol's and Wald's, the three-component theory of retinal photochemistry is now accepted as fact.

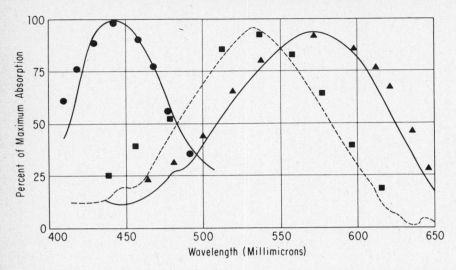

FIGURE 4-9.   Smoothed curves from the microspectrophotometer showing peaks in the blue, green, and "red" regions of the spectrum. (From "Three-pigment color vision" by Edward F. MacNichol. Copyright © 1964 by Scientific American, Inc. All rights reserved.)

Afferent Coding

The direct measurements of single receptor cells and the discovery of three photochemical transducers that we have been discussing are convincing evidence for the essential validity of the Young-Helmholtz theory, at least at the receptor level. But there are many remaining questions concerned with how information arising in the retina is transduced into neural energy from photochemical energy and how neural impulses arising in the retina reach the brain. Our present level of knowledge does not permit any firm conclusions on how the process of transduction occurs.

However, we are in a much better position to make generalizations about the afferent coding process, which has been discovered at the level of the lateral geniculate body. The discovery of afferent coding has revived interest in the Hering theory and has led to the suggestion that the Young-Helmholtz and Hering theories are not necessarily incompatible. Hurvich and Jameson (1957) have offered a modification of the Hering theory in the form of a model (Figure 4-10) that assumes the existence of three different receptor processes in keeping with the Young-Helmholtz theory. These are linked with the neural units in such a manner as to account for all possible responses, including black and white.

It should be noted that the model assumes that red and green are coded as opposites, not combinations. Therefore, the red-green system receives input from both red and green cones. If the input from the red predominates, the output of the red-green system is positive, resulting in an increased neural response. If green predominates on the input side, the output response is negative. Note that the red-green system also receives some input from the blue absorption process. This

Neural Responses (Output)

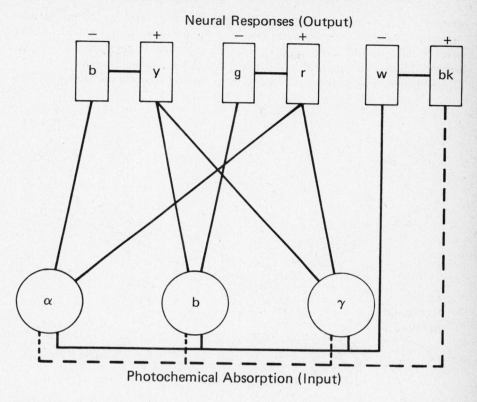

Photochemical Absorption (Input)

FIGURE 4-10. The Hurvich-Jameson model of the photochemical processes in color vision. For explanation see text. (Redrawn from Hurvich, L. M., and Jameson, D. An opponent-process theory of color vision. Psychological Review, 1957, 64, p. 388. Copyright 1957 by the American Psychological Association.)

accounts for purple and, more important, for the fact that in color mixing it is necessary to add a little blue to the red-green mixture in order to get a complement. Similarly, the blue-yellow system is an opposite one, with yellow arising as an excitation of the system while blue is a decrease in excitation. White arises as the simultaneous excitation of all three receptors, and black is a complex experience arising from simultaneous or successive contrast following or during light stimulation of some part of the retina. The absence of stimulation yields a homogeneous or neutral gray, such as what we may perceive in a darkroom after adaptation. Finally, it might be noted that spectral-sensitivity curves drawn from the Hurvich-Jameson theory account better for the facts of color mixing experiences than those derived from the Young-Helmholtz.

Support for the essential validity of some type of color coding process in the neural centers comes from studies of the responses of the cells in the lateral geniculate body. Typical of such research is the work of De Valois and Jacobs (1968). In these investigations, microelectrodes placed directly into the lateral geniculate bodies (Figure 4-11) of monkeys allowed recording of the responses of these cells to the entire spectrum of wavelengths. The neural units of the lateral geniculate body were found to exhibit a resting level of activity when not under stimulation. Under such conditions the rate of firing is quite slow and somewhat irregular.

When the eye is stimulated, the response pattern changes as a function of the

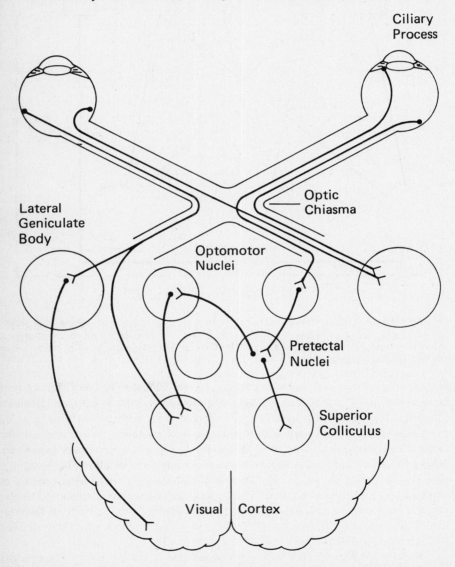

FIGURE 4-11. The central visual pathways. The optomotor and pretectal nuclei function in visual reflexes. The superior colliculi are believed to be involved in intensity discrimination. The main pathways to the visual cortex are by way of synapsing neurons in the lateral geniculate bodies.

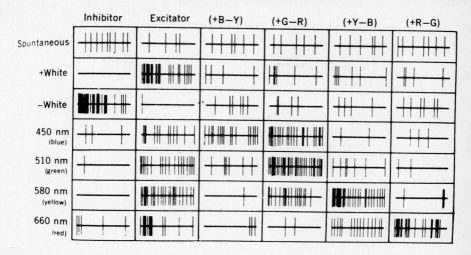

FIGURE 4-12.   Discharge patterns of the six principal types of macaque lateral geniculate cells in response to light flashes. (+ white) = increment in white light; (− white) = decrement in white light. (From DeValois, R. L., and Jacobs, G. H., Science, Vol. 162, pp. 533–540, Fig. 5, 1 Nov. 1968. Copyright 1968 by the American Association for the Advancement of Science.)

wavelength of light employed. For some cells the onset of stimulation by short wavelengths increased the firing rate, which then subsided upon the cessation of stimulation. Long wavelengths, on the other hand, resulted in an increased rate of firing when the stimulus was turned off. Thus a cell may be blue-excitatory and yellow-inhibitory (+ B − Y), another may be yellow-excitatory and blue-inhibitory (− B + Y).

Figure 4-12 shows six principal types of lateral geniculate cells in the macaque monkey. In general, it may be noted that the opponent pairs are complementary. When blue excitatory cones are active, the yellow are inhibited, and vice versa. The same relationship holds for red and green types. That some such opponent process must occur is demanded by the law of complementary colors; since if complements are aroused simultaneously, the resultant experience is a complete desaturation or gray.

It should also be noted that in addition to the opponent-type cells, nonopponent types are also present in the lateral geniculate body. These showed excitation for all wavelengths tested. The nonopponent cells are probably responsible for brightness or whiteness sensitivity. Thus, high levels of nonopponent activity would result in desaturated or very light colors, accounting for saturation phenomena as well as for hue.

Cortical Mechanisms in Vision

The lateral geniculate nuclei are only partial processing centers for visual information. It has been known for some time that retinal cells are connected to the visual areas of the occipital cortex in a highly localized manner. However, the

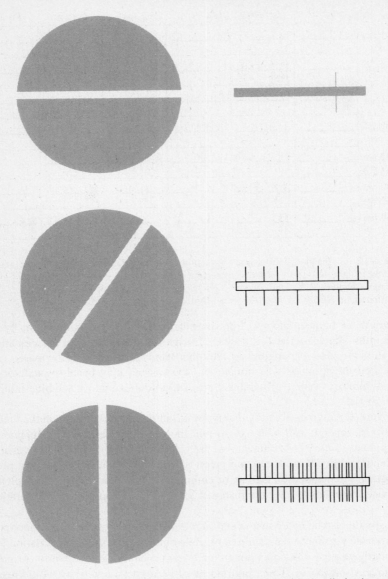

FIGURE 4-13. The importance of orientation for the simple cortical cells is shown by the varying responses to a slit of light. The horizontal slit produces almost no response; tilting produces a weak response; and placing the stimulus in the preferred vertical orientation produces a strong response. (From "The visual cortex of the brain" by David H. Hubel. Copyright © 1963 by Scientific American, Inc. All rights reserved.)

organization and processing functions of the cortical centers for vision have been little understood until the recent work of Hubel and Wiesel in the United States and that of R. Jung and his associates in Germany (see Grossman, 1973, p. 87, for a bibliography) provided information about the response mechanisms of cells in the primary visual cortex (area 17) and associated areas (areas 19 and 20).

Hubel and Wiesel (Hubel, 1963a, 1963b; Hubel & Wiesel, 1965, 1971), whose work will be summarized here, have identified two types of visual cells in the primary visual cortex (area 17) that process visual information. The first they call a "single" cortical cell. This cell responds selectively to a line stimulus presented to the eye, such as a slit, bar, or edge. Each simple cortical cell has a specific receptive field orientation and the degree to which the cell fires is determined by the position of the visual stimulus relative to the specific orientation (Figure 4-13). A simple cortical cell with a vertical orientation will respond minimally when the light stimulus is horizontal but will respond maximally when the light stimulus is vertical. As the light stimulus is displaced from the vertical, the cell will decrease its firing rate. Other simple cortical cells sensitive to other orientations will, however, increase their rate of firing.

The second variety of cortical cell has been called the "complex"; like the simple cell, the complex also responds to bars or edges but will respond with sustained firing to a moving bar, provided that it maintains the proper orientation. If the cell is sensitive to vertical edges, it will respond when the vertical edge is moved left and right, but there will be no response to an up or down movement.

Other types of cells have also been discovered in the visual association areas of the cortex (areas 18 and 19). These have been labeled "hypercomplex" by Hubel and Wiesel. Both lower-order and higher-order hypercomplex cells have been discovered in the visual area. The lower-order cells, like the complex cells, respond to either a bar, slit, or edge, but the length of the stimulus must be limited in one or both directions to be effective. The adequate stimulus, then, is a critically oriented line falling within a given region of the retina. The higher-order hypercomplex cell resembles the lower-order cell in requiring that a line stimulus be limited in length at one or both sides; however, it will respond to a line in either of two orientations 90 degrees apart.

All cells in the visual system may be viewed as receiving and building upon the information provided at the immediately preceding cellular level. The simple cortical cell receives and organizes the input from several on-off lateral geniculate cells and responds only to an edge of specific orientation. The complex cortical cells organize the input from several simple cortical cells and respond to a moving edge in a specific orientation. The lower-order hypercomplex cell organizes the input from several complex cells and responds to a moving line of specific length.

Neurons in the visual cortex tend to be concentrated and patterned depending on how they are coded. Single neurons in area 17 are coded for simple lines. The arrangement of others in columns in the cortex suggests that there is a topographic representation on the cortex of the retinal mosaic as well as a possible cortical mechanism for depth perception.

We should also like to call attention to the work of Lettvin and his associates (1959) on visual coding in the frog. In an article provocatively entitled, "What the Frog's Eye Tells the Frog's Brain," they showed that movement coding can be detected in the frog's optic nerve by applying microelectrodes directly into the optic tract. Some fibers, they found, respond only to stationary edges, others to moving edges. Some fibers respond with a burst of light only when illumination is first shut off. Others respond at increasingly more rapid rates the longer the darkness continues. The most interesting fiber type was found to be one that responded to small, dark, moving objects, suggesting a mechanism for the frog's well-known ability to catch flies on the wing. This research has provided evidence that even in relatively simple organisms a high level of information can be provided to the brain directly from the sense organ through retinal coding.

In summary, the brilliant technical achievements that we have just outlined show that modern visual research is dealing with more and more complex events, thus closing the traditional gap between sensory or receptor processes and perceptual or cortical processes. This work is also an excellent illustration of the value of good theory, since the early theories of visual sensation stimulated generations of researchers along what have proved to be highly fruitful lines.

Contemporary Trends in Auditory Theory

As is true of visual theory, auditory theorists have generally taken as their point of departure one of the classical theories. The most famous and influential of these are the resonance, or place, theory formulated by Helmholtz in 1863, and the frequency theory formulated by William Rutherford (1839–1899). Before considering these two theories, let us bear in mind the basic auditory phenomena for which any theory must account if it is to be comprehensive. Briefly, these phenomena are as follows:

1. Frequency discrimination, or the ability of the ear to distinguish between differen. frequencies of sound.
2. Intensity discrimination, or the ability of the ear to distinguish between different intensities of sound.
3. Timbre, or the ability to sense differences in tonal quality produced by different sounding bodies.
4. Beats, or the periodic fluctuation of sound intensity produced when two tones differing slightly in frequency are sounded simultaneously.
5. Combination tones, or tones generated when two frequencies are sounded simultaneously.
6. Transduction, or the conversion of mechanical energy in the cochlea into nervous impulses.
7. Organization and functioning of the higher auditory pathways.

Helmholtz argues that the basilar membrane, including the organ of Corti with its hair cells (Figure 4-14), functions as a resonator. That is, the fibers of the membrane vibrate in sympathy with external sounds coming into the ear by way of the tympanic membrane and auditory ossicles. Because the basilar membrane is trapezoidal in shape—that is, narrow at one end, increasing gradually to maximum width at the other end—Helmholtz reasoned that the narrow end, which is near the

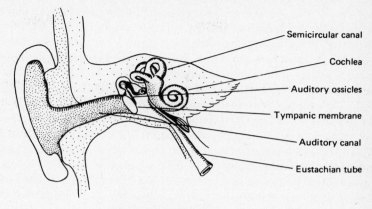

A. Gross Anatomy of the Ear

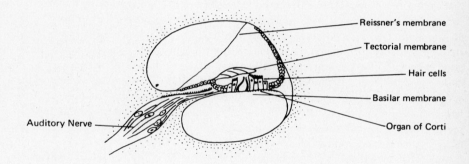

B. Cross Section of Cochlear Canal

FIGURE 4-14. (a) Semidiagrammatic drawing of the ear. (b) Cross section of the cochlear canal.

base of the cochlea, is tuned to high frequencies while the wide end, near the tip of the cochlea, vibrates in resonance with low frequencies.

By assuming that pitch is dependent on the *place* of stimulation, Helmholtz accounted for the *quality* dimension of auditory experience. The mechanism for the appreciation of loudness or the intensity dimension of audition remained to be explained. Helmholtz eventually accounted for this by assuming that (a) auditory nerve fibers respond with more nervous impulses per second to more intense sounds or (b) more fibers respond per unit of time to sounds of greater intensity. He accounted for timbre by assuming that the ear was capable of analyzing complex tones into fundamentals and harmonics. He explained beats by postulating that sounds close together in frequency set up vibrations in overlapping portions of the basilar membrane. Finally, combination tones were accounted for as artifacts or subjective experiences arising in the auditory ossicles.

We have stated the Helmholtz theory in its definitive form as if all major facets of the theory had been worked out by 1863. In reality, the theory was originally announced in an incomplete form, and nearly a decade passed before Helmholtz evolved his theory as it now stands. However, it was the more definitive form of the theory to which criticism was directed and that also served as a reference point for the formulation of alternative theories. For this reason we have avoided any attempt to trace the theory from its inception to its final form.

As Boring (1942, p. 408) points out, very little criticism was leveled at Helmholtz's theory during its first twenty years. Then a variety of criticisms and alternative theories were suggested (and are still being suggested) as more and more factual knowledge accumulated about the auditory mechanism. By 1942, a little over a century since Helmholtz had announced the place theory, twenty-one theories of hearing were summarized by Boring in his historical account of sensation and perception.[7] Many of these came into existence as a result of Helmholtz's theory. Of the post-Helmholtzian theories those that stand most directly in opposition to the original are the pure-frequency theories. In essence, a pure-frequency theory holds that the cochlea responds like a telephone transmitter to sounds entering the external ear; that is, the cochlea simply transmits nervous impulses along the auditory nerve at the same rate as incoming stimulus frequencies. For this reason the original frequency theory formulated by William Rutherford in 1886 is known as the "telephone theory." Boring suggests that Rutherford was influenced by two factors in choosing a frequency hypothesis to account for auditory mechanisms. One was the invention of the telephone in 1886, and the other was his experiments on frog nerve-muscle preparations. In the course of his investigations he found that muscle preparations gave off tones when stimulated with sufficient rapidity to result in tetanic or sustained contractions.

A frequency theory such as Rutherford's places the entire burden of analysis of wave form on the auditory cortex, in contrast to a resonance or place theory, which assumes that analysis takes place in the cochlea. In reality, either alternative is theoretically possible. However, the chief difficulty with Rutherford's theory is its failure to account for loudness. Because the intensity dimension of sensation is traditionally associated with the frequency of nervous discharge, Rutherford's theory, by attributing pitch to frequency, leaves no mechanism by which to explain loudness.

However, the real limiting factor in the understanding of auditory mechanisms during the several decades following Helmholtz's announcement of his theory was too much theorizing in the absence of adequate neurophysiological knowledge. Any valid body of information on the physiology of the auditory nerve and higher centers had to wait for the development of modern electronic equipment. The problem involved is very similar to that met with in vision. Dozens of *logical* theories of either visual or auditory mechanisms can be postulated. But theorizing in the absence of adequate anatomical or physiological information adds only to the fund of theories, not to factual knowledge.

---

[7]For a critique of the place and frequency theories of hearing, see Gulick (1971, chap. 5).

With the invention of techniques capable of probing the mysteries of nervous transmission from the cochlea to the brain, auditory research developed in a new direction in which the search for basic factual information took precedence over theory. The high-fidelity amplifier and the oscilloscope make it possible to pick up, amplify, and photograph the nervous impulses that arise in the cochlea, travel over the auditory nerve, and eventually terminate in the auditory cortex after passing through several subcortical centers.

Much of the recent neurological work in audition stems from an ingenious experiment conducted by Wever and Bray (1930a, 1930b). These investigators were studying the behavior of the auditory nerve in cats. Their technique consisted of placing electrodes on the exposed auditory nerve of the anesthetized cat so as to pick up electric potentials, which were then amplified and eventually fed into a telephone receiver in a separate room. The dramatic moment in the experiment occurred when Wever and Bray discovered that both human speech and various tonal frequencies up to 500 Hz could be heard in the receiver after being directed into the cat's ear. There they were changed into nervous impulses and were picked up and amplified by the electronic equipment. The implications of the experiment were far-reaching, for if the auditory nerve were faithfully following the frequency of incoming sounds, Helmholtz's popular resonance theory appeared inadequate to account for this phenomenon.

Further research by Wever and Bray and by Davis (see Stevens & Davis, 1938, chaps. 13 and 14) revealed that although the auditory nerve does follow the stimulus frequency within certain limits, also present was an entirely different phenomenon, which has since come to be known as *cochlear microphonics*. Let us consider the latter phenomenon first and then return to the question of transmission along the auditory nerve.

Cochlear microphonics are electric potentials generated by the cochlea as it is converting sound waves into nervous impulses. Perhaps the most interesting aspect of the cochlear microphonic is its localization along the cochlea to correspond in a general way with what might be expected from Helmholtz's analysis of pitch localization on the organ of Corti. This phenomenon is shown in Figure 4-15, which reproduces a map of cochlear microphonics as determined by Culler (1935) for the guinea pig's ear.

It is now believed that cochlear microphonics are essentially generator potentials originating in the hair cells and functioning as excitors of the afferent neuronal endings of the auditory nerve, which terminate in the hair cells. The (1960) research of Georg von Békésy (1899–1972), for which he was awarded the Nobel prize, shows that during acoustic stimulation a traveling wave or bulge moves along the cochlea and exerts a shearing force at the point where the hair cells are attached to the basilar membrane. Békésy has also shown that the wave travels along the cochlea according to its frequency, with low-frequency waves traveling farther toward the apex than high-frequency waves, as would be predicted by a place theory. Although low-frequency waves exert a broad stimulating influence on the cochlea, Békésy has utilized models to demonstrate that localization is sufficiently sharp to account for frequency discrimination.

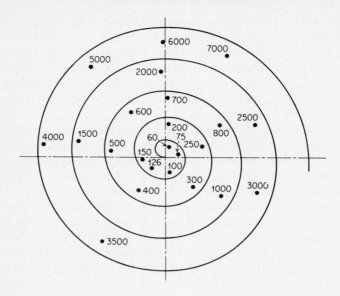

FIGURE 4-15.   Frequency localization in the cochlea as determined by the position where the cochlear microphonic is maximal. (After Culler, 1935. Reproduced by permission from *Physiological Psychology*, by C. T. Morgan and E. Stellar, Copyright 1950. McGraw-Hill Book Company, Inc.)

In summary, then, acoustic stimulation generates a traveling wave in the cochlea. The pressures exerted by that wave stimulate the hair cells at particular locations to generate transducer potentials, which, in turn, generate auditory impulses along the VIIIth (acoustic) nerve.

Although Wever and Bray's original experiment failed to separate cochlear microphonics from auditory nerve impulses, this has been done since. An analysis of the two phenomena reveals that the VIIIth nerve does follow stimulus frequencies, but not so faithfully as Wever and Bray were led to believe by the results of their original experiment. The situation is this: Synchronization of stimulus and VIIIth-nerve action potentials is very close at frequencies to 1000 Hz; good to 3000 Hz; poor to 4000 Hz; and lacking above 4000 Hz. The surprising, and at the same time puzzling, aspect of these findings is that there should be any following above 1000 Hz, since neurons are not capable of firing at such high rates of speed. Whereas different types of neurons do respond faster than others, it is doubtful that even the largest, most high-speed fibers can exceed 500 Hz (Morgan, 1965, pp. 69, 213). Speeds such as these are far lower than the minimum "following" frequency of the VIIIth nerve.

To account for synchronization at speeds above the refractory period of the auditory neurons, Wever and Bray postulated a volley theory, in which it is assumed that the neurons of the VIIIth nerve fire in "volleys" analogous to the way platoons in an infantry company might fire their weapons in successive volleys. In other words, instead of firing in a stepwise manner, the neurons of the VIIIth nerve fire in rotation, and in this way are able to transmit more impulses over a given period of time than if fired all at once.

In order to clarify the picture, the reader might imagine a large number of infantrymen, each with a single-shot rifle requiring reloading after discharge in much the same way that a neuron must "reload" following an all-or-none response. Obviously, if all our soldiers fire at once, reload, fire again, and so on, we shall have an "intense" discharge but a slow rate of fire. If, however, number 1 fires, instantly followed by 2, then 3, and so on, we shall have a much faster but weaker volley of shots. Let the first squad fire, followed by the second squad, and so on, and while the second squad is firing let the first squad reload and fire, and we shall have both high speed and a choice of intensity of fire according to the number of soldiers making up the squads.

The importance of postulating "squad firing" in the case of the auditory nerve is this: *It accounts for the mechanism of intensity,* and in this way avoids the stumbling block that Rutherford's frequency theory could not avoid. Indeed, Wever and Bray's volley principle has been woven into a duplex theory of hearing that accounts for pitches up to 3000 to 4000 Hz in terms of the frequency principle and for pitches higher than 4000 Hz in terms of the place or resonance principle.

There are, however, many traps and pitfalls awaiting the auditory theorist in the behavior of the cochlea, auditory nerve, and cortical centers. For this reason no contemporary theory of hearing can account for all the phenomena discovered in recent years by researchers in the field. We now seem to have a reversal of the original situation where there was too much theory and too few facts; now there are too many facts for any one theory to comprehend. Still, one set of facts that stands out above all the rest has to do with localization throughout the entire auditory system. There is, as we have already shown, localization in the cochlear response. But there is also a complex kind of localization or specialization of fibers in the auditory nerve. Roughly speaking, fibers from the basal, middle, and apical portions of the cochlea preserve their identity by forming bundles as they travel toward the medulla and cortex. Moreover, it has been found that some *tonotopic,* or spatial, organization persists at the level of the subcortical and cortical centers for hearing, as would be demanded by a place theory.

Galambos and Davis (1943), using microelectrode techniques, have found specialization of fibers for a restricted band of frequencies in the auditory system of the cat. In the thalamus (Figure 4-16), the great relay station for sensory fibers on the way to the cortex, Ades, Mettler, and Culler (1939) discovered a tonotopic organization of responses to frequency. Finally, a number of investigators have offered evidence for such organization in the auditory cortices of various animals; see Figure 4-17 for a tonotopic map of the auditory cortex that represents a synthesis of recent findings. It will be noted that the cochlea appears to be "unrolled" on the surface of the cortex, although the relationship is a complex one, with the cochlea being represented by two areas that are spatially the mirror images of each other with respect to localization (see also Morgan, 1965, pp. 217, 233; and Stevens, 1951, pp. 1119–1133). For a highly technical but comprehensive summary of research on auditory mechanism by leading experts in the field, see Békésy (1960,

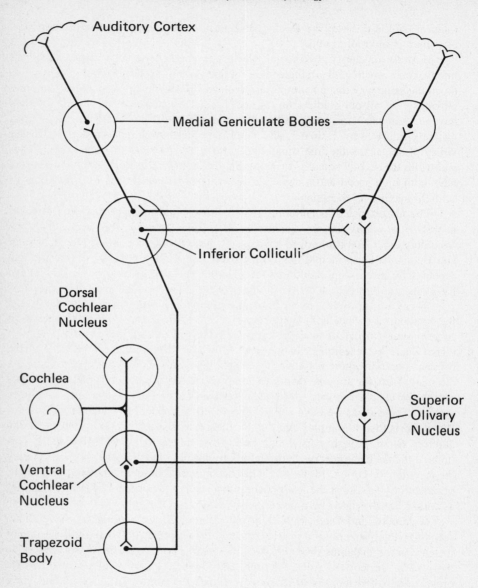

FIGURE 4-16.   Central auditory pathways. Note that impulses from each ear go to both auditory areas in the cerebral cortex.

especially chaps. 9, 10, and 12, which deal with problems of organization). Also valuable is Uttal's (1973) analysis of auditory coding and cortical localization.

Finally, we might note that Wollberg and Newman (1971), utilizing techniques similar to those of Hubel and Wiesel, have found that the auditory cortex of the squirrel monkey is highly specialized. Over 80 percent of the neurons respond to

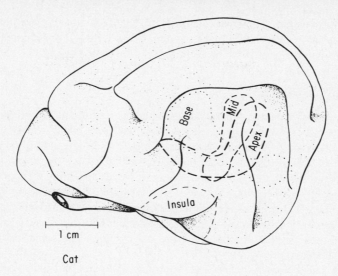

FIGURE 4-17.   Tonotopic organization of the temporal cortex of the cat. (Reprinted from Sensory Communication by W. A. Rosenblith by permission of the M. I. T. Press, Cambridge, Massachusetts.)

species-specific vocalizations. However, some neurons are more specialized than others. Some fire in response only to clicks or noises and some fire only to vocalizations, showing that the auditory cortex is highly adapted for selective coding of stimuli that are vital to the organism's survival.

In summary, the weight of the evidence from recent electrophysiological studies of the ear has confirmed *in principle* Helmholtz's theory that quality or pitch depends on the locus of stimulation of the hair cells along the basilar membrane. Moreover, this tonotopic organization of auditory mechanisms is preserved in some degree all along the conduction pathways and in the auditory cortex itself. What remains is to reconcile these findings with the fact that the auditory nerve shows synchronization of firing with outside frequencies at least along a restricted range of stimuli. There can be little doubt that this problem will eventually be resolved—perhaps in the form of a resonance-frequency theory. Meanwhile, we may conclude our survey of contemporary auditory theory with the comment that recent research has carried us far along the road to a comprehensive understanding of our second most important sensory modality.

Specialized Receptors and the Other Senses

It will be recalled that both Müller's doctrine of the specific energies of nerves and von Frey's specific end-organ theory of cutaneous sensitivity predicted that for each of the senses a specialized receptor organ would be discovered. It would be beyond the scope of a general account such as ours to attempt to review the extensive literature and vast body of empirical research for which these theories have been responsible. However, in order to round out our survey of sensory processes, it may prove worthwhile to summarize briefly the present status of the special end-organ theory for the more important remaining senses.

The Chemical Senses

The two most important chemical senses are gustation and olfaction. Because of its greater accessibility, the sense of taste has been more widely and more definitively investigated than has the sense of smell. As Figure 4-18 shows, there is good reason to believe that the taste buds are specialized for the mediation of the primary tastes of sweet, salt, sour, and bitter. However appealing this commonsensical assumption might be, direct microelectrode stimulation of taste buds does not reveal such a high degree of specificity. Moreover, largely through the work of Pfaffmann (1959), we also know that there are certain fiber types in the taste nerves that mediate those sensations, but the types are complex and some mediate more than one quality (Figure 4-19).

Briefly, one fiber may respond to solutions of hydrochloric acid, potassium, salt, quinine, and sucrose. However, different fibers show a maximum response to a given substance. One fiber may respond maximally to acid, another to sucrose, another to salt, and so forth (see Figure 4-19). Apparently, the *pattern* of firing of

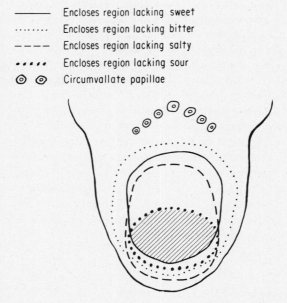

FIGURE 4-18.   Regions of the tongue sensitive to the primary gustatory stimuli. (From Woodworth, R. S., and Schlosberg, H., Experimental psychology. New York: Holt, Rinehart and Winston, Inc. Copyright 1954.)

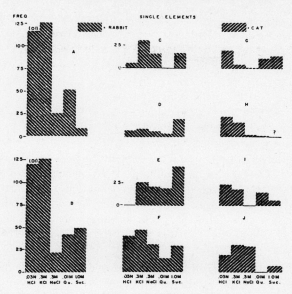

FIGURE 4-19. Responses of six individual elements in rabbit and cat to five types of taste stimuli on the tongue. (After Pfaffmann, J. Neurophysiol. 18:435, 1955—Fig. 9.)

the taste neurons is the important factor, with the brain in some as yet not understood manner being able to decode the complex message from the taste nerve.

There are many theories of olfactory sensitivity, none of which is definitive. The inaccessibility of the olfactory epithelium makes it extremely difficult to investigate this sense. Henning's well-known classification of salient odors is given in Figure 4-20. Little is known of the central olfactory pathways. The difficulty with

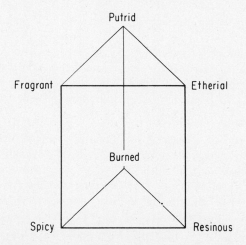

FIGURE 4-20. Henning's classification of the salient odors.

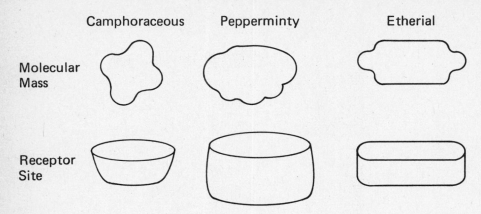

FIGURE 4-21.   A diagrammatic representation of Amoore's molecular theory of olfaction. The clusters of molecules are analagous to keys which fit into the receptor sites (locks).

Henning's classification is its lack of supporting evidence in known specialized receptor mechanisms mediating the salient odors.

More attractive is Amoore's theory (1964), based on the molecular shapes of odorous substances. Amoore lists seven primary qualities: camphoraceous, musky, floral, minty, ethereal, pungent, and putrid. Based on his studies of the molecular shapes of representatives of these qualities, he argues that receptors with corresponding shapes must exist in the olfactory epithelium into which the molecules fit, much as a key fits a lock. For this reason the theory is known as a stereochemical theory (stereo = three dimensionality). Molecules for camphoraceous substances, for example, form bowl shapes and are presumed to fit into a corresponding concave depression in the olfactory epithelium (Figure 4-21). Minty substances are shaped like a rectangle rounded at the corners. Similarly, each of the other receptors and its stimulus is assumed to have a distinct pattern into which the appropriate molecular shape fits.

Some empirical proof for the theory has been offered by Amoore, who has synthesized substances of key receptor shapes and demonstrated that they smell as they should according to the theory. Some, however, do not. Therefore, no theory of olfactory sensitivity is completely acceptable at the present time.

The Cutaneous Senses

Much more is known about the peripheral and central mechanisms of the somatic senses. For the cutaneous senses the specific end-organ theory has held up well except in the case of thermal sensitivity, which has proved puzzling to generations of researchers. Encapsulated or specialized end organs serve touch and deep pressure. For touch, basket endings and Meissner corpuscles mediate touch (Figure 4-22). Deep pressure is mediated by Pacinian corpuscles. Traditionally, pain is believed to be mediated by free nerve endings. Support for this hypothesis comes from studies of the cornea of the eye, which is richly endowed with free nerve endings and is also a structure capable of generating a great deal of pain if injured.

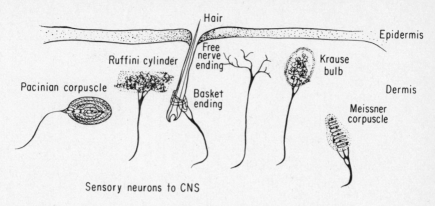

Sensory neurons to CNS

FIGURE 4-22.   A diagrammatic representation of the more important subcutaneous receptors.

However, the exact nature of the neural coding for pain remains controversial. Because any intense stimulus may give rise to pain and because pain can be blocked in many ways (for example, by acupuncture, by feeding loud music into the ears, by hypnosis), it has been suggested (Melzack, 1961; Melzack & Wall, 1965) that pain may be related to the pattern of fibers firing in the spinal cord. The gate control theory, as it is called, assumes that the substantia gelatinosa (an area of the spinal cord where interneurons synapse with fibers conducting pressure and pain impulses) acts as a gate, either allowing pain impulses to travel up the cord or inhibiting them.

The critical factor determining whether inhibition of impulses occurs or whether impulses are allowed to continue up the cord is the behavior of A and C fibers entering the cord. Activity in A fibers mediating pressure inhibits the substantia gelatinosa, while activity in C fibers mediating pain decreases the inhibitory effects of the substantia gelatinosa, allowing the gate to open. The effect of distracting stimuli, acupuncture needles, and the like would block pain by inhibiting the firing of the pain-conducting neurons in the spinal cord or higher centers. Temperature sensitivity has traditionally been assigned to Krause bulbs (cold) and Ruffini cylinders (warmth). The evidence for this, however, is inconclusive. The Krause bulbs are located at the proper depth (0.1 millimeter) to serve as cold receptors as judged by the reaction time to cold stimuli. The greater depth of the Ruffini cylinders (0.3 millimeter) correlates positively with the fact that the reaction time to warm stimuli is longer than to cold.

In addition to the evidence from reaction time studies, it has been possible to show that there is some correspondence between cold- and warm-sensitive areas of the body and the presence of Krause bulbs and Ruffini cylinders. However, the correspondence is by no means perfect. Some thermally sensitive areas have no specialized end organs—only free nerve endings. It has been suggested that these types of fibers—particularly those associated with the minute blood vessels—may mediate thermal sensitivity. For a recent review of the evidence bearing on the specific end-organ doctrine and temperature sensitivity, the reader is referred to Geldard (1972), Kenshalo (1971), and Uttal (1973).

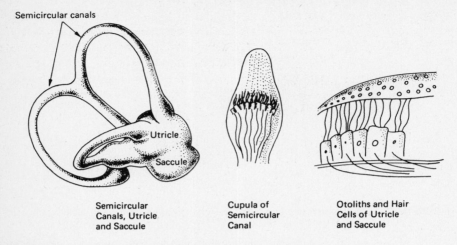

Semicircular canals

Semicircular
Canals, Utricle
and Saccule

Utricle

Saccule

Cupula of
Semicircular
Canal

Otoliths and Hair
Cells of Utricle
and Saccule

FIGURE 4-23.   The semicircular canals, utricle, and saccule.

Proprioception and the Static Sense

For proprioception and static sensitivity, the specialized end-organ theory has held up quite satisfactorily. It is generally agreed that Pacinian corpuscles are responsive to movements of the joints and that a variety of muscle spindles and tendon organs are responsive to stretch of muscles and tendons. Static sensitivity is associated with two receptor centers. The semicircular canals mediate the sense of acceleration-deceleration, and the receptors in the utricle and saccule mediate the sense of head position (Figure 4-23).

SUMMARY AND EVALUATION

In casting a backward glance over the evolution of theory and research in sensation, one is immediately struck by a strong sense of the historical depth of sensory psychology. Along with associationism, sensory psychology formed the core of the prescientific psychologies and, in terms of a descriptive system, reached its culmination in Titchener's structuralism. Then for a time sensation faded into the background of psychological research and systematizing. This in part was the result of its displacement by interest in other aspects of behavior and experience and in part because evolution slows down or stops temporarily when there is no place for further improvement because of technical limitations.

When modern electronic techniques became available, a burst of progress followed immediately; in fact it is still going on. But the direction of research has shifted from the description and measurement of sensation on a purely psychological level to a concerted attack on the underlying neurophysiology of the sense organs themselves. We have attempted to show the general lines of advance of the new approach in the areas of vision and audition. Much the same pattern has been typical of recent research on the gustatory, olfactory, and cutaneous senses—where significant gains are being made in accounting for the physiological substrata of these modalities. It seems fair to say that even though this type of neurophysiological research is reductionistic in nature, a new kind of reductionism has permeated the field. Researchers are dealing with far more complex stimulus patterns and are finding that *patterns of coding* rather than discrete, one-for-one neural correspondence is the typical way the nervous system operates for sensory processes.

Perception: The Classical Heritage

5

In his *New Theory of Vision* the philosopher Berkeley likened sensations to the sounds of language: They have no intrinsic meaning but must be interpreted by the listener. From this point of view, sensations have no inherent meaning. They are the raw materials of experience to which mind contributes understanding. But, it may be objected, we do not hear "sounds" in everyday life that have to be "translated" into meaningful concepts; nor do we experience masses of qualities, extents, and intensities from which we consciously construct a world of objects and events. Instead, under ordinary conditions, meaning comes instantaneously. It is as if we never *sense* stimuli out there but *perceive* objects, space, time, and events; our brains, it seems, are geared for perception, not sensation.

Naturally, this does not deny the obvious fact that we must sense before we can perceive. Rather, it means that the entire process of observation is so telescoped that we are rarely aware of sensory activity as such. Just as a good reader grasps ideas and meanings instead of words and letters, so the observer perceives meaningful objects instead of experiencing crude sense impressions. And this principle brings us to the fundamental problem for classical perceptual psychology: *to account for the orderly arrangement of objects in space and time in the world of the perceiver*.

The British empiricists, it will be recalled, taught that all knowledge comes to mind by way of the senses. But as an explanation of the meaningfulness of experience, this doctrine begs the question, since the empiricists also held that sensations in and of themselves are not knowledge but only the elements from which knowledge is derived. Thus far we seem to have a variation on the old puzzle of the primacy of the chicken or the egg. To resolve the dilemma the empiricists employed the principles of the association of ideas to account for meaning. Their argument ran somewhat as follows: Simple sense experiences eventually "go together" through repetition and contiguity. For example, the experience of a certain wavelength of light stimulating the eye of the child is frequently accompanied by a second experience, the spoken color name, and eventually each comes to mean the other. Sensation, then, is only the foundation for perception; the role of experience in providing meaning is crucial.

On a more complex level, general or abstract ideas can also be explained by means of associationism. The philosopher Hume asks us to consider the concept of a triangle. How do we come to have such a general idea that applies to a diversity of geometric forms? His answer is that the concept of triangularity is built up slowly on the basis of individual sensory experiences with particular triangles. The general or abstract concept is the result of the association in memory of many experiences with various kinds of triangles.

For many years the empirical account of perceptual meaning was accepted as a valid explanation of the process. However, the adequacy of the associational account of perceptual meaning was eventually challenged on the ground that it failed to take into consideration motivational and other dynamic factors. For example, in abnormal perceptions, such as hallucinations or delusions, the effect of powerful motivational factors is evident. In these cases, frustration, conflict, or strong desire determines the meaning of a percept just as surely as the stimulus factors or past experiences that may be involved.

Similarly, in recent decades a great deal of emphasis has been put on attitudes, physiological states, personality traits, even cultural factors as perceptual determinants. Because of the gradually increasing range of recognized determinants, perceptual theory has grown broader over the years to include more and more such factors. Today it is fair to say that virtually every other mental process has been investigated in terms of its possible role in influencing perception. Finally, modern technology with its emphasis on computer programming and information processing has had a significant impact on perceptual theory, further broadening its scope.

Because perception has come to occupy so prominent a position in contemporary psychology, we shall devote this and the following chapter to tracing its evolution from sensory psychology to its present status as one of the most important and central areas in the entire field. In this chapter we shall deal with the origins of perceptual psychology in philosophy, its subsequent development in the early experimental period, and its place in the systematic structures of the schools. In Chapter 6 we shall be concerned exclusively with contemporary perceptual systems developed during the past half-century.

PERCEPTION IN PRESCIENTIFIC PSYCHOLOGY[1]

The Scottish philosopher Thomas Reid (1710–1796) first formulated the distinction between sensation and perception. He held sensations to be the activities of the sense organs as these are experienced in consciousness. Perception he held to be dependent on, but different from, sensation in that the perceiver is aware of objects

---

[1]Our account has been drawn from a variety of secondary sources: Boring (1942, 1950), Brett (1953), Heidbreder (1933), F. S. Keller (1937), Murphy (1949), Warren (1921), and Woodworth (1948).

or events in his or her environment and not merely sense impressions. Moreover, he pointed out that awareness of what is in the environment carries with it a strong sense of conviction of the objective character of events, situations, time, and space. Reid called this objective aspect of perception an "invincible belief" in the existence of external objects. The objectifying of percepts is, therefore, a product of mind. Going beyond his descriptive definition of perception, Reid tried to account for the *why* of perceptual experience, and in doing so posed a fundamental question that subsequent generations of philosophers and psychologists have sought to answer. Reid's own solution was simple and forthright but not very satisfying to the modern reader. He attributed the "existence quality" of perception to an "instinctive tendency" in the human constitution. He considered the perception of both spatial extension and temporal duration—two fundamental dimensions of perception—to be "intuitive."

Although Reid failed to formulate an acceptable explanation for perceptual meaning, he did set the stage for further inquiry into the problem along two major lines: *nativism* and *empiricism*. The nativists, following Reid, postulated innate ideas or hereditary predispositions as the explanation of the perceptual processes. The empiricists, in general, subscribed to associationism as the key to perceptual meaning. The empirical view was sponsored by Berkeley, Lotze, Helmholtz, and Wundt, and nativism was championed by Kant, Johannes Müller, Hering, and Stumpf.

We shall examine the specific contributions of each of these representatives of the empirical and nativistic traditions in more detail in the following sections. However, a word of explanation is in order for the contemporary student of psychology in regard to the emphasis on space and object perception in prescientific and early scientific writings on the subject. The modern reader, fresh from a general psychology course, is likely to think of perception in terms of motivational and emotional influences, consciousness expansion, self-perception, information processing theory, or some similar topic of current interest. In the face of these highly challenging contemporary developments, it may be difficult to appreciate that the *fundamental* problem of perceptual psychology is to account for the perception of objects in space. It was natural, therefore, that early perceptual theorists expended most of their efforts on this primary problem. With this in mind, let us begin by examining the contribution of the empiricists, who were particularly concerned with the specific cues employed in space perception.

PERCEPTION AND THE EMPIRICAL TRADITION

We have already seen (Chapter 2) how the empiricists, starting with Hobbes, brought the doctrine of innate ideas under attack. It was natural, therefore, for Berkeley in his *New Theory of Vision* to account for space perception on the basis of experience. He argued that distance, or the third dimension, is not directly perceived, since the stimuli that come to the eye terminate in a point on the retina, which in no way varies in depth with the distance of the stimulus object. It makes no difference as far as the depth of the retinal image is concerned whether the point of light on the fovea originates in a star a million light-years away or comes from a source a few yards from the observer. Having only two dimensions itself, the retina has no mechanism for the direct appreciation of depth.

Depth, then, must be the result of experience—experience of past contacts and movements employed in dealing with objects in space. Moreover, Berkeley argued that the kinesthetic strains set up in the extrinsic and intrinsic ocular muscles could serve as cues for distance. Again, the process is essentially one of association, for if we frequently experience the tensions associated with strong convergence of the eyes on near objects, these tensions presumably come to mean "near," while relaxed muscles and low tensions stand for "far." A similar reasoning holds for the belief that accommodation of the lens is a possible cue of depth.

In addition to reducing distance perception to nonspatial cues, Berkeley undertook an analysis of object size or magnitude, which is of course closely correlated with distance. Object size, he pointed out, varies with the distance of an object from the retina; but in spite of variation in distance, the perceived size of objects remains relatively constant (size constancy). Berkeley related perceived size or magnitude to distance by arguing that the observer takes into account his own distance from the object, thus making for relative constancy in perceived size despite wide variations in viewing distance.

Finally, Berkeley came to grips with the problem of perceptual meaning, which he explained in terms of associationism. Specifically, he held that any given perception is meaningful only in the light of past perceptions, whose meaning is carried into the present in the form of memories. Similarly, present perceptions become the ideas of the future to be associated with tomorrow's perceptions.

The empirical tradition, as reported in Chapter 2, continued in British philosophy from Berkeley to Mill. But empiricism also took root on the continent of Europe and eventually found a place in Wundt's psychology. Because Wundt's system is in the mainstream of our evolutionary approach, we shall turn our attention to Continental empiricism, beginning with a study of Lotze's theory of space perception, a position that strongly influenced Wundt's.

Lotze and "Local Signs"

Rudolf Lotze (1817–1881), an early German philosopher-psychologist, is in many ways reminiscent of Gustav Fechner. Like Fechner, Lotze was a blend of humanist and scientist. He was attracted, on the one hand, to the freedom of philosophical and metaphysical speculation and, on the other, to the exactitudes and discipline of science. Although Lotze had been trained as a physician, he devoted a great deal of time to philosophical study and, as was true of Fechner, became interested in the mind-body problem. His interest in psychology eventually resulted in a book entitled, *Medical Psychology*. It was in this volume in the section on space perception that Lotze presented his famous "local-sign" theory—a theory that proved to be highly influential in nineteenth- and early twentieth-century psychology. In fact, Boring (1950) argues that Lotze was responsible for the great interest in empiricism shown by Wundt and his immediate predecessors.

Lotze assumes that mind is inherently capable of perceiving space. However, space perception depends on sensory cues, which in and of themselves are non-spatial. For example, when the surface of the body is stimulated by anything larger than a point, the individual is able to perceive the spatiality of the stimulus. This perception of spatiality, Lotze argues, depends on cues generated by the pattern of excitation of the skin receptors. Objects larger than a point excite many receptors simultaneously, thus giving rise to experiences of length and breadth. Moreover, because the skin is elastic, it is depressed by tactile stimuli; but the degree to which it is depressed is related to underlying conditions in the subcutaneous tissues. Over bony areas the pattern of depression (and its attendant sensory excitation) differs from the pattern over more yielding fatty or muscular tissues. These differential intensity patterns are *local signs* that furnish the basis for cutaneous space perception.

In applying his theory to vision, man's most highly developed spatial modality, Lotze places great emphasis on eye movements as cues for the appreciation of space. That is, our visual apparatus is in almost continuous motion as we attempt to bring external objects into clear focus on the fovea, and because of the effort involved, patterns of kinesthetic sensations are continually arising from the eye muscles. These sensations Lotze calls "changing feelings of position." The kinesthetic sensations generated as the eye sweeps around an arc of regard establish the local signs for the retinal points associated with such movements. If the quiescent eye is subsequently stimulated at two or more separate points, the associations of frequently experienced "feelings" of movement from the past come into consciousness, and the result is a sense of experienced space. In essence, the perception of space is learned through associations of movement in space with the activity of local sensory spots that are stimulated in the course of such movements.

Lotze explains auditory spatiality by assuming that stimuli that are not in the midplane of the head affect the two ears differentially and so become local signs for space localization.

Clearly, Lotze's theory is limited to explaining spatial perception for those senses in which movement of the sensory apparatus is possible (vision) or for those modalities where stimuli may be moved over the sense organs or may stimulate spatially separated organs (touch, audition). For this reason the adherents of a strict local-sign theory do not attribute spatiality to olfaction or taste.

The publication of Lotze's theory generated a controversy. The empiricists, as had been stated, claimed the theory for their side; but the nativists, by pointing to Lotze's original premise that the brain is inherently capable of perceiving space, could argue that spatiality is an inherent or native process. We shall consider the opposite, or nativistic, view in more detail in a later section of this chapter. But the point to be emphasized here is that Lotze's theory was by no means unambiguously empirical. However, it was an attractive theory; and the early texts in psychology, whether on the side of empiricism or nativism, gave it extended consideration.

Indeed, traces of the theory in a highly modified form can be found in contemporary associationistic accounts of perception.

Helmholtz and "Unconscious Inference"

Helmholtz, with whom we are already familiar from our study of his famous theories of hearing and color vision, became involved in perceptual problems through his interest in sensation and optics. In his publications on these subjects, he clearly and forthrightly embraced empiricism, thereby placing himself in opposition to the strongly nativistic German tradition.

In essence, Helmholtz's theory of space perception was developed around the concept of "unconscious inference." By the latter he meant that the experience of space is not an inherent characteristic of mind, but an *inferred* quality brought to present perception from the individual's past experiences with objects in space. Just as when ice is perceived visually we infer that it is cold because of memories of past tactual experiences with ice, so we may infer "seen" space on the basis of our past interaction with objects in space. Thus, if we are touched on the arm with our eyes closed, we can tell whether the right or left arm was touched and the approximate location of the contact. This spatial localization is possible because of many prior experiences of the same kind in which touching the arm has acquired a local sign.

Helmholtz, moreover, believed in local signs in that he held that the various sense organs and nerves have their characteristic qualities, or as Müller had argued, "specific energies." But such specific sense qualities are not in themselves spatial or intrinsically meaningful. They are bare sense impressions to which associations must be added (unconsciously inferred) to render them meaningful. Actually, in the child or in novel experiences in the adult, such associations would at first be conscious. It is frequent repetition that makes them rapid and automatic to the point where they eventually become "unconscious." For example, as children we were conscious of the greater strain associated with lifting large objects than small objects. If as adults we are confronted with two objects identical in weight but greatly differing in size, the larger will seem much *lighter* than the smaller because we unconsciously associate greater effort with lifting large objects. Our "surprise" at the speed with which the larger rises makes it seem abnormally light. A pound of feathers can be made to appear lighter than a pound of lead through unconscious inference! Helmholtz referred to the compelling quality of such inferences as their "irresistibility."

In summary, Helmholtz extended Lotze's local-sign theory and at the same time attempted to make it congruent with Müller's doctrine of specific nerve energies. But of even greater importance was his clear-cut stand on the issue of nativism and empiricism itself. His strong support of empiricism carried great weight with the physiologists and embryonic psychologists of his day. Consequently, it is not surprising that Wundt, who was Helmholtz's assistant for four years at Heidelberg (1858–1862), was strongly influenced not only by the desirability of empiricism as a general point of view in psychology but also more specifically by the utility of a modified doctrine of unconscious inference for explaining perceptual meaning (Boring, 1950, p. 309).

Wundt on Perception

In this section we shall take up only a special aspect of Wundt's perceptual theory, since we shall be considering the overall structuralistic treatment of perception in detail when we discuss Titchener's system. In general, Wundt adhered to the empirical-associationistic tradition, which held that mind is a compound of elemental processes bound together by associations. Since he considered perception a complex process involving sensations and meaning, he had to face the problem of showing how meaning accrues to sensory experience, and it was his effort in this direction that led to his special "doctrine of apperception." By apperception Wundt means awareness of any conscious content that is clearly comprehended or grasped. Stated differently, he argues for a distinction between a passive "pure perception" without logical meaning, and the more active "apperception," which is pure perception plus preexisting ideas. It is the preexisting ideas that make perceptions meaningful. The total complex of preexisting ideas, or memories, make up what Wundt calls the "apperceptive mass."

But it would be a mistake to think of apperception as a passive process that automatically accrues to perception. On the contrary, apperception is accompanied by a conscious feeling of activity—an awareness of tension and excitement. It is, so to speak, a reflection of the excitement of "discovery" experienced as one clearly grasps the meaning of a perceptual situation and its relationship to the totality of present and past experience. Therefore, *feeling* is an integral part of apperception from Wundt's point of view.

Finally, an important aspect of the doctrine of apperception is the role played by attention in the overall process. Wundt distinguishes between the whole range or field of consciousness on the one hand, and the focus or momentary "point" on the other. Because apperception involves a clear grasp or comprehension of conscious content, only those processes at the focus of attention are apperceived. However, to avoid confusion, it is important to note that the heart of the doctrine is his belief that *the complex of ideas from past experience* form "apperceptive masses," which give meaning to present consciousness.

Wundt took the doctrine of apperception from Johann Friedrich Herbart (1776–1841),[2] one of the Continental philosopher-psychologists of the nineteenth century. Herbart, in turn, got the idea from the mathematician Leibnitz. Therefore, the doctrine of apperception was already well entrenched in psychology when Wundt made it a part of his system. Moreover, the doctrine crept into systems other than structuralism and became a lively controversial issue in early German and

---

[2]Herbart was deeply interested in education and urged that teachers strive to develop apperceptive masses in their pupils for the better comprehension and understanding of new experiences.

American psychology. What we wish to emphasize here, however, is the fact that Wundt made experience and an active consciousness the central themes in his psychology of perception. His explanation of meaning in terms of past experience is clearly on the side of empiricism.

In summary, the empiricists—whether dealing with the relatively simple matter of space perception or the more general process of perceptual meaning—sought to demonstrate the validity of empirical explanations of the perceptual processes. Moreover, even in this brief summary of the empirical position, it is possible to recognize the tendency for perceptual psychology to broaden, gradually allowing for the inclusion of more and more complex processes. In fact, William James might well have been criticizing contemporary perceptual psychology when he complained that perception in becoming apperception allowed "innumerable" individual factors to enter into the meaning of perceptual experience. In short, James felt that the concept of perception had become so broad as to be meaningless.

Whatever the merits of the case, the empiricists had claimed that the explanation of all perceptual processes was to be found in experience—not only for simple visual extents but for the complex cognitive processes as well. But there was another side to the argument, the nativistic, with an equally strong tradition—a tradition that has its counterpart in contemporary psychology. We must now consider this side of the controversy.

NATIVISM AND PERCEPTION

As we pointed out earlier in this chapter, nativism was supported by Kant, Müller, Hering, and Stumpf. Before we consider the individual contributions of these men, a brief general statement of the concept of nativism itself will be presented to serve as a frame of reference for the discussion of individual nativist contributions.

Nativism originated in philosophy as a parallel concept to rationalism and, like rationalism, is frequently employed as a bipolar opposite to empiricism in accounting for perceptual meaning. Nativism opposed the *tabula rasa* view of mind in which sensation gives rise to memory, and, by association, memory in turn gives rise to ideas. The rationalists, on the contrary, believed that mind possesses inherent or a priori ideas—ideas of right and wrong, of space, of time, and, some believed, of God. If this conception of mind were correct, then the materialistic philosophy of the empiricists would be founded on error. The "pure reason" (to borrow Kant's famous phrase) of the empiricists failed to take into account the limitations of their own philosophy.

Because the doctrine of empiricism occupied a central place in prescientific psychology, it was natural that an opposition movement arose to question the idea that mind is derived from experience. Moreover, it is understandable that the controversy began in the field of perception—the key process in the understanding of mind. Finally, we might note that the controversy did not await the formal founding of psychology but got under way as a result of the publication of Kant's great philosophical treatise *The Critique of Pure Reason*.

Kant and Nativism

In choosing the title *The Critique of Pure Reason,* Kant (1724–1804) did not mean to imply that he was against reason. Rather, he took as his thesis the argument that the British empirical school of philosophy represented by Locke and his followers had fallen into the error of erecting their systems on false premises. Specifically, he charged that they had failed to realize that philosophy and science must recognize the validity of absolute truths arising out of the innate content of mind. These truths, Kant believed, are not only independent of empirical proof but are true *before* experience, or in other words, are true a priori. Kant went on to argue that mathematics is replete with such absolute, a priori truths. The basic axioms of the mathematician are not dependent on experience for proof, but are the inevitable consequence of the nature of the human mind.

Space and time, to cite examples more relevant to psychology, are not born of sensations but are a priori forms of perception that coordinate and make meaningful incoming sensations. Sensations arising from objects in the environment do not, as the empiricists believed, automatically take on a kind of unity or order and so become meaningful perceptions. Rather, according to Kant, *mind* imposes a selectivity on sensations, accepting some and rejecting others, depending on its purpose. "Mechanical" principles of association, such as frequency, recency, and contrast, are inadequate to account for the order of mind. For Kant, mind is the master of sensations; sensations are not the masters of mind.

Kant's philosophy becomes psychology in the sense that two of his a priori attributes of mind are space and time. Because mind is inherently spatial, sensations are ordered on a continuum of space; and since mind can appreciate time, then time, too, lends order to experience. Mind therefore contributes to experience as much as it takes. But in another sense Kant's views are not psychology at all, for it is impossible to subject a priori ideas or innate "givens" to experimental tests. As a psychology, Kant's *Critique* provided no advantage over Descartes' doctrine of innate ideas. For this reason Kant's importance to psychology consisted primarily of his having provided a focus for empirical attacks on the nativistic point of view. However, this is not to say that nativism itself stands or falls with Kant, for in some form or other it has persisted in psychology up to the present time, especially in the Gestalt tradition.

Johannes Müller

Müller came into the empirical-nativistic controversy by way of his doctrine of the specific energies of nerves, which we considered in connection with the historical development of physiology (see Chapter 2). The argument that special experiential qualities are associated with specific nerves is, of course, far removed from Kant's doctrine of innate categories of mind or a priori truths. Instead, it simply states that nerves impose their innate or structurally determined qualities on mind. Since nerves are native equipment, Müller's doctrine is necessarily a kind of nativism.

To relate the doctrine to perception, it can be argued that mind has no direct contact with the environment but instead is aware only of the activities of nerves. Because of the spatial arrangement of the nerves that make up the optic tract, space is directly perceived from the tract. More specifically, the image from an external object is projected on the retina, and the retina, by way of the optic tract, "projects" the resulting nervous impulses on the brain in a pattern that mirrors the objective stimulus complex. Finally, it should be noted that Müller accepted the Kantian doctrine that mind is spatial. Such an assumption is a necessary part of Müller's argument since patterns of nervous impulses cannot in themselves give a sense of space unless mind in some way *interprets* the pattern as spatial.

Although Müller accepted a Kantian-nativistic view of perception, it would be unfair to think of him as a pure nativist. His overall orientation was closer to empiricism than nativism. As Boring (1942, 1950) points out, the complicating factor running through the entire empirical-nativistic controversy is that every nativist is something of an empiricist and every empiricist something of a nativist. In this connection, one is reminded of the heredity-environment controversy of more recent vintage, in which, as it turns out, no one is willing to ascribe all individual differences to either factor but must admit that both play a part. In fact, it is typical of psychologists' controversies that they revolve around questions of emphasis rather than absolute differences.

Hering and Stumpf

Ewald Hering (1834–1918) is most famous in the annals of psychology for his theory of color vision, which we summarized in Chapter 4, whereas Carl Stumpf (1848–1936) is best known for his pioneer studies in the psychology of tone. We shall consider Hering's and Stumpf's theories of space perception only briefly, for two reasons. First, both accepted the local-sign theory formulated by Lotze, with which we are already familiar, although both argued for a nativistic interpretation of Lotze's signs. Second, theories, such as Hering's and Stumpf's, that attributed inherent spatiality to the retina did not win general acceptance in the face of the far more popular empirical explanations. As a result, the strictly nativistic point of view on retinal spatiality failed to evolve into an acceptable form in contemporary psychology. The nearest thing to nativism in modern perceptual theory is represented by the Gestalt point of view, which will be considered later in this chapter.

Hering holds that the retina, besides furnishing sensations of light and color, is capable of imparting three spatial qualities: height, breadth, and depth. These in turn he relates to retinal points or local signs. While adopting the local-sign foundation of space appreciation, Hering stipulates that spatiality is an inherent property of the retina. In elaborating the theory, he takes into account directional ability, binocular factors in depth perception, and the relationship between depth perception and kinesthetic cues arising from the eye muscles. We need not enter into the details of the theory here. It is exceedingly complex and has no counterpart in contemporary perceptual theory. The interested reader may consult Titchener (1910) for a summary and critical interpretation of this theory.

In regard to Stumpf's theory we need only mention that, like Hering, he argued for a nativistic interpretation of Lotze's local signs. Moreover, Stumpf accepted Hering's argument that the retina possesses an inherent mechanism for the appreciation of visual space. Indeed, Stumpf took the position that space is just as directly perceived as sensory quality.

The difficulty with these theories is the a priori nature of their assumptions. The nativist, by making space inherent, more or less cuts the ground from under the opposition. Theoretically, in order to evaluate the nativistic position, one would have to test the infant's perceptual ability to determine whether or not he or she has an inherent sense of space.[3] The empiricists, however, labor under no such limitations. And because the empiricists' hypotheses could be subjected to experimental tests, their viewpoint found favor in the experimentally oriented atmosphere of the late nineteenth century.

As we take leave of this old controversy, let us point out that it has some value for the contemporary student of psychology in its emphasis on the desirability of appealing to experimentation, instead of speculation and authoritarian doctrine, for the resolution of theoretical issues. The controversy is an excellent, albeit unfortunate, example of too much theorizing and too little research. Moreover, the influence of the "weight of authority" is clearly evident as a factor that served to intensify and prolong the controversy.

Kant's and Müller's great stature undoubtedly influenced Hering and Stumpf on the nativist side, just as Locke's and Helmholtz's fame must have attracted followers to the empirical camp. But, in a sense, neither personal stature nor authority has any place in science—which, theoretically at least, is impersonal. However, being a product of the human mind, science cannot completely free itself from the limitations of human nature.

PERCEPTUAL PSYCHOLOGY AND THE SCHOOLS

The leaders of the schools of the late nineteenth and early twentieth centuries varied widely in their general approach to perception and in the emphasis that they gave the perceptual process in their systems. For Wundt and Titchener, perception was a crucial problem. Watson, in keeping with his strict behaviorism, ignored perception. The Gestalt school, having originated as a result of a perceptual experiment, went on to make the study of the perceptual processes the very heart of its psychology. Moreover, each of the schools that developed systematic interpretations of perception took a stand on the empiricist-nativistic controversy, which, in a sense, was their heritage from prescientific psychology. The lines of division were no longer so clearly drawn, and the exponents of the schools did not employ traditional terminology. Nevertheless, whether implicitly or explicitly, each had to resolve the issue for his or her system.

Finally, it should be noted that perception proved to be a critical test of the old method of mental analysis. In fact, the whole question of the validity of perceptual

---

[3]In Chapter 7 we shall see that psychologists have recently made an attempt to do just this.

analysis became one of the central issues in the disputes among the schools. But we shall let the schools speak for themselves, beginning with Titchener's structuralism, which in many ways represents a culmination of the tradition of interpreting perception in terms of associationism.

Titchener and Structuralism[4]

Titchener, it will be recalled, developed his system around the three elements of consciousness—sensations, images, and affective states. In view of his elementalism, not only perception, but the other higher mental processes as well, posed a critical test for structural psychology. If the perceptual process could be resolved into a single element or a combination of elements by introspection, then the original elements would be adequate to explain perception. If, on the other hand, perception proved to be irreducible, a new element, "perception," would have to be granted coequal status with the original three. However, Titchener found that his elements were equal to the task of accounting for perception and announced his position in his famous "core-context" theory.

Titchener (1910) begins his exposition of the theory by asking his readers to assume with him that perception might be analyzed into sensations "without remainder." It would then have to be admitted that such a "mere enumeration" of sensations would be inadequate to account for perception. To begin with, the particular sensations involved in any perception form a cluster or special group of impressions, which are selected out of the total possible complex of stimuli impinging upon the individual at any given moment. This selective aspect of perception Titchener explains on the basis of attention. The grouping, the clarity, and the focusing involved in perception are reducible, therefore, to the determinants of attention.

Although this may account for selectivity, it still fails to render a complete picture of perception. Common experience tells us that perceptions are *meaningful;* and in attempting to explain meaning, Titchener comes to grips with the heart of the problem: "Perceptions are selected groups of sensations, in which images are incorporated as an integral part of the whole process. But that is not all: The essential thing about them still has to be named; and it is this—that perceptions have meaning" (1910, p. 367). In the next paragraph he defines meaning as "context." In other words, one mental process is the meaning of another.

In essence, Titchener's core-context theory is this: Sensations are the core of perceptions, but images accrue to the core to lend meaning to the complex of sensations. In contemporary terms this could be further simplified to read that memory or past experience makes present experience meaningful.

In elaborating his theory, Titchener argues that meaning is originally a kinesthetic process. At first the individual takes a bodily attitude when confronted with a situation. For example, a child who comes too close to a fire and burns himself or herself will take the bodily attitude of withdrawal and at the same time

---

[4]The exposition of Titchener's position is taken from his *Textbook of Psychology* (1910).

will experience pain. Fire, then, *means* withdrawal accompanied by pain in this concrete situation. In future experiences the original sensations of pain and muscular movement (which in the meantime have become memory images) are added to the perception of a fire with the result that the meaning of "pain," "burn," and "get away" instantly come to the child's consciousness. These memory images *are* the context that makes the child's present perception meaningful.

Titchener admits that verbal as well as concrete images play an equally important role in conveying meaning. However, he argues that words at first are only meaningful as kinesthetic attitudes in the form of gestures or other overt responses. But with the passage of time, overt attitudes become abstract images. Thus, irrespective of whether the imagery is kinesthetic or verbal, the process is the same— namely, one of telescoping or abstracting. In fact, Titchener points out that the whole process can become so telescoped that meaning itself is conveyed unconsciously, as is true in the auditory perception of a well-learned foreign language. Upon first becoming acquainted with the language, we consciously and laboriously "translate" what we hear, but as our facility with the language improves, meaning comes swiftly and without conscious effort.

To summarize, Titchener's core-context theory is subsumed under four cardinal points. First, sensations form a cluster or group according to the principles of the selectivity of attention. Second, the sensations are supplemented by images. Third, the context provided by the imagery that accrues to the sensory complex *is* meaning. Fourth, in well-established perceptual situations, meaning may "lapse from consciousness" and instead be mediated by habitual nervous sets.

Titchener also deals with the more specialized problem of space perception. In general, he explains depth perception in terms of the physiological cues furnished by retinal disparity, accommodation, and convergence, and by the secondary cues of linear and aerial perspective, interposition, apparent magnitude, and so on. In all essential respects the discussion closely parallels contemporary texts; hence, we need not go into the details of his account here.

In this same connection, it might be noted that Titchener is a mixture of nativist and empiricist in the sense that he accounts for extensity or spatiality as inherent capabilities of mind. But at the same time he emphasizes the importance of learning or experience in depth perception. Titchener, therefore, was attempting a synthesis of the traditional empiricist-nativist controversy. However, he is most famous for the core-context theory of meaning and not for his attempted resolution of nativistic and empirical factors in depth perception. His highly characteristic treatment of the complex processes involved in perception bears testimony to the versatility of his elements and to his own ability as a systematizer.

Functionalism and Perceptual Psychology[5]

Harvey Carr, who is our representative of the functional point of view, was deeply interested in the area of perceptual psychology. Besides treating it at consid-

---

[5]Our account follows Carr's *Psychology* (1925) and *An Introduction to Space Perception* (1935).

erable length in his general text (1925), he wrote an advanced textbook (1935) on perception. Since functionalism emphasizes mental activities from the point of view of their adaptive significance and because attention and selectivity as attributes of perception are crucial in adaptation to the environment, it is no surprise that a functionalist would show considerable interest in perception.

In his general text, from which we are drawing the functionalist account of perception, Carr begins with a definition that sets the tone of the two chapters he devotes to the perceptual processes. To quote Carr: "Perception may be defined as the cognition of a present object *in relation to some act of adjustment*" (1925, p. 110; italics added). The characteristically functional part of the definition is, of course, the italicized half. Carr is making the definition of perception commensurate with his original definition of psychology as the study of mental activities that are "concerned with the acquisition, fixation, retention, organization, and evaluation of experiences, and their subsequent utilization in the guidance of conduct" (1925, p. 1).

Carr further points out that every act of perception involves two stages. First, there is a preliminary phase of attention that ensures selectivity and clarity of incoming sense data. Second, perception involves an interpretive phase in which there is an arousal of meaning. Meaning, in turn, is dependent on both past experience and present or contemplated conduct. In essence, then, perception is *selective, organized,* and *meaningful.* Let us consider each of these aspects in more detail from the functionalistic point of view.

As has already been pointed out, for Carr attention is the process that ensures selectivity of perception. This is accomplished partly by suppression or inhibition of some stimuli and in part by the synthesis of other stimuli. Suppression or inhibition functions in eliminating irrelevant or distractive stimuli such as noise. By synthesis Carr means the whole complex of cooperative adjustments in the sense organs (such as turning the eyes for foveal fixation) and in the body in general (such as bending over when searching for a lost object). All such activities must be synthesized into an integrated whole for maximal effectiveness and efficiency of perception.

The organization of incoming sensory data depends on past experience. The force of this process is best revealed in negative examples. When first experienced, picture puzzles and the sounds of an unfamiliar language are disorganized jumbles of visual and auditory sense data. Irrespective of how attentive the observer may be, until he or she has had sufficient experience with the stimuli in question, they remain disorganized and meaningless. When the observer is shown (or discovers) the hidden figure in the puzzle or when he or she learns the language, the organizing effect of experience is so strong that the individual cannot *avoid* seeing the hidden figure or, in the case of the language, hearing meaningful words.

Meaning is also dependent on the arousal of previous experiences. However, associations from past experiences need not be in the form of complete redintegrations of experience in order for meaning to occur. In many cases a partial or indirect reactivation of associations is sufficient to arouse meaning. Precisely how complete a reactivation of previous experience takes place for any given perception depends on how well practiced the associations in question are. Small segments of well-established associations need not be reactivated completely to carry meaning; the first few notes of "Yankee Doodle" are sufficient to redintegrate the perception of the entire piece. Finally, the nature of the whole perceptual complex is dependent on such additional factors as the environmental situation, the individual's purposes and activities at the moment of perception, and the sensory modality involved.

Although Carr did not elaborate on the importance of O variables such as purposes or goal sets, he did include these factors as possible perceptual determinants. His recognition of such motivational influences is highly significant, for this marks the beginning of a trend that became a central theme in psychology during the 1940s and 1950s.

Turning to Carr's analysis of space perception, we may begin by noting that his account follows the familiar empirical-associationistic tradition. He introduces the topic by arguing that space perception depends on local signs. Consequently, the essential problem for the psychologist is to enumerate and describe these signs for each of the senses that mediate spatiality. In his general text (1925) Carr confines his discussion to visual and auditory localization. Let us consider each of these modalities briefly.

In audition the cues for distance perception are *intensity* and *tonal complexity*. In other words, the nearer the sound, the more complex and intense it will be when it reaches the ear. Distant sounds, on the other hand, are weak and lacking in complexity by the time they reach the observer. Auditory localization is dependent on differential binaural stimulation. In this case Carr emphasizes phase differences in sound waves as the chief binaural cues.[6]

In the section on visual space perception the familiar cues for depth perception of accommodation, convergence, interposition, and perspective are each discussed briefly. Carr's treatment of this topic is not different in any essential respect from Titchener's or other standard texts from 1900 to the 1930s. Apparently space perception had ceased to be a controversial issue. Although this must not be interpreted to mean that psychologists of that period considered all the facts to be in, it does mean that the main outlines were clear. The empiricists, for the time being at least, had won the day. The Gestalt movement had yet to be felt in its full force; and when it was, the old controversy had a rebirth.

Finally, Carr faces the question of how space perception is acquired and holds that the weight of the evidence favors learning. He cites studies of individuals blind from birth who recover their sight in maturity as a result of surgery. In such cases the individual's visual space perception is poor, and cues for space must be interpreted in terms of the more familiar modalities of touch and hearing. In addition, he points to Stratton's classic experiment on the inversion of the retinal image.

Stratton wore a lens designed in such a way as to "turn things upside down" and reverse right and left. At first his movements were confused and uncoordinated. Objects seen on the right were heard on the left. Objects perceived to be below eye

---

[6]It is now believed that differences in time and intensity are of greater importance than phase differences. Phase differences can be reduced to time differences (Stevens & Davis, 1938).

level were in reality above. In reaching for objects, Stratton had to employ a trial-and-error process of approximations. But after only three days his initial helplessness and confusion gave way to unpremeditated, skilled movements in the new visual frame of reference. In fact, he became so familiar with his new visual world by the end of the experiment (eight days) that he felt the world was right side up. This must not be interpreted to mean that he *saw* things right side up. Rather, objects were felt, seen, and heard in a coordinated, logical relationship to each other.

In his book on space perception (1935), Carr argues that Stratton's experiment, if it had been conducted on an infant from birth onward to adulthood, would have demonstrated that the subject as an adult would see the world as right side up. In other words, he concludes that objects have no spatial significance for the infant. Rather, the child *learns* up, down, right, left, and other spatial frames of reference as a result of his experience with objects in space. Despite the inversion of the retinal image, touch, kinesthesis, and vision are gradually coordinated so that what is *felt* in one position in space is also *seen* in that position.[7]

By way of summarizing Carr's position on perception, we need only reiterate the principle that perception is a form of mental activity in which the meaning of present situations, objects, and events is determined in part by past learning. But meaning is also related to a present or contemplated act of adjustment. The initial stage in perception is the attentive phase, characterized by receptor and bodily adjustments that make for selectivity of perception. Past experience provides organization and interpretation for the incoming stimuli. For Carr, then, perception is a highly functional or useful process in adaptation.

Behaviorism and Perception

The student of systematic psychology will search in vain for the term "perception" throughout John B. Watson's *Behavior: An Introduction to Comparative Psychology* (1914) or his *Psychology from the Standpoint of a Behaviorist* (1919). However, the omission should not come as a complete surprise in the light of our previous discussion of his aims and methods.

Yet, despite his stand that concepts such as "meaning," "perception," and "images" are mentalistic and consequently unworthy of a scientific psychology, Watson had two possible avenues of approach to perception had he elected to use them. His verbal-report method and the techniques of discriminative conditioning both can be adapted for behavioristic investigations of perception. For example, the contemporary psychologist who is interested in studying personality by means of projective techniques obtains a verbal report of the subject's reactions to inkblots, pictures, cartoons, or similar material. The subject's verbal productions are treated as raw data to be evaluated by the psychologist according to objective and preestab-

---

[7]This experiment has been repeated several times both with human and animal subjects. The results are not in agreement. For a critical account of a number of such experiments, see Munn (1965, pp. 259–265), and the following chapter.

lished criteria. Similarly, if an animal or human subject can learn to discriminate between two stimuli, this may be taken as evidence that the subject is able to perceive the stimuli, or at least the difference between them.

Although classical behaviorism did not exclude the possibility of the study of the perceptual processes, both Watson and those who followed in the behavioristic tradition were primarily interested in response, or *R,* psychology. In effect, this has meant an emphasis on learning as opposed to perception among the proponents of the school. As is true of all generalizations, the foregoing is an oversimplification of the picture. Still, on the whole it represents the behavioristic attitude toward this area; and because of their preoccupation with other aspects of psychology, the behaviorists failed to make significant contributions in the field of perception. For this reason we shall pass on to the Gestalt school, which, by way of contrast, made its greatest contributions in the area of perceptual psychology.

Perception and Gestalt Psychology[8]

There is general agreement among contemporary psychologists that the Gestalt school exerted a greater influence on the evolution of modern perceptual psychology than any other. As we pointed out earlier in this chapter, the Gestalt movement developed out of Max Wertheimer's study of perceptual phenomena; and its leaders went on to devote a great deal of their research efforts to the field of perception. This must not be taken as an implication that Gestalt psychologists have failed to make significant contributions to other areas of psychology. Rather, it means that the school's *most* significant and *characteristic* contributions were in the field of perception.

It will be recalled from our discussion of the aims and methods of Gestalt psychology in Chapter 3 that the starting point of the movement was Wertheimer's research with apparent movement, the results of which led him to challenge the tradition of elementalism that had dominated the thinking of the structuralists. In Chapter 3 we also brought out additional "protests" on the part of Wertheimer and his associates, Köhler and Koffka, which were directed against behavioristic psychology. We must now turn to the positive side of the Gestalt program. First we shall examine the basic, classical principles that the school offered in support of its systematic approach to perception, and then we shall discuss more recent developments in Gestalt psychology.

The fundamental law and *raison d'être* of Gestalt psychology is revealed by the school's name. *Gestalt* psychology is *form* psychology. According to its proponents, our perceptual experiences arise as *gestalten* or *molar* configurations, which are not mere aggregations of sensations but organized and meaningful wholes.

The "bundle hypothesis"—a term used to characterize the structuralistic position on perception—is completely fallacious according to the Gestalt psychologists,

---

[8]For primary sources, see Koffka (1935) and Köhler (1929). Good secondary accounts may be found in Heidbreder (1933), Michael Wertheimer (1970, 1972), and Woodworth and Sheehan (1964).

since it treats complex perceptions as though they were nothing more than bundles of simple sensations. Similarly, the meaning accruing to a complex percept cannot be treated as a "bundle" of simple meanings.

The determinants of perceptual organization and meaning are related in turn to certain fundamental laws of gestalten, the most important of which is isomorphism. The principle of isomorphism states that there is no one-to-one relationship between stimuli and percepts, but that the form of experience corresponds to the form or configuration of the stimulus pattern. Gestalten, then, are "true" representations of the physical world, but not photographic copies of it. They are not identical in size and shape. Just as a road map is not a literal copy of the geographical terrain that it represents, so an experience is not a literal copy of the outside world. There are point-for-point correspondences, it is true, and each feature of the terrain is represented on the map. But there are also distortions. The map is only a fraction of the size of what it represents. Curves in the road map may be less sharp in reality. Minor features may be omitted altogether. But, because the map is *iso* (identical in) *morphic* (form or shape), it can be used as a guide for travel. Similarly, mental or cognitive maps must "mirror" the form of the physical world or life would be chaos.

Isomorphism also frees psychology from treating the percept as nothing more than the collection of sensations from which it arises. Everyday experience is good Gestalt psychology in the sense that we see objects that are perceived as objects and not as aggregates of sensations. The perception of a table is the perception of a molar object, not a collection of color patches, intensities, spatial extents, and the like. Moreover, it is important to recognize that this holds true even for the child who has not yet acquired the concept "table." Provided he or she is attending to the table at all, it is an object—an object that is perceived against a background.

Gestalt psychology looks upon the world as psychophysical. As we have seen, the world of experience is not the same as the physical world; and to emphasize the distinction, Gestalt psychologists are in the habit of referring to the *psychological field* to represent the perceiver's view of reality. In contrast, the world of the physicist is referred to as the *physical situation*. By way of illustration, see Figure 5-1, which shows an old perceptual illusion. No matter how long one looks at it, the lines appear to spiral in toward the center. The spiral effect is the observer's psychological field. However, if the observer starts at point *A* and follows the twisted line 360 degrees, he or she will arrive back at *A*. The spirals, it turns out, are all circles. This is the physical situation.

Although illusions provide dramatic and extreme illustrations of the absence of any one-to-one relationship between the situation and field, we need only to go to everyday experience for hundreds of equally valid, if less obvious, instances. Mother's valuable antique chair may be perceived as a piece of junk by her modern-minded daughter-in-law. Or consider the strikingly different reactions shown by people of opposite political persuasions as they listen to a politician during the heat of a campaign.

We are now in a position to consider certain subprinciples under the general law of isomorphism. These are the well-known Gestalt principles of perceptual

FIGURE 5-1.   The spiral illusion. For explanation see text. (From E. G. Boring, H. S. Langfeld, and H. P. Weld, Foundations of Psychology, New York: John Wiley and Sons, Inc., 1948.)

organization. The laws have sometimes been called *laws of primitive organization* because they are presumed to describe inherent features of human perception. Put somewhat differently, the Gestalt psychologists argue that everyone, including the child or the savage, experiences meaningful, patterned perceptual fields on the basis of these principles.

The most fundamental of these principles of primitive organization is that of *figure-ground*, which states that every perception is organized into a figure that stands out from a background. The figure not only stands out but also has well-defined contours, depth, and solidarity. It must be emphasized, however, that these figural characteristics are not properties of the *physical* stimulus-object but are characteristics of the psychological field. An object such as a block of ice has solidity, contours, depth, and other qualities in the physical sense; but if the object is not in the focus of attention it is part of ground and consequently lacks solidity, well-defined contours, and depth. If the observer turns his or her attention toward the block of ice, it will then become the figure—taking on solidity, depth, and the like; and objects previously in the foreground of consciousness will become ground.

We do not mean to give the impression that the Gestalt principle of figure-ground is merely the equivalent of attention in other systems. It must be borne in mind that the traditional treatments of attention and perceptual meaning emphasized the role of experience as an explanatory concept. The Gestalt psychologists, on the other hand, emphasize figure-ground as a spontaneous and native organization that does not depend on learning but is an inevitable consequence of human perceptual apparatus.

The Gestalt position on the fundamental nature of figure-ground perception was strengthened by experiments with animals that responded to test situations in such a way as to suggest that they were able to perceive a figure on a ground. In a test of the European jay's ability to respond to a figure-ground pattern, Hertz (1928) arranged a number of inverted flowerpots in a large ellipse, placing an additional "odd" pot outside the ellipse. On test trials the bird watched the experimenter put food under one of the pots and was then allowed to fly to the pattern and search for the reward. If the food was placed under the "figure" or odd pot, then the jay had no difficulty; if it was placed under any of the "ground" pots in the circle, the bird became confused and experienced great difficulty in selecting the correct pot.

The Gestalt position on isomorphism and figure-ground perception puts the school in the nativistic camp. However, contrary to a widespread misconception, the Gestalt psychologists did not take an extreme position in which the role of learning in perception was ignored. Rather, they de-emphasized learning in favor of contemporaneous principles that emphasize immediate, spontaneous percepts and meanings. This position is further brought out by certain less fundamental but equally compelling organizing factors, which can be readily illustrated by simple visual diagrams (see Figure 5-2).

Proximity refers to perceptual experiences involving groups of stimulus objects. Those that are proximate or close together tend to form distinct groups; see Figure 5-2(a). *Continuity* refers to the tendency to perceive lines as unbroken or continuous even though they are interrupted by other lines; see Figure 5-2(b).

More characteristically, Gestalt is the principle of *Prägnanz,* which holds that percepts take the best form possible under the circumstances. They make, so to speak, good gestalten. In Figure 5-2(d), for example, the figure on the right is perceived as a square despite the fact that physically it is four disjointed lines. Figure 5-2(c) illustrates a corollary principle, that of *closure,* which is a special case of the law of *Prägnanz.* The gaps, so to speak, are "closed" by the perceiver. More generally, *Prägnanz* and closure operate in all sensory modalities to give the best definition, symmetry, and form to perceptual figures.

Prägnanz and closure also occur in everyday life as organizing factors in complex experiences that may depend on the simultaneous contribution of both present and past experiences. Sets, past experiences, present motivations, and other *O* factors are all determinants that influence the perceptual field. We shall consider these at length in the next chapter, but it is worth noting here that the Gestalt psychologists did not confine their perceptual principles to simple drawings. There is a tendency to form this impression because of the widespread use of simple visual illustrations in texts that deal with Gestalt principles.

FIGURE 5-2 (a).   Proximity. The three birds on the left form a group while the two on the right form another group.

FIGURE 5-2 (b).   Continuity. Both the straight line and the wavy line are seen as continuous despite the fact that each is broken by the other.

FIGURE 5-2 (c).   Prägnanz. A vague, disjointed figure is perceived as "good" as circumstances will permit.

FIGURE 5-2 (d).   Closure. In spite of gaps the figure on the left is seen as an arrow and the figure on the right as a square.

Finally, among the fundamental laws[9] of the classical Gestalt school is the law of *transposition*. This principle states that because gestalten are isomorphic to stimulus patterns, they may undergo extensive changes without losing their identity.

---

[9]There are literally hundreds of laws, principles, and corollaries in Gestalt source books if the various offshoots of the Gestalt school are included. We have included only the basic laws in our summary.

For example, a tune transposed to another key remains the same tune even though the elements (notes) making up the melody are all different. In a classic and often verified experiment, Köhler (1927) trained apes and chicks to respond to the darker of two shades of gray for a food reward. Let us call the brighter stimulus A and the darker B. After a number of repetitions, a new gray, C, was introduced where C was darker than B. The animal immediately responded to C, even though this meant shifting from the shade that was so well practiced in previous trials.

Perception, then, is flexible; and, just as a map may be expanded, shrunk, or presented in different types of geographic projections and remain recognizable as the same map, so the elements of our perceptions may be changed—often markedly—and still yield the same perception. Naturally, there is a limit beyond which change in elements may not go without producing a complete transformation in the percept. The structuring of the elements may be changed markedly without destroying the gestalt only so long as the *relative* spatial and temporal relationships are preserved.

The principles summarized in the preceding paragraphs are closely related to a broad and fundamental concept which runs through the whole of Gestalt psychology—that of *equilibrium*. Perceptual fields are dynamic wholes that, like a magnetic field of force, tend toward equilibrium. And, as is true of a magnetic field, when the psychological field is "disturbed" by the introduction of new forces, the whole undergoes a realignment of forces until equilibrium is once more established. In short, it is a fundamental property of percepts to tend toward stability and to remain as stable as conditions permit.

RECENT GESTALT THEORY

Our summary of Gestalt theory in the preceding section has covered the fundamental laws of gestalten. By employing these principles, the Gestalt psychologists attempted to account for the organized and meaningful nature of perceptual processes. But carried to this point, the theory is incomplete. There remains the problem of relating perceptual phenomena to underlying cortical processes in accordance with the principle of isomorphism. Isomorphism, it will be recalled, is the Gestalt psychologist's answer to the traditional mind-body issue, in which they seek to link the neurological and psychological fields.

Isomorphism and the Brain

In formulating a theory of the neurological correlates of perceived gestalten, Gestalt psychologists were attempting to substantiate the general hypothesis that cortical fields behave according to Gestalt-like principles. It will be recalled from our previous discussion that in order to clarify their position, the Gestalt psychologists contrasted isomorphism with the "machine" view (Köhler, 1929) of the nervous system. The latter is a more or less "static" conception of cortical processes that likens nervous activity to the workings of a machine incapable of organizing or modifying what is fed into it. Thus, a "memory machine" or computer would faithfully reproduce a percept without distortion. Moreover, a machine view, according to the Gestalt psychologists, implies a one-to-one correspondence in size, form, and configuration between the percept and its cortical counterpart.

Carried to its logical extreme, such a view would postulate that an exact cortical "picture" corresponding to the physical stimulus configuration would be generated in the brain in every perception. Specifically, if one were looking at a cross, the cortical neurons in the visual area would be activated in the form of a cross with a one-to-one correspondence between the retinal image and the cortex, and with a similar correspondence of retinal image and stimulus figure. It was in opposition to any such literal mirroring of percept and cortical field that isomorphic brain fields were postulated to relate percepts to their neurological foundations.

For many years Wolfgang Köhler, one of the original founders of Gestalt psychology, conducted a research program designed to investigate various facets of the Gestalt conception of isomorphism and cortical brain fields. In formulating his hypotheses, Köhler took as a point of departure the concept that cortical processes behave in a manner that is analogous to fields of electric force. Perhaps the simplest illustration is the behavior of an electromagnetic field of force around a magnet (see Figure 5-3).

In undisturbed magnetic fields the lines of force are in equilibrium; if a disturbance is introduced, the field will be temporarily thrown into a state of disequilibrium. However, a rapid realignment of the lines of force will occur, and equilibrium will be reestablished. It is also important to recognize that such a field is a continuum, and whatever affects one part of the field affects all parts to some degree.

As applied to the cerebral cortex, Köhler (1940) suggests that electromechanical processes in the brain may establish fields of neuronal activity in response to sensory impulses coming in over afferent neurons. For example, if one fixates a simple figure-ground stimulus, such as a white cross on a background of uniform gray, electrochemical events in the visual area of the occipital cortex that are isomorphic to the stimulus pattern will be activated. The cross would be represented by rather strong electromotive forces in the cortex shading off from the boundary outward. In effect, then, a neurological figure-ground would be set up in the cortex because of the potential differences existing between adjacent areas of tissue. The

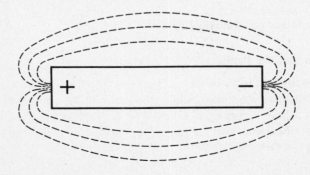

FIGURE 5-3.   A magnetic field of force.

cortical figure-ground would in turn correspond isomorphically to the phenomenally observed figure and ground.

Now the only *direct* proof of such a theory would have to be nothing short of an examination of the living brain with oscilloscopes sensitive enough to demonstrate such effects, if they do indeed occur. Since at that time (1940s) there was no feasible way of carrying out such experiments, the appeal had to be to indirect methods.

The nearest thing to a direct demonstration of cortical fields is Köhler and Held's electroencephalographic studies (1949), in which potential differences in the visual cortex were shown to occur as a test object was moved across the subject's visual field. To some extent the expected configuration was found, but unfortunately the electroencephalogram can measure only relatively gross and complex electrical signs of cortical activity as they appear on the surface of the head and is therefore unable to trace the outline of a "cortical" figure-ground, if such in fact exists.

However, Köhler and Wallach (1944) have also approached the problem from the phenomenological side. Their logic in brief is this: If it can be shown that the brain behaves *as if* it were developing cortical fields isomorphic to test patterns, then it will be demonstrated that the theory of isomorphism is at least plausible and consistent with perceptual phenomena. Such demonstrations have been made in

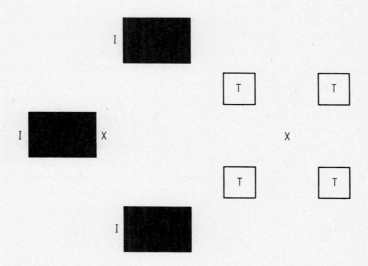

FIGURE 5-4.   A demonstration of the figural aftereffect. (After Köhler and Wallach, 1944.) Fixate the X in the inspection figure for 35 to 40 seconds. Shift the fixation directly across to the X in the test figure. The left-hand squares of the test figure will be seen to be spread apart while the right-hand squares will appear closer together. Since the black rectangle in the extreme left of the inspection figure falls between the left-hand test squares when the gaze is shifted, the test squares "move away" from the satiated area. Similarly, when the gaze is shifted, the two black rectangles on the right-hand side of the inspection figure fall outside the test squares on the extreme right and "squeeze" them together. It may be necessary to repeat the experiment if it does not work the first time.

terms of *satiation* phenomena, especially interesting aspects of which are *figural aftereffects,* first studied by J. J. Gibson (1933).

Köhler further proposes that if the visual cortex does develop electric fields isomorphic with stimulus configurations, then such fields in the cortex should undergo changes if kept active for long periods of time. This effect can, in fact, be shown in isolated neurons in which various electrotonic changes can be demonstrated to occur with prolonged stimulation. Going back to the perceptual side, let us suppose that a figure is fixated for a much longer period of time than is normally true in the course of our rapid everyday glances at objects around us. Will changes in the appearance of such figures occur that are explicable in terms of cortical processes? Köhler and Wallach (1944) believe this to be true of figural aftereffects. The reader may demonstrate the phenomenon of figural aftereffects by following the directions accompanying Figure 5-4.

In relating such aftereffects to cortical events, Köhler and Wallach propose that the cortical area stimulated by the black squares becomes "satiated," and as a consequence the white squares are distorted away from the area of original stimulation. Or, in physiological terms, the part of the cerebral cortex that is polarized becomes satiated with direct currents as a result of prolonged stimulation from the visual receptors as the inspection figure is fixated. Increasing resistance develops in such areas; and when new stimulation arrives at the cortex as a result of examining the test figure, the resulting cortical currents will flow away into less satiated areas of lower resistance. A similar explanation is utilized in accounting for the reversible figures (see Figure 5-5). When the visual cortex becomes satiated, the figure "escapes" by changing both phenomenally and cortically.

Other equally striking demonstrations have shown that fixation of curved lines will make a subsequently observed straight line appear curved. Angles can be made to change and even illusions may disappear (Köhler & Fishback, 1950) because of such satiation effects. These findings have been extended to other sensory modes. For a review of the research in this area, see Spitz (1958).

Not all psychologists have been willing to accept figural aftereffects as convincing demonstrations of the reality of isomorphic processes in the cortex. This critical literature is too extensive to review here. The interested reader is referred to F. H. Allport (1955), Ganz (1966), and Spitz (1958). As is usual in cases of

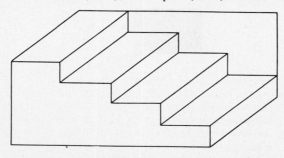

FIGURE 5-5.   The reversible staircase. Fixate on the figure for a few moments, and the staircase will be seen as "upside down."

conflicting opinion in regard to the validity of research findings, only time and further experimentation will provide the final answer.

It seems appropriate in bringing our discussion of Gestalt perceptual theory to a conclusion to indicate that even though the school as such no longer exists, the Gestalt influence continues to leave its impression on contemporary perceptual research and theory. We have already mentioned (Chapter 4) the research of Hubel and Wiesel on higher-order visual processes—research whose spirit and interpretation is in the nativistic vein. Similarly, a considerable Gestalt influence can be detected in information theory analyses of perception to be considered in the following chapter. Neisser's award-winning book on cognitive psychology (1967), though not entirely in agreement with Gestalt psychology, has been strongly influenced by it. That the broad phenomenological orientation to the study of mental and behavioral processes championed by the Gestalt psychologists continues to be viable is further revealed by developments in existential and humanistic psychology, again to be met with later in this volume. Finally, we can point to developments in perceptual theory in social psychology (see Chapter 16), particularly those that emerged from Lewin's circle, as revealing a Gestalt orientation.

Psychoanalysis and Perception

It should come as no surprise to anyone with some knowledge of psychoanalysis that Freud showed no concern with perceptual psychology in the sense in which we have been using the concept throughout this chapter. The traditional pre-Freudian psychology was a cognitive psychology emphasizing sensory and perceptual processes and thinking, whereas Freudian psychology is a conative psychology. Freud emphasized drives, instincts, personality development, and unconscious processes; hence his system de-emphasized perception. In general, we traditionally associate perceptual processes with conscious processes; but Freud considered the perceptual conscious relatively unimportant in comparison with preconscious and unconscious aspects of mental life. Man the rational became man the irrational in Freudian psychology. As Frenkel-Brunswik (1951, p. 357) puts it, there was a shift from "surface to depth" in Freud's account of the dynamics of human behavior. (See also Chapter 11 on motivation.)

However, it would be a serious mistake to dismiss the whole of the clinical movement as lacking in interest in perceptual psychology. Starting with Alfred Adler, a one-time associate of Freud's in the early days of the psychoanalytic movement, a radically different view of human nature has been elaborated by those who dissented from Freud's teachings but are nevertheless considered to belong broadly within the psychoanalytic movement. This psychotherapeutic school has (either directly or indirectly) put a great deal of emphasis on perceptual factors in both normal and abnormal patterns of psychological development. Such practitioners as Karen Horney, Harry Stack Sullivan, and Erich Fromm, who constituted the vanguard of the group called the "social psychoanalysts," emphasized *goal perception* and *self-perception* in relation to the individual's life goals as basic factors in psychological development and adjustment to the environment. Moreover, psychologies of self-actualization and existential points of view emphasize perceptual processes. In Chapter 17 we shall discuss these viewpoints at some length.

SUMMARY AND EVALUATION

An overview of the evolution of perceptual theory during the period covered in this chapter reveals that the field has undergone both intensive and extensive development from its first formulation in the writings of Reid. Nevertheless, the central theme of perceptual psychology—to account for the meaning of human experiences—has remained unchanged. In the early stages of its development as a separate field, the problems of perceptual psychology were narrowly conceived in the sense that most writers undertook the task of explaining the mechanisms of space perception. We have seen how the philosophers and psychologists of the prescientific period sought the answer to this question along two major lines: empiricism and nativism.

With the development of the academic schools, the field of perception broadened to include the study of cognitive factors such as sets, habits, and attitudes. However, this was only a hint or foretaste of the great expansion of perceptual psychology that was to occur in recent decades. In their stand on the nativistic-empiricistic controversy most of the schools recognized the importance of *both* native and empirical factors, though each tended to place more emphasis on one set of variables than on the other. In our account of the academic schools, we have emphasized the contributions of the structuralists because of their core-context theory—historically important in grappling as it did with the difficult problem of perceptual meaning—and of the Gestalt psychologists for their unique reformulation of the entire field of perceptual psychology. Finally, we have touched on the place of perception in the psychoanalytic school in order to point out basic differences in emphasis between the Freudians and post-Freudians. Whereas Freud minimized perception, the post-Freudians have made self-perception and interpersonal perceptions of central importance in their theories.

Perception: Recent Trends

6

Kurt Koffka, the Gestalt psychologist, once observed that the basic problem of perceptual psychology was to answer the question: Why do things look as they do? Koffka did not, of course, intend to restrict perception to visual processes. Rather, he meant that, fundamentally, to perceive is to experience objects—to see, hear, taste, feel, and smell—that is, to discriminate among things and to experience a meaningful world. The perceptual psychologist, then, searches for processes that make our world organized and meaningful.

We have seen how classical perceptual psychology emphasized the problem of spatiality and the organization of stimuli into meaningful groupings. Following this tradition the schools maintained the close relationship between sensory and perceptual psychology. The answer to Koffka's question was sought entirely within the framework of the associationistic-empirical tradition—except of course for the Gestalt group, who favored a nativistic interpretation of perceptual processes.

But from time to time there were hints of dissatisfaction with the state of perceptual psychology by those who favored broadening its scope to include the study of how central determinants—motives, emotions, attitudes, and the like—influence our interpretations of raw sensory data. Perceptual experience, these critics pointed out, is only partly a function of stimulus conditions and the associations that are called up from memory to make them meaningful. However, it was not until after World War II that the field of perception underwent a revolution in the course of which the traditional types of perceptual experimentation and theorizing were overshadowed by the search for central determinants. For some years the field was dominated by the investigation of the role of both relatively simple central determinants, such as mood and motives, and highly complex determinants, such as attitudes and personality traits.

Moreover, the old problems of analysis and synthesis underwent reformulation. Analysis was carried farther and farther away from the sense organs and sensation to higher brain centers and to more complex mental processes. Half a century after William James had pointed out that a significant part of what we

145

perceive comes out of our own heads, the postwar psychologists were emphasizing that meaning, which is the end product of perception, does not derive from stimuli but is largely contributed to it by the observer. Things, therefore, are not what they seem. Our perceptions of the world and the people in it are determined by attitudinal, emotional, motivational, and evaluational factors as surely as they are determined by stimuli from the external world.

However, in scientific (as in political) revolutions, radical changes may be temporary, and the reassertion of more traditional or conservative modes of thought often follows periods of dramatic change. In the field of perception, widespread interest in central determinants of the 1940s and 1950s began to wane in favor of a return to a more limited concern with the traditional problems of space perception and with the role of sensory information as a fundamental determinant of perception. In the latter case much of the theory and research has been oriented around information processing theory, whose development arose from the rapid technological advances in the detection, processing, and storage of information that began near the end of World War II and is still going on.

Because the broadly functionalistic point of view encompasses several of the important theoretical research programs of the past half-century of experimental psychology, we shall consider these first. Then we shall summarize the directive state and information processing approaches to perception.

FUNCTIONALISM IN RECENT PERCEPTUAL THEORY

The functionalistic point of view is broad enough to support a variety of viewpoints in any area of psychology, including the field of perception. It will be recalled from our discussion of classical functionalism in Chapter 3 that this system favors the study of mental processes or behavior patterns as they are instrumental in functioning in humans' adaptation to their environment. Because perception is inevitably involved in all adaptive behavior, *any* perceptual theory might logically be included under the category of functionalism. However, there is the danger of broadening a point of view to such an extent that it loses all meaning. We shall avoid the latter danger by selecting for presentation three recent perceptual theories that in our opinion have been formulated in the original spirit of the functionalistic point of view. Specifically we refer to "transactional functionalism," a system formulated by Ames and his associates at the Hanover Institute for Associated Research; Gibson's theory of the senses considered as a perceptual system; and Helson's adaptation level theory.

Ames and his associates[1] not only have drawn heavily upon classical functionalism in erecting their theoretical structure but also have devised some of the most remarkable perceptual experiments in the history of experimental psychology. The experiments themselves are highly functionalistic in design in the sense that the

---

[1]See F. H. Allport (1955), Ames (1953), Brunswik (1943), Ittelson (1952), Ittelson and Cantril (1954), and Kilpatrick (1952).

subject is put in the position of interacting with experimental setups that are so elaborate that they virtually constitute "environments." In short, the Ames group has wed theory to practice as closely as possible under the necessarily artificial conditions of the laboratory.

Let us begin with their best-known experimental demonstration, shown in Figure 6-1. It should be noted that in taking the photograph the camera was placed in the same position as a subject's eye in viewing the room. Clearly, something is wrong. The boy appears to be taller than the adult, while the room *looks* normal. However, the room is far from the rectilinear room of everyday experience; instead it was constructed with trapezoidal floors and walls (the left wall being higher than the right) and the left side of the rear wall sloping back away from the observer, so as to *reproduce the retinal image of a room as seen by an observer standing in the left corner of a normal room*. With this background information we can explain the distortions experienced by an observer or demonstrated in photographs. Our past experiences with rooms tell us that when we are viewing a room from a corner angle, the room has equally high walls with a rectangular floor and ceiling *in spite of the fact that our retinal image is distorted*. Relating this to the Ames experiment, our experiences with past rooms at the moment of looking into the experimental

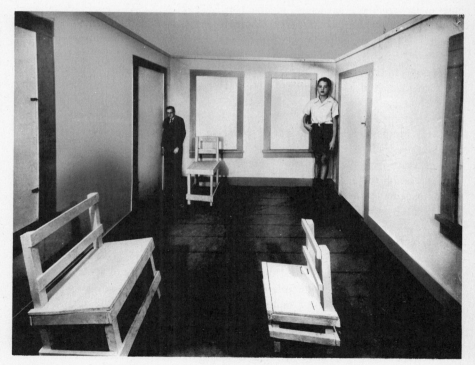

FIGURE 6-1.   Distorted perception induced by the Ames room. When the camera is placed in eye position so that light rays from the right and left walls reflect equally on the film, the walls are perceived as equal in size. The people in the room are then distorted to conform to our past experience with "normal" rooms. (Eric Schaal, Time-Life Picture Agency.)

room are all in favor of the room's being perceived as normal—so much so that the people in it are distorted.

By means of similar experimental setups, the Ames group has devised demonstrations where marbles appear to roll uphill, familiar objects are distorted in size and shape, jumbled patterns look like meaningful objects, and a window that seems to be oscillating back and forth is, in reality, rotating 360 degrees.

At first glance, such experimental demonstrations seem to be in opposition to the functional point of view, which holds that perception aids in the organism's adjustment to its environment. However, illusory perceptions actually demonstrate the strength to which normal human beings develop perceptual constancies and interact with their environments on the basis of these constancies. This is entirely consistent with functionalism, for in dealing with rooms, it makes sense that we perceive them as rectangular in spite of distortions in our retinal image. After all, with the exception of "crazy houses" at carnivals and psychologists' experimental rooms, rooms *are* rectilinear. The exceptions in this case only serve to demonstrate the worth of the rule. If our perceptions changed with every change in viewing conditions, the world, as James once said, would truly be "one great booming buzzing confusion." Or, as Stagner and Karwoski put it, "Illusions are the price we have to pay for this (constancy) mechanism" (1952, p. 229).

The theoretical explanation employed by Ames and his associates to account for the results of the experiments just described is relatively straightforward. It is formulated in a system of concepts that are directly related to the philosophical antecedents of the classical school of functionalism championed by Dewey, Angell, and Carr discussed in Chapter 3. Going back one step, it will be recalled that the intellectual antecedent of Dewey, Angell, and Carr was William James, exponent of the philosophy of pragmatism, which holds that ideas that work in practice are true. To put it another way, the real test of the value of principles, concepts, or ideas is how well they actually serve us in daily living. As James once said in his inimitable style, "Truth is the cash value of an idea."

Returning to functionalism in perception, it may be argued that our perceptions, especially the constancies that we develop through experience, are "pragmatic truths" in the sense that they work for us in practice. And in a very general way this principle is the bulwark of functionalistic perceptual theory. As Brunswik (1943)[2] has pointed out, our perceptions are never completely valid representations of the physical world of objects, sizes, shapes, colors, and the like. On the other hand, neither do we "distort" objects to the extent of achieving perfect constancy. Our give-and-take relations with the environment are a compromise wherein things are perceived neither as demanded by the retinal image nor as perfectly constant. As Brunswik puts it, we come to establish "hypotheses" or "probabilities," which we unconsciously bring to perceptual situations.

---

[2]Brunswik was not a member of the Ames group. His "probabilistic functionalism" is very close to transactional functionalism, and we are making use of some of Brunswik's concepts in the present discussion.

Applying this argument to the distorted-room situation, we find that our assumptions about the rectangular character of a room are so strong that the probabilities are virtually certain that it will be seen in terms of perfect constancy. In more lifelike situations, however, constancies are not so perfect. Colors have a way of appearing different on our living room walls after we make a "perfect" match at the paint store. Similarly, near objects do look somewhat larger than distant objects, and if we go out of our way to choose odd or unusual viewing conditions, constancy is very poor indeed. Anyone who has looked down from a tall building at people and cars in the street below will recall how small and antlike they appear. Presumably a child reared in such a way that he or she experienced objects only from the vertical perspective of tall buildings would have trouble on street level. In such cases the old hypotheses and probabilities about the perceptual world do not apply.

The theoretical assumptions underlying the preceding argument ought to be testable from a frame of reference other than that of devising illusory demonstrations. Since the theory places a heavy burden on learning and experience, it should be possible to demonstrate that (1) perception follows a developmental trend in children and (2) through learning, it ought to be possible to overcome illusions or distorted percepts. These problems, apparently simple of solution, have proved difficult to answer in a straightforward manner. Bower (1964, 1965, 1966) by means of ingenious operant conditioning techniques has shown that infants possess some degree of object constancy, although there is modification of the process with increasing age (see Chapter 7). In part the difficulty is the old one in psychology of obtaining different results with different experimental designs and equipment (E. J. Gibson, 1969, pp. 363–368).

I. Kohler (1964) and his associates, W. von Kundratitz and T. Erismann, in a series of experiments known as the Innsbruck studies, wore a variety of distorting prisms or mirror spectacles that rearranged the visual world. Unlike the somewhat primitive telescopic lens employed by Stratton in the pioneer experiment described in the preceding chapter, Kohler's sophisticated apparatus consisted of goggles that could distort laterally the visual input by use of built-in wedge prisms or "turn the world upside down" by attached mirrors through which all visual input was received. We shall summarize the results of the latter experiment as typical of the series.

The effects of so gross a reversal of normal input were dramatic during the first several days of the experiment. As Stratton had found 50 years earlier, errors were made in attempting to touch objects, walking unaided was impossible, and perceptions of objects appeared upside down. However, by the fourth day of the experiment the subject could ride a bicycle, and on the sixth day, could ski—activities that require a high level of skill and eye-motor coordination. Moreover, after several days, perceptions appeared to be right side up under certain conditions, particularly when a point of reference such as a plumb line was present in the perceptual field. And, as was true in Stratton's case, when the distorting mirror was removed at the end of the experiment, things and people appeared upside down, as if suspended from above. This effect, however, wore off quickly (within about 30 minutes).

We may at this point ask: Is space perception a matter of simple learning in adapting to whatever optics are present—natural or artificial—as the functionalists and the empiricists have insisted? At first reading, the fact that Kohler and his associates could adapt so quickly to a variety of distorting lenses and mirrors suggests that it is. However, experiments such as these are by no means as simple or unambiguous as they appear. Does the subject's *perception* actually change so that he or she sees objects in the environment differently? Or are there proprioceptive and vestibular changes that result from the subject's interactions with the new environment so that he or she senses parts of the body in new ways and therefore sees the environment from a new *perspective?*

A considerable literature has developed around the problem.[3] Invoking the rule of one independent variable, experimenters have attempted to separate out the visual and motor components subjects employ in adaptation to rearranged visual space. As typical of these experiments, Held and Hein (1958) required subjects to wear distorting prisms for three minutes under three different conditions: (1) while the hand was stationary; (2) while watching the hand perform a self-initiated task; (3) while having the hand perform the task by being moved mechanically by the experimenter. In each case the test task was to mark the position of intersecting lines with dots over a series of trials. It was found that passive stimulation produced no adaptation, whereas active movement of the arm produced almost perfect adaptation within 30 minutes. Similar results have been obtained by other experimenters who involved the subject's entire body.

These experiments suggest that proprioceptive and vestibular information is a component part of visual space perception and that complex experiments such as Stratton's or Kohler's involve both optic and nonoptic components. We cannot at this time come to definitive conclusions about the relative role of various input and response systems in visual space perception. We shall return to the problem from a somewhat different point of view in the chapter to follow.

The experiments of the Ames functionalistic group and to some extent those carried out by Kohler and others who were stimulated by the Innsbruck studies may be criticized on the grounds that the apparatus employed and the environment selected are to some degree artificial.

To summarize, the transactional functionalists, true to their tradition, emphasize *learning* as basic to perception. In effect, they are empiricists rather than nativists in their thinking. In this sense they are in opposition to Gestalt theory, at least to the extent that Gestalt psychologists claim so much for inherent organizing factors while tending to ignore the role of experience and the importance of interactions between stimuli and observer that occur in perception. In fact, the interactive nature of perceiving is so heavily emphasized in the Ames variety of functionalism that the theory is aptly called "transactional" functionalism. In other words, perception is developed out of the transactions of humans with their environment.

To avoid misunderstanding it should be emphasized that transactional

---

[3]See Haber and Hershenson (1973), Harris (1965), Hochberg (1971), Kaufman (1974), and Richards (1975) for interpretive reviews of the theoretical and experimental literature.

functionalists do not propose that in our interactions with environmental objects, distances and the like, we *consciously* say to ourselves, "My past experience tells me rooms are square; therefore this room must be square." On the contrary, the whole process is an unconscious and instantaneous *inference* rather than a conscious rationalization of the situation. Moreover, it would be wrong to give the impression that Ames and his associates are solely interested in looking backward to account for present perceptions. Although this is a necessary part of their interpretation of the experimental work, they also emphasize that the "transactions" of individuals with their environment determine their future course of action. Thus, the theory attempts to be predictive in addition to accounting for present behavior. And in this respect the theory once again demonstrates a close relationship to its ancestral philosophy of pragmatism, for James once wrote, "Habit is the great flywheel of society." In terms of contemporary perception, James' statement can be taken to mean that constancies found to be expedient in the past become habitual and are carried into the future.

THE SENSES AS A PERCEPTUAL SYSTEM

James J. Gibson, with his wife and professional collaborator, Eleanor J. Gibson, has contributed an impressive body of empirical and theoretical research to the area of perceptual psychology. J. J. Gibson's experimental work in visual perception spans four decades. E. J. Gibson is equally well known for her research in perceptual development and learning. J. J. Gibson's theoretical contributions, with which we shall be concerned here, have been directed primarily toward demonstrating that traditional theories of perception, which depend on the principle that sensations must be "translated" into perceptions, are in error. In their place he offers his own challenging and unique interpretation of the senses as a perceptual system—a system that does not require the utilization of associations or other intervening variables to make percepts from raw data.

Gibson defines *perception* as the process of maintaining contact with the world. The term *stimulation* refers to the types and variables of physical energy to which the sense organs respond. The basic hypothesis underlying the system is that perception is a function of stimulation whenever the pattern of stimulation is of sufficient complexity to permit the perceptual process to occur. In his own words:

> The explicit hypothesis is that for every aspect or property of the phenomenal world of an individual in contact with his environment, however subtle, there is a variable of the energy flux at his receptors, however complex, with which the phenomenal property would correspond if a psychophysical experiment could be performed. (J. J. Gibson, 1959, p. 465)

To assume that perception is a function of stimulation and stimulation a function of the environment—and consequently that perception is a function of the environment—is a radical departure from tradition. The classic view of perception with which we are familiar sharply delineated the physical environment from the individual's awareness of it. Thus Müller held that we are not directly aware of the world, only of the states of nerves—and that, further, each nerve has its specific energy or quality. The quality of sensation, therefore, is not the quality of the stimulus but of the nerve. Gibson disagrees with the contention that we cannot be directly aware of the source of information. Müller's doctrine may hold for the senses. However only as they are

> . . . considered as channels of sensation but not for the senses considered as detection-systems. Information about the cause of arousal may not get into a nervous system through a single receptor but it may well get into the nervous system through a combination of receptors. We may be "aware of the state of a nerve" as Müller put it, but we are more likely to be aware of patterns and transformations of input that specify the causes of arousal quite independently of the specific nerves that are firing. (J. J. Gibson, 1966, p. 38)

Sensations in Gibson's view are neither the prerequisites of perception nor the raw data of perception; that is, they are not all that is given for perception. If the validity of this point of view is granted, traditional psychophysics is, in reality, more physiology than psychology, and the core-context theory and all its modern derivatives are in error. In Gibson's view, *all* processes for converting sensory data into perception are superfluous. This is not to deny that people have sensations. In the laboratory the subject can experience pure colors, tastes, bright or dull pressures, and the like, but such experiences are not the basis of phenomenal experience. Instead they are the artifacts of introspection.

> The phenomenal world is not composed of colors, sounds, touches, tastes, and smells as we have for so long assumed, but of such properties as surface, edge, slant, convexity, concavity, of rising, falling, beginning, ending, moving, and changing. Sensations are the occasional symptoms of perception, not the cause of it. (J. J. Gibson, 1959, p. 460)

Turning from the negative, or what perception is not, to the positive, or what perception is, Gibson develops what he calls a "stimulus ecology," which deals with the physics of ambient stimuli. By ambient is meant those stimuli that surround or encompass the individual—the optics of slanting and reflecting surfaces in a sunlit room or field, or the gravitational force we all experience in walking, sitting, or lying down. It is the world of acoustics in a symphony hall, the odorous environment of a smoke-filled room.

Space as perceived is not the abstract geometric space describable in mathematical coordinates. Visual space is perceived in terms of what fills it—things, objects, surfaces, and edges—but not the isolated stimuli emphasized by the traditional psychophysicists.

Gibson distinguishes between *imposed* and *obtained* perceptions. Imposed stimulation or perception arises from the skin, nose, ears, eyes, or other organs when these are passively stimulated, as occurs in the laboratory. Obtained perception arises when the sense organs are oriented toward the environment and are actively seeking information. It is these active senses that Gibson calls perceptual systems.

From this point of view the classical senses are viewed as modes of attending—listening, touching, smelling, tasting, and looking. No definitive list of senses or sense organs is offered by Gibson. Indeed, the failure of classical sensory psychology to catalogue sensation definitively is taken by him as evidence in favor of his view that potential stimulus information is unlimited.

Throughout Gibson's most recent and definitive statement of the theory, *invariance* is emphasized as the aspect of the environment to which the organism responds. Invariance means that the active organism finds that the environment provides a continuous and stable flow of information to which it can respond. For this reason stimulus equivalence, so long a problem in traditional perceptual psychology, offers no problems for Gibson.

> Different stimulus energies—acoustical, chemical and radiant—can carry the same stimulus information. The equivalence of different "stimuli" for perception and behavior has long been a puzzle, but it ceases to be puzzling if we suppose that it results from equivalent stimulus information being carried by different forms of stimulus energy. (J. J. Gibson, 1966, p. 55)

In order to maintain maximum invariance of stimulus information, the organism maintains a kind of automatic tuning or attentiveness to those properties of the environment that are significant for adaptation. Moreover, learning is postulated as an important factor in the organism's ability to discriminate environmental information. Gibson, however, is careful to make it clear that he does not mean to utilize the doctrine of associationism.

> In this theory, information about the world can be obtained with any perceptual system alone or with any combination of perceptual systems working together. It is not required that one sense be *validated* by another, as vision is supposed to require confirmation by touch. It is not required that one sense get meaning from another, as visual sensations are supposed to get objective meaning by having been associated with tactual sensations. (J. J. Gibson, 1966, p. 55)

In his *Senses Considered as a Perceptual System* (1966), Gibson devotes three introductory chapters to a general statement of his theory, a summary of which has been presented above. The following eleven chapters are a detailed exposition of how the theory applies to the various sensory systems. We cannot undertake even a summary of so far-ranging an exposition here, but to give some idea of how the theory applies to one sensory system, we shall outline its application to visual perception.

The stimulus for vision is an optic array that has textural properties because of the structure of surfaces. An important and basic property of surfaces is that of texture *gradients* (see Figure 6-2). A texture gradient is a continuous change in the visual field in which regions closest to the observer appear coarser and more de-

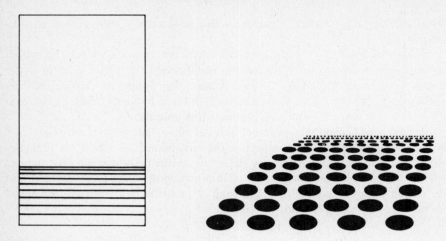

FIGURE 6-2.   Texture gradients.

tailed, whereas those farther away have a finer and finer gradation in size and show correspondingly less detail. Such a patterning of information is not a learned cue but immediately provides direct depth perception.

Similarly, an edge and a corner may be demonstrated by means of plane surfaces and lines, such as those shown in Figure 6-3. The discontinuity of the lines gives an immediate perception of an edge in the figure on the left and of a corner in the figure on the right.

Another fundamental concept in Gibson's theory as it applies to visual space perception is that of *transformations* in the optic array which impinge on the eye

FIGURE 6-3.   An edge and corner demonstrated by an arrangement of plane surfaces and lines. (From The Senses Considered as Perceptual Systems, by James J. Gibson. Houghton Mifflin Company, 1966. Used by permission of the publishers.)

(J. J. Gibson, 1959, pp. 482–485). These are of particular importance in the perception of motion. Traditional theories of perception emphasize simple movements of a stimulus across the retina, which arouse discrete receptors in serial order. Because the eye can also move relative to a stimulus, the problem of how we perceive motion resulted in a "theoretical morass" in Gibson's words. However, if higher-order arrays of continuous transformations are utilized, the problem of explanning motion perception is simplified. Figure 6-4 shows some of the changes in the flow of information stimulating the eye in various types of motion perspective.

The *stability* of the visual world is discovered in observations of the fact that it does not turn, tilt, appear upside down, or rotate—even though the head assumes these positions. This stability of the perceptual world again demonstrates that the observer is not the passive victim of stimulus properties but is attuned to relational patterns of incoming information that lend constancy to the world view.

As these examples[4] from Gibson's theory suggest, perception is a direct apprehension of the flux and flow of information that has stability and is adaptively

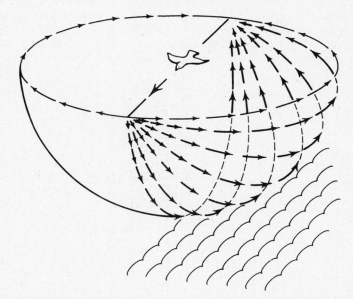

FIGURE 6-4.   The flow of the optic array during locomotion in a terrestrial environment. When a bird moves parallel to the earth, the texture of the lower hemisphere of the optic array flows under its eyes in the manner shown. The flow is centrifugal ahead and centripetal behind—that is, there are focuses of expansion and contraction at the two poles of the line of locomotion. The greatest velocity of backward flow corresponds to the nearest bit of the earth and the other velocities decrease outward from this perpendicular in all directions, vanishing at the horizon. The vectors in this diagram represent angular velocities. The flow pattern contains a great deal of information. (From The Senses Considered as Perceptual Systems, by James J. Gibson. Houghton Mifflin Company, 1966. Used by permission of the publishers.)

---

[4]For references to experimental tests of the theory, see J. J. Gibson (1950, 1959, 1966).

useful to the organism. If the organism is not the passive recipient of stimuli that must be "translated" into perceptions by means of associated memories, what then does learning contribute to perception? It provides for the differential selectivity of perception. Invariants are extracted and features that distinguish one object or event from another are developed through experience. Figure 6-5, taken from E. J. Gibson's *Principles of Perceptual Learning and Development* (1969), summarizes the developmental interrelationships of perceptual and cognitive processes. That her view of perceptual learning complements J. J. Gibson's is revealed in the following statement of what is learned in perceptual learning:

> In an earlier discussion of perceptual learning (Gibson & Gibson, 1955), the view to be presented was called the specificity theory. Let us consider the reasons for choosing this term. Perceptual learning was defined as an increase in the ability of an organism to get information from its environment, as a result of practice with the array of stimulation provided by the environment. This definition implies that there are potential variables of stimuli which are not differentiated within the mass of impinging stimulation, but which may be, given the proper conditions of exposure and practice. As they are differentiated, the resulting perceptions become more specific with respect to stimulation, that is, in greater correspondence with it. There is a change in what the organism can respond to. The change is not acquisition or substitution of a new response to stimulation previously responded to in some other way, but is rather responding in any dis-

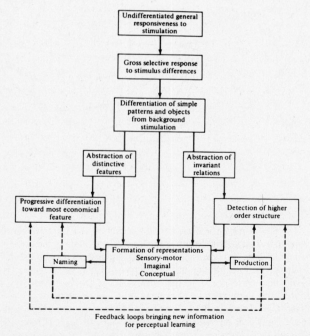

FIGURE 6-5.   The developmental interrelationships of perceptual and cognitive processes. (From E. J. Gibson, Principles of Perceptual Learning and Development. Reprinted by permission of Prentice-Hall, Inc. Englewood Cliffs, N.J. © 1969.

criminating way to a variable of stimulation not responded to previously. The criterion of perceptual learning is thus an increase in specificity. What is learned can be described as detection of properties, patterns, and distinctive features. (E. J. Gibson, 1969, p. 77)

By way of concluding, we may observe that J. J. Gibson's theory of perception as a function of stimulation is a challenging departure from the traditional account. It is both an impressive theoretical formulation and a body of empirical research. Not all predictions made by the theory have been verified by experimental tests (Hochberg, 1971, pp. 505–506). Moreover, the theory remains not an account of perception in general, but a limited theory of space and form perception.

J. J. Gibson does not deny that recollection and imagination may, in the absence of any external stimulation, arouse perceptual activities. Nor does he deny that set, errors of perception (as in hallucinations and illusions), and other central factors give rise to what have been called perceptual processes. However, the theory does not hold that these processes are fundamental to an account that has been able to demonstrate veridical perceptions as a function of stimulation. How far such a theory can be broadened to include central factors, particularly the higher nervous processes that are presumed to mediate perception of the environment, remains a problem for future theorizing and research.

ADAPTATION LEVEL THEORY

We shall conclude our survey of contemporary functionalism in perception with a brief summary of Helson's adaptation level theory. The theory had its origins in psychophysical observations that demonstrated that the contextual or background stimuli against which a judgment is made affect the perceived magnitude, brightness, or hue of the stimulus being judged. As early as 1860 Fechner found that when a subject lifted a weight the kinesthetic sensation involved persisted in the form of a trace. If another objectively equal weight was then hefted, it appeared heavier than the first. Apparently the fading trace of the original weight acted as a kind of residual stimulus against which the comparison weight was judged, and because of the former's fading, the second was overestimated. Helson's own observations of the effect of contextual stimuli on perceptual judgments began in 1924 (Helson, 1959) with experiments to determine the effect of background illumination on the perception of hues. Further experiments with lifted weights convinced him that the concept of *adaptation level,* or AL, would be useful to explain the interaction of present and background stimulation affecting the organism in various types of behavior. He defined the AL quantitatively as the weighted log mean of all stimuli affecting the organism.

Particularly significant in determining the AL are *anchoring stimuli,* or the contextual series of stimuli against which other stimuli are compared. An informal experiment on thermal sensitivity attributed to Aristotle convincingly demonstrates the strong effects of anchors on sensory experiences. The subject has before him three vessels of water, the left one hot, the right one cold, and the middle neutral, or

TABLE 6-1   Theoretical and Experimental Values of Adaptation Level to Show Effect of a Stimulus as Member of a Series and as a Comparison Stimulus[a]

Condition	Theoretical Adaptation Level	Observed Medium
Single stimuli (200, 250, 300, 350, 400 grams)	253.9	250.0
Single stimuli with 900 grams included	314.0	313.0
900-gram anchor	349.0	338.0
Single stimuli with 900 grams included in series	202.0	211.0
90-gram anchor	180.0	185.0
Single stimuli (88, 92, 96, 100, 104 grams)	92.8	96.2
Single stimuli with 40 grams included in series	79.9	92.7
40-gram anchor	74.0	77.0
260 grams included in series [b]	110.2	
260-gram anchor	120.0	

[a]From H. Helson, "Adaptation level as a frame of reference for production of psychophysical data." *American Journal of Psychology, 60*:1-29, 1947. Reprinted by permission of the author.
[b]The values were so far below 5.0 that a reliable figure for the medium could not be obtained.

at skin temperature. If the left hand is submerged in the hot water and the right hand in the cold for a sufficiently long interval to allow physiological adaptation to occur, and then the hands are plunged simultaneously into the middle vessel of neutral water, the water in it will feel cool to the left hand and warm to the right.

Helson's AL, however, is not concerned with physiological adaptation but with more complex perceptual and judgmental processes. Table 6-1 shows the results of an experiment on perceptual anchoring in which the perceived size of weights is biased or distorted depending on the subject's exposure to extreme stimuli. It will be noted that the theoretical and observed adaptation levels were first calculated for a series of single stimuli. The subjects were then required to lift the weights again, this time including a 900-gram weight. The effect, of course, was to raise both the theoretical and observed adaptation levels. These first two experimental runs were carried out for the purpose of establishing levels for comparison when an anchor weight of 900 grams was introduced. Clearly, the anchor significantly changed the adaptation level, as the theoretical and observed values indicate. The results of the second series involving weights of 88, 92, 96, 100, and 104 grams are to be interpreted similarly.

It is important to recognize that AL phenomena are not confined to psychophysical experiments or to sensory processes. Helson (1964a, 1964b) has extended AL theory into the areas of personality, social behavior, motivation, and other psychological processes. As Table 6-2 shows, the judgments of subjects in social situations are significantly influenced by the reports of the group in which such judgments are made. In this case the subjects were given attitude scales

TABLE 6-2.   Changes in Attitudes by Ascendant, Average, and Submissive Subjects as Shown by Movement Toward or Away from Background Group in Terms of Number of Category Steps[a]

Subject Type	Steps Toward Group	Steps Away from Group
Ascendant	10.5	2.2
Average	15.5	1.3
Submissive	17.1	1.7

[a]From H. Helson, Blake, Mouton, and Olmstead, "Attitudes as adjustments to stimulus, background, and residual factors." *Journal of Abnormal and Social Psychology, 52*:314-322, 1956. Copyright 1956 by the American Psychological Association. Reprinted by permission.

followed by experimental manipulation in a group situation, and their degree of attitude change was evaluated by readministration of the attitude scale. By using this technique the effect (positive or negative) of the group experience on the subjects' attitudes can be measured.

Similarly, most of the recent laboratory studies on conformity and on the establishment of group norms show the influence of experimentally manipulated social contexts on such processes.

Returning to more theoretical issues, Helson's assumptions or postulates (1959, 1964a) underlying AL theory are as follows: First, all behavior centers on the AL of the organism. This reflects a kind of behavioral homeostasis against which each act deviates to some degree up or down from a theoretical neutral along the adaptation level scale. Second, the AL depends on the interaction of all stimuli confronting the organism at the present time plus the residual pool of past stimulation. Third, the value of the AL is a weighted mean of the stimuli confronting the organism. Thus, it follows that fixed stimuli cannot have constant effects, but depend on their relationship to previous levels of stimulation. Fourth, group behavior as well as individual behavior is assumed to be affected by the AL.

The assumption that present judgments and perceptions are influenced by contextual and relational factors appears valid. However, the theory raises certain fundamental questions about its applicability in perception. One question centers on the issue of whether it is the immediate experience or the perception of stimulus patterns that is undergoing change as a result of AL or whether it is the individual's judgment about the placement of a comparative stimulus. Another problem revolves around the issue of how the concept of the AL differs from older concepts such as contrast, assimilation, sensory adaptation, homeostasis, aftereffects, and constant and variable errors in scale judgments. Issues such as these—involving, as they do, intervening variables that have been postulated to account for various aspects of behavior—may in the long run turn out to be different names for the same or similar phenomena. The resolution of these issues is in the hands of psychologists of the future.

CENTRAL DETERMINANTS IN PERCEPTUAL THEORY

As we pointed out in the introduction to the present chapter, one of the strongest trends in perceptual research immediately following World War II was to put the O back into the old S-R formula. Indeed, it might be said that the same perceptual determinants that the classical psychophysicists sought to eliminate from their experiments became the experimental variables in a large segment of this research. In the days of Weber and Fechner any psychologist who allowed the subject's attitudes, needs, values, or similar O factors to affect the experimental results would be considered a poor experimentalist. In the 1940s and 1950s experiments on the effect of such variables were in the forefront of research in the field of perception. This movement appeared so radical when it first got under way, after World War II, that it was dubbed ''the New Look'' in psychology. By now it already has receded into history, so rapid has been the flow of events in contemporary psychology during the past quarter-century.

Speaking somewhat more technically, this movement is known as ''directive-state'' theory (F. H. Allport, 1955) on the assumption that the *direction* of perceptual experience is influenced by such O factors as sets, attitudes, values, needs, and similar intervening variables. In reality this conception of central determinants is not new, for both literature and philosophy are full of allusions to inner ''determinants'' in perception. Among the classical psychologists, Helmholtz and the Gestaltists also emphasized the significance of such determinants.

Needs and Sets as Perceptual Determinants

The general design of experiments falling under this category is as follows: The experimenter chooses some measurable verbal or motor reaction that is dependent on perception and establishes the subject's average level of response under ''normal'' conditions. Then, he or she induces a need, set, or motive in the subject and repeats the measurements. The difference in response is attributed to the influence of the induced determinant on the subject's perception. In this type of experimental design the subject serves as his or her own control. It is also possible to use equated groups and to measure the difference between the performance of the experimental group, which is under the influence of the determinant, and of the control group, which is not subjected to the experimental variable.

In experiments on *needs,* for example, there have been several in which subjects are deprived of food until hungry and then tested for their tendency to perceive food-relevant objects in perceptual test fields. Even before the era of the New Look in perception, Sanford (1936a, 1936b) showed that hungry subjects completed word stems in such a way as to make more food-relevant words than did nonhungry subjects. For example, the word stem ME____ was more likely to be completed as MEAT or MEAL by hungry subjects than by nonhungry. There have been a number of similar studies by subsequent investigators, the results of which have been in general agreement with Sanford's (see F. H. Allport, 1955; Levine, Chein, & Murphy, 1942; Postman & Crutchfield, 1952; Schafer & Murphy, 1943).

Since sets are temporary states of motivation that alert the subject to perceive or respond in accordance with the set, it might be predicted that such states would exert perceptual influences of the same type as just discussed in connection with needs. A study by Siipola (1935) demonstrates that sets influence perception as expected. In the experiment the subjects were required to respond to words presented tachistoscopically for 0.10 second. The stimulus words were as follows:

1. horse
2. baggage
3. chack
4. sael
5. wharl
6. monkey
7. pasrort
8. berth
9. dack
10. pengion

Subjects in one group were told they would be dealing with words having to do with *animals or birds,* while members of the other group were informed they would be responding to words in the category of *travel or transportation.* Since all "words" except numbers 1, 2, 6, and 8 are ambiguous, the hypothesis was that the responses would be in keeping with the set. For example, the first group might report *sael* as *seal, wharl* as *whale,* and so on, whereas the second group might report the same words as *sail* and *wheel,* respectively.

The results confirmed the hypothesis. Subjects in the first group reported six times as many *animal-bird* words as did the subjects in the second group, who, incidentally, reported five times as many *travel-transportation* words as the first.

Emotional States as Perceptual Determinants

Folk wisdom has recognized that emotional states and moods tend to influence perception. We say: "The lover looks at the world through 'rose-colored glasses.' " "Misery loves company." "The child's happy optimism makes the world appear to be his oyster." Although such generalizations may seem to have face validity, we must appeal to the experimental literature for the precise relationships involved.

Experiments designed to investigate the influence of moods and emotional states are relatively straightforward. The experimenter induces a mood or emotional state in the subject and then compares the responses in a perceptual test situation either to the subject's normal responses or to those of a matched control group that is not under the influence of an emotional state. We may illustrate the problems in research on emotional states by discussing perceptual defense, the most controversial of the directive-state issues.

The literature of this problem goes back to a study by McGinnies (1949) in which subjects were presented with a list of words, eleven of which were neutral and seven of which had emotional connotations. Among the emotional words were the following: *raped, whore, penis,* and *bitch;* and among the neutral, *apple, child, river, music,* and *sleep.* Eight male and eight female college students were presented with the eighteen words in a scrambled order. The words were viewed by the subject in a tachistoscope, which allowed McGinnies to expose the words for duration periods of 0.10 second upward. At the same time, a psychogalvanometer (GSR) was connected to the subject to record emotional reactions, if any. The subjects were instructed that they would be shown words and were to judge what the word was, but not report until signaled to do so by the experimenter. In this way the subject's psychogalvanic response could be noted *before* they reported. Thus, two measures were possible: the subjects' thresholds, in seconds, for recognition and the galvanic responses for the trials preceding correct recognition. Presumably, if the emotional words resulted in high galvanic responses *before* they were correctly recognized on a conscious level, this would indicate prerecognition on an unconscious level. Finally, McGinnies was also able to make a qualitative study of the kinds of verbal responses made to the neutral as opposed to critical words. If there were more cases of misperceiving emotional words, especially in the direction of making them "harmless," this, too, would indicate the operation of an unconscious perceptual determinant. An example of such misrepresentation would be reporting *whose* for *whore* or distorting it into an entirely dissimilar word or even into a nonsense syllable.

In short, McGinnies found significant differences between the neutral and critical words along all three dimensions measured. Specifically, the thresholds for emotional words were higher, the GSR responses greater, and there were more distortions among the emotional words than the neutral words. He interpreted his findings as an anxiety-avoidance reaction in the form of a "perceptual defense" mechanism that protected the subjects from the unpleasant meanings of the critical words.

The critics[5] were quick to charge that McGinnies had failed to control for several possible factors. Solomon and Howes (1951) pointed out that the critical words appear less frequently in writing, speaking, and reading and on this basis alone might be harder to recognize, consequently, generating mild emotional reactions that could be mistakenly interpreted as "perceptual defense." Aronfreed, Messik, and Diggory (1953) found that in cases where the subjects were females and the experimenter a male, the recognition threshold was longer and the emotional reaction greater for emotional words, thus demonstrating that embarrassment might be a factor.

To obviate some of these difficulties, McCleary and Lazarus (1949) utilized

---

[5]The critical literature on perceptual defense is extensive. It has been estimated that the controversy generated over 1000 technical papers and theoretical articles. For detailed expositions, see Vernon (1970), Dixon (1971), and Erdelyi (1974). The last paper attempts to deal with perceptual defense in terms of information processing theory.

nonsense syllables half of which were accompanied by shock in a pretest conditioning series. When the shocked syllables were subsequently presented with non-shocked syllables, the emotional reactions were found to be higher for the crucial syllables. But again the critics have pointed to additional difficulties of interpretation and control. Bricker and Chapanis (1953) argued that subliminal presentation of nonsense syllables does convey some information to the subject and that syllables more similar to the shocked syllables result in an increased galvanic skin response. Murdock (1954), utilizing nonsense syllables, also demonstrated the possibility of partial recognition—a factor that other investigators had not taken into account in experiments involving all-or-none recognition thresholds.

Finally, in any discussion of word frequency in relation to subception or perceptual defense, the work of C. W. Eriksen (1956a, 1956b, 1960) should be mentioned. Eriksen has criticized the use of the Thorndike-Lorge word list as a source of materials for constructing balanced lists of equally familiar neutral and taboo words for perceptual defense experiments. He believes that the Thorndike-Lorge list is inadequate in that it underestimates the frequency of the so-called taboo words in the language. Thus experimenters using this list might not find evidence for perceptual defense simply because their taboo words were not, after all, taboo to the subjects. Eriksen has also pointed out that there may be statistical artifacts in subception experiments that have not been controlled adequately.

Another objection raised against the perceptual defense hypothesis has been that subjects were delaying or withholding their responses rather than failing to perceive taboo words. Research bearing on the issue has been carried out by Siegman (1956), who reported that nearly 80 percent of his subjects said they had withheld responses. That subjects may, in fact, dislike to report taboo words orally is suggested by the results of Postman, Bronson, and Gropper (1953), who found less inhibition when the subjects were allowed to write down the terms rather than utter them aloud. Finally, perceptual defense has been objected to on logical grounds. How can one be unaware of perceiving what must be defended against and yet perceive it?

Clearly, in view of the variable nature of the phenomena, the issue of perceptual defense and subception remains unsettled. The falling off in the literature of research in the area in recent years suggests that psychologists in general are less convinced that these phenomena are a reality apart from artifacts of experimental design. There appears to be at least a tacit admission that if all variables, such as embarrassment, problems relating to threshold measurements, short-term memory, frequency of neutral as opposed to emotion-provoking words, partial recognition, and response bias are taken into account, there is no hard evidence that perceptual vigilance or subception exists.

The problem here is analogous to that found in research on extrasensory perception. Statistically, the phenomenon of ESP was easily shown in early and loosely controlled experiments, but it has not been demonstrated to the satisfaction of psychologists in general in more recent experiments in which controls are rigid and when experimental errors are ruled out (Hansel, 1966).

Attitudes and Values as Perceptual Determinants

In dealing with such complex cognitive processes as attitudes or values, the experimenter must first screen his or her subjects by means of a test or socioeconomic survey in order to set up two groups that are widely divergent along some attitudinal or value dimension. Then he or she brings the experimental variable to bear in order to determine whether or not the preexisting intervening variables of value, attitude, and the like have a demonstrable effect on the subject's reaction. We shall present the classic experiment by Bruner and Goodman (1947) to illustrate the methodology involved.

Bruner and Goodman selected two groups of 10-year-old children, one group from "rich homes" and one from "poor homes." The subjects' task was that of estimating the physical size of coins ranging from 1 to 50 cents. Estimations were made by the manipulation of a knob, which in turn controlled a diaphragm regulating the size of a circular patch of light on a ground-glass screen. The actual sizes of the coins were the standards, and the averages of the subjects' light settings were compared to the standards in order to obtain a measure of the magnitude of under- or overestimation. Essentially the technique was the old psychophysical method of

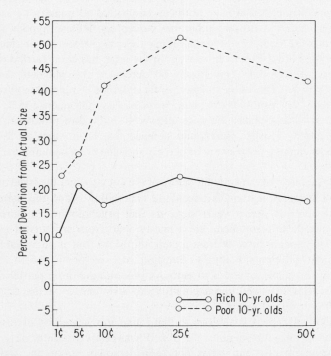

FIGURE 6-6. The deviation in the perceived size of coins by rich and poor children. (From Bruner, J. S., and Goodman, C. C. Value and need as organizing factors. Journal of Abnormal and Social Psychology, 1947, 42, p. 40. Copyright 1947 by the American Psychological Association. Reprinted by permission.)

average error. A control group made similar estimations using cardboard disks as the standard stimuli.

The "poor" children overestimated the size of every coin to a greater degree than the "rich" children, although all subjects tended to overestimate coins, especially the 5-, 10-, and 25-cent denominations. There is less overestimation, incidentally, when the coins are absent and estimations are made from memory. Figure 6-6 shows the subjects' estimations in terms of deviations from physical size.

This experiment has been repeated with other valued objects and with adults as well as with children. The results have not always been in agreement with Bruner and Goodman's, but in general, valued objects or objects that have acquired temporary value through experimental manipulation have been overestimated in respect to size. Objects with no value or with negative values induced by experimental manipulation have been underestimated. Thus, the directive-state theorists have shown that the relation between size and value can be manipulated experimentally and may be mediated by motivational and culturally determined values.

Personality Traits and Perception

The final aspect of the problem of central determinants in perception that we shall examine in this chapter is the research in the area of personality variables as influences on perception. Because our aim in this volume is to relate theory and empirical research, we shall once more invoke the "sampling technique," and we shall present the results of a series of investigations spanning nearly two decades in which basic experimental investigations of the interaction of sensory and motor processes in perception have led to broad techniques for the investigation of personality.

The fundamental research on sensory-motor interaction in perception is the work of Werner and Wapner (1949, 1956, 1965) and their associates. Its extension into the area of personality is the work of H. A. Witkin and his associates.

In the preface to *Personality through Perception,* Witkin, Lewis, Hertzman, Mackover, Meissner, and Wapner describe their study as one "concerned with the way in which personal characteristics of the individual influence his perception" (1954, p. XXI). The report, they add, "represents a ten-year labor, and parts of it required the services of a sizable group of investigators, each having a specialized psychological skill." In keeping with the comprehensive nature of their aim, Witkin and his associates employed a battery of space-orientation tests, most of which were developed in a long series of experimental investigations carried out by Witkin. In brief, there were three main space-orientation tests.[6]

In the first, subjects adjusted a luminous vertical rod presented within a frame in a dark room. The frame was tilted 28 degrees from vertical, and the subject's task

---

[6]A two-hand coordination test, a body steadiness test, and a figure embeddedness test were also employed. However, our summary is confined to the more important perceptual tests. The interested reader may consult Witkin and his associates (1954) for results on the other tests.

was to set the rod to true verticality by instructions to the experimenter, who slowly moved the rod until the subject was satisfied that it was vertical. In essence, the subject's problem was to overcome the effect of the distorted frame of reference created by the tilted frame.

In the second, the tilting-room–tilting-chair test, the subject might be tilted while the framework remained vertical. Or the subject could be kept vertical while the "room" and frame were tilted. On some trials the subject was instructed to make the room upright; on others he or she was required to adjust the chair to true verticality. In this way the subject's use of his or her own bodily orientation in perception could be evaluated.

The third test was a rotating-room test, in which essentially the same tasks of adjusting the room and chair to verticality were presented, but with the additional complication for the subject of having to take into account the pull of gravity—partly downward and partly outward—due to the centrifugal force created by the room's rotation at 18.8 revolutions per minute. In every case the measures employed were the subjects' deviations in degrees from true vertical of the rod, room, or chair for a series of trials.

The perceptual adjustments involved in the three tests are far more complex than appear at first glance. Essentially they involve, first, "part-of-a-field" tasks, such as the rod-and-frame test and, second, "field-as-a-whole" tasks, as represented by the room-adjustment problems. Thus, when the subject is confronted with a part-field problem, there is the advantage of a normal frame of reference which he or she may employ to correct the item that appears to be distorted. On the other hand, when the whole field is distorted, if the subject "accepts" the whole field as a frame of reference, then objects in it will suffer distortion. However, it must be emphasized that the subject in the space-orientation tests is not *compelled* to accept the whole field "passively" as is the case in the Ames demonstrations. In the experiments under discussion, the subject at least has the possibility of adjusting the field as a whole—for example, by moving the room instead of the rod or his or her own body. The room is the field-as-a-whole, whereas the rod or the subject's body is the bit or part of the field-as-a-whole.

We shall return to the space-orientation tests later. First, we shall summarize the chief techniques used to evaluate the personality dimensions involved in the study. There were an autobiography, a clinical interview, a personality questionnaire made up of items selected from the Minnesota Multiphasic Personality Inventory, a sentence completion test, a figure drawing test, a word association test, and the Rorschach and thematic apperception tests. Thus, a multidirectional design was employed in order to ensure a relatively complete analysis of each subject's personality.

Witkin and his associates found that, on the average, the visual field in each test exerted a significant effect on the subject's perception of the task involved as revealed by his or her adjustments of the apparatus. For example, in the rod-and-frame test, subjects generally did not adjust the rod to true vertical, but moved it instead in the direction in which the frame was tilted. It is interesting to note that on this and the other perceptual tests, male subjects showed smaller deviations in their adjustments than did females. We shall return to this sex difference shortly; meanwhile, several other findings will be considered first.

On the various perceptual tests, the influence of the visual field was greater when the "position of the field as a whole was to be determined than when the position of an item within the field was to be established . . ." (Witkin et al., 1954, p. 60). To illustrate, if the room in the tilting-room–tilting-chair test were being adjusted by the subject, the deviations were greater than if the subject were adjusting the position of his or her own body in the adjustable chair. This seems reasonable, since the larger portion of our perceptual environment is apt to dominate what we see.[7]

Another general result from the experiments involving body adjustment (the tilting-chair test) was the finding that the body was less influenced by the visual field than was an external item such as the rod. The authors suggest that the strong kinesthetic sensations from the body may cause the subject to resist displacement in this case, whereas in the rod test the subject gets only visual cues arising from external sources that are consequently overcome more readily.

It will be recalled that Witkin and his associates (1954) also studied children and hospital patients. The hospital patients, as might be expected, were more deviant in their adjustments than normals. Indeed, the statistical analyses showed that these individuals tended toward opposite extremes on the space-orientation tests in the sense that there was a greater proportion of individuals in this group who were either highly *dependent* on the visual field, on the one hand, or extremely *independent* and *analytic,* on the other hand, with proportionately few cases falling in the intermediate range. Put another way, normals in general tend toward dependence on the visual field but show a normal range of reactions from great dependence to relative independence. However, only a few cases are represented at the extremes among normals; most are in the intermediate range of deviations. The hospital cases, on the other hand, tend to group themselves on the more extreme ends of the range of individual differences.

Perhaps the most significant general finding with the children was a tendency for field dependence to decrease with age. Evidently the adult is less likely to accept things as they are and takes instead a more analytic attitude toward his or her environment. As was true with adult women, the female subjects among the children were more "passive" in accepting the visual field and as a result made more deviant adjustments at all ages. The authors suggest that this may be due to the more passive cultural and biological roles imposed upon the female in our society.[8] At any rate, there is no evidence to suggest that such differences are inherent.

---

[7]An everyday example occurs when large fluffy clouds are racing across a moonlit sky. Frequently it is the moon that appears to be racing. The large clouds are "forcing" the small moon to move, since they provide a more stable frame of reference.

[8]Iscoe and Carden (1961) have reported parallel findings for 11-year-old boys and girls. Interestingly, field-independent boys were more popular and showed less anxiety than field-dependent boys. The reverse was true for female subjects suggesting the effects of social conditioning of sex differences on personality.

Turning to the personality tests, we shall outline a sample of the findings based on the interview, the Rorschach test, and the figure drawing tests.

In the clinical interview, the field-dependent subjects showed a lack of insight into their own mental processes, tended to repress their feelings and impulses, and were inclined to suffer from inferiority feelings. This finding was generally confirmed by the subjects' figure drawings. The field-dependent subjects drew immature, inadequate figures of people, whereas the analytic, independent subjects drew more capable-looking and mature-appearing figures.

On the Rorschach, the field-dependent subjects tended to be dominated by the blot as a whole, or, to put it another way, yielded to their "environment" as represented by the blots, without analyzing or looking beyond the "popular," more obvious interpretations. In fact, a "coping" score, which can be derived from the Rorschach responses, showed that those who demonstrated relatively low deviations on the space-orientation tests were high in the ability to cope with their environments, whereas the field-dependent or high-deviation group on the space tests had low coping scores.

Finally, we might note that field-independent subjects select and do better in courses in analytic subjects, such as mathematics and the sciences, whereas field-dependent subjects tend to select and do best in areas such as the social sciences, testing and counseling, and courses that involve interactions with people (Witkin, 1973; Witkin, Dyk, Faterson, Goodenough & Karp, 1962).

In evaluating the research program of Witkin and his associates, we must bear in mind that although this work began with the focus on general or nomothetic cognitive processes whose measurement grew out of experimental work on perception, it is more properly characterized as correlation research, whose recent emphasis has been on the assessment of individual differences or idiographic factors. To put it another way, we cannot at the present time establish cause and effect or independent-dependent relationships among the perceptual and personality variables studied. Rather, we can only justify the conclusion that the individual's cognitive style (whether global or analytic) is correlated with his or her performance on personality measures and interests. Whether one causes the other or both are related to still a third set of variables we cannot say.

PERCEPTION AND INFORMATION PROCESSING THEORY[9]

As we indicated in Chapter 3, the field of perception has undergone rapid expansion and change in the decades following World War II. As the New Look perception of the 1940s and 1950s matured, the technology of information processing and computer programming was also undergoing rapid development. Each passing year witnessed the birth of more sophisticated techniques for detecting, processing, and

---

[9]The reader who wishes to review the more technical aspects of information processing may wish to consult Chapter 15 at this point. For an excellent collection of primary source material, see Haber (1969). For a discussion of information processing theory and perception from the cognitive point of view, see Neisser (1967).

storing information. Inevitably, psychologists recognized the many parallels that can be drawn between the human organism and information processing. In physical devices designed for data processing, information must be detected, stored, and processed according to a predetermined program. Later it may be retrieved upon command of an operator. Similarly, the human organism can detect, store, process, and retrieve information. Since the individual is his or her own programmer, the parallel is not exact, and this and other differences—as Neisser (1967) and Haber (1969) have pointed out—intrude into theoretical interpretations. However, many perceptual psychologists have found the information processing analysis of perception productive, and a large proportion of recent research in the area has been directly or indirectly influenced by information processing theory.

Perhaps the simplest way to introduce the analysis of perception as information processing is to utilize the example of the old reaction-time experiment. The subject sits before a panel with two lights, a red and a green, and two keys, one near his or her right hand and one near the left. The subject is instructed to press the right-hand key if the green light comes on and the left-hand key if the red light appears. The problem can be analyzed into an information processing sequence as follows. The subject must first sense the light (detection). Second, the signal must be transduced from light energy into neural energy, encoded, and transmitted to the brain. There it must be processed in terms of already stored information ("When the green light comes on, press the right key; when the red light comes on, press the left key") and an appropriate response (output) made after retrieval of this stored information.

As simple as this experiment seems, the processes are, nevertheless, complex. Their complete understanding would necessitate nothing short of a comprehensive description of all the traditional cognitive processes—sensing, attending, perceiving, remembering, and thinking. As Haber has said:

> Sensation, perception, memory, and thought must be considered on a continuum of cognitive activity. They are mutually interdependent and cannot be separated except by arbitrary rules of momentary expediency. Further, to understand how these processes function and interact, they should be subjected to an information-processing analysis, rather than be viewed as static structural systems. Such an analysis makes it clear that a proper explication of thought processes must begin with perceptual behavior just as thought cannot prosper in the absence of stimulation. Equally as important, it is not possible to understand perception, especially recognition, identification, and perceptual memory, without understanding the whole range of cognitive activity. (1969, p. 1)

Because information processing theorists treat the cognitive processes as a continuum, it is not surprising that their research and interpretive literature span the entire spectrum of the traditional sensory-perceptual and higher mental processes. Broadly speaking, the following have been the most significant research areas in the past two decades: (1) span of apprehension; (2) short-term visual storage of information; (3) masking effects, or the change in effectiveness brought about in one stimulus by the presence of another; (4) scanning and searching; (5) encoding, storage, and retrieval of information, involving the memory processes.

Because the information analysis of cognitive processes involves stages beyond perception, we shall arbitrarily consider only the perceptual processes in this chapter and defer further discussion of the information analysis of the so-called higher mental processes until Chapter 15, after we have considered memory and thinking. Since the literature in the area of perception from an information processing point of view is far too extensive to summarize in its entirety, we shall report on representative experiments from the several research areas in order to illustrate the experimental designs and theoretical interpretations characteristic of this new approach.

Span of Apprehension

In a now classical article entitled, "The Magical Number Seven, Plus or Minus Two: Some Limitations on Our Capacity for Processing Information," G. A. Miller (1956) reexamines the old problem of the span of apprehension. The span of apprehension experiment is one of the oldest in psychology. As reported by Woodworth (1938), as early as 1859 Sir William Hamilton, the famous Irish mathematician and astronomer, threw marbles on the floor in a random pattern and requested his subject to estimate the number. On the average, somewhere between six and eight marbles could be estimated correctly, hence the "magic number seven." A number of subsequent experiments by psychologists have confirmed the finding that most people can apprehend between five and nine items at a single exposure, with the average number about seven.

Experiments on the span of apprehension or the absolute judgment of multidimensional stimuli at first centered on finding out how many discrete objects could be apprehended correctly at a single exposure. As G. A. Miller points out in the article referred to above, these experiments have become far more sophisticated, raising such questions as the effects of the nature of the material, luminance, duration of exposure, and grouping of the items. We shall briefly summarize the effects of two of the factors on the number of items that can be correctly apprehended at a single exposure: (1) grouping and (2) exposure time.

As pointed out by G. A. Miller (1956) in reviewing a number of experiments, the amount of information that can be apprehended in a single exposure ranges from five to nine depending on the kind of material being tested. However, if the information is grouped or chunked, the number of items that can be apprehended is greatly increased. In Figure 6-7 the nine dots in A are randomized and cannot easily be estimated correctly at a single glance. If, however, the dots are grouped as in B, the nine are readily apprehended. In fact, in C, sixteen items of information—a number far above the normal span—can be apprehended without difficulty, provided the dots are grouped in an easy-to-apprehend pattern.

The factor of duration of exposure was tested in an experiment by Averbach (1963). Subjects seated before a uniform white field with a fixation point in the center were instructed to press a switch, whereupon anywhere from one to thirteen dots appeared. After an interval of time another field consisting of a large random number of dots appeared (the "erasing" field), and the subject was then requested

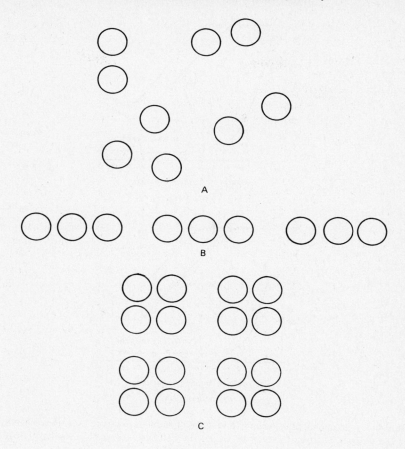

to give the number of dots that had appeared in the first field. We need not concern ourselves with the significance of the erasing field, since we shall be examining the effects of sequential stimulus interaction in the section to follow. Here our concern is limited to the number of correct dots apprehended as a function of duration of exposure.

As Figure 6-8 shows, the span of apprehension is a function of stimulus exposure time. At very short exposure times of 40 milliseconds, the number correct drops off rapidly, whereas at relatively long exposure times of 150 and 600 milliseconds, the number correct can be as high as thirteen in 50 percent of the test exposures. It is interesting to note that the differences between exposure times of 150 and 600 milliseconds are not large. Obviously a law of diminishing returns is operating for exposure times of increasing duration.

The results of experiments such as these raise interesting questions about the relationship between perception and memory. Are the dots being perceived as a unitary visual image or remembered from a sequence of silent counting? To put it in the language of information processing, how much information can be apprehended

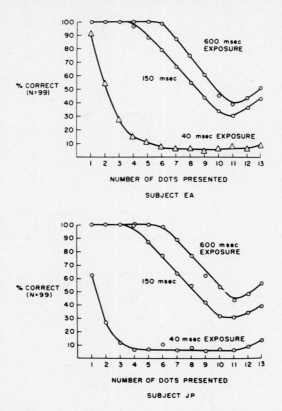

FIGURE 6-8.   Span of apprehension as a function of stimulus exposure time. (From Averbach, B., and Coriell, A. S. Short-term memory in vision. The Bell System Technical Journal, 1961, No. 3756.)

by parallel processing and how much by sequential processing? We shall begin to answer the question in the following section and return to it again in Chapter 15.

Short-Term Visual Storage

Averbach and Coriell (1961) presented subjects with a 2×8 randomly chosen array of letters. The exposure time was 50 milliseconds. Then after a variable delay interval a black bar marker of 50-millisecond duration was presented either above or below one of the letters in the top or bottom rows respectively; see Figure 6-9(a). A black circle was also employed as an indicator in a second phase of the experiment to be discussed subsequently. Figure 6-9(b) shows the experimental sequence in a typical trial. Figure 6-10 shows the average performance of three well-practiced subjects, revealing the decay in visual storage with increasing time. Averbach and Coriell hasten to point out that the curves are not valid descriptions of time-storage decay in general, since the latter would be expected to decay to zero over very long periods, whereas storage decay in the present experiment only reached about 30

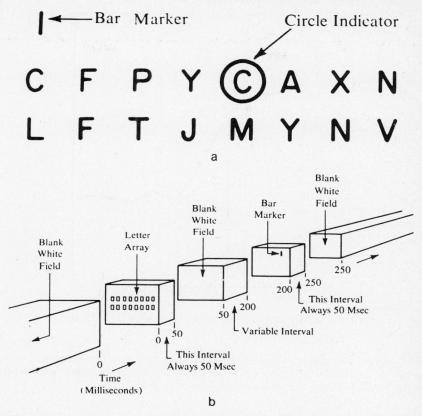

FIGURE 6-9. (a) The stimulus pattern in the Averbach and Coriell experiment. (The Bell System Technical Journal, 1961, No. 3756.) (b) The procedure diagrammed.

percent, indicating that under the conditions of the experiment a long-term storage process had evidently taken place.

It is important to note that in experiments such as Averbach and Coriell's the subjects report that they can "look at" the letter even after it is no longer present (Sperling, 1960). Therefore, a true visual image is present, not merely a remembered verbalization. Neisser (1967) has called such images *iconic memory* in order to avoid the varying implications of the traditional term "image."

We may now ask how long iconic memory lasts. The answer suggested by experiments such as Averbach and Coriell's is about 1 second. Factors such as intensity, exposure time, and, as we have seen, the nature of the postexposure field are important variables in determining how long iconic images persist. In general, the results of Averbach and Coriell's experiment (1961) and related experiments by other investigators show that the visual process demonstrates a high capacity for acquiring and storing information almost instantaneously in addition to the ability to retain it and utilize it over a relatively long decay period, during which time it can be converted into visual memory.

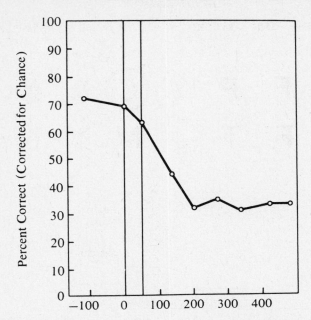

Time in Milliseconds Between Array and Bar Marker

FIGURE 6-10.   The decay in visual storage with increasing time. (From Averbach, E. Span of apprehension as a function of exposure duration. Journal of Verbal Learning and Verbal Behavior, 1963, p. 62. Reprinted by permission of Academic Press, Inc.)

Masking

The concept of visual *masking* refers to situations in which the effect of the test stimulus is reduced by the presentation of another (the masking stimulus) in close temporal contiguity. When the masking stimulus follows the test stimulus, we have backward masking. When the masking precedes the test stimulus, we have forward masking.

In the second part of the Averbach and Coriell experiment described above, we have an example of backward masking. In that experiment, it will be recalled, either a bar marker or a circle was used to indicate to the subject that he or she should report the letter indicated. When the circle was employed, the subject's performance was significantly poorer. The proximity of the circle as compared to the bar was held to be the responsible factor, the exposure of the circle in effect erasing the storage of the letter.

Masking effects, as implied in the definition, need not result in complete obliteration of the original iconic memory. Instead, its effectiveness may be reduced or it may be modified in some significant way. In an interesting experiment by Guthrie and Wiener (1966), a drawing of a seated man was given brief exposure. In one exposure the man was given angular outlines, in another, rounded contours.

Then a second figure of the man was exposed for 450 milliseconds. The second figure was a vague, broken-line figure. The subjects were requested to make mood and character judgments of the latter. The test figure was judged to be more hostile and aggressive when preceded by the angular figure. Even the presence of a gun in the hand of the rounded figure did not have a greater effect on the judgments of negative traits than the angular figure without the gun. Guthrie and Wiener conclude that it is the *figural* properties and not the meaning of the stimulus that affect the course of processing.

Scanning and Searching

So far we have been dealing with cases where information is presented to the subject directly. Neisser and his associates (Neisser, 1963, 1964; Neisser & Beller,

a.	b.
EHYP	ZVMLBQ
SWIQ	HSQJMF
UFCJ	ZTJVQR
WBYH	RDQTFM
OGTX	TQVRSX
GWVX	MSVRQX
TWLN	ZHQBTL
XJBU	ZJTQXL
UDXI	LHQVXM
HSFP	FVQHMS
XSCQ	MTSDQL
SDJU	TZDFQB
PODC	QLHBMZ
ZVBP	QMXBJD
PEVZ	RVZHSQ
SLRA	STFMQZ
JCEN	RVXSQM
ZLRD	MQBJFT
XBOD	MVZXLQ
PHMU	RTBXQH
ZHFK	BLQSZX
PNJW	QSVFDJ
CQXT	FLDVZT
GHNR	BQHMDX
IXYD	BMFDQH
QSVB	QHLJZT
GUCH	TQSHRL
OWBN	BMQHZJ
BVQN	RTBJZQ
FOAS	FQDLXH
ITZN	XJHSVQ
VYLD	MZRJDQ
LRYZ	XVQRMB
IJXE	QMXLSD
RBOE	DSZHQR
DVUS	FJQSMV
BIAJ	RSBMDQ
ESGF	LBMQFX
QGZI	FDMVQJ
ZWNE	HQZTXB
QBVC	VBQSRF
VARP	QHSVDZ
LRPA	HVQBFL
SGHL	HSRQZV
MVRJ	DQVXFB
GADB	RXJQSM
PCME	MQZFVD
ZODW	ZJLRTQ
HDBR	SHMVTQ
BVDZ	QXFBRJ

FIGURE 6-11. Materials used in scanning and searching experiments by Neisser and his associates. (From "Visual search" by Ulric Neisser. Copyright © 1964 by Scientific American, Inc. All rights reserved.)

1965; Neisser & Lazar, 1964; Neisser, Novik, & Lazar, 1963) have carried out a
series of experiments on visual searching where the subject must search for a target
letter that is presented in an unpredictable place in a list of letters. Or the target may
be a line from which a certain letter is missing (Figure 6-11). When the subject has
identified the target, he or she presses a switch, stopping a clock that measures the
time elapsed from the beginning of the search until its termination. From the
subject's total time, the time per line can readily be calculated. Neisser (1967, p.
68) reports that practiced subjects can reach speeds of ten lines per second. Naturally the difficulty of the discrimination in part determines speed, as even a superficial comparison of Figure 6-10a and 6-10b reveals.

Interesting questions of interpretation are raised by experiments such as Neisser's. Does the subject have a model or template of the target in mind, so that he or
she stops searching when a fit is found? Neisser reports that subjects insist that they
do not ''see'' the individual letters. Rather, the lines are a ''blur'' from which the
target ''stands out.'' Moreover, multiple searches—looking for both a Z and a K,
for example—take no longer for practiced subjects than simple searches. Positive
identification of a letter—such as is necessary when a response is contingent upon
its absence—takes longer than a simple search for the presence of a letter, indicating
the necessity for more complex analyzers in the cognitive system.

Theorists are not yet certain about the nature of the underlying perceptual
processes involved in search. The retina and brain must contain feature analyzers
that enable the individual to recognize certain letters and shapes. In Chapter 4 we
found that the cat's cortex has analyzer cells sensitive to certain line and edge
orientations. In the frog, evidence was discussed for a complex set of detectors in
the retina, one of which is responsive to motion—a useful analyzer for a species
whose livelihood depends on catching moving insects (Lettvin, Maturana, McCulloch, & Pitts, 1959). We shall have more to say about perceptual analyzers in
Chapter 15.

Encoding and Storage

The process of encoding perceptual information involves such variables as the
effect of set (already familiar to us from directive-state theory), frequency of words
in the English language, and repetition of exposures. In an experiment designed to
test several of these factors, Haber (1965) had subjects tachistoscopically view
words of three syllables and seven letters in length. Some words were from the
rarest third of those appearing in the Thorndike-Lorge word-count list and some
from words taken from *Webster's Unabridged Dictionary* (1939 edition). The
frequent words were all selected from those above the median of the Thorndike-
Lorge list. The words were randomly divided into nine lists of sixty-four words
each, each list to be presented at one of nine exposure sessions. Every list had an
equal number of randomly ordered rare and familiar words.

Each word was assigned one of two duration values (either high or low), one of
eight exposure trial numbers (1, 2, 3, 4, 5, 10, 15, or 25) representing the number of
times it would be flashed, and one of two conditions of prior knowledge (complete

or no knowledge). Complete prior knowledge was provided by exposing the word for 5 seconds before the first trial, requiring the subject to spell out the word. For no prior knowledge the subject first saw the word during the experimental series proper. The subjects were required to report the letters and their respective positions; and all analyses of results were based on letters, not words, in order to minimize guessing. The subject was scored as having perceived a word when he or she reported correctly all seven letters on the last exposure given for that word. Subjects, however, did not know that words were to be shown repeatedly. Otherwise they might have withheld reporting until they were certain.

The results of the experiment are shown in Figure 6-12. It will be noted that both word frequency and prior knowledge affect the results. Both prior-knowledge means are significantly above no-prior-knowledge means. The differences between rare and frequent words were significant only when the subject had no prior knowledge. Thus prior knowledge obliterates differences between rare and frequent words. Haber believes that the findings support a perceptual rather than a response interpretation:

> The findings regarding the effect of trials clearly support the "perceptual" rather than the response interpretation. This was seen most clearly for the low duration, where there was no ceiling. Here all four curves showed nearly identical effects of trials, regardless of the frequency of the words or the prior knowledge of S. The same tendency is apparent for the high-duration curve, even though the prior knowledge words reach the ceiling first. Consequently, even when S knows exactly what the stimulus will be, his ability to see all of the letters grows gradually with repeated exposures, just as it does when he does not know the stimulus. (1965, p. 766)

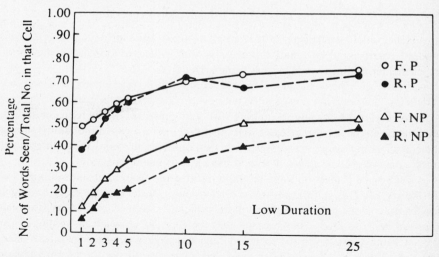

FIGURE 6-12. The influence of word frequency and prior knowledge on encoding and storage. R = rare; F = frequent; NP = no prior exposure; P = prior exposure. (From Haber, R. N. The effect of prior knowledge of the stimulus word on recognition processes. Journal of Experimental Psychology, 1965, 69, p. 284. Copyright 1965 by the American Psychological Association. Reprinted by permission.)

Subjective reports obtained from the subjects also supported a perceptual interpretation of the results. On the first flash the subjects saw nothing—neither parts of letters nor complete letters. After several flashes, parts then whole letters became visible. As the trials went on, there was an increasing clearness and development of the percept of the rest of the letters. Haber does not suggest precisely what mechanism underlies the growth of perception in such experiments but does indicate that the process is remarkably similar to what Hebb's theory would predict in terms of the development of cell assemblies and phase sequences. (See Chapter 14.) The results strongly indicate that the development of some such neural mechanisms must parallel the development of perceptual processes.

In concluding this brief overview of perception from the point of view of information processing, we have shown how psychologists working in this new area have utilized designs that reveal variables that are significantly related to span of apprehension, visual storage, masking, encoding, and storage and retrieval of information. Literally hundreds of research and theoretical articles have appeared during the past two decades within this recently developed area of psychology. This effort continues at the present time at more and more complex levels. It is obviously impossible to assess the ultimate place in psychology of information processing analyses of the cognitive processes. In Chapter 14 we shall be returning to information theory as it applies to the higher cognitive processes of thinking and memory. Following a summary of the recent work in these areas, we shall attempt at least a tentative assessment of these revolutionary new developments in psychology.

A Generalized Model for Perceptual Information Processing

Haber and Hershenson (1973, pp. 161–167) have provided a generalized model for perceptual information processing that will serve to integrate the various experimental findings we have just summarized.

Figure 6-13 shows the model in schematic form. It will be noted that the model is developed around the most significant general characteristics involved in perceptual information processing, beginning with light projected on the retina or auditory stimulation in the ear (or by extension other types of sensory stimulation), through the encoding and storage processes, to the response output stage. We shall comment briefly on each of the stages and their channels of interconnection.

The retinal projection stage refers to information from light sources impinging on the retina. This is followed by a brief (iconic) visual storage stage lasting no longer than a second but perhaps more typically confined to 250 milliseconds' duration because of eye movements, and the flux and flow of changing environmental stimulation. From the iconic storage stage the processing may take one of two possible channels—a visual image stage or directly to short-term memory. However, in practice both of these channels operate in parallel. Thus, for example, in looking up an unfamiliar telephone number in a directory, one glances at it, forms a visual image and dials, utilizing short-term memory. A failure to complete the call usually necessitates another look, since short-term memory is not permanently encoded and stored in the retrieval system.

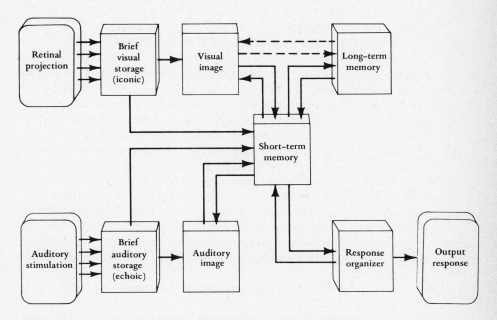

FIGURE 6-13. The Haber and Hershenson model for information processing. From Haber and Hershenson The Psychology of Visual Perception. New York, Holt, Rinehart and Winston. Copyright, 1973.

As the model indicates, the visual image and or short-term memory may progress into long-term memory. Note, too, that long-term memory may in turn act back upon the visual image (as in recognition, for example) whereupon meaning may accrue to the image.

Similarly, auditory stimulation generates a brief storage or echoic process which becomes an auditory image. The auditory image can develop a short-term auditory memory, and here again this can become a long-term memory or, if circumstances favor such an interaction, may interact with information arriving by visual channels.

Finally, all channels ultimately lead to some kind of response organization and output as shown in the lower right-hand side of the model. These responses involve motor processes, such as looking, pointing, articulating words, and the like.

It is important to note that although information processing theory appears to emphasize stimulus-response units and describes the organism in the technical symbolization of machine processing, the organism is nevertheless not treated as a passive machine. The internal processes of visual or auditory imagery with their interconnections to long-term memory make possible active selection of stimuli, recognition, meaning, and decision making. Moreover, as Haber and Hershenson point out, room is provided in the input stages for the operation of the principles of perceptual organization emphasized by the Gestalt school. And so it is interesting to note in concluding that these highly technical developments in recent perceptual theory are in no way inconsistent with the work of those pioneers who paved the way for their contemporaries.

A NOTE ON EXTRASENSORY PERCEPTION[7]

In all of the perceptual processes that we have discussed up to this point, awareness of objects and events is presumed to be mediated by the senses. This fundamental principle is the heritage of the empirical school of philosophy dating back to Aristotle, and no modern school or system of psychology has seriously questioned its validity. However, although they remain apart from traditional systems, there is a group of psychologists who believe in the possibility of extrasensory perception or that knowledge or influence can be transmitted directly from one individual to another or to an object without the mediation of the senses. Included under extrasensory perception or ESP are (1) telepathy or direct thought transfer from one individual to another; (2) clairvoyance or the ability to know objects or events without sensory mediation; (3) precognition or the knowledge of a future event. Another subject for investigation by those whose research interests lie in the area of ESP is psychokinesis, or PK, which is the ability to influence a material object through direct willing or mental effort.

The phenomena of ESP are generally investigated by means of a special pack of cards, called Zener cards, which consist of 25 cards with 5 different symbols imprinted on the face—square, star, cross, circle, and wavy lines. In telepathy experiments the sender takes a card from the shuffled deck and upon a signal concentrates on it while a receiver attempts to form an impression of what he or she is attempting to transmit. Elaborate precautions may be taken to prevent direct sensory signals or inadvertent errors, such as isolating the sender and receiver, allowing only electronic signals to indicate the beginning and end of trials, and having sealed records scored by a third party.

In tests for clairvoyance a subject simply attempts to guess the order of a shuffled face-down pack of cards. In precognition experiments the situation is the same as in telepathy except that the subject tries to guess what will be sent on the next trial, clearly an attempt to predict a future event.

In all these instances, statistical analyses are used to determine whether or not the subject's guesses exceed the level expected by chance. For example, in a telepathy experiment using Zener cards, the subject's chance level is 5 correct out of the 25 total. Anything consistently above that on a series of runs would be evidence in favor of ESP. For research on psychokinesis, dice are usually employed. As these are thrown on the surface of a table by a mechanical thrower, the subject attempts to

---

[7]The literature on ESP is extensive. Rhine's books (1964, 1970, 1971) contain summaries of the pioneer experiments from the Duke laboratory as do the twenty volumes of the *Journal of Parapsychology*. Rawcliffe (1959) has an excellent critical chapter on Soal's research. More recently, Hensel (1966) has reviewed the entire field critically. For recent pro-ESP accounts, see McConnell (1969) and Van de Castle (1969).

influence which faces will come up. Again any consistent level above chance is taken as evidence for psychokinesis.

In the United States, Joseph B. Rhine has for many years pioneered in experiments on ESP and has written extensively on the phenomena. He and his associates at Duke University were convinced that their experiments provided sound statistical evidence in favor of ESP. Similarly, Samuel G. Soal in England became the European pioneer in ESP, conducting hundreds of experiments with a variety of subjects. In general, European investigators, including Russians, are convinced of the reality of ESP. In the United States, by contrast, only a small number of psychologists believe that ESP has been scientifically established. In the United States those interested in investigating ESP have stood apart from the experimentalists as parapsychologists, publishing their own journal and never winning recognition by the traditional systems or schools.

The critics of ESP offer several serious reservations about experiments in parapsychology. Early criticism revolved around loose control of sensory cues that might inadvertently have been used by receivers, the possibility of fraud, and unintentional errors on the part of recorders (Hensel, 1966). As a result of these criticisms, a general "tightening up" of controls took place with a consequent sharp reduction in results favorable to ESP. In fact, the alleged ability involved, called Psi, is unique among psychological abilities in *decreasing* with repeated practice, even in "good" subjects. ESP has also been criticized on the grounds that individual subjects show considerable variability under different conditions of testing—the presence or absence of believers, whether telepathy or clairvoyance is under investigation, and whether or not the subject is fatigued. Such variability has seriously called into question the reliability of ESP findings. The critics have also pointed out that those who are convinced of the reality of ESP have no acceptable theoretical explanation of how it occurs. Finally, some psychologists remain unconvinced of the reality of a phenomenon that is based primarily on statistical analyses, particularly analyses that have often been manipulated in ways that tend to favor ESP. Most scientists are highly sceptical of any phenomenon or process that can *only* be inferred from probability studies. For these reasons the old Scotch verdict of "not proven" is rendered by most psychologists. This is not to say that they believe ESP to be an improper subject for study, only that after many decades of research they remain unconvinced that it is a worthwhile area for investigation. Its appeal to the layman remains strong, often on the basis of a single personal experience that seems unexplainable by conventional means. Popular belief in ESP has also been strengthened by the fact that prominent individuals, such as Carl Jung, William James, Arthur Conan Doyle, and Aldous Huxley seemed favorably disposed toward belief in the reality of Psi.

It appears likely that the reality of ESP will remain controversial for years to come. That it has never become part of the traditional body of experimental and systematic psychology does not in itself prove that it does not exist. Rather, psychologists' unwillingness to accept paranormal phenomena in general reflects a strong belief that any class of phenomena that falls outside of the ordinary must be viewed with greater than normal scepticism and consequently, must be subjected to more stringent scientific tests than are usually applied.

SUMMARY AND EVALUATION

With this summary of developments in information processing theory, we shall take leave of perception. In this and the preceding chapter, we have witnessed a continuous (and recently rather remarkable) broadening that has taken place in this area of psychological theory and research. Specifically, the shift has been in the direction of emphasizing the interrelations among organism factors or intervening variables. Beginning with the postwar directive-state psychology, motivational and personality variables were emphasized in research designs. During the latter half of the 1950s and throughout the 1960s the emphasis has been on information processing analyses of perception. Here again the emphasis has been on the continuity of the psychological processes in perception, starting with sensation and the dynamic factors that directly influence the encoding and storage of information and relating these in turn to memory and retrieval. In general, the predominant trend in the past several decades has been to treat perception as an *active* rather than a static process.

Developmental Psychology

7

In the preceding chapter we pointed out that the field of perception has experienced two revolutions during the past quarter-century. First, there was the impact of post–World War II central determinants theory and second, the proliferation of models utilizing information processing theory with its allied technological advances. Something of the same rapid acceleration in theoretical and research programs has been enjoyed by the field of developmental psychology. Until comparatively recent years the field was commonly known as child psychology, reflecting a long and fruitful history of interest in the human child, in terms of his or her capacities and sensorimotor, emotional, and social development.

Indeed, it is correct to trace the origins of child psychology to Plato in ancient Greece, who formulated the first systematic theory of how children should be educated as future citizens of the ideal state. Speculation about the mental capacities and limitations of the child continued until the third quarter of the nineteenth century when pioneer empirical studies of children supplanted philosophical speculation.

Beginning with the pioneer studies and continuing until the mid-1950s a great deal of the theoretical emphasis and research data in developmental psychology was of the *normative* type. That is, investigators were interested in establishing the age of onset of a behavioral process, and the range of individual differences in behavior found among groups of children, and in assessing the relative role of heredity and environment as determiners of behavior. In a sense, then, a major portion of traditional child psychology might be characterized as *differential* psychology, since the emphasis was on differences among children and groups of children of different ages.

It is true that a small but significant number of psychologists considered children as experimental subjects for the study of general mental or behavioral processes, but for the most part emphasis was on the establishment of normative or differential data, the problems of child rearing, and on the traditionally strong interest in the child as father of the adult, especially as reflected in the literature of the psychoanalytic and allied schools.

The strong shift of interest away from normative child psychology to the developmental point of view during the 1950s is the result of several factors. First, as Wohlwill (1973) has recently pointed out, there has been an "invasion" of experimental psychologists into the field. These researchers are less interested in normative data or differential studies than in utilizing children to investigate the development or growth of a behavioral process. To put it somewhat differently, the emphasis is not so much on the child per se as on the process, with the child as a research subject ideally suited for revealing the nature, growth, and in some cases, decay of the process over the trajectory of development.

Second, there has been a great deal of interest among psychologists in the general area of the cognitive processes in recent decades—perception, thinking, language, and learning. Because the onset of these processes and the period of their most rapid development occurs during childhood, the developmental psychologist quite naturally turns to children as subjects.

Third, the field of gerontology, or the study of old age from the medical, psychological, and social points of view, has burgeoned in recent decades and in doing so has broadened interest in development to include the later decades of life.

We shall make no attempt here to trace the history of child psychology[1] as it evolved from philosophy and medicine. The normative type of studies to which it gave rise do not reflect the strong systematic and theoretical orientation that is the theme of this volume. We shall, however, sketch the evolution of the developmental point of view by summarizing several pioneer studies that have become classics in the field and at the same time attempt to grapple with the broad question of the relative contribution of heredity and environment to development. Following this, we shall examine the attitude and contributions of the schools toward developmental psychology. Finally, we shall offer a sampling of contemporary trends as representative of ongoing theory and research in the field.

PIONEER STUDIES OF MATURATION AND LEARNING AS BASIC FACTORS IN DEVELOPMENT

We are already familiar with the heredity-environment or nature-nurture controversy from the theories of the nativists and empiricists in perception (Chapter 5). However, nowhere in the entire field of psychology is the question of the relative contribution of hereditary and environmental factors in behavior more relevant than in the area of developmental psychology. Indeed, by its very nature, the question is a developmental one. But, as we observed in discussing the nativist-empiricist controversy in perception, the question is meaningless if formulated in absolute or either-or terms, since all behavior is dependent on both factors. Realizing this, pioneer developmental psychologists attempted to reformulate the question more definitively in terms of the *relative* contribution of maturation and learning as basic processes in development.

---

[1]For a comprehensive treatment of the older, normative literature in child psychology, the reader is referred to the second edition of *Manual of child psychology* (1946), edited by Leonard Carmichael. See also R. I. Watson (1965) and Dennis (1949) for historical accounts of child psychology.

The concept of maturation was borrowed from biology, where it originally referred to the ripening of the germ cells. As employed in psychology it included the growth and development that is prerequisite to the appearance of unlearned behavior or to the growth and development necessary before the learning of a particular behavior can take place. By adopting the term maturation, developmental psychologists hoped to make the question of the biological factors in behavioral processes more identifiable and more specific. The question of the relative contribution of heredity could then be reformulated into what neural, hormonal, metabolic, and other factors are basic to a given behavior.

Learning, on the other hand, was simply defined as any relatively permanent modification in behavior that results from practice or experience. This definition would, of course, eliminate changes due to maturation or to such irrelevant conditions as diseases or drugs. With these definitions in mind, we are now ready to summarize the work of two pioneers on the development of locomotor behavior.

THE MATURATION OF SWIMMING BEHAVIOR

Leonard Carmichael (1898–1973) devoted his long and productive career in developmental studies to the investigation of prenatal behavior, reflecting his conviction that development does not begin at birth but at conception, with birth the end of the first stage in the trajectory of development that ends at death. Early in his career Carmichael became interested in determining whether locomotor behavior was primarily the contribution of maturation or of learning. Utilizing tadpoles, which offer the advantage of a ringside seat during their development from fertilized egg to adult frog, Carmichael (1926) took a mass of fertilized frog's eggs as his experimental group and allowed them to develop in an anesthetic solution, which prevented practice but allowed development to proceed in the sense of normal growth and differentiation of parts. A control group of eggs was allowed to develop under natural conditions in ordinary water.

When the members of the control group were swimming freely, Carmichael removed the experimental tadpoles from the anesthetic solution and dropped them into water. Within 20 minutes all members of the experimental group were swimming freely, showing that locomotor behavior in this species is dependent on maturation, not learning.

The experiment, however, can be criticized as not entirely valid in its design on the grounds that the anesthetized tadpoles did have a 20-minute period in which to learn to swim. Carmichael (1927) therefore performed another experiment to control for this factor by placing freely swimming tadpoles in the anesthetic solution to determine how long it took the effect of the anesthetic to wear off when the subjects were once again placed in ordinary water. The answer: 20 minutes, on the average. Therefore, the 20-minute period needed for members of the original experimental group to begin swimming freely was one in which the anesthetic was wearing off and was not a period of rapid learning.

Neural Mechanisms in Locomotor Behavior

Carmichael's studies of tadpoles do not tell us precisely what mechanisms are responsible for the development of locomotor behavior. G. E. Coghill (1872–1941), whose developmental studies of maturational processes span a period of over thirty years, carried out a long series of experiments on *Ambylostoma,* a common salamander. Careful observation of the behavior patterns of the developing salamander revealed that locomotor behavior went through five stages (Coghill, 1929): (1) the nonmotile stage; (2) the first flexion or C-stage; (3) the coil stage; (4) the S-stage; (5) the free-swimming stage (Figure 7-1).

In the nonmotile stage the salamander, whose brain, spinal cord, and muscle segments are fully developed by this time, does not react to a stimulus applied to the head region. However, in the first flexion or C-stage there is the reaction of flexing the body sharply away from the direction of stimulation. During this stage of development the salamander is still unable to swim.

The coil stage may be considered a further development of the C-stage in which more of the muscle segments lower down the spinal cord have become capable of responding.

With the S-stage a significant change has taken place in the development of the salamander. It is now able to flex both the head and tail regions in sequence. Clearly, it is only a short time later in development when the organism will be sufficiently mature to utilize S-flexions in free swimming.

Coghill next attacked the problem of what neural changes had occurred in the developing organism to make the observed behavioral changes possible. Sectioning, staining, and mounting hundreds of specimens in various stages of development for the purpose of making microscopic examination of their nervous systems, he found that it was the progressive maturing of synapses in the spinal cord that enables the observed behaviors to occur in sequences. In the first flexion or C-stage the growth of a sensorimotor synapse by only 1/100 mm made the difference. In other words,

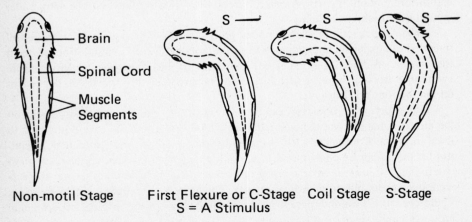

FIGURE 7-1.   Developmental stages in the salamander. 1. the non-motil stage; 2. the first flexion or C-stage; 3. the coil stage; 4. the S-stage; 5. the free-swimming stage.

during the nonmotile stage, receptors in the skin were sending impulses into the spinal cord but these impulses could not stimulate motor neurons controlling the flexion muscles, since these synapses were not yet sufficiently developed. When they had grown a fraction of a millimeter, impulses were able to cross, making a reflex muscular reaction possible.

Studies of sections of salamanders in the coil stage revealed that additional synapses had matured further down the spinal cord. This head to tail progression of maturation came to be generalized into the principle of *cephalocaudal* development, and can be observed in all species including man. A corollary principle is that of *proximodistal* development, also widely observable in members of the phylogenetic series (Figure 7-2).

The significant change from simple flexion and coiling to the S-stage basic to locomotion is the result of the maturation of the proprioceptive system in the salamander. The proprioceptive sense is one whose receptors are located in muscles, tendons, and joints. For the sake of simplicity, let us consider how the system is organized for the muscle segments in the salamander. As Figure 7-3 shows diagramatically, contraction in a muscle segment sets up sensory impulses over the proprioceptive pathways, which cross the cord (dotted lines) to synapse with motor neurons innervating muscle segments on the opposite side. Thus, a reaction at A not only can cause flexion on that side but, by proprioceptive reflex reaction, on the opposite side. Differential histological studies of salamanders in the coil stage and the S-stage showed that those in the coil stage possessed proprioceptive pathways,

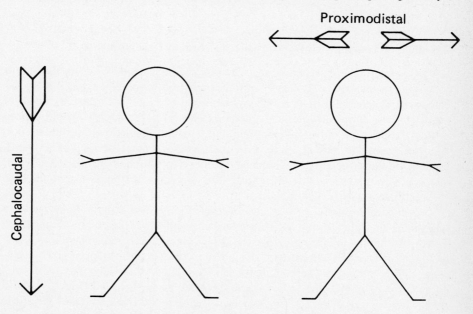

FIGURE 7-2. A. Cephalocaudal development. B. Proximodistal development. The arrows show the direction of development.

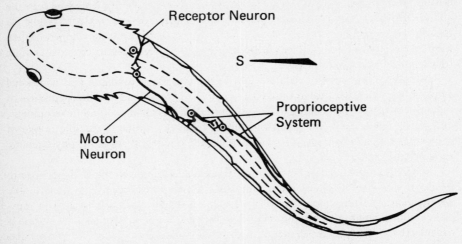

FIGURE 7-3.   The development of the proprioceptive system in *Ambylostoma*. For explanation see text.

but because the synapses were not fully developed, the pathways were nonfunctional. With the maturation of the synapses, impulses could cross the spinal cord and S-flexions take place. The free swimmimg stage depends on the further maturation of proprioceptive pathways.

The Role of Learning and Maturation in Human Development

The experiments of Coghill and Carmichael are acceptable as demonstrations of the role of maturation in locomotor development in amphibians, but it would be dangerous to generalize these results to human children without further evidence in support of the dominant role of maturation. Ideally, psychologists should experimentally restrict the opportunity for learning to occur, thus allowing maturation to take place normally. However, ethical considerations preclude such experiments because of the possibility of permanent damage to the subjects. Fortunately for research purposes, societies sometimes create conditions that approximate the kind of experimental design just suggested.

Dennis and Dennis (1940) utilized the Hopi Indian culture of Arizona to investigate the relative role of maturation and learning in locomotor behavior in babies. At that time most mothers in the Hopi villages used cradle boards, in which their infants were bundled by strips of cloth after being tightly wrapped in a blanket. Typically the infant was kept on the cradle board most of the day, except for brief periods when cleaned. The baby was carried on the mother's back or hung on a bush if she was engaged in an activity such as gathering food. The restriction, therefore, was severe and the child did not get the opportunity to practice sitting, creeping, and walking that unbundled children enjoyed. After 6 to 14 months, the cradle board was discarded.

The question may be raised as to the effect of such severe restriction on the average age of walking in bundled as compared with unbundled children. The Hopi children could be compared with white American children. However, racial and social differences would make such a comparison invalid. But several of the villages at the time of the Dennis and Dennis study had given up use of the cradle board as a result of becoming "Americanized." This group of children, free to practice locomotor behavior, yet of the same racial and general social background, served as an ideal control group. On the average, the age of walking in the control group was 15 months. For the cradle board babies it was also 15 months. Clearly, it takes little or no practice for the human baby to develop the fundamental locomotor skills of sitting up, creeping, standing, and walking.

It would be a mistake to assume that long continued restriction has no effect on locomotor behavior. Motor response systems that are given no opportunity to function at or near the time that they normally appear may suffer permanent retardation. This time period when behavior normally appears and when practice is most effective is called the *critical period*. The same serious retardation has also been observed in language development and socialization in orphan children (Dennis, 1960; Goldfarb, 1943, 1945). In language and social development, retardation may be more severe than in simple motor behavior since the former functions are more heavily dependent on adult stimulation.

The Effect of Special Training

It seemed natural for the pioneer developmental psychologists to raise the question of the role of special practice in accelerating development. Would such practice leave the child with some degree of permanent advantage over one not so practiced? Utilizing the method of co-twin control in order to rule out hereditary differences, numerous investigators have found that early special practice can give a temporary advantage in basic locomotor skills, but the effect is not great nor is it long lasting. For example, Gesell and Thompson (1929) used as subjects two identical twin girls. One girl, T, was trained in special activities, such as climbing, and the other, C, was given no opportunity to practice such activities.

By the end of a six-week period of practice, twin T had progressed from not being able to climb stairs at all to climbing five stairs in 26 seconds. Control twin C was now allowed to try, and on her first attempt climbed the five stairs in 45 seconds. With two weeks of training she had improved her performance to the point where she could climb the same number of stairs in 10 seconds.

The early investigators of the relative role of maturation and learning were not so scientifically unsophisticated as to conclude that practice played no role in the perfection and extension of basic locomotor skills. Moreover, they recognized that practice plays a major role in the acquisition of more culturally determined skills, such as language. In this case, incidentally, the role of special early practice can show advantages that last for decades. Granting these complexities, the experimental literature on the study of development during the first half of the twentieth century left a rich heritage to serve as a foundation for contemporary studies of development. We shall consider these after examining the role of the schools in developmental psychology.

STRUCTURALISM AND FUNCTIONALISM IN DEVELOPMENTAL PSYCHOLOGY

Neither the structuralists nor the functionalists made significant contributions to developmental psychology. For all practical purposes, the method of introspection favored by the structuralists ruled out the utilization of children as subjects. Although Titchener did suggest that introspection by analogy might be employed in the study of the consciousness of children, no such program was ever undertaken.

Similarly, the functionalists did not develop experimental programs that utilized children as subjects. This was an unfortunate omission, since the point of view they espoused—that mental processes should be studied in terms of their usefulness in adapting the organism to its environment—is in no way inconsistent with developmental viewpoints. Indeed, the child would seem an ideal subject for the study of the process of adaptation. However, preoccupied as they were with establishing psychology as the study of the normal human adult, little attention was given to developmental processes or to children as subjects.

BEHAVIORISM AND CHILD PSYCHOLOGY

John Watson, founder of behaviorism, evidenced keen interest in child psychology. His strongly environmental point of view led him to assume that learning played the major role in development. His famous statement about training any infant to become any kind of specialist (which we quoted in Chapter 3) reflects this point of view, or if you prefer, bias. Watson, of course, never carried out any such utopian program, but he did publish a kind of pioneer guide for parents on the care and handling of children (Watson, 1928), and his most eminent successor in behaviorism, B. F. Skinner (1948a, 1948b, 1953, 1971), has been writing for many years of experimentally designed societies in which children would be reared according to principles of behavioral conditioning. This, however, is getting ahead of the story.

In an attempt to demonstrate the validity of his position, Watson carried out a study on the development of the emotions in infants that has become a classic despite a fatal weakness in its design. We shall summarize both the original study and the criticisms of it.

Watson defined an emotion as a *"hereditary 'pattern-reaction' involving profound changes of the bodily mechanism as a whole, but particularly of the visceral and glandular systems"* (1919, p. 195). By "pattern-reaction" he refers to the various response components that appear with some degree of regularity each time the appropriate stimulus situation arises. He believes that there are three such fundamental patterns in the human infant: *fear, rage*, and *love*. The appropriate stimulus situation for the evocation of fear is either a sudden loss of support or a loud sound. For rage, the stimulus is hampering the infant's movements; and for love, stroking or manipulating one of the erogenous zones.

The hereditary reaction-pattern characteristic of fear consists of a sudden catching of the breath, closing of the eyes, puckering of the lips, and random clutching movements of the hands and arms. For rage, the responses are stiffening of the body, screaming, and slashing or striking out with the arms and legs. For love, the responses consist of smiling, cooing, and extending the arms as if to embrace the experimenter.

Again, Watson faced the problem of demonstrating how the vast panorama of human emotions develops from these basic three reaction-patterns. Once more the answer is through conditioning and habit. Environmental conditioning, first of all, brings about a partial inhibition of the more obvious external emotional responses. Thus, the violent responses of the infant become the implicit glandular and smooth muscular reactions of the adult. The second effect of environmental conditioning is the attachment of the basic hereditary responses to a variety of stimuli not originally capable of eliciting them. Watson, himself, proceeded to show how this was possible by conditioning an 11-month-old boy to fear a rat. Watson's description of his famous experiment follows:

(1) White rat suddenly taken from the basket and presented to Albert. He began to reach for rat with left hand. Just as his hand touched the animal the bar was struck immediately behind his head. The infant jumped violently and fell forward, burying his face in the mattress. He did not cry, however.

(2) Just as his right hand touched the rat the bar was again struck. Again the infant jumped violently, fell forward, and began to whimper.

In order not to disturb the child too seriously no further tests were given for one week.

Eleven months, ten days old. (1) Rat presented suddenly without sound. There was steady fixation but no tendency at first to reach for it. The rat was then placed nearer, whereupon tentative reaching movements began with the right hand. When the rat nosed the infant's left hand the hand was immediately withdrawn. He started to reach for the head of the animal with the forefinger of his left hand but withdrew it suddenly before contact. It is thus seen that the two joint stimulations given last week were not without effect. He was tested with his blocks immediately afterwards to see if they shared in the process of conditioning. He began immediately to pick them up, dropping them and pounding them, etc. In the remainder of the tests the blocks were given frequently to quiet him and to test his general emotional state. They were always removed from sight when the process of conditioning was underway.

(2) Combined stimulation with rat and sound. Started, then fell over immediately to right side. No crying.

(3) Combined stimulation. Fell to right side and rested on hands with head turned from rat. No crying.

(4) Combined stimulation. Same reaction.

(5) Rat suddenly presented alone. Puckered face, whimpered, and withdrew body sharply to left.

(6) Combined stimulation. Fell over immediately to right side and began to whimper.

(7) Combined stimulation. Started violently and cried, but did not fall over.

(8) Rat alone. The instant the rat was shown the baby began to cry. Almost instantly he turned sharply to the left, fell over, raised himself on all fours and began to

crawl away so rapidly that he was caught with difficulty before he reached the edge of the table. (J. B. Watson, 1919)

Watson went on to demonstrate that Albert, though originally conditioned to fear a rat, generalized his fear to a variety of furry animals and also showed fear of a fur coat and Santa Claus whiskers. Watson suggests that many adult aversions, phobias, fears, and anxieties for which the individual has no rational explanation may well have arisen years before by a process of conditioning.

Finally, the native or fundamental emotions and their substitute derivatives become combined and consolidated into more and more complex emotions through learning. Love, by such an evolutionary process, gives rise to tenderness, sympathy, lovesickness, and related emotions; fear to embarrassment, anguish, anxiety, and similar derivatives; and rage to hate, jealousy, anger, and similar emotions.

Watson's insistence on a behaviorist approach to the emotions, along with his interest in the physiological changes that accompany emotional behavior, was highly influential in stimulating a great deal of research on emotional development in children and on the specific reaction-patterns in specific emotions. However, subsequent experiments failed to substantiate the specific responses postulated by Watson. When the experimenter is unaware of the stimulating situation, infantile reactions do not necessarily conform to those announced by Watson. If observers are aware of the stimuli applied to the infant, their agreement as to the emotional nature of the infant's reaction is much better (Sherman, 1927a, 1927b). Apparently, adults tend to read their own feelings into the child's behavior. Consequently, if an adult *observes* the infant being dropped, he or she assumes that the child's reaction is fear.

In addition to the likelihood that Watson fell victim to this error, his observations were limited to a relatively small number of infants. Bridges (1932), who observed a large number of infants and young children over a wide age range, believes that infants show only general excitement, which, with increasing age, differentiates into the basic emotions of distress and delight. The latter, in turn, undergo differentiation into more and more complex emotions.

Similarly, a number of studies of the physiological changes accompanying emotional behavior have failed to verify the hypothesis that a specific pattern of changes is correlated with specific emotions. The one clear-cut exception is the startle pattern studied extensively by Landis and Hunt (1939). Unexpected stimuli result in a rapid "hunching" of the body. The head is thrown forward; the eyes blink; the mouth widens. However, in the case of other emotions, the degree of activation of the various organ systems appears to be the only reliable index of differentiation.

GESTALT PSYCHOLOGY AND THE DEVELOPMENTAL POINT OF VIEW

The fundamental law of Gestalt psychology, that the phenomenal whole or molar behavior must be the unit of analysis, is consistent with the developmental point of view. No psychologist would seriously argue that to reduce a child or any other organism to a collection of unrelated behaviors, stages of development, or processes would be psychologically meaningful. Each child is a unique whole. And yet, if one is interested in studying mental or behavioral processes, one can, of course, ignore the concrete individual in favor of the abstract process. It will be recalled that although the Gestalt psychologists were interested in processes, they nevertheless attempted to make their units of observation holistic and to avoid reductionism.

Only one of the original founders of the Gestalt school, Kurt Koffka, attempted to relate Gestalt theory to child development. In a book entitled, *The Growth of the Mind* subtitled, *An introduction to child-psychology* (1928), Koffka discusses such familiar topics as infant behavior, the role of maturation and learning in development, and various aspects of sensorimotor and cognitive development. However, in no way does the volume provide a truly developmental psychology. Rather, it is an attempt to take an already structured general theory and to graft it onto the existing literature of child psychology—a literature that was still in its infancy. For these reasons Koffka's work failed to make an enduring contribution to the field of child development.

Köhler and Wertheimer, although they employed children as research subjects in some of the classic Gestalt experiments, also failed to formulate Gestalt-oriented theories of child development.

It would be a mistake, however, to assume that the Gestalt school was lacking in influence on theoretical and research programs in developmental or child psychology. The most notable of the attempts to extend the Gestalt point of view into child psychology was that carried out by Kurt Lewin (1890–1947). Although it must be admitted that Lewin's field theory was primarily a general theory of behavior, and Lewin himself was best known as a social psychologist, he did write a chapter in Carmichael's *Manual of Child Psychology* (1946) in which he attempted to show that the principles of field theory can be applied to child behavior. We shall be considering field theory at length in Chapter 12, which deals with motivation, since this theory is largely concerned with dynamic psychology. However, we shall now summarize several principles from Lewin's 1946 account in order to give the flavor of his theoretical approach to child psychology.

First, he emphasizes that the individual child must be studied in relation to the existing environment. Behavior, therefore, is a function of the total situation, or in abstract terms, $B = F(P, E)$ where B represents behavior, F a function, P the person or child, and E the environment. This formula may be said to represent the child's *life space*. Lewin's insistence on psychology as the study of the interaction of the individual with the psychological field is clearly opposed to systems that tend to overemphasize environmental influences, such as Watson's, or on the other hand, to overemphasize inner determinants, such as Freud's. Since it also assumes that there are discoverable laws that apply to the individual case, it is an idiographic system.

According to Lewin, the most important psychological process that occurs during development is increasing differentiation of various dimensions of the life space. For the newborn the life space is relatively undifferentiated:

No definite objects or persons seem to be distinguished. No area called ''my own body'' exists. Future events or expectations do not exist; the child is ruled by the situation immediately at hand. (1946, p. 796)

The differentiation of those cognitive structures that make up the life space may be described along numerous dimensions, including those involving the body: feeding and elimination, time, and reality-irreality. The dimensions of time and reality-irreality are significant throughout the entire life of the individual.

As Figure 7-4a shows, the infant's cognition of time is the relatively simple division of past, present, and future. However, early in development, the cognition of events differentiates into the level of reality *(R)* and irreality *(I)* for past, present, and future. As Figure 7-4b shows, the mature individual exhibits not only more complex past, present, and future cognitions as suggested by the breaking up of the ellipses into more divisions, he or she also can deal with the more distant future and past. Moreover, there are individual differences in the fluidity or rigidity of the cognitive structures, with older individuals showing increasing rigidity. Development may stop temporarily or even move in the opposite direction, in which case the child's behavior retrogresses to patterns more appropriate to an earlier age.

Lewin also emphasized another Gestalt principle with which we are already familiar from perception, that of equilibrium. As applied to the child, the life space at any given moment in time may be compared to a *field of forces* seeking equilibrium. The hungry child, for example, is in a state of disequilibrium. Eating cookies will return the child to a state of equilibrium. He or she will therefore engage in

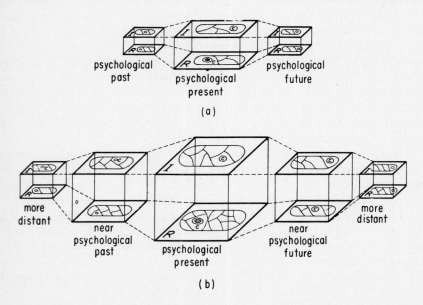

FIGURE 7-4.   Diagrams representing the life space of the individual at two different levels of maturity. (From Lewin, K. Behavior and development as a function of the total situation. In Carmichael, L. (ed.) Manual of child psychology. John Wiley & Sons. Copyright © 1946.)

locomotion, Lewin's term for movement within the life space that tends toward a goal and the restoration of equilibrium. In this case locomotion is toward the cookie jar. If the child's locomotion is blocked by parental threats of punishment, he or she may become frustrated and engage in a variety of behaviors in an attempt to overcome the feelings attendant upon frustration.

Utilizing the basic concepts of the life space, cognitive structures, differentiation, field forces, equilibria and disequilibria, Lewin (1946, pp. 806–840) elaborates his theory of motivation with specific reference to the literature of child psychology as it existed at that time. We shall be considering the dynamic aspects of his theory in Chapter 12 and need not follow it further here. We should like to point out, however, in concluding this brief summary of Lewin's major developmental concepts, that there are close parallels in his definition and use of the concept of differentiation and those employed by Heinz Werner (1948) in his organismic system of development, a Gestalt-related point of view, and in the psychology of Jean Piaget, which we shall be considering later in this chapter.

FREUD'S PSYCHOANALYTIC THEORY OF CHILD DEVELOPMENT[2]

Sigmund Freud's views on the psychosexual development of the child are at one and the same time the most controversial and influential of the twentieth century. The controversy which the theory generated resulted from Freud's assumptions that the infant and young child exhibit adult forms of sexuality—indeed, that the fundamental motive in the child's entire life processes is the elaboration of his or her personality in psychosexual development. The strong influence the theory exerted on the twentieth-century view of the child centered around the impetus that the theory lent to research and to focusing on childhood as the period during which adult patterns of adjustment are developed and fixated. These views were of particular significance in changing educational, pediatric, and psychiatric practices during the 1920s to 1940s, a period when Freud's influence was at its peak.

Freud utilized the concept of the *libido* to refer to the basic motivating instinct with which every child is born. At first the libido is diffuse, raw sexuality, but as the child grows older, the libidinal instinct broadens to include other types of sexual love, including romantic love, filial love, religious feeling, and patriotic and other complex sentiments.

From the point of view of Freudian psychoanalytic theory, the most important phase of development occurs during the early years, especially the infantile period, which Freud defined as lasting until 5 or 6 years of age. During the very early infantile period, the child, according to Freud, is "autoerotic." That is, the child derives erotic or sexual satisfaction from stimulation of his or her own body or from having the "erogenous" zones such as the lips, cheeks, nipples, or genital organs stimulated by the mother incidental to feeding and bathing. More specifically, the

---

[2]See Freud (1920, 1924, 1933, 1938a, 1938b) and Munroe (1955) for both primary and secondary sources.

early infantile period can be subdivided into three stages: (1) the *oral stage,* in which stimulation of the mouth gives rise to pleasurable sensations; (2) the *anal stage,* in which libidinal pleasure is obtained in connection with the activities of the lower bowel; and (3) the early *phallic stage,* in which manipulation of the sexual organs is the chief source of erotic pleasure.

Throughout these early stages, the child's libido is said to be undergoing localization in increasingly more pleasurable regions of the body. But at the same time, the libido seeks "object attachment," or attachment to a human being. Obviously, during the autoerotic stages, the object choice is the child's own body. Because the infantile libido is centered on the child during the autoerotic stage, Freud referred to the infant as narcissistic, after the legend of Narcissus of Greek mythology, who was in love with himself.

During the genital stage, however, the child becomes attached to the parent of the opposite sex. This early parental attachment Freud described as the *Oedipus complex* after the Greek tragedy *Oedipus Rex,* which tells of Oedipus' murder of his father and marriage to his own mother in fulfillment of the decree of the Fates. Eventually the child overcomes the Oedipus complex because of increasing fear of retaliation on the part of his or her "rival," that is, the parent of the same sex.

In overcoming incestuous impulses, the child uses three mechanisms: *repression, sublimation,* and *identification.* Repression is the forceful ejection from consciousness of forbidden impulses or of shameful, traumatic experiences. Sublimation involves the conversion of sexual impulses into socially acceptable forms of behavior. It is a kind of transformation of energy from one form to another in which the progression is from a baser to a more "sublime" type of motivation. Identification involves the child's putting himself or herself in the place of the parent of the same sex and thereby obtaining vicarious sexual satisfaction from that parent's sexual relations with the spouse.

When the child has successfully resolved the Oedipus complex, he or she enters upon the second major stage of motivational development, namely, the *latent period.* During this stage, which lasts from the end of the infantile period to the onset of puberty, the child is primarily engaged in the development of social feelings. Narcissism is diminished, autoeroticism declines further, and—as the term *latent* implies—sexuality as such is not evident.

After the onset of puberty, the genital organs become capable of sexual functioning and a revival of erogenous zone sensitivity occurs. A resurgence of narcissism and autoeroticism accompanies the development of the sexual organs. Autoeroticism takes the form of masturbation at this stage of development. There may also be a revival of interest in the Oedipal-object choice (the parent of opposite sex) at puberty; but in the normal course of events a heterosexual choice is made outside the family, and marriage follows.

During the course of psychosexual development, *fixations* may occur at any stage, with the result that the child's motivational system will fail to develop properly and personality growth will be seriously hampered. For example, if fixation occurs during the early oral stage because the mother has overindulged the child, the fixated child or adult will be excessively carefree, generous, overoptimistic, and will behave in general as if the world owed him or her a living. Presumably, the individual expects a continuous flow of pleasure from life—just as he or she experienced an overabundant flow of milk from the mother's breast. However, if the child is frustrated during the early oral stage, he or she will become pessimistic, demanding, and socially dependent on others. If fixation occurs at the anal stage, the child may develop into an excessively orderly adult, whose concern for detail, cleanliness, and possessiveness reflects parental overemphasis on bowel training and parental evidence of emotional revulsion or disgust at the sight of feces.

Freud believed that the normal frustrations that accompany weaning, bowel training, and the suppression of the Oedipus complex strengthen the child's character. This assumes that the training is not carried out in a harsh manner and that the child has an adequate supply of libidinal energy to maintain repressions as well as to meet the demands of reality. In an atmosphere of warmth and affection, the expanding personality of the child derives more and more pleasure from the stimulation afforded by dealing with reality and less from indulgence in primitive bodily satisfactions. Thus, in the normal adult, crude sexual curiosity has been sublimated into mature intellectual interests.

The characteristic broadening of interests that goes with the process of maturation indicates, in effect, that the libidinal energy is becoming attached to more and more objects. Moreover, with changing situations and varying age levels, the type of object attachment changes. The young adolescent in the first throes of love is at a stage of development when all libidinal energy is attached to one object. The mature individual with diverse intellectual interests shows a constellation of libido attachments that spread far beyond primary sexual satisfaction.

Although Freud's constructs were instrumental in launching more research in child psychology than that stimulated by any other theoretical system, the results have thus far yielded only partial or ambiguous support for psychoanalytic theory. This lack of clear-cut evidence in support of Freud's position is not an unexpected outcome in light of the complex and sometimes ill-defined nature of psychoanalytic concepts. Those kindly disposed toward psychoanalysis have attempted to formulate certain of Freud's concepts more precisely and to test them under controlled, experimental conditions, again with mixed results (Baldwin, 1967; S. White, 1970).

RECENT AND CONTEMPORARY THEORIES OF CHILD DEVELOPMENT

Erikson's Developmental Theory

The most influential variant of Freudian psychoanalysis is Erik Erikson's development theory of personality, which we shall summarize briefly to demonstrate how the classic psychoanalytic position has become more ego-oriented and has evolved to recognize the importance of social factors in development.

Erikson, a leading American psychoanalyst, has outlined his position in a number of technical papers and books, including *Young Man Luther* (1958), *Child-hood and Society* (1963), *Insight and Responsibility* (1964), and *Identity: Youth and Crisis* (1968). In *Childhood and Society,* from which this summary has been taken, Erikson presents his famous theory of psychosexual stages in development, in which he emphasizes the interaction between biological and social factors in personality development during childhood and adulthood.

Erikson's first four stages (see Figure 7-5) resemble Freud's early stages of sexual development. The first stage, the *oral-sensory,* begins the child's *encounter* between his or her instincts and the demands of society. During the oral stage the child is in his or her most helpless stage, entirely dependent on others (normally the mother) for nurturance and protection; and it is in this primary relationship with the mother that the child acquires a basic orientation of trust or, in an abnormal pattern of development, of mistrust. Basic trust or mistrust becomes an attitude that carries over into later stages of development and determines the direction that the

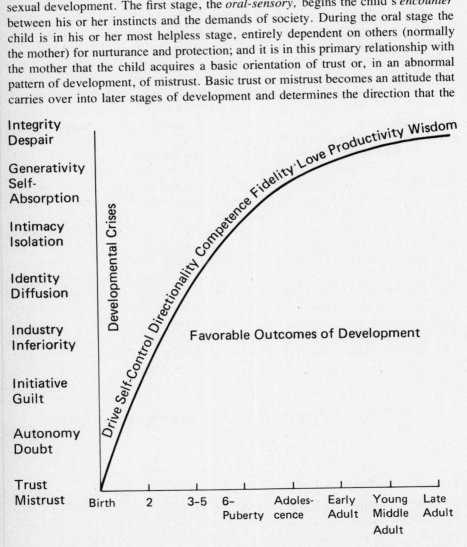

FIGURE 7-5.   Erikson's stages of psychosexual development. After Erikson, *Childhood and Society,* Second Edition, Revised, 1950.

ego takes toward others. The trusting child becomes the trustworthy and trusting adult. The mistrustful child develops into an adult who distrusts others because he or she failed to experience the deep, meaningful relationship of a mother's love.

In the second, or *anal* stage, the crisis the child must resolve is again biosocial. He or she must master muscular control of the eliminative organs and so gain a sense of autonomy or freedom of choice. Attitudes of shame and doubt are the consequence of failure to do so. He or she develops into an obsessive adult whose personality is characterized by strong drives to possess and control (Freud's anal character). Similarly, in the third *locomotor-genital* stage (Freud's phallic stage) the child must learn to cope with genital impulses—in other words, to channel urges into socially acceptable behavior. Erikson, following Freud, believes that the child at first becomes sexually assertive toward the parent of the opposite sex, whom he or she wishes to possess sexually. During the years from three to five the child must learn to turn these impulses into an acceptable form. In Erikson's words:

> In the boy, the emphasis remains on phallic-intrusive modes; in the girl it turns to modes of "catching" in more aggressive forms of snatching and "bitchy" possessiveness, or in the milder form of making oneself attractive and endearing.
> The danger of this stage is a sense of guilt over the goals contemplated and the acts initiated in one's exuberant enjoyment of new locomotor and mental power: acts of aggressive manipulation and coercion which go far beyond the executive capacity of organism and mind and therefore call for an energetic halt on one's contemplated initiative. (1950, pp. 224–225)

Erikson's fourth stage, the *latency period,* parallels Freud's latency stage, but emphasizes the importance of the child's moving away from the family constellation into society, as first represented by the school. Success means that the child acquires traits of industry and competence; failure is burdened with feelings of failure and inferiority.

During the fifth stage of *puberty* or *adolescence,* which merges into the sixth stage of *young adulthood,* the child must face an *identity crisis,* which, if resolved, provides a sense of who he or she is and what his or her goal in life is. The child must also resolve problems centering on developing sexuality and learning to control impulses in relation to others. Failure means role confusion and isolation and that the child cannot become a fully functioning adult with a clear sense of identity and the capability of experiencing meaningful relationships with members of the opposite sex.

Erikson's seventh stage is *adulthood,* a time of productive (generative) and socially meaningful parental and social working relationships with children and others. Failure at this stage leads to stagnation, or an inability to progress beyond the concerns of adolescence and young adulthood. In the final stage, *maturity,* the individual achieves a sense of ego integrity if he or she has successfully resolved all the preceding crises. If he or she has failed, the result is a sense of despair.

Throughout this brief summary of Erikson's developmental stage theory we have pointed out his emphasis on the interaction between the child and the world.

This contrasts with Freud's emphasis on internal conflicts. Erikson also goes beyond Freud in stressing development in later life and in focusing on the problems of identity and integrity in ego development. Although Erikson begins with basic instinctual conflicts, he goes beyond these to stress the achievement of competency and the resolution of existential crises during development and in this respect deviates significantly from Freud. In pursuing this course, Erikson follows Adler, Horney, Erich Fromm, White, and others who have transcended Freud's instinct theory to develop psychosocial theories of personality.

Behavioristic Programs[3]

Much of the early research on *S-R* or behavioristic theories of child development centered around the study of psychoanalytic concepts as translated into the language of learning theory, where they could be studied experimentally. More recently, emphasis has been on the use of social learning theory as a framework for research in child development. Since the earlier work was primarily concerned with the concept validation of psychoanalytic constructs and less with processes in child development, our sample of *S-R* theory will utilize the social learning model first offered by N. E. Miller and Dollard in *Social Learning and Imitation* (1941) and more recently elaborated and extended by Albert Bandura and his associates.

The early model of social learning developed by Miller and Dollard made use of four fundamental concepts: drive, cue, response, and reward. A drive is defined as any strong stimulus that arouses an organism to action. Drives may be either primary and unlearned, such as the physiological drives, or they may be secondary and learned, such as the need for affection. Secondary or learned drives are based on primary drives. The infant, for example, has a need for food—a primary drive. He or she is fed by the mother typically in an affectionate manner. The reduction of the hunger drive is rewarding to the infant, and because the mother's presence and behavior is associated with the reward of hunger reduction, it too becomes rewarding. Thus the mother is demanded for her presence and behavior such as cuddling even though the infant may not be hungry.

Cues are stimuli that guide the responses of the organism. In Pavlov's famous experiment with the bell and salivation in the dog, the bell or conditioned stimulus (CS) became the cue for salivation after a number of trials in which it was presented along with food. In the infant, the sight of the breast or bottle becomes a cue for the cessation of struggling and crying and the transition to sucking behavior.

Responses are behavior patterns that may be either innate or derived. The struggling, crying, and sucking of the infant that attends hunger is a hierarchy of innate responses that become associated with the cue—that is, the bottle or breast. But the crying of the infant as a demand for the mother when the infant is not hungry is an acquired response.

Reward, as the concept was defined by Miller and Dollard, is any agency that

---

[3]For more extensive treatments of the behavioristic point of view in developmental psychology, see S. White (1970) and Baldwin (1967).

reduces or partially reduces a need, such as food in the case of hunger or the mother's cuddling in the case of the need for affection.

Thus far, Miller and Dollard's analysis is reminiscent of Watson's pioneer experiment showing how an innate fear response can, through learning, be associated with various types of cues. But Miller and Dollard went beyond Watson's model to emphasize *matched-dependent behavior* as a source of much social learning in children.

Matched-dependent behavior is a form of imitative behavior in which one individual is aware of the cues in the environment leading to rewards while the other is not. Children, for example, are often dependent on parents for the recognition of reward-related cues and therefore match their behavior to that of the parents and so obtain rewards. Similarly, younger children may match their behavior to that of older children and obtain rewards. Miller and Dollard (1941) give the following illustration:

Two brothers are playing. The older child hears the father's footsteps, indicating that he has come home from work. The older child runs to meet the father, since he usually brings home candy. The younger child did not hear the footsteps, and he does not generally run because his brother runs. However, on this occasion, by chance, he does follow his brother and receives a reward. The reward increases his tendency to imitate his brother's running. In terms of the drive, cue, response, reward paradigm:

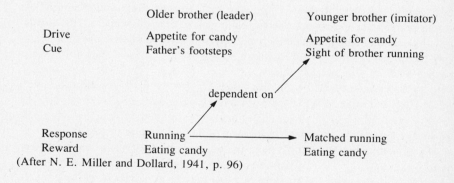

(After N. E. Miller and Dollard, 1941, p. 96)

In an experimental test of this paradigm using rats, a leader was trained to run a maze for food. One group of animals was trained to run in the same direction as the leader, while the other group was rewarded for running in the opposite direction. Only the leader, however, was aware of the cues leading to food. The group that was trained to run in the same direction as the leader learned to imitate the leader's running and when put into other situations continued to imitate the behavior of the leader. Members of the other group did not show imitative behavior.

By extension, Miller and Dollard are suggesting that much social behavior in children can be accounted for as the rewarding of specific imitative behavior whose effects generalize to other situations.

Bandura and his associates have carried out a long series of experiments on modeling behavior in which the work of Miller and Dollard was broadened and extended (Bandura, 1965a, 1965b, 1965c; Bandura & Mischel, 1965; Bandura, Ross, & Ross, 1961; Bandura & Walters, 1963). Of particular interest are their studies of aggression, since Freud has postulated that aggression is an instinctive component of human nature and so would appear without learning in children. Bandura and his associates believe that the behavioral learning model can account for this type of behavior without the necessity for assuming an instinct of aggression.

In an experiment typical of the series, young children watch a woman playing with a set of Tinker Toys and a large BoBo doll (an inflatable plastic doll of nearly adult dimensions that when knocked down returns to upright). After playing quietly with the Tinker Toys for a short time, the adult begins to act aggressively toward the doll, striking it, kicking it, sitting on it, and throwing it around. While engaged in these acts she shouts such phrases as "Sock him in the nose," "Boom, boom, boom," "Pow," and the like. This is the training phase of the experiment. Later the child is brought into the room with toys, alone, and allowed to play with them. Children who had observed the aggressive model behaved much more aggressively than those who did not. Tests showed that observing adult aggression on film by means of closed circuit television heightened aggression in test situations just as much as watching live models.

In another experiment (Bandura, 1965a) children watched a similar performance on film involving aggression toward a BoBo doll, but this time there were three experimental conditions: (1) ending the film with the adult model being given generous praise and candy by an observer who walked onto the scene; (2) ending the film with the adult being punished by being referred to by an observer as a bully and having the observer's finger shaken at him; (3) showing neither of the above conditions, for a no-consequence condition.

Immediately afterward the children spent time in the experimental room with the BoBo doll and other toys and were observed for aggressive behavior. Following this, some children received no additional incentive for attempting to remember the adult acts of aggression previously witnessed and some were given positive incentives for remembering the adult's acts in the form of fruit juice and attractive pictures.

Children exposed to the model-rewarded and to no-consequence conditions performed about the same in the play test and in the absence of any incentive. However, when the model was punished, imitative behavior diminished significantly. But when positive incentives were introduced for remembering the adult's aggressive actions, the differences were not significant, showing that there had been an equivalent amount of learning under conditions of model-punished, even though performance was diminished. The reinforcement administered to the model influenced the observer's performance but not the acquisition of matched responses. The results of this experiment further suggest that direct drive reduction (as in the Miller-Dollard design) is not a necessary condition for learning. Cognitive factors may be of equal importance in the acquisition of a response.

A number of other conditions have been investigated by Bandura and others, including the relative effectiveness of live versus televised models, peer versus adult models, high-versus low-status models, and the presence or absence of weapons in the aggressive situation. However, many additional questions remain, particularly with regard to the carry-over of laboratory induced aggression to the world outside and the permanency of such effects, when found. Again, ethical considerations stand in the way of direct investigations of such variables. However, as these limited samples show, the behavioral approach has been shown to provide a fruitful method for assessing aggressive behavior in children and for demonstrating the importance of learning in the acquisition of such behavior.

Jean Piaget and the Development of Understanding in the Child

Jean Piaget (b. 1896) is a "school" unto himself. For many years he has been associated with the University of Geneva, where he has carried out elaborate investigations on the development of the child's understanding of the physical and social environments. The results of this research and his challenging theoretical interpretations have appeared in over a dozen books since 1926. In addition, he has contributed a large number of articles to French technical journals. These publications range over such varied subjects as the development of language, judgment, intelligence, play, number concepts, and appreciation of reality in the child. In recent years Piaget has extended his work into the experimental areas of perception and thinking in order to search out the more fundamental processes that underlie his descriptive categories and modes of thinking.

Although Piaget stands aside from the traditional British-German-American schools of psychology, his work has made itself felt throughout the psychological world and has stimulated a considerable amount of research. Consequently, we have decided to include it here. We should also point out that both his results and theoretical interpretations are considered controversial.[4] We might also note that the best original introductions to Piaget's early work are his *The Child's Conception of the World* (1929), *The Child's Conception of Physical Causality* (1930), and *The Origins of Intelligence in Children* (1952, originally published in French, 1936). His more recent work is represented by his *Play, Dreams, and Imitation in Childhood* (1962) and by *The Psychology of the Child* (1969, with Barbel Inhelder). The present account has been drawn largely from these sources.

In his investigations of children's conceptions of the world, Piaget employed three general, but not entirely independent, methods. First, he followed the purely verbal procedure of asking the child questions about his or her relations to other people, to environmental objects, and to natural phenomena; in the same category were questions designed to test the child's understanding of physical causality. For example, the child might be asked, "Where does the wind come from?" "What makes you dream?" "Is the air outside alive?"

---

[4]We shall make no attempt to review the extensive literature bearing on the controversy. For references to the older literature, see Jersild (1954, chaps. 13, 14). See also G. G. Thompson (1952, pp. 234–238). For more recent surveys see Berlyne (1965) and Phillips (1969).

The second method was half verbal and half concrete. Concrete descriptions of natural phenomena were presented orally to the child, who was then asked questions designed to test his or her understanding of the phenomena in question.

The third method was primarily concrete. Piaget and his associates arranged miniature experiments designed to demonstrate fundamental physical relationships. For example, children were shown a toy engine run by steam generated by means of a small alcohol lamp. Water was placed in the boiler and the fire was lighted in the child's presence. When sufficient steam had been generated, a small piston caused a flywheel to rotate rapidly. The fire was then extinguished, and the flywheel gradually stopped. The child was then asked to explain the energy transformations involved.

Stages of Cognitive Development

In recent decades[5] Piaget has cast his theoretical explanations of children's thinking into a developmental form involving several age periods ranging from preconceptual stages to sophisticated, operational stages of thinking characteristic of adolescents and adults. In the first stage, which lasts from birth to age 2, there are no concepts or true representative processes. This stage Piaget calls the *sensorimotor stage*. The child is learning the bare rudiments of space and time in reference to his or her own bodily reactions in the environment, which, at this stage, consist largely of inborn reflexes. The sensorimotor stage is succeeded by the *period of preconceptual thought,* which lasts until approximately age 4.

During the period of preconceptual thought the child cannot generalize meanings; nor can he or she think inductively or deductively. Thinking is transducive or simply specific from one experience to another. The child may, for example, have a protoconcept of *cat* from experiences with the family cat but not a true generalized idea of "catness" such as that possessed by a high school student. For this reason many young children mistake similar animals (skunks, porcupines, and the like) for cats—sometimes to the children's considerable embarrassment and dismay.

From 4 to 7 the child enters a period of *intuitive thought* in which he or she can reason, but only on a limited basis. At this stage of development the child is still dominated by perceptions and so comes to erroneous conclusions if given abstract problems. For example, if the child watches the experimenter pour water from one glass into a taller and thinner glass, he or she is likely upon being questioned to say that there is now more water in the second glass than there was in the first because the level is higher or that there is less because the second glass is narrower (Figure 7-6).

From 7 to 11 years of age, the child enters the stage of *formal operations,* during which he or she is acquiring a set of operational concepts which are organized into systems of thought. The process, if developed more formally, starts about age 12 and becomes the kind of thinking that is characteristic of the adult.

---

[5]For a summary of Piaget's earlier work on the child's concepts of reality and physical causality, see the second edition of this book (Chaplin & Krawiec, 1968).

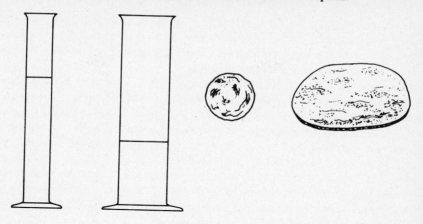

FIGURE 7-6.   The conservation problem. The volume in the two cylinders is the same. The mass of the two shapes of modeling clay is identical.

The Matrix of Development

Piaget's theory of stages is built around certain general principles that he believes are characteristic of the development of all children. These are *organization, equilibration,* and *adaptation.* Organization refers to the interrelationships among the elements of mental life, which he calls *schemata.* The latter are essentially mediating processes, and as development proceeds they provide a structure into which incoming sensory data can fit. Therefore, schemata become organized patterns of thought and action. They structure the child's world and make possible an orderly intake of new information—a process Piaget refers to as *assimilation.*

Cognitive organizations made up of schemata tend toward states of equilibrium, or equilibration; in other words, they become sharper, better delineated, and capable of forming higher-order cognitive organizations that allow for better adaptation. Therefore, in Piaget's view, the child is not a passive sponge who assimilates new information willy-nilly but an active, selective recipient of stimulation from the world around him or her.

Moreover, in cases in which existing organizations of cognitive schemata are incapable of assimilating new information the process of *accommodation* takes over. This means that a new organization of schemata will be formed. Even though there is a tendency for the child to seek equilibration, he or she does not do so at the expense of excluding information that will help him or her adapt better to the changing world.

By adopting a sequential maturational theory of the development of thinking in the child, Piaget clearly puts himself on the side of nativism. The reader will also have noted the resemblance between Piaget's accounts of hierarchies of cognitive organizations and those formulated by the Gestalt school discussed earlier in this chapter.

It must be emphasized that not all psychologists are in agreement with Piaget's analysis of the child's conception of physical causality. Attempts to repeat his early studies with American children have been inconclusive. Some investigators have found similar concepts of the physical world and of physical causation in the children studied; others have failed to confirm Piaget's findings. Some have even found evidence of animistic thinking in adults.

It has been suggested that cultural and educational differences between European and American children may, in part, account for the differences.[6] However, studies of children from Western nations have generally supported Piaget's contention that fixed and stable sequences of development occur during the sensorimotor, preconceptual, intuitive, and formal operations stages. Whatever the final outcome of research on the development of understanding in the child, Piaget's studies are unexcelled for the richness and spontaneity of children's verbalizations of their own experiences and attempts to understand the world around them. And because of his profound influence on the literature of developmental psychology, Piaget is considered a giant among contemporary psychologists.

Kohlberg's Studies of Moral Development in Children

Basing his work on Piaget's recent theory of cognitive stages and an earlier study entitled, *The Moral Judgment of the Child* (Piaget, 1932), Lawrence Kohlberg (1967, 1969) has carried out a series of studies to determine whether there are universal stages of moral development in children. His technique involves presenting short stories to children where the characters involved are faced with a moral dilemma, in which conforming behavior would be followed by punishment and deviant acts by reward.

One such story involved a husband whose wife was dying and who could only be helped by a medicine discovered and sold by a druggist in the same town. However, even though the medicine was inexpensive to make, the druggist charged $2000 for a small amount—a sum which the husband could not afford. Desperately, the husband borrowed half the money, offering it to the druggist with a promise to pay the remainder later. The druggist refused, and the husband broke into the store and stole the drug. The child is then asked whether the husband should have behaved as he did and whether his behavior was right or wrong.

The children's responses were evaluated not in terms of whether they considered the behavior in the stories right or wrong, but in terms of the reasons given for the decision rendered as to whether the behavior was right or wrong. Kohlberg believes that he has evidence for three levels of moral values, which are revealed in six stages of development—two stages within each level.

The first level is called the *premoral level,* in which the child is guided in his or her judgment by immediate hedonism; that is, whether the act will result in the avoidance of punishment and the obtaining of rewards. In stage 1 of the first level, rules are obeyed to avoid punishment; in stage 2, conformity to rules is seen as the way to rewards. The premoral level is characteristic of children under 7 years of age.

---

[6]Berlyne (1965), Phillips (1969).

Level II is the *morality of convention,* the "good boy" or "good girl" morality (stage 1) that avoids disapproval and wins approval, or (stage 2) the morality of authority. Children from 7 years of age on tend to evaluate moral acts in terms of this level of morality—which, it might be noted, is still closely allied with considerations of reward and punishment but on a more long-range basis than in level I.

Level III is the morality of *individual principles,* with two stages: first, the morality of the social contract or of individual rights as democratically established in law; and second, the morality of individual principles of conscience as illustrated by the behavior of Henry Thoreau in defying what he considered to be amoral tax laws. In the case of stage 1, conformity to moral principles is seen as desirable for the common welfare. In stage 2, conformity is to self-accepted principles in order to avoid self-condemnation, even in the face of almost certain social disapproval. This later stage of moral development, Kohlberg finds, is rare, exhibited by less than 10 percent of his subjects.

Not all psychologists are in agreement with Kohlberg, particularly insofar as his moral stages are presumed to evolve from parallel stages of cognitive development. The psychoanalytic school, as we have seen, emphasizes the process of identification with the parents as important models in moral development. Social anthropologists have emphasized cultural relativity in moral behavior, pointing out that what is ethical or moral in one society need not necessarily be in another. Finally, a distinction must be made between "pencil and paper morality" as revealed on tests and behavior in real life. Studies going back to the classic work of Hartshorne and May (1928), who employed real-life situational tests in their investigations of deceit in children, showed that there are often wide discrepancies in what children say they will do and what they actually do when confronted with specific real-life situations.

However, even though Kohlberg's results are controversial, they do raise interesting questions for the education of children in our time, when as adults they may be faced with the kind of moral dilemma that Lt. Calley or the draft resisters made the great moral issue of our time.

THE STUDY OF AGING[7]

One of the most dramatic changes in developmental psychology in recent years has been the sharp increase in interest in the psychology of late adulthood. Early developmental psychology was concerned almost exclusively with young children and adolescents. Experimental psychologists centered their attention on young adults. This narrowed perspective resulted partly from the fact that both these

---

[7]A voluminous literature has recently come into existence on aging. The best single overview of papers on the developmental, clinical, experimental, and social aspect of aging is the volume by Eisdorfer and Lawton (1973), commissioned by the American Psychological Association in recognition of the growing interest in the field. A shorter collection of important studies is contained in Chown (1972). For a review of recent perspectives on death, dying, and bereavement, see Schultz (1978).

classes of individuals are easily accessible through college, university, and school populations. In part, interest in the young was related to the fact that psychologists recognized that learning and maturation, the basic processes in development, progressed most rapidly in the early years. Finally, psychologists' attitudes toward the aging process reflected, in part, the attitudes of Western society—namely, one of neglect and disinterest. Now with the increasingly large proportion of older people in our society, psychologists, sociologists, and medical practitioners have focused their attention on the later years, even on that traditionally taboo subject, death and dying.

Early studies of the developmental process during the later years emphasized quantitative differences in learning, sensory, sexual, and intellectual functions with increasing age. Most of these investigations were predicated on the assumption that the decline of psychological capacities parallels the general senescence of the individual as a whole. In some cases the assumption was confirmed; in others it was not.

As an example of one of the classic studies in the field, Wechsler (1958), developer of the widely used Wechsler intelligence scales, investigated the decline of intellectual ability with age. Variations on the total score and various scores of the scale's subtests were studied from ages 16–74, utilizing the Wechsler Adult Intelligence Scale (WAIS).

As Figure 7-7 shows, the decline in total score begins around age 30 and is progressive up to age 74. However, as Figure 7-8 reveals, the total curve is misleading, since the rate of decline varies with each subtest. From these studies Wechsler developed the concept of "hold" and "don't hold" tests. Among the hold tests on the WAIS are vocabulary, information, object assembly, and picture completion. Among the don't hold tests are digit span, similarities, digit symbol, and

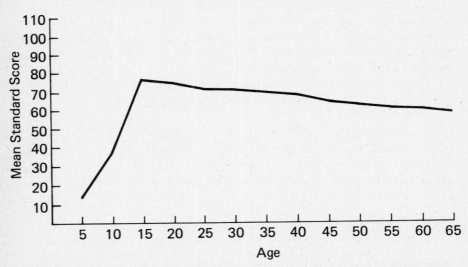

FIGURE 7-7. The decline in total score on the Wechsler Adult Intelligence scale as a function of age. After Wechsler, Mental health in later maturity. Supplement No. 168 to Public Health Report, U.S. Public Health Service. Washington, U.S. Government Printing Office, 1942.

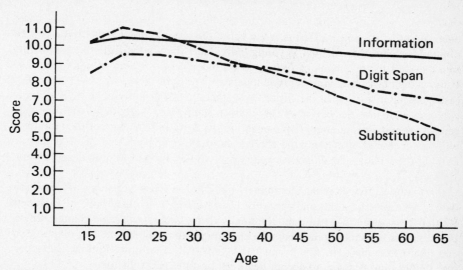

FIGURE 7-8. Three sub-tests of the Wechsler Scale plotted against age. Note that Information (a hold test) does not decline rapidly with age while Substitution and Digit Span (don't hold tests) decline rapidly. After Wechsler, Mental health in later maturity. Supplement No. 168 to Public Health Report, U.S. Public Health Service. Washington, U.S. Government Printing Office, 1942.

block design. He concluded that the scores on tests revealing minimal deterioration with age can be employed by clinicians to assess the level of the individual's original ability. Deterioration can then be measured in terms of difference scores between the hold and don't hold subtests.

In general, quantitative studies of older individuals showed some loss of capacity in learning, memory, intelligence, sensorimotor capacity, and sexual behavior. However, the degree of loss is often found to be far less than expected on the basis of preconceived notions about older people. Aside from a slowing down that mainly affects speed tests, older people who are physically healthy do not show sharp declines in learning, retention, and performance on other cognitive tasks. In fact, on some tests, such as vocabulary and comprehension, older individuals may continue to improve well into the sixties (Chown, 1972). Similarly, Kinsey and others found in surveying sexual behavior, that older people typically continue to have sexual relations, although the frequency of intercourse may be diminished.

Early studies of creativity emphasized that the creative process was largely a function of youth, pointing out that great inventors, scientists, and artists showed their genius early in life. However, as Dennis (1966) has shown, creative thinking and productivity persist into the later years as revealed by many outstanding examples, such as Will and Ariel Durant, Pablo Casals, Pablo Picasso, Bertrand Russell, and Thomas Edison.

More recent studies of aging have tended to stress the social and personality aspects of aging rather than variations in ability functions. Among the areas of investigation that have been emphasized are retirement, self-concept, family life, and attitudes toward death and dying. The general picture that is emerging from these studies is one reemphasizing the old principle that individual differences exceed group differences. That is, great variations among individuals exist along the dimensions investigated. Just as young individuals show great differences in ability to cope with the problems of living, so do older people, some of whom succeed better at their tasks than younger individuals do. For some there is evidence of gradual disengagement starting in the fifties. For others vigorous activity and engagement continue well into the seventies, or eighties with many individuals building successful second careers after retirement from the first. Whether or not the individual will be successful in meeting the challenges of aging appears to depend largely on attitudes and habits developed during youth and adulthood (Cuming and Henry, 1961).

Finally, a considerable literature is building on the psychology of death and dying. Stimulated by the pioneer work *On Death and Dying* (1969) of Elizabeth Kübler-Ross, attitudes toward the terminally ill are undergoing rapid change. Physicians, nurses, and family members are encouraged to recognize the fact that patients are aware that they are dying and need help in overcoming attitudes of anger, resentment, and despair, to accept death as the final phase of life.

These marked shifts of emphasis in developmental psychology have not yet consolidated into an integrated theory of the developmental process. The nearest thing to a complete theory is Erikson's. However, its emphasis on psychoanalytic concepts and personality variables means that many traditional areas of interest are neglected by him. While a vigorously growing area from the point of view of empirical studies of the aging process, developmental psychology is weak in theoretical and systematic points of view.

SUMMARY AND EVALUATION

There are two main threads running through theories and allied research programs in child development. One is the familiar issue of native versus empirical factors in behavior, cast in this instance into the maturation-versus-learning dichotomy. In general, the research of the twentieth century has supported the position that all behavior is a joint function of both processes, with some basic locomotor skills relatively independent of learning. However, it is also clear that even those behaviors that are primarily maturated must be given an opportunity for practice at the critical stage of development when they normally appear; otherwise, permanent retardation may result.

The second theme running through the literature on development is that of stages. Most of the early research on the cognitive and sensorimotor capacities of the child utilized the concept of normative stages in development with, of course, individual differences in the actual time of appearance of the behavior in question. A similar point of view has permeated the work of the psychoanalytic school, both the classical Freudian and the contemporary theory of Erikson, as well as Piaget's long series of studies of the development of understanding in the child.

Learning I: The Classical Heritage

8

In introducing the topic of sensation (Chapter 5), we pointed out that the study of the sensory processes dominated psychology during its formative years. We also emphasized the close relationship that existed between sensationism and associationism. Philosophical empiricism treated sensations as the elementary processes out of which ideas are formed, and ideas in turn coalesce into more and more complex ideas because of the attractive power of associations. But we also indicated that introspective sensory psychology suffered a decline with the collapse of structuralism.

Associationism, on the other hand, continued its progressive evolution into modern learning theory. Through the work of Hermann Ebbinghaus (1850–1909) in the late 1880s on human verbal learning, philosophical associationism became experimental associationism; and experimental associationism, in turn, evolved into the field of contemporary verbal learning around the turn of the century. Largely as a result of the pioneer efforts of Edward L. Thorndike (1874–1949) and Ivan P. Pavlov (1849–1936), experimental comparative psychology became established as one of the fundamental fields within the science. Because early comparative psychologists favored the study of learning, they contributed heavily to both theory and methodology within the field. In the decades that followed, the field of learning enjoyed a steady growth until it became one of the largest areas of psychology in terms of productive research and theory construction.

Because learning came to occupy such a central position in modern psychology, three chapters will be devoted to tracing its evolution from its origin in classical philosophy to its modern status in psychology. In this chapter we shall first consider in some detail the pioneer experimental programs of Ebbinghaus, Thorndike, and Pavlov. We shall then trace the development of learning theory as it underwent further evolution within the schools of psychology. In Chapter 9 we shall deal with the learning theories that were stimulated by the earlier schools and developed into "miniature" systems, and in Chapter 10 we shall examine theories in human verbal learning—a field that has absorbed the experimental and theoretical interests of an enormous number of psychologists in the United States.

We have already discussed the associationistic point of view in Chapters 2 and 3, and it will be recalled that associationism was a well-established system in British empirical philosophy by the middle of the eighteenth century.[1] Philosophers such as Locke, Berkeley, Hume, and Hartley had undertaken the Herculean task of reducing the complexities of mind to the sensory-association continuum. In doing so, they set the stage for the evolution of modern learning theory and for an experimental attack on the higher mental processes.

Although no one would deny the importance of these contributions, the chief weaknesses of associationism as a psychology were threefold. First, the highly general nature of its claims broadened the doctrine to the point of superficiality. To reduce ideas, memories, space perception, and thinking to associations greatly oversimplifies the complexity of the mental processes. Second, little or nothing was offered by way of explaining the processes of acquisition and forgetting, both topics of great importance in modern learning theory. Third, such variables as the influence of motivation, individual differences, and methods of learning on the formation of associations were not systematically explored by the philosophers— largely because the investigation of such problems demands the use of experimental techniques that had not yet been developed.

In summary, the associationists set the stage for the experimental attack on the higher mental processes. What remained was for someone to turn speculative philosophical empiricism into scientific experimentalism. A German psychologist, Hermann Ebbinghaus, undertook the pioneer labor of forging the necessary techniques.

EBBINGHAUS AND THE EXPERIMENTAL STUDY OF MEMORY

While engaged in a program of independent study, Ebbinghaus became interested in the quantitative investigation of the mental processes as a result of reading a copy of Fechner's *Elements of Psychophysics.* The experience marked a turning point in Ebbinghaus' career. He was deeply impressed by Fechner's careful experimental analysis of the sensory processes and became convinced that the same techniques could be adapted to the study of the higher mental processes. During an extended period (1879–1885), Ebbinghaus devoted himself to this self-appointed task, and in 1885 he published the results of his experiments in a little volume entitled, *Über das Gedächtnis,*[2] a book that was destined to become a landmark in the literature of experimental psychology.

Ebbinghaus launched his research program by devising a revolutionary kind of material, the nonsense syllable, for use in learning sessions by combining consonants (C) and vowels (V) into CVC triads in such a way as to avoid meaningful words. For example, *vol, rux, noz,* and *lut* are readily pronounceable syllables that

---

[1]See Boring (1950), Brett (1953), Murphy (1949), Woodworth (1948), for more complete accounts of associationism.

[2]An English translation is available under the title *Memory* (Ebbinghaus, 1913).

have little resemblance to real words. By utilizing such material, Ebbinghaus could "start from scratch" and thereby avoid the ever-present danger involved in using meaningful material, namely, the possibility of inadvertently selecting passages once studied but not "forgotten." As his own results subsequently demonstrated, material once learned may be relearned with less effort and fewer errors, even though it has been forgotten in the conventional sense.

It should be noted that psychologists' sustained interest in the utilization of nonsense syllables for the study of learning is based on the assumption that the principles of learning as revealed by lower levels of verbal learning will also be valid for higher levels. This assumption, which underlies almost a century of work by those who followed in Ebbinghaus' tradition, may be incorrect. Much the same difficulty occurs when *any* elementary process is taken as a model for more complex processes.

Essentially, what is being assumed is that the differences are quantitative rather than qualitative. But maze learning, conditioning, and the learning of nonsense syllables may be different qualitatively as well as quantitatively from their more complex counterparts in human and animal learning. The problem of the possible differences in the processes employed in different learning tasks is a difficult one, which we shall meet again and again. The student should be aware of the possible limitations that it places on generalizations made from the simple to the complex.

Ebbinghaus designed a research program to test the influence of various conditions on both learning and retention. In these experiments he served as both experimenter and subject. His work, carried out without the stimulation from a university environment, was a model of precision and, when published, of clarity in exposition. We shall consider his findings under two main headings: first, his studies of factors influencing learning; second, his investigations of conditions influencing retention.

Before presenting Ebbinghaus' results, it will be worthwhile to formulate a distinction between learning and retention, since we will be dealing with both processes in this and the following chapters. Retention is being measured when an interval has elapsed following the learning trials. The interval may be long or short, but it is traditionally assumed to be longer in duration than any of the intertrial intervals. Moreover, retention is assumed to be a consequence of prior learning and comparisons are typically made between subjects who have been exposed to learning trials and those who have not. Obviously, in order to measure learning, the psychologist must measure retention, since it is the test of learning. Consequently, the distinction between the two is often blunted, and the question of what is being measured is one of emphasis. Is the emphasis on the conditions under which the response is acquired? Or is the emphasis on the conditions favoring its retention once it has been acquired? While Ebbinghaus was most interested in the retention process, he necessarily studied it through varying the conditions of original learning.

Ebbinghaus found that increasing the length of his lists greatly influenced the number of repetitions necessary for an errorless reproduction and, of course, increased the time required to learn a given list. Analyzing his data further, he also

TABLE 8-1.   Learning Time and Length of List[a]

Number of Syllables in List	Number of Readings Required	Time for Total List (seconds)	Average Time per Syllable (seconds)
7	1	3	0.4
12	17	82	6.8
16	30	196	12.0
24	44	422	17.6
36	55	792	22.0

[a]After Ebbinghaus, H., *Memory: A Contribution to Experimental Psychology.* New York: Teachers College Press, Columbia University. Copyright 1913.

found that the *average time per syllable* was markedly increased by lengthening the list. His results are summarized in Table 8-1.

Although most high school students could have predicted the outcome of Ebbinghaus' experiment *in a general way,* its significance lies in his careful control of conditions, his *quantitative* analysis of his data, and the not so readily predictable finding that *both* the total time for learning *and* the time per syllable increase with longer lists. Indeed, the magnitude of the difference in time for memorizing longer lists is surprisingly large. An examination of Table 8-1 will show that adding only five syllables to a list of seven items increases the total time for learning 27-fold and the average time per syllable 17-fold. This finding—that proportionately more time is required per unit of material in longer lists—has been confirmed by subsequent investigators, although the relationship between the variables depends on the nature of the material and the degree of learning (Woodworth, 1938). The greater number of repetitions and increased total time required for learning longer lists is explicable on the basis of intrasyllable inhibitory effects. That is, the longer the list, the greater the likelihood of both forward and backward interference effects between associations.

Ebbinghaus also investigated the relationship between the degree of original learning and subsequent retention. Since his criterion for mastery was one errorless repetition,[3] he repeated the lists from memory a number of times beyond bare mastery in order to test the effect of overlearning. His measure of overlearning was the saving in time to achieve once again a perfect repetition of the original list following a 24-hour retention period. This technique is now known as the *savings method,* or *method of relearning.* Table 8-2 reproduces Ebbinghaus' results with various lengths of lists.

Many repetitions and variations on Ebbinghaus' experiment have since been carried out by psychologists, and the results are in general agreement. Overlearning, up to a point, results in a saving of both time and errors upon relearning. In fact, the

---

[3]Contemporary psychologists who work in the field of learning generally require two or three perfect consecutive repetitions.

TABLE 8-2.   Savings in Repetitions and Percent of Requirement for Original Learning after a 24-Hour Interval for Three Lengths of Lists[a]

Number of Syllables in Series	Number of Repetitions for Original Learning	Saving in Repetitions in Relearning after 24 Hours	Savings in Percent of Requirement for Original Learning
12	16.5	5.5	33.3
24	44	21.5	48.9
36	55	32	58.2

[a]After Ebbinghaus, H., *Memory: A Contribution to Experimental Psychology.* New York: Teachers College Press, Columbia University. Copyright 1913.

savings method is so sensitive an index of retention that some saving in subsequent learning may appear years after the material has been "forgotten" in the ordinary sense (Burtt, 1941).

Ebbinghaus proceeded to investigate a number of additional variables that influence the curves of learning and retention, such as the effects of near and remote associations within lists, the review or repeated learning, and the passage of time. We shall make no attempt to summarize all of his results. The interested reader may consult the original work or Woodworth's excellent summary (1938), which also includes the subsequent studies bearing on these same questions.

It would be a grave omission not to mention Ebbinghaus' famous curve of retention, which has been used to illustrate the general process of forgetting in every major textbook of experimental and general psychology published within the last three-quarters of a century. The curve is presented in Figure 8-1 as drawn from Ebbinghaus' original data (1913, p. 76). Its equation is

$$r = \frac{100K}{(\log t)^c + K}$$

where r is the percent retained, t is the time elapsed, and K and c are constants.

Ebbinghaus' curve of retention is interesting not only because it shows the general nature of forgetting—the initial rapid dropoff followed by decreasing increments of loss with the further passage of time—but also because it is one of the major pioneer attempts in psychology to reduce experimental data to mathematical form.[4] Ebbinghaus' logarithmic relationship is known as an *empirical* equation because it was based on an actual set of experimental data to which an equation was fitted by the method of least squares. In effect, this means that the parameters (constants or variables determining the shape of a curve) employed by Ebbinghaus

---

[4]The Ebbinghaus curve may represent a spuriously rapid loss because of his extensive work with nonsense syllables leading to the buildup of considerable proactive inhibition. See Chapter 10 for a further analysis of the problem of retention in highly practiced subjects.

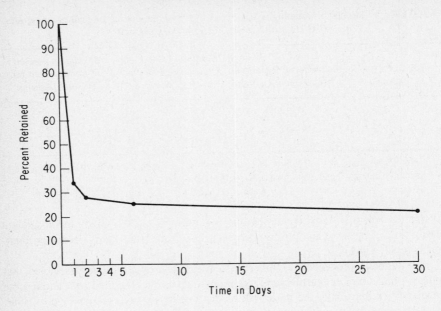

FIGURE 8-1.   Ebbinghaus' curve of retention for nonsense syllables. (Plotted from Ebbinghaus, H. Memory: A contribution to experimental psychology. Teachers College Press, Columbia University. Copyright 1913.)

have no rational significance. They are, as the modern phrase puts it, "purely empirical."

By way of contrast, there have been a number of attempts to formulate *rational* equations for learning curves—equations that are not merely descriptive of the data obtained but are based on a study of the fundamental nature of learning and retention and attempt to provide a rational basis for the type of parameters selected. We shall have more to say about such equations in the next chapter, but we are introducing the concept here partly to clarify the nature of Ebbinghaus' equation and partly to reveal its limitations. Clearly, it is a dubious procedure to make predictions beyond the limits of an empirical curve since there is no assurance that additional samples will yield similar results. With rational curves, on the other hand, deductions and hypotheses can be made by extrapolations beyond the observed limits of the data. Hypotheses formulated on the basis of such extrapolations can and should be subjected to subsequent verification by experimental tests.

In a sense, Ebbinghaus' failure to formulate a rational basis for his results reveals his limitations as a theorist, for the essence of theory *is* to go beyond observed data by hypothesis and deduction. But Ebbinghaus was not a theoretician on the order of Fechner. His great strength lay in his careful sense of controlled experimentation and (within the limits of the times) experimental design. In the last analysis we can only reiterate what has often been said before, that those who provide the instruments and methods of research contribute just as significantly as those who provide theories and systems.

THORNDIKE AND THE EXPERIMENTAL STUDY OF LEARNING

In turning from Ebbinghaus to Thorndike we are making a transition from European psychology to a system developed within the United States and, at the same time, are turning from experiments on human verbal learning to studies of animal learning. Moreover, the contrast between the work of these two men is heightened by the fact that, whereas Ebbinghaus is known for his model experiments, Thorndike's fame in the field of learning is primarily the result of his theoretical explanations of his research findings.

Indeed, it may be said that Thorndike offered the psychological world the first miniature system of learning—a system that proved to have a profound influence on the development of learning theory for the next half-century. In fact, Thorndike's theory may be considered a *contemporary* theory of learning, and is so treated by Hilgard in the several editions of his *Theories of Learning* (1948, 1956, 1966). From the point of view of the present account, Thorndike's theory is *transitional*—characterized, on the one hand, by its associationistic foundations and, on the other hand, by its behavioristic approach to experimentation. For this reason we have chosen to include it in this, rather than in the following, chapter.

Thorndike's theory of learning grew directly out of the results of his own experiments with chicks, cats, fishes, dogs, and monkeys. Of these, the most famous and influential are those in which the subjects were cats and chicks. It was on the basis of the experiments with cats that Thorndike described *trial-and-error learning* as a fundamental type of learning, while the chick experiments, as we shall see, had profound significance in assessing the validity of his laws of trial-and-error learning.

Let us first consider the experiments with cats. Thorndike employed a variety of puzzle boxes, which required different kinds of manipulations on the part of the animal for a successful solution. The simplest box required only that the cat pull a loop in order to open the door, whereupon the animal could escape from the box and obtain a reward of fish. One of the more complex boxes is illustrated in Figure 8-2. In this case three separate acts were required to open the door. Both bolts had to be raised, one by depressing the hinged platform, the other by clawing the exposed string; and either of the bars outside the door had to be turned to the vertical position. The door then opened automatically as a result of the pull exerted by a weight attached to a string fastened to the outside of the door.

The following description of the animals' behavior in the puzzle box is quoted from Thorndike's *Animal Intelligence* (1911). It is a general summary of his results with twelve cats ranging from 3 to 19 months of age.

When put into the box the cat would show evident signs of discomfort and of an impulse to escape from confinement. It tries to squeeze through any opening; it claws and bites at the bars or wire; it thrusts its paws out through any opening and claws at everything it reaches; it continues its efforts when it strikes anything loose and shaky; it may claw at things within the box. It does not pay very much attention to the food outside, but seems simply to strive instinctively to escape from confinement. The vigor with which it

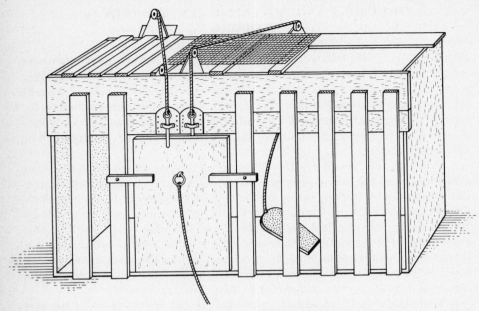

FIGURE 8-2.   One of Thorndike's puzzle boxes. (Redrawn from Thorndike, E. L., Animal intelligence. The Macmillan Company. Copyright 1911.)

struggles is extraordinary. For eight or ten minutes it will claw and bite and squeeze incessantly. The cat that is clawing all over the box in her impulsive struggle will probably claw the string or loop or button so as to open the door. And gradually all the other non-successful impulses will be stamped out and the particular impulse leading to the successful act will be stamped in by the resulting pleasure, until, after many trials, the cat will, when put in the box, immediately claw the button or loop in a definite way. (1911, pp. 35–40)

Thorndike's description of the cats' behavior epitomizes what has since been known as trial-and-error learning. Reduced to the fundamental stimulus-response patterns involved, trial-and-error learning means that the animal must learn to associate one or more responses with a certain stimulus pattern. It is important to note that the animal does not learn a new response. Rather, an appropriate response must be *selected* out of the animal's repertoire of responses, and the cat must learn to associate this response with a certain stimulus pattern. The gradualness with which the appropriate response is selected convinced Thorndike that the animal does not reason out the solution, but proceeds in a blind or random manner. Finally, his assumption that "unsuccessful responses will be stamped out" and "the successful act will be stamped in by the resulting pleasure" is an informal statement of his highly influential Law of Effect, which we shall consider as a formal law after a brief description of his experiments with chicks.

     Figure 8-3 is a reproduction of the floor plan of several of the "pens" Thorndike employed in studying the course of learning in chicks. These were

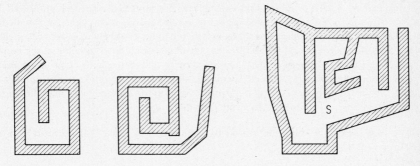

FIGURE 8-3.   Three mazes used by Thorndike in his studies of trial and error learning in chicks. (Redrawn from Thorndike, E. L., Animal intelligence. The Macmillan Company. Copyright 1911.)

constructed of books set on end. In contemporary terms they were simple mazes, which in a more elaborate form have been widely used in learning experiments with rats. In studying the chick's behavior, Thorndike placed the bird somewhere in the center of the maze (say, at S), and the problem was to find the exit that led to food and other chicks. In general, Thorndike found that the chicks' behavior was of the same trial-and-error variety as that exhibited by cats in puzzle boxes. The main differences, according to Thorndike, were that (1) the chicks were "very much slower in forming associations" and (2) they were less able to solve difficult problems.

Finally, Thorndike's interest in comparative psychology led him to test dogs and monkeys on a variety of problems. In general, an animal's performance correlated closely with its phylogenetic level. That is, the monkeys solved problem boxes with relative ease and rapidity and at the same time showed more planning in their attack on the escape mechanism. Dogs were more comparable to cats in their behavior; yet their learning curves were somewhat smoother than those for the cats, indicating that the dogs were less variable in their problem-solving ability. However, it is important to note that the higher animals' greater speed and superior performance in no way led Thorndike to modify his view that animals in general do not solve problems by a process of reasoning. In Thorndike's own words, "There is also in the case of the monkeys, as in that of the other animals, positive evidence of the absence of any general function of reasoning" (1911, p. 186).

Thorndike's findings with the various species that he tested were sufficiently consistent to formulate into two fundamental laws of learning—perhaps the most widely known and influential laws ever formulated in this area of psychology. These were the "Law of Effect" and "Law of Exercise."

The statement of the laws follows that given in *Animal Intelligence:*

The Law of Effect is that: Of several responses made to the same situation, those which are accompanied or closely followed by satisfaction to the animal will, other things being equal, be more firmly connected with the situation, so that, when it recurs, they will be more likely to recur; those which are accompanied or closely followed by discomfort to the animal will, other things being equal, have their connections with that situation weakened, so that, when it recurs, they will be less likely to occur. The greater the satisfaction or discomfort, the greater the strengthening or weakening of the bond.

The Law of Exercise is that: Any response to a situation will, other things being equal, be more strongly connected with the situation in proportion to the number of times it has been connected with that situation and to the average vigor and duration of the connections. (Thorndike, 1911, pp. 244–245)

Thorndike explains what he means by "satisfaction" and "discomfort" in the following sentences:

By a satisfying state of affairs is meant one which the animal does nothing to avoid, often doing such things as attain and preserve it. By a discomforting or annoying state of affairs is meant one which the animal commonly avoids and abandons. (1911, p. 245)

In *Animal Intelligence* Thorndike added a principle which in a subsequent publication[5] was to become the "Law of Readiness." In the account we are following, he gave it only the status of a "provisional hypothesis." As originally formulated, the hypothesis held that neuronal synapses are capable of modification through exercise. This, he believed, might be brought about by chemical, electrical, or even protoplasmic changes that could be the consequences of exercise. The Law of Readiness was subsequently formulated in terminology closely paralleling that of the Law of Effect. As given in Thorndike's *Educational Psychology,* the law states: "For a conduction unit ready to conduct to do so is satisfying and for it not to do so is annoying" (1913a, p. 128). Thorndike also added, "For a conduction unit unready to conduct to be forced to do so would be annoying" (1913a, p. 127).

Although Thorndike spoke about neurons in his early formulations of the Law of Readiness, the law makes little sense if taken literally. Indeed, it is actually contradictory to speak, on the one hand, of "forced" conduction as detrimental to the establishment of bonds and, on the other hand, of neuronal connections being established through exercise—since conduction, whether forced or "voluntary," would be a form of exercise and should therefore strengthen connections. Moreover, there is no physiological basis for the neurological hedonism implied by the law. Broadly speaking, Thorndike's Law of Readiness makes sense only if interpreted to mean that a preparatory set on the part of the organism as a whole is an important condition influencing learning. If the animal is set for a given kind of behavior, then engaging in that behavior pattern is rewarding or reinforcing. Conversely, when an animal (or a person) is forced to do what he or she does not want to do, the experience is annoying. The foregoing modification of the principle of readiness is the one generally utilized by psychologists who consider readiness an important condition of learning.

In addition to his three primary laws of exercise, effect, and readiness, Thorndike advocated various subsidiary laws and principles over the years (1913a,

---

[5]*Educational Psychology* (1913a, 1913b).

1913b, 1931; Thorndike & Lorge, 1935), several of which are sufficiently important to warrant our attention. These are the principles of (1) *multiple response,* (2) *set or disposition,* (3) *selective responses,* (4) *response by analogy,* and (5) *associative shifting.* Each of these will be discussed briefly.

The principle of *multiple response* states that when one response fails to produce a satisfying state of affairs, it will trigger a new response. For this reason the animal continues to respond until some response finally results in satisfaction. Thus, the cat in the puzzle box described earlier unleashes its repertoire of responses until one releases the latch. The adaptive significance of the animal's ability to vary responses is obvious. The animal that gave up after the first failure would die of starvation, if not released by the experimenter. In some cases, as Thorndike points out, fatigue or extraneous factors may intervene to distract the animal from its attempts to escape. As a rule, however, the animal's own varying behavior pattern brings about release.

The principle of *set or disposition* is Thorndike's equivalent of the concept of motivation or drive in contemporary learning systems. The hungry cat will struggle to get out of the box; the satiated animal is likely to go to sleep. Consequently, set, or disposition to engage in activity, is fundamental for the initiation of responses and, indirectly, for learning.

The law of *selective responses* holds that as learning proceeds, the animal responds selectively to certain elements in the problem situation while ignoring others. The cats in the problem boxes, for example, concentrated on the general area of the door, the latch, or the pulley, as the case might be, even in the first few trials. The relevance of such selectivity of response and discrimination is obvious. An animal that is incapable of discrimination will never learn an escape route.

Response by analogy is a transfer principle. The cat that has experienced one problem box will, when placed in a different box, utilize whatever responses are appropriate—provided that the new situation contains some elements that are identical with elements in the previous situation. In formulating the principle of analogy, and in his more general treatment of transfer of training, Thorndike devised an "identical elements" theory. This is to say that transfer will occur if, and only if, there are elements in common between the two learning situations involved. More generally, his theory of learning was permeated with "connectionism," the doctrine that the functional bonds between stimulus and response or between associations are mediated by neural links, which can be either inherited or formed by learning. The concept of connectionism, which is basic to transfer, spread into his writings on intelligence, educational applications of learning theory, and social psychology.

Associative shifting is the Thorndikian equivalent of conditioning. In essence, the principle states that responses learned to one set of stimulus conditions may be learned to a new set of stimuli, provided the overall situation is kept relatively intact during the substitutive learning. By way of illustration, the reader may call to mind any of the many tricks animals can be taught to perform. If, for example, a child wishes to teach a dog how to sit up at command, he or she proceeds by holding a biscuit out of the dog's reach (or forces the animal into a sitting position) and at the same time verbally orders the dog to sit up. After a number of trials the animal sits up on command, even when the child does not offer food. Associative shifting is a form of conditioning that is no different in principle from Pavlov's bell-salivation experiment.

The five subsidiary principles just discussed—plus the three fundamental laws of exercise, effect, and readiness—constitute Thorndike's fundamental systematic views on learning. Most of the laws and principles were elaborated on the basis of his early animal experiments, but with slight modifications they are theoretically applicable to human learning situations. In fact, Thorndike himself generalized his laws to the human level; and his growing interest in educational psychology eventually led him into research in the field of human learning. However, as Thorndike continued with his experimental program, his own findings made it clear that the laws of exercise and effect required modification. In fact, the Law of Exercise as originally stated had to be abandoned, and the Law of Effect turned out to have a much narrower range of generality than Thorndike originally believed.

The Law of Exercise was disproved by Thorndike in experiments in which exercise was made the independent variable while other factors were held constant. For example, he had college students draw a 3-inch line while blindfolded. Some subjects were allowed more than a thousand trials, and the measure of learning was the increase in accuracy from the beginning to the end of the session. On the average there was no improvement from the first to the final trial. Practice without knowledge of results failed to produce improvement.

The line-drawing test employed by Thorndike would be exactly parallel to requiring soldiers to shoot at targets without informing them of their scores. No improvement could be expected. For the human subject, knowledge of results acts as a correctional and reinforcing agent, or, in terms of Thorndike's system, provides an opportunity for the operation of the Law of Effect. Despite these negative findings on the value of practice itself, Thorndike did not take the absurd position that learning could occur in its absence. Rather, he held that exercise or practice provides an opportunity for other factors to operate. In short, it is *rewarded practice*—not practice alone—that strengthens bonds.

The Law of Effect came under fire as a result of experiments designed to test the relative efficacy of reward and punishment in strengthening and weakening connections. It will be recalled that the law is a two-part law, wherein a connection is strengthened if it leads to satisfaction or weakened if it leads to annoyance. In his often-cited experiment with chicks, which we described earlier, Thorndike employed a simple maze where the correct pathway led to "freedom, food, and company," while incorrect choices led to confinement for a period of 30 seconds. In terms of the Law of Effect, the responses that led to a large enclosure where there was food and "company" (in the form of other chicks) should have been stamped in, while incorrect responses should have been stamped out—since they led to a state of solitary confinement as well as to the annoyance of prolonged hunger.

By keeping track of the tendency of the chicks to repeat preceding correct choices if rewarded and to avoid preceding choices if punished, Thorndike was able to test both aspects of his Law of Effect. The outcome of this experiment and a number of other experiments along similar lines with both animal and human subjects was clear. Reward strengthens connections, but punishment fails to weaken connections. As a result of these negative findings with respect to punishment, Thorndike had to abandon the second half of the law insofar as any direct effects of punishment are concerned. He did continue to hold that punishment retains some *indirect* value in the sense that it may cause a "shift to right behavior" for which there is a reward. Or, in the case of undesirable behavior, punishment can act as a barrier to the attainment of a reward, thus indirectly weakening a connection. But even in the case of such indirect effects, the influence of punishment is in no way comparable to that of reward.

Meanwhile, Thorndike formulated a new principle, *belongingness,* and discovered a phenomenon (the spread of effect) that he believed to be a crucial and independent test of his modified Law of Effect. We shall consider each of these more recent aspects of Thorndike's position in turn.

Belongingness is a principle that was formulated on the basis of verbal learning experiments with human subjects. In a typical experiment bearing on belongingness he read the following sentences to his student subjects ten times:

> Alfred Dukes and his sister worked sadly. Edward Davis and his brother argued rarely. Francis Bragg and his cousin played hard. Barney Croft and his father watched earnestly. Lincoln Blake and his uncle listened gladly. Jackson Craig and his son struggle often. Charlotte Dean and her friend studied easily. Mary Borah and her companion complained dully. Norman Foster and his mother bought much. Alice Hanson and her teacher came yesterday. (Thorndike, 1932, p. 66)

Immediately after the last reading the subjects were asked the following questions:

> 1. What word came next after rarely?
> 2. What word came next after Lincoln?
> 3. What word came next after gladly?
> 4. What word came next after dully?
> 5. What word came next after Mary?
> 6. What word came next after earnestly?
> 7. What word came next after Norman Foster and his mother?
> 8. What word came next after and his son struggle often? (Thorndike, 1932, p. 66)

If contiguous repetition was the only principle governing the formation of bonds, then all sequences of words should have been remembered equally well. However, this was not the case. Even though *Edward* follows *sadly* just as frequently as *Davis* follows *Edward,* the "belongingness" of *Davis* to *Edward* outweighs the mere contiguity of the *Edward-sadly* connection. In summary, the average percentage of correct associations from the end of one sentence to the beginning of the next was 2.75, while 21.5 percent correct responses were obtained, on the average, for the first and second word combinations in the same sentences. Obviously, we are more accustomed to associating words within sentences than between sentences, and, in addition, there is the functional belongingness of subjects and their verbs. In summary, Thorndike is arguing that rewards and punishments, to be maximally effective, must be relevant to the situation to which they apply.

The spread-of-effect principle states that reward strengthens not only the connection to which it belongs but also the connections that precede and follow the rewarded response. So strong is the spread of effect that even *punished* responses three to four steps removed from the rewarded connection are made with greater than the expected frequency (Thorndike, 1931). There is, however, a gradient involved, so that the effect on any given response becomes weaker the further that response is from the rewarded connection.

The gradient effect was demonstrated in experiments where a number of possible responses could be given to certain stimuli. For example, Thorndike presented stimulus words to which the subject responded by saying any number between one and ten. The experimenter arbitrarily "rewarded" responses to certain stimuli regardless of the response given and, in the same series, "punished" other responses. The reward was simply hearing the experimenter say "Right," and the punishment, "Wrong." A typical series might be diagrammed as follows: W W W W R W W W. In general, findings from such experiments show that the effect of the reward is strongest on the rewarded connection but may spread or scatter to connections several steps removed from the rewarded connection.

By discovering the spread of effect, Thorndike believed he had come upon independent evidence for the Law of Effect (Thorndike, 1933) and at the same time had strengthened his position that rewards operate mechanically—a position consistent with his fundamentally behavioristic trial-and-error conception of learning. However, Thorndike's interpretation of his results has been questioned by other investigators. Furthermore, a long-standing controversy has developed over the reality of the phenomenon itself (some investigators have failed to find it in attempts to duplicate Thorndike's original experiment) and over its interpretation in those cases where such effects have been duplicated. We cannot undertake to review this extensive literature here. The interested reader is referred to Hilgard and Bower (1966), McGeoch and Irion (1952), and Postman (1947) for a variety of experimental tests and interpretations of the spread-of-effect phenomenon.

Whatever the ultimate status of Thorndike's basic laws and principles, there is general agreement among psychologists that his theory of learning heralded the rise of modern learning theory to its position of preeminence in modern psychology. The greatest strength of the theory lies in the fact that the various tenets were stated with sufficient specificity to render them subject to experimental investigation. But in a sense this same specificity proved to be the greatest weakness. Thorndike's emphasis on bonds or connections, his elementalism in accounting for transfer, the mechanical operation of the Law of Effect, and his rote-drill conception of human learning have—in the opinion of many psychologists—greatly oversimplified the nature of the learning process. This, of course, does not mean that psychologists disapprove of exactitude in the exposition of theoretical and systematic positions. Rather, it means that subsequent experimentation failed to confirm Thorndike's expectations.

Although this may be disappointing to the theorist, it is of enormous value to the science as a whole in the sense that research has been stimulated and alternative hypotheses and interpretations have been offered to account for experimental findings. In this respect Thorndike's pioneer efforts rank among the greatest in the history of psychology. As will be demonstrated more fully later, his theoretical interpretation of learning has profoundly influenced two generations of psychologists.

PAVLOV AND THE CONDITIONED REFLEX

Ivan P. Pavlov, the distinguished Russian physiologist, ranks with Ebbinghaus and Thorndike as one of the great pioneers in the early study of learning. He was awarded the Nobel prize in medicine in 1904 for his experimental investigations on the physiology of digestion, particularly the reflex secretions of the salivary, gastric, and intestinal glands. During the course of this work he had observed—as had many children who owned pet dogs—that an animal will sometimes salivate *in anticipation* of receiving food, such as when it is approached by its owner or a laboratory assistant with a feed pan. Pavlov called these "psychic secretions," reflecting the fact that they had been learned in the course of the animal's experience and were to be distinguished from unlearned secretions made in response to food taken into the digestive organs.

Pavlov became intrigued with these learned responses and began their systematic investigation utilizing the process of conditioning. This research, begun when he was 50 years of age and continued into his eighties, became world-famous and has exerted a profound and continuing influence on American as well as Russian psychology.

Because he found psychic secretions to be variable from dog to dog and readily influenced by external stimuli, Pavlov and his associates developed a rigidly controlled experimental procedure for their investigation (see Figure 8-4). The animal was lightly suspended in a harness facing the experimenter, who made his observations from an adjacent room by means of a periscope. Food was presented automatically through a pneumatic tube. Saliva was collected by means of a cannula or small tube attached to the outside of the animal's jaw. The cannula was connected to a tube that conveyed the saliva to an apparatus for measuring the number of drops secreted as well as the total amount in cubic centimeters. The experiments were conducted in a windowless, soundproof room in order to minimize the effect of extraneous stimuli on the subject.

Following a period of pretraining designed to accustom the animal to the apparatus, conditioning was initiated by introducing an arbitrary stimulus, such as a buzzer, called the *conditioned stimulus,* or CS. As the stimulus was presented, the dog was given a puff of meat powder or a squirt of weak acid, called the *unconditioned stimulus,* or US. The latter, of course, initiated an *unconditioned response,* or UR, namely, salivation. And after a number of pairings of CS and US, the CS elicited a *conditioned response,* or CR, which was salivation to the buzzer alone. Pavlov referred to the US as the *reinforcement,* since its effect was to strengthen the CR. Indeed, in its absence CR would not occur at all.

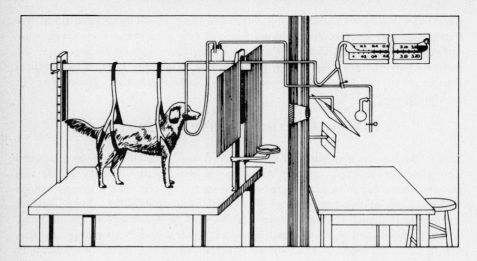

FIGURE 8-4.   Pavlov's experimental arrangement for conditioning dogs. (Redrawn from Lectures on Conditioned Reflexes by Ivan P. Pavlov (1928). © International Publishers Inc. 1967.)

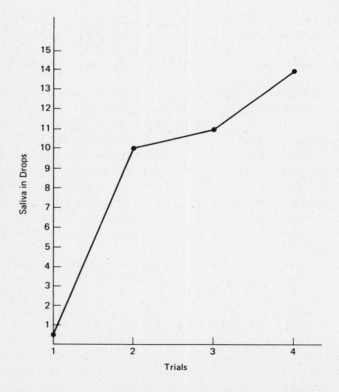

FIGURE 8-5.   The acquisition of a conditioned response. (After Pavlov, 1927.)

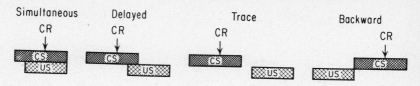

FIGURE 8-6. Temporal relationships in conditioning. For explanation see text. (Reprinted from Elements of Psychology by David Krech and Richard S. Crutchfield, by permission of the publisher, Alfred A. Knopf, Inc., Copyright 1958 by David Krech and Richard S. Crutchfield.)

Pavlov's experimental findings can be conveniently summarized under five basic laws, each of which will be formally stated and illustrated.

The Law of Acquisition

A conditioned response is established by a series of contiguous pairings of CS and US (Figure 8-5). Contiguity as here defined means simultaneity or near simultaneity of the presentation of CS and the reinforcing US. In practice there are several possibilities, as shown in Figure 8-6. In simultaneous conditioning, CS and US are presented at the same time and continue together until CR occurs. In the delayed conditioned response, CS is presented anywhere from a few seconds up to a minute before US and may continue with it for a few seconds. In trace conditioning, CS is presented first, then after a brief delay US follows; and in backward conditioning, US is given before CS. Pavlov and his associates found that simultaneous, trace, and delayed procedures were effective in conditioning (provided the interval between CS and US was not too great in trace conditioning) but were unable to establish backward conditioned responses. For this reason the CS in Pavlovian conditioning is spoken of as a signal heralding the onset of the US. Naturally in backward conditioning, CS, occurring after US, cannot assume such a role and is therefore ineffective.

The Law of Experimental Extinction

If CS is repeated without reinforcement, CR gradually weakens and disappears (Figure 8-7). That the disappearance of CR is not a permanent abolition of the habit but, rather, its inactivation is revealed in *spontaneous recovery,* which is the reappearance of CR after an interval of rest following experimental extinction. As Figure 8-8 shows, the recovery is typically not complete but shows a *gradient,* or dropoff in magnitude. Moreover, the spontaneously recovered response can be quickly extinguished with a few unreinforced trials. We shall examine the theoretical nature of extinction more fully after first considering several additional basic laws.

The Law of Generalization

CR once established may be elicited by stimuli similar to the original CS. A CR established to a tone may also be elicited by a soft buzzer. Or if a tone with a

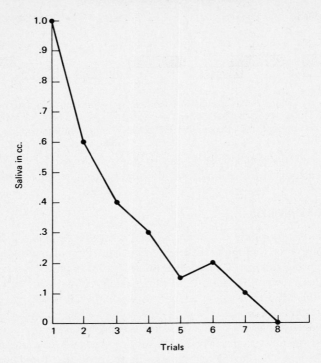

FIGURE 8-7.   Experimental extinction. (After Pavlov, 1927.)

frequency of 256 Hz is employed in establishing CR, a tone of 356 Hz will probably also elicit CR. As was true of spontaneous recovery, a generalized CR shows a gradient with a greater magnitude of response to stimuli of a higher degree of similarity and an increasingly weaker response to stimuli of decreasing magnitude.

The Law of Differentiation

Differentiation can be established by differential reinforcement. If a CR has been established to a tone of 256 Hz and has shown generalization to a tone of 356 Hz, and the 256-Hz tone is reinforced while the 356-Hz tone is never reinforced, CR to the 356-Hz tone will undergo extinction. Basically, the situation is this: the 256-Hz tone may be thought of as CS$^+$ which is always followed by the UCS, while the 356-Hz tone is CS$^-$ never followed by the UCS. With this procedure of presenting one stimulus that is consistently reinforced with another that is nonreinforced, we have discrimination learning. This important discovery gave Pavlov a powerful tool for investigating sensory discrimination in animals and for the investigation of "experimental neuroses" brought about by presenting the animal with discrimination problems beyond its ability.

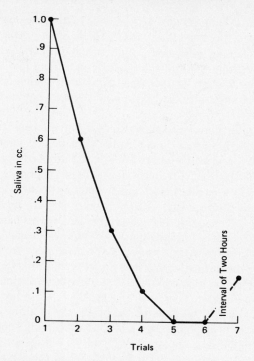

FIGURE 8-8.   Spontaneous recovery. (After Pavlov, 1927.)

The Law of Higher Order Conditioning

A CS after having acquired the ability to elicit a CR may acquire reinforcing properties. By way of illustration, let us assume that CS is a buzzer which has been used to elicit salivation with US being, of course, the food. After CR or salivation to the buzzer is well established, CS_1 (the buzzer) may now be paired with a flashing light (CS_2). After a few trials CS_2 will elicit salivation to the light alone (CR_2). In the technical language of conditioning, a higher-order conditioned response has been established.

Higher-order conditioned responses are difficult to establish in animals and are unstable, since the process of establishing them necessitates a kind of series of extinction trials for CS_1. Because of difficulty in developing and maintaining higher-order conditioned responses, the Pavlovian model is essentially limited to the establishment of original CRs and therefore has serious problems accounting for the acquisition of complex skills—problems not experienced by operant models, as we shall find in the following chapter.

In presenting his empirical findings, Pavlov attempted to establish a theoretical basis in the nervous system for the basic laws of conditioning. Acquisition was explained as the establishment of a new functional connection or association between two centers in the brain. In the experiment involving the dog salivating to the sound of a buzzer, the CS at first elicits activity in the auditory cortex and the US in the motor center governing salivation. Upon successful conditioning, the CS is capable of directly exciting the salivatory center, indicating that a new functional pathway has been established in the brain. Obviously, some kind of potential anatomical connection must preexist between two centers before they can become functionally related.

Pavlov did not offer a precise explanation of how these new functional connections were established. He wrote of some kind of attraction of impulses taking place between the unconditioned neural centers and the conditioned centers. Other early conditioning theorists spoke of "drainage of impulses" occurring from one center to another analogous to what takes place in a hydraulic system where water flowing under high pressure will bleed off, or drain, water flowing under low pressure, assuming an appropriate connection between the two. Devices based on this principle are sold in retail outlets for draining basements by means of water flowing through a garden hose with a suction line placed in the flooded area. As we shall see in Chapter 14, the problem of what occurs in the central nervous system during learning is a difficult one, which continues to occupy the attention of physiological psychologists and neurologists.

Experimental extinction was interpreted by Pavlov in terms of the concept of inhibition. The process of inhibition is a new kind of learning superimposed on the original response. Inhibition is the ability to hold the old response in abeyance or temporarily to suppress it altogether. The fact that spontaneous recovery occurs and that reconditioning after extinction is more rapid than original conditioning, is positive evidence that extinction is a temporary suppression by inhibition rather than the abolition of the original response. Again the precise anatomical and physiological nature of inhibition was not delineated by Pavlov. He believed that in some way inhibitory impulses arose as "signals" in the cerebral cortex in response to lack of reinforcement.

Generalization he explained by *irradiation,* or the spread of excitation over the cortex from a center of high activity to areas of lower activity. Selective conditioning would therefore indicate that inhibition of such irradiation had taken place.

In experiments on generalization and selective conditioning in which the animal is confronted with an impossible discrimination, a breakdown in the ability to discriminate occurs and symptoms of *experimental neuroses* are likely to appear. For example, the animal confronted with a discrimination between a circle and an ellipse where the major and minor axes of the ellipse are made closer and closer in magnitude will eventually be unable to make the discrimination. The previously quiet and well-adapted dog begins to whine, barks at the apparatus, attempts to bite the harness and to escape from the situation. Moreover, the animal's "breakdown" becomes general. The dog salivates to any arbitrary stimulus and can no longer make previously easy discriminations. Pavlov described such a condition as the "inhibitory brake" giving way. The animal must be removed from the laboratory and allowed a "rest cure" if it is to be employed in further conditioning experiments. The analogy between experimental neuroses in animals and the psychoneurotic breakdown and readjustment in human beings brought about by confrontations with impossible or difficult problems of adjustment seems clear.

Pavlov also believed that in the concept of inhibition he had a theoretical explanation of sleep. Sleep is the spread, or irradiation, of inhibition over the cortex, inducing a trancelike or anesthetic state. This explanation was originally offered to account for the discovery that animals kept in the experimental harness during long waits in the conditioning procedure slumped in the traces, became drowsy, and eventually went to sleep. A lack of stimulation renders the cortex inactive. A free animal, on the other hand, will generate its own activity by exploration and will remain alert.

Pavlov's important empirical work on the laws of conditioning is a landmark contribution to psychology. Less important are his theoretical explanations of the laws in terms of the reciprocal processes of "irradiation" and "inhibition." These terms do not describe known anatomical or physiological processes in the nervous system but remain on the level of what has been called the *conceptual nervous system*—that is, a system of constructs that explains by translating the facts of behavior into the language of neuroanatomy and physiology. As we shall see in studying other systems of learning, this process has been employed—often with questionable results—by learning theorists as well as by those in other areas of psychology. Pavlov's conceptualizations fail to explain observed behavioral events and remain themselves to be explained. This is not to denigrate their value as initiators of research, but only as explanatory devices.

Finally, Pavlov's inclusion of the concept of language in his principles of conditioning as a "second signal system," as Hilgard and Bower (1966) point out, made conditioning theory an open-ended system capable of dealing with humans' unique linguistic and thinking ability without reducing these complex processes to the mechanistic levels that are invoked to explain learning in animals.

Pavlov's work contributed most richly to the behavioristic schools and systems of psychology, particularly to those of J. B. Watson, Guthrie, Hull, and, indirectly, Skinner (see Chapter 9). Whether conditioning can be validly considered as a model for all learning, as Pavlov and other early investigators thought, remains controversial. However, no learning theorist can ignore the technical and theoretical discoveries of this great Russian physiologist.

LEARNING AND THE SCHOOLS

Following our usual plan, we shall next consider how the topic of learning was handled by the representatives of structuralism, functionalism, behaviorism, and Gestalt psychology. (Because psychoanalysis failed to treat the learning process in any systematic way, we have not included that school's views here.) However, in beginning our survey with Titchener, it will seem as if we are moving backward; for although Thorndike's and Pavlov's were associationistic psychologies in principle, they looked beyond traditional associationism. Titchener's psychology of learning, on the other hand, is old-fashioned by comparison. It would be difficult to conceive of systems founded on the same basic principles of associationism that are more different in all essentials. Titchener's associationism has an aura of eighteenth- and nineteenth-century British philosophy about it, whereas Thorndike's connectionism and Pavlov's conditioning have all the earmarks of a contemporary experimentally oriented system.

Undoubtedly the primary explanation of the great difference between these systems lies in the general aims and methods of their proponents. Titchener's analytic introspectionism favored associationism—but associationism as a conscious higher mental process involved in perception, ideation, attention, and other mental processes. Thorndike's and Pavlov's objectives, especially in the early years, were akin to Watson's. Therefore, Thorndike and Pavlov, like Watson, hoped to demonstrate that by the study of behavior within the *S-R* framework, the science of psychology could be objectified. Since Titchener's account of learning was developed in terms of the older associationism, we shall give it only summary treatment and pass on to the other schools, where the topic of learning found a more congenial atmosphere for its development.

Titchener and Associationism[6]

Titchener (1910) introduces his chapter on association by briefly recapitulating the history of the concept in British philosophy. He reviews the traditional laws of association and the empiricists' attempts to reduce them to the single law of contiguity. He then summarizes Ebbinghaus' work, stating that "the recourse to nonsense syllables, as a means to the study of association, marks the most considerable advance, in this chapter of psychology, since the time of Aristotle." Ebbinghaus' results are presented with considerable emphasis on the conditions under which associations are formed. In the course of the discussion it becomes clear that Titchener favors contiguity as the primary condition for the formation of associations. Mention is also made of forward and backward linkage in serial associative learning, and, surprisingly, even such matters of contemporary interest as retroactive inhibition, associative interference, and mediated associations are briefly touched upon.

An entirely separate chapter is devoted to retention, but the treatment bears little resemblance to that found in modern texts. The entire section emphasizes introspective descriptions of memory images, afterimages, types of imagery, and similar processes. In spite of his high regard for Ebbinghaus, very little of Ebbinghaus' experimental results found a place in Titchener's account; and what is presented is put into fine print as if Titchener felt that experimental findings were of minor importance compared to his own lengthy descriptions of the associative and retentive consciousness.

We shall make no attempt to present Titchener's account of memory. The material has little relevance to the understanding of contemporary learning theories. The interested reader will find an excellent summary of the memorizing process

---

[6]The exposition follows Titchener's *Textbook* (1910).

from the introspective or impressionistic point of view in Woodworth (1938, pp. 23–35). Meanwhile, we shall go on to consider the functionalistic treatment of learning.

Functionalism and Learning[7]

Carr, it will be recalled, defined mental activities as those processes concerned with "the acquisition, fixation, retention, organization, and evaluation of experiences, and their subsequent utilization in the guidance of conduct" (1925, p. 1). Clearly, this strongly functional definition of psychology places great emphasis on learning as a key process in adaptation. Carr recognized that the theoretical problems involved in animal learning and those in human verbal learning are different. Because of this he treats the process of learning under two headings: (1) learning as an adaptive act and (2) learning as association.

Learning as an Adaptive Activity

Learning is defined as the "acquisition of a mode of response" in a problem situation. Problems, in turn, are the result of a lack of adjustment brought about in one of several ways. First, the environment may be lacking in some needed substance or the individual may be confronted by obstructions that must be circumvented if a goal is to be reached. Second, an organism may lack the required skill to respond to a situation. The human infant, for example, lacks the motor skills to satisfy his or her needs. Finally, problems often arise out of conflicting response tendencies such as curiosity and fear. As an illustration, Carr offers the example of the nesting bird torn between the impulse to stay on her eggs and her fear of an approaching intruder.

In solving problems of adaptation, the organism employs a "variable, persistent, and analytical motor attack." All previously useful modes of behavior are tried since, as Carr puts it, "the world is so constituted that acts that are adapted to one situation are usually somewhat appropriate to similar situations" (1925, p. 89). Carr goes on to state that the animal's attack on the problem is neither aimless nor random but relevant to the situation and, moreover, "selective and analytical." He believes—and he must have had Thorndike in mind—that other psychologists overemphasize the trial-and-error nature of animal learning.

Carr then considers the knotty problem of how the correct responses in adjustmental learning are fixated while the incorrect responses are eliminated. He begins by stating the Law of Effect as a *descriptive* statement of what takes place, but does not agree with Thorndike that the sensory consequences of an act can either "stamp in" pleasant acts or "stamp out" unpleasant acts. Carr offers the alternative hypothesis that the organism's behavior is controlled by the character of the sensory stimuli encountered by the animal *during* the problem-solving attack.

---

[7]Based on Carr's *Psychology* (1925), except as otherwise indicated.

All acts alter the sensory situation, and the sensory stimuli necessarily exert some effect upon the subsequent behavior of the organism. Successful and unsuccessful acts can be differentiated on the basis of these effects. In the first case, the resultant sensory stimuli tend to reinforce, direct, and continue the act until the objective is attained, while the sensory stimuli resulting from an unsuccessful act operate to inhibit, disrupt, and discontinue that mode of attack. For example, a rat soon desists from further digging when the hard floor is reached, and the sensory results of gnawing at the wire mesh are not conducive to a continuance of this mode of attack. On the other hand, the sensory consequences of a successful act function to direct that act to the attainment of its objective. The rat lifts the latch, the open door entices the animal to enter, the rat approaches the food and begins to eat, and this act of eating is then continued until the animal's hunger is appeased. In fact, the continuance or discontinuance of any line of attack is almost wholly a function of the character of the sensory stimuli that are encountered during this time. (Carr, 1925, pp. 93–94)

Carr concludes his discussion of learning as adaptive behavior by considering the problems of *transfer, association,* and *habit,* and by relating these processes to his overall account of adjustmental learning. In dealing with transfer, he points out that all learning involves the utilization of previous experience: A dog that learns how to carry a cane through a gate by grasping it at one end instead of in the middle can transfer the solution to similar objects and situations. Or the child who is frightened by a specific dog will exhibit fear of dogs in general.

Carr also points out the practical utility of transfer and argues that as the organism is confronted with new situations it both utilizes and modifies habitual modes of behavior. In this sense, transfer is basic to all learning, for even from the beginning the organism is endowed with a "congenital repertoire of movements" that provide the basis of all future learning.

Learning as Association

The functionalists' point of view on associative learning is developed in two classic expositions by Carr and Edward S. Robinson, a former student and associate of Carr's. We have already mentioned Carr's article (1931), from which our summary of the functionalistic position will be taken. Robinson's views are to be found in a book published in 1932. In most respects the two statements represent a common viewpoint; hence we have chosen to base the following summary on Carr's statement.

Carr begins by proposing a distinction between *descriptive* and *explanatory* laws. Descriptive laws are those that state the conditions under which sequences of associations tend to occur. For example, the traditional law of similarity states that the thought of one object tends to arouse the idea of a similar object. Explanatory laws are those that state relations of dependence between the observed variable and the antecedent condition(s) that are capable of being observed independently. Carr cites the law of contiguity as an example of an explanatory law. Theoretically, the conditions or factors that make for contiguity (temporal and/or spatial sequences) are prior to, and are measurable independently of, the associations to which they give rise. In Carr's view this independence justifies the designation "explanatory." Similarity, on the other hand, cannot be regarded as an explanatory law because similarity is merely a characteristic or attribute of a thought sequence and therefore cannot be observed independently of, or apart from, that sequence.

Descriptive laws are of little importance to psychology. They are great in number and are reflections of all sorts of logical and grammatical relationships among words and consequently, are of little interest to the psychologist. Explanatory laws, on the other hand, are of considerable importance for psychology and can be divided into three classes.

The first class deals with the *origin* or *formation* of associations. The law of contiguity belongs to this class and, in Carr's opinion, is the most important law of association. In conditioning theory, he points out, the law of simultaneity is the equivalent of the law of contiguity.

The second class of laws deals with the *functional strength* of associations. Simply stated, laws subsumed under this class purport to explain why some associations are stronger than others. The *law of frequency* is a specific example of this class of laws. The law states that associative strength increases as a function of the relative frequency of repetition.

However, there is a point of diminishing returns beyond which frequency of repetition does *not* increase associative strength. Fatigue, boredom, and a host of other factors may make the operation of the law of frequency ineffective. Moreover, the various conditions of learning, such as distribution of practice, whole versus part learning, and ordinal position in a list of the items, are also factors that influence the functional strength of associations. In fact, Carr states that the conventional associationistic laws of frequency, recency, and primacy "must be expanded to include many of the factors that are discussed under the heading of 'laws of learning.' "

A third class of laws is needed to explain the frequently observed phenomenon of variability in learning. The *law of assimilation*[8] exemplifies a very broad principle subsumed under this class. The law states that "any novel sense impression will tend to elicit those responses that are already connected with a similar sensory stimulus." The operation of the law may be exemplified in conditioning experiments where "incidental stimuli" are often associated with the conditioned response.

Pavlov, for example, found that the buzzing of a bee that had accidentally flown into his laboratory during a conditioning experiment elicited the salivary response in a dog that had been conditioned to the sound of a tuning fork. Pavlov and his followers referred to this phenomenon as stimulus generalization.

The law of assimilation, however, goes far beyond such cases of incidental learning, since, as Hilgard and Bower (1966) point out, it is the framework in which the functionalist can investigate transfer—the equivalent of Gestalt insight and transposition—as well as generalization phenomena. In short, it is an all-inclusive

---

[8]Compare Thorndike's principle of response by analogy.

law broad enough to include virtually everything that may be subsumed under the topic of ''learning.'' It is also important to recognize that Carr, by including the law of assimilation, denies that associative learning is explicable on a purely *S-R* basis. In order to include the factors subsumed under the law of assimilation, the *S-R* formula would have to be modified to become an *S-O-R* formula. In Carr's own words, ''the character of the associations that are established is not wholly determined by the sequence of objective events, but . . . is also materially influenced by the reaction of the organism to its environment'' (1931, p. 223).

Finally, it must be emphasized once again that Carr was not seeking to formulate a definitive set of laws of learning, but *classes* of laws organized on the basis of their function—of which the laws of contiguity, frequency, and assimilation are but specific examples. In other words, Carr sought to make the functionalist framework broad enough to include additional laws as needed.

We shall return to the functionalistic point of view in the chapters to follow on contemporary trends in learning theory. Meanwhile we shall examine the classical behavioristic position on learning, as formulated by J. B. Watson. Before considering Watson's point of view, however, we shall summarize the background of behaviorism in animal psychology, a tradition that exerted a profound influence on Watson's entire system and research program, as well as on subsequent behavioristic systems.

Animal Psychology as a Forerunner of Behaviorism

Animal psychology as a formal discipline originated with the work of Charles Darwin. Upon the publication of his *Origin of Species* in 1859, man could no longer claim unique status in the animal kingdom. The wide divergence in both anatomical forms and behavior patterns that had lent support to the dogma of the individual creation of each specific species could now be accounted for on the basis of chance variation and selection by survival of the best-adapted variants. And once the problem of the evolution of the body had been brought under attack, it was only a question of time until the possibility of the evolution in mind came to the foreground of scientific investigation. In fact, Darwin himself brought the hypothesis of mental evolution under scientific scrutiny in his *Expression of Emotions in Man and Animals* (1873). In this volume he accounted for the overt aspects of human emotions by postulating that they are vestigial carry-overs from ancestral animal behavior. The human rage pattern, for example, bears a striking relationship to that found in lower forms.

More direct support for the hypothesis of mental evolution was offered by one of Darwin's countrymen, George Romanes, whose *Animal Intelligence* (1883) was the first book devoted to comparative psychology. Romanes collected and organized what amounted to anecdotal accounts of the behavior of fishes, birds, domestic animals, and monkeys. Because his work was based on anthropomorphic speculations, Romanes' conclusions fell far short of modern scientific standards. Nevertheless, he is respected for his pioneer efforts and the stimulation he provided to those who followed.

One of the outstanding British scholars who took up the challenge of animal psychology was C. Lloyd Morgan. Lloyd Morgan is famous for his "Canon," which was formulated as a criticism of Romanes' anthropomorphic interpretations of animal behavior. The Canon states that an animal's behavior must not be interpreted as the outcome of higher mental processes if it can be interpreted in terms of lower mental processes. In effect, the Canon is a law of parsimony in scientific explanation.

Lloyd Morgan published several books dealing with animal behavior and the relation of the animal to the human mind. In these publications he cites the results of studies and observations of animal behavior carried out by himself and others. His work was not truly experimental in the modern sense of controlled laboratory investigations, but it was a great step forward for the times.

Interest in animal psychology grew rapidly toward the end of the nineteenth century. By this time Thorndike had started his program of animal experiments in the United States. Loeb had announced his theory of tropisms in 1890 and had launched his mechanistically oriented studies of the life processes. In France, Henri Fabre's world-famous studies of insects appeared, beginning in 1874; and in England, L. T. Hobhouse published his *Mind in Evolution* (1901), a volume that summarized his experiments on animals ranging in size from cats to elephants. Some of Hobhouse's experiments are quite modern in design, one of his investigations being strikingly similar to Köhler's studies of insight in chimpanzees. A monkey, "the Professor," was confronted with the problem of getting a banana out of a large pipe. By using a stick supplied by Hobhouse, the animal succeeded in solving the problem after a few trials by pushing the reward completely through the pipe. Though Hobhouse does not use the term "insight," he credits the monkey with "articulate ideas" (1901, p. 247).

Of all the influences that lent impetus to the behavioristic movement in psychology, the work of Ivan P. Pavlov, the Russian physiologist, stands out most prominently. His careful systematic series of experiments, his objectivism in interpreting his results, and his use of conditioning as a technique for investigating sensory and higher mental processes were highly influential in determining the direction of Watson's behaviorism and its associated systems.

With this brief historical sketch of the forerunners of behaviorism in animal psychology, we now turn to Watson's treatment of learning, which, like much of the rest of his system, remained more of a program than a concrete set of accomplishments.

Watson on Learning[9]

Watson's initial interest in animal research stemmed from his early association with the functionalists at the University of Chicago, where he obtained his Ph.D. degree. His doctoral research was concerned with the investigation of sensory

---

[9]Our account is based on J. B. Watson's *Behavior* (1914) and *Psychology from the Standpoint of a Behaviorist* (1919).

mechanisms in maze learning in rats. His first book, *Behavior: An Introduction to Comparative Psychology,* reflects his early interest in animal psychology, but, strangely enough, gives only slight emphasis to Pavlov's conditioning experiments. Watson merely reports the method as useful chiefly for investigating animals' receptor processes. He even expresses doubt that "the method could be worked upon the primates" (1914, p. 68), thereby proving himself a poor prophet.

With the publication of *Psychology from the Standpoint of a Behaviorist* in 1919, there could be little doubt that Watson's reservations about conditioning had disappeared. It was now one of the chief methods of the behaviorist and was employed by Watson himself in the famous experiment where the child was conditioned to fear a rat (see Chapter 13). Moreover, by this time, Watson had come to lay unlimited stress on learning in the development and modification of human behavior.[10]

Despite this enthusiastic beginning and the favorable *Zeitgeist* Watson himself helped to create, it comes as something of an anticlimax to learn that Watson never developed a satisfactory theory of animal learning. In his early work on maze learning in rats, he formulated a kinesthetic reflex theory to account for the animal's ability to run the maze successfully. In essence, he argued that the execution of one movement became the kinesthetic stimulus for the next movement (1914, p. 212). However, he had to admit that the evidence for this view was largely negative in that it was based on his own experiments in which the other senses were systematically destroyed with no significant effect on the animals' maze-learning ability. Since the kinesthetic sense had not been destroyed, he concluded that it must be the crucial sense in maze learning.[11] The question of how correct responses are fixated is discussed in the seventh chapter of his comparative text (1914). He holds that the animal learns the correct responses primarily through the operation of the law of frequency (exercise) and secondarily through the law of recency. He justifies his argument on the grounds that the animal runs along the true path more frequently than it enters the various blinds. The animal *must* run the true path at least once per trial, but it often skips blind alleys, thus gradually eliminating them. The principle of recency, Watson felt, applied more to problem boxes than to mazes. Since the last of a series in the problem box *is* the correct one, it tends to decrease the probability of the occurrence of all other activities.

Therefore, in his early accounts of animal learning, Watson favored the age-old associationist principles, even as he denied the broader implications of associationism as it had been traditionally applied to ideation, memory, and imagination. He specifically denied the validity of the Law of Effect, calling it no law but "Thorndike's conviction." Watson, of course, objected to Thorndike's terminology, since phrases such as "satisfying state" and "followed by discomfort to the animal" were cast in the language of consciousness.

---

[10]See the quotation in Chapter 3.

[11]Watson was wrong. He failed to make *combination* destructions, which reveal that the animal deprived of one sense falls back on those that remain. Thus, a blind, deaf, or anosmic animal can still learn a maze. But a blind-deaf-anosmic animal shows no significant learning. See Honzik (1936).

In his later work with the method of conditioning, Watson again emphasized the repetition of *S-R* sequences and failed to recognize what subsequently became a key issue in conditioning theory—reinforcement. In summary, then, despite his interest in the objective methods for the study of animal learning, Watson belongs with the pre-Thorndikian associationists. Consequently, his views on learning failed to evolve into a form acceptable to contemporary behaviorists. With this rather paradoxical conclusion, we shall leave Watson and turn our attention to Gestalt contributions to learning theory.

Gestalt Psychology and Learning Theory

The Gestalt psychologists evidenced little interest in empirical research on learning and made few significant contributions to learning theory. Despite this harsh evaluation, it is something of a paradox that any enumeration of the most significant experiments in the literature of psychology would have to include Köhler's studies of problem solving in apes. Nevertheless our initial statement stands. As we pointed out earlier, the school's chief interest was in the field of perception and thinking, whereas learning remained a subordinate issue. Moreover, from its very inception, Gestalt psychology was antagonistic to the Thorndikian and Watsonian types of analysis. Indeed, the members of the Gestalt school considered that one of their major contributions to psychology was the attack on associationistic and *S-R* theories of learning. It might also be noted that Köhler's experiments on apes, significant as they are, are in many ways more properly classified as experiments in the area of thinking or reasoning rather than learning. However, it has become conventional to treat these experiments under the topic of learning, and we shall follow tradition and summarize them here.

Köhler's experiments with chimpanzees were carried out at the University of Berlin Anthropoid Station on the island of Tenerife (one of the Canaries) during the years 1913–1917. The results were published in German in book form in 1917, and an English translation was issued in 1925 under the title *The Mentality of Apes*. The following account has been drawn from a later edition (1927) of this work. In this volume Köhler describes four types of problems he employed in testing the apes' ability to solve complex problems. These were (1) detour problems, (2) problems involving the use of ready-made implements, (3) problems in which the animal must construct implements, and (4) building problems.

A detour problem requires the subject to make an initial turn away from the goal in order to reach it eventually (see Figure 8-9). To be credited with insight, the animal must, according to Köhler, show evidence of perceiving the relationships involved by adopting the detour route quickly and smoothly. Köhler describes his human subject's solution for a similar problem as follows:

> A little girl of one year and three months, who had learned to walk alone a few weeks before, was brought into a blind alley, set up *ad hoc* (two meters long, and one and a half wide), and, on the other side of the partition, some attractive object was put before her eyes; first she pushed toward the object, i.e., against the partition, then looked around slowly, let her eyes run along the blind alley, suddenly laughed joyfully, and in one movement was off on a trot round the corner to the objective. (1927, p. 14)

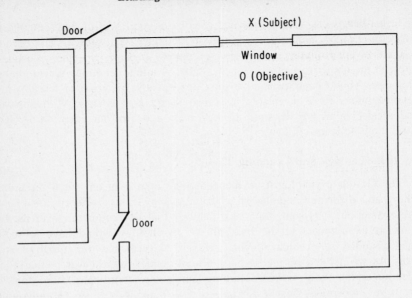

FIGURE 8-9.   A detour problem. (Redrawn from Köhler, W. The mentality of apes. Humanities Press, and Routledge & Kegan Paul, Ltd. Copyright 1927.)

But when tested on the same type of problem, hens showed no evidence of reasoning or insight. The birds spent most of their time "rushing up against the obstruction." Some eventually achieved the solution in simplified problems if they extended their running sufficiently to hit upon the opening accidentally, where they could then see a direct route leading to the goal.

The dog and the chimpanzee did solve the detour problem in an insightful manner. Köhler reports that his subjects' behavior clearly revealed the dramatic moment at which insight occurs.

Köhler's second and third types of problems involved both the use of ready-made implements and the making of implements. In either case, the successful solution to the problems involves the animal's understanding the implement as a tool. For example, if a banana is placed out of reach outside the animal's cage and several hollow bamboo sticks are provided inside the cage, then the animal must perceive the sticks in an entirely new manner, not as playthings but as tools to be used as extensions of himself or herself.

When Sultan, Köhler's brightest ape, was confronted with a related problem, he failed at first. He tried to get the banana with one stick (it was too short), then brought a box toward the bars and immediately pushed it away again. He next pushed one stick out as far as it would go, took the other stick and pushed the first with it until the first touched the banana. Sultan, Köhler adds, exhibited considerable satisfaction at this actual contact with the fruit. However, despite the fact that Köhler gave Sultan a "hint" by putting his finger in the bamboo stick while the animal watched, the ape did not succeed in solving the problem in the course of an hour-long trial. But immediately after that trial, Sultan suddenly solved the problem in the course of playing with the sticks. The following report is by Sultan's keeper, who happened to be observing the animal at the critical moment.

> Sultan first of all squats indifferently on the box, which has been left standing a little back from the railings; then he gets up, picks up the two sticks, sits down again on the box and plays carelessly with them. While doing this, it happens that he finds himself holding one rod in either hand in such a way that they lie in a straight line; he pushes the thinner one a little way into the opening of the thicker, jumps up and is already on the run towards the railings, to which he has up to now half turned his back, and begins to draw a banana towards him with the double stick. I call the master; meanwhile, one of the animal's rods has fallen out of the other, as he has pushed one of them only a little way into the other; whereupon he connects them again. (1927, p. 127)

In subsequent experiments, Sultan solved the problem quickly and was not confused even when given three sticks, two of which could not be fitted together. Köhler reports that the animal did not even try to put the wrong sticks together.

We may interpret the significance of this and similar tests with implements as follows: The chimpanzee does not exhibit "pure insight" in solving such problems in the sense that he needs no experience with the implements before demonstrating their use in an insightful manner. *Some* trial-and-error behavior is a necessary prelude before insight can take place.[12] Once the animal grasps the problem, he exhibits a high degree of understanding and good transfer.[13]

We shall conclude our summary of Köhler's studies by reporting briefly on the box-stacking problem—perhaps the best known of all of Köhler's experiments. The situation confronting the animal is to utilize properly one or more boxes to obtain a banana that is suspended too high for the animal to reach directly or to grasp by jumping.

It turned out that apes have considerable difficulty with this problem. Sultan needed repeated trials and several demonstrations of box stacking by the experimenter before succeeding. However, Köhler argues that the animal was actually confronted with two problems in one. First, he had to solve the problem of the gap between the floor and the banana. Essentially, this was a perceptual problem necessitating the recognition of the box as a gap filler. The second aspect of the problem was the mechanical one of actually building the box structure, and it was in this phase of the problem that the animals experienced the greatest difficulty. They were, so to speak, poor builders. Even on the first trial, Sultan quickly demonstrated that he knew how to bridge the gap by dragging boxes under the suspended fruit, but he stacked the boxes in so wobbly a manner that his structures kept collapsing. It is, after all, unnecessary for a chimpanzee to be a skilled builder in his natural surroundings when he is so agile in climbing trees. However, several of Köhler's animals eventually managed a three- to four-box tower that remained in place long enough for them to scramble up and seize the banana before the structure collapsed.

---

[12]See Birch (1945) for a similar interpretation and an experimental confirmation.
[13]See Chapter 10 for a discussion of Harlow's work on learning to learn, which is relevant to the problem of interpreting experiments on insight.

Köhler concluded that the building problem was solved only by trial and error, but the perceptual problem was solved by insight.

By way of summary, let us try to abstract from these experiments what the Gestalt psychologists mean by insight. Certainly, as Köhler himself points out (1927, pp. 22–24), an important condition of insight is the nature of the experimental situation. *The animal must be able to see the relationships among all relevant parts of the problem before insight can occur.* Köhler criticizes Thorndike's work on the grounds that the cats in the puzzle boxes were frequently confronted with problems in which a survey of the entire release mechanism was impossible. Köhler believes that the various elements or parts of the problem must be perceived by the animal or it will be impossible for the subject to reorganize them into a coherent whole.

Second, these experiments clearly point out that insight follows a period of trial-and-error behavior, by which is meant not the "blind, random attack" of Thorndike's cats, but a procedure more akin to what we might call "behavioral hypotheses," which the animal is trying out and discarding. In this connection, the animal's previous experience with either the specific elements involved in the problem under attack or with similar problems in the past is crucial. Past experience with similar problems leads to fruitful hypotheses in future problem solving.

Third, once the animal solves the problem by insight, there is a high degree of transfer to similar problems. Moreover, the animal shows a high level of retention and understanding, which, of course, makes for good transfer.

Finally, insight is closely related to the animal's capacity to learn. Not *all* chimpanzees can solve the same problem. And there are differences among different species of animals. It will be recalled that dogs could readily solve the detour problem, whereas hens could not. No one has made an exhaustive study of the matter, but it is doubtful that anything akin to "reasoning" or "insight" can be demonstrated lower on the phylogenetic scale than the rodents; and even there the problems must be so simple that whether they can be properly characterized as "reasoning" problems is a controversial matter (Morgan, 1965).

To conclude, Köhler's studies of insight lent support to the Gestalt psychologists' molar interpretation of behavior, as opposed to associationistic and behavioristic elementalism. Köhler's results were subsequently used to support the contention that learning of the insightful variety is essentially a perceptual reorganization or restructuring of the psychological field. The animal confronted with a problem is in a state of disequilibrium. There is a "gap" in the animal's psychological field that closes at the moment insight occurs. Thus an insightful solution is analogous to closure in the area of perception.

SUMMARY AND EVALUATION

In this chapter we have attempted to show how philosophical associationism evolved into experimental associationism and eventually into the modern experimental psychology of learning. In our opinion the most significant events that took place during the period covered were the investigations of memory by Ebbinghaus, the theoretical interpretations of acquisition and forgetting by Thorndike, and the experiments utilizing the conditioned reflex conducted by Pavlov. Ebbinghaus' work evolved into the highly active field of verbal learning—a field that is basically functionalistic in spirit. Thorndike's and Pavlov's animal researches were part of the developing behavioristic movement, which favored studies of animal subjects. The tradition of animal research has been continued up to the present time among behavioristically oriented psychologists. However, although contemporary behaviorists in general have no fault to find with Thorndike's trial-and-error *description* of animal learning, they have been far less sympathetic to his theoretical *interpretation* of how learning takes place. It remains something of a paradox that Thorndike's Law of Effect has probably stimulated more controversy and research in the area of learning than any other single theoretical principle.

As we noted earlier in this chapter, Ebbinghaus was not a theorist. He was content to account for verbal learning by the principle of frequency of repetition as related to amount retained over time. Thorndike, while utilizing frequency, added the concept of effect at the same time strongly rejecting traditional mentalistic explanations of how associations or connections are formed in the course of learning. Pavlov contributed a powerful tool for investigating not only learning but sensory and discriminative capacities in animals. As will be more fully developed in chapters to follow, the nature of reinforcement—a concept first used by Pavlov—proved to be a challenge to the generation of psychologists who followed.

The Gestalt psychologists, as we pointed out, were more attracted to the field of perception than learning. Since perceptual psychology was the stronghold of the structuralists, the Gestalt psychologists wanted to demonstrate the incorrectness of their point of view. Gestalt psychologists also found themselves in opposition to the traditional associationistic views favored by the other schools. However, ignoring evolutionary trends, Köhler's experiments on insight, along with his studies on transposition in learning discussed in Chapter 6, are numbered among the classics in the entire field of psychology. Moreover, the Gestalt movement as a whole has made its influence felt in contemporary learning theories, as will be brought out in the next chapter.

Learning II: Miniature Systems

9

The great leap forward by Ebbinghaus, Thorndike, and Pavlov in developing an experimental psychology of learning evolved into the work of their successors in the behavioristic tradition, men whose names became famous for "miniature systems," as their theories came to be called. These were first formulated in the 1930s and 1940s, and reached their maturity in the 1950s. In contrast to the leaders of the traditional schools, the originators of the miniature systems of learning strove for comprehensiveness in a specific area of interest rather than in attempting to encompass the entire field of human behavior—although, as we shall discover, it is sometimes impossible for the theorist to resist generalizing the principles of behavior discovered in the learning laboratory to the world outside. However, the initial thrust of the generation of learning theorists that followed Ebbinghaus, Thorndike, and Pavlov was the establishment of the laws of learning and, for some, to go beyond description and seek an explanation of how learning occurs.

The theorists of the 1930s through 1950s shared several common characteristics. First, all were attracted to the behavioristic point of view, although some were more rigid than others in their insistence on excluding variables that are not directly observable. Second, all shared the belief that the principles of learning can best be discovered in animal subjects, because of the possibility of better control of conditions and because the less complex behavior of animals is more likely to reveal basic principles than the highly complex behavior of human subjects. None of these theorists, however, hesitated to generalize their results from animals to human beings. Third, these scientists held in common a conviction that learning is the key process in behavior, pervading as it does the organism's entire developmental history. In taking this position they shared something of the excitement Watson must have felt when he first announced that conditioning would prove a technique capable of producing any kind of adult the psychologist might desire to mold, provided he were given control of him or her as a child.

Not all the expectations of the 1930s and 1940s were fulfilled, and by the latter part of the 1950s, some of the theories had already shown signs of serious deficiencies and had to be greatly modified. However, on the positive side, all theorists made significant contributions that proved enduring not only in the primary area of learning but in related areas of behavior modification and educational, clinical, and developmental psychology. Indeed, one of the theories, B. F. Skinner's operant conditioning, has achieved a position of preeminence in contemporary psychology and may be said to have long since passed from a miniature theory of learning to a major psychological system.

Before taking up specific theories, we should like to outline our scheme for the exposition of the several theories with which we shall be concerned in the pages to follow. First, we shall indicate the theorist's overall systematic position—behavioristic, Gestalt, and others. Second, for each theory we shall summarize the chief laws or principles that bear upon the acquisition of learned responses. More specifically, we shall delineate the theorist's position on the relative role of practice and reinforcement (or reward) as determinants in learning. Third, the laws of generalization or transfer will be considered wherever applicable. Fourth, the laws of extinction, or forgetting, will be examined in light of the author's overall position. Finally, other important variables or laws not included in the preceding categories will be discussed briefly. In this way we hope to facilitate cross-comparisons between the several points of view represented.

GUTHRIE'S CONTIGUOUS CONDITIONING:[1]
A PURE CONTIGUITY THEORY

We have Edwin Guthrie's (1896–1959) own admission that he had long favored the behavioristic approach in psychology. However, the designation ''behaviorist'' immediately brings to mind J. B. Watson and the revolution he directed against structuralism and functionalism. In contrast to Watson's iconoclastic program, Guthrie's is a mild-mannered and sober account of an associationistic-contiguity theory of learning. Indeed, at first reading the theory appears simple and uncomplicated to the point of superficiality. This effect is heightened by Guthrie's engaging style and frequent use of anecdotes and homespun examples. But although the system appears simple in the sense that Guthrie (in contrast to most learning theorists) makes little use of formal laws, it is anything but simple in the range of phenomena it attempts to encompass and in the careful attention that Guthrie gives to measuring his position against those held by other prominent theorists. But let us turn to the theory itself, considering first Guthrie's laws of acquisition.

The Laws of Acquisition

The framework of Guthrie's system is based on conditioning; consequently, the development of the theory centers on the principle that learning occurs through

---

[1]The exposition is based on two primary sources: E. R. Guthrie's *Psychology of Learning* (1952) and E. R. Guthrie and G. P. Horton's *Cats in a Puzzle Box* (1946). For bibliography of critical summaries, see E. R. Guthrie (1952, p. 81).

contiguity of stimulus and response. Early in his book on learning, Guthrie makes his position clear by announcing his primary and only formal law of learning: *"A combination of stimuli which has accompanied a movement will on its recurrence tend to be followed by that movement"* (1952, p. 23). The implications of the terms "movement" and "tend" in the law require further comment. As a behaviorist, Guthrie is interested in the observable responses of animal or human subjects. However, he makes a distinction between responses as acts and responses as movements. Psychologists ordinarily measure acts which consist of a series of movements that accomplish a result. Thus, the act of hitting a baseball involves a pattern of movements that theoretically can be recorded and measured, but in practice are not. Only the act is considered important.

From Guthrie's point of view, however, particular movements, not acts, are the true conditioned responses and therefore the raw material of the system. Moreover, it must be emphasized that movements produce proprioceptive stimuli, and these stimuli serve as the conditioned stimuli to further movements. If we bear in mind that any learning situation involves both environmental stimuli and those internal stimuli carried by the organism from situation to situation, the stimulus pattern for any given learning situation is highly complex and difficult to identify. The use of the qualifying term "tend" recognizes the common finding that expected responses do not always appear because of a variety of "conflicting" or "incompatible" tendencies, as will be further elucidated later in this discussion.

It should be emphasized that Guthrie does not accept either a law of effect or reinforcement as an important condition of learning. He finds it unnecessary to postulate any kind of "confirmatory" explanation of conditioned associations, whether these take the form of Thorndikian satisfiers or reinforcers in the sense of drive-reducing agents. In short, *learning depends on contiguity of stimulus and response patterns alone*.

Let us illustrate Guthrie's law of acquisition by introducing Guthrie and Horton's experiment (1946) on cats in puzzle boxes. The experiment under consideration involved the use of a puzzle box of special design, in which the front of the box was made of glass to provide for complete freedom of observation and photographic recording. A second feature was the inclusion of a special release mechanism consisting of a post suspended from the top (or in some models standing on the floor of the box). The post was designed so that slight pressure by the animal *from any direction* caused the door to open. Movement of the post simultaneously activated a camera, which took the cat's picture at the moment of responding. In order to control the subject's approach to the post, the cats were always introduced into the box from a starting compartment in the rear. Finally, a dish of fish was placed outside the puzzle box. The glass door enabled the cat to see the fish at all times.[2] Let us follow a typical animal's progress in escaping from the box.

Guthrie tells us that upon entering the puzzle box the cat exhibited the tradi-

---

[2]The reader should compare the design of the Guthrie-Horton box to Thorndike's. See Chapter 8, Figure 8-2.

tional "trial-and-error" behavior expected of cats that have found themselves in psychologists' puzzle boxes since Thorndike's pioneer studies of this variety of behavior. To quote Guthrie:

> In general the cats, on being admitted to the box, paused at the threshold, entered cautiously, proceeded to the front door and clawed, sniffed, looked about. Any outstanding features such as the crack around the door got attention and were pushed at or bitten at. Approximately an average of fifteen minutes was spent in such exploratory behavior. This meant many excursions about the box.
>
> Eventually, most cats did something that moved the pole and opened the escape door. The noise of the door was followed by the cat's looking at the door and then (usually) by its leaving the box through the open door. (Guthrie, 1952, p. 265)

Guthrie and Horton were struck by several features of the cats' behavior. First, there was a strong tendency for the animals to repeat the precise movements leading up to and including the escape movement. Some cats exhibited several "routines" or sequences of movements during the early trials but typically settled on one routine during later phases of the experiment. Guthrie and Horton call the tendency for the animal to repeat successful movement patterns "stereotypy." Figure 9-1, taken from original photographs, shows the stereotyping of one animal's responses during the course of a series of trials. The significance of this repetitive behavior is interpreted by Guthrie and Horton as strong evidence in favor of contiguity learning. The pattern of escape movements is repeated because it removes the animal from the box, *thereby preventing new and contradictory associations from being formed.*

In some of their animal subjects, Guthrie and Horton occasionally found patterns of behavior that involved the appearance of entirely new solutions. Such idiosyncratic behavior is also accounted for by the principle of contiguity. Evidently, because the animal entered the puzzle compartment from a slightly different direction or angle, thereby setting up new proprioceptive and external stimuli patterns, *a new learning situation requiring a new escape response* was involved. The animal then went on to repeat the new sequence rather than the old; the latter, in effect, had been *unlearned* by the acquisition of the new pattern of responding. Guthrie and Horton believe that the priority of new over old responses supports the principle that associations *reach their full associative strength upon the first pairing*. In other words, learning is complete in one trial!

If, as Guthrie and Horton believe, learning occurs on the first successful trial, why, it may be asked, are so many trials necessary in the typical animal learning situation? The answer, Guthrie believes, lies along these lines: First, the simplest learning situation is, in reality, highly complex. Second, many stimuli are confronting the animal. Some arise from external sources, others from proprioceptive organs in the animal's own muscles, tendons, and joints. Guthrie argues that "every action performed by the cat in the puzzle box is conditioned on the contemporary cues from the cat's own movements from the box and other external stimuli" (1952, p. 271). Therefore, following the initial successful trial, the cat repeats the entire routine, including "errors" or irrelevant movements as well as the "correct" re-

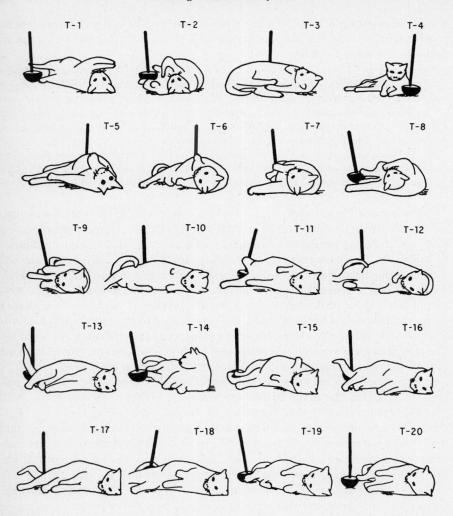

FIGURE 9-1.   Stereotyping of a single cat's responses over 20 trials in the puzzle box. From Trial 5 on, the animal uses its rear leg or tail to activate the release mechanism. Reproduced from tracings of the original photographs made at the time of release. (From Guthrie, E. R., and Horton, G. P. Cats in a puzzle box. Holt, Rinehart and Winston, Inc. Copyright 1946.)

sponse. That irrelevant movements are gradually eliminated in favor of the increasingly stereotyped correct response is the result of relearning. The observer sees the cat shortening the time of escape, reducing irrelevant movements, and attaching the appropriate movement to the appropriate cue. Any given correct movement is learned on the first occasion it occurs; but with each new trial some movements drop out if they are not recurrent or essential to the action pattern.

The cat in the puzzle box is judged by the external observer to have "learned" only when the animal's performance is a smooth sequence of the essential acts involved in the solution to the problem. In effect, the animal has eliminated all the associations that, from the observer's point of view, are useless. Thus, practice results in improvement *only in the outcome* of learning but does not affect the strength of any given association. In learning highly complex skills, such as typing, driving an automobile, or playing basketball, so many movements must be attached to their appropriate cues that the learning of the tasks takes many trials.

The Role of Reward and Punishment

It will be recalled from the preceding description of the puzzle box experiment that a dish of fish was placed outside the box. At the same time we also indicated that Guthrie does not hold that the Law of Effect or reinforcement is a necessary condition of learning. The cat learns the correct movements by *S-R* contiguity. What, then, is the role of reward? Rewards, according to Guthrie, prevent the animal (or human) subject from engaging in behavior patterns that could break up previously learned patterns. Therefore, if it were feasible, putting the cat in a "cataleptic trance" the instant the animal escaped from the box would be just as effective in preventing forgetting as allowing it to eat the salmon. The act of eating the fish keeps the cat from moving about and establishing new (and possibly disruptive) *S-R* connections. In summary, then, the effect of reward is the purely mechanical one of preventing unlearning. It might be noted in this connection that Guthrie and Horton observed that their cats often failed to eat the fish after escaping from the box.

This raises the related problem of the role of drives or motives in learning. Why, it might be asked, make the animal hungry in the first place? The answer lies in the fact that the hungry animal is the more restless animal whose higher rate and greater variety of responses are more likely to lead to movements that will result in escape. Thus, drive for Guthrie does nothing more than energize behavior in a general way and provide for vigorous movements. It has no place in his learning system other than as an overall regulator of behavior.

Transfer

Guthrie's position on transfer is virtually identical with Thorndike's. It will be recalled that Thorndike treated transfer in terms of identical elements. If two learning situations, *A* and *B*, have elements in common, then transfer from *A* to *B* can occur. Guthrie deals with the problem of transfer in much the same way. If certain *S-R* relationships are identical from one situation to another, then, and only then, is there a possibility of transfer.

Forgetting

Despite his general orientation in favor of conditioning, Guthrie does not agree that extinction results from nonreinforced practice, or forgetting from disuse. In regard to extinction, it will be recalled that he does not subscribe to reinforcement theory; consequently, "extinction" has no meaning in this system. However, forgetting and the related problem of breaking undesirable habits are treated at considerable length. Forgetting occurs because new learning takes the place of what has been previously learned. If an established *S-R* connection is not displaced by a new association, it will persist indefinitely. To support his position, Guthrie cites the stability of conditioned responses in dogs. Such responses may last for months, provided the dog is not subjected to bells, buzzers, tuning forks, or other stimuli similar to those used in conditioning experiments. Then there is nothing in the dog's normal routine to expose him to new learning that could interfere with what has been previously learned in the relatively artificial laboratory situations. Similarly, Guthrie points out that certain human skills such as skating or swimming may persist over years of disuse simply because nothing occurs to interfere with them.

Breaking Habits

A problem closely related to the process of forgetting is that of unlearning undesirable habits. Life is full of instances where the individual's goal is to get rid of habits rather than to acquire them. The parent, clinician, animal trainer, and teacher frequently desire to "break bad habits" in those under their control. Guthrie was long interested in such practical applications of learning theory to problems in the guidance and control of behavior. Indeed, he conceives of much of the "undesirable behavior of the nervous breakdown, the anesthesias, paralyses, compulsions, tics, seizures, that make life a burden to the psychoneurotic" as habits (Guthrie, 1938, p. 71).

Although Guthrie's analysis of the problem is too extensive to be done justice here, we shall briefly outline the substance of his argument. For a complete discussion of this interesting application of learning theory, the reader should consult Guthrie (1938, chaps. 5, 7; 1952, chap. 11).[3]

The fundamental rule for breaking a habit is *to discover the cues that initiate the undesirable action and then to practice a different response to the same cues.* Guthrie offers several specific techniques for achieving this end. In the first technique the conditioned stimulus is introduced so gradually that the associated response is not evoked. For example, in helping an individual overcome a fear of cats, one would have him or her acquire a tiny kitten whose helplessness and small size fail to evoke the usual antagonistic reactions. Since the kitten's growth is so gradual, the individual acquires tolerance for adult cats. The second technique involves repeating the stimulus cues until the response is fatigued. For example, by allowing the child to have his or her temper tantrums or the bucking horse to tire himself out, the subject is rendered temporarily tractable to reconditioning. The final technique involves pairing the undesirable response with a mutually contradictory response. Guthrie gives the rather macabre example of tying a dead chicken around the neck of a dog habitually guilty of chasing chickens. The ani-

---

[3]Guthrie was a pioneer in behavior therapy. See the discussion of his approach to Skinner's theory later in this chapter.

mal's violent reactions under these conditions will result in the development of an avoidance response.

Conclusion

Because of limitations of space, many aspects of Guthrie's system of contiguous conditioning have been neglected in our highly condensed discussion. However, within the limitations intrinsic to such an account, we have attempted to present the broad outlines of his theory.

Independent attempts to test Guthrie's system in experimental situations have, as is so often the case in psychological experiments, turned out to be divided in their support—some providing positive, some negative evidence. For example, V. W. Voeks—a student of Guthrie's who formalized the theory in a series of postulates (1948, 1950)—carried out experiments designed to assess the validity of the postulates. The best known of her postulates is the *principle of postremity,* a formalization of Guthrie's assumption that what the animal does last is learned. This assumption was tested by studying the learning of human subjects in finger mazes. The experimental hypothesis was cast into the form of a test of the relative predictability of frequency of prior choices at a choice point versus postremity, or the last choice made. For all but one of fifty-seven subjects postremity was a better basis for prediction than frequency.

However, Seward (1949) tested two groups of rats in a bar-pressing situation in which members of one group were permitted to eat the food, while members of the other group were quickly removed from the situation after making the correct response. In this case the experimental design was obviously intended as a test of Guthrie's hypothesis that reward is irrelevant and that only contiguity produces learning. Indirectly, the experiment also is a test of postremity, since the animals that did not engage in eating behavior should be superior according to the principle. But Seward found that although both groups learned to press the bar, the rewarded group progressed significantly faster than the unrewarded group.

These two examples are only representative of many contradictory sets of results that might be cited pro and con Guthrie's position. Hilgard and Bower (1966, pp. 98–101) summarize a number of experiments bearing on the theory, and Osgood (1953, pp. 370–372) presents a critical analysis of the results of several experiments, including Voeks'. In general it is fair to say that the apparent simplicity of the theory has proved illusory. Its very generality makes it difficult to subject the theory to a critical experimental test; and in those cases where its postulates have been cast into more precise form, results have been divided—some supporting, others failing to support the theory. Until future research assigns it a permanent place in learning theory, Guthrie's theory will remain a challenging example of the wide range of phenomena that a pure contiguity theory can account for without invoking the principle of reward.[4]

---

[4]For a final statement of Guthrie's theory by its originator, including a biographical summary, see E. R. Guthrie (1959, pp. 158–195).

HULL'S HYPOTHETICODEDUCTIVE SYSTEM: A DRIVE
REDUCTION THEORY

Clark L. Hull's (1884–1952) learning theory represents the work of a lifetime. He began to elaborate his theory in preliminary form as early as 1915, and at the time of his death in 1952 the system was still incomplete. By 1943 the theory was in a sufficiently advanced stage to be published in book form in a volume entitled *Principles of Behavior*. (A mathematical exposition of a part of the theory having to do with rote learning, by Hull, Hovland, Ross, Hall, Perkins, & Fitch had been published three years earlier, in 1940.) In 1951 Hull published a revision of his system, entitled *Essentials of Behavior;* and in 1952 his final publication, *A Behavior System,* appeared posthumously. Hull had planned an additional volume in which he intended to report continued extension of his theory into the area of social phenomena. As a result of his death before the completion of his plans, the system remains unfinished in the sense that its author never got to apply the basic theory to a wide range of behavioral phenomena not covered in the last statement of the theory.

We have chosen to base our exposition of Hull's system on his *Principles of Behavior,* which, while more restricted in range than *A Behavior System,* can be rendered intelligible to the student with a background in general psychology. Moreover, our choice offers the additional advantage of minimizing the oversimplification of Hull's original statements. In dealing with systems based on a highly integrated and logically deduced set of postulates, there is considerable risk in any attempt at simplification, since both the precision of the original language and the originator's symbolization are necessarily sacrificed for simplicity. However, after we have summarized the tenets of the original core theory, we shall attempt to indicate the major areas in which Hull sought to extend his theory and at the same time point out any important changes in the fundamental postulates. In this way it will be possible to present the theory without unduly sacrificing the precision that Hull himself believed to be one of its most important contributions. At the same time, with this introduction as a background the serious student should be able to consult the primary sources or more advanced secondary sources.

Laws of Acquisition

In order to take the stimulus or antecedent conditions into account, as well as the possibilities of central nervous interaction, Hull's first two postulates are concerned with (1) afferent impulses essential for the appreciation of stimuli and (2) central nervous interaction. In his first postulate Hull states that sensory impulses generated in receptor organs excite nervous tissue rapidly, but the effects gradually decrease and eventually die out altogether after stimulation has ceased. The most significant concept in the postulate is that of the gradual decay of nervous excitation. *This slow decay allows for the possibility of association by contiguity.* Thus, even though thunder follows lightning, association of thunder *with* lightning is possible, since the nervous excitations generated by the lightning persist for some time and thereby allow it to be experienced contiguously with the subsequent thunder. In conditioning, much the same process occurs. The excitations from CS persist long enough to overlap with those generated by US.

The second postulate, which deals with afferent neural interaction, states that sensory impulses occurring together in the nervous system interact and, in the process of interacting, modify each other. The manner in which impulses are modified varies with any given set of impulses, whether they occur in simple pairs or in combinations. The degree to which one impulse influences another depends on the strength of the first.

The importance of this postulate lies in the fact that it allows for the synthesizing effects of cortical processes; thus it permits Hull to deal not only with *patterns* of stimuli but also to account for the configurational effects to which the Gestalt psychologists devoted so much attention. For example, if one fixates a small yellow square against a gray background, the resulting color experience is quite different from the sensation resulting when a yellow square is fixated against a blue background. More generally, combinations of stimuli are continually bombarding our receptors, but the effects are not isolated in our nervous system. Rather, each stimulus influences every other stimulus because of the resulting neural interaction.

Hull next relates his system to needs by arguing that the general function of effector systems is that of bringing about need satiation. However, because environmental conditions vary a great deal, no one response can always be guaranteed to bring about needed relief. Consequently, Hull postulates that organisms are capable of demonstrating "hierarchies of response" in problem situations, thus ensuring a range of varied activities that have a high probability of successfully reducing needs. This process might be exemplified by the remarkable behavior of the excised fetal guinea pig described by Carmichael (1946). If the animal (which is kept alive in a warm saline solution) is stimulated by having its cheek touched with a horsehair, it will make avoidance movements with the entire head region. If the stimulus persists, the animal will make brushing movements with its paws, and finally under continuing stimulation will swim away with its attached placenta. Here, indeed, is a strikingly adaptive hierarchy of responses.

Thus far we have been examining the groundwork for what may be regarded as the most basic postulate in Hull's system, Postulate 4. We shall quote the postulate as originally given, followed by a simplified statement.

Postulate 4

Whenever an effector activity $(r \rightarrow R)$ and a receptor activity $(S \rightarrow s)$ occur in close temporal contiguity $(_s C_r)$ and this $_s C_r$ is closely associated with the diminution of a need (G) or with a stimulus which has been closely and consistently associated with the diminution of a need $(\dot{G})$, there will result an increment to a tendency $(\Delta_s H_R)$ for that afferent impulse on later occasions to evoke that reaction. The increments from successive reinforcements summate in a manner which yields a combined habit strength $(_s H_R)$ which is a simple positive growth function of the number of reinforcements (N). The upper limit (m) of this curve of learning is the product of (1) a positive growth function of the magnitude of need reduction which is involved in primary, or which is associated with secondary reinforcement; (2) a negative function of the delay (t) in reinforcement;

and (3) (a) a negative growth function of the degree of asynchronism (t') of S and R when both are of brief duration, or (b), in case the action of S is prolonged so as to overlap the beginning of R, a negative growth function of the duration (t'') of the continuous action of S on the receptor when R begins. (Hull, 1943, p. 178)

Let us break this postulate into its two component parts, considering first the aspect that deals with temporal contiguity as an important condition of learning and second, the part concerned with the role of reinforcement. In simplified form the first part of Postulate 4 states that habit—or, more precisely, habit strength—depends on close temporal contiguity of the receptor and effector activities involved. Hull is patterning this aspect of his postulate on the familiar conditioning experiment where CS (bell) must be closely associated with UR (salivation to food) before conditioning can occur. However, it must be emphasized that although contiguity is a necessary condition for learning, it is not a sufficient condition. Consequently, we must next consider the critical role of reinforcement contained in the statement of the postulate.

Hull distinguishes between primary and secondary reinforcement. Primary reinforcement, as Hull originally formulated the concept, is a process of need reduction.[5] The animal that jumps from a charged grid into a "safe" area as one of a number of possible reactions to the shock, quickly establishes the habit of jumping and no longer exhibits the variety of other responses typical in such situations, such as urinating, biting the bars, and trying to climb the walls. The jumping reaction is reinforced because it is closely followed by need reduction—the need in this case being to avoid the injurious effect of the shock. Similarly, food in Pavlov's conditioning experiment is a primary reinforcer because it reduces the animal's need for food.

Secondary reinforcement results when stimuli closely associated with primary reinforcement become effective reinforcers in their own right through learning. The infant, for example, stops crying when it is fed. But because the mother typically picks up the infant and cuddles it during the process of feeding, the cuddling stimuli become associated with the primary reinforcement (food); and after a number of such experiences the infant will stop crying upon being picked up. The cuddling, then, may be said to have become a secondary reinforcer.

Turning to the aspect of the postulate that deals with habit strength, Hull specifies the manner in which summation of increments of habit strength depends upon repetitions of reinforcement. In addition, three variables that limit habit strength are stated. Figure 9-2, taken from Hull (1943, p. 116), shows a theoretical representation of habit strength as a function of successive reinforcements. The curve is a typically negatively accelerated learning curve in which gains are initially high and gradually diminish with successive reinforcements. A word of explanation is in order with regard to the steplike pattern of the curve; this pattern is attributed to the fact that each reinforcement is a unit and is therefore theoretically indivisible in its effect on learning.

---

[5]Hull subsequently changed his mind and defined primary reinforcement as drive-*stimulus* reduction. See "Major Revisions of Hull's Theory" later in this chapter.

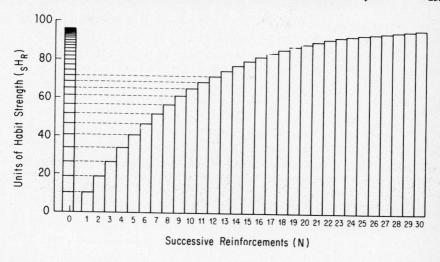

FIGURE 9-2.   A diagrammatic representation of habit strength as a function of successive reinforcements. (From Clark L. Hull, Principles of Behavior. Copyright, 1943, D. Appleton-Century Co. Inc. By permission of Appleton-Century-Crofts, Inc.)

The limit of habit strength depends upon (1) the magnitude of need reduction, (2) the delay between response and reinforcement, and (3) the time interval between the conditioned stimulus and the response. The variable of magnitude of need reduction theoretically operates as follows: The greater the quantity and the higher the quality of reinforcement, the higher the upper limit of the curve of habit strength.[6] Delay in reinforcement is negatively correlated with habit strength, which means that the longer the reinforcement is delayed, the weaker its effect.

The problem of temporal patterning in conditioning is complex and has already been discussed in Chapter 8 in connection with Pavlov's experiments. The reader may refer to Chapter 8, particularly Figure 8-5, for a discussion of temporal factors in conditioning.

With this discussion of the role of contiguity, primary and secondary reinforcement, and temporal patterns in conditioning, we have come to the core of Hull's theory: *The basic condition under which learning takes place is contiguity of stimuli and responses under conditions of reinforcement.* Because of its emphasis on reinforcement, Hull's has been called a "need reduction" theory, in contrast to Guthrie's contiguity theory and Tolman's purposive behaviorism, which is known as a cognitive theory and is discussed next in this chapter.

The student should also compare Hull's reinforcement principle to Thorndike's Law of Effect (Chapter 8) and to Carr's theory of adaptive learning (Chapter 8). Hull, in fact, has attempted to integrate the Law of Effect into Pavlovian conditioning. Finally, we would like to point out that although Hull's is a behavioristic theory, his use of the intervening variable of reinforcement represents a departure

---

[6]See also discussion at the end of this chapter.

from a strict behavioristically oriented S-R psychology, which employs only the principles of frequency and recency to account for learning. J. B. Watson surely would have objected to the O factor of reinforcement on the same grounds that he objected to consciousness, sets, motives, and other "unobservables."

Drives

Hull relates drives to learning by stating that drives activate effective habit strength into "reaction potentiality" ($_sE_R$). In essence, this means that learned habits are evoked only in the presence of drives, or that drive regulates performance. In Hull's terms, the relevant postulates are stated as follows:

Postulate 6

   Associated with every drive (D) is a characteristic drive stimulus (S_D) whose intensity is an increasing monotonic function of the drive in question. (Hull, 1943, p. 253)

Postulate 7

   Any effective habit strength ($_s\bar{H}_R$) is sensitized into reaction potentiality ($_sE_R$) by all primary drives active within an organism at a given time, the magnitude of this potentiality being a product obtained by multiplying an increasing function of H by an increasing function of D. (Hull, 1943, p. 253)

Since the original wording of Postulates 6 and 7 is relatively simple, we need only emphasize that the magnitude of reaction potential is a multiplicative function of drive and habit strength. Therefore if drive is zero, reaction potential will be zero. If drive is maximum, reaction potential will be high—how high depending, of course, on habit strength. Finally, we might note that because drives carry characteristic stimulus patterns (Postulate 6), the animal can learn to discriminate on the basis of drives.

Let us illustrate the factors given in Postulates 6 and 7 by means of simple examples. A rat that has been conditioned to press a bar to obtain a pellet of food will be stimulated to respond by a high level of drive, whereas the satiated animal will give few responses irrespective of how well it may have learned the bar-pressing habit. If the learning situation demands discrimination, as is true in the case of a maze in which the animal when hungry must turn right for food and when thirsty must turn left for water, then the stimuli associated with these visceral drives will evoke the proper response in proportion to the strength of the drives and the degree of effective habit strength.

Transfer

Conditioning theorists prefer to speak of generalization rather than transfer. It will be recalled that the concept of generalization comes from the classical Pavlovian conditioning experiment in which the animal, after having been conditioned to respond to a certain stimulus, will respond to similar stimuli. In general, the greater the similarity between the stimuli, the greater the magnitude of the generalized response; and the more dissimilar the stimuli, the weaker the response. Consequently, there is a *gradient* of generalization that is directly related to the degree of similarity between CS and the generalization stimulus. In all essential respects, Hull's position on transfer is the same as Pavlov's.

The Problems of Inhibition, Extinction, and Forgetting

Thus far we have discussed the critical role of contiguity and reinforcement in habit strength. However, common experience tells us that the presence of adequate habit strength and drive is sometimes insufficient to assure an effective reaction. There are occasions when inhibition may prevent the appearance of an otherwise readily evoked response. If, for example, an animal has been responding for a long period of time in a conditioning experiment, fatigue will set in. In and of itself fatigue will generate a form of inhibition that Hull calls *reactive inhibition,* and the animal will cease to respond. If an arbitrary stimulus is presented at the same time that the response is gradually diminishing because of fatigue, *conditioned inhibition* will develop, and the associated stimulus will become capable of inhibiting the response. Because of the ever-present factor of variability in behavior, Hull also postulates that inhibitory potentials oscillate from instant to instant. The relevant postulates follow:

Postulate 8

Whenever a reaction (R) is evoked in an organism there is created as a result a primary negative drive (D); (a) this has an innate capacity (I_R) to inhibit the reaction potentiality $(_sE_R)$ to that response; (b) the amount of inhibition (I_R) generated by a sequence of reaction evocations is a simple linear increasing function of the number of evocations (n); and (c) it is a positively accelerated increasing function of the work (W) involved in the execution of the response; (d) reactive inhibition (I_R) spontaneously dissipates as a simple negative growth function of time (t'''). (Hull, 1943, p. 300)

Postulate 9

Stimuli (S) closely associated with the cessation of a response (R) (a) become conditioned to the inhibition (I_R) associated with the evocation of that response thereby generating conditioned inhibition; (b) conditioned inhibitions $(_sI_R)$ summate physiologically with reactive inhibition (I_R) against the reaction potentiality to a given response as positive habit tendencies summate with each other. (Hull, 1943, p. 300)

Postulate 10

Associated with every reaction potential $(_sE_R)$ there exists an inhibitory potentiality $(_sO_R)$ which oscillates in amount from instant to instant according to the normal "law" of chance, and whose range, maximum, and minimum, are constant. The amount of this inhibitory potentiality associated with the several habits of a given organism at a particular instant is uncorrelated, and the amount of diminution in $_s\bar{E}_R$ from the action of $_sO_R$ is limited only by the amount of $_s\bar{E}_R$ at the time available. (Hull, 1943, p. 319)

In addition to what has already been said in the introductiom to Postulates 8 and 9, it should be noted that in Postulate 8(d) reactive inhibition spontaneously dissipates with time after the cessation of practice. A simple example may be found in the case of spontaneous recovery in conditioning experiments. In such cases the animal is extinguished by repeated nonreinforcement but recovers following a rest period. It should also be emphasized that conditioned inhibition does *not* spontaneously dissipate with time. Conditioned inhibition is *learned* inhibition, and, according to Hull, time per se has no effect on learned reactions. Only unreinforced repetition of conditioned reactions (including conditioned inhibition) could cause a diminution in response. Finally, it should be noted that according to Postulate 9, reactive and conditioned inhibition are additive in their effects in diminishing reaction potential.

Postulate 10, as previously pointed out, deals with the oscillation of reaction potential. Hull believes there is evidence to show that these variations in inhibition take place according to the laws of chance and, when plotted, follow the normal probability curve. Finally, the second sentence in the postulate contains the hypothesis that two or more inhibitory potentials existing within the individual at the same time are not correlated, and the extent of the effect of inhibitory potentials is limited only by the amount of effective reaction potential available at the time.

Hull points to two important implications of the oscillation principle. First, he believes that it explains the frequently observed phenomenon that stimuli may elicit reactions that have never been conditioned to them. More specifically, such variable reactions occur because the oscillation process results in variations in the intensity of muscular contractions, thus making every coordinated act slightly different from every other. Second, oscillation implies that behavior can never be predicted with certainty at any given point in time. However, prediction is nevertheless possible since oscillation follows the law of chance. As a result, predictions can be made in terms of the central tendency of behavior; of course, this procedure involves collecting data from a large number of observations.

Hull has no postulate dealing directly with either extinction or forgetting. However, Postulate 4 deals with the problem of extinction in the sense that it *implies* that unreinforced repetitions of CS will lead to the disappearance of the conditioned response. In such cases extinction will follow a negative growth function. Data and curves are presented by Hull both from animal and human experiments demonstrating the occurrence of extinction under conditions of unreinforced repetition. However, it is important to recognize that in such cases the cause of extinction is *the building up of conditioned and reactive inhibition*. In other words, extinction results not from unreinforced repetition but from inhibitory effects.

Hull presumes forgetting to be the result of a decay function. This is implied by one of Hull's corollaries, which states: "*In the case of rote series learned by massed practice, reminiscence will rise at first with a negative acceleration, which will presently be replaced by a fall*" (1943, p. 296). Figure 9-3 shows a hypothetical retention curve for the rote learning of nonsense syllables. The brief rise in the curve following the cessation of practice is the result of reminiscence. The reminiscence effect is most marked, as Hull implies in the corollary quoted above, when practice is massed, presumably because of the more rapid buildup of inhibition under such

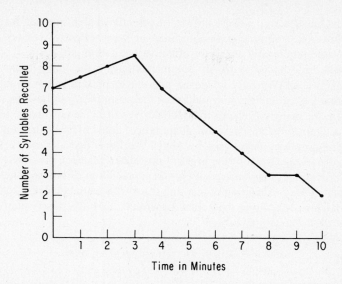

FIGURE 9-3. Reminiscence. The subject practices until he or she can repeat seven syllables correctly. Reminiscence is shown by the initial rise in the curve without further practice.

conditions. A further study of the curve shows that the material undergoes a gradual decay with time, following the appearance of reminiscence.

Reaction Thresholds and Response Evocation

The final concept we wish to introduce from Hull's 1943 system is that of the reaction threshold $(_s\bar{E}_R)$. It will be remembered that Hull's system of intervening variables is anchored to antecedent conditions, such as receptor stimulation and other general conditions essential for learning. However, in Hull's own words, "The pivotal theoretical construct of the present system (around which the various factors described in the postulates are oriented) is that of the effective reaction potential $(_s\bar{E}_R)$" (1943, p. 342). In his final six postulates, Hull attempts to anchor effective reaction potential to certain variables not yet considered which influence responses. At the same time several basic problems of measurement are considered.

The two most important variables that govern the evocation of responses are thresholds and incompatible responses. Other things being equal, if the effective reaction potential is above threshold, then a response will appear. In the case of incompatible responses, the response whose reaction potential is greatest will be the response evoked.

Several of Hull's postulates deal with quantitative problems involved in the measurement of responses. Briefly, Hull advocates probability of response, latency, and resistance to experimental extinction as measures of effective reaction potential. Clearly, the stronger the habit, the greater the probability of response, whereas short latency and high resistance to extinction indicate a high degree of effective reaction potential, and indirectly, a high degree of effective habit strength $(_s\bar{H}_R)$. Long latency and low resistance to extinction indicate weak effective reaction potential and at the same time a low degree of effective habit strength.

We have now traced in highly summarized form the major assumptions of Hull's 1943 system. We have made no attempt to present much of the detailed reasoning that lies behind the formulation of the postulates, nor have we attempted to summarize the many corollaries that Hull derives from the postulates. Finally, we have not attempted to discuss the quantitative units of measurement and the mathematical constants developed by Hull. We hope that despite these gaps a sufficiently detailed account of the primary postulates has been presented to convey the flavor of Hull's system and to give some appreciation of his hypotheticodeductive approach to the formulation of learning theory. In a final glance at the postulate system as a whole, the major theoretical constructs in Hull's theory may be related in terms of the following equation:[7]

$$_s\dot{\bar{E}}_R = {_s\bar{H}_R} \times D - (I_R + {_sI_R}) - {_sO_R}$$

where $_s\dot{\bar{E}}_R$ represents the momentary effective reaction potential or Hull's observable measure of learning, $_s\bar{H}_R$ is habit strength, D is drive, I_R is the amount of reactive inhibition, $_sI_R$ is the amount of conditioned inhibition, and $_sO_R$ is oscillation potential associated with $_s\bar{H}_R$.

The formula may be interpreted as follows: The momentary effective reaction potential (in short, performance) depends first upon effective habit strength (learning) multiplied by drive. Thus, if *either* effective habit strength *or* drive is zero, no response can be evoked. Second, the product of effective habit strength and drive is diminished by the addition of two antagonistic factors, reactive and conditioned inhibition. The relationship is such that if either is zero or very weak in magnitude, then reaction potential is high. Since $I_R + {_sI_R}$ is *subtracted* from $_s\bar{H}_R \times D,$ if either reactive or conditioned inhibition is present, effective reaction potential will be adversely affected. Finally, the influence of the oscillatory potential $(_sO_R)$ is subtractive in its effect. Consequently, as oscillation decreases, effective reaction potential increases, and vice versa.

Major Revisions of Hull's Theory

Hull's revisions took several forms. In some cases postulates were dropped, and in other cases they were revised. Several new postulates were substituted for those dropped. Without attempting to go into detail, we shall indicate the direction that the major changes took.

First, it will be recalled that habit strength $(_s\bar{H}_R)$ increases as a function of reinforcement. The magnitude of the increase depends, in turn, upon the degree of

---

[7]We are indebted to B. B. Murdock, Jr., for this formulation.

need reduction and the temporal factors involved (see Postulate 4). In the 1952 system these factors are no longer held to influence habit strength. Rather, only the number of reinforced contiguous repetitions of S-R relationships influences habit strength.

The second major revision involves increased emphasis upon secondary reinforcements, along with a closely related change in attitude toward the essential factor in reinforcement. It will be recalled that Hull emphasized primary reinforcement as the critical condition in habit formation in the 1943 system and, further, defined primary reinforcement as need reduction. In the 1952 edition *drive-stimulus reduction* is the essential factor in reinforcement. To clarify the point, let us consider the case of a hungry animal. It needs food, and its restless behavior indicates the operation of a drive for food. Accompanying the drive process are stimuli arising from the viscera, such as hunger pangs, which Hull refers to as "drive stimuli." Now the critical factor in reinforcement may be considered to be either the reduction of the hunger drive, in the sense of diminution of the need for food, or the reduction of the drive stimuli themselves. It is the latter process that the 1952 system held to be crucial. Under most conditions, secondary reinforcement is more effective in reducing drive stimuli than primary needs; consequently, secondary reinforcement becomes of much greater importance in the revised system.

Hull also emphasized two factors associated with $_s\bar{E}_R$, or the response tendency. These were: V, or the stimulus-intensity dynamism, and K, or incentive reinforcement. In the case of stimulus-intensity dynamism, it is assumed that for any given level of habit strength, or $_s\bar{H}_R$, the greater the stimulus intensity, the greater the reaction potential, or $_s\bar{E}_R$. In the form of an equation:

$$_s\dot{\bar{E}}_R = V \times {_s\bar{H}_R}$$

Similarly, for any given level of habit strength, the greater the magnitude of the reinforcement, or K, the greater the reaction potential. In the form of an equation,

$$_s\dot{\bar{E}}_R = K \times {_s\bar{H}_R}$$

If we introduce these new variables into the basic equation for performance in a learning situation, then,

$$_s\dot{\bar{E}}_R = {_s\bar{H}_R} \times D \times V \times K - (I_R + {_sI_R}) - {_sO_R}$$

By introducing incentive motivation into his system, Hull allowed for the empirical finding that incentives regulate performance and, incidentally, brought his system closer to Lewin's field theory and other systems that emphasize incentives as arousers of drive and regulators of behavior.

Finally, we should like to quote Postulate 17, the last stated by Hull is his 1952 system:

Postulate 17

The "constant" numerical values appearing in equations representing primary molar behavioral laws vary from species to species, from individual to individual, and from some physiological states to others in the same individual at different times, all quite apart from the factor of behavioral oscillation ($_sO_R$). (1952, p. 13)

Clearly, by including a special postulate devoted to individual differences, Hull is giving formal recognition to an age-old problem in psychology. Individuals differ in respect to intelligence, learning ability, motivation, and so forth; and all theories of learning must take such individual differences into account. In practice, Hull and his associates had already done this for the portions of the 1943 system for which quantitative constants had been developed. This was accomplished by repeated measurements on large groups of animal or human subjects in order to eliminate individual variations statistically.

With regard to extensions or applications of the system into areas other than simple learning situations, the major portion of *A Behavior System* is devoted to this task. It is impossible in this chapter to do more than broadly indicate the fields involved.

First, Hull extended his theory into the area of discrimination learning. He discusses both generalization of stimulus qualities and stimulus intensities and concludes that the primary factor underlying discrimination learning of either type is differential reinforcement. In accounting for discrimination learning in this manner, Hull follows classical conditioning theory, for Pavlov found that by selective reinforcement, differential conditioned responses could be established after generalization had occurred.

Second, Hull extends the system into the area of maze learning. In dealing with this favorite topic of the animal psychologist, Hull reintroduces one of his early concepts, that of the *goal gradient*. The goal-gradient hypothesis holds that learning will be more effective the closer the animal gets to the goal. Therefore, the hypothesis predicts that, other things being equal, the animal will eliminate blind alleys in reverse order. Similarly, long blind alleys are eliminated faster than short ones, and short mazes are learned more readily than long mazes. Hull believes that the empirical evidence collected by himself and others supports the validity of the goal-gradient hypothesis (1952, p. 304). Moreover, he argues that the principle of experimental extinction may be applied to maze learning, although—because of the complexity of factors operating concurrently in the maze situation—it is difficult to isolate experimentally.

Third, Hull seeks to extend his theory into the area of problem solving, a traditional stronghold of the Gestalt psychologists. Laying great stress on the stick-and-banana problem as a model, Hull believes that behavioral oscillation coupled with stimulus-and-response generalization can account for what the Gestalt school calls insight learning. Insightful behavior, according to Hull, is not as sudden as it appears to be but occurs only after various stages of subgoals have been mastered through repetitive reinforcement. Birch's experiment with apes is cited in support of

Hull's position. It will be recalled that, in Birch's study, apes who had no previous experience with sticks were unable to solve the stick-and-banana problem.[8]

Hull's final extension of his system is in the area of values. After reviewing a number of philosophical approaches to the problem, Hull outlines his suggestions for a natural-science approach to the theory of values in terms of learning theory, but we shall make no attempt to summarize his tentative conclusions in this highly complex area.

Summary and Evaluation

The central concept in Hull's system remains reinforcement. Around this basic concept he erected a tightly knit logical structure supplemented by empirical studies. The system is elaborated in the form of postulates, theorems, and corollaries. Although it was originally based on conditioning principles, Hull was confident that his system could be broadened sufficiently to include such complex processes as problem solving, social behavior, and forms of learning other than conditioning. He lived only long enough to see part of his ambition realized; and it is, of course, a highly controversial matter whether the extensions contained in *A Behavior System* will prove to be significant contributions to psychological theory.

More generally, the validity of Hull's entire system has been a controversial issue in the professional literature for several decades.[9] To attempt any final evaluation of Hull's theory would, of course, be premature, but it is generally agreed that his attempt to formulate precise quantitative laws of learning represents a significant step forward over the older schools. The latter were largely programmatic in the sense that they attempted to define the field of psychology and specify the general approach to the study of all psychological processes. Hull, on the other hand, sought to formulate a precise, self-correcting system within a limited field—a system capable of evolution into broader and broader areas. As Hilgard and Bower (1966, p. 185) have pointed out, a theory formulated in a highly precise postulate form is more vulnerable to attack than theories whose aims are broad and whose purpose is largely programmatic.

Perhaps the two most controversial aspects of Hullian theory are (1) the assumption that drive reduction is the basic process in learning and (2) the generality of his parameters, many of which are founded on the basis of limited sets of data derived from animal experiments. In regard to the problem of generality, a theory that seeks to discover principles applicable to the entire range of mammalian behavior ought to utilize a wide range of representative species in establishing its constants, whereas much of Hull's system is based on experimental findings involving white rats.

In regard to drive reduction, as we pointed out earlier, the current trend in

---

[8]See "Gestalt Psychology and Learning Theory" in Chapter 8.
[9]For a detailed criticism, see Hilgard (1956) and Koch (1954).

learning theory is away from drive reduction and toward contiguity. However, even his severest critics admit that Hull's Herculean effort to formulate a deductive theory of learning represents a brilliant achievement irrespective of what the final outcome may be with respect to the particulars within the system. As we shall see, Hull's theory had a profound influence on a generation of contemporary learning theorists and many who followed.

EXTENSIONS OF HULL'S SYSTEM

A large number of psychologists who became prominent in their own right were associated with Hull as students or as colleagues in the Department of Psychology at Yale University during Hull's long and distinguished career at that institution. His students and professional associates all felt the impact of Hull's research and theorizing. It is beyond the scope of this volume to attempt any inclusive summary of Hull's influence in derivative or competitive systems, but we shall summarize the work of two theorists, Kenneth W. Spence (1907–1967), and Neal E. Miller (b. 1909), both of whom became widely influential in the area of learning. Spence was a student and later an associate of Hull's who subsequently took academic positions at the University of Iowa and at Texas. Miller, holder of numerous academic appointments, most recently at Rockefeller University, was influenced by Hull as a colleague but unlike Spence did not remain within the confines of classical conditioning theory. His wide range of experimental and theoretical works spans the areas of drive acquisition, conflict, reinforcement, the operant conditioning of autonomic responses, and the application of S-R theory to personality development.

Spence's S-R Reinforcement Theory

While Spence accepts the validity of the Hullian stimulus response analysis of learning within the larger framework of a conditioning model, he differs with his former teacher and associate both on general theoretical issues and on the interpretation of empirical findings. In his *Behavior Theory and Conditioning* (1956, pp. 54–59) he brings his points of disagreement with Hull to the foreground.

First, Spence believes that Hull's attempt to utilize the hypotheticodeductive method is an erroneous conception of the method and gives a misleading impression of the state of development of psychology as a science. He argues that Hull's is, in reality, an intervening variable system and not a hypotheticodeductive system. Second, Spence does not believe that it is useful to define intervening variables in neurophysiological terms. Third, unlike Hull, Spence did not attempt to specify the nature of reinforcement, believing that it is nonproductive to attempt to explain reinforcement by translating it into neurophysiological concepts. Finally, Spence criticizes Hull for his willingness to build an elaborate system on the basis of a minimal set of empirical data. He prefers instead to move cautiously in developing a limited theory based on a step-by-step elaboration of hypotheses which are followed by experimental verification, rejection, or modification.

Turning to Spence's positive contributions to basic Hullian theory, we may begin by introducing the concept of the fractional anticipatory goal response, or r_g, first developed by Hull but elaborated into a major construct in conditioning theory by Spence and his associates. The fractional anticipatory goal response is an antedating response—a response that occurs earlier in a sequence of events than it had originally occurred, particularly a response that occurs prior to the appearance of the stimulus that originally evoked it. To begin with a very simple example of an antedating response, we may consider the case of an animal learning a maze, who upon arriving at a certain point in the entering arm of a Y segment (let us assume the first point where the two arms diverge), begins to bend toward the right. But as the learning progresses, the animal begins to veer right—hugging the wall immediately upon entering the Y. The animal is now showing an antedating, or anticipatory, response. In terms of a cognitive theory, the subject is showing expectancy. Indeed, the concept of the antedating response is the analogue of expectancy in cognitive theories of learning. Similarly, the fractional anticipatory goal response is a reaction that occurs progressively earlier in a response chain during the acquisition of a conditioned response.

In his last book, *A Behavior System,* Hull (1952) referred to the complete unconditioned response, or UR, as the goal response, or R_g, and any portion of it as the fractional response, or r_g. The rat that begins chewing movements upon approaching a goal compartment is showing a fractional anticipatory response. Now, because the r_g occurs in contiguous association with proprioceptive stimuli arising from the musculature and produced by r_g, Hull argued that $r_g \rightarrow s_g$ sequences become important mediators and integrators of behavior.

Spence and his associates at the University of Iowa elaborated the concept of the fractional anticipatory goal response as an explanation of latent learning as revealed in experiments with a simple Y-type maze (Spence, Bergmann, & Lippitt, 1950). These investigations had been undertaken in an attempt to find a crucial experiment in which the hypothesis that learning occurs in the absence of reinforcement could be tested. As it turned out, "motivationless" animals refused to run the maze and "social" motivation in the form of a cage of rats at the goal end of the maze had to be provided to ensure activity on the part of the experimental subjects. During the course of the training, satiated animals were given an opportunity to experience finding water in one goal compartment and food in the other. Forced trials were employed to ensure that the animals entered both compartments the same number of times. On the first test trial, in which the animals were either hungry or thirsty, there was a significant tendency to choose the correct or appropriate side. The results of a second test trial in which the motivation was reversed again leaned in the direction of latent learning, although in this case the results were not statistically significant.

In experiments such as that just described, Spence and his associates stressed the importance of $r_g \rightarrow s_g$ sequences as integrators and organizers of behavior. Essentially, the act of reinforcement at the end of the maze produces the conditioning of fractional anticipatory goal responses to stimulus cues through the response chain. It is assumed that the sight or smell of food is mildly reinforcing even to a satiated animal. It can be further assumed that the evocation of an $r_g \rightarrow s_g$ sequence to food $(r_f \rightarrow s_f)$ is different from that evoked by water $(r_w \rightarrow s_w)$. It is also necessary to assume that when the animal arrives at a choice point in a Y or T maze, it looks to the right and left, thus making motor responses. These motor responses need not be obvious; in fact they may be so weak or tentative as to be only implicit. Because these proprioceptive responses have been associated with eating or drinking—or, in the case of latent learning experiments, with the sight and smell of food, hence with r_g's—the induction of a thirst or hunger drive leads to the appropriate fractional anticipatory goal response and, at the choice point, to movement toward food or water. Therefore, in essence, *the r_g is a special response inasmuch as it produces reinforcing effects and is capable of influencing the motivational level of the organism.*

More simply, in the typical maze experiment the animals' sight and smell of food and water antedate the behavior patterns involved in manipulating or ingesting the same objects. The sight and smell of the goal objects come to elicit antedating fractional portions of the total goal reaction, and it is these reactions that come to signify the "eatability" or "drinkability" of the objects. The association of these antedating reactions with proprioceptive stimuli at choice points is assumed to be strengthened by the presence of reinforcement. On subsequent trials the presence of drive stimuli arouses the appropriate sequence of responses, so the correct choice is made.

Closely related to the concept of the r_g is the concept of K, or incentive motivation, which was adopted by Hull largely as a result of Spence's insistence on its central importance in learning. Whereas Hull simply identified K with incentive motivation and therefore with the level of habit strength, depending upon its reinforcing value, Spence identified it with the fractional anticipatory goal response or r_g. In effect, K is the anticipated response based on $r_g \rightarrow s_g$ that the "food is near." In this sense K becomes very similar to Tolman's concept of the sign gestalt to be discussed later in this chapter.

Spence holds that the relationships between habit strength, drive, and K are additive—not multiplicative, as Hull believed. Thus, even when the level of drive is at zero or near zero (such as in a latent learning experiment), learning can occur, even though it may not be revealed in performance. The evidence to support this contention is complex and incomplete. It is reviewed by Spence in the sixth chapter of his *Behavior Theory and Conditioning* (1956). Essentially, the evidence revolves around the related questions of whether or not the degree of learning and the level of performance vary as a function of the level of drive and the nature and the amount of the reward. The problem is therefore part of the larger issue of whether or not contiguity or reinforcement is essential for learning. Spence, in disagreement with Hull, believes that these are unsettled questions and cannot be resolved by the postulation of simple multiplicative relationships between habit strength and drive for all forms of learning.

In summary, then, Spence's theory is a stimulus-response reinforcement theory based on Hullian model, but a modified reinforcement theory in which considerable emphasis is placed on $r_g \rightarrow s_g$ and K. With the introduction of r_g as essentially a cognitive anticipation of the reward, Spence included in his system an important element of cognitive theory and thus brought the two camps closer together.

Miller's Reinforcement Theory

We may illustrate the learning process according to N. E. Miller's *S-R* analysis by describing his basic and widely cited experiment on fear as an acquired drive (1948). Figure 9-4 shows the acquired-drive apparatus in which white rats were

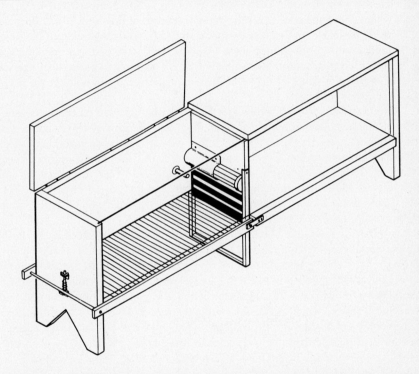

FIGURE 9-4.   Miller's apparatus for utilizing anxiety as a drive. (From Miller, N. E. Studies of fear as an acquired drive. Journal of Experimental Psychology, 1948, 38, p. 90. Copyright 1948 by the American Psychological Association. Reprinted by permission.)

used as subjects. The animals were first put in both the white and black compartments, where they could explore freely. They showed no fear of either compartment or of the grid on the floor of the white compartment. Next, Miller administered shocks to the animals who were placed singly in the white compartment. The rats were allowed to escape the pain by running into the black compartment, the experimenter meanwhile raising the door (painted with white and black stripes) by remote control. So far the experiment demonstrates only the well-known fact that animals can learn to escape a noxious stimulus. But Miller went on to demonstrate that later, without the grid being electrified, the animals being put into the white compartment showed signs of fear (urinating, defecating, crouching, and the like) and ran to the black compartment. The *stimuli* (cues) in the white compartment, consisting of the compartment plus the strong responses made by the animal itself, which also serve as cues, had become associated with the *response* of running to the black compartment as a result of the fear *drive*. The *reinforcement* in this case was the reduction of the fear drive.

To demonstrate that the acquired fear of the white box could serve as a drive in itself to motivate new learning, Miller arranged the experimental situation in such a way that the animals could only escape from the white compartment by turning a small wheel above the door. This the animals learned to do—not, it will be recalled, in response to shock, but to fear of shock. Indeed, Miller was able to demonstrate that a lever could be substituted for a wheel as the device opening the door leading to the black compartment. The animals quickly learned to extinguish the wheel-turning response in favor of the lever-pushing response, again without the necessity of additional shocks.

This experiment with white rats suggests that similar mechanisms are also operative in the course of human development. Fear, a primary reaction to a noxious or painful situation, produces responses that we call emotional reactions, which, in turn, through learning can serve as cues that guide or control behavior in subsequent situations. Phobias, anxieties, and other ''irrational'' fear responses in conflict situations in adults may thus develop through learning during childhood. We call such fears and anxieties irrational only because we have not observed their development in the individual's childhood.

Similarly, if we did not know that the rats had been shocked in the white compartment, their behavior would seem irrational. Moreover, it should be obvious that such fears can be eliminated only by repeating the original situation (in which the organism was induced to make the fear response) and by withholding reinforcement. Thus, if the rat is placed in the white compartment often enough without receiving a shock, it will gradually extinguish its fear responses and running reaction. Verbal psychotherapy, by analogy, is the expression of anxieties in the presence of a permissive therapist who helps to bring about extinction by nonreinforcement— reinforcement in this case being verbal statements or criticisms from the patient's friends and family that strengthen his or her fear reactions.

Miller has also adopted S-R theory in an analysis of conflict situations (1959). The theoretical foundation involves five basic assumptions. First, it is assumed that the tendency to approach a goal increases as the distance to the goal decreases. Second, the tendency to avoid a negative stimulus becomes stronger with decreasing distance between the organism and the stimulus. Third, it is assumed that the gradient for avoidance or negative stimuli is steeper than for approach or positive stimuli. Fourth, increase in drive increases the level of gradients of either approach or withdrawal. Fifth, if two response tendencies are in competition, the stronger will occur in behavior.

Figure 9-5, 9-6, and 9-7 show theoretical representations of several types of conflict analyzed according to gradients of approach and avoidance and the strength of the tendency operating in the organism at any given time. A number of empirical

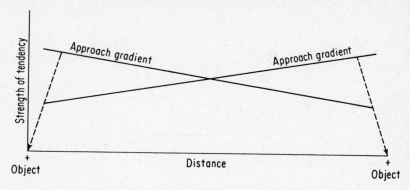

FIGURE 9-5.   A diagrammatic representation of the approach-approach gradient. As either positive object is approached, the gradient of approach becomes steeper.

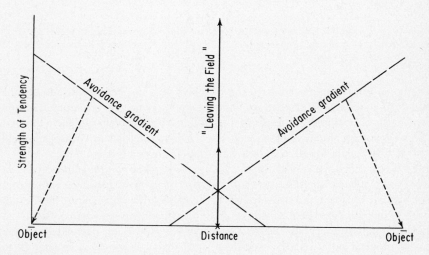

FIGURE 9-6.   A diagrammatic representation of an avoidance-avoidance gradient. As either object is approached, the gradient of avoidance becomes steeper. The gradient is least steep at maximum distance from the two negative goals. The arrow labeled "leaving the field" indicates a tendency for the subject to resolve such conflicts by escaping the situation.

studies by Miller and others (summarized by Miller, 1959) show that this type of analysis is a valid extension of the drive aspects of S-R learning theory into the area of conflict and personality.

Dollard and Miller (1950) have elaborated their extension of Hullian theory into an entire system of personality development and psychotherapy. In doing so, they follow the tradition set by Pavlov, Guthrie, and Skinner, who also attempt to utilize the basic principles of conditioning theory to account for the infinite complexities of behavior found in life outside the laboratory. The validity of such efforts to extend and generalize basic learning theory has been and remains a controversial

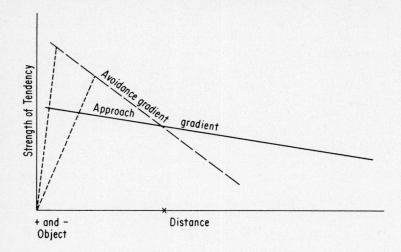

FIGURE 9-7. Approach-avoidance gradients. As the individual approaches an object with both positive and negative qualities, the avoidance gradient becomes steeper and steeper eventually to overcome the approach tendency.

issue among both learning theorists and psychologists in general. Essentially the conflict lies in the fact that physiology and biological science have a strong tradition of explaining the complex in terms of the simple or elementary. In fact, this has been one important tradition of science since it first emerged in Greek empirical philosophy, although not all scientists subscribe to elementarism.

It has also been traditional for psychology to explain complex phenomena in terms of more elementary processes from the days of the British empiricists (except for John Stuart Mill) and the structuralists to the present time (except for the Gestalt and other phenomenological schools). But the opponents of such systems of explanation either reject the *method* outright—as do those persuaded of the phenomenological point of view—or they argue that it is too soon to attempt to generalize from the laboratory to life. Spence is representative of the latter group, Miller of the former. Whatever the merits of the issue, we doubt that the critics will have their way. The desire to make psychology relevant to real human problems is too strong to be overcome by scientific caution. Few psychologists would disagree that at *some* stage of the development of psychology such an attempt should be made.

The Instrumental Learning of Autonomic Responses

In recent years Miller has turned his attention from theoretical issues in the area of learning to a series of investigations of central motivational processes in the brain utilizing electrode implantation techniques and to the possibility of operant conditioning of autonomic responses. We shall be concerned with Miller's motivational studies in Chapter 14. Here we shall summarize evidence for the dramatic discovery that autonomic or visceral processes can be instrumentally conditioned. Pavlov was, of course, the first investigator to utilize an autonomic or visceral process—salivation—in conditioning. However, conditioned salivation as Pavlov studied it is a classical or type-S conditioned response. Miller's research, by contrast, involves operant models. Let us illustrate the techniques involved by presenting two examples from recent research by Miller and his associates.

In an experiment (Miller & DiCara, 1968) designed to test the hypothesis that heart rate can be instrumentally conditioned utilizing reinforcement in the form of electrical stimulation of the medial forebrain (''pleasure centers''), twenty-four albino rats were prepared with bilaterally implanted electrodes, at least one of which was subsequently proved to be effective as a reward upon mild electrical stimulation. This effectiveness was shown by shaping the animals' behavior in a bar-pressing situation so that each bar-press response was rewarded by a mild shock to the forebrain. The experimental animals all displayed high rates of bar pressing for a forebrain reward, indicating that the reward was effective.

In the second phase of the experiment, the animals' skeletal muscles were completely paralyzed by doses of d-tubo-curarine chloride (curare) in order to prevent the possibility that fluctuations in heart rate might be mediated by the skeletal muscles, in the animals' moving about, struggling, and so on. It was also necessary to respirate the animals artificially, since the diaphragm and intercostal muscles are affected by curare.

When each animal's condition had stabilized, it was assigned to a fast- or slow-rate reward group by chance. If the animal was in a fast-reward group, fluctuations in heart rate above normal or average were rewarded, and if in a slow-rate reward group, slower than normal rates were rewarded. Eleven out of twelve rats rewarded for fast-rate fluctuations showed significant increases in rate during the training series, and ten out of eleven rewarded for slow rate showed significant decreases. The results of this phase of the experiment are shown graphically in Figure 9-8.

It is obvious that during the 90-minute training session, conditioning occurred, with progressively faster or slower rates being established by reward. This result is clearly operant or instrumental conditioning, since no arbitrary stimulus was employed and the reinforcement was contingent upon the animal's performance.

Miller and his associates not only have demonstrated the possibility of the operant conditioning of visceral responses such as heart rate, rate of intestinal contraction and relaxation, and urine output; they also have presented evidence that animals can respond *differentially* to different stimuli. For example, in a third phase of the experiment just summarized, the animals were conditioned to respond differentially (that is, with faster or slower rates) depending on the presence or absence of a tone.

In a subsequent experiment, Miller and DiCara (1968) showed that animals conditioned to modify vasomotor responses could be trained to respond differentially in distinct organ systems to an appropriate signal.

First the animal subjects had electrodes implanted in the forebrain and were conditioned to respond with vasodilatation or vasoconstriction in the ears as meas-

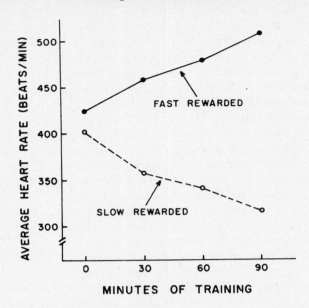

FIGURE 9-8.   Instrumental learning by the heart in groups rewarded for fast or slow rates. Each data point represents average of beats per minute during 5 minutes. (From Miller, N. E., and DiCara, L. V. Instrumental learning of heart rate changes in curarized cats. Journal of Comparative and Physiological Psychology, 1967, 63, p. 14. Copyright 1967 by the American Psychological Association. Reprinted by permission.)

ured by a sensitive electronic plethysmograph. The procedure was essentially the same as in the heart rate experiment—some animals being rewarded for vasodilatation and others for vasoconstriction. Again, the animals' skeletal muscles were completely paralyzed with curare to prevent artificial vasomotor responses from voluntary movements.

In the crucial phase of the experiment, half of the animals were rewarded for relatively greater vasodilatation of the right ear and the other half for relatively greater dilatation of the left ear. It was then possible to condition vasodilatation to the presence or absence of a 1000-Hz tone, the subject obtaining a reward for making the proper response—a differential dilatation—only during periods when the tone was on. The results are shown in Figure 9-9, with an explanation in the accompanying legend.

It is too early to attempt to assess the overall theoretical and practical significance of results such as these. Despite early confirmation of visceral learning from several laboratories, more recent research by Miller and others has failed to replicate the early findings on curarized animals. They have been repeated with success, however, with non-paralyzed animals, including rats, baboons, and monkeys. Intensive research by Miller and others directed toward improving techniques and controlling the possible effects of the skeletal muscles on visceral learning

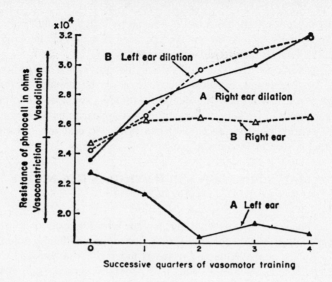

FIGURE 9-9. Learning a difference between the vasomotor responses of the two ears. Group A was rewarded for relatively more dilatation of the right ear. Group B was rewarded for relatively more dilatation of the left ear. (From DiCara, L. V., and Miller, N. E., Science, Vol. 159, pp. 1485–1486, Fig. 1, 29 March 1968. Copyright 1968 by the American Association for the Advancement of Science.)

continues. A general review of the area of visceral learning and biofeedback may be found in a review by Miller in the 1978 *Annual Review of Psychology*.

Biofeedback

The work of Miller and his associates and research on the conditioning of brain waves (Kamiya, 1968; Morrell, 1959) may be considered instances of *biofeedback*. Biofeedback refers to changes in the functioning of an organism or a physiological system as a result of receiving information from an outside source. For example, the alpha wave of the electroencephalogram, or EEG, can be conditioned to an outside signal such as a tone or light. The alpha rhythm is an 8–12-Hz high-voltage wave from the occipital region of the cerebral cortex. It is most prominent when the subject is relaxed with his or her eyes closed. The subject can learn to increase or decrease the frequency of the alpha rhythm by being reinforced during spontaneous periods of high or low alpha activity. Eventually the subject learns to link high or low alpha activity with a signal and finally to dispense with the signal, voluntarily increasing or decreasing the rhythm. Kamiya in a semipopular article (1968) reports that his research indicates that yogis and persons trained in Zen meditation are particularly adept in inducing changes in the alpha rhythm.

The significance of conditioned EEG rhythms is not yet clear. It is possible that in the future various states of consciousness might be correlated with brain waves. These electrical signs of cortical activity may be useful in exploring euphoria, anxiety, depression, or psychedelic states induced by drugs. Whatever the wave of the future, experiments such as these have provided new and challenging methods of investigating relatively inaccessible processes.

Miller's results may also help to explain the previously mysterious effects demonstrated by yogis and shamans who appear to be capable of controlling metabolic processes to a remarkable degree. Although some of these effects are undoubtedly the result of trickery or illusion, others appear to be authentic. Perhaps through years of training, the practitioner can bring visceral processes under the control of subtle bodily or ideomotor cues.

TOLMAN'S PURPOSIVE BEHAVIOR: A COGNITIVE THEORY

In the heyday of the schools of psychology, anyone who suggested that behaviorism and Gestalt psychology could achieve a productive rapprochement would have been considered a jokester or a madman. Yet this is precisely what Edward C. Tolman (1886–1959) attempted to achieve—and, it is generally agreed, with considerable success.

Tolman's system evolved slowly over the course of a quarter century. The first important exposition of the system was his *Purposive Behavior in Animals and Men,* published in 1932. The system continued to evolve in a series of articles and two books, *Drives toward War* (1942) and *Collected Papers in Psychology* (1951), the latter being made up largely of material previously published as journal articles. Tolman's final statement, entitled "Principles of Purposive Behaviorism," was published in 1959 in the second volume of *Psychology: A Study of a Science* (S. Koch).

However, Tolman's system held fast to certain basic principles stated in *Purposive Behavior.* It was in this first important exposition of the system that he announced his general orientation, programmatic aims and methods, and the systematic framework around which he believed experimental studies of animal learning could be organized. Indeed, so comprehensive was Tolman's initial statement that it can be considered as either a complete system of psychology analogous to Carr's, Watson's, or the Gestalt psychologists', or it may be treated as a theory of learning. The latter treatment is justified in the sense that the learning process is heavily emphasized within the system as a whole. Having chosen the latter course, we shall restrict our discussion of Tolman's system to the learning theory within the overall system. Our exposition will be based largley on *Purposive Behavior* (1932) and certain significant articles[10] that have appeared in support of Tolman's position.

As has been implied, Tolman's general orientation is at the same time behavioristic and Gestalt. Because this is something of a paradox, let us attempt to delineate the relative roles of each of these traditional systems as they appear in Tolman's synthesis.

---

[10]Tolman (1949, 1959) and Tolman and Honzik (1930a, 1930b).

Tolman is a behaviorist in the sense that he is strongly opposed to a psychology of consciousness or pure phenomenology. In the prologue to *Purposive Behavior,* he states: "The motives which lead to the assertion of a behaviorism are simple. All that can ever actually be observed in fellow human beings and in the lower animals is behavior" (1932, p. 2). Moreover, in keeping with this behavioristic orientation, he favors the study of animals. Indeed, his *Purposive Behavior* is dedicated to *Mus norvegicus albinus,* the albino rat, whose kith and kin have given so generously to psychological research.

But despite his predilection for animal research and objective observation, Tolman is *not* a Watsonian behaviorist. He makes it clear that behavior in his system will be treated as a *molar* rather than a *molecular* phenomenon. A molar definition of behavior implies that the *behavioral act* is the unit for psychological study *without regard to underlying molecular components in the nerves, muscles, and glands.* Moreover, the molar orientation envisages behavior as goal seeking or purposive. The particular movements the animal makes in getting out of puzzle boxes or in running through mazes are of far less consequence than the fact that these movements lead to goals.

Molar behavior is also characterized "by the fact that it always involves a specific pattern of commerce-, engagement-, communion-with such and such intervening means-objects, as the way to get thus to or from" (Tolman, 1932, p. 11).[11] In less technical terms, molar behavior makes use of environmental objects—tools, pathways, signs, and the like—in arriving at goals. Finally, molar behavior is characterized by selectivity toward "means-objects"; that is to say, the animal will make use of shorter rather than longer routes in reaching goals.

Tolman's system is a Gestalt system in the sense that he characterizes molar behavior as *cognitive.* Evidence for the cognitive nature of purpose behavior is found in the animal's reactions to environmental means-objects in arriving at goals. He asks us to consider the well-practiced rat "dashing through the maze." As long as the maze is not altered, the rat's rapid, sure performance is operational evidence of the animal's cognitive expectancy that the maze is as it always has been. If the maze is altered, the rat's behavior breaks down. To anticipate a little in order to make the matter of cognition clear, Tolman's explanation of learning is centered on "sign learning." The animal in the maze or puzzle box learns the significance of signs along the route. For this reason, Tolman's theory is often called a "sign-ge-stalt" theory.

Finally, by way of orientation, Tolman emphasizes that molar behavior is "docile" or, in other words, teachable. The molecular reflex cannot be taught about goals; moreover, reflexes are not characterized by purposes. But, says Tolman, behavior "reeks of purpose." That is, behavior in the sense of behavioral *acts* is characteristically purposive. The importance of docility lies in the fact that it provides objective support for Tolman's contention that behavior is purposive. The

---

[11]Tolman's *Purposive Behavior* is sprinkled with neologisms and peculiar phrases, which are at once colorful and annoying.

animal that varies its behavior and shows the ability to select shorter and easier paths to goals *is* demonstrating cognitive and purposive behavior, in the Tolmanian sense.

In summary, Tolman's orientation is at once behavioristic and Gestalt. To use one of his own phrases, he is unwilling to have "commerce with" subjective or molecular approaches. Thus, he attempts to break through two traditions: the tradition of objective psychology as molecular (Watson, Titchener) and the tradition of subjective psychology as molar (Gestalt). In short, he believes that he can build a valid system by taking the best of the older traditions and discarding the worst.

With this brief discussion as a guide, we shall now consider Tolman's position on the major variables in learning—acquisition, transfer, extinction, and so on.

Laws of Acquisition

After a sixteen-page review of the experimental literature on the role of practice in learning, Tolman concludes that "the law of exercise, in the sense of differentially more frequent or recent repetitions of one of the alternative responses as against any of the others as the cause of learning, plays little, if any role" (1932, p. 362). Later in the same chapter, he goes so far as to suggest that *some* practice on *incorrect* choices in learning situations is probably necessary (1932, p. 346). However, lest we have given the impression that Tolman discounts the value of practice altogether, we must emphasize that he believes practice to be necessary for the building up of *sign gestalts*. With this statement we have come to the heart of Tolman's theory of learning, for sign learning is the core around which the system revolves.

Sign gestalts are cognitive processes that are learned relationships between environmental cues and the animal's expectations. In the maze the untrained animal has many cues available—auditory, visual, olfactory, tactile. If the animal is hungry it will move around the maze, sometimes on the true path, sometimes in blinds, and eventually will discover the food. In subsequent trials the goal gives purpose and direction to the animal's behavior, so that as it comes to each choice point, the animal builds up expectations that such and such a cue will lead to food. If the animal's expectancy is confirmed, the sign gestalt of cue expectancy is strengthened. The entire pattern of sign gestalts thus builds up what Tolman calls a "cognitive map." In the long run, then, the animal learns a cognitive map of the maze, *not* a set of motor habits. The role of practice is to provide an opportunity for building the map, and the role of reward is to lend purpose to the animal's behavior.

The evidence upon which Tolman has erected his sign-gestalt theory of learning comes from experiments designed to test the relative role of motor habits versus sign learning in the maze. These experiments may be considered under three headings: (1) "place learning" experiments, (2) "reward expectancy" experiments, (3) "latent learning" experiments. We shall exemplify each type and attempt to show how the results support Tolman's sign-gestalt theory.

Place Learning

If, Tolman argues, we consider the question of what the animal learns in the maze, the alternatives appear to be (1) some kind of motor habit, possibly a chain of conditioned responses to either kinesthetic or external cues or (2) a cognitive map made up of sign gestalts. Now a test of these alternatives was designed by Tolman and Honzik (1930a) as follows: A maze was constructed in the form of a cross with two possible starting points and two alternative goals (see Figure 9-10). One group of rats was trained so that its members always found food *at the same place,* say, F_1, irrespective of whether they started at S_1 or S_2. Another group was required to make the *same response,* turning right, at the choice point, C, irrespective of their starting point. The first group, or the "place learners," were significantly better in their performance than the "response learners." This result supports the cognitive theory in the sense that learning a place presumably requires a cognitive map of that place rather than a specific set of motor responses. By analogy, the individual who is thoroughly familiar with his town or city can take a variety of routes to a given goal and not be lost if his usual path is blocked.[12]

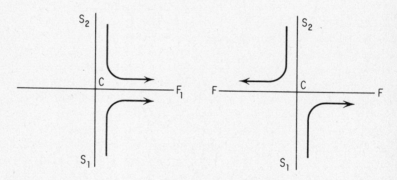

FIGURE 9-10.   A schematic representation of the place learning experiment. One group of animals always found food at the same place irrespective of the starting point. The other group was trained to make the same response at choice point C. Place learning was found to be superior to response learning.

Reward Expectancy

Reward expectancy in its simplest sense means that the learner comes to anticipate the presence of a reward (or in some cases a certain type of reward), and if that reward is absent or changed, behavior is disrupted. One of Tolman's associates,

---

[12]This early experiment on place learning has been repeated a number of times under various conditions and with modifications in the apparatus. The results have not always supported Tolman's position. For a more detailed analysis of place learning with additional examples and bibliographic references to critical interpretations, see Hilgard and Bower (1966, pp. 196–199).

M. H. Elliott (1928), employed a T maze in which two equally hungry groups of rats were trained to find a reward of bran mash and sunflower seed, respectively. Elliott called the bran mash group the experimental group and the sunflower seed group the control group. As Figure 9-11 shows, when sunflower seed was substituted for bran mash on day 10 for the experimental group, learning was disrupted, as demonstrated by a marked increase in errors. The hypothesis is that the animals had come to *expect* the bran mash—a more desirable reward, as demonstrated by the more rapid learning of this group—and when their expectation was not confirmed, behavior was disrupted. This experiment, among others, provides Tolman's operational definition of reward expectancy and, at the same time, serves as objective support for the importance of reward expectancy as a factor in learning.

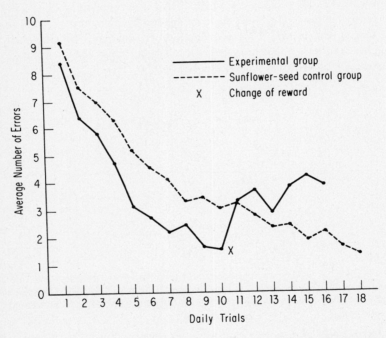

FIGURE 9-11.   The effect of change of reward on learning in the T-maze. For explanation see text. (From Edward Chace Tolman, Purposive Behavior in Animals and Men. Copyright 1932, The Century Co. By permission of Appleton-Century-Crofts, Inc., and the University of California Press.)

Latent Learning   Tolman

Latent learning is a fundamental concept in Tolman's system and continues to be a controversial topic in contemporary learning theory. As the term implies, "latent learning" is hidden learning; it goes on unobserved but can be revealed under certain conditions in performance. One of the classics in the experimental literature is Tolman and Honzik's study (1930b) of latent learning in rats. Three groups of rats were used: a no-reward group that was allowed to wander around in the maze but found no food in the goal compartment; a regularly rewarded group; and a delayed-reward group that received no reward for the first ten days but from the eleventh day on found food in the goal compartment. As Figure 9-12 shows, no reward results in little apparent learning. But—as the curve for the delayed-reward group demonstrates–learning was taking place, although it was not manifested in performance until the introduction of the reward.

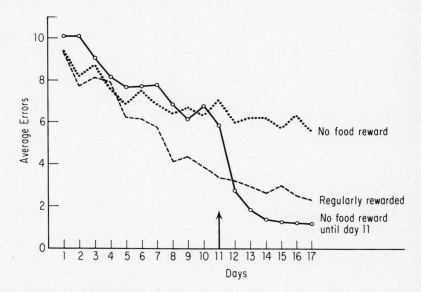

FIGURE 9-12. Evidence for latent learning. For explanation see text. (After Tolman and Honzik, 1930. From Ernest R. Hilgard, Theories of Learning. © 1956, Appleton-Century-Crofts, Inc., and the University of California Press.)

The importance of Tolman and Honzik's findings lies in its opposition to the older concepts of drive reduction through reinforcement, or the Law of Effect. If reward acts as a reinforcer of responses leading to the goal, then traditional reinforcement theories simply cannot account for the learning of the delayed-reward group. Tolman, on the other hand, argues that the exploratory behavior of the animals in the delayed-reward group provided an ideal opportunity for the formation of sign gestalts, since the animals thoroughly explored blind alleys as well as the true path.

Reinforcement theories, such as Hull's 1952 version, argue that the *amount* of reinforcement is irrelevant. They attempt to account for latent learning by pointing to the operation of subtle but significant incentives, such as "curiosity" and the desire to return to the living cage, which are operative even though the animal is not hungry and no food is present. In such cases, learning is reinforced, but *performance* is poor because of the lack of direction provided by a single goal with a relatively high incentive value such as food.

Since the Tolman-Honzik study, there have been literally dozens of latent learning experiments with wide variations in design. A review of this large body of material has been provided by Thistlewaite (1951), who cites seventy-six relevant studies. A more recent review of the relevant literature is available in G. A. Kimble (1961). The controversy is far too extensive to be reviewed here, but there is no longer much doubt about the reality of the phenomenon. The main problems with which most investigators are now concerned are (1) under what conditions latent learning is demonstrable and (2) in the light of those conditions, the bearing of latent learning on drive reduction theories versus cognitive theories.

Transfer

The problem of transfer—including the conditions under which it occurs—has not been one of the central issues in Tolman's system. However, the topic is not completely neglected, since transfer is considered as the carrying over of a sign-gestalt readiness from one situation to another. "Sign-gestalt readiness" is defined by Tolman as follows:

> . . . the organism is possessed of a generalized "universal" propensity whereby, in order to get to or from a given demanded type of goal-object, he is ready to have such and such positive or negative commerce with such and such means-objects (sign-objects) whenever particular instances of (i.e., the appropriate stimuli for) the latter are present. (1932, p. 454)

In simplified language, Tolman is arguing that, if two situations are similar, the animal will carry appropriate sign gestalts from one situation to another. He cites an experiment by Gengerelli wherein animals trained in one T maze were able to transfer learned habits to a similar but not identical maze (1932, pp. 33–34). Because Tolman favors a cognitive theory of learning, he would expect a high degree of transfer as a matter of course—provided that the problem situations were such that a general understanding of the essential elements was possible.[13] In practice, however, Tolman devotes very little space to the topic of transfer; and, as a consequence, the problem does not loom large in his system.

Forgetting

The topic of forgetting does not appear in the index of Tolman's *Purposive Behavior* (1932). This omission is indicative of the fact that both he and his associates were more interested in the process of *acquisition* than in forgetting. Moreover, psychologists whose research has been primarily with animals have traditionally shown little interest in forgetting, as compared with those who work with human subjects. It seems likely that this difference in interests can be explained

---

[13]See also the Gestalt view of transfer discussed in "Gestalt Psychology and Learning Theory" in Chapter 8.

by the fact that verbal material lends itself to experiments on retention more readily than do mazes, problem boxes, and the like. Furthermore, verbal materials are learned under conditions that favor forgetting. After learning a list of nonsense syllables, for example, the typical human subject goes from the laboratory to situations in everyday life where new learning is required. And, as has been abundantly demonstrated in retroactive inhibition experiments, new learning interferes with the recall of old.

The animal subject, on the other hand, is in a more isolated or "protected" environment where it is not confronted by the necessity of learning additional material once its responsibilities to the experimenter have been discharged. Forgetting, therefore, is less rapid in the animal subject and, for this reason, less often studied. *Purposive Behavior* does contain a brief reference to retentivity, however. Retention is treated under capacity laws as an ability that promotes more rapid learning (1932, p. 375).[14]

Other Laws of Purposive Behaviorism

In addition to the principles enumerated in the preceding sections, Tolman postulated a large number of "laws" of learning during his long and distinguished career to account for various types of learning within the sign-gestalt orientation. In keeping with psychological opinion in general, Tolman's laws vary with the nature of the learning situation. There are laws for conditioned-reflex learning, trial-and-error learning, and "inventive learning." The list of laws is far too extensive for detailed discussion here. Briefly, Tolman believes that three types of laws are needed to account for learning: (1) capacity laws, relating to traits, aptitudes, and characteristics of the learner that determine types of tasks and situations that can be mastered successfully; (2) stimulus laws, which deal with conditions inherent in the material itself, such as the belongingness of its parts and how well it lends itself to insightful solutions; (3) laws relative to the manner in which material is presented, such as frequency of presentation, distribution of practice, and use of rewards.

Moreover, in revisions of his system, Tolman (1949, 1959) emphasizes that there is not one kind of learning but a number of types involving not only sign gestalts but the learning of motor patterns, discriminations, and complex ideational processes. It must be emphasized, however, that by broadening his position to include diverse forms of learning, Tolman is not departing from his original emphasis on cognitive factors. Rather, just as conditioning theorists, such as Hull, came to recognize that they had to modify their systems to include important phenomena of learning if they wished to maintain comprehensiveness, so Tolman softened his original position to admit the relevance of types of learning emphasized by rival theorists.

---

[14]In his *Drives toward War* (1942) Tolman accepts repression as a special case of forgetting.

Concluding Statement

There can be little doubt that Tolman and his associates have contributed a significant body of research to the field of learning. In general, Tolman's experiments directed toward the support of the place learning hypothesis and those intended to demonstrate latent learning have excited the widest interest among psychologists and, even more important, have stimulated a great deal of independent research by psychologists not affiliated with him. Tolman's many fruitful experiments in animal learning stand apart as significant contributions to the field, irrespective of the acceptability of his interpretation of the results or the ultimate fate of his system.

It was Tolman who first distinguished clearly between learning and performance on the basis of the latent learning experiments. By so doing he brought to the attention of learning theorists the importance of motivational variables as energizers and regulators of learned behavior. Tolman's early insight was to reach a definitive formulation in Hull's postulate (Postulate 7) relating performance to drive and habit strength:

$$_S\dot{\bar{E}}_R = {}_S\bar{H}_R \times D$$

Tolman is also known for his concept of the intervening variables, which are O factors or unobservable entities postulated to account for behavior. Generally speaking, experimental psychologists have found explanations of behavior in terms of intervening variables to be a major step forward in the precise formulation of experimental designs developed to test such variables.[15] Indeed, the heart of the experimental psychology of learning has become the search for the relationship among intervening variables. It is to Tolman's great credit that he was the first to define clearly and to point out the importance of this orientation to the study of behavior.

It is somewhat paradoxical that the most frequently criticized aspect of Tolman's system is his own set of intervening variables. Psychologists in the area of learning have found such variables as "sign gestalts," "means-end-capacities," "cognitions," and "expectations" difficult to accept. By their very nature, such intervening variables are difficult to anchor to measurable stimulus-response variables with any degree of precision.

The molarity of Tolman's concepts makes them widely applicable but at the same time insufficiently definitive to test experimentally.[16] Perhaps time will deal kindly with this aspect of Tolman's system, and once the more elemental or molecular variables involved in learning have been clearly identified, it will prove possible to reformulate Tolman's more global variables as complexes of simpler variables. It may be that once the processes entering into cognitions, capacities, expectancies, and so on are better known, their manifestations in molar form can be subjected to more precise experimental manipulation.

---

[15]As exemplified by Hull, who adopted the concept of intervening variables from Tolman.

[16]For an attempt to render Tolman's programmatic principles into definitive laws, see MacCorquodale and Meehl (1954, pp. 177–266).

SKINNER'S OPERANT CONDITIONING: REINFORCEMENT THEORY

B. F. Skinner's (b. 1904) system of operant conditioning is a *descriptive* behaviorism devoted entirely to the study of responses. Since Skinner leans toward an empirical system that does not demand a theoretical framework around which behavioral data are organized, his is an *R* psychology in contrast to Hull's *S-O-R* psychology. At first glance, therefore, Skinner's orientation to learning seems to be essentially the same as Guthrie's. However, Guthrie formulated an elaborate theoretical statement of contiguous conditioning some years before his main supporting experiments were carried out, while Skinner's objective descriptions of his experimental results are atheoretical—representing a system that is descriptive rather than explanatory in its aims. Moreover, a central concept in Guthrie's system is the role of stimuli, especially kinesthetic stimuli, as mediators of learned behavior sequences. Skinner, on the contrary, believes the inclusion of stimulus analysis to be both unnecessary and undesirable. Here, then, is behaviorism strictly descriptive in its approach, based on the study of responses and opposed to the analysis of intervening variables.[17]

Despite Skinner's conviction that learning psychologists need not commit themselves to a theoretical system in which explanation plays the major role, they nevertheless should find some framework necessary around which to organize empirical data from their learning experiments. This framework is conditioning. However, he favors a special variety of conditioning known as *operant conditioning,* which he believes to be clearly distinguishable from classical Pavlovian conditioning and which he holds to be more representative of learning in everyday life.

In his first attempt to write a system of behavior (1938), Skinner distinguished between "type-*S*" and "type-*R*" conditioning. Type-*S* conditioning is the classical Pavlovian variety wherein a known stimulus is paired with a response under conditions of reinforcement. In type-*S* conditioning the behavioral response is *elicited* by the stimulus and may be called a *respondent.* In contrast, type-*R* conditioning, the stimuli, if identifiable in the first place, are irrelevant to the description and understanding of operant behavior.

Skinner believes that most behavior is emitted behavior, for which we either do not know the stimuli correlated with the response or for which we must postulate them in order to account for the observations. For example, suppose we observe someone writing a letter. The responses are certainly observable, but what are the stimuli that gave rise to the writing responses? Perhaps the letter was initiated by glancing at a picture of an absent loved one. Perhaps it was the receipt of a letter from the person to whom the subject is writing. Or the subject may have been impelled by "an impulse." Whatever the case, the example points up the difficulty of attempting to pinpoint the stimuli that give rise to everyday behavior.

---

[17]For a defense of Skinner's position opposing the use of intervening variables in psychology, see his article in *Behaviorism and Phenomenology* (Wann, 1964). This symposium also contains contrasting viewpoints on behaviorism and phenomenology by other prominent psychologists.

Skinner grants that in classical conditioning experiments conducted under highly circumscribed laboratory conditions, the stimulus that elicits the response may be identifiable; indeed, it must be identifiable before the experiment can proceed. The bell in Pavlov's experiment is clearly correlated with the conditioned response of salivation. But, Skinner points out, the learned modification of visceral reflexes is not the type of behavior of greatest theoretical and practical interest to psychologists. In Skinner's opinion, the traditional conditioning theorists have greatly overemphasized type-S conditioning. Skinner hopes to correct this imbalance. In his own words:

> The early contention that the concepts applicable to spinal respondents and to conditioned reflexes of Type S could be extended to behavior in general has delayed the investigation of operant behavior. There is, therefore, good reason to direct research toward obtaining a better balance between the two fields, especially *since the greater part* of the behavior of the intact organism is operant. (1938, p. 45; italics added)

Because Skinner made operant responses the basic behavioral data in his system, he adopted an instrumental conditioning experiment as the model for the study of variables that influence operants. The experiments are based upon the well-known "Skinner box," an early form of which is shown in Figure 9-13. In this case the operant behavior studied is bar pressing in rats. The lever is a small brass rod that moves downward in response to slight pressure, activating a food magazine (not shown) in such a way that a small pellet of food is released into the tray. The lever can be connected to a pen or stylus for recording each movement of the lever. Finally, it may be noted that the construction of the box is such that all extraneous stimuli are eliminated as far as possible.

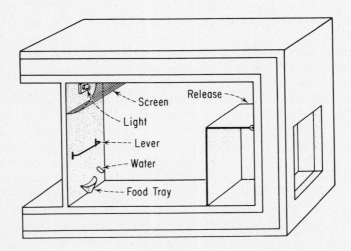

FIGURE 9-13.   An early form of the Skinner box. (From B. F. Skinner, The behavior of organisms. Copyright, 1938. D. Appleton-Century Co., Inc. By permission of Appleton-Century-Crofts, Inc.)

In choosing bar pressing as his operant, Skinner states that this particular response has certain advantages over other possible choices. First, it is a relatively easy response for the animal to make. Second, an untrained animal will, on the average, press the lever up to a dozen times an hour, thereby demonstrating sufficient "spontaneous" behavior upon which to base operant conditioning. Third, it is not included in other behavior patterns crucial for the organism, and therefore it can be isolated and recorded. If, for example, scratching were chosen as an operant, its high frequency of spontaneous occurrence and significant role in grooming would obscure the results. Fourth, the bar-pressing response is unambiguous; hence there is little difficulty in deciding whether or not it has occurred.

The bar-pressing experiment, then, is Skinner's "model" experiment, just as puzzle boxes were models for Thorndike and Guthrie. In recent years Skinner has worked with human subjects and animals other than the rat. However, the design of his recent experiments involving species other than rats is not essentially different from that employed in the original Skinner box. For example, pigeons have been used as subjects where the operant under investigation is pecking at a spot that acts as a key to trigger the reinforcement (see Figure 9-14) and human subjects where the operant is problem solving. For the pigeons, food is the reinforcement just as it is for the rat in the box; but with human subjects the reinforcement may be getting the right answer or a verbal expression of approval. However, because the designs are essentially the same, the following discussion of the laws of acquisition, extinction, and so on will be based on the rat experiments from which Skinner's system originally evolved.

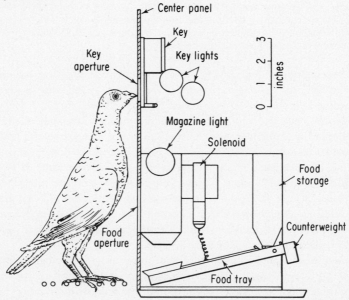

FIGURE 9-14.　The Skinner box as adapted for the pigeon. (From B. F. Skinner and C. B. Ferster, Schedules of reinforcement. Copyright 1957. By permission of Appleton-Century-Crofts, Inc.)

Laws of Acquisition

The bar-pressing operant is conditioned by first allowing the unconditioned but hungry animal to explore the box. As previously indicated, the operant of bar pressing will be emitted a number of times "spontaneously." This establishes the preconditioned level of operant behavior. Following such a series of preconditioned operants, the experimenter now places food in the magazine so that the lever is connected to the food magazine in such a way that whenever the bar is pressed the animal obtains a pellet of food. From this point on, conditioning proceeds rapidly. Figure 9-15 shows the results from one of Skinner's experiments. As the slope of the curve indicates, the first few reinforcements are relatively ineffective, but after the fourth reinforcement, the rate of response is extremely rapid.

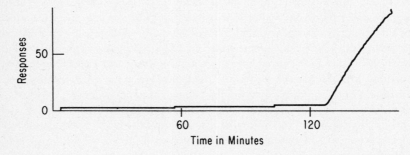

FIGURE 9-15.   A learning curve for original conditioning where all responses were reinforced. Note the rapidity of conditioning after the first few reinforcements which were relatively ineffective. (From B. F. Skinner, The behavior of organisms. Copyright, 1938, D. Appleton-Century Co., Inc. By permission of Appleton-Century-Crofts, Inc.)

The experiment just described illustrates the law of acquisition, which is stated by Skinner as follows: *"If the occurrence of an operant is followed by presentation of a reinforcing stimulus the strength is increased"* (1938, p. 21).

Clearly, both practice and reinforcement are basic in the establishment of high rates of bar pressing. However, practice itself does not increase rate of response but merely provides an opportunity for repeated reinforcement to occur. At first glance, Skinner's law of acquisition might appear to be essentially the same as Thorndike's Law of Effect or Hull's Postulate 4. However, it must be borne in mind that Skinner makes no assumptions about the pleasure-pain consequences of reinforcement as Thorndike did; nor does he believe it desirable to interpret reinforcement as drive reduction—a position favored by Hull. Thorndike's and Hull's are *explanatory* systems, while Skinner's is a *descriptive* system.

If the question is pressed as to why reinforcers are reinforcing, Skinner points to the obvious biological significance of reinforcers such as food and water. From a broad evolutionary point of view, any response that reduces deprivation is likely to be reinforced and thus lead to the repetition of the response. However, Skinner does not find that attempts to analyze the nature of reinforcement are of practical benefit to his system.

In a descriptive system such as Skinner's the problems of units of measurement and of recording the data are of crucial importance. The data *are* the system, provided that they can be demonstrated to be lawful and predictable. Skinner's objective recording system has already been described. His measure of the progress of conditioning is *rate of response*. For any given animal the rate of response is obtained by finding the number of responses per unit of time by direct measurements taken from the animal's data curve, as illustrated in Figure 9-16.

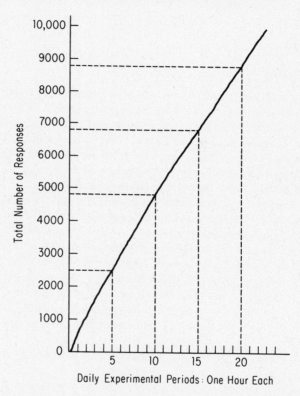

FIGURE 9-16. A cumulative response obtained with reinforcement at three-minute intervals. Note the high rate of conditioning. At 5 days the animal has given approximately 2,500 responses; at 10 days, 4,800; at 15 days, 6,800; and at 20 days, 8,800. (From B. F. Skinner, The behavior of organisms., Copyright 1938, D. Appleton-Century Co., Inc. By permission of Appleton-Century-Crofts, Inc.)

Data curves are automatically drawn by a *cumulative recorder,* a device in which a pen marks a continuously moving strip of paper. Because the pen moves toward the side of the strip as it marks, the slope of the curve of conditioning can be recorded over a time baseline. Steeply rising curves indicate rapid rates of responding, and slowly climbing curves indicate slow rates. When curves of responding flatten out, the rate of response is falling off. Such a record will be obtained if the reinforcement is withdrawn. The slope of the curve under these conditions will drop to zero or nearly zero. In technical terms, extinction has occurred when the rate of response is equal to that observed before conditioning. Clearly, then, cumulative curves in operant conditioning experiments cannot be interpreted in the same way as ordinary learning curves, which upon flattening out indicate that the subject has reached mastery or is approaching his or her physiological limit.

As we have seen, the laws of Skinner's descriptive behaviorism are the laws that govern the rate of response; and the basic law is the law of reinforcement. However, before continuing with a discussion of the variables associated with reinforcement, we should like to indicate briefly the role of drives as related to reinforcement.

The Role of Drives

According to Skinner, drive in animals is governed by depriving the animal of food or water—usually food. In his purely descriptive system Skinner defines drive in terms of the *number of hours of deprivation* and does *not* consider drive as a "stimulus" or "physiological state." Hours of deprivation can be measured; drive cannot. Following Skinner's reasoning, drive is simply a set of operations that affect behavior in certain ways. The appropriate question concerning the role of drive becomes: How do x hours of deprivation influence rate of response? This is the only legitimate question that can be asked about drive in a purely descriptive system and has been answered by a number of experiments (Skinner, 1938, pp. 341–405), in which hours of deprivation are correlated with rate of conditioning.

In general, the *rate* of conditioning is increased with increasing length of deprivation. It has also been demonstrated that the rate of extinction (another favorite measure of operant strength) is highly correlated with the *number* of reinforcements during learning but not with the degree of deprivation during conditioning. Thus drive has been shown to affect rate of response but not strength of the operant, as measured by the number of trials to extinction under conditions of nonreinforcement.

A closely related problem in learning systems is the role of punishment in the acquisition of responses. It will be recalled that Thorndike first considered punishment as a negative reinforcer that stamped out undesirable responses, but subsequently modified his position in favor of regarding punishment as having no effect other than an inhibitory action in preventing a response. Skinner regards punishment in essentially the same way as did Thorndike in his later formulation. In other words, punishment affects the rate of response but does not weaken operant strength. Thus, if a rat has been well conditioned to press a bar for food and is then shocked for a number of trials every time it touches the bar, rate of response will rapidly fall off to approach zero. If the bar is then rendered harmless, rate of bar pressing will once again go up sharply. Moreover, it has been demonstrated in extinction experiments that the total number of responses to extinction is not affected by punishment.

However, Skinner emphasizes *negative reinforcement* is not to be confused with punishment. Regardless of whether a reinforcer is positive or negative, it increases the strength of the operant. Thus, a negative reinforcer (or aversive stimulus) increases the strength of the operant to avoid that stimulus. A further discussion of aversive conditioning will be presented later in this chapter.

Variables Associated with Reinforcement

Aside from his basic experiments with bar pressing or key pecking, Skinner is best known for his investigations of various schedules of reinforcement (Skinner & Ferster, 1957).

Let us approach the problem of schedules of reinforcement by considering the typical reinforcing situation in a classical conditioning experiment. CS is presented and followed by US. During the period of acquisition, the US is always presented, and for this reason the reinforcement is continuous. But Skinner points out that in the operant behavior more characteristic of everyday life, reinforcement is anything but continuous. Consider the gambler, for example, who for years responds to the lure of the horse races despite the fact that reinforcement in the form of picking a winner is all too infrequent. In more ordinary cases, life is replete with examples of partial or intermittent rewards. The factory worker gets raises only periodically; the housewife does not expect paeans of praise for *every* culinary effort; and the mature scientist or artist may be willing to work for years with only occasional recognition.

The question immediately arises: Which is more effective—continuous or intermittent reinforcement? Similarly, the related problem of what types of intermittent reinforcement are most effective in learning must also be considered.

To begin with, the least complicated situation is that in which the animal is reinforced according to a certain predetermined time schedule, say, every two minutes or every five minutes. Skinner classifies such schedules under the category of *fixed-interval reinforcement,* since the fundamental variable is the *time interval* involved. Figure 9-17 shows a graphic record of lever responses made by rats under four conditions of fixed-interval reinforcement. The records show lawful and relatively uniform rates of responding, which are inversely proportional to the intervals between reinforcements. Clearly, the shorter the interval, the more rapid the rate of response, with rate of response falling off rapidly with the very long intervals. If, by a simple calculation, the rate of responding is related to the number of reinforcements, it can be shown that over a considerable range of intervals the animal makes about eighteen to twenty responses per reinforcement.

In regard to extinction, Skinner found that the curves for extinction fall off much more slowly where interval reinforcement is employed during acquisition than for those cases where reinforcement has been continuous. In one experiment, a pigeon gave 10,000 extinction responses after a special schedule of intermittent reinforcement. Skinner believes the explanation for this finding lies in the fact that with intermittent reinforcement the extinction trials resemble the conditioning trials much more closely than is true in continuous reinforcement. In the latter case, the animal moves from continuous reinforcement to zero reinforcement, but in the former many of the conditioning trials were not reinforced. Therefore the animal's responding is not rapidly disrupted by a series of nonreinforced trials at the begin-

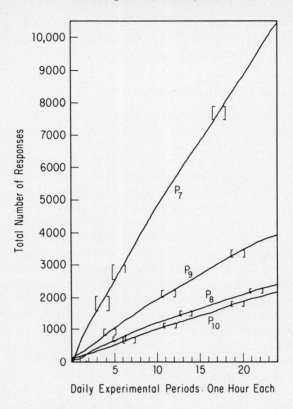

FIGURE 9-17.   A record of lever responses for 24 daily experimental periods of one hour duration. For P_7 responses were reinforced every three minutes; for P_9 every six minutes; for P_8 every nine minutes; and for P_{10} every twelve minutes. (From B. F. Skinner, The behavior of organisms. Copyright 1938, D. Appleton-Century Co., Inc. By permission of Appleton-Century-Crofts, Inc.)

ning of extinction. The situation is analogous to the case of the small boy, following a long period of finding cookies in a certain jar, never finds them after his mother decides to hide them elsewhere. Extinction of ''Looking for the cookies'' would be quite rapid. On the other hand, if another boy occasionally finds cookies in a jar and then does not find them, it is reasonable to suspect he will go on responding much longer than the first child, since ''not finding'' has occurred before in the second child's experience.

A second type of intermittent reinforcement makes use of *fixed-ratio* schedules. Here an animal determines its own schedule of reinforcement in the sense that after so many trials—say, twenty—the animal is reinforced. The essential contingent is the *rate* of responding. It must then press the bar another twenty times to obtain another reinforcement. The surprising result is that with low rates of reinforcement, relatively high rates of response are obtained.

Figure 9-18 shows several curves obtained under ratio reinforcement, where

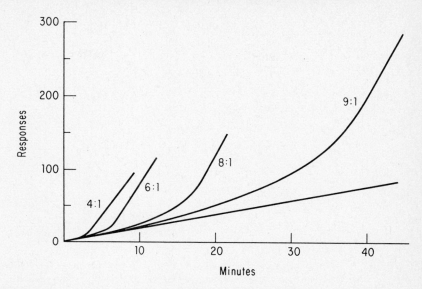

FIGURE 9-18.   Calculated curves from various fixed ratio reinforcement schedules. (From B. F. Skinner, The behavior of organisms. Copyright 1938, D. Appleton-Century Co., Inc. By permission of Appleton-Century-Crofts, Inc.)

cumulative responses are plotted against time. It may be noted that in this case the four-to-one ratio results in the most rapid rate of responding. It should also be noted that ratio schedules typically result in higher rates of responding than interval schedules. Because rapid rates of response on a ratio schedule bring larger amounts of reinforcement, whereas rapid response rates on an interval schedule do not, it is not surprising that animals on ratio schedules respond rapidly.

Both fixed-interval and fixed-ratio reinforcement schedules have a scalloping effect on the cumulative record curves. This is caused by the fact that rate of responding is slow after a reinforcement has occurred and then speeds up, reaching a maximum as the next reinforcement is due. Figure 9-19 shows a typical scalloping effect obtained with a fixed-ratio reinforcement schedule. It appears obvious in these cases that the animal has become conditioned to respond to the time intervals involved.

It is also possible to set up schedules of reinforcement making use of variable intervals, variable ratios, and a variety of mixed schedules. Discussion of these more complex varieties of reinforcement schedules is beyond the scope of this book. For detailed presentations of acquisition and extinction rates under a variety of schedules of reinforcement, the reader is referred to Skinner and Ferster's *Schedules of Reinforcement* (1957).

Secondary Reinforcement

The Skinner box is well adapted to the study of secondary reinforcement. In secondary reinforcement a stimulus that is originally neutral may become reinforc-

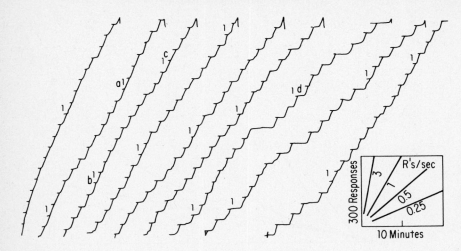

FIGURE 9-19.   The scalloping effect obtained with fixed ratio reinforcement. Every eleventh reinforcement was followed by a two-minute time-out period. (From B. F. Skinner and C. B. Ferster, Schedules of reinforcement. Copyright 1957. By permission of Appleton-Century-Crofts, Inc.)

ing by being associated with a reinforcing stimulus. Let us suppose that when the animal presses the bar, a light comes on, followed by a pellet of food. The bar pressing is, of course, reinforced by the food. Let us further assume that several trials with the bar-light-food sequence are given, following which the bar pressing is virtually extinguished by nonreinforcement. The bar is then connected to the light in such a way that pressing the bar activates the light, but no food appears in the tray. The rate of bar pressing immediately increases, showing that the light alone has become a reinforcer. The number of times that the animal will respond to the secondary reinforcing stimulus is proportional to the number of times it has been paired with the primary reinforcer.

In discussing secondary reinforcement, Skinner prefers to emphasize the concept of *generalized reinforcers* (1953, especially pp. 77–81), by which he means a variety of conditions that may become associated with primary reinforcers. Skinner suggests money as "the generalized reinforcer par excellence" (1953, p. 79), because it becomes associated with a variety of primary reinforcers of great significance to the individual, such as food, clothing, and shelter. The significance of generalized reinforcers lies in the fact that they strengthen responses other than the original response used in conditioning and can transfer to drive conditions other than the original drive.

In dealing with secondary or generalized reinforcers, Skinner points out that such reinforcers may be either positive or negative depending on the original emotional situation in which conditioning occurs. If the primary reinforcement is negative, then any secondary reinforcers associated with it will be negative, and their *withdrawal* will strengthen the probability of response. If the original primary reinforcer is positive, then the generalized reinforcers must also be positive.

Moreover, Skinner notes that generalized reinforcers are effective, even though the original reinforcers from which they were developed are no longer present.

By making use of these principles, Skinner can account for behavior that, on the surface, appears to be unrelated to reinforcement, such as the irrational emotional reactions that commonly occur in phobias. In the case of phobias, the original or primary conditions of reinforcement may no longer be present or remembered, but the presence of stimuli associated with the original reinforcement reactivate the original emotional response. In such instances the original traumatic experience need not recur in order to generate the anxiety. Rather, anxiety will occur if stimuli associated with the original fear-producing situation are present to act as secondary reinforcers.

Generalization

Skinner's equivalent for generalization or transfer is *induction*. By induction he means the tendency for stimuli with common properties to be effective in arousing behavior. If, for example, a pigeon has been conditioned to peck at a red circle in the Skinner box, a yellow spot will evoke pecking behavior but at a much slower rate. An orange spot will evoke a more rapid rate of response than a yellow spot, but not as rapid a rate as did the original red spot. Skinner refers to this decrement in rate as the "induction gradient."[18]

Induction is explained by Skinner on the basis of the presence of "identical" elements in both the original and new stimulating situations. Similarly, induction can occur on the response side, provided that identical responses are possible in the two situations. In reinforcing a given response, similar responses are strengthened—that is, responses with "identical elements." A common example of response induction may be found in mirror drawing, where the individual who acquires skill with one hand "transfers" a great deal of the acquired skill to the other hand without intervening practice.

In discussing stimulus and response induction, Skinner makes it clear that he believes that other theorists have placed too much emphasis on the discreteness of stimuli and responses. He suggests that neither stimuli nor responses are separate, discrete units but, instead, are *classes* of events. Skinner finds it "difficult to conceive of two responses which do not have something in common" (1953, p. 94);[19] similarly, "a discrete stimulus is as arbitrary a notion as a discrete operant" (1953, p. 132). Clearly, Skinner allows for a much greater degree of transfer than has been traditional in previous conditioning theories.

Finally, we might note that Skinner's own usage of the concept of "identical elements" is very similar to Thorndike's conception of transfer as dependent upon identical elements (see Chapter 8). However, Skinner provides for both discrimination among stimuli and differentiation among responses. Discrimination in operant

---

[18]In classical conditioning the parallel process is called gradient of generalization.
[19]See Skinner (1938, Chapter 5; 1953, pp. 94–95).

conditioning is brought about in much the same manner as in Pavlovian conditioning, namely, by selective reinforcement. For example, if the experimenter trains a pigeon to attack another pigeon when a green light appears and to stop attacking when a red light appears by selectively reinforcing attack behavior only if it occurs in the presence of the green light, then discrimination among stimuli has been established. At the same time the *response* can be said to be differentiated on the basis of selective reinforcement.

Extinction

We have already included a number of Skinner's graphs showing cumulative responses during conditioning (see Figures 9-17, 9-18, and 9-19). It has been noted that in the cumulative responses records employed by Skinner, extinction is demonstrated when the curve bends toward the baseline, or abscissa, and eventually flattens out. This indicates that rate of response is zero, and extinction has taken place. Skinner has demonstrated that rate of extinction varies with various schedules of reinforcement. Generally speaking, extinction is more rapid with continuous, as opposed to intermittent, reinforcement.

Forgetting is distinguished from extinction in much the same manner in which Hull differentiated between the two processes. That is, extinction results only from nonreinforcement, whereas forgetting is due to slow decay with the passage of time. Skinner (1953, p. 71) reports that forgetting, under controlled laboratory conditions is indeed a slow process. Pigeons may show operant responses six years after conditioning, even though no reinforcement has been given during the interim.

COMPLEX SKILLS AND THE METHOD OF SHAPING OR SUCCESSIVE APPROXIMATIONS

Skinner and his associates have taken cognizance of the fact that learning theories must account for more complex behavior than bar pressing and pecking at spots, particularly novel behavior not ordinarily observed in the animal's repertory of responses. However, the Skinnerians believe that the principles of operant conditioning are sufficient to account for novel or highly complex motor skills and have demonstrated the validity of their claim in ingenious experiments with seriatim problems (Skinner, 1951). For example, a rat may be trained to obtain a marble from a magazine by pulling a string. It must then pick up the marble in its paws and carry the marble to a tube that projects above the floor of the cage and deposit it there before obtaining reinforcement.

The *method of shaping or successive approximations* must be employed to accomplish so complex a program of training. That is, the animal is first reinforced for approaching the string. It is then reinforced for pulling on the string. Reinforcement is then given as the animal approaches the released marble and later upon picking up the marble, and so on until only the complete act brings reinforcement. In an informal way the method has been used by animal trainers for centuries.

Skinner (1948a) has shown how shaping can account for the hitherto uniquely human behavior of superstitions. If a pigeon is reinforced according to a fixed-interval schedule regardless of what it is doing, some operant will be reinforced. Suppose, for example, that the bird happens to be bobbing its head when it is reinforced the first time. The response will tend to be repeated. If this occurs several times with reinforcement, head bobbing will come to dominate the pigeon's behavior during the course of conditioning.

The situation just described for the pigeon is exactly parallel to that found in human superstitions. For example, if a mother happens to be in her son's room looking at his picture and experiences a strong premonition that some misfortune has happened to him at the moment his picture happens to fall from the wall, she will identify pictures falling from the wall as a sign of bad luck if she subsequently hears that her son indeed came to some misfortune at the time of her observation.

Behavior Modification

It will be recalled that Guthrie[20] introduced several techniques for the modification of behavior—particularly for breaking undesirable habits. With the growing impact of Skinner's system of operant conditioning, a vast research effort developed in the area of what has come to be called behavior modification. The most important aspect of this effort has been the development of behavior therapy, which we shall discuss in Chapter 17 in connection with personality and psychotherapy.

Verbal Behavior

Skinner's interest in verbal behavior spans over three decades and embraces such divergent problems as the design of the now famous teaching machine, the verbal summator (a device for producing vague, speechlike sounds that are interpreted by subjects as meaningful words and phrases, just as inkblots or other unstructured stimuli may be seen as meaningful objects), and an analysis of language in terms of operant conditioning. Although any attempt to summarize Skinner's extensive work in this area would move us far from the focus of this chapter, we may point out that speech sounds are behavioral responses that can be reinforced by verbal reinforcers in the same manner that bar pressing or spot pecking can be reinforced by food. Which sounds will be reinforced will depend, of course, upon the culture. Any normal human infant has the potentiality to learn any language in the world. In Chapter 11 we shall have more to say about the possibility of interpreting verbal behavior in terms of conditioning. Meanwhile we shall conclude our summary of Skinner's theory with a few general observations.

---

[20]Knight Dunlap was another pioneer in behavioral therapy. He introduced the method of negative practice, in which an undesirable behavior is deliberately practiced to the point of fatiguing it, thus setting up inhibitory tendencies.

Concluding Statement

In our brief survey of Skinner's descriptive behaviorism we have attempted to summarize his position on the more important variables in simple learning. As we have indicated, Skinner takes as his point of departure what might be called "raw behavior"; and to the extent that the raw data are lawful and consistent, they form a system. It seems unlikely that anyone would argue that Skinner's raw materials fail to demonstrate the kind of lawfulness upon which a descriptive system can be built. Moreover, Skinner has done a remarkable job of demonstrating the wide range of applicability of principles derived from operant conditioning research.

However, even though Skinner has developed a large following, not everyone agrees that his system of behavioral analysis is applicable to the entire range of human behavior. Chomsky (1959) in a review of Skinner's *Verbal Behavior* (1957) goes far beyond the task of a book reviewer to call into question the validity of Skinner's entire system. In a particularly noteworthy passage, Chomsky observes:

> The notions "stimulus," "response," "reinforcement" are relatively well defined with respect to bar-pressing experiments and others similarly restricted. Before we can extend them to real-life behavior, however, certain difficulties must be faced. We must decide, first of all, whether any physical event to which the organism is capable of reacting is to be called a stimulus on a given occasion, or only one to which the organism in fact reacts; and correspondingly, we must decide whether any part of behavior is to be called a response, or only one connected with stimuli in lawful ways. Questions of this sort pose something of a dilemma for the experimental psychologist. If he accepts the broad definitions, characterizing any physical event impinging on the organism as a stimulus and any part of the organism's behavior as a response, he must conclude that behavior has not been demonstrated to be lawful. In the present state of our knowledge, we must attribute an overwhelming influence on actual behavior to ill-defined factors of attention, set, volition, and caprice. If we accept the narrower definitions, then behavior is lawful by definition (if it consists of responses); but this fact is of limited significance, since most of what the animal does will simply not be considered behavior. Hence the psychologist must admit that behavior is not lawful (or that he cannot at present show that it is—not at all a damaging admission for a developing science), or must restrict his attention to those highly limited areas in which it is lawful (for example, with adequate controls, bar-pressing in rats; lawfulness of the observed behavior provides, for Skinner, an implicit definition of a good experiment) (1959, p. 30).

Chomsky goes on to develop a 32-page critique of Skinner's account of the acquisition of language in terms of operant conditioning, at the same time criticizing each of the system's basic concepts. It would be impossible to summarize Chomsky's brilliantly reasoned article fairly, and the interested reader is referred to the original. We need only note here that Chomsky calls into question (1) the generality of application of concepts derived from the relatively restricted type of behavior that Skinner has studied in his experimental programs; (2) Skinner's unwillingness to take into consideration structural and hereditary factors in the development of psychological processes, particularly language; (3) the failure of operant-reinforcement systems to account for spontaneity, curiosity, and creativity; (4) Skinner's tendency to lapse into subjective explanations (for example, self-reinforcement, or being reinforced by one's own behavior, thinking, utterances, and so on); (5) Skinner's failure to take into account the known facts about the development of language. We shall return to the last issue in Chapter 10. Meanwhile, we may briefly note Skinner's attempts to extend his system into social engineering.

Beginning with his now-famous novel, *Walden II* (1948b), Skinner has written a series of technical and semipopular articles and books in which the problem of controlling human behavior in society is the central issue. Essentially, Skinner is a utopianist who believes that the principles of behavioral analysis can be successfully applied to the design of society. In *Science and Human Behavior* (1953), *Contingencies of Reinforcement* (1969), the best-selling *Beyond Freedom and Dignity* (1971), and *About Behaviorism* (1974), Skinner develops the principles of how behavioral analysis may be applied to the control of human behavior in a designed society. He believes that the problems of the present social order are in large measure the result of an erroneous set of values wherein the dignity and freedom of the individual are held to be paramount. The individual is assumed to be self-determining; and because he or she is held to be a rational creature capable of distinguishing right and wrong, social control is achieved through setting up laws to be enforced by aversive techniques—punishment and the threat of punishment—that at best are imperfect.

If we are to solve "the terrifying problems that face us in the world today," we must reorient our values in such a manner as to make the survival of the species paramount. If this fundamental change is accepted, then individual autonomy will be sacrificed for designed control. In *Walden II,* the country of the future, the behavioral analyst will apply the principles of operant conditioning to the rearing and education of children and shape them "with due regard for the lives they are going to lead." The basic materialism, the arts, and the sciences necessary to the good life would be made to flourish without all the ills attendant upon rampant individualism and technology. The psychologist-director (or board of directors) would determine which behaviors ought to be reinforced. Presumably, aggressive behavior, excessive materialism—with its environmentally destructive technology—and gluttonous life-styles would be replaced by the somewhat monastic, albeit biologically and psychologically healthy, behavior portrayed in *Walden II*.

When the experimental scientist becomes the philosopher and designer of Utopias, he or she subjects himself or herself to the criticisms not only of professional colleagues but of literary critics, popular writers, and philosophers. Skinner is no exception. Because the fundamental issue with which he grapples is the problem of control, the question raised by his critics—particularly by humanists—is: Who shall control the controllers? They envision the application of behavioral methods as leading to the realization of an Orwellian 1984, in which the individual freedom so cherished by democratic tradition will be crushed under the boot of authoritarianism.

Skinner counters by pointing out that the goals of democratic humanism are not necessarily antagonistic to those of species survival in a designed society and that the controllers themselves would be shaped by the environment in which they live—presumably in the same desirable direction as the people of the community at large. The alternative, as Skinner sees it, may be a society in which the free individual is destroyed by the social diseases created by failure to control rampant individualism. In any event, Skinner points out that much of our alleged freedom is illusory. We are in large measure already controlled by laws, institutions, advertising, and the gadgetry of twentieth-century technology. Why not designed control?

The issues between Skinner and his critics are fully joined but so far are unresolved and are likely to remain so until the distant future. Moreover, what the final evaluation of Skinner's system *as a psychology* will be, only history will reveal. It is impossible to attempt an evaluation of a vigorously developing system while it is in the process of evolving. Nevertheless, it seems safe to say that Skinner's emphasis on operants is a significant and salutary departure from the traditional emphasis on Pavlovian conditioning. Skinner's greatest contribution may ultimately be what he hoped for his system nearly a generation ago—to turn the attention of psychologists to a new conception of learning as operant behavior.

ENDURING ISSUES IN LEARNING THEORY: CONTIGUITY, EFFECT, AND EXPECTANCY[21]

In glancing over the many theories of learning we have reviewed, the persistent question that overshadows all others is the nature of learning itself. How is a stimulus-response bond learned? Or, speaking more generally, how is any acquired association learned? In the last analysis, most of the controversies in learning theory revolve around this basic question. Beginning with Aristotle and stretching into the present and, no doubt, the future, we have seen that the principle of contiguity has either implicitly or explicitly played an important role in learning theory. Another influential view, popularized by Thorndike, has been that some form of the Law of Effect strengthens associations or *S-R* connections. And a third major principle has been expectancy. Because differences among theories as to the relative role of these factors or conditions play a major part in recent research and theorizing in learning, we shall conclude this chapter with an examination of each of these principles and attempt to indicate the trends that research has taken over the past decades.

Contiguity Theory

Contiguity theorists hold that the essential condition for the occurrence of learning is the simultaneous (or nearly simultaneous) presentation of a neutral stimulus and the response with which it is to be associated. Such a position is most

---

[21]Within the past decade a great body of literature has developed around current issues in learning. *The Annual Review of Psychology* and the *Psychological Review* are excellent sources for following year-by-year developments. Hilgard and Bower (1966) devote two chapters of their *Theories of Learning* to current developments. See also H. Goldstein, Kranz, and Rains (1965) and Marx (1970).

explicitly held by classical conditioning theorists. The CS and the US must occur simultaneously or nearly so, or the desired association will fail to develop. In classical conditioning, learning is theoretically a process of stimulus substitution, so the CS comes to be the equivalent of the US. Either is then capable of evoking the desired response. In Pavlov's experiment, the bell (or tuning fork) came to elicit the salivation reaction normally elicited by food in the mouth. Pavlov saw no necessity for invoking a principle of motivation or effect in order to account for learning. His conception of learning was both behavioristic and mechanistic. Contiguity was held to be both a necessary and a sufficient condition for learning in the conditioning situation.

However attractive conditioning may be to the classical conditioning theorist, critics have pointed out that even though Pavlov, Watson, and their successors believed that classical conditioning was the key that would unlock the door to the fundamental laws of learning, their hopes have never been realized. No one has denied that the conditioned response is a *form* of learning, but many psychologists would argue that it is not the only form; indeed, some (Skinner, for example) would go so far as to argue that it is a very special type of learning applicable only to autonomic processes.

Moreover, many theorists have pointed out that a contiguity theory of stimulus substitution as an explanation of conditioning is, in itself, insufficient to account for the facts. The conditioned response is not a mere substitute for the unconditioned response. The conditioned response is typically not as strong; it is more variable and is likely to show a longer latency period than the unconditioned response. Indeed, a strict stimulus-substitution theory would demand that the animal behave toward the CS in the same way that it behaves toward the US; for example, the dog would attempt to eat the CS. No such literal substitution of stimuli has been observed in conditioning research.

Turning away from conditioning, a pure contiguity theory should also be able to account for latent learning. However, the reality of latent learning is itself controversial, as we have indicated. Certainly it does not occur in a clear-cut and unmistakable manner, as would be demanded by strict contiguity theory. As Spence has pointed out, completely "motivationless" animals are not impelled to traverse mazes in order to provide psychologists with tests of the contiguity (or expectancy) principle. Similarly, studies of "incidental" learning (Osgood, 1953) and learning during sleep—a kind of acid test of incidental learning (Emmons & Simon, 1956)—have been disappointing in providing satisfactory evidence in favor of pure contiguity as a sufficient condition for learning.

Paradoxically, despite the lack of agreement about the sufficiency of contiguity for learning, few psychologists would seriously question its necessity. Long delays between CS and US are not conducive to learning; and common sense tells us that if thunder followed lightning by several days instead of seconds, human beings might well still be wondering what causes celestial booms after summer storms. And everyone who has engaged in the rote learning of verbal materials, such as a foreign-language vocabulary assignment, knows that contiguous repetition of the stimuli is the essence of learning. Thus contiguity seems a *necessary* condition for certain kinds of learning, even though it fails to be a sufficient condition. The remaining questions concern the relative role contiguity plays in various forms of learning.

Effect

Some form of the Law of Effect has played a major role in learning theory since it was first clearly formulated by Thorndike about three-quarters of a century ago. Thorndike, it will be recalled, stated his law in both physiological and hedonic terms: Connections are strengthened by satisfiers; connections are weakened by annoyers. We have already seen in Chapter 8 how quickly the negative half of the law had to be abandoned and also how varied has been the fate of the positive half.

Initially much of the controversy centered on the Law of Effect was concerned with the use of the concepts of satisfaction and annoyance. The behaviorists were particularly scornful of mentalistic terminology, and even the most favorably disposed saw a circularity in the reasoning that satisfying states are what the animal seeks to prolong and annoying states are what the animal seeks to curtail. The explanation, they argued, is similar to an explanation in terms of instincts. What is an instinct? An instinct is an unlearned form of behavior, such as nest building in the wasp. What is nest building in the wasp? An instinct. The circularity of such reasoning is obvious. Because of dissatisfaction with the original wording of Thorndike's Law of Effect, numerous substitutions were offered by those favorably disposed toward the law in the hopes of finding a more operationally defensible statement. *Reward, reinforcement, tension reduction, maintaining stimuli, drive reduction,* and *homeostatic equilibrium* are some of the terms that have been used and have played a role in theoretical explanations of learning.

Some theorists have attempted to meet the problem by distinguishing between an *empirical law of effect* and a *theoretical law of effect*. The empirical law of effect states only that the occurrence of a response followed by some effect is necessary for learning to take place. About this fundamental fact of behavior there is no disagreement, even among such antidrive reductionists as Guthrie and Skinner. The controversy centers on whether some kind of drive reduction or drive-stimulus reduction is a necessary part of reinforcement or reward. Those who maintain that it is endorse a theoretical law of effect. Their research is designed to demonstrate that in the absence of drive reduction or drive-stimulus reduction, learning does not occur. There is, more simply, no such thing as latent learning or learning by pure contiguity.

An enormous body of research has been devoted to attempts to formulate a "critical" experiment that will reveal the precise nature of reinforcement. Such experiments may take the form of Tolman's place-learning experiments, whose purpose was to show that drive-conditioned habits are not necessary to account for learning; or they may take the form of research designed to show that animals can learn in the absence of drive reduction.

In an early experiment, Sheffield and Roby (1950) showed that animals can learn with saccharine as a reward. Similar results were found by Kraeling (1961), who, using sucrose, showed that variations in the strength of drive as measured by speed of learning are a function of the concentration of sucrose employed. Since saccharine is inert metabolically, it theoretically should not reduce drive. The Sheffield-Roby experiment seems to give a clear instance of reward without drive reduction. In Kraeling's experiment, taste rather than drive appears to be the critical factor. Unfortunately, the matter is not as simple as it first appears. E. J. Murray (1964, p. 31) has pointed out that rats prefed on saccharine do not eat as much and do not press a bar as often for food as rats not prefed. Similarly, white rats will show learning when rewarded with copulation, but not with drive-reducing ejaculation (Kagan, 1955).[22] However, such behavior becomes aversive if ejaculation is never permitted.

Some experimenters have approached the problem by designing a situation in which animals can be given drive-reducing reinforcement but in which any possibility of "reward" or stimulation from the head receptors is ruled out. This can be accomplished by preparing the animals in such a manner that a food (such as milk) can be introduced directly into the stomach by way of a fistula, or opening to the outside. Meanwhile the members of a comparison group receive their reinforcement in the usual manner, that is, by eating or drinking. N. E. Miller and Kessen (1952) showed that rats prepared in this way can learn a discrimination problem where the reinforcement is milk injected directly if the animal makes the appropriate choice in a T maze—the incorrect choice leading to an injection of saline solution. And Kohn (1951), one of Miller's associates, has shown that food eaten normally is less effective in a bar-pressing experiment than food injected directly via fistula. Food introduced into the stomach quickly reduces drive and depresses rate of bar pressing.

To complicate the picture still further, we have the discovery of the "pleasure centers" in the subcortex of the brain by Olds and Milner (1954). Animals will press bars for hours in order to stimulate these centers with mild shocks. Stimulation of the centers can also be utilized as a reward in maze learning. In this case we have a situation where no need existed or where sensory pleasure via the receptors can be ruled out. And it must also be borne in mind that the studies by Harlow (1950) and others have shown that monkeys will learn to operate complex puzzles with the only reward being the successful solution of the problem.[23] Clearly, if the satisfaction of the curiosity or manipulatory drive can serve as a motive for learning, it will be difficult to test for "pure" contiguity or expectancy, since curiosity or manipulation may operate as "hidden" motives.

To attempt to resolve an issue here that can only be decided in the laboratory by future research would be futile. We can only confess that we do not know why

---

[22]It is characteristic of the male rat that mounting and insertion of the penis (intromission) may occur several times before ejaculation, or discharge of seminal fluid, takes place and sexual behavior ceases. In order to study the role of intromission as a reward, the animals are allowed intromission, but not ejaculation and the drive reduction that it would provide.

[23]See Chapter 14 for a further discussion of the brain implantation studies and Chapter 12 for the experiments bearing on curiosity and manipulatory motives.

rewards are rewarding, but only that both drive reduction and drive-stimulus reduction are effective in producing learning. We must also admit that nonnutritive substances associated with stimulation of the receptors are also reinforcing. Thus, as is so often true in complexities of behavior, there appear to be several reasons why reinforcement increases the probability of the recurrence of a response.

Expectancy

As we have already pointed out, expectancy theory was first formally espoused by Tolman and then moved into the camp of the drive-reduction theorists and won converts there. Expectancy is related to incentive motivation and as such has roots in Gestalt psychology and field theory. Because our survey of expectancy theory has been largely within the confines of the present chapter, we need not review the evidence again. What we wish to emphasize is this: Expectancy, a cognitive variable, has gained status in recent years to take its place along with effect and contiguity as a major explanatory construct in learning.

It may be fairly said that most of the issues in learning theory divide themselves between S-R theory and cognitive theory, of which expectancy is one form. Although the latter had its origins as an explanatory concept in learning in the animal studies of the Gestalt school and in Tolman's work, the greatest opportunity to utilize cognitive theory arises in studies of human learning. For this reason our final look at cognitive theory will be deferred until the end of Chapter 10, which deals with selected theoretical issues in human verbal learning.

In summary, then, we have a "three-factor" learning theory—contiguity, effect, and expectancy—with most psychologists willing to grant some validity to each point of view. Which factor plays the greater role may, in the long run, turn out to be a function of the situation utilized as an experimental design. All we can safely conclude at the present time is that all three are significant variables in learning.

Learning III: Selected Theoretical Issues in Verbal Learning

10

THE FIRST HALF-CENTURY

A casual glance over the two preceding chapters would give the impression that psychologists are more interested in the process of learning in animals than in man. And, although Ebbinghaus and Thorndike were interested in human learning, it would have to be admitted that the preponderance of *theories of learning* has developed around animal models. This, in part, is a reflection of the strong interest among American psychologists in conditioning—a learning paradigm that has dominated research and theory for nearly half a century. But it also reflects the psychologist's hope that in the study of relatively simple forms of animal learning lies the key to the more complex forms of human learning. This, it will be remembered, was the firm conviction of Pavlov, Watson, and Hull and remains the goal of the Skinnerians and others interested in the analysis of operant behavior.

However, a moment's reflection will also suggest that the associationism that lies at the heart of conditioning theory did not begin with the analysis of animal learning but with attempts to explain memory and the cognitive processes. Originating in the speculations of Aristotle and continuing through British empirical philosophy, associationism found its experimental justification in the research programs of Ebbinghaus and Thorndike.

We pointed out in Chapter 3 that American psychology remained functionalistic in spirit with the passing of the schools, although it adopted the methodology of behaviorism. This characterization of the field is nowhere more valid than in the area of modern verbal learning over the first half-century of experimental psychology. Psychologists working in this area approach their research objectively—with the rigorous experimental methods and statistical analyses that are the hallmarks of contemporary psychology and a reflection of the behavioristic influence. During this period most verbal learning psychologists showed little interest in elaborating complex theoretical structures or systems comparable to those we have reviewed in the immediately preceding chapters. Instead of seeking to establish basic laws of learning, they concentrated on the experimental investigation of variables associated with the acquisition of responses and the course of retention and forgetting.

In the late 1950s a revolutionary change became apparent in the field of human verbal learning and memory. The half-century tradition of investigations of long-term memory generated by the work of Ebbinghaus shifted to the study of short-term memory—the kind of memory involved in the immediate memory span we employ when we attempt to remember a telephone number. Characteristic of this new look in verbal learning is the assumption that the nature of memory can best be investigated through the direct study of memory rather than indirectly through an analysis of the variables associated with learning or acquisition. Moreover, in contrast to the primarily atheoretical position assumed by the investigators of the first half-century, those involved in the study of short-term memory have generated a rapidly growing theoretical literature on the nature of the memory process. Utilizing conceptual tools developed by those interested in information processing and computer technology, short-term memory theorists have formulated a number of models of memory that draw close analogies between the input, processing, storage, and retrieval of information from machines and from human memory.

In the first part of the chapter we shall summarize the traditional studies of long-term memory that were stimulated by the work of Ebbinghaus and that made up so large a proportion of the total experimental literature in psychology for over half a century. In the latter part of the chapter we shall turn our attention to recent developments in the experimental and theoretical studies of short-term memory.

In keeping with the purpose of this volume, we shall avoid any attempt to review the complex and massive literature in this field of psychology;[1] instead, we shall confine ourselves to selected issues that involve theoretical differences in interpretation. Wherever possible we shall attempt to relate these to familiar systematic positions.

THE FUNCTIONAL ANALYSIS OF ACQUISITION

To provide a perspective or overview for our first major topic, the functional analysis of acquisition, it will be helpful to outline the type of problems investigated in this area. First, beginning with the work of Ebbinghaus, the variable of mean-

---

[1]For recent exhaustive interpretive review of verbal learning, see Horton and Turnage (1976) and Hulse, Deese, and Egeth (1975). The older literature is summarized by McGeoch and Irion (1952).

ingfulness of the material learned has been an important area of research. Second, the distribution of practice—the size of the block of the material and the length of the practice period and interpolated rest periods—has come in for a large share of the investigators' attention. Third, the whole-versus-part variable (whether the material is gone over as a whole or in parts) has been extensively investigated for all kinds of material. Fourth, the question of various motivational variables, such as active recitation and knowledge of results, has been analyzed both in theoretical and practical learning situations. We shall begin our discussion with the first variable, meaningfulness.

Meaningfulness of Material

Classical associationism would predict that meaningful material is more readily mastered and retained than meaningless material. If memory consists of ideas held together by bonds developed through such principles of association as similarity, contrast, and belongingness, then meaningless, disjointed material with no relationship among its elements should not only be more difficult to learn but also should be more quickly forgotten. Common sense and common experience seem to verify the associationistic position. The average person if given a choice between memorizing a Shakespearian sonnet and a list of nonsense syllables would choose the former, knowing in advance that it would be easier to master.

However, the question immediately arises whether or not it is proper to compare poetry and nonsense syllables or any other such dissimilar material. It is theoretically possible that variables other than the relative meaningfulness of the material might account for any observed differences in relative ease of learning. This possibility can be avoided, at least in part, if nonsense syllables are compared to words of equal length or to digits. Moreover, nonsense syllables themselves vary in association value and have been calibrated for the use of psychologists interested in the variable of meaningfulness. For example, a list of syllables of high association value, such as LUV, LOS, RUF, can be compared to syllables which are relatively meaningless, such as XUY, ZER, YUT.

In an early study by McGeoch (1930) the learning of three-letter words was compared to the learning of nonsense syllables with varying association values. Three-letter words were significantly easier to learn than nonsense syllables with 100 percent association value; and as association value decreased, nonsense syllables became increasingly harder to learn.

More recently, J. F. Hall (1966) used the Thorndike-Lorge Word Frequency List to investigate the influence of association value or familiarity on learning. Four lists of twenty words each varying in frequency were employed as shown in Table 10-1, which also shows that the mean recall value varies as a function of the frequency of the word count, with the words that have a high frequency in the English language being more easily remembered. Hall employed discrete lists of words; however, when items are presented in the form of paired associates, the same results are obtained. For example, Cieutat, Stockwell, and Noble (1958) employed paired associates made up of dissyllables and nonsense syllables scaled

TABLE 10-1.   Learning as a Function of Thorndike-Lorge Word Frequency[a]

T-L Frequency Count	Mean Recall
1 per million	12.04
10 per million	13.31
30 per million	15.02
50–100 per million	15.04

[a]From J. F. Hall, *The Psychology of Learning*. Philadelphia: J. B. Lippincott Company, 1966. Copyright © 1966 by J. B. Lippincott Company.

for meaningfulness. Pairs of H-H, or high-high, meaningfulness were much easier to learn than L-L pairs, or low-lows. In general, numerous other studies (Cofer, 1971, pp. 852–859; Hilgard & Bower, 1966, pp. 292–329; McGeoch & Irion, 1952, pp. 468–480), both of long-term and short-term memory, reveal that on the whole there is a positive correlation between meaningfulness and ease of learning and retention.

In attempting to account for the relationship between meaningfulness and ease of learning, some psychologists have invoked the concept of positive transfer. Positive transfer, it will be recalled, refers to those situations where the learning of *A* facilitates the learning of *B*. Thus, learning to drive a Ford ensures that with little additional training the subject can drive any other make of automobile. The transfer is both positive and almost complete.

McGeoch and Irion (1952) assume that the same process accounts for the relative ease of learning meaningful as opposed to meaningless material. To encounter a word such as *love* or a nonsense syllable such as LUV (which a typical subject actually remembers as *love*) is to recognize something already learned and is therefore a case of positive transfer of identical elements. The subject's only task is to remember the serial order of the list under study. On the other hand, to encounter such syllables as XEV, YIW, NEX (or lists of unrelated digits) is to begin learning practically from scratch.

In accounting for the greater ease of learning meaningful material in paired-associate learning, Underwood and Schultz (1960) have suggested that verbal learning involves two stages: a response-integration stage and an association stage. In the response-integration stage the subject learns to identify the responses that he or she is called upon to make. If these are meaningless combinations such as XER, the task is made more difficult, since the subject must learn the letter sequences. If meaningful words are employed, the more familiar they are the less difficult and protracted the response-integration stage is likely to be, since more familiar words have a higher response availability to the subject.

An alternative theoretical explanation for the advantage of meaningful material in serial learning has been offered by the Gestalt-oriented psychologists in the form of the principle of differentiation. Differentiation refers to the fact that familiar terms have been discriminated from other terms in past experience, whereas meaningless terms, because they have not been discriminated in past experience, do not stand out from other such terms until considerable practice has made them familiar. Evidence for this hypothesis comes from studies of serial learning in which the middle portion of the series proves the most difficult to master whether the material be nonsense syllables, lists of common words, or a maze. Figure 10-1 shows this effect as it is revealed in verbal rote learning (Hovland, 1938).

Taking cognizance of this effect, von Restorff (1933) showed that a two-digit number was more readily learned if placed in a list of nonsense syllables than if mixed in with other digits. Similarly, if a nonsense syllable in the middle of a list is printed in red, it will be easier to learn than if printed in ordinary black (Van Buskirk, 1932). The Gestalt psychologists attribute these findings to *isolation*, or perceptual differentiation, a special case of the figure-ground effect.

An alternative hypothesis to account for the serial order phenomenon has been offered by learning theorists who favor interference effects as the cause of forgetting. They argue that the serial order effect is the result of inhibitory effects that build up as the subject progresses further and further into the list. Figure 10-2 shows Hull's hypothetical analysis of such effects for a list of nonsense syllables. Presumably, the more meaningless the material, the greater the interference effects. The von Restorff effect is accounted for simply on the basis that printing the middle syllable in a distinctive color is the equivalent of breaking the list into two parts and thereby reducing intralist interference.

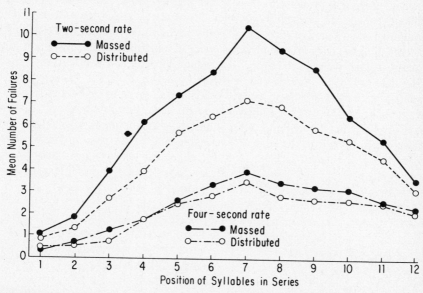

FIGURE 10-1. A family of curves showing the effect of massed and distributed practice on the serial order position of nonsense syllables under two different presentation rates. Note the significantly increased difficulty of learning with massed practice under a high rate of presentation, especially for syllables in the middle of the list. (From Hovland, C. I. Experimental studies in rote learning III. Journal of Experimental Psychology, 1938, 23, p. 178, Fig. 2.) Copyright 1938 by the American Psychological Association. Reprinted by permission.

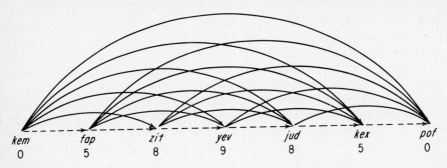

FIGURE 10-2.   A diagrammatic representation of both immediate and remote forward excitatory tendencies. The straight broken arrows represent immediate excitatory tendencies; the curved solid arrows, remote excitatory tendencies. The number of remote excitatory tendencies spanning the syllables is given below each. (From Hull, C. L., The conflicting psychologies of learning. A way out. Psychological Review, 1935, 42, p. 502, Fig. 1.) Copyright 1935 by the American Psychological Association. Reprinted by permission.

Distribution of Practice

The importance of inhibitory and interference effects on learning is further emphasized by studies of massed versus distributed practice. In massed practice the learner is required to master the material in a single session. In distributed practice, blocks of practice are interspersed with blocks of rest. If the absolute learning time is computed, distributed practice is generally found to be superior to massed practice. This, at least, has been the preponderance of experimental findings in the older literature. Again, we refer to Figure 10-1, which shows a family of curves obtained by Hovland (1938) for massed and distributed practice under two different rates of presentation. In both situations, massed practice was found to be inferior to distributed practice. Similar effects, it might be noted, have been found with motor tasks such as in rotary pursuit learning, which consists of attempting to keep a stylus on a dot that is revolving near the edge of a turntable similar to a phonograph turntable. In fact, the phenomenon is more readily and reliably observed in motor or skill learning situations than in verbal learning, perhaps because in motor learning more inhibition is likely to be induced by long periods of work or practice.

Distribution effects vary considerably with the nature of the task to be learned and with the relative length of practice periods and rest intervals. Unfortunately, at present it is not possible to generalize as to what the most economical distribution of practice and rest is for various types of learning. Those interested in reviewing the conflicting evidence in this area are referred to McGeoch and Irion (1952, chap. 5).

One aspect of the distribution of practice about which there appears to be little doubt is the phenomenon of "reminiscence." As ordinarily used, the term means to remember the past, informally recalling scenes or events. As used in verbal learning, however, the concept refers to a temporary improvement in performance without intervening practice. Thus, if a subject reaches a point where he or she can correctly anticipate seven out of ten nonsense syllables and then gives nine correctly after a few minutes' rest, reminiscence has occurred. Similarly, a subject following a target in a rotary pursuit task will, if given a rest period, typically show an improved performance on the next trial.

The phenomenon of reminiscence has been recognized for many years. William James took note of it when he observed that we learn to ice skate in summer and to swim in winter. James was not referring to laboratory studies of learning but to the common observation that after a rest period we often feel we are doing better at a task. Most people who have tried to master a sport or motor skill know that if they try too hard, the learning progresses poorly. This suggests that the maximum amount of reminiscence might be found in laboratory studies where the learning is massed or where the task is presented at a rapid rate. Such, in fact, is typically the case (Hovland, 1938), which further suggests that reminiscence may be due to some kind of interference or inhibitory effect. Hovland, who did a considerable amount of the early work on reminiscence, adopted this hypothesis. It will be recalled that in his study of the serial position effect, more errors were found under conditions of massed practice than under conditions of distributed practice (see Figure 10-1).

Massed practice favors reactive inhibition, and intralist interference effects are maximal near the middle portion of the list. Because reactive inhibition and interference effects dissipate with rest, distribution of practice favors reminiscence and therefore makes for efficient learning.

More generally, the benefits of distribution of practice have been accounted for by a number of theoretical alternatives. One widely favored theory is the retroaction or interference theory just discussed in connection with reminiscence. Other investigators have assumed that motivation and fatigue are important variables in acquisition and that massing practice tends to tire the subject, with a consequent drop in motivation. The discovery that reminiscence is most striking in motor tasks supports the importance of these variables as possible causative factors, since fatigue is more likely to occur in motor skills—particularly during the early stages of learning.

Another theory that found favor among the older investigators was the perseveration hypothesis (McGeoch & Irion, 1952, pp. 178–180). Perseveration theory postulates that some form of persistent activity is necessary in the nervous system for consolidation of the memory traces to take place. We shall go into this hypothesis more fully when we examine theories of retention later in this chapter. Here we need only note that the concept has been invoked to account for distribution of practice effects. Clearly, if practice trials are massed or if high rates of presentation are used, the neural circuits will have little time for perseveration; consequently, the traces cannot become established. Rest, on the other hand, would obviously favor consolidation, since it would permit continued neural activity immediately following the cessation of practice.

Finally, brief mention may be made of rehearsal as a possible factor in accounting for distribution effects. If not otherwise instructed, the subject may rehearse during rest periods in verbal learning situations and thus show superiority on the next trial without formal intervening practice. Unless some sort of "implicit" or "symbolic" rehearsal is assumed, it is more difficult to understand how rehearsal can occur in motor tasks.

In summary, the majority of opinion favors explaining the inferiority of massed practice in terms of interference or inhibitive effects and using the dissipation of such effects to account for both reminiscence and the general superiority of distributed practice.

It must be emphasized, however, that neither reminiscence nor superior performance under conditions of massed practice are consistently found in studies of learning. In several investigations, Underwood (1957) has been unable to find an advantage for distributed practice in verbal learning under certain conditions, particularly in paired-associate learning. It now appears that the subject's level of sophistication in learning experiments and the response habits that he or she brings to the laboratory from everyday life may have an important bearing on the results obtained. We shall have more to say about this problem when we examine retroactive and proactive inhibition as variables in retention and forgetting. Here we need only add that no one theory of distribution effects has proved adequate to account for the laboratory findings; and as is so often true in psychology (and science in general), the effects obtained are a function of the operations or experimental arrangements used to obtain those effects.

Whole versus Part Learning

Whole learning means attacking the entire task and going over it in its entirety until it has been mastered. In part, learning the material is subdivided, and each subdivision is mastered separately. For example, a poem may be memorized as a whole by reading the entire poem from beginning to end until mastery is reached, or it may be learned in parts, stanza by stanza.

It has been difficult to obtain clear-cut results on the whole-versus-part issue in laboratory studies utilizing a variety of materials. Moreover, the issue has generated very little theoretical controversy and does not appear to be related in any meaningful way to proactive and retroactive inhibition theories, which play such prominent roles in the analysis of laboratory findings. In addition, the dichotomy of whole learning versus part learning is somewhat artificial to begin with, since, as Woodworth and Schlosberg (1954, p. 786) have pointed out, the task must eventually be performed as a whole even when the parts are learned separately. This would apply not only to poetry and similar verbal materials but also to mazes and other tasks involving serial learning.

Disregarding these difficulties, it seems fair to summarize the experimental findings as follows: For tasks of short and moderate length the whole method has generally been found to be superior. For tasks of increasing length the part method has been found to be more economical of learning time. The issue is, however, a complex one, and many other variables need to be studied before the problem can be definitely resolved.

Motivational Variables

There is an enormous literature on the role of motivational variables in learning. However, the motivational studies of theoretical interest have largely been in the area of animal models. For this reason a considerable portion of our discussions of the classical, miniature, and derived theories of learning in the preceding chapters was devoted to the role of motivation, drive, drive-stimulus reduction, and incentives.

In human verbal learning, relatively little attention has been paid to the role of motivational variables. We know that an active attitude where the subject participates by reciting and being aware of his or her progress favors learning (Woodworth & Schlosberg, 1954, pp. 779–782). Also, intentional learning is more efficient. As early as 1933, J. G. Jenkins had students act as experimenters reading nonsense syllables to subjects who were instructed to learn the lists. A test of recall showed that although the experimenters learned some of the syllables, they did not show the high degree of learning typical of the subjects. More generally, in verbal learning experiments, the experimenter attempts to motivate the subject by the instructions and in some cases by offering tangible rewards, such as monetary payments. However, assuming that the subject is willing to participate, the experimenter makes little further effort to motivate him or her beyond giving some indication of progress made. Typically, no mention is made of motivational variables in the analysis and discussion of the data.

The dearth of motivational studies reflects, in part, the difficulties encountered in attempting to control human subjects. The psychologist is usually not in a position to deprive his or her subjects of food, water, or other physiological reinforcers; and even if this were the case, the situation would be an artificial one, since such states are not typical of how subjects are motivated to learn in everyday life. The experimenter is also limited in the use of incentives, and those that have been employed tend to have an artificial quality. However, in industry and education, rewards and incentives have been utilized for generations. It is assumed that to some degree there is a direct relationship between motivational variables and the speed of learning or performance. Few of the studies qualify as direct investigations of the role motivation plays in learning. Most are concerned with regulating performance, and there seems to be little doubt of the efficacy of motivational variables as regulators of performance. Unfortunately, the lack of rigid experimental controls makes the results of such studies of limited use to the theoretician or experimental psychologist.

Some psychologists have approached the problem indirectly by studying the effect of levels of anxiety on learning by using questionnaires such as the Manifest Anxiety Scale. These instruments are given to large samples, and high- and low-anxiety subjects are selected as experimental and control groups in learning situations (Deese, 1958, p. 117). A number of such studies have been carried out with eyelid conditioning as the learning variable. The results generally favor the conclusion that conditioning does occur more readily in individuals with high anxiety drives. However, we must be cautious in generalizing these results. Very high levels of anxiety disrupt learning in more complex situations (I. Sarason, 1956; S. B. Sarason, Mandler, and Craighill, 1952). Most of us would expect such a result from our everyday experiences, since we know it is difficult to learn during periods when we are emotionally upset.

Level-of-aspiration studies (P. S. Sears, 1940) also show that subjects who constantly experience failure become discouraged and show lower levels of aspiration on subsequent trials. However, the exact relationships between motivational variables, on the one hand, and learning, performance, and retention, on the other hand, are exceedingly complex and will require much more research.

TRANSFER OF TRAINING

When learning in one situation influences learning in another situation, we have evidence of transfer of training. In general, there are two types of transfer. First, learning in situation A may favorably influence learning in situation B, in which case we have *positive transfer*. Second, learning in situation A may have a detrimental effect on learning in situation B, in which case we have *negative transfer*. Both types of transfer are readily observable in everyday life. We learn to drive one automobile, confident that the skills acquired will transfer positively to other automobiles. We learn to roller skate and discover that it helps us in learning to ice skate, although in this case we find that the degree of transfer is not so great as in learning to drive.

We may also observe negative transfer when we carry out a skilled act such as attempting to do something for the first time while looking in a mirror. Our movements are jerky and uncoordinated. We may block completely and find ourselves unable to move at all. We are bringing to the mirror situation all our previous practice in eye-hand coordination under normal conditions, with the result that severe interference occurs.

Transfer has been studied in the laboratory in a wide variety of situations using perceptual-motor skills and verbal materials. Although we are primarily concerned with the latter in this chapter, we shall refer to other types of transfer to illustrate principles or to provide support for hypotheses of transfer.

The general design for a transfer experiment may be diagrammed as follows:

Experimental group: Learn task A → Learn task B
Control group: Rest → Learn task B

The experimental and control groups must be equated.

The degree of transfer, whether positive or negative, can be determined by finding the difference in the learning time, or trials for task B, for the experimental group. If the transfer has been positive, then the experimental group will take fewer trials to learn B. If the transfer is negative, the experimental group will require more trials than the control group to reach the criterion.[2]

In verbal learning, typical studies of transfer have employed paired associates, which can be either S-R pairs of nonsense syllables, meaningful words, or mixtures

---

[2]There are many other possible designs for studying transfer. The interested reader may consult Postman (1971, pp. 1022–1030).

of the two. In general, there are two extreme possibilities. The stimuli can be completely different in task B with the responses remaining the same; or the responses in task B can be changed completely with the stimuli remaining identical.

In schematic form the first possibility might be illustrated with the following pairs:

	Task A				Task B	
S		*R*	*S*			*R*
glass	$- - - \rightarrow$	bell	nail	$- - - \rightarrow$		bell
sand	$- - - \rightarrow$	chair	boy	$- - - \rightarrow$		chair
cloud	$- - - \rightarrow$	book	pin	$- - - \rightarrow$		book
	and so on			and so on		

The second design would look like the following illustration:

	Task A				Task B	
S		*R*	*S*			*R*
girl	$- - - \rightarrow$	desk	girl	$- - - \rightarrow$		car
paper	$- - - \rightarrow$	floor	paper	$- - - \rightarrow$		dog
man	$- - - \rightarrow$	brick	man	$- - - \rightarrow$		toy
	and so on			and so on		

In general terms, the first situation is an $S_1 \rightarrow R_1 : S_2 \rightarrow R_1$ design, while in the second situation, we have $S_1 \rightarrow R_1 : S_1 \rightarrow R_2$. The first situation gives slight positive transfer—the transfer arising from the subject's already having learned the responses. He or she must still learn the new stimuli, but the task is easier than if both stimuli and responses had to be learned.

When subjects are tested in $S_1 \rightarrow R_1 : S_1 \rightarrow R_2$ situations, the transfer is strongly negative. The learning of competing or conflicting responses causes severe interference effects. If both the stimuli and the responses are identical ($S_1 \rightarrow R_1 : S_1 \rightarrow R_1$) from task A to task B, the transfer will, of course, be strongly positive. All the subject has to overcome is whatever degree of forgetting may have occurred between the cessation of task A and the initiation of learning task B.

There are, of course, other possibilities. The stimuli may be made similar and the responses identical, whereupon strongly positive transfer will be obtained. If the stimuli remain identical and the responses similar, there will be slightly positive transfer.

Some studies (J. Jung, 1962, 1963) have suggested that the general principles given above and based on work extending over the first half of the century may have to be modified somewhat. In some instances, attaching an old response to a new stimulus may result in slightly negative transfer. Since the effect has been confirmed by several investigators, we must accept a modification of the general rule that

$S_1 \rightarrow R_1$: $S_2 \rightarrow R_1$ designs always lead to positive transfer. The reasons for this effect are not fully understood, but it has been suggested (J. Jung, 1963) that the relative meaningfulness of the material is a factor in determining whether negative transfer will occur. If highly meaningful S-R pairs are used, the transfer is more likely to be negative—no doubt because the S-R connections are more unified when meaningful materials are used than when nonsense syllables are employed.

Mediation Theory

In recent years a large number of studies of *mediational processes* in transfer have been carried out. Mediation occurs when one member of an associated pair is linked to the other by means of an intervening element. Thus, when a man remembers his wedding anniversary by linking it to his house number, he is employing mediation. In laboratory studies a variety of paradigms or designs have been employed involving forward and backward chains, stimulus equivalence, and response equivalence. Table 10-2 summarizes the various possibilities of the three-stage mediation paradigm.

In Table 10-2 the letters A, B, and C represent the material learned, which may be nonsense syllables, meaningful words of low frequency, or meaningful words of high frequency. By changing the order of the elements, up to eight three-stage paradigms may be obtained. Experimenters who utilize nonsense syllables and low-frequency words do so to prevent the subject from utilizing associations that might have been learned outside the laboratory.

In an elaborate investigation of the eight possible paradigms shown in Table 10-2, Horton and Kjeldegaard (1961) found that all eight facilitated subjects' performance in stage 3, in comparison to the learning of control groups where the material for stage 3 was unrelated to that learned in stages 1 and 2. However,

TABLE 10-2.   Types of Three-Stage Mediation Paradigms[a]

Forward chain	Stage 1:	Learn A-B	B-C
	Stage 2:	Learn B-C	A-B
(A → B → C)	Stage 3:	Test A-C	A-C
Backward chain	Stage 1:	Learn B-A	C-B
	Stage 2:	Learn C-B	B-A
(A ← B ← C)	Stage 3:	Test A-C	A-C
Stimulus equivalence	Stage 1:	Learn A-B	C-B
	Stage 2:	Learn C-B	A-B
(A → B ← C)	Stage 3:	Test A-C	A-C
Response equivalence	Stage 1:	Learn B-A	B-C
	Stage 2:	Learn B-C	B-A
(A ← B → C)	Stage 3:	Test A-C	A-C

[a]Reproduced with permission from E. Saltz, *The Cognitive Basis of Human Learning.* Homewood, Ill.: The Dorsey Press, 1971, p. 279.

significant differences in the degree of learning among the various paradigms were not found, which indicates that for the material used—in this case, nonsense syllables—the direction of chaining was unimportant.

Studies employing real words (Cramer & Cofer, 1960; Horton & Hartman, 1963) show that mediation experiments using natural language associations give essentially the same results as those found by Horton and Kjeldegaard employing nonsense syllables. In the Horton and Hartman experiment there was also evidence that forward chaining is somewhat more effective than other conditions, as might be predicted on the basis of everyday experience where forward associations such as table-chair, grass-green, sky-cloud, are developed and strengthened by frequent repetition. Nevertheless, a number of studies have shown that backward mediation is also effective.

It is also possible to test four-stage mediated chains. The general paradigm is as follows: (1) A-B, (2) B-C, (3) C-D, and (4) A-(B-C)-D. Note that in the final test for mediation two associated elements (B-C) are necessary for mediation. A comprehensive experiment by J. J. Jenkins (1963) that involved sixteen possible paradigms failed to show evidence of significant mediation in four-stage paradigms. Other studies have found evidence for mediation in such paradigms, but the effects are weak and unstable. Apparently the increase in the number of elements required to mediate weakens the implicit mediator (B-C) to the point of ineffectiveness.

Clearly, mediation or chaining is a special case of transfer that may be explained in terms of *S-R* theory. Indeed, the results of mediation studies have been used to support classical associational explanations of transfer to which we shall turn next.

Theoretical Explanations of Transfer

Theoretical explanations of transfer have emphasized two broad classes of responsible factors: general and specific. General factors include understanding, insight, and learning sets as explanations of positive transfer. Specific factors consist of stimulus-response elements, which, as we have just seen, can be correlated with positive and negative transfer effects depending upon their arrangement and degree of similarity from one task to another.

Very early experiments (Jost, 1897) on transfer of principles showed that subjects could transfer a general understanding of a task from one situation to another. We found (Chapter 8) that the Gestalt psychologists strongly emphasized this factor in their experiments on insight learning in both animal and human subjects, and contemporary cognitive theorists continue to stress understanding and other higher-order processes as factors in transfer. Although few psychologists would disagree that a general understanding of a situation can be transferred from one situation to another, they are by no means in agreement that such concepts as "insight," "transfer of principles," or "understanding" add anything by way of explanation.

Working with monkeys, Harlow (1949) showed that the general transfer effect from one situation to another may be accounted for by the concept of "learning how to learn,'' or learning sets. In a number of experiments the animals were given a series of discrimination problems consisting of positive and negative cue-objects presented in a random order over food cups. The animal obtained food only if the ''positive'' cue-object was chosen. On a large number of trials the monkey had to learn to pick up the positive object in spite of its varying position. Hundreds of pairs of such objects were used. On the second trial following the presentation of the first few problems, the monkeys were only 50 percent correct—no better than chance—in selecting the proper object. By the time 100 tasks had been mastered, the monkeys were 80 percent correct on trial 2. By the end of 300 tasks they were 95 percent correct. A man from Mars entering the laboratory at this point might well have attributed insight to the animals, whereas a more parsimonious explanation in terms of learning to learn, or learning sets, is adequate to account for the data.

Similar results have been obtained by Postman (1964) in verbal learning. Subjects who engage in the learning of paired associates and serial lists of nonsense syllables will do better on subsequent tests involving not only these specific tasks but others as well. However, while there is general transfer in these situations, the effect is limited. No evidence was found to indicate that rote learning improves the memory process in general. Rather, learning in the laboratory is a process that requires the development of certain skills and attitudes. Subjects who engage in nonsense syllable learning for the first time often lack confidence. They have not yet learned how to learn. When they acquire confidence and the necessary skills, these carry over into subsequent learning situations (Ward, 1937). See Figure 10-3.

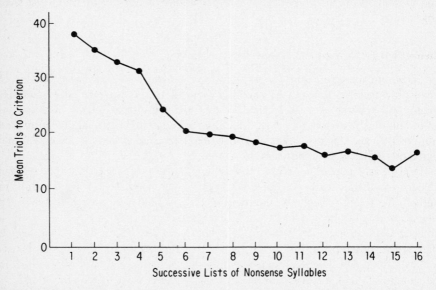

FIGURE 10-3.   The cumulative positive transfer effect in learning successive lists of nonsense syllables. (From Osgood, 1953, after Ward, L. B. Reminiscence and rote learning. Psychological Monographs, 1937, 49, No. 220, p. 13, Fig. 3.) Copyright 1937 by the American Psychological Association. Reprinted by permission.

However, another word of caution is in order. Too much prior learning may result in proactive inhibition effects. Proactive inhibition refers to the learning of A having a detrimental effect on the learning of B. It is a negative transfer effect. Of this we shall have more to say in the following section which deals with forgetting.

Specific theories of transfer assume that any special skills or responses that can be carried from one situation to another will result in positive transfer if similar or identical and in negative transfer if dissimilar or antagonistic. This hypothesis was first formulated by Thorndike. Since we have already extensively analyzed this type of transfer, we need not discuss it further here.

In summary, then, we have considered two main theoretical explanations of transfer: (1) transfer of general principles, including learning sets, and (2) transfer by means of identical elements. We also mentioned, incidentally, that generalization in conditioning (induction in operant conditioning) is invoked by some theorists to account for transfer. The conditioning theorist may account for positive transfer in cases of stimulus similarity by assuming stimulus generalization, and in cases of response similarity by assuming response generalization. Negative transfer would presumably be the result of conflicting or incompatible responses.

RETENTION AND FORGETTING

Research on the nature and conditions of retention and forgetting began with the work of Ebbinghaus and has continued to be a challenging and well-developed empirical and theoretical area for almost a century. We are already familiar with Ebbinghaus' famous curves of retention, which he obtained with nonsense syllables utilizing the savings method. Ebbinghaus' work was quickly followed by studies of retention as a function of (1) the different methods of measurement, (2) the conditions under which the original learning took place, (3) the type of material learned, (4) the extent and nature of related activity prior to original learning or interpolated between original learning and recall, and (5) the influence of various pathological and psychological conditions.

Different Methods of Measurement

A representative study of different measurement methods is Luh's classic investigation (1922) of retention curves obtained under different conditions of measurement. These curves are presented in Figure 10-4. Luh's results clearly demonstrate that retention is a function of the method by which it is measured. Recognition is the most sensitive of the various measures employed, with anticipation the least sensitive and also the most difficult for the subject. The curve for the relearning method, it will be noted, first falls more rapidly than those for recognition and reconstruction and then levels out. This is undoubtedly due to the fact that the relearning method is actually a combination of two methods—recall and relearning—that are negatively correlated, since the greater the recall at the first presentation, the less relearning is required.

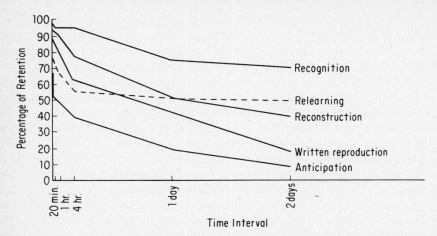

FIGURE 10-4.   Retention curves obtained with different methods of measurement. (From McGeoch, J. A., and Irion, A., The psychology of human learning, 1952; after Luh, C. W., The conditions of retention. Psychological Monographs, 1922, 31, No. 142, p. 22, Fig. 10.) Copyright 1922 by the American Psychological Association. Reprinted by permission.

Conditions of Original Learning

Typical of studies concerned with the conditions of original learning are those that investigate the effect of overlearning. "Overlearning" is defined as practice beyond one (or two) perfect recitations. Numerous studies have shown that over-learning up to a point of diminishing returns aids in retention (Krueger, 1929).

Even more striking results are obtained when additional learning is spread over a long period of time in the form of reviews (see Figure 10-5). The results of such

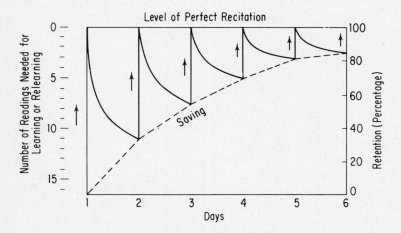

FIGURE 10-5.   A diagrammatic representation of Jost's Law. Each successive review (represented by the arrows) causes the curve of retention to fall less steeply and the savings in time needed to relearn increases sharply. (From Woodworth, R. S., and Schlosberg, H. Experimental psychology, 2nd ed. Copyright © 1954 by Holt, Rinehart and Winston, Inc., Reprinted by permission.)

studies have been formulated by Jost (1897) into a law stating that given two associations of equal strength but different ages, practice is more beneficial to the older of the two. Jost's law is a reflection of the shape of the curve for retention. Clearly, a recent association is on a steeper part of the curve than an older association; consequently, the recent association will undergo a more rapid decline.

We have indicated earlier that under most conditions of learning, distributed practice is superior to massed practice. A similar general statement can be made for learning under conditions demanding active participation (Woodworth & Schlosberg, 1954, pp. 779–782). Thus, the basic principle underlying these results is that whatever favors efficiency in original learning also favors retention.

Type of Material Learned

Attempts to measure differential forgetting as a function of the types of material learned are fraught with difficulties of methodology and interpretation. Can the learning of a poem be directly compared to the learning of a list of nonsense syllables? Do motor skills undergo slower decay in retention than verbal skills, as seems to be the case from everyday observation? Can we compare insightfully learned problems to rote learning? In attempting to answer these questions, psychologists are not certain that investigators who have attempted to compare poetry, prose, nonsense material, and the like have achieved sufficient control over the original degree of learning. We are not sure that a poem learned to the criterion of one errorless repetition has been learned to the same degree of mastery as a list of twenty nonsense syllables learned to the criterion of one errorless repetition. The same problem is accentuated when investigators attempt to compare retention for motor skills to retention for verbal skills.

Nevertheless, despite the formidable difficulties in the way of any final answer, the question has not gone begging. Figure 10-6 shows a composite curve reflecting a relative comparison of several types of material (Guilford, 1939). It will be observed that materials that lend themselves to insight learning are retained better than poetry, connected discourse, and nonsense syllables. Poetry with its rhyme schemes and rhythm has an advantage over prose; and prose, in turn, over nonsense syllables.

In addition to studies such as these, researchers working with animals have found that very simple motor skills, such as those acquired in conditioning experiments, are retained over very long periods (six years) if the animals are not subjected to additional training (Hilgard, 1956). This suggests that retention is influenced not only by the type of material but also by what happens to the subject during the retention interval. We shall develop this point further in the next section.

We may add here that two reasons have been suggested why verbal materials are not retained as well as perceptual-motor habits. First, the latter are typically overpracticed. A boy or girl does not learn to ride a bicycle to the point of bare mastery and then stop practicing. Considerable overlearning occurs. Second, there is more opportunity for interference effects in the area of verbal learning than in motor learning, particularly among young adults who are in school and therefore amassing large blocks of verbal materials daily. The isolated laboratory animal, on

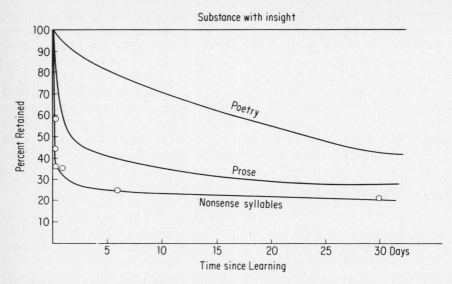

FIGURE 10-6. Theoretical curves for material with varying degrees of meaningfulness from insightful to nonsense. (From Guilford, J. P. General psychology. Van Nostrand, 1939.)

the other hand, is subjected only to the highly restricted environment of its living cage. If the animal is not the subject of research, there is little in its behavioral routine to interfere with a learned habit.

In discussing the type of material learned, it will be recalled that the Gestalt psychologists (Chapter 8) emphasized that tasks that could be interpreted in a meaningful manner resulted in more efficient learning and better retention. In his book *Organizing and Memorizing* (1940), Katona, a Gestalt psychologist, reported on a number of ingenious experiments in which tasks could be learned either by rote memorizing or could be organized in such a way as to lead to understanding. For example, the series 156879468576 can be learned by straight rote or it can be organized into the numbers 156, 879, 468, 576 by coding it into one hundred fifty-six billion, eight hundred seventy-nine million, and so on. Even this minimal degree of organization makes the task a little easier. Consider the following series: 149162536496481. Again the series can be learned by rote; but a high degree of understanding is possible if it is recognized that the series is not a collection of random numbers, but the squares of the single digits 1, 2, 3, 4, 5, 6, 7, 8, and 9. In his report, Katona presents experimental evidence to show that not only is learning made more efficient by such organizing techniques, but retention is greatly improved (a result in keeping with the Gestalt position).

Interpolated Material

In studying the influence of extraneous or interpolated material on retention, the psychologist is investigating what is technically known as proactive and retroactive inhibition. Retroactive inhibition, as the name implies, refers to inhibitory effects generated by the interpolation of material between the original learning and recall. In terms of an experimental design, retroactive inhibition is studied by means of two equated groups as follows:

Experimental group: Learn A → Learn B → Recall A
Control group: Learn A → Rest → Recall A

The difference in recall is the measure of retroactive inhibition.

Proactive inhibition refers to the influence of previously learned material on the retention of the experimental material. In terms of a design:

Experimental group: Learn B → Learn A → Recall A
Control group: Rest → Learn A → Recall A

Prior to World War II retroactive inhibition received the major share of research and theoretical attention as the factor primarily responsible for forgetting and interference effects. A wide variety of subjects ranging from cockroaches to humans were studied by varying a number of parameters such as the degree of original and interpolated learning, the nature of the interpolated material, and the temporal placement of the interpolated material close to the original learning or just prior to recall.

Studies of the relationship between similarity of original and interpolated material (McGeoch & Irion, 1952) have generally shown that the learning of moderately similar materials results in maximum interference, whereas if the interpolated materials are either identical to the original or entirely dissimilar, interference is absent (identical material) or minimized (dissimilar material). Taking account of a series of his own experiments and those of E. B. Skaggs, E. S. Robinson formulated what has come to be known as the Skaggs-Robinson hypothesis, which states, "As similarity between interpolation and original memorization is reduced from near identity, retention falls away to a minimum and then rises again, but with decreasing similarity it never reaches the level obtaining with maximum similarity" (Robinson, 1927, p. 299). The principle is shown in schematic form in Figure 10-7. Some of the early research carried out by Robinson and by Harden (1929) verified the first half of the law, but not the second. Dissimilar materials cause more interference than would be predicted by the hypothesis. However, a vast experimental literature has grown up around the problem of similarity and interference since 1941, and the problem itself has proved to be far more complex than Robinson's assumptions led him to believe. As we noted in connection with negative-transfer experiments, not only must general similarity be taken into account, it is also important to specify whether we are referring to stimulus similarity or response similarity.

A number of studies (Briggs, 1957; McGeoch, 1929; Postman & Riley, 1959; Robinson, 1927) have shown that the degree of original learning is inversely related to the degree of mastery of interpolated learning. In other words, if task A is thoroughly mastered, task B has less detrimental influence than if A is only incom-

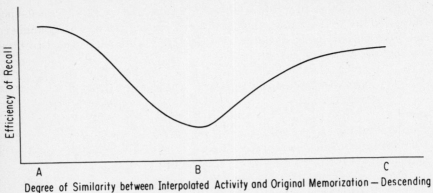

FIGURE 10-7.   The Skaggs-Robinson hypothesis relating efficiency of recall to degree of similarity between interpolated activity and original memory. At A similarity is maximal; at B similarity is intermediate; at C similarity is minimal. (From Robinson, E. S. The "similarity" factor in retroaction. American Journal of Psychology. 1927, 39, 299.)

pletely mastered. This suggests that in cases of incomplete mastery the memory traces have not become completely consolidated and hence are subject to disruption—an important hypothesis to be evaluated in any complete theory of learning.

However, it is important to recognize that although retroactive inhibition effects increase with the degree of interpolated learning, these effects are measured *relative* to the level of a control group. The *absolute* difference between the experimental and control groups tends to remain about the same with increasing degrees of original learning (Briggs, 1957). Consequently, the decline in retroactive inhibition—as measured by comparing the relative levels of performance of the experimental group and a control group—is a function of the higher level of performance of the latter and its greater degree of mastery of the original material.

It seems logical to assume that the degree of interpolated learning would also influence the amount of retroaction, with greater degrees of interpolated learning causing more interference. McGeoch (1929) tested this hypothesis by varying the number of trials of the interpolated learning while holding the number of trials of the original learning constant. The original material was presented for 11 trials, the interpolated for 6, 11, 16, 21, or 26. Retroactive interference increased from between 6 and 11 trials but not beyond that, suggesting again that recency effects in retroaction may be the most important variable.

McGeoch's early findings utilizing nonsense syllables have, in general, been confirmed by subsequent investigators utilizing a variety of meaningful materials. For a review of these findings, as well as for additional factors bearing on retroactive inhibition, the reader is referred to Postman (1971).

Theoretically it might be assumed that placement of interpolated material directly after the original learning would maximize interference, whereas placement later in the interval near recall time would result in less interference, with a possible increase near recall time. Unfortunately, the results are conflicting, with some investigators finding peaks of maximal interference at various points along the curve of retention (Figure 10-8). However, the tentative conclusion that interference is maximized when the interpolated material is learned just after the original learning session appears to be justified, thus lending support to an anticonsolidation hypothesis (Postman & Alper, 1946).

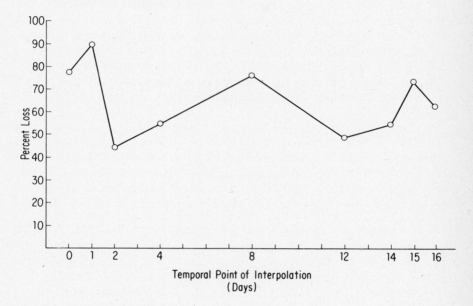

Temporal Point of Interpolation
(Days)

FIGURE 10-8. The relationship between loss in retention and the temporal point of interpolation of interpolated material. (From Postman, L., and Alper, T. G. Retroactive inhibition as a function of time of interpolation of the inhibitor between learning and recall. American Journal of Psychology. Copyright 1946 by the American Psychological Association. Reprinted by permission.)

Theories of Retroactive Inhibition

The discovery of retroactive inhibition stimulated learning theorists to attempt to account for the phenomenon. As indicated in the discussion of the effects of interpolated learning, the perseveration hypothesis offered in the early 1900s suggested that immediately after practice the memory traces need a period of consolidation before becoming fixed. McGeoch in his influential book *The Psychology of Human Learning* (1942) offered an alternative explanation of retroaction as an inhibition effect, since numerous studies had shown retroaction to vary with intertask similarity. If activity alone—activity that theoretically disrupts perseveration—were responsible, retroaction would not vary with the similarity of the interpolated material. Essentially, McGeoch's hypothesis assumes that because retroaction varies with interlist similarity, direct competition is set up during recall between the original responses and those from the interpolated material. This hypothesis, as we have seen, finds support in negative-transfer designs where $S_1 \rightarrow R_1 : S_1 \rightarrow R_2$.

However, the only *direct* evidence for an inhibition theory would be the actual verbal intrusion of the competing responses during recall. This, in fact, does occur but not to the extent necessary to account for the amount of retroaction obtained. Indeed, Melton and Irwin (1940) found that the number of intrusions increases rapidly during early trials on the interpolated list but then falls off, indicating that some other factor is operating. This factor has been identified as *unlearning*, or the extinction of the original list associations during the interpolated practice. Considerable support for the unlearning hypothesis has been found in a variety of experimental designs. However, the issues involved in accounting for retroaction are complex and remain unsettled. For a recent review of the theoretical and experimental literature the reader is referred to Postman (1971, pp. 1090–1102).

Proactive Inhibition

Since World War II a number of studies of proactive inhibition have been carried out by B. J. Underwood and his associates. Figure 10-9, which was formulated by Underwood (1957) from the results of several studies, shows the effect of prior learning on recall. Figure 10-10 provides a comparison of the effects of

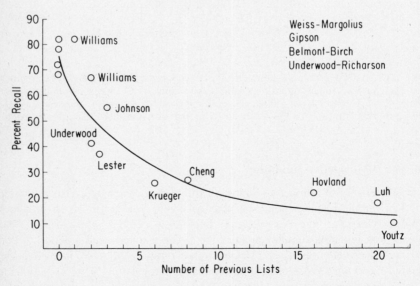

FIGURE 10-9.   The effects of prior learning on recall. Note that with increasing numbers of prior lists, recall becomes less efficient. (From Underwood, B. J. Interference and forgetting. Psychological Review, 1957, 64, p. 53, Fig. 3. Copyright 1957 by the American Psychological Association. Reprinted by permission.)

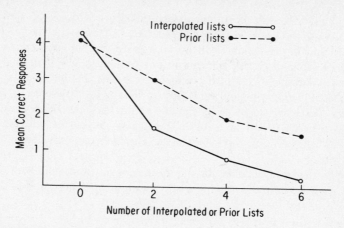

FIGURE 10-10. Retention as a function of the number of interpolated lists (retroactive inhibition) and prior lists (proactive inhibition). (From Underwood, B. J. The effects of successive interpolations on retroactive and proactive inhibition. Psychological Monographs, 1945, 59, No. 3, p. 22, Fig. 5.) Copyright 1945 by the American Psychological Association. Reprinted by permission.

proactive and retroactive inhibition on retention (Underwood, 1945). Although retroaction causes the greatest amount of interference, the two curves are similar in all respects.

The importance of Underwood's findings for a theory of forgetting lies in his showing that the retention of any given set of materials is a joint function of (1) what has gone on before and (2) interpolated learning, which may come afterward.

His work further suggests that some of the early literature utilizing well-practiced subjects (Ebbinghaus, for example) may show abnormally steep losses in retention following learning because of hidden proactive inhibition. Although the precise mechanisms of proactive inhibition are not yet understood, we must now recognize that any theory of forgetting must take both types of interference—retroactive and proactive—into consideration. Underwood, moreover, has emphasized the subject's extralaboratory experiences as possible influences on the course of forgetting, particularly in the case of college student subjects who are likely to be engaging in verbal learning tasks similar to those demanded of them in the laboratory.

Pathological and Other Conditions

Any theory that ascribes a major share of forgetting to activities interpolated between learning and recall needs to take into account the influence of various psychological states on retention. If, as interference theories presuppose, the failure of trace consolidation because of interpolated activities is the primary cause of forgetting, then studies that investigate the role of level of activity following learning should provide direct evidence on the validity of these theories.

The classic studies on the problem were carried out by J. G. Jenkins and Dallenbach (1924) and by Van Ormer (1932), who investigated the influence of sleep on retention. In the Jenkins-Dallenbach experiment, subjects learned lists of ten nonsense syllables and then engaged in one to eight hours of normal waking activity (control subject) or sleep (experimental subject). Figure 10-11 shows the comparative level of forgetting during sleep and waking for two subjects. It will be noted that the curve for sleep drops rapidly—though not as sharply as that for waking—and then levels off at a higher level than the curve for waking. The experiment furnishes no direct evidence as to why the sleep curve should show a rapid initial loss.

Indirect evidence to account for this result comes from studies of the electroencephalographic recording of brain waves during sleep. These studies show that

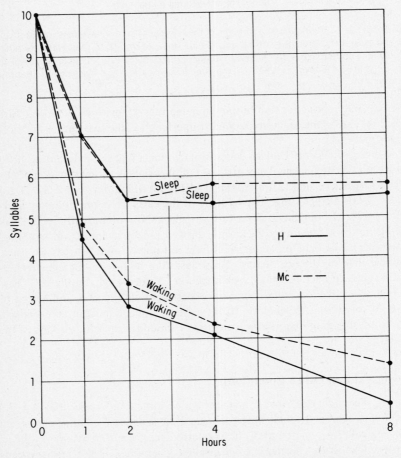

FIGURE 10-11.   Retention as a function of sleep and waking for two subjects. (From Jenkins, J. G., and Dallenbach, K. M. Obliviscence during sleep and waking. American Journal of Psychology, 35. Copyright 1924 by the American Psychological Association. Reprinted by permission.)

deep sleep is not achieved instantly. Presumably, the cortex remains more active for the first hour or so of sleep than during deep sleep. The Jenkins-Dallenbach results clearly demonstrate that the differential forgetting during the waking state is due to the cerebral activity going on and not to mere "disuse" with the passage of time. These findings were confirmed in all essentials by Van Ormer, who utilized the savings method rather than direct recall, and more recently by Ekstrand (1967).

Attempts to control the activity level of animal subjects to the point of "freezing" them physiologically immediately after learning have given mixed results. Drugs and anesthetics have been used for this purpose, but retention level is not improved by anesthesia, possibly because of the deleterious physiological effects of the drug. In an attempt to circumvent this difficulty, Minami and Dallenbach (1946) utilized the propensity of the cockroach to become inactive when subjected to extensive bodily contact, such as when crawling into a box containing tissue paper. Comparison of an experimental group and a control group (which was permitted activity in a small cage) on a simple maze problem showed that the active insects were significantly inferior to the inactive insects in retention, the inactives showing only a very moderate loss in retention.

It would be unwise to generalize from maze learning in cockroaches to verbal learning in humans to prove that complete inactivity in humans would result in better retention. However, the results are interesting as a confirmation of the work with human subjects and as a striking example of the great phylogenetic range of this fundamental principle of retention.

Equally instructive in accounting for the mechanism of retention are clinical studies of retrograde and anterograde amnesia. Both of these conditions can result from blows to the head, which produce varying periods of forgetting. In retrograde amnesia the events immediately before the injury are forgotten. In anterograde amnesia events following the injury are forgotten. In either case, the theoretical explanation is given in terms of interference from the physiological disturbance adversely affecting the consolidation of the memory traces.

Similar results are obtained when human or animal subjects are subjected to electroshock immediately after learning. If human patients under electroshock therapy are given lists of verbal materials to learn, they cannot retain these following shock (Zubin, 1948). Similar results have been obtained by investigators who subject animals to cerebral shock following learning (Morgan, 1965, pp. 547–548). We do not know why shock causes amnesia (or why it brings about remission of symptoms in certain psychiatric conditions). It has been suggested that the attendant convulsions cause temporary anoxia in the brain, thereby disrupting the neuronal pathways that mediate recent memories.

MOTIVATED FORGETTING

We are indebted to Sigmund Freud for the first systematic theory of motivated forgetting. In his famous *Psychopathology of Everyday Life* (1938a) he called attention to many instances of slips of the tongue *(lapsis linguae),* forgetting of appointments, functional amnesias, and similar states that seem to have a psychological function in protecting the ego. Thus, forgetting a name associated with an unpleasant experience is an adjustive mechanism designed to protect the self from a painful memory. Similarly, a husband who forgets the opera tickets when he really does not want to attend may be expressing a subconscious wish by his behavior.

More generally, Freud and his followers postulated that in cases of memory involving painful or shameful experiences a process of *repression* inhibits memories from reaching consciousness. Repression, it must be emphasized, is not forgetting; repressed memories are only inhibited and constantly strive to find disguised expression in dreams, neurotic symptoms, slips of the tongue, and the like.

Although it is not possible for psychologists to experiment on repression directly by having children undergo threatening or humiliating experiences, it has been possible to design analogues of repression using verbal materials. Zeller (1950a, 1950b, 1951), who has done considerable work in this area, utilized the broad outlines of a retroaction experiment to investigate repression. His experimental group learned task A, then was given practice on task B with ego deflation and embarrassment (the experimenter informed the subjects they had failed). There followed a recall test for task A to determine whether repression had occurred. The subjects were then given more practice on task B with praise from the experimenter (broadly analogous to a therapeutic session), and finally, a test of task A to discover if repression had been successfully removed. Zeller has reported that he obtained evidence of repression by comparing experimental groups with control groups who did not undergo ego deflation. Similar experiments carried out by Aborn (1953) gave similar results.

It is also possible to interpret repression in terms of conditioning models of learning. In operant conditioning situations (Chapter 9), when a response is followed by punishment, behavior will be depressed or inhibited. However, it is not "forgotten" or eliminated from the organism's repertoire of responses, since if the punishment ceases, the response can quickly revert to its original level. If repressed responses are considered as suppressed or inhibited by punishment in the form of parental threats, social prohibitions, or "feelings of guilt," then therapy being a nonpunishing situation will allow the responses to recur as they were originally learned.

However, the experimental conditions in these experiments fall short of those demanded by Freudian theory, which presumed repression to be the result of an extremely traumatic experience, such as a sexual assault or a child's witnessing parental intercourse. Clearly, ego deflation, while embarrassing and humiliating for some subjects, does not measure up to such highly charged experiences. More generally, in repression we may have an instance of a psychoanalytic concept that is almost universally accepted by psychologists but for which there is little concrete experimental evidence, largely because of ethical barriers to research on the problem.

Problems of experimental design and interpretation are also sources of controversy in attempting to evaluate the famous *Zeigarnik effect,* or the tendency for subjects to remember interrupted tasks better than completed tasks. Zeigarnik

(1927), a pupil of Lewin's, gave subjects a series of twenty simple tasks. Half of the tasks were interrupted, and the rest were allowed to go on to completion. At the end of the session the subjects were asked to recall all tasks. On the average, about 50 percent could be recalled; but of the remembered tasks 68 percent of the unfinished tasks were recalled as against only 43 percent of the finished. This differential recall of unfinished tasks is known as the Zeigarnik effect and was attributed by her to the tensions associated with a subjective state of disequilibrium because of lack of completion or closure of the task.

The experiment has been repeated a number of times with positive results. However, in some cases reversals of the effect may occur, with completed tasks being recalled better if the subject believes his or her intelligence is being measured. Failure becomes humiliating, and it is accompanied by an apparent tendency to wish to forget the "failed" tasks. Ego defense, then, may be the critical factor rather than "tension" or "disequilibrium." A number of experiments bearing on the problem are interpretively reviewed by Osgood (1953, pp. 582–587). Here we need only note that regardless of the theoretical interpretation of the Zeigarnik effect, it appears to lend support to motivated factors in forgetting.

AN INTEGRATED THEORY OF FORGETTING IN LONG-TERM MEMORY

Any theory of forgetting that pretends to completeness would have to take into account not only the factors reviewed in this chapter but others as well. Let us briefly discuss these by way of a summary of this section.

1. Disuse. Disuse has never proved to be a popular theory of forgetting. Nevertheless, we mention it as a possibility. It seems logical to believe that *some* degree of forgetting could be the result of disuse, especially because of fading traces caused by metabolic changes in the cerebral cortex.
2. Interference effects. Of these we have discussed (a) retroactive inhibition, which has played a prominent if not the major role in theories of forgetting since the work of Ebbinghaus and (b) proactive inhibition, which also has come into increasing prominence with the studies of Underwood and his associates since World War II.
3. Pathological and other states. Under this variable we have included retrograde and anterograde amnesia, shock effects, and the like as special kinds of forgetting that more generally support a perseveration or consolidation theory of trace formation.
4. Motivational variables. Important here are clinical cases of forgetting because of functional amnesia and because of repression, which reveal the role of personality and ego-defense mechanisms in retention.
5. Gestalt factors. The reader will recall that the Gestalt psychologists emphasized that memories undergo systematic changes with the passage of time in accordance with the principles of perceptual organization (Chapter 5). These, too, would have to be included in a complete theory of forgetting.

Of these five possible causes of forgetting, we may add that interference effects are currently believed to be the single most important factor in ordinary forgetting.

Moreover, retroactive and proactive theory has received the widest general experimental support.

CONTEMPORARY TRENDS: SHORT-TERM MEMORY

Within the past two decades considerable interest has developed around the concept of short-term memory and its possible differences from long-term memory. A short-term memory is illustrated by the memory span or the number of digits that can be recalled after a single presentation. Such a unit of material has been called a "chunk" (G. A. Miller, 1956) and may represent a maximal amount that can be encoded in the brain from a single brief exposure. Individuals with long memory spans may be able to encode larger masses of information into a limited number of chunks by grouping techniques.

L. R. Peterson and M. J. Peterson (1959) studied short-term memory by presenting the subject with a three-letter nonsense syllable followed by a number. When the subject heard the number, he or she was instructed to count backward from it by threes until given a stop signal. This was done to prevent rehearsal of the syllable. At the signal the subject tried to recall the syllable. Intervals between the presentation of the syllable and the signal for its recall were 3, 6, 9, 12, or 18 seconds. The frequencies of correct recalls are shown in Figure 10-12. It will be noted that forgetting is rapid, with nearly complete forgetting occurring by 18 seconds. These results show the very limited time in which storage can take place. Confirmation of these results was obtained by Murdock (1961), who utilized paired associates made up from the Thorndike-Lorge Word Frequency List. No difference was found in the subject's ability to remember three words as opposed to three digits, both being made up of an equal number of chunks.

Since these early experiments on short-term memory were reported, many investigators have carried out studies involving primarily the effects of proactive and retroactive inhibition on the process. The effects of intralist similarity, the amount of interpolated material, and the buildup of proactive inhibition under conditions of repeated testing have all been investigated. In general, the same effects are obtained in short-term as in long-term retention. Repeated testing of subjects leads to proactive inhibition; the interpolation of material results in retroactive inhibition; and the degree of similarity of the original and interpolated tasks is important. In retroactive inhibition, acoustic similarity of the original and interpolated materials is extremely important, since materials in short-term memory experiments are pronounced orally.

Many of the experiments on short-term memory involve methodological investigations in this relatively new field, and there are differences of opinion over the interpretation of different investigators' results. As yet, it is impossible to conclude that long- and short-term memory are identical, even though they do exhibit many of the same phenomena in experimental programs (Murdock, 1967a, 1967b).

However, there are also certain measurable differences in short-term as opposed to long-term memory, and these have led some theorists to assume that two different processes are involved. First, the free recall of a series of unrelated words gives evidence of two different kinds of memory in that the beginning, middle, and

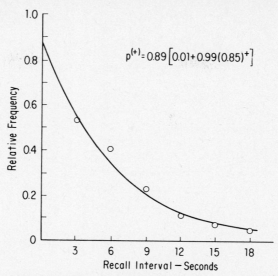

$$p^{(+)} = 0.89 \left[0.01 + 0.99(0.85)^{+} \right]$$

FIGURE 10-12.   A curve for short-term memory. Note that the relative frequency (of correct recalls) has dropped to nearly zero after only 18 seconds. (From Peterson, L. R., and Peterson, M. J. Short-term retention of individual items. Journal of Experimental Psychology, 1959, 58, p. 195, Fig. 3. Copyright 1959 by the American Psychological Association. Reprinted by permission.

end items in the list show varying probabilities of recall. In such experiments (Glanzer & Cunitz, 1966) the subjects are presented with the words one at a time and then asked to recall as many as possible in any order that they please.

When the probability of recall is plotted against the serial position of the items in the list, a curve is obtained that shows the best retention is for items near the end of the list, the next best retention for items near the beginning of the list, and the poorest for items in the middle of the list (see Figure 10-13).

The recency effect, which describes the better recall of items near the end of the list, has been attributed to short-term memory. Retention in the early part of the curve, the primacy effect, is attributed to long-term memory, as is retention as measured by the middle of the curve. Additional support for the assumption that the recency effect is the result of short-term memory comes from studies where the recall is delayed (Bartz, 1969; Craik, 1970) or when the subject is required to perform an interpolated task, such as solving arithmetic problems immediately after presentation and before recall.

A second body of evidence in support of a two-process theory of memory comes from two kinds of interference effects known as *acoustic* and *semantic* similarity. These effects are tested by constructing lists of synonyms (semantic similarity) and homophone[3] pairs (acoustic similarity). Acoustic similarity between items has a significantly detrimental effect on short-term memory, whereas semantic similarity has little effect.

---

[3]Homophones are words that are pronounced approximately the same but are different in meaning: led-lead; bare-bear; hair-hare.

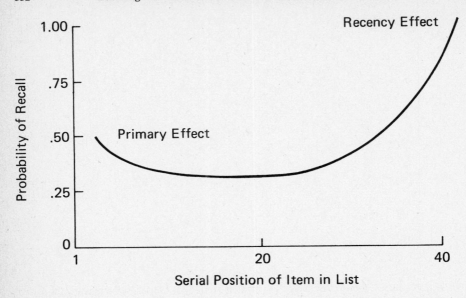

FIGURE 10-13.   Probability of recall as a function of serial presentation position.

In an experiment designed to test the differential effects of semantic and acoustic similarity, Kintsch and Buschke (1969) used word lists of two types. One list consisted of sixteen unrelated words and the other of eight pairs of synonyms. The words were presented in random order. In a parallel experiment the two lists were unrelated words and pairs of homophones. It was found that semantic similarity had a negative effect on long-term memory, but acoustic similarity had a detrimental effect on the recency portions of the curves. The underlying assumption is that the semantic meanings of common words are well established in long-term memory and so would have little effect on short-term memory, whereas acoustic similarity arises purely through the arbitrary pairing of words without regard to meaning and so depends more on immediate memory processes. Because of sound similarities there is more chance for interference effects among such pairs.

Finally, striking evidence for a two-process theory of memory comes from clinical studies of persons suffering from hippocampal lesions. The hippocampus is part of the limbic system, a phylogenetically older part of the brain buried deep below the cerebral cortex. We know that it is involved in emotional reactions (see Chapter 14), but we also know (Milner, 1959; Scoville & Milner, 1957) that patients with hippocampal lesions show serious deficits for recent memories even though their memory for events in the more distant past may be intact. Memory for recent events is so deficient that such patients are unable to learn the names of new acquaintances, new telephone numbers, or street addresses even though they are repeated hundreds of times.

These disabilities strongly suggest that something is seriously wrong with the encoding process for short-term memory, making it impossible for these to be converted into long-term memories.

A number of theorists have attempted to account for the differential nature of long- and short-term memory by assuming that there are two related but separate storage mechanisms. Atkinson and Shiffrin (1971), for example, believe that the key mechanism in short-term memory is a *rehearsal buffer* process, which provides for rapid rehearsal of selected items during the short-term memory phase that then become encoded into long-term memory given sufficient rehearsal. Obviously, a selective process is involved in which only a limited number of items (memory span) can be processed and rehearsed at a given time. Consequently, much incoming information never gets encoded and so is discarded.

INFORMATION PROCESSING THEORY AND MEMORY

There is a strong trend among contemporary learning theorists to adopt an information processing model of learning and memory (see, for example, Murdock, 1974). It will be recalled that a similar trend has been dominant in perceptual theory for the past two decades. For this reason a kind of rapprochement has developed between the two fields in that theorists in both areas are employing similar concepts and models. Thus, one may speak of perceptual experiences, which are detected → coded → stored → retrieved, or of memory experiences, which are similarly processed through input → short-term memory → rehearsal → long-term memory → retrieval. Fundamentally, the two sets of processes are the same.

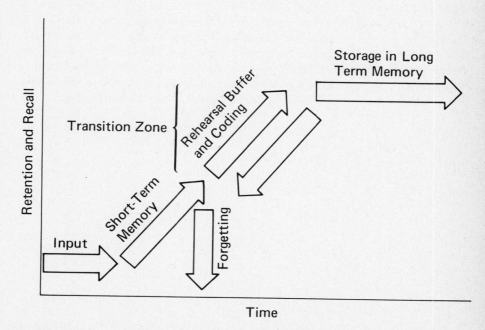

FIGURE 10-14. An information processing model of the flow of information for short and long term memory.

To further relate the two, we may think of incoming information entering a sensory input system (Figure 10-14), there to undergo iconic storage. If it is not interfered with by new information, it enters short-term memory processing. Again it is subjected to a selective process (the rehearsal buffer) that encodes some information for permanent storage in long-term memory. In either case the retrieval system can reactivate long-term memories or permanently encoded perceptual experiences. As Figure 10-14 shows, the time spectrum involves an extensive continuum—ranging from a few milliseconds to days, weeks, months, and even years.

The feedback loops shown in Figure 10-14 reflect the fact that information processing models must take into account underlying neural mechanisms. As first suggested by Hebb (1949), perceptual processing and short-term memory probably depend upon some kind of reverberatory neural circuits (Chapter 14). Functionally speaking, these are circular chains of neurons in which stimulation sets up activity that may persist for a period of time without further input. If activity persists long enough, consolidation takes place, either into short- or long-term storage. Retrieval circuits may be activated by outside stimulation—as remembering a name when we see an acquaintance—or by self-generative processes, as when we can remember our friend's name even though he or she is not present. Because channel capacities are limited, and since there is always the possibility of interference effects (both immediate and long-term), the successful functioning of the system depends on a high degree of selectivity both in the input and encoding stages.

There remain many gaps between the data from psychological studies of the memory function and neurophysiology. The concepts and models that rely on information processing theory are models. They do not necessarily have truth value. Their usefulness lies in their ability to summarize and schematize what we know about the flow of information from the environment and in their potential for generating research. Even the most superficial glance at the experimental literature in perception and learning in recent years demonstrates the enormous stimulation psychologists have received from the technology of information processing.

Thinking and Language

11

Thinking is closely allied with the process of learning, inasmuch as our chief tools of thought—concepts—are learned. Moreover, a great deal of our thinking in everyday life is based on memories, recollections, and memory images. Indeed, much of what is called thinking is actually remembering. For example, when an individual exclaims, "I wish I could think of his name," he or she is trying to remember something learned in the past.

However, there are other cases in which thinking is clearly different from simple memory. The farm boy resting on a haystack and building castles in Spain is engaging in reverie, a form of thinking which depends upon memory, but goes far beyond memory to the imagining of events that have never happened and probably never will. Or consider a scientist who is engaged in seeking the solution to a problem. He or she utilizes learned concepts, but the characteristic thing about this variety of thinking is the discovery of new relationships. Thinking, then, takes many forms. Here at the outset let us attempt to classify the more important types in order to have working definitions for the discussion of the systematic views on thinking that constitute the remainder of this chapter.

VARIETIES OF THINKING

Perhaps the simplest and most fundamental type of thinking is simple association, of which there are two varieties: *free* and *controlled*. Free association occurs whenever the thinker allows the stream of consciousness to wander where it will, as so often happens at night when we are dropping off to sleep. Frequently under these conditions memory seems to drift from one thing to another, to the point where the individual may be surprised at the long chain of loosely related events that has passed through consciousness. It is also interesting to note that free association is employed in psychoanalysis. Theoretically, the freely associating patient's "guard" is down; and, as a consequence, memories and impulses ordinarily not admitted to consciousness can come to the foreground.

By contrast, in controlled association thinking is restricted, since the subject is instructed to respond with a certain type or class of possible responses. For example, he or she may be told to respond to a set of stimulus words by giving their opposites. Thus, if the stimulus word "light" is spoken by the experimenter, the subject responds with "dark." In the case where opposites must be given, the degree of restriction is great. However, where the subject is required to give synonyms a somewhat greater degree of latitude is permitted.

In reverie, fantasy, and dreams (both day and night), associations flowing through consciousness are not directed by conscious efforts of the thinker. However, in any of these varieties of thinking, thought patterns are more highly organized and interrelated than is true of thinking in free association. There is, so to speak, a theme running through the thinker's mind. In fact, as common experience tells us, nocturnal dreams may be so highly structured and realistic that, upon awakening, the dreamer is not certain whether he or she has been dreaming or has experienced real events. Most psychologists believe that the theme or story in reverie, fantasy, and dreams is related to the thinker's motivational processes. Often these varieties of ideational activity are wish fulfilling in the sense that the individual is obtaining satisfactions in imagination that he or she cannot achieve in reality; or, as is so often true in reverie, the function may be purely recreational. One cannot focus on reality all the time!

Autistic thinking is dominated by the thinker's needs rather than by the demands of reality. In this sense, autistic thinking is closely related to reverie, fantasy, and dreaming; and, for this reason, some psychologists use the terms more or less interchangeably. However, there are occasions when autistic thinking can be distinguished from reverie, fantasy, and dreaming. For example, let us suppose that a scientist has a strong prejudice (and scientists do have prejudices) in favor of a particular theory. Quite unconsciously his or her interpretations of empirical findings may be distorted in favor of a theoretical position, even though every effort has been made to be objective.[1] Therefore, in contrast to fantasy, reverie, and dreaming, which are usually conscious, autistic thinking is frequently an insidious, unconscious process that is difficult to detect.

Animism is thinking in which the individual projects life, or the attributes of life, into inanimate objects. As we shall see, this form of thinking is common in young children, who are prone to attribute life or conscious awareness to clouds, astronomical bodies, the wind, and other natural phenomena.

Problem solving and creative thinking are highly directed, goal-oriented types of ideational activity. In some cases the subject may be engaged in reasoning to find new relationships; or he or she may simply be trying to remember a formula that will solve a mathematical problem. Or perhaps the thinker is a philosopher at work in an armchair trying to improve on a traditional ethical system. In still another instance the thinker might be an artist attempting to develop a new school of painting. As these few examples show, problem solving and creative thinking take many forms—so many, indeed, that an extensive breakdown of this broad category of thinking alone would constitute an entire volume.

Our brief outline of the chief types of thinking should serve to demonstrate that ideation is a process with many facets; and, as a consequence, it is often necessary

---

[1]Darwin once observed that he was always careful to record any information unfavorable to his theory of evolution, since, if he failed to do so, he often forgot it.

to specify what *type* of ideational activity is under consideration rather than to employ the loose term "thinking." As will be apparent in our examination of the systematic psychology of thinking, investigators, aware of the many varieties of the thought processes, have developed different theories or systems in an attempt to explain certain types or aspects of thinking, rather than encompass the thought processes as a whole in a single, comprehensive theory.

HISTORICAL BACKGROUND

Much of what we had to say about the early psychology of perception and learning is, of course, equally relevant to thinking. The philosophers and pioneer experimental psychologists who sought to learn the nature of the higher mental processes through the study of elements were confident that thinking could be reduced to simpler processes. As we have pointed out in previous chapters, mental chemistry was popular among the empiricists and associationists, and—besides being responsible for the development of associationism as a school of philosophy—also led to the structuralist psychology of Wundt and Titchener. Because the basic aim of the structuralists was the analysis of mental contents, we may include Wundt, Titchener, and their followers under the broad rubric of "content" psychologists.

The Austrian and Würzburg Schools

However, during the same period that Wundt and Titchener were developing structuralism, two opposition movements were growing in psychology, both of which found support on the continent of Europe and in the United States. In Europe the chief opponent of content psychology was a group in southern Germany and Austria collectively known as the Austrian school. This school stressed the study of mental *acts* and *functions* as the proper subject matter for psychology as opposed to conscious content. The act school of psychology, as it also came to be known, was founded by Franz Brentano (1838–1917), a man of diverse interests and strong theoretical leanings. Brentano held that the subject matter of psychology should be acts, not contents; or to put it another way, psychology ought to be the study of mental processes, not structures. For example, the mental activity of seeing a color must be distinguished from what is seen. The sensory content of redness is not the same as the experience of sensing red. Mental acts must be thought of as verbs—seeing, sensing, feeling, thinking, and so forth—and not as nouns—sensations, affective states, images, and the like.

As we have seen, the American functionalists James, Dewey, Angell, and Carr—who were also opposed to structuralism—held that the subject matter of psychology should be the study of mental and behavioral processes and not conscious contents. Consequently, they found common cause with the act psychologists in opposing structuralism, although they were not members of the Austrian school.

Another opposition group that became famous and influential in its opposition to Wundt and Titchener was led by Oswald Külpe (1862–1915), a former follower of Wundt who broke away to found what came to be known as the Würzburg school, the name taken from the University of Würzburg where Külpe accepted a position of professor of psychology in 1894 and where he established a laboratory, which for a time rivaled in importance Wundt's at Leipzig.

Unlike the Austrian group, Külpe and his associates did not reject conscious content as the subject matter of psychology; nor did they abandon the introspective method. They remained content psychologists but expanded the study of contents to encompass the higher mental processes, including thinking, which Wundt had said could not be successfully studied by introspection.

In their early introspective work, Külpe and his students attempted to find an element of thinking that would be coequal to Wundt's elements of sensation and affective states. They failed and concluded that thinking is an imageless process. This finding led to the concept of *imageless thought* to represent the fact that thinking can carry meaning without conveying specific images. We shall see that this finding led to a controversy with Titchener and the Wundtian school, but first we must note two other concepts developed by the Würzburg school, *conscious attitudes* and *set,* or *determining tendency*. Conscious attitudes were described by Karl Marbe, a student of Külpe's, who found that in judging weights, subjects exhibit conscious contents—hesitation, doubt, vacillation, relations, confidence, and so on—which were not considered to be sensations or images but new states called conscious attitudes.

Determining tendencies were described by Narziss Ach as a set or readiness that persists during a course of thought. In solving a problem, for example, one has an initial set to cope with the task, called by the Würzburg school the *Aufgabe*. The task exerts an immediate controlling tendency over consciousness, but the tendency persists or continues until the solution is complete. Ach held that determining tendencies need not be conscious in order to have an influence, agreeing with Külpe's and Marbe's stand on imageless thought.

It might be noted that the Austrian and Würzburg schools arrived at similar positions despite their initial differences in approach. That is, they agreed that thinking is a *sequential process,* which cannot be profitably studied merely by examining its conscious content. In this they received support from the functionalists, as we have already noted, and from the Gestalt school with its emphasis on directionality in thinking.

This, then, was the climate of psychological opinion on the thought processes when Titchener undertook the challenge of resolving the differences between structuralism and its rival schools.

THE STRUCTURALIST VIEW OF THE THOUGHT PROCESSES

Titchener's account of "thought,"[2] which is the title of the ninth chapter of his *Textbook,* begins on a strongly controversial note. Titchener, it will be recalled, taught that consciousness was reducible to three basic elements: sensations, images,

---

[2]Our exposition is based on Titchener's *Textbook of Psychology* (1910).

and affections. Reports emanating from the Austrian and Würzburg laboratories to the effect that introspection of the thought processes revealed the existence of "conscious attitudes," "imageless thoughts," and "elementary processes of relation" had come to his attention. None of these ideational activities appeared to be explicable in terms of the structuralists' traditional three elements; and, even more disturbing, these activities might have to be regarded as new elements.

The greater part of Titchener's account of thinking is an attempt to refute this challenge to structuralism rather than to develop an original point of view on the thought processes. We do not mean to impute prejudice to Titchener. He is fair in concluding that opinion alone is not sufficient for resolving issues that can be decided upon only after further experimentation. What we wish to emphasize is the weakness of the structuralist contribution to the psychology of thinking. Titchener's simple elementalism was no match for the variety and richness of the cognitive processes. But let us summarize his arguments on the old controversies of the day, for it will help to introduce us to the issues that were central in the early systematic viewpoints on thinking.

Conscious attitudes may be exemplified by such everyday concepts as "hesitation," "vacillation," or "dissent." Can a strong conscious state of the attitude "this is novel" be analyzed into the familiar elements of consciousness? The initial introspective reports generally favored the stand that such an attitude was unanalyzable. Titchener holds the contrary view that such conscious attitudes are analyzable and that the difficulties experienced by other investigators were the result of several experimental errors.

First, he believes that psychologists working in the area of thinking had become victims of suggestion, so that when observers found conscious attitudes unanalyzable, others took their findings more or less for granted and failed to pursue their own investigations with sufficient rigor. Second, Titchener points out that attitudes "thin out" with repetition, so the visual and verbal images that originally mediate attitudes are no longer present when an attitude is brought under laboratory investigation. As a result, the thought processes involved seem to be imageless and sensationless. It was precisely this finding that supported the argument for new elements; for if thought is not dependent upon the elements of consciousness, it must stand alone as a new element coequal with the original three. Third, Titchener believes that some observers had fallen into the error of reporting their ideas or attitudes *as ideas* instead of looking beyond to the elements out of which the idea or attitude is formulated. The situation here is similar to that found in describing an object in terms of its ordinary meaning (the stimulus error),[3] instead of the raw conscious processes that are generated by stimuli from the object.

Other difficulties connected with the analysis of ideational processes are discussed by Titchener, but the three we have summarized are a sufficient indication of the problems and pitfalls of the introspective approach to the thought processes. Titchener, however, is certain that the difficulties are experimental artifacts and that

---

[3]See Chapter 3 of this volume.

more carefully controlled observations will eventually resolve them in favor of the structuralist point of view. Indeed, he reports positive results from his own laboratory, where a large number of attitudes were "pounced upon" at the moment they came to the observer's consciousness and "made focal and examined as carefully as the circumstances allowed" (1910, p. 516). In Titchener's opinion there was little doubt of the result: "All the reports show the same features: visual images, pictorial or symbolic; internal speech; kinesthetic images; organic sensations. Nowhere a sign of the imageless component!" (1910, p. 516). Thus the problems of "conscious attitudes" and "imageless thoughts" are resolved by Titchener at one and the same time.

The "alleged elementary process of relation" is described by Titchener as the conscious state which arises when such concepts as "if," "and," "but," and "is to" occur in the observer's consciousness. Some introspectionists were convinced that the conscious relations mediated by such terms are elementary thought processes not reducible to sensations, images, and affections. In Titchener's own words, the problem and its possible solutions are described as follows:

> The observer was asked, for instance, "London is to England as Paris is to _____?" or: "Eyes are to face as a lake is to _____?" He was required to answer these questions, in the sense of the relation obtaining between the first pair of terms, and then, afterwards, to give an introspective account of the whole experience. The results were of three kinds. The blank may be filled up, under pressure of the instruction, without any consciousness of relation; the transferred relation may be carried in visual images, or in internal speech; and, lastly, the relation may be present in consciousness, without any imaginal component, simply as an "imageless thought." From these results the conclusion is drawn that "the feelings of relation are of the same order as feelings of sensory qualities; each feeling of relation is a simple quality." (1910, p. 512)

Titchener and his associates tackled the problem of ideational relations in their characteristically forthright manner, and the results from the laboratory in no way favored the supporters of "imageless relations" or "elementary processes of relation." Rather, the consciousness of relations was, in the great majority of introspective reports, accompanied by sensory or verbal images.

At the end of his discussion, Titchener concluded that the structuralists' position that there are only three elementary processes—sensations, images, and affections—stands. He then goes on to deal with other cognitive processes such as language, abstract ideas, and judgment. We need not trace the development of his position on these topics, since we would only be multiplying examples. As he saw it, the problem throughout is the same: how to analyze the complex and often elusive thought processes into more elementary components. It is truly a psychology of content, whose fundamental method is mental chemistry. Nothing original was added to the psychology of thinking by the structuralists. Instead, ideational activities are reduced to the familiar, well-established elements from which all complex conscious processes are derived.

Summary

This, then, was the state of the structuralist psychology of thought. Titchener, trained in the Wundtian tradition, championed the point of view that the thought processes could be successfully analyzed into the traditional elements of the structuralists without the necessity for postulating a new "thought element." Külpe, from the same academic background, gained wide support for the "imageless thought" interpretation of the ideational processes and, as a result, gradually moved toward a functionalistic position. Consequently, the structuralists were under attack by their German colleagues as well as by the American functionalists, whose position we shall consider next.

FUNCTIONALISM AND THE THOUGHT PROCESSES

William James, the brilliant precursor of the American school of functionalism, sets the tone for the functionalist view of the thought processes in one of the most famous passages in the literature of psychology. We refer to the ninth chapter of the first volume of his *Principles of Psychology* (1890), entitled, significantly, "The Stream of Thought." A few quotations from it are worth including, both for their excellent descriptive value and functionalist flavor. Here, for example, is the famous paragraph in which James defines thought as a stream of consciousness:

> Consciousness, then, does not appear to itself chopped up in bits. Such words as "chain" or "train" do not describe it fitly as it presents itself in the first instance. It is nothing jointed; it flows. A "river" or a "stream" are the metaphors by which it is most naturally described. *In talking of it hereafter, let us call it the stream of thought, of consciousness, or of subjective life.* (1890, p. 239)

A few pages later James writes of the "flights" and "perchings" of thought:

> As we take, in fact, a general view of the wonderful stream of our consciousness, what strikes us first, is this different pace of its parts. Like a bird's life, it seems to be made of an alternation of flights and perchings. The rhythm of language expresses this, where every thought is expressed in a sentence, and every sentence closed by a period. The resting-places are usually occupied by sensorial imaginations of some sort, whose peculiarity is that they can be held before the mind for an indefinite time, and contemplated without changing; the places of flight are filled with thoughts of relations, static or dynamic, that for the most part obtain between the matters contemplated in the periods of comparative rest. (1890, p. 243)

Finally, in one of the best-known passages from the *Principles,* James describes the consciousness of a set or tendency:

> Suppose we try to recall a forgotten name. The state of our consciousness is peculiar. There is a gap therein; but no mere gap. It is a gap that is intensely active. A sort of wraith of the name is in it, beckoning us in a given direction, making us at moments

tingle with the sense of our closeness, and then letting us sink back without the longed-for term. If wrong names are proposed to us, this singularly definite gap acts immediately so as to negate them. They do not fit into its mould. And the gap of one word does not feel like the gap of another, all empty of content as both might seem necessarily to be when described as gaps. (1890, p. 251)

As descriptive psychology, James' prose is without parallel. However, we must take the long jump from James to Carr in order to examine the functionalists' position on ideation after functionalism had developed from an embryonic psychology into a mature school. The leap, however, does not represent an extensive historical period, for only thirty-five years elapsed between the publication of the *Principles* and Carr's *Textbook;* but, in the meantime, functionalism had become experimental and developed the strong systematic point of view that *mental activities* were to be studied as they functioned in enabling the organism to adapt to its environment.

Carr's[4] treatment of the nature and function of ideas strongly reflects the school's adaptive frame of reference: "An idea or thought," Carr begins, "is a cognitive process in that it involves the apprehension of an object in the interest of some subsequent reaction in reference to it" (1925, p. 164). The final phrase in the quotation conveys the potential utility value assigned to ideas by the functionalists in keeping with their overall orientation. After discoursing at length on various types of ideas, Carr returns to the characteristically functional position in a section entitled "The Function of Ideas." Here ideas are treated as substitutes for perceptual stimuli. Now if we bear in mind that he defines perception as "The cognition of a present object in relation to some act of adjustment," then it is clear that ideas are capable of arousing response patterns that have adaptive value for the individual. Carr exemplifies his argument by suggesting that the thought of a coming lecture may induce more adequate preparation, or that the individual in walking home at night may utilize his or her cognitive knowledge of the streets by taking advantage of a shortcut.

Ideas, therefore, have the same consequences in adaptive activity as perceptions. More particularly, Carr suggests three ways in which ideas may function in adaptive conduct. First, the object of thought may be the end or goal of adaptive behavior. The dress designer or architect has an ideational conception of the end product of his or her activities in mind from the beginning.

In this same connection, Carr adds that it is by means of ideas that we are able to strive for remote goals. Because of the ability to look ahead, the human organism is capable of creative ideational behavior. Inventions, bridges, dams, and similar complex and remote goal-adaptive projects can be undertaken for human betterment. Second, thoughts may serve as means to ends. To illustrate, we may think of a tool that will facilitate the completion of an ongoing do-it-yourself project and thus utilize an idea in bringing about a more nearly adequate adjustment. Finally, ideas may serve a vicarious function in taking the place of actual behavior. The chess

---

[4]Our exposition follows Carr (1925, chap. 8).

player, for example, often makes many moves ideationally in order to foresee, if possible, their consequences when carried out in actuality.[5]

In addition to his treatment of ideas in general, Carr devotes a chapter to the specific topic of reasoning. The treatment, however, is so similar to his earlier account of perceptual motor learning (see Chapter 8) that one wonders why he bothered to separate the two. In essence, he considers reasoning as identical in all important respects to perceptual-motor learning. The reasoner is confronted with a problem that can be either perceptual or ideational. The solution is achieved by a "variable, persistent, and analytical ideational attack which is continued until the solution is more or less accidentally discovered" (Carr, 1925, p. 202).

This definition of reasoning is virtually identical with that given previously by Carr for perceptual-motor problems, save in the latter the term "motor" is used instead of "ideational." Carr, indeed, goes a step further in arguing for the similarity of the two types of problem solving by emphasizing that reasoning problems require considerable repetition before the solution is fixated.[6] Finally, he briefly discusses the process of *generalization* of ideational solutions. Generalization corresponds to transfer as he employs the latter concept in his previous discussion of perceptual-motor learning.

While the parallel is complete, Carr does not, of course, consider the two processes to be literally identical. Both the advantages and disadvantages of reasoning are pointed out by Carr and compared with those for motor behavior. In general, the great advantages of ideational problem solving over perceptual-motor solutions are its efficiency and the fact that abstract problems can be dealt with only in ideational thinking. However, he also points out that the consequences of our acts cannot always be foreseen, and in such cases we must fall back on a motor trial-and-error attack. And so, as we are leaving Carr's treatment of the reasoning process, we must again emphasize the strong affinity that exists for him between motor and ideational activity. Undoubtedly, much of the identity in the two processes is the result of his emphasis on the adaptive nature of the activities in question. The goal of adaptation, therefore, is the important consideration from the functionalists' point of view; the nature of the ideational processes involved is of less consequence.

BEHAVIORISM AND THE GREAT REVOLT

When we come to examine John B. Watson's views on thinking, we are face to face with one of the most characteristic, challenging, and controversial of all his doctrines. We refer to his famous "peripheral theory of thinking." Since Watson's viewpoint is often contrasted with the "centralist" theory of thinking, it will be convenient to consider the two together. As Figure 11-1 shows, the centralists contend that thinking is exclusively a cerebral affair, whereas the peripheralists

---

[5]Tolman coined the colorful phrase "behavior feints" to describe such processes.

[6]In reading Carr, one is impressed by his implicit lack of belief in insight and rather strong tendency to favor a trial-and-error conception of learning.

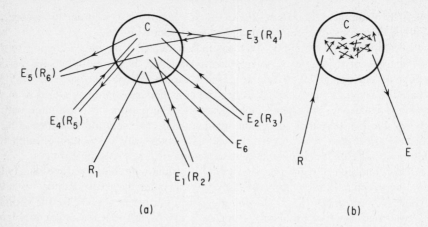

(a)   (b)

FIGURE 11-1.   The peripheralist (a) and centralist (b) views of the role of the brain in thinking.
(From J. F. Dashiell, Foundations of General Psychology. Boston: Houghton Mifflin, Co., 1949.)

consider ideation to be a function of the body as a whole. The centralist position is, of course, the older, traditional point of view supported by common experience; that is, we seem to think with our heads. Moreover, we found that the structuralists argued that the image—a central, conscious process—is the mediator of ideas. All such central processes were held to be dependent on the brain.

As early as 1914 Watson had attacked "central images," or "centrally aroused sensations," in the introductory chapter of his *Behavior: An Introduction to Comparative Psychology.* In this book he defined the image as a form of *implicit behavior,* although he had to admit that no method was then available to demonstrate the existence of any such implicit-behavior patterns, and he doubted that one would ever be devised. However, he strongly suggests that the muscles of the larynx and tongue are the probable foci of much of our implicit behavior because of the close association between language and thought. In his *Psychology from the Standpoint of a Behaviorist* (1919), published only five years after *Behavior,* Watson proves himself a poor prophet; for the behaviorists *had* found a way to measure responses of the laryngeal musculature.

The procedure he describes for recording implicit behavior is simple. A tambour, or small drum, is attached to the subject's neck in the region of the larynx. Whenever muscular movements occur, pressure changes are set up within the tambour and are transmitted to a recording device. Moreover, Watson reports investigations on deaf-mutes. He found that their hands and fingers frequently move, just as the normal individual's lips are often active while reading or deeply engaged in thought. Even though Watson's investigations of normal and deaf-mute implicit muscle movements sometimes failed to yield positive results, he was confident (1919, pp. 324–326) that such movements existed in all cases of thinking and awaited only the discovery of better instrumentation in order to be revealed.

Clearly, Watson recognized and emphasized the close correspondence between language and thinking. Indeed, "laryngeal habits" *are* his equivalent for "thinking.'' Laryngeal habits are developed in early childhood out of the vocalizations that all infants display during the first year of life. Through conditioning, such vocalizations become words. For example, the child's ''Da-da'' is attached to the father by conditioning and, through selective reinforcement, eventually becomes ''Daddy.'' As the child's verbal habits grow stronger, he or she no longer needs to speak the word ''Daddy,'' but may simply ''think'' it upon seeing the parent. However, the child's ''thinking'' is nevertheless motor as revealed by his or her *subvocal* pronunciation of words.

In addition to laryngeal habits, the language function may also be mediated by gestures, frowns, shrugs, and the like, all of which ''stand for'' more overt reactions to situations. Similarly, writing, drawing, dancing, painting, and sculpturing may be considered forms of motor communication that represent ideas. Indeed, Watson goes so far as to argue that there is really little value in attempting to record thinking experimentally, because ''it finally eventuates in action and in the second place most of it in mankind is worthless from the standpoint of society—any consistent series of thought processes which is of any social interest will, if sufficiently well-integrated with other bodily action systems, take issue finally in overt action'' (1919, p. 327).

Watson left the field of academic psychology before modern techniques for recording muscle potentials, brain waves, and nerve impulses were developed. It has since been demonstrated without doubt that the entire body and not the brain alone is involved in thinking (Humphrey, 1948; Jacobson, 1929, 1932). The muscles of the arms, legs, and trunk are in constant tension, or tonus; but during mental activity the tensions are increased—especially in the muscles closely associated with the content of the thought pattern. For example, if a man imagines lifting a weight, strong bursts of action potentials can be recorded from his arms, even though these limbs are apparently quiescent. The extrinsic muscles of the eyes are especially rich sources of such potentials during periods of waking thought and, even more dramatically, can be used as an objective index of dreaming (Dement & Wolpert, 1958).

Despite abundant confirmation that peripheral mechanisms are involved in thinking, contemporary psychologists are inclined to take a middle ground on the centralist-peripheralist continuum, recognizing that *both* cortical and peripheral processes are involved in ideational activity. There is increasing evidence to show that consciousness, thinking, and muscular processes are complementary. Ideational activity often initiates muscular activity, but the relationship is reciprocal; and muscular contractions, by stimulating lower brain centers, indirectly affect the cortex. We are getting ahead of our story, however, and must return to the teachings of the systematists, turning our attention to the contributions of the Gestalt school.

GESTALT PSYCHOLOGY AND THE THOUGHT PROCESSES

Generally speaking, the work of three Gestalt psychologists stands out in the area of thinking. We refer to Köhler's research on insight in chimpanzees, which we have already considered in Chapter 8; Max Wertheimer's analysis of productive thinking

(1959); and Duncker's classic experimental work on problem solving (1945) carried out on University of Berlin students. We shall examine both Wertheimer's and Duncker's research programs and their theoretical interpretations. The reader may wish to review the account of Köhler's experiments on insight (Chapter 8).

Experiments with Insightful Learning

In introducing his experiments with young schoolchildren, Max Wertheimer asserts that "productive thinking" in children is the exception rather than the rule. In large measure, he lays the blame for this unsatisfactory situation on the educational system, which, he believes, has been dominated by traditional logic and association theory. Traditional logic analyzes thinking in terms of formal definitions, propositions, inferences, and syllogistic reasoning. Since the days of Aristotle, logicians have sought to ensure correct thinking by insisting on precise definitions, exact judgment, carefully formulated concepts, and the like. According to the logicians, the individual who is able to carry out the operations laid down by the science of logic *is* able to think correctly.

But Wertheimer finds that in comparison with "real, sensible, and productive" thinking, the examples of traditional logic seem "barren, boring, empty, unproductive" (1945, p. 10). Even more important, logical thinking does not guarantee either correct or productive thinking. One may be exact in one's thinking if logical procedures are followed, but thinking may nevertheless be senseless and sterile.

Similarly, from Wertheimer's point of view, traditional association theory leads to blind drill, chance discovery of the correct answers, and fixation of whatever is "reinforced" regardless of whether or not that something is meaningful and productive. Wertheimer argues that the educational system is operating under the philosophy of associationism and so is dedicated to the inculcation of rules and principles by rote memory. The result is that pupils' thinking is rarely productive and more often is a blind repetition of procedures dictated on a priori grounds by their teachers. When subsequently confronted with a variation of a problem learned under this system of education, the child is unable to solve it, even though the same basic procedure applies.

To exemplify his argument, Wertheimer investigated the technique usually employed for teaching pupils how to find the area of a parallelogram. The procedure was as follows: (1) The teacher first reviewed the process for finding the area of a rectangle where area = altitude × base; (2) a parallelogram such as that shown in Figure 11-2 was then drawn on the blackboard; (3) the pupils were next shown how to drop perpendicular lines, *ab* and *cd*, at the ends of the parallelogram, and to extend the bottom side *de;* (4) they were then told that the area is equal to the base times the altitude, since the parallelogram had been transformed into a rectangle.

Following the demonstration outlined above, the pupils had no difficulty solving a variety of similar problems. But when confronted with the situation illustrated in Figure 11-3, many of the pupils either refused to attempt a solution or proceeded with logical but incorrect solutions such as those illustrated in Figure 11-4. A few rotated the figure to "normal" position and obtained the correct solution.

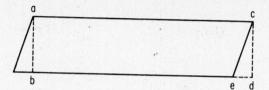

FIGURE 11-2.   From Productive Thinking, Enlarged Edition, 1959 by Max Wertheimer, edited by Michael Wertheimer. Copyright © 1945, 1959 by Valentin Wertheimer. Reprinted by permission of Harper & Row, Publishers, Inc.

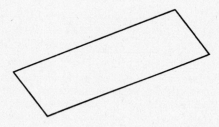

FIGURE 11-3.   From Productive Thinking, Enlarged Edition, 1959 by Max Wertheimer, edited by Michael Wertheimer. Copyright © 1945, 1959 by Valentin Wertheimer. Reprinted by permission of Harper & Row, Publishers, Inc.

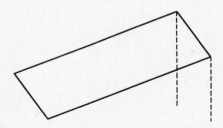

FIGURE 11-4.   From Productive Thinking, Enlarged Edition, 1959 by Max Wertheimer, edited by Michael Wertheimer. Copyright © 1945, 1959 by Valentin Wertheimer. Reprinted by permission of Harper & Row, Publishers, Inc.

Going a step further, Wertheimer found that some children, after being instructed on how to find the area of a parallelogram by the method outlined above, were able to find acceptable solutions for problems involving trapezoids and similar figures such as those shown in Figure 11-5. In general, among children who attempted solutions, Wertheimer found two types of responses, which he calls "A-responses" and "B-responses," respectively. In A-responses the children essentially shifted the triangles by proper use of auxiliary lines to arrive at a correct solution. In B-responses previously learned operations (dropping lines) were indiscriminately applied to arrive at incorrect solutions. These are illustrated in Figure 11-5. On the other hand, some children refused to attempt solutions, asserting that they had never been instructed in the proper procedure for solving such problems.

A - responses:

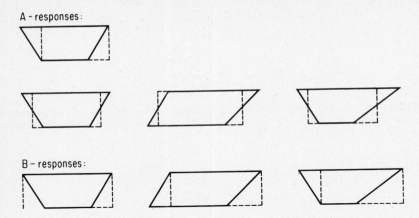

B - responses:

FIGURE 11-5.   Problems and solutions involving trapezoidal figures. In the A responses the subjects change the figures into rectangles by shifting the triangles. In the B responses previously learned operations are applied indiscriminately. (From Productive Thinking, Enlarged Edition, 1959 by Max Wertheimer, edited by Michael Wertheimer. Copyright © 1945, 1959 by Valentin Wertheimer. Reprinted by permission of Harper & Row, Publishers, Inc.)

Finally, Wertheimer presented other types of geometric figures in which "A-solutions" were possible by drawing auxiliary lines, and some in which A-solutions were not possible (see Figure 11-6). In the A-figures the child must realize that when lines are dropped to make rectilinear forms, the "remainders" do not matter, since they are equal in area to the indentations. No such solution is, of course, possible with the B-figures. Nevertheless, Wertheimer found that some children (indiscriminately) attempted to apply A-solutions to B-problems.

Wertheimer is convinced that children do not necessarily approach geometric problems such as those we have illustrated in a blind, inappropriate manner, but have become victims of a pedagogic tradition that relies on a teacher-taught "correct" procedure that does not offer any real insight into the problem. Wertheimer adds that the validity of his interpretation is supported by the results of studies where pupils who had been instructed in the traditional manner were asked for proofs of their solutions. The children, he found, were either dumbfounded or attempted to "prove" the solution in terms of specific measurements for a particular case.

What is lacking in such instances, Wertheimer continues, is a knowledge of the *inner relationships between the size of the area and the form of the figure*. He exemplifies his argument with a simple rectangle which is subdivided into little squares (see Figure 11-7). The squares are immediately organizable into an integrated whole. The solution then becomes meaningful in terms of the relations between area and form. The thinker perceives that the total area is equal to the total number of smaller squares, which can readily be obtained by multiplication.

For the application of the "squares solution" to trapezoids, the figures must be restructured in such a way as to produce a "better figure," that is, a rectangle. Wertheimer found that children who had never been given formal training in geometry (and adults who had forgotten theirs), when shown how to obtain the area

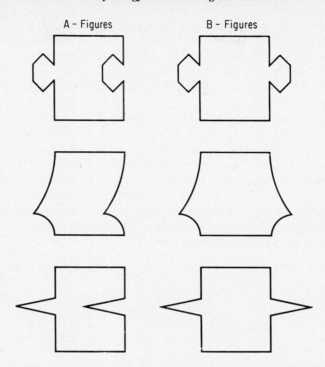

FIGURE 11-6. Examples of figures in which A solutions cannot be applied to B figures. Some children saw no difference between A and B figures, attempting to apply the same solution to both. (From Productive Thinking, Enlarged Edition, 1959 by Max Wertheimer, edited by Michael Wertheimer. Copyright © 1945, 1959 by Valentin Wertheimer. Reprinted by permission of Harper & Row, Publishers, Inc.)

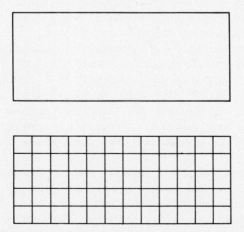

FIGURE 11-7. From Productive Thinking, Enlarged Edition, 1959 by Max Wertheimer, edited by Michael Wertheimer. Copyright © 1945, 1959 by Valentin Wertheimer. Reprinted by permission of Harper & Row, Publishers, Inc.

of a rectangle by the squares method, arrived at solutions to parallelograms and trapezoids with little or no assistance. "Some children reached the solution with little or no help in a genuine, sensible, direct way. Sometimes, after strained concentration, a face brightened at the critical movement. It is wonderful to observe the beautiful transformation from blindness to seeing the point!" (Max Wertheimer, 1945, p. 48).

Wertheimer cites dozens of interesting examples of solutions of geometric problems by children—some as young as 5 years—all of which showed structural changes involving transformations of the figure. Moreover, he studied the thought processes involved in other types of problems, such as proving the equality of the angles formed by the intersection of straight lines (see Figure 11-8); how to solve the series $1 + 2 + 3 + 4 + 5 + \cdots + n$ quickly and without adding the entire series; and finding the sum of the angles of a polygon. In each case, he analyzed the types of solutions employed by his subjects in terms of the productiveness and insightfulness of the thinking involved.

FIGURE 11-8.   From Productive Thinking, Enlarged Edition, 1959 by Max Wertheimer, edited by Michael Wertheimer. Copyright © 1945, 1959 by Valentin Wertheimer. Reprinted by permission of Harper & Row, Publishers, Inc.

Professor Wertheimer (1945) also devotes a chapter to an account of the thought processes the great physicist Albert Einstein utilized in developing his limited and general theories of relativity. The account is of special interest, since it is based on a series of personal interviews with Einstein.

As a result of his investigations, Wertheimer formulated a theory of productive thinking, which constitutes the concluding chapter in his book. He begins by summarizing his general findings on the various types of problems he utilized in his investigations (1945, pp. 189–190). First, he finds that the individuals studied showed many instances of "genuine, fine, clean, direct productive processes—better than some might have expected." Wertheimer is convinced that productive thinking is the natural way to think but is often absent because of blind habits, bias, and school drill.

Second, his subjects employed processes such as "grouping," "centering," and "reorganization" that had not been recognized by logicians and associationists in their analyses of the thought processes. Third, productive solutions were not perceived piecemeal but were related to "whole characteristics." This was true even though some operations favoring the traditional analyses were found; they, too, were utilized in a functional relationship to the whole characteristics of the problem.

Finally, and perhaps most importantly, productive solutions showed a "structural truth." They did not partake of "cheap plausibility," but were honest and sincere attempts to verify or prove the solutions utilized in solving problems. Moreover, Wertheimer strongly emphasizes that thinking cannot be conceived of as a purely intellectual operation, but as a process in which attitudes, feelings, and emotions also play a significant role. There must be a willingness to adopt an honest and sincere attitude that takes cognizance of the demands of the situation rather than a blind, egocentric view (1959, p. 179).

On the basis of his findings, Wertheimer is convinced that productive thinking involves a grasp of the inner structural relationships of the problem followed by grouping the parts of the problem into a dynamic whole; any "gaps" or "disturbances" must be understood and dealt with in terms of the structural unity of the problem. The thinker must realize the difference between peripheral and fundamental aspects of the problem and arrange each type in a structural hierarchy.

Wertheimer is fully aware of the inherent difficulty and lack of definiteness in his terminology, but points out that his research was undertaken more in the expectation of exposing problems for further research than of providing answers to already formulated hypotheses. In fact, he had hoped to publish two additional volumes on thinking, but his goal was never realized.[7]

Duncker's Studies of Problem Solving

Karl Duncker's studies of problem solving (1945) were highly similar to Wertheimer's, in terms both of experimental design and theoretical interpretation of the results. Duncker worked with college students rather than elementary school children and employed more "practical" problems than Wertheimer's abstract geometric examples. His overall aim, however, was quite similar to Wertheimer's in that he sought to reveal the essential nature of the thought processes.

Duncker's most thoroughly investigated problem was the following: Given an inoperable stomach tumor and rays that at high intensity will destroy tissue (both healthy and diseased), how can the tumor be destroyed without damaging surrounding tissue? Typically, the subjects were also shown a sketch of the problem while it was being presented verbally. Duncker's drawing is reproduced in Figure 11-9.

The following experimental protocol is quoted from Duncker's monograph to illustrate a subject's thought process in arriving at a solution.

Protocol
1. Send rays through the esophagus.
2. Desensitize the healthy tissues by means of a chemical injection.
3. Expose the tumor by operating.

---

[7]*Productive Thinking* was published posthumously. An enlarged edition including other types of problems illustrative of Wertheimer's research and theoretical interpretations was edited by his son, Michael Wertheimer, and published in 1959.

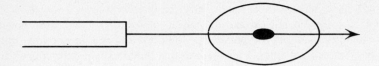

FIGURE 11-9.   A schematic representation of Duncker's tumor problem. The ellipse represents a cross section of the diseased area with the tumor in the middle. If the body is rotated, the
radiation will be maximized in the center and minimized on the periphery. (From Duncker, K. On
problem solving. Psychological Monographs, 1945, 58, No. 270, p. 2, Fig. 1.) Copyright 1945 by
the American Psychological Association. Reprinted by permission.

4. One ought to decrease the intensity of the rays on their way; for example would this
   work?—turn the rays on at full strength only after the tumor has been reached.
   (Experimenter: False analogy; no injection is in question.)
5. One should swallow something inorganic (which would not allow passage of the
   rays) to protect the healthy stomach-walls. (E: It is not merely the stomach-walls
   which are to be protected.)
6. Either the rays must enter the body or the tumor must come out. Perhaps one could
   alter the location of the tumor—but how? Through pressure? No.
7. Introduce a cannula.—(E: What, in general, does one do when, with any agent, one
   wishes to produce in a specific place an effect which he wishes to avoid on the way
   to that place?)
8. (Reply:) One neutralizes the effect on the way. But that is what I have been
   attempting all the time.
9. Move the tumor toward the exterior. (Compare 6.) (The E repeats the problem and
   emphasizes, ''. . . which destroys *at sufficient intensity*.'')
10. The intensity ought to be variable. (Compare 4.)
11. Adaptation of the healthy tissues by previous weak application of the rays. (E: How
    can it be brought about that the rays destroy only the region of the tumor?)
12. (Reply:) I see no more than two possibilities: either to protect the body or to make
    the rays harmless. (E: How could one decrease the intensity of the rays en route?)
    (Compare 4.)
13. (Reply:) Somehow divers . . . diffuse rays . . . disperse . . . stop! Send a broad
    and weak bundle of rays through a lens in such a way that the tumor lies at the focal
    point and thus receives intensive radiation. (Total duration about half an hour.)
    (Duncker, 1945, pp. 2–3)

Duncker analyzed the protocols obtained from his subjects according to stages
revealed by the subject's reactions. First, there is the discovery of the ''general or
essential properties of a solution.'' Using the protocol quoted above as an example,
when the subject begins thinking about the problem, he or she suggests sending the
rays through the esophagus, desensitizing healthy tissue, or lowering the intensity of
the rays on their way to the tumor. None of these solutions is practical, but they
reveal a general grasp of the problem and a reformulation of it in a goal-oriented
direction.

Upon being advised of the impracticality of his or her first general proposals,
the subject continues to formulate solutions that are still broad but which are more
truly *solutions* as opposed to mere reformulations of the problems. These solutions

Duncker groups under the heading of solutions with "functional value." Out of functional solutions the subject develops specific solutions, one of which is acceptable—focusing the rays by means of a lens.[8]

Of course, not every subject clearly showed all three stages during the course of problem solving, nor did each come up with the same functional and specific solutions. But Duncker argues that however primitive the solutions offered, they were not describable "in terms of meaningless, blind, trial-and-error reactions" (1945, p. 2). A little further on he emphasized that

> . . . what is really done in any solution of problems consists in formulating the problem more productively. . . . The final form of a solution is typically attained by way of mediating phases of the process, of which each one, in retrospect, prossesses the character of a solution, and, in prospect, that of a problem. (1945, p. 9)

Put more simply, problem solving consists of organization of the problem into hierarchically related stages, starting with general solution-oriented reformulations of the problem and progressing to increasingly more specific solutions. Because each stage is related to those that have gone before as well as to those that lie ahead, the process is a dynamic whole rather than a blind, trial-and-error affair.

Duncker went on to investigate mathematical problem solving, insight, learning, and the process of transfer of solutions to new problems. Even a summary of his complete experimental program is far beyond the scope of a single chapter. However, because of its intrinsic interest and importance in thinking, we shall include a brief description of his concept of "functional fixedness" in problem solving. Functional fixedness is illustrated on a simple level by apes who, after mastering a banana-stick problem cannot solve the problem without a stick because they fail to perceive that they can break off a small branch from a nearby tree. The animals have become "fixated" on unattached sticks and are blind to the possibilities of utilizing other sticks that may be available.

On the human level, the same phenomenon has been investigated in *Einstellung* (set) experiments, wherein the subject is shown how to do a series of problems, all of which involve a certain fixed series of stages. If similar problems are introduced where the correct solution *cannot* be attained by the now familiar approach, subjects tend to continue to use the inappropriate method because of the strong set built up by the initial series of successful solutions. For example, Duncker requested his subjects to suspend several cords from a wooden shelf for "perceptual experiments." On a table were screw hooks, the cords, and a gimlet. The subjects readily used the gimlet to bore holes for starting the screw hooks but found there were one too few hooks to hang the required number of cords. They failed to perceive that the gimlet could be employed as a support after it had been used to start the holes for the

---

[8]The idea is only correct in principle. X rays, for example, are not deflected by a lens. In medical practice, several weak rays coming from different directions are made to focus on the tumor, or the patient is rotated to minimize the exposure of healthy tissues and maximize the exposure of malignant tissue.

screw hooks. The subjects' set toward the gimlet was as a tool and not as a support, even though nothing in the instructions prevented the latter use. In Duncker's terms, the subjects' search for an additional screw hook was *unprägnant,* because restructuring of the problem failed to occur as a result of fixation.

Summary and Evaluation

The experimental programs and theoretical interpretations offered by Köhler, Wertheimer, Duncker[9] and other Gestalt psychologists strongly emphasized the *perceptual* nature of problem solving. The problems employed have typically called for creative or reasoned solutions, as opposed to trial-and-error solutions. Therefore, to some extent, their interpretations in terms of Gestalt principles have been favored by the Gestalt-like nature of the problems chosen, just as a "reinforcement" interpretation of animal learning experiments is favored if the initial design and conditions of the experiment preclude the possibility of insightful solutions. Because we have tried to follow closely Wertheimer's and Duncker's rather difficult original wording and interpretation, we shall conclude this section by attempting to bring together the essence of the Gestalt viewpoint in a highly summarized and simplified set of principles which we hope will clarify the Gestalt position without doing violence to the spirit of the original.

1. *Productive or creative thinking occurs when the organism is confronted with a problem that cannot be resolved by habitual means.* Köhler's and Duncker's problems are excellent illustrations of this principle. Apes do not habitually obtain their food with the aid of tools, nor do college students treat tumorous patients. Both are "original" problems, and both lend themselves to "thoughtful" solutions, in the sense that all elements of the problem are in the subject's perceptual field.

2. *Thinking takes the form of a perceptual reorganization of the problem in a series of hierarchically related solutions, which tend to become increasingly more specific.* Both Wertheimer's and Duncker's protocols revealed such step-by-step transformations in the subject's thought processes. It is impossible to know whether Köhler's apes were engaged in hierarchical thinking because, of course, it was not possible to obtain verbal reports from the animals.

3. *Perceptual reorganization during thinking tends in the direction of centering and focusing, of filling gaps, and seeking better gestalten.* Köhler's apes, Wertheimer's children, and Duncker's college students all demonstrated behavior that suggested increased focusing on the "missing parts" of the problem. The apes had to perceive the boxes as filling the gap between the floor and the banana before they were able to "solve" the problem. This the animals perceived early in the experiment, as revealed by their dragging the boxes under the fruit. However, the more difficult problem of statics (box stacking) remained to be solved. In his studies of human thinking, Wertheimer found that his pupils often referred to something

---

[9]N. R. F. Maier, an American psychologist, has conducted a number of similar experiments on reasoning in both animals and human subjects. His results and interpretations are entirely congruent with Wertheimer's and Duncker's.

"missing" or something "messy" on the ends of parallelograms and trapezoids. A similar process occurred in Duncker's students, who often realized "something was needed" to protect healthy tissue, even though they could not yet suggest just what.

4. *The readiness with which the solution is found is related to the fixity of the perceptual field, motivational factors, and the subject's previous training.* Here we must rely mainly on Wertheimer's work with children who had been given rigid, formal training in geometric problems. They experienced more difficulty in the solution of parallelograms than did naive subjects. However, Duncker's studies of fixedness are also pertinent since subjects with the incorrect set had difficulty with experimental problems.

5. *The final solution tends to occur as a sudden reorganization or transformation of the perceptual field.* "Suddenness" is, of course, a byword in Gestalt interpretations of problem solving. Once again, we must emphasize that suddenness is not to be confused with rapidity. Some of Duncker's subjects required more than thirty minutes for the solution of the tumor problem. What is meant is that the subject's reorganization of the perceptual field is done step by step; he or she "jumps" from one possible solution to another.

6. *A high degree of transfer to similar problems may be expected if the subject is allowed to work out his or her own solutions to cognitive problems.* Both Köhler's apes and Wertheimer's subjects demonstrated high transfer, provided they achieved insightful solutions. Such solutions depended in turn upon grasping the principle of the problem. Though not discussed in this chapter, Duncker's results on transfer are consistent with the work of other Gestalt psychologists.

Selected Current Trends in the Psychology of Thinking

In the second half of the first century of experimental psychology, research in the area of thinking has developed along diverse lines, some of which go back to the early part of that century. One approach that has proved highly challenging is the study of the development of thinking in children, much of which we owe to the work of Jean Piaget, whose research was summarized in Chapter 7. Another line of investigation centers on the role of the brain in abstracting, an approach that has drawn upon both clinical studies of human patients and work with animals. Studies of concept formation also loom large in the areas of experimental investigations of thinking. And during the past fifty years a long tradition of research has evolved from studies of creative thinking. Finally, in recent years psycholinguistics, or the study of language, has become an important theoretical and research area in the field. We shall summarize representative contributions in each of these areas, starting with clinical and experimental studies of abstracting ability and cortical functions first investigated during the second half of the nineteenth century.

Studies of Abstraction and Representative Factors

Studies of abstraction and representative factors are best exemplified by the work of Goldstein and his associates on human patients with brain injuries and by the research of neuroscientists on animals. We shall briefly outline the general findings in these areas.

Goldstein's work spans half a century. He became interested in the conceptual abilities of soldiers suffering from brain injuries (especially injuries in the frontal lobes) during the first World War. Such patients, he found, were unable to think in abstract terms. For example, when asked to classify skeins of wool of assorted hues into appropriate *classes* of colors, they were unable to do so. Obvious greens or reds could be grouped correctly by such patients, but they were unable to deal with hues that deviated markedly from the standard.

By way of interpretation, Goldstein postulated two levels of conceptual ability, *concrete* and *abstract*. The concrete functions are not seriously impaired in brain-injured patients, but abstracting ability is either deficient or absent. The greatest impairment to abstracting ability occurs in cases of injury to the frontal lobes.

In 1941 Goldstein and Scheerer reported a further series of studies of hospital patients with brain injuries in the frontal regions. The studies in question involved the administration of various tests of abstracting ability to the patients. Some of the tests were standardized by Goldstein and his associates for clinical use. Descriptions of these may be found in the 1941 Goldstein-Scheerer monograph. Others were simple qualitative tests improvised by the investigators.

Among the tests used were those requiring the patient to assume a set and then shift it from one task to another. Subjects were also asked to keep two tasks in mind simultaneously as they alternatively performed one and then the other. Additional tests involved putting together jigsaw puzzles, abstracting out the common denominator of a series of fractions, or drawing maps of familiar places. All of these tasks are readily accomplished by the normal individual but only with difficulty or not at all by the brain-injured.

Goldstein and Scheerer's reports have, in general, been confirmed by clinical studies carried out by other investigators, notably by Teuber and his associates (Teuber, Battersby, & Bender, 1960; Teuber & Weinstein, 1956). Consistent losses in scores on a hidden-figures test, such as the Gottschaldt or Bender-Gestalt were found in brain-injured individuals. On these tests the subject is required to pick out a simple geometric form hidden in a complex of similar forms. Interestingly, deficits in this type of ability may occur as a result of injuries almost anywhere in the cerebral cortex and not just in the frontal lobes alone; this finding indicates that this kind of perceptual problem solving is less well localized than those investigated by Goldstein and Scheerer.

Goldstein's clinical investigation of human subjects has been paralleled by animal research directed toward discovering the symbolic processes or representative factors that mediate thought. The investigations most closely related to Goldstein's studies are experiments on the memory trace in monkeys. These experiments originated out of the finding that animals have the ability to make delayed reactions. For example, a normal monkey can be shown where a reward is hidden under one of two cups that are placed some distance apart and in front of the animal. Even though forced to delay up to 30 seconds, the monkey can still go to the correct cup. But Jacobsen (1934, 1935) found that monkeys with bilateral lesions in the frontal lobes were unable to delay more than a few seconds, if at all.

Jacobsen believed his animals had suffered an amnesia of the "representative factor" by means of which they remembered the cues utilized in finding the reward. However, a number of investigators have challenged Jacobsen's interpretation on the basis of their own investigations of brain-injured (prefrontal) animals. Finan (1942), for example, gave prefrontal monkeys "predelay reinforcement," which took the form of allowing the animals a little food on the correct side just before the delay period. Despite their lesions, the reinforced animals could delay successfully. Finan's results suggest that the basic loss in prefrontal animals is not one of memory but of attention. The prefrontal monkey is excitable and readily distracted; it is therefore possible that Jacobsen's animals were not sufficiently attentive to the experimenter's activities and as a consequence had no cues to remember.

Additional evidence that the deficiency is in the area of attention comes from a number of studies in which prefrontal monkeys were given sedatives, kept in the dark during the delay, or otherwise rendered less distractable during the test situation (Jacobsen, 1934; Malmo, 1942; Mishkin & Pribram, 1956; Spaet & Harlow, 1943; Wade, 1947). The general findings suggest that the disturbance is, indeed, in the process of attention.

However, Pribram (1969) has suggested that deficiencies in prefrontal monkeys on delayed-reaction problems may reflect a deficit in information processing or short-term memory. According to this view, the frontal regions serve to break experiences into discrete periods. Animals with lesions in the frontal regions cannot do this. Consequently, in delayed-reaction situations separate experiences are run together, and the animal is unable to "set aside" information presented a short time before the discrimination test.

If we stretch a point and look for the common factor running through studies of human and animal subjects whose frontal lobes have been injured, the general picture is a deficiency in the *planning, management, and control of behavior*. The human patient's lack of abstracting ability is, in part, the result of an inability to concentrate, keep a set, and maintain a consecutive series of activities without constant guidance from the physician. Thus, the frontal lobes exercise a restraining, guiding influence on other brain centers—especially emotional centers—as is also revealed by the personality changes accompanying prefrontal lobotomy in psychotics.

Although both animal and human studies have led to an increased knowledge of the functions of the frontal lobes, no real theory of thinking has emerged from these investigations. Goldstein and Scheerer admit that their eight criteria of abstracting ability are descriptive rather than explanatory. Similarly, the animal studies tell us nothing about the nature of the representative factors animals utilize in making delayed reactions.

Concept Formation

Contemporary studies of concept formation can also be said to be more descriptive than explanatory. Three representative studies will be cited to illustrate the experimental approach to the study of concept formation. The classic study of concept formation carried out by Hull in 1920 laid the groundwork for subsequent research; hence we shall outline his experiment first. Hull presented his subjects with a series of twelve packs of cards. Each card carried a Chinese character, and one of the characters in each pack included a "concept" (see Figure 11-10). For example, the concept "oo" was represented by a checklike character as illustrated for each series in Figure 11-10. The subjects were practiced on a given series until they could give the correct concept. In a later part of the experiment (Series VI to XII) the subjects were tested for the ability to generalize the learned concepts, or, in other words, to recognize them in new situations.

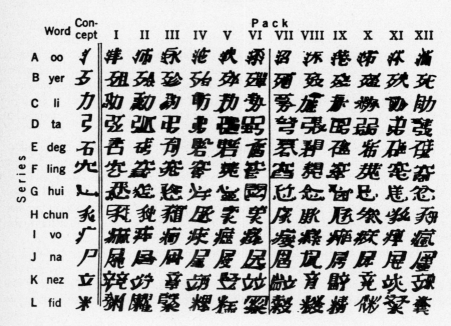

FIGURE 11-10.   Chinese characters used in studies of concept formation. For explanation see text. (From Hull, C. Quantitative aspects of the evolution of concepts. Psychological Monographs, 1920, 28, No. 123, p. 11, plate I.) Copyright 1920 by the American Psychological Association. Reprinted by permission.

Hull analyzed his results in terms of ordinary discrimination learning. The subject, he argues, learns to discriminate the *common element* in the characters and, on the basis of his or her experiences, can recognize and utilize similar elements when they appear in new settings. Thus, the child comes to understand the meaning of "round" from experiences with apples, oranges, balls, beads, and similar objects and is thus able to recognize roundness in unfamiliar situations. Obviously, Hull's interpretation reduces concept formation to the principles of conditioned learning—reinforcement, generalization, and selective discrimination.

In a later and extensive series of studies utilizing the discrimination model, Heidbreder (1946a, 1946b, 1947, 1948) investigated the formation of various *types* of concepts. Utilizing a series of drawings presented on a memory drum, she instructed her subjects to anticipate nonsense names for the concepts embedded in the drawings. For example, when Series I was presented, the subject watched as the experimenter pronounced the name of each figure (see Figure 11-11). On the next trial the subject tried to give the name associated with the picture and was prompted by the experimenter whenever necessary. In each series of sixteen figures, nine concepts were embedded. In Series I, faces were always named RELK, and buildings LETH. After the subject had learned the first series, he or she began the second series and so on, until all were learned. At some point during the experiment, the subject recognized concepts learned in previous series and began to anticipate all faces by responding with RELK, all buildings by responding with LETH, and so on.

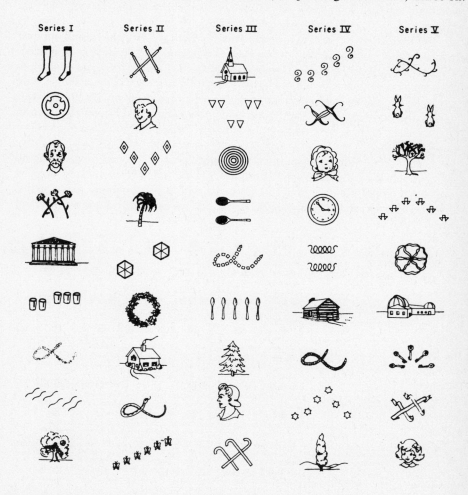

FIGURE 11-11. Materials used by Heidbreder to study concept formation. For explanation see text. (From Heidbreder, E. The attainment of concepts: I. Terminology and methodology. Journal of General Psychology, 1946, 35, p. 182, Fig. 1.)

Three general types of concepts occurred in Heidbreder's series: *concrete objects, spatial forms,* and *abstract numbers.* She found that concrete concepts are readily attained. Spatial forms are intermediate in difficulty and abstract numbers most difficult to learn. By way of interpretation, Heidbreder suggests that concrete forms are not only the concepts first experienced in childhood but also are the concepts that occur most frequently in the everyday life of the adult. At first a ball is a concrete object to be manipulated by the child and is only secondarily thought of as round or something to be counted. Thus, there is an order of "dominance" in human thinking ranging from the concrete to the abstract, with the latter type requiring more than mere perception. The parallels between Heidbreder's hypothesis and Goldstein's analyses of thinking into concrete and abstract levels are obvious.

The third study of concept formation that we shall present was carried out over a period of five years by a team of Harvard investigators and resulted in an influential book, *A Study of Thinking* (Bruner, Goodnow, & Austin, 1956). In contrast to Hull's and Heidbreder's conditioning-discrimination paradigms, the Harvard team emphasized cognitive interpretations of the process of concept attainment. In their investigation they employed eighty-one cards (see Figure 11-12), which varied in four attributes: number of borders, color of figures, shape of figures, and number of figures.

The subjects were instructed that a concept might be formed by grouping all cards that showed a particular set of attributes. On the simplest level, cards with one green circle could define a concept. Or cards with a single border could define another. However, as the authors point out, we do not ordinarily attain a concept or

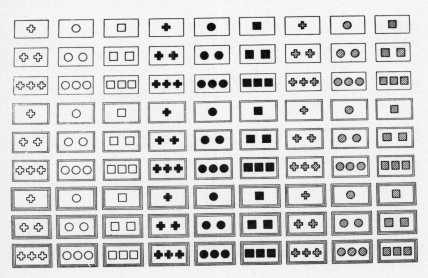

FIGURE 11-12.   Cards used in a study of concept formation by Bruner, Goodnow, and Austin. (From Bruner, Goodnow, and Austin, A study of thinking, 1956, p. 42, Fig. 1. By permission of John Wiley & Sons.)

identity from a single attribute but from several taken together. And so in the case of the cards shown in Figure 11-12, a more complex concept might involve "all cards possessing the same number of figures and borders." Or another might be defined in terms of "all green cards with three squares."

In discussing types of concepts that may be investigated with such materials, the authors identify *conjunctive, disjunctive,* and *relational* concepts. A typical conjunctive category or concept would involve the combination of several attributes—for example, three red circles, of which there are only three instances in the experimental cards. The attainment of such concepts is not difficult for most individuals.

Disjunctive concepts involve at least one element from a number of elements. In Figure 11-12 the class of cards possessing three red squares or any constituent element thereof is a disjunctive concept. Thus, any card would qualify if it possessed three figures, red figures, squares, three red figures, or red squares, or three squares. In everyday life a disjunctive concept might be illustrated by a strike in baseball. As Bruner and his associates (1956) point out, it may be any pitch in the strike zone; a pitch that is struck at regardless of zone but that is not hit out into the field; a foul ball, provided that there are not already two strikes on the batter; or even a foul bunt after two strikes. Disjunctive concepts are difficult to achieve, partly because of their arbitrary nature. There is often a lack of any obvious relationship between the attributes, as in the example given above. Relational concepts depend upon the relationships among elements in a situation. For example, all cards in Figure 11-12 with fewer figures than borders would constitute a relational concept or category. Another might be all cards with an equal number of figures and borders.

The concepts illustrated thus far can be inferred with certainty from experiences with objects (such as the cards) that possess the defining properties of a concept. Bruner, Goodnow, and Austin point to another interesting type of concept—the probabilistic—where inferential certainty from experiencing defining attributes cannot be achieved (1956, pp. 182–230). As an example they give the instance of a battlefield undergoing artillery bombardment. Some shells falling are live and some are duds. Assuming 70 percent are live and 30 percent are duds, the question may be raised as to what a particular soldier might do. If he takes cover every time, he will, of course, never be killed. If, on the other hand, he always stays exposed, his chances become 70:30 of being killed. If he stays exposed only part of the time, his chances of survival are increased.

In less deadly instances—for example, gambling—the individual may attempt to work out a strategy. Subjects look for patterns or make fallacious assumptions, such as if heads have come up five times in a row in coin tossing, the chance of tails on the next toss is greater than 50:50. In a larger sense, however, all perceptual or cognitive learning may be considered probabilistic as emphasized by the transactional functionalists and Brunswik (see our discussion in Chapter 6).

Bruner, Goodnow, and Austin found that subjects in their experimental situations utilized four *selection strategies:* (1) simultaneous scanning, (2) successive scanning, (3) conservative focusing, and (4) focus gambling.

In simultaneous scanning, the subject tries to keep all possibilities in mind simultaneously while attempting to eliminate as many as possible with each card choice. He or she is in somewhat the same position as the bridge player or the chess master who must strive to hold in mind dozens of possible plays while judging the impact of any given play. Because of the difficulty of such a strategy, subjects ordinarily do not use it.

In successive scanning the subject assumes a "hypothesis" and then checks the validity of his or her hypothesis with each successive trial. Thus, if he or she thinks, "It's three red squares," and is called correct each time three red squares come up, he or she quickly verifies his or her hunch and can demonstrate its validity to the experimenter. Obviously, if the hypothesis is disproved by a negative instance, another must be adopted and verified or discarded.

Conservative focusing may be described as finding a positive instance to use as a focus and then making a sequence of choices, each of which alters one attribute value of the first focus card, and testing to see whether the change yields a positive or negative instance (Bruner et al., 1956, p. 87).

Conservative focusing may be illustrated by citing an instance where the focus card is one red circle with no borders. If the concept is red circles, the sequence of choices might be as follows:

1. Focus card: one red circle, no borders.
2. Two red circles and no borders; positive choice, therefore number of figures may be eliminated.
3. One green circle; negative choice, therefore retain red as relevant.
4. Two red crosses; negative choice, therefore retain circle as relevant.
5. Two red circles and two borders; positive choice, therefore eliminate borders and the concept is red circles.

In focus gambling the subject jumps to conclusions, changing more than one attribute at a time. Sometimes the strategy pays off, as for example, if he or she is shown two green squares in a single border and the guess is two figures. If the next card is two crosses in a double border, and he or she is informed that the answer is correct, the gamble has paid off. However, if the assumption is incorrect, the subject must then revert to simultaneous scanning, having wasted the time already devoted to gambling.

It is impossible within the limitations of a summary such as this to adequately demonstrate the richness and scope of the experimental investigations of Bruner and his associates or the growing body of literature[10] that emphasizes cognitive processes in concept formation. However, we hope that this brief summary has provided a significant glimpse into this challenging new approach to concept formation and thinking.

----

[10]For an extended discussion of cognitive theory in concept formation with an extensive bibliography, see Saltz (1971, chap. 2). For studies of concept learning from other viewpoints, see Bourne, Eckstrand, and Dominowski (1971), H. H. Kendler and T. S. Kendler (1967, 1975), and Vinacke (1974).

Creative Thinking

Interest in creativity and creative thinking had its scientific origins in studies of individual differences in abilities and their genetic transmission. During the second half of the nineteenth century, Sir Francis Galton (1822–1911), the great British scientist and cousin of Charles Darwin, published a series of studies on genius and creativity that have become classics. In *Hereditary Genius* (1869) he demonstrated by means of careful biographical and ancestral studies that genius tends to run in families. This work was followed by *English Men of Science* (1874) and by *Inquiries into Human Faculty and Its Development* (1883).

Galton's studies are not inquiries into the nature of creative thinking as such. Much the same can be said for James McKeen Cattell's famous study of eminent American scientists, which was stimulated by Galton's work. But these and similar biographical investigations reveal a deeply rooted interest in the outstanding intellectual ability and other personal characteristics that are associated with creative thinking.

More direct attempts to get at the process involved in creative thinking originated in anecdotal accounts of original thinking provided by such outstanding men as Helmholtz and the brilliant French mathematician Poincaré. Both stressed the sudden, seemingly ''inspired'' nature of many of their solutions to difficult problems—inspirations that came only after arduous preparation followed by several unsuccessful attempts to solve the problem by more or less habitual techniques. These impressionistic reports were supplemented during the 1930s by questionnaires sent to eminent scientists asking for descriptions of their methods of work. Earlier, Graham Wallas (1926) had formalized the results of some of the early studies into a four-stage theory of creative thinking, which held that periods of preparation, incubation, illumination, and verification were characteristic of such thought.

In preparation, the thinker ''loads up'' on all relevant information that is pertinent to the problem and may attempt tentative solutions. If an immediate solution is not forthcoming, a period of incubation follows during which the thinker makes no deliberate efforts to solve the problem, having temporarily ''given up.'' But, according to Wallas, ''unconscious cerebration'' is going on, leading to a sudden illumination, which often occurs at unexpected times and places. This ''Eureka experience''—as Wallas termed it—must, of course, be followed by an attempt to verify its validity by observation or experimentation.

In an attempt to subject Wallas' four stages to an experimental test, Patrick (1935, 1937) had poets and painters come to the laboratory, where they were assigned to a creative task to be carried out during a living-in period. They were asked to write impressionistic reports of their mental processes during creative activities; and these, upon analysis supported Wallas' theory, particularly the interesting hypothesis that incubation or unconscious cerebration occurs during creative thinking. About three-fourths of the subjects testified to experiencing incubation periods followed by sudden and unexpected illuminations. However, Patrick found that many admitted that the incubation period was by no means free of thinking. The problem recurred from time to time with tentative stabs at a solution. It has also been pointed out that many people experience a change of perspective on a problem after a period of no active work. This change may lead to a sudden solution. The combined effect of these factors of rehearsal and change of perspective appears less mysterious than "unconscious cerebration."

More recently, the study of creativity has returned again to the approach pioneered by Galton and Cattell—that is, the study of individual differences. However, the work to which we shall refer involves large-scale analysis of the intellectual and personal characteristics of creative persons who were studied directly. Our summary is based on a report of a team project carried out by Barron (1965) at the University of California at Berkeley.

In this multifaceted approach under the leadership of Donald W. MacKinnon and Frank Barron, measurements of the personal and intellectual traits of outstanding architects, research scientists, writers, engineers, and mathematicians were carried out using a variety of tests and rating scales.

In one set of studies the method of "living-in assessment" was employed. An assessment typically involved a Friday to Sunday weekend in which the research staff and the subjects being evaluated actually lived together in a former fraternity house near the Berkeley campus. Meals were taken together, and every effort was made to create a friendly atmosphere in order to make the situation as natural as possible. At the end of an assessment session each member of the staff wrote down impressions of each subject, utilizing several checklists to aid in completeness and objectivity. In other sessions scientists and creative writers took a variety of standardized tests designed to measure personality traits and intellectual abilities. For a complete description of the method, tests, and results, the reader is referred to Barron's article (1965). Here we shall attempt to give only a sample of the extensive results.

We may begin with a summary of Q-sort items,[11] which were found to be correlated with creativity. As Table 11-1 shows, creativity is positively correlated with such traits as unconventionality of thought and behavior, positive evaluation of intellectual values, and high intellectual capacity and is negatively correlated with dependability, sympathy, and conventional morality. Table 11-2 also shows some of the composite Q-sort descriptions for the two highest categories (8 and 9 on a 9-point scale) associated with creative writers; Table 11-2 also reveals such traits as high intellectual capacity, independence, fluency in thinking and expression, and high esthetic reactivity. A similar profile was obtained for creative architects, although the latter were more socially conventional and practical-minded, as is no doubt necessitated by the demands put upon them in the world of business.

Data obtained from personality inventories—such as the Minnesota Multiphasic Personality Inventory, the California Psychological Inventory, and the

---

[11]As used in this study, the Q-sort technique refers to a personality assessment in which raters sort a number of statements into piles representing the degree to which the statements apply to the subjects. Each statement can then be given a score representing the degree of strength to which a given subject possesses traits. The Q sort is also widely used as a technique for having subjects judge their own traits.

TABLE 11-1.   Clinical Q-Sort Items Correlated with Creativity[a]

r with Creativity Rating	Q-Sort Item
Positive correlations:	
0.64	Thinks and associates to ideas in unusual ways; has unconventional thought processes.
0.55	Is an interesting, arresting person.
0.51	Tends to be rebellious and nonconforming.
0.49	Genuinely values intellectual and cognitive matters.
0.46	Appears to have a high degree of intellectual capacity.
0.42	Is self-dramatizing; histrionic.
0.40	Has fluctuating moods.
Negative correlations:	
−0.62	Judges self and others in conventional terms like "popularity," the "correct thing to do," "social pressures," and so forth.
−0.45	Is a genuinely dependable and responsible person.
−0.43	Behaves in a sympathetic or considerate manner.
−0.40	Favors conservative values in a variety of areas.
−0.40	Is moralistic.

[a]From F. Barron, The Psychology of Creativity. In F. Barron, W. C. Dement, W. Edwards, H. Lindman, L. D. Phillips, and J. and M. Olds (Eds.), *New Directions in Psychology.* Vol. 2. Copyright © 1965 by Holt, Rinehart and Winston, Inc. Reprinted by permission of Holt, Rinehart and Winston, Inc.

TABLE 11-2.   Composite Staff Q-Sort Description of Creative Writers[a]

9's:
Appears to have a high degree of intellectual capacity.
Genuinely values intellectual and cognitive matters.
Values own independence and autonomy.
Is verbally fluent; can express ideas well.
Enjoys esthetic impressions; is esthetically reactive.

8's:
Is productive; gets things done.
Is concerned with philosophical problems, for example, religion, values, the meaning of life.
Has high aspiration level for self.
Has a wide range of interests.
Thinks and associates to ideas in unusual ways; has unconventional thought processes.
Is an interesting, arresting person.
Appears straightforward, forthright, candid in dealing with others.
Behaves in an ethically consistent manner; is consistent with own personal standards.

[a]From F. Barron, The Psychology of Creativity. In F. Barron, W. C. Dement, W. Edwards, H. Lindman, L. D. Phillips, and J. and M. Olds (Eds.), *New Directions in Psychology.* Vol. 2. Copyright © 1965 by Holt, Rinehart and Winston, Inc. Reprinted by permission of Holt, Rinehart and Winston, Inc.

Type Indicator based on Carl Jung's types—show consistently more psychopathological deviation among creative persons than among members of control samples. However, Barron and his associates strongly emphasize that the creative individual also possesses greater ego strength and self-control, thus being able to contain his or her tendencies toward deviation. No evidence was found to support the popular contention that creative individuals show psychotic traits or the "madness of genius."

Finally, we may briefly note a composite characterization of the productive young research scientist so important in our scientific and technocratic culture, as revealed by a number of studies whose authorship is given by Barron (1965, p. 85). Table 11-3 shows these characteristics, which—as we may judge for ourselves—bears a close resemblance to many of the traits revealed in the Berkeley studies.

TABLE 11-3.   A Unified Picture of Traits Found in Productive Scientists[a]

1. High ego strength and emotional stability.
2. A strong need for independence and autonomy; self-sufficiency; self-direction.
3. A high degree of control of impulse.
4. Superior general intelligence.
5. A liking for abstract thinking and a drive toward comprehensiveness and elegance in explanation.
6. High personal dominance and forcefulness of opinion, but a dislike of personally toned controversy.
7. Rejection of conformity pressures in thinking (although not necessarily in social behavior).
8. A somewhat distant or detached attitude in interpersonal relations, though not without sensitivity or insight; a *preference* for dealing with things or abstractions rather than with people.
9. A special interest in the kind of "wagering" that involves pitting oneself against the unknown, so long as one's own effort can be the deciding factor.
10. A liking for order, method, exactness, together with an excited interest in the challenge presented by contradictions, exceptions, and apparent disorder.

[a]From F. Barron, The Psychology of Creativity. In F. Barron, W. C. Dement, W. Edwards, H. Lindman, L. D. Phillips, and J. and M. Olds (Eds.), *New Directions in Psychology*. Vol. 2. Copyright © 1965 by Holt, Rinehart and Winston, Inc. Reprinted by permission of Holt, Rinehart and Winston, Inc.

It is also of considerable theoretical and practical importance to recognize and measure creative ability in children. Its theoretical importance lies in the possibility of distinguishing between creativity, on the one hand, and high general intelligence, on the other hand. From the practical point of view, it is important to recognize highly creative children in order to encourage their special talents.

J. P. Guilford (1967, pp. 161–170) has distinguished between *divergent-production abilities* and *convergent-production abilities*. Divergent abilities describe the modes of thinking involved in the development of novel resolutions of a problem or the generation of new ideas, such as is found in creative thinking. Convergent abilities describe the kind of thinking that goes into the solution of problems that have a single correct resolution, such as are commonly found in the educational curriculum or on standard intelligence tests. The divergent ability tests developed by Guilford have no one correct answer. Rather, they are scored in terms of novelty and diversity of response. For example, the subject may be requested to embellish outlined pieces of furniture with decorative lines. Or he or she may be asked to suggest a number of uses for a brick or to think up titles for a short story. Creative children's drawings and responses are more elaborate, less stereotyped, and revealing of novel thinking than are average children's.

In an elaborate investigation of 151 fifth-grade children, Wallach and Kogan (1965a), utilizing both standard intelligence tests (Wechsler) and five creativity measures based on Guilford's divergent-thinking tests, found that the creativity measures correlated highly with each other (average $r = + 0.40$) but were not significantly correlated with standard intelligence test scores (average $r = + 0.10$). Children who scored high on creativity tests and also on general intelligence tests were high in both self-confidence and self-esteem. However, high-creativity children who scored low on general intelligence tests tended to be hostile toward other children. They suffered from feelings of inadequacy and found it difficult to relate to their peers.

Children who scored low on creativity tests but high on general intelligence tests tended to be addicted to school achievement. The possibility of failure was perceived by these children as catastrophic. Those low in both general intelligence and creativity were described as "basically bewildered." Some attempted useful compensatory behavior; others became passive or developed psychosomatic complaints.

These interesting and provocative investigations of creative persons' traits are, it must be remembered, largely descriptive. Much more research will be needed before we have a complete picture of the dynamics of creative thinking and how it is related to intellectual and personality traits. We do not know, for example, to what extent being a successful creative thinker generates some of the modes of behavior measured and described in these studies. Correlations, we must always bear in mind, are not necessarily revealing of causation. We do not mean to imply anything as extreme as the generalization that one could *become* intelligent by engaging in creative thinking over a long period of time, but it is possible that under the same circumstances one might become unconventional, more interested in abstract impersonal activities, and less interested in warm, personal contacts. Certainly, there is much biographical data to show that many famous writers and artists became increasingly unconventional as they became more successful and withdrew from ordinary society.

We do not, however, mean to call into question the general validity of studies such as these. Rather, we commend the entire report to the interested reader for many additional facets of methodology and results. Moreover, we shall be considering the problem of outstanding individuals again in connection with Maslow's theory of motivation.[12]

---

[12]The reader who wishes to anticipate will find Maslow's theory discussed in Chapter 12.

LANGUAGE BEHAVIOR

Until relatively recently, language behavior was one of the most neglected areas in the field of psychology. Psychologists had not failed to appreciate its significance, but the extraordinary complexity and difficulty of study relegated language behavior to an inferior status in both research and theorizing. However, within the past two decades the area of language behavior has become one of the most active in the entire field. A subfield of psychology, *psycholinguistics,* has evolved, and its adherents have generated an enormous body of research and theory.[13]

From a theoretical point of view, this complex and diverse effort can be categorized most simply in terms of its adherents' position on nativism and empiricism in language development during childhood. Nativistic psycholinguists believe that human language is predicated on biologically determined neural processes, which provide every human child with a kind of species-specific ability to organize sounds into words and, further, words into sentences with a crude but highly efficient grammar. Through further maturation and learning, adult speech patterns evolve. The empiricists, on the other hand, believe that language is primarily learned by a conditioning process and that the child acquires words, phrases, and sentences through reinforced repetition of the adult speech patterns to which he or she is exposed. We shall summarize both points of view, starting with the empirical.

Classical Conditioning and Language Development

Floyd Allport in his popular *Social Psychology* (1924) formulated a widely cited classical conditioning paradigm of language acquisition (see Figure 11-13). According to his model, the child, at a critical level of maturation, utters random syllables such as *dada, mama, googoo.* These unconditioned responses (UR) are heard both by the child and the parents. In order to encourage the child to speak the first word, the parent speaks a word (such as *doll*) which is similar to one of the child's vocalizations *(da).* The adult's spoken word is an unconditioned stimulus (US) that serves to elicit an imitative response in the child. When the US is paired with the object, doll, which serves as a conditioned stimulus (CS), the latter will come to evoke *doll* from the child—a conditioned response (CR). Presumably, the child's entire language development, including words, phrases, sentences, and grammatical rules are acquired in this same manner.

---

[13]Skinner's *Verbal Behavior* (1957) is pivotal on the side of empiricism in psycholinguistics. On the nativistic side the "classic" works are Chomsky's *Syntactic Structures* (1957) and *Aspects of the Theory of Syntax* (1965). Lenneberg's *The Biological Foundations of Language* (1967)—with an appendix on generative theory by Chomsky—is ranked with Chomsky's works as a contemporary landmark on the nativistic point of view. For representative studies of language development in children—a crucial issue from either point of view—see R. Brown (1973) and McNeill (1967, 1968). For excellent general introductions to psycholinguistics, see Deese (1970), Foder, Beven, and Garrett (1973), and Slobin (1971). For a review of recent theoretical positions, see Houston (1971).

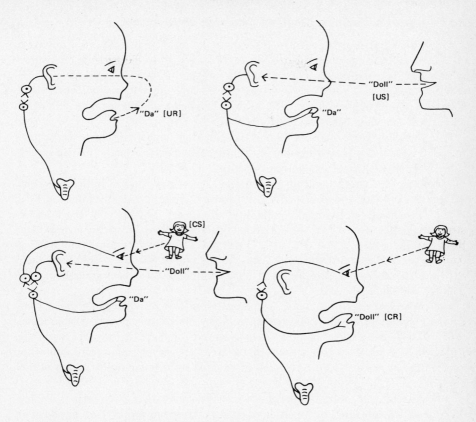

FIGURE 11-13. The development of language habits in the infant. (Redrawn from Allport, F. H. Social Psychology, 1924.)

More recently, Mowrer (1960) has restated and elaborated the classical conditioning paradigm of language acquisition. Utilizing a Hullian point of view, he holds that the child's imitation of adult language is a consequence of the reinforcement of sounds because of their pleasurable association with sensations accompanying feeding, cuddling, bathing, and so on. Through generalization and selective conditioning, further language development goes on throughout the trajectory of life.

Both Floyd Allport's and Mowrer's views are strongly empirical in the sense that the major burden of acquisition is put on learning. Naturally, through biological endowment the child must have a working vocal apparatus that is sufficiently mature for learning to take place, but the rest is up to learning.

The classical conditioning model of language development is elegant in its simplicity. It also accounts very satisfactorily for the obvious fact that the child learns the language of the environment and that deaf children do not spontaneously learn a language. And it also has the advantage of being able to relate linguistic development to conditioning paradigms of concept formation, such as those discussed earlier in this chapter.

An Operant Conditioning Model of Language Development

It is not surprising that as operant conditioning reached maturity, its proponents advocated an instrumental or operant model of language development in opposition to the classical conditioning paradigms. As early as 1934, B. F. Skinner began a tentative analysis of verbal behavior as part of his research program in operant behavior. Twenty-three years later *Verbal Behavior*, a detailed and extensive analysis of language behavior, was published.

In *Verbal Behavior* (1957), Skinner classifies language according to the manner in which it functions as instrumental or operant behavior. Essentially, human speech consists of *mands, tacts, echoic reactions, and autoclitics*.

Mands, a neologism coined from *demand, command*, and so forth, are verbal operants "in which a response of a given form is characteristically followed by a given consequence in a verbal community" (Skinner, 1957, p. 35). From an instrumental point of view, a mand is a verbal operant where the response is reinforced by a specific consequence and so is under the control of certain conditions of deprivation or aversive stimulation. Thus, to use one of Skinner's examples, *Pass the salt!* specifies an action followed by a reinforcement—the former being the passing, the latter, the salt.

Similarly, *Thank you, Look out! Stop doing that! Give him the book*, and similar expressions are all common mands. Some mands are expressive of superstitions, such as the expression *Seven, come eleven!* of the dice thrower. Some are "magical" or expressive of wishes, since they have never occurred or could not occur. *May he roast in hell!* or *Go and catch a falling star* exemplify mands of this class.

Tacts refer to a "verbal operant in which a response of a given form is evoked (or at least strengthened) by a particular object or event or property of an object or event" (Skinner, 1957, pp. 81–82). Tact functions are involved in the process of learning to name objects. Parents and teachers reinforce children for using tacts, and so these are strengthened as operants. The reinforcement may be simply the spoken word *Right!* or it may be more subtle, as when the tact *chair* is reinforced by pointing to the object it represents. However, Skinner emphasizes (1957, p. 90) that tacts or names of objects or events do not depend upon the physical presence of what they signify. Generalized reinforcement makes tacts independent of specific-stimulus control or elicitation. Tacts, moreover, may be under the control of private stimuli (Skinner, 1957, pp. 130ff.). The verbal behavior *I have a toothache*, is an example. The terms *familiar* and *beautiful* are further examples of tacts for which private stimulus control resides in the speaker. Familiarity and the sense of beauty are generated during the individual's history of reinforcement.

A similar principle holds for past, future, or potential events expressed verbally (Skinner, 1957, pp. 142–146). Clearly, a large and important class of tacts is subsumed under these categories.

Echoic operants refer to the simple cases where "verbal responses generate a sound-pattern similar to that of the stimulus" (Skinner, 1957, p. 55). Echoic behavior is basically direct verbal imitation on the part of a listener to something said by a speaker. The child, then, learns what is differentially reinforced by the verbal community, and a significant proportion of vocabulary development in childhood can be accounted for in this manner.

Autoclitics are operants involved in assertions *(It is going to rain)*, in negations *(No, I cannot do as you request)*, in quantifications of response *(I guess so; I estimate)*, and in the complex relations in grammatical and syntactical ordering in sentences. The English-speaking community reinforces the autoclitics involved in spoken English so that the distribution of nouns, verbs, objects, and so on is correct *(The boy hit the ball)* and are built into the child's speech in the proper sequence. In a different verbal community (say, French or German) similar processes would occur, ensuring the appropriate sequence of syntactical structures for that language.

Our brief definitions and examples cannot do justice to Skinner's detailed account of language development. However, we hope that they have served to emphasize the fundamental principle underlying his analysis of verbal functions; that is, verbal behavior—whether simple naming, imitation, or complex sentence composition—is basically operant behavior that has been reinforced and shaped by the verbal community. The same principles of operant conditioning derived from the analysis of behavior utilizing rats and pigeons in Skinner boxes are invoked to account for the processes involved in reinforcing, generalizing, discriminating, and so on in verbal behavior. It is Skinner's assumption that verbal behavior can be accounted for without the necessity for mentalistic concepts or nativistic assumptions about organismic factors in the causation of behavior. In turning to the nativistic account of language development we shall find that Skinner's assumption has been called into serious question.

Nativism and Language Development

As we indicated earlier, the nativists assert that although learning undoubtedly plays a role in language development, it is not the major one that Skinner and other conditioning theorists believe. In criticizing the empirical position, representatives of the nativistic point of view argue that language is not built out of conditioned responses. For example, Deese observes:

> Yet the most important aspect of language is that it is creative. We can and do in almost every sentence that is not a stereotyped cliché say what has never been said before. Nor is what we say when we say something new simply a random or stochastic perturbation of our fixed associations. When we say something new we say it according to the system of rules that is the language. In short, the essential features of sentences are determined by rules, not by conditioned reactions. . . . There is, then some embodiment of the abstract rules of language, and this embodiment is psychological, and, we must suppose, neurophysiological. (1970, pp. 5–6)

Chomsky, one of America's leading psycholinguists, in reviewing[14] Skinner's *Verbal Behavior* comments on the issue as follows:

---

[14]Chomsky's review (1959) goes far beyond an analysis of *Verbal Behavior* to call into question most of Skinner's fundamental concepts in operant conditioning. It is highly recommended for those interested in a critique of Skinner's systematic position.

One would naturally expect that prediction of the behavior of a complex organism (or machine) would require, in addition to information about external stimulation, knowledge of the internal structure of the organism, the ways in which it processes input information and organizes its behavior. These characteristics of the organism are in general a complicated product of inborn structure, the genetically determined course of maturation, and past experience. (1959, p. 27)

Finally, Lenneberg, another leading psycholinguist of the nativist school, writes:

Why do children normally begin to speak between their 18th and 28th month? Surely it is not because all mothers on earth initiate language training at that time. There is, in fact, no evidence whatever that any conscious and systematic teaching of language takes place, just as there is no special training for stance or gait. . . . The central and most interesting problem is whether the emergence of language is due to very general capabilities that mature to a critical minimum at about eighteen months to make language, and many other skills, possible, or whether there might be some factors specific to speech and language that come to maturation and that are somewhat independent from other more general processes. (1967, pp. 125–126)

As Lenneberg points out, there is no direct experimental way to explore the contribution of maturation to children's development. Consequently, the psycholinguist must evaluate the role of maturation by inference. It will be convenient first to develop the nativists' position on maturation and language development around their criticisms of the empirical position.

To begin with, Chomsky (1959), Lenneberg (1967), and others have stressed the fact that a high degree of competence in language is acquired by the child in a very short time. The child normally begins to speak between the eighteenth and twenty-eighth month, and language development is virtually complete by the end of the fourth year. It is difficult for the nativist to believe that the acquisition of vocabulary, syntax, and the subtleties of stress and intonation (particularly important in certain languages other than English) could all be acquired through conditioning in so short a time. As G. A. Miller (1965) has pointed out, even to hear all the possible combinations of twenty-word sentences in the English language would require millions of years.

Second, the child's initial grammatical constructions are not crude approximations of adult speech, as conditioning theory would demand. Rather, the child possesses a language acquisition device, or LAD (Chomsky, 1965), which enables him or her to process the verbalizations that are heard in the environment in such a way as to produce an implicit grammar, which can then be utilized in generating new sentences.

Third, the nativists also point out that there is no evidence to show that parents train a child in the use of language by systematically setting up schedules of reinforcement. Indeed, few parents the world over would have any idea how to proceed with such a project. Instead, the child acquires a language spontaneously. The child's initial sentences are two and three words in length and resemble adult telegraphic language but are not copies of it. Some examples provided by McNeill (1967) follow: *More milk, All gone boat, Pretty fan.* The child's grammar is therefore not modeled on adult grammar but employs fewer structural parts of speech and, most important, *can be used to generate new, nonimitative sentences.*

Returning to our discussion of nativistic theory, a fourth criticism of conditioning theory is offered by Lenneberg (1967, pp. 137–141) who has studied children who are deaf, whose parents are deaf, or who have severe congenital defects of the speech mechanism that prevent articulation. Children with such severe problems show a surprisingly well-developed comprehension of language, which obviously could not be acquired through reinforcement. Naturally, a child who is deaf cannot acquire language spontaneously; and children from severely handicapped verbal environments are retarded in their linguistic development, thus revealing the role of learning. However, that good comprehension—not only of words but of correct grammatical structure—can occur in the absence of usage is evidence against a strict conditioning paradigm, which requires that responses be overtly made before learning can occur.

Aside from these specific criticisms of the empirical point of view, Chomsky (1957, 1959, 1967) has taken the general position that in order to understand language development in children, psychologists must first understand the nature of language itself. His *generative theory,* a major positive contribution to psycholinguistics, holds that one must first understand the sentence and the syntactical substructure that makes the sentence possible before the elements of sentences or the development of language can be understood. Following his own precepts, Chomsky has undertaken an extensive analysis of language from the syntactical, semantic, and phonological points of view.

His work thus far suggests that all children have an innate "theory of language" that enables them to utilize speech in the verbal community. The child possesses a general and highly analytical linguistic structure, which results in linguistic development appearing as a series of hierarchies that reflect the unfolding of maturational processes as they interact with learning. More startling still is the possibility that at a deep level there may be a universal grammar or at least a few restricted classes of grammar.

Lenneberg (1967), also writing on the general level, states that the appearance of linguistic stages in children's speech the world over and their correlates in general development strongly indicates that language development is basically maturational. He conceives of the period of childhood—particularly the early period—as a critical one (1967, pp. 176, 371–379) for language acquisition. In this connection he emphasizes the commonly known fact that adults have considerably more difficulty in learning a language than do children and that even when adults succeed, they typically speak the new tongue with a noticeable accent.

Finally, Lenneberg also emphasizes the relative independence of language and IQ as a point in favor of the nativistic position. Admitting that vegetative idiots do not learn to speak, he stresses the fact that children within the normal range of IQ—and it is a wide one—all acquire language at about the same time, regardless of the level of their IQ's. Again it is difficult to justify such findings on a purely empirical basis. Of course, there are differences in the speech of dull and bright children. This, admittedly, is the result of learning. However, the uniformity of hierarchical development of language suggests a basic biological process that is "released" at appropriate stages in the level of development.

Support for the hypothesis that the language acquisition process goes through similar stages of development in all children has recently been reported by Slobin (1970) and his associates, who studied the speech of a number of children from different cultures, involving eight languages: German, Russian, French, Luo (a language of Kenya), Samoan, Japanese, Serbian, and Bulgarian. A study of the data collected thus far indicates that children everywhere go through approximately the same stages of development—beginning with babbling, progressing to one- and then two-word phrases. As early as two-word phrases, a rudimentary grammar has developed, even though not directly presented by adults. The universality of stages in language development, though not inconsistent with learning theory, nevertheless, strongly suggests a nativistic process.

Additional support for the nativistic point of view comes from recorded conversations between children and their mothers. These recordings reveal that contrary to what empiricists have suggested, the child does not imitate adult speech in the manner that reinforcement theory would demand. R. Brown (1965, 1970, 1973), a social psychologist who has worked extensively in the area of psycholinguistics, summarizes several differences from a study of three children called in the report Adam, Eve, and Sarah, whose conversations with their mothers were extensively recorded and transcribed.

First, the child, as indicated above, uses short sentences of two to four morphemes, or basic linguistic units of meaning (see Table 11-4). The length of the child's utterances is not constrained because of vocabulary limitations but because of limitations on the planning and programming ability of the language acquisition function at early ages. Second, it may be noted from Table 11-4 that the child does not omit nouns and verbs, which are the fundamental parts of speech. The omissions occur among prepositions, articles, pronouns, plurals, possessives, and connectives. It is the omission of these more abstract parts of speech that gives children's speech its telegraphic characteristics. Third, Brown emphasizes that the order of words is preserved, indicating that *the child is processing the model sentence as a whole* rather than dealing with it as a list of words. If the sentence were not treated as a sentence, there is no reason that the child might not reverse the order of words and give the most recent first.

Finally, Brown and his associates have emphasized that adults imitate children—more so, indeed, than children imitate adults. Table 11-5 shows examples of expanded children's sentences produced by mothers. As these examples indicate, the mother preserves the child's word order. She adds connectives, articles, pronouns, and so on to make the child's sentences grammatical. The expansion of the child's speech serves both as a confirming reaction and a tutorial. That is, to repeat the child's utterances is, in effect, to ask, Is this what you mean? At the same time the mother is offering a model of correct adult speech. However, Brown cautions us to remember that imitation remains only a model. The child is not slavishly shaped

TABLE 11-4. Imitations Produced by Adam and Eve[a]

Adult Model	Child's Imitation
Tank car.	Tank car.
Wait a minute.	Wait a minute.
Daddy's brief case.	Daddy brief case.
Fraser will be unhappy.	Fraser unhappy.
He's going out.	He go out.
That's an old-time train.	Old time train.
It's not the same dog as Pepper.	Dog Pepper.
No, you can't write on Mr. Cromer's shoe.	Write Cromer shoe.

[a]From R. Brown, *Social Psychology*. Copyright © 1965 by The Free Press. Reprinted with permission of The Macmillan Company.

TABLE 11-5. Expansions of Child Speech Produced by Mothers[a]

Child	Mother
Baby highchair.	Baby is in the highchair.
Mommy eggnog.	Mommy had her eggnog.
Eve lunch.	Eve is having lunch.
Mommy sandwich.	Mommy'll have a sandwich.
Sat wall.	He sat on the wall.
Throw Daddy.	Throw it to Daddy.
Pick glove.	Pick the glove up.

[a]From R. Brown, *Social Psychology*. Copyright © 1965 by The Free Press. Reprinted with permission of The Macmillan Company.

ultimately to imitate the parents' speech. Instead, the child's speech remains open-ended and generative.

Our brief discussion of this challenging new area of psychology does not enable us to decide between nativistic and empirical theories. Any such choice would be both premature and self-defeating. The fundamental question that remains for future research to resolve is not which theory is correct, but what are the relative contributions of biological and environmental factors in language development. All we can say with assurance at this time is that the nativists have provided an impressive body of fact and theory that redresses the imbalance between the older, simplistic conditioning theories and contemporary psycholinguistics.

Current Research and Issues

In concluding this discussion of psycholinguistics, it seems appropriate to comment briefly on current areas of high research interest and the issues that this research is designed to resolve. First, the nature of language itself continues to be investigated intensively by a number of linguists and psycholinguists who are studying the fundamental syntactical relationships in speech, the relationships between thought and language, and semantic and grammatical relationships (R. Brown, 1970; Chomsky, 1968; Slobin, 1971).

A second area of research interest is concerned with investigations of communication among animals. The best known of these efforts is that carried out by Gardner and Gardner (1969) with Washoe, a female chimpanzee whom they taught American Sign Language. The animal acquired an astonishingly large vocabulary of 150 signs. The importance of such projects lies in testing the limits of communication among the various species and in discovering the fundamental nature of communication in its simplest form, stripped of its complex human characteristics.

Another area of active research is the subcultural differences found in language performance, particularly among black children in the United States. Contrary to widespread assumptions among public school teachers, black children's speech is not deficient when observed and tested in the home or among the children's peers (Houston, 1970). That black children may perform in an inferior manner when observed in school situations reflects social conditioning and disadvantage rather than intrinsic linguistic deficits. In effect, the black child is bilingual. He speaks black English at home and among peer groups and standard English in school. These differences found in black children are of considerable practical and theoretical importance in intelligence testing. This problem will be discussed in more detail in Chapter 15.

Interest among psycholinguists (Slobin, 1971) continues concerning cultural differences among peoples of widely disparate cultures. In a classic book, *Language, Thought, and Reality,* Whorf (1956) suggested that language determines the manner in which we perceive and think about the world. That something approaching a functional equivalence between thought and language exists is supported by the fact that peoples in different cultures think about their environments in different ways depending upon their language. The Eskimos, for example, have twenty words for snow; we have only one. R. Brown (1965) reports that one Indonesian tribe has eighty words for rice, indicating a richness of thought about an important source of food. A somewhat different but related view of thought and language has been provided by Vygotsky (1962), who emphasizes the close relationship between thought and inner speech. Because so much of our thinking depends upon inner speech, Vygotsky's views support Whorf's.

The areas of recent and current research noted above—along with the work of Piaget, Skinner, and those working in concept learning—have raised fundamental systematic and theoretical issues concerning the relationship between thinking and language. Skinner's position that the basic problem for psycholinguists is to discover the *behavioral* consequences of language and to understand the manner in which reinforcement shapes language and thought is close to the positions of Whorf and Vygotsky, in that all take the view that thinking and language behavior are functionally equivalent or identical. Some, but not all, investigators in the area of concept learning hold the same view.

The point of view held by Piaget, Chomsky, Lenneberg, and Brown and his associates stresses the development of conceptual processes that make language acquisition and development possible. This approach is strongly cognitive and emphasizes the child's use of rules and sequential development of the matrices of thinking. However, it also leaves room for environmental and social influences in shaping language, not only in the sense that each child obviously acquires the language of the environment but also in the sense that cultural, subcultural, economic, and other influences play upon the basic language acquisition process to determine the final outcome of linguistic performance.

The issue, in conclusion, is not a simple one of what proportion of language behavior is empirically determined and what proportion is nativistically determined, but an ongoing investigation of structural, motivational, cognitive, and environmental factors in the acquisition and utilization of language.

Motivation

12

In this and the following chapter we are entering upon the study of systems and theories in *dynamic psychology*. As used in the language of everyday life, the term *dynamic* has the implication of *power, energy, force,* or *action*. In the technical literature of psychology the concept has the same connotation, but its denotation is much more specific. Technically, dynamic psychology is the psychology of motivation and emotion. The two processes are grouped under the broad heading of *dynamic psychology* because psychologists look upon motives and emotions as *conditions that arouse, regulate, and sustain behavior*. It is also interesting to note that both terms come from the same Latin root, *movere,* meaning to move or incite to action. Thus, psychological usage is sanctioned by etymological tradition.

In psychological research and in the systematic literature, however, motivational and emotional processes are conventionally treated separately, partly for practical reasons and partly on theoretical grounds. We shall follow the convention of considering the two processes independently, devoting the present chapter to motivational theory and the following one to systematic theories of emotion.

Before we begin our examination of historical conceptions of motivation, it will be helpful to consider what has traditionally been included within this area. As we examine the scope of motivational psychology, it will become apparent that the field is both broad and complex, in the sense that motivation is intimately related to a number of other psychological processes.

First, the psychology of motivation is concerned with *changing physiological states* associated with hunger, thirst, sex, and so forth. Therefore many of the early experimental studies of motivation were directed toward the investigation of the strength of drives known to be related to bodily needs and physiological processes. More recently, a great deal of research and theorizing has been directed toward understanding the fundamental neurological, metabolic, and physiological factors underlying the primary drives.

Second, *emotional states,* as already indicated, are sometimes treated as motivating conditions. Psychologists have demonstrated experimentally that emotional states, through learning, can act as drives. Moreover, as common experience tells us, emotions often reinforce motives in progress. When we strongly desire something, the accompanying emotional tone increases the strength of our desire to attain our goal.

Third, *habits* enter the realm of motivational psychology because of the fact that well-established habits can incite the individual to action. The professional man or office worker who has spent thirty or forty years on the job often finds retirement an exceedingly difficult adjustment. He reminds us of the proverbial fire horse who, though officially retired, charged off at the sound of the alarm. Habits are also considered to be at the heart of social motives. It is generally agreed that such motives as prestige, affection, the desire for possessions, security, and the like are learned patterns of behavior, or, as some authorities prefer to put it, culturally determined.

Fourth, *sets, attitudes,* and *values* are complex cognitive processes compounded, in part, of motivational factors and, because of this dynamic component, are considered to be within the scope of motivational psychology. Sets may be defined as temporary states of motivation that make for greater selectivity of perception and increased specificity of response. Attitudes are more enduring cognitive states that are motivational in the sense that where they are strongly held they predispose the individual to react in a certain way, as is so clearly illustrated by racial and religious prejudices. Values, too, may be thought of as enduring cognitive processes that function as guides to conduct and as goals toward which the individual directs his behavior.

Fifth, *incentives* and other *environmental influences* that play upon motivational processes are properly included within the scope of both theoretical and experimental studies of motivation. Lewin, for example, made incentives and general environmental conditions an important aspect of his system of dynamic psychology.

Our brief outline of the major areas of motivational psychology should serve to indicate the complexity of the task facing psychologists who undertake the formulation of a comprehensive theory of motivation. However, the broad scope of the field is by no means the only problem confronting the systematist. Motivational processes are hidden states, often outside the conscious awareness of the individual and, as a consequence, must be inferred from behavior. Although the same is true of learning, perception, intelligence, and other mental processes, the problem is accentuated in motivational studies because of the difficulty of establishing "anchoring points" on the stimulus and response sides.

Finally, we should like to point to another factor that retarded the development of motivational psychology during the first quarter of the present century. We refer to the dominance of the structuralist psychology of consciousness, which did not recognize motivation as an area of investigation. Moreover, the molecular approach of the early behaviorists, directed as it was toward externally observable behavior, failed to develop the orientation required to experiment on inferred processes. It was not until the impact of Freud's psychoanalytic theory was felt in academic circles that psychologists began to turn their attention to the development of techniques for the investigation of motivation.

Because the representatives of the early academic schools of psychology had little to say about motivational processes in their systematic literature, we shall present a brief historical introduction and then consider Freud's theory of human motivation. Following our discussion of his system, we shall examine several modern academically nurtured systems in which motivational theories have played a significant role. Finally, we shall discuss recent trends in motivational theory and discover that they are developing rapidly along many diverse lines.

MOTIVATIONAL PSYCHOLOGY IN THE PRESCIENTIFIC ERA

Ever since people first began to speculate about human nature, the question of motives has inevitably arisen. In ancient philosophical and theological works, human nature is treated as a "problem" in the sense that ethical philosophy and moral theology traditionally sought to guide and control the individual for the betterment of society. Consequently, the reasons that people do the things they do and want the things they want became of paramount importance. Closely related to the question of human wants and desires is the problem of freedom of will—a question that is still an issue in philosophy, theology, and psychology. Are we free to act as we will? Are we pawns of fate? Or are we puppets of hereditary and environmental forces over which we have no control?

In seeking the answers to the basic driving forces in human nature, the ancient Greek philosophers favored a humoral, or bodily, basis for motivation. Perhaps it was the enlightened, scientific approach to knowledge characteristic of the Golden Age of Greece that was responsible for the Greek biological analysis of human motives, or it may have been the rapidly developing interest in medicine. Whatever the reason, Greek philosophical speculation on human motivation took the form of relating patterns of action and thought to differences in physique and underlying physiological states. We have already touched upon Plato's physiological theory of human nature in Chapter 1, but the most influential of all classical theories of human motivation was Hippocrates' fourfold typology. The Father of Medicine believed that people could be classified according to their temperaments and held that there are four basic personality types, each of which is related to a different bodily "humor." The "sanguine" individual's optimistic and hopeful attitude is associated with a predominance of the "blood humor." The "melancholic" temperament is caused by a predominance of "black bile," while an abundance of "yellow bile" gives rise to the "choleric," or irascible, disposition. Finally, the "phlegmatic" temperament is associated with an excess of "phlegm."

Typological theories of individual differences have persisted down through the ages with incredible pertinacity and remain a part of modern psychology. But because they attempt to encompass the whole of personality, typologies are only tangential to the psychology of motivation. The point at which the two overlap is in the search for the underlying energetics of behavior. The typologist is rarely satisfied with formulating broad descriptive categories of personality or temperament, but also typically endeavors to explain individual differences in terms of the biological substratum of motivation—usually on the basis of bodily build or the endocrine system.

Another motivational doctrine that has played a considerable role in both ancient and modern accounts of human motivation is psychological hedonism. The doctrine of hedonism developed out of ethical philosophy, where it took the form of affirming that the attainment of happiness is the highest good in life. For this reason, ethical hedonism is an unscientific, philosophical value system, and, as such, has little relevance to psychology. Psychological hedonism, on the other hand, does not impute value judgments to the pursuit of good or evil, but simply postulates that humans seek pleasure and avoid pain.

The philosopher Bentham was the first to formulate clearly psychological hedonism as the basis for human motivation. Largely as a result of the applications of his doctrine to criminal law, our present penal code is based on the assumption that punishment acts as a deterrent to crime by balancing the pleasure to be gained from the commission of a crime with an equal degree of pain. Thus, in British common law, the problem for jurists was "to make the punishment fit the crime."

However, it eventually became apparent that the doctrine of hedonism was an oversimplification of human motivation. More and more severe penalties had to be written into law in an effort to deter criminals, until some 250 offenses carried the supreme penalty. Pickpocketing was one of the infractions calling for the death penalty. But at the public hangings of convicted pickpockets, those still out of custody gathered in large numbers to ply their trade among the excited spectators. Obviously, hedonism as an explanation of human behavior proved defective and in its original form no longer occupies an important place in most systems of motivation. Hedonism is now considered not so much a *determiner* of conduct as an emotional accompaniment of motivated behavior. Pleasantness of hedonic tone indicates an overall attitude of approach and acceptance, whereas unpleasantness implies a tendency to reject and withdraw.

The next historical development of importance in motivational psychology was the rise of the instinct school of motivation. Largely as a result of growing interest in animal behavior around the middle of the nineteenth century, biologists and early comparative psychologists were impressed with the repertoire of complex unlearned behavior patterns exhibited by lower forms. The concept of instinct achieved widespread popularity among those attempting to account for behavior patterns that are unlearned and for which the organism has no foresight of the consequences. Thus, the wasp, without education or insight into the nature of its activities, builds a complicated cellular nest. Similarly, yearling birds migrate thousands of miles without guidance or foreknowledge of their ultimate goal.

The doctrine of instinct as an explanatory concept was given support by the theory of evolution and the science of genetics. Once the mechanisms of heredity had been identified, the somatic, or bodily, basis of instinct could, with considerable logical justification, be attributed to propensities for certain patterns of behavior mediated by inherited "chains" of reflexes or "prepotent" nervous pathways. At a particular stage in the organism's development certain stimulus patterns "trigger off" a sequence of behavior that, taken as a whole, is described by the outside observer as an "instinct." Because of its apparent explanatory power, the concept of instinct became highly popular in late nineteenth-century biology and psychology. Undoubtedly, a great deal of its attractiveness lay in the fact that it offered a mechanistic explanation for behavior, apparently reducing complex acts to simpler elements in hereditary nervous and glandular processes.

However, as is so often true in the history of science, first explanations lose their attractiveness as mature reflection displaces initial enthusiasm. It became increasingly clear that accounting for behavior in terms of instincts had accomplished nothing after all. To attribute the wasp's nest-building activities to an instinct for nest building is a circular explanation. Basically, the difficulty arises from the fact that instinctive behavior is defined as behavior that is unlearned and unlearned behavior is, in turn, "explained" as instinctive. As an example, we say that the wasp's ability to build a nest must be instinctive, since the wasp has no opportunity to learn the behavior in question. But if we then ask what enables wasps to build nests and accept instinct as the answer, the circularity of the reasoning involved is apparent. Moreover, to explain instincts as hereditary propensities is to substitute one mystery for another. As a result, the concept of instinct fell from its position of preeminence to become, for a time, a bad word in psychology—especially from the point of view of the behaviorists, with their distrust of the unseen.

But as has already been pointed out, there are cycles of ascendance and descendance in psychological theory. In the past several decades the investigation of instinctive behavior has enjoyed a resurgence of interest, largely as a result of the work of European ethologists seeking to discover environmental-physiological relationships in the behavior of lower forms. We shall return to the problem of instincts later in this chapter when we discuss this new and challenging approach to comparative psychology, but we must first consider several important motivational systems that reached their development during the early decades of the present century.

FREUD AND THE LIBIDO THEORY[1]

In many ways Freudian psychoanalysis is an outgrowth of instinct psychology. As his biographers emphasize, Freud was strongly attracted to both Darwin and Goethe, whose evolutionary systems appealed to his biological interests. As a young man, Freud studied medicine at the University of Vienna, where a brilliant academic staff numbered among its members some of Europe's outstanding biologists, physiologists, and neurologists. Darwinism was in the air in Viennese academic circles; and Freud, finding himself drawn more and more toward psychology, believed he saw a way to keep the science of mind on a firm biological basis by founding the motivational aspect of his psychoanalytic system on a modification of the reproductive instinct, which he called the *libido*.

The term *libido* is best understood as a psychophysical concept meaning both the *bodily and mental aspects of the sex instinct* (1924, vol. 2, pp. 282–283). In other words, the libido is at once raw sexuality and the mental desire or longing for sexual relations. Freud, however, emphasized the mentalistic aspect of the libido in his writings; and for all practical purposes, libidinal energy may be equated with mental or psychic energy. Moreover, he employed the term to cover a range of

---

[1]See Freud (1920, 1924, 1933, 1938a, 1938b) and Munroe (1955) for both primary and secondary sources.

behavior and motivational phenomena ordinarily not considered sexual in the narrower sense. Self-love, a mother's love for her child, religious love—in fact, any pleasurable activities in which the individual engages—are broader aspects of the basic desire to achieve sexual satisfaction.

In his later writings, Freud further generalized his libido theory into an all-inclusive "life instinct," *eros*. Eros includes self-love, love for others, the instinct for self-preservation, the desire to propagate the species, and the tendency to grow and realize one's potentialities. In short, eros is the creative force that underlies life itself. However, Freud also observed in his patients the urge to destroy—sometimes to destroy the self, sometimes others. Man, he believed, is inevitably drawn toward death. If the death instinct is turned inward, it results in suicide; if outward, in hate or aggression or, in its worst form, murder. This all-embracing instinct of death and destruction he called *thanatos*.

Since eros and thanatos exist side by side, we are all driven by conflicting unconscious forces. Love, then, is a fusion of eros and thanatos. In fact, every human motive is an alloy of both constructive and destructive impulses. Freud agreed in principle with the poet Oscar Wilde, who said that in wish or deed each man kills the things he loves.

On the basis of these fundamental instincts, Freud built his entire system of motivation. As the child develops, the elaboration of eros and thanatos determines his or her relationships with members of the family constellation and the child's reactions to the social order into which he or she is born and to those with whom he or she will have interpersonal relations during adulthood. As we pointed out in Chapter 7, the libido goes through oral, anal, and genital stages of development in infancy followed by a latent period during which the child is being socialized.

Since Freud's theories range over such diverse phenomena as infantile sexuality, neurotic behavior patterns, the structure of primitive societies, and the Judaeo-Christian tradition, a *complete* discussion of his motivational system would require several volumes rather than a section in a single chapter. However, even a summary of Freud's theory of human motivation would be incomplete without some mention of the interesting and highly characteristic methods he employed to assess the motivational structure of his patients. Indeed, as the historical accounts of psychoanalysis reveal, methodology and theory marched hand in hand throughout the evolution of the Freudian system.

As Freud has pointed out (1938a), psychoanalysis began with Breuer's discovery[2] that patients under hypnosis reveal memories for experiences that they are unable to recall in the waking state. In treating his own patients, Freud eventually dispensed with hypnotically induced states in favor of free association. Theoretically, the free-associating patient's "guard" is down, and unconscious material is therefore able to escape the "censorship" normally exerted during directed, conscious thinking. This does not mean that the patient's associations are entirely lacking in direction or are unrelated to an overall goal. The very fact that he or she is

---

[2]Breuer was a Viennese physician who pioneered the therapeutic use of hypnotism in the cure of hysteria.

a suffering human being who is voluntarily seeking help lends a general purpose to the analytic session; the patient is there to explore the inner self, not simply to reminisce idly. Consequently, his or her associations tend to be concentrated within emotional and motivational areas. Indeed, if the patient wanders too far afield, the analyst interprets this as a sign of "resistance" and strives to bring him or her back to more significant productions.

An important submethod within the larger technique of free association is dream analysis. So critical is the process of analyzing dreams that it is sometimes considered a separate method of uncovering unconscious motivational processes. However, in practice, dreams are analyzed by having the patient free-associate around the content of the dream so that its dynamics may be revealed. Because Freud considered dreams as a "royal road to the unconscious," it will be necessary to go into the process of dream analysis in some detail.

To begin with, it is important to recognize that, upon analysis, dreams reveal two distinct types of content, the *manifest content* and the *latent content*. The dream as remembered by the dreamer upon awakening is the manifest content. Psychoanalytically, the manifest content is not the significant portion of the dream, since in the process of becoming conscious, it has undergone considerable distortion in order to make it acceptable to the dreamer. The hidden, or latent, content of the dream, therefore, must be discovered by searching deep below the surface of the manifest content. This depth analysis is accomplished in two ways. First, the patient is required to associate around elements within the dream. If, for example, the dream involves swimming, the patient may be asked to associate on "water." Presumably, water in the manifest content has some hidden significance for the dreamer, and the memories and impulses that it stimulates during free association help to reveal just what that significance is.

The second method for discovering the latent meaning of dreams is symbol analysis. Since symbolism in dreams is largely a private affair, the meaning of symbols must be determined in relation to the psyche of the individual dreamer. This involves the discovery of partial or incomplete identities between the manifest symbols and hidden wishes or impulses buried in the patient's unconscious. In general, the majority of symbols in dreams are sexual (Freud, 1920, p. 161). Because sexual impulses are "forbidden," the *dream work* utilizes several processes to convert them into acceptable, and apparently harmless, symbols. A number of these are common from individual to individual and may therefore be considered "universal" symbols.

For example, the male sex organ appears in the form of sticks, poles, steeples, snakes, or other pointed objects. The female genitals are symbolized as pocketbooks, trunks, caves, or enclosed places. The process of birth is symbolized as running water or swimming. The dreamer's body takes the form of a house—if the dreamer is male, the walls of the house will be smooth; if female, the house will have ledges and balconies (breasts).

In the foregoing examples the partial identities are easily recognized. But in many dreams the manifest content is extremely distorted and sometimes bizarre. In such cases the symbolism in the dream and the events depicted have undergone considerable modification by the dream work. The first, and one of the most important processes of the dream work, is *condensation,* in which the manifest content is translated into a highly abbreviated form. Some elements of the dream are omitted, and others only appear in fragmentary form. In other cases several elements may be blended into one. Frequently, in the latter instance, one person in the manifest content may stand for several individuals in the latent content.

A second process employed by the dream work is *displacement.* This takes two forms: First, a latent element may be replaced by something more remote—something that is virtually an allusion instead of a direct representation of a significant event in the dreamer's life. Second, the latent accent may be displaced in the manifest content. For example, latent accent on the male genital organ may appear in the dream as accent on the nose. Not infrequently, displacement takes the form of accenting opposites. Thus clothing often represents nakedness, or love may be a disguise for hate, and vice versa. Finally, the process of *secondary elaboration* helps to disguise the real significance of dreams. In secondary elaboration the dreamer, upon awakening, makes a "good story" out of the dream. He or she tends to add elements that were not in the original dream and omits others. In some cases elaboration may modify the dream to such an extent that its significance is totally misunderstood (Freud, 1920, p. 190).

In general, the process of dream interpretation is designed to reverse the dream work. In other words, the purpose of the analysis is to reveal precisely what the dream work is trying to repress. Basically, what is repressed is a wish—a wish strongly desired by the dreamer's unconscious but incompatible with the dreamer's evaluation of himself or herself. Because unconscious repressed impulses are at the root of the patient's symptoms, the importance of their identification for successful therapy is obvious.

Freud was also convinced that slips of the tongue, errors in writing or behaving, and accidental or symptomatic acts reveal hidden motivation. Of special importance in indicating a strong desire to repress or hide unconscious motives is the process of *resistance,* which is encountered in neurotic patients during therapy. The operation of resistance is revealed when the patient's free associations become unproductive, when he or she refuses to go on, "forgets" appointments, or otherwise behaves as if he or she were on the defensive. According to Freud, the appearance of resistance indicates that a sensitive, painful area of the unconscious is being approached; and for protection from the anxiety attendant upon the exposure of deeply repressed impulses or experiences, the patient strengthens his or her defenses. In such cases the analyst moves slowly, reassures the patient as the analysis proceeds, and helps him or her to understand the meaning of defensive behavior.

Finally, neurotic symptoms themselves reveal the operation of unconscious motives. The unsatisfied libido, frustrated by reality, is forced to seek its satisfaction in other ways, and the symptoms become substitutes for the suppressed urges of the libido. Symptoms are less shocking to the individual's conscious than the direct wishes lurking in the unconscious. Thus, compulsive symptoms such as hand washing, counting steps, or touching certain objects are symbolic, disguised wish fulfillments of repressed desires. By carrying out the compulsive act, the individual achieves tension reduction. Consequently, symptoms act as safety valves for relieving pent-up libidinal energies that might otherwise explode catastrophically.

We shall have more to say about Freud's concepts of human motivation when we consider his theory of personality structure in Chapter 17. Meanwhile we shall briefly consider the motivational aspects of several of the more important variants of Freudian theory.

ADLER AND INDIVIDUAL PSYCHOLOGY[3]

Alfred Adler was an associate of Freud's from 1902 to 1911, at which time psychoanalysis was still in its formative stages. After making a number of contributions to psychoanalytic theory, Adler disagreed with Freud on certain fundamental issues and thus resigned from the International Association for the Promotion of Psychoanalysis that Freud had established some years earlier. After his departure from the Freudian circle, Adler founded a rival school of Individual Psychology, wrote extensively on his theoretical views, and, in collaboration with his colleagues, founded a number of clinics for the treatment of children and adults.

Adler's theory of human motivation takes as its point of departure the initial weakness and helplessness of the child. Although the child is aware of his or her comparative inferiority, he or she possesses an inherent urge to grow, to dominate, to be superior. The child's goal is the goal of security and superiority, and he or she is driven toward this objective by insecurity and feelings of inferiority. Children with organic defects, female children, and those born into minority groups bear an added burden of inferiority and are likely to develop "inferiority complexes."[4] In striving to overcome inferiority feelings, the child adopts compensatory patterns of behavior, which in extreme cases take the form of overcompensation. Thus, the child with an inferior body may, by a supreme effort, become a great athlete. A girl with poor eyesight might strive to become an artist or dress designer. Adler pointed to many outstanding men of past ages—Julius Caesar, Demosthenes, Alexander the Great, Theodore Roosevelt—who overcame serious organic defects to be numbered among the great leaders of history.

Not all compensation, however, is direct and socially useful. The neurotic, the psychotic, and the delinquent are striving to overcome inferiority feelings indirectly and according to a "style of life" that is socially unacceptable or even destructive. Such individuals, Adler believed, are lacking in "social interest" and are overly preoccupied with individual goals. He was firmly convinced that no human being can achieve happiness in the pursuit of egocentric, fictional goals. Therefore, the

---

[3]For sources, see Adler (1927, 1929) and Ansbacher and Ansbacher (1956).

[4]In his later writings, Adler put less emphasis on feelings of inferiority as negative states that must be overcome by compensatory mechanisms. Rather, he came to interpret feelings of inferiority as states of imperfection or incompletion. He saw restlessness and incessant striving not so much a desire to rid oneself of deficiencies as a more positive process in which one seeks to grow and to move forward to higher things.

focal point of therapy is the patient's style of life. Adler helped his patients explore the various ramifications of the neurotic style of living to which they had become habituated. The patient's energies being directed toward the unrealistic, fictional goals must be revealed, understood, and redirected toward socially useful goals. In this connection Adler laid special emphasis on the exploration of the marital, vocational, and social aspects of the patient's life-style, since each of these areas is so crucial in the individual's adjustment.

It is also important to note that Adler, in contrast to Freud, never practiced psychoanalysis. Adler's was a face-to-face technique in which the therapist and patient were on an equal footing. During the course of the therapeutic conversations, Adler explored with his patient the latter's early recollections and present dreams, since he felt both were highly significant in revealing the patient's life-style. He also stressed the patient's position in the family constellation and relationships to the parents. In general, Adler's therapeutic technique was more "permissive" than Freud's and more directed toward contemporaneous as opposed to genetic problems. In modern psychiatric practice, Adler's therapy would be characterized as "ego therapy" as opposed to the deeper Freudian procedures.

Like Freud, Adler stressed the family situation and the early years as the critical factors in the development of the child's character structure. Unlike Freud, however, Adler did not assign a fundamental role in personality development to sexuality. He believed that Freud had greatly exaggerated the importance of the sex motive while neglecting the child's social relationships with parents and siblings. Both the pampered child and the rejected child are in danger of becoming maladjusted. Pampered children cannot develop confidence in themselves, expect too much from others, and attempt to dominate others just as they dominated their mothers. Rejected children become insecure, anxious, or in some instances hostile and rebellious. In any event, both overprotected and rejected children never acquire the spirit of cooperation that makes for sound, productive human relationships.

In summary, Adler's theory of human motivation emphasizes social as opposed to biological factors. The individual's style of life as it impinges upon his or her interpersonal relations in marriage, work, and community living is the reflection of his or her basic motivational structure. Adler, therefore, in contrast to Freud, advocated a molar rather than a molecular approach to human behavior. The individual's entire program of living—not the sexual side of life alone—is the focus of therapy. In Adler's system, the self is a central concept. In many ways Adler anticipated the neo-Freudian psychoanalysts, whose theories will be summarized later in this chapter.

JUNG AND ANALYTICAL PSYCHOLOGY[5]

Carl Jung (1875–1961) was another close associate of Freud's during the early period of psychoanalysis, but he ultimately disagreed with the master on theoretical

[5]For sources, see C. Jung (1923, 1931, 1933).

issues and, like Adler, founded his own school. Jung's school, known as Analytical Psychology, is (as the name implies) a system that is closer in both spirit and practice to Freud's than is Adler's.

Jung's major point of disagreement with Freud was over the nature of the libido. Years before Freud had integrated the concept of the libido with eros, Jung had defined it as a general life urge. He held that Freud's conception of infantile sexuality was incorrect and that the child's libido expresses itself in terms of growth and the urge to excel rather than in direct sexuality. Moreover, Jung disagreed with Freud on the nature of the unconscious, arguing that it exists on two levels, the *individual unconscious* and the *collective unconscious*. The former arises from repressions, whereas the latter consists of inherited neural patterns that predispose the individual toward primitive modes of thought such as autistic thinking and belief in magic or superstitions. Because it is a racial instinct, the libido is contained in the collective unconscious.

It is also important to note that Jung believed that the sexual instinct is not of primary importance. In primitive societies the hunger drive plays a more important role than sexuality, and in civilized societies the drive for power is of more importance to many individuals than sexual satisfaction. In addition to these biocentric instincts which link man and the animals, the archetypes of the collective unconscious play a dynamic role in the individual's behavior. They are not mere intellectualizations but impulses to action and freighted with feelings and emotions. Thus, when a man suddenly falls in love with a woman at first sight and feels that he is helplessly in the grip of an emotion over which he has no control, he is correct. She is the archetype of the woman in the man's collective unconscious or in another sense is his *anima* or the feminine aspect of his personality. Consequently, she is "perfect" for his unconscious even though consciously he may wish that he could free himself from his emotional involvement with her. More generally, archetypes play an important role in much of our personal and social behavior, and so we are in a signficant measure creatures of the racial or collective unconscious.

Jung is most famous for his concepts of *introversion* and *extroversion,* terms which have become part of our everyday speech. The motivational and interest patterns of the individual whose orientation is introverted dispose him or her toward self-centeredness. In dealing with the physical and social worlds, such individuals will be governed by the relationship of things and other people to themselves. He or she is also inclined to be rigid in behavior, and if he or she develops a neurosis, it will most likely be of the obsessive-compulsive variety. The individual whose orientation is extroverted, on the other hand, is adaptable, sociable, and is governed by objective reality rather than by subjective considerations. Those whose orientation is extroverted tend to develop hysteria if they become psychoneurotic. It is important to note that the concepts of introversion and extroversion as Jung employed them do not imply distinct types of people but, rather, orientations toward life.

Jung, like Freud, tended to think in terms of opposites or polarities. The individual whose dominant personality pattern is introversion is unconsciously extroverted, and vice versa. The male has in his makeup elements of femininity; and, correspondingly, the woman has masculine tendencies in her unconscious. To complicate the picture even further, mental activity takes four dominant forms: *sensation, thinking, intuition,* and *feeling* (see Figure 12-1). Thinking and feeling are polar opposites, and both tendencies are always present in the individual at the same time. If his or her dominant mental activity is thinking, the individual's unconscious tends toward feeling. Similarly, sensing and intuition are opposites; and, as is true of the other polarities, both are operative in the individual at the same time.

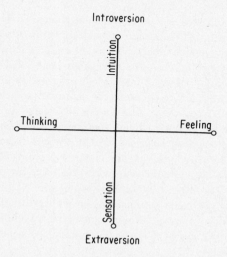

FIGURE 12-1.   Jung's fundamental polarities of introversion-extroversion and modes of response.

Clearly, where so many diverse and conflicting tendencies are present, there is a great danger of one-sided development. One aspect of the individual's personality tends to become dominant, totally overshadowing the unconscious, latent self. If the extroverted masculine-thinking aspects of the self gain a unilateral ascendance, the individual cannot utilize the introverted, more feminine, and intuitive potentialities that remain untapped in the unconscious. In such cases the therapist must help the individual to realize these hidden potentialities and to integrate them with the more active side of the self.

Moreover, the Jungian therapist must help the patient explore the collective unconscious in order to achieve a sense of oneness with the entire human race. One of the most powerful factors in the collective unconscious is man's religious instinct. Jungians, therefore, encourage their patients to strengthen their religious sense and search for their souls. A cure is not achieved until the patient is able to integrate and harmonize the personal and collective unconscious and to arrive at a working synthesis of the complementary polarities that divide him or her from the true self.

MOTIVATIONAL THEORY IN POST-FREUDIAN
PSYCHOLOGY

By the third decade of the present century, psychoanalysis had made its impact felt in every department of human thought. Its influence, however, was most marked within the arts, social sciences, and medicine. The violent reaction of conservatism and prudery during the first two decades of the twentieth century had given way to enthusiastic acceptance in some quarters, and to at least a limited recognition of the value of the Freudian insights in others.

However, Freud's influence on the arts and sciences was no longer a one-way process. Developments within the rapidly expanding fields of anthropology, sociology, social psychology, and medicine began to exert a reciprocal influence on psychoanalysis. Cultural anthropologists were discovering that many of the taboos and other social practices Freud had interpreted in terms of libido theory and the Oedipus complex either did not occur in all primitive social orders or took an entirely different form from those making up the warp and woof of civilized societies. Malinowski, for example, found that incest taboos among the Trobriand Islanders were directed against relations with the sister rather than the mother. Moreover, Freud's general hypothesis that neurotic symptoms and modes of thought in civilized Westerners are similar to attitudes and behavior patterns in primitive peoples could not be confirmed. However, the validity of his general theory of unconscious dynamics did receive support from anthropological and sociological field studies. At the same time, sociologists and social psychologists were compiling evidence that much of our behavior is determined by social conditioning rather than by biological factors.

Within psychoanalysis itself, the impact of the cultural sciences resulted in a strong so-called neo-Freudian[6] movement quite different in spirit and purpose from the various splinter movements that had occurred earlier within Freud's international association. In most cases the earlier schisms grew out of disagreements over methodology or theoretical emphasis and were not the result of fundamental differences in libido theory and psychosexual development.

The post-Freudians, on the other hand, rejected both the libido theory and Freud's general emphasis on sexuality. Instead, neuroses were envisioned as being partly a product of cultural conflicts and partly the result of unsound social development. The child was no longer considered to be at the mercy of biological instincts. Instead, normal development was believed to be contingent upon secure and affectionate family relationships, on the one hand, and the cultural and social influences that play upon him or her, on the other hand. Moreover, the very definition of what is normal and what is abnormal was held to be culturally determined.

An outstanding exponent of the post-Freudian point of view is Karen Horney (1885–1952), who for many years was associated with the New York Psychoanaly-

---

[6]Since many psychoanalysts of the post-Freudian period rejected Freud's emphasis on sexuality, either in whole or in part, we believe the group should be referred to as post-Freudian rather than neo-Freudian.

tic Institute. In her book, *The Neurotic Personality of Our Time* (1937), she emphasizes her dissatisfaction with orthodox Freudian theory. In the first chapter, entitled significantly, "Cultural and Psychological Implications of Neuroses," Horney strongly emphasizes the cultural definition of neurosis as a deviation from a pattern of behavior commonly accepted in a given society. She believes that the driving force behind the neuroses is "basic anxiety" generated originally by a genuine lack of love and affection in childhood. In striving to overcome anxiety, the child develops "neurotic trends," which are essentially compensatory behavior patterns whose purpose is to promote security. In a later book, *Our Inner Conflicts* (1945), she argues that there are three fundamental and mutually incompatible neurotic trends: (1) moving toward people, (2) moving against people, and (3) moving away from people.

If the child's dominant compensatory trend is moving toward people, he or she is attempting to overcome anxiety and insecurity through excessive demands on others for love and affection. If the child's predominant mode is moving against people, he or she seeks to overcome insecurity by the excessive development of power, prestige, and dominance. Finally, moving away from people implies a search for security through withdrawal. The child who is hurt and rejected retreats from the source of pain and eventually refuses to try at all lest he or she fail.

In her own clinical experience, Horney found that neurotic trends do not exist in isolation in the individual but occur together, thus giving rise to inner conflicts. For example, if a neurotic's predominant trend is moving against people, he or she nevertheless unconsciously wishes to move *toward* people. Because his or her hostile behavior antagonizes others, it becomes more and more difficult for the neurotic to make friends despite the fact that they are desperately needed, albeit unconsciously. The result is increased anxiety, leading to greater hostility, which in turn is accompanied by rapidly deteriorating interpersonal relations. The neurotic, to employ Horney's phrase, is caught in a "vicious circle." The problem for the therapist is to help the patient realize his or her inner conflicts and the various secondary defense mechanisms to which they give rise. This is accomplished through psychoanalysis.

A detailed examination of post-Freudian theory is beyond the scope of this volume.[7] However, the brief sketch that has been presented here is representative of the strong socially oriented nature of the new movement. While retaining Freud's methods—his emphasis on determinism, unconscious motivation, repression, and conflict—the post-Freudians show considerably more theoretical and methodological flexibility than is characteristic of conservative Freudians. In the last analysis, this new spirit of freedom and experimentation that the post-Freudians have brought to psychoanalysis may prove to be more significant than the specific theoretical and methodological issues that now divide them. Certainly, the willingness of the post-Freudians to recognize the relevance of contributions from the social sciences has

---

[7]For a detailed comparative study of both Freudian and post-Freudian schools of psychoanalysis, see Munroe (1955).

commanded respect from the academic psychologists who work in the areas of motivation and personality. These psychologists have found the study of recent psychoanalytic theory both stimulating and enlightening, and many post-Freudian concepts of personality development have close parallels in contemporary theories of motivation and personality.

LEWIN'S FIELD THEORY[8]

As was pointed out in Chapter 5, Lewin may be considered as a member of the Gestalt school or as the developer of a separate system. Neither characterization is correct if taken literally, since Lewin's system is Gestalt in its overall orientation and at the same time differs strikingly in its emphasis on needs, will, personality, and social factors from orthodox Gestalt psychology. The founders of the Gestalt school stressed the study of perception and, to a lesser degree, learning, emphasizing in their theoretical writings physiological constructs in accounting for behavior. Lewin's orientation, on the other hand, is toward psychology as a social science. In their experimental work Lewin and his associates emphasized the study of behavior as a function of the total social and physical situation. Much of this research was carried out on children; and it often utilized elaborate experimental setups in an attempt to control (or at least get detailed information about) the child's total environment during the course of the investigation. We shall give examples of Lewin's experimental techniques as we examine his theoretical position.

Lewin lays the foundation for his theoretical system by analyzing the basic structure of science in general. He believes that science has evolved over three developmental epochs, which he designates as *speculative, descriptive,* and *constructive*. Early Greek science exemplifies the speculative stage of scientific evolution; its goal was to discover the fundamental elements or processes underlying natural phenomena. A science in this initial phase of development is friendly to speculative theorizing. In general, scientific systems at this stage of development are characteristically "all-inclusive" and are derived from a few basic concepts. Plato's mind-body dichotomy, Heraclitus' reduction of all things to fire, and Aristotle's laws of association are all illustrative of science during the speculative epoch of scientific evolution.

In its descriptive phase, science seeks to accumulate as many facts as possible and to describe them with precision. Classifications take the form of broad abstractions, and theorizing is looked upon with disfavor. Perhaps the best illustration of this mode of scientific development is found in pre-Darwinian biology, in which classification of plants and animals into phyletic categories and descriptions of their life cycles were the subject matter of zoology and botany. Similarly, structuralism as a system of psychology was largely a descriptive science held together purely by a logical ordering of phenomena with little or no underlying theory.

The constructive—or, as Lewin also calls it, "Galilean"—mode of science has

---

[8]Our account is drawn primarily from Lewin's *Principles of Topological Psychology* (1936). See also Ellis (1938), Lewin (1938, 1946), and Lewin, Lippitt, and White (1939).

as its goal the discovery of laws by means of which the scientist can predict individual cases. The scientist is no longer satisfied with descriptive categorization, but envisions the system in terms of a group of interrelated concepts held together by laws. Constructive, or Galilean, science is friendly to empirical theories and laws but does not demand that either be treated as "universals." Events are lawful even if they occur only once in an individual. The proof of a law depends upon the "purity of the case" and not necessarily upon the frequency with which it occurs.

Reduced to its simplest terms, Lewin's argument holds that psychological laws need not be formulated solely on the basis of statistical averages. Rather, the individual case is equally important. Even if all general psychological laws were known, we would still need to understand the specific individual and the total situation in which he or she exists before we could make any predictions about his or her behavior. Thus, Lewin favors an *idiographic* psychology in which the focus is on the *individual*, as opposed to a *nomothetic* psychology where the emphasis is on the statistical average. Lewin reduces his thesis to the following formula: $B = f(PE)$, where B represents behavior, f is a function (or, in the more general case, a law), P is the person, and E is the total environmental situation.

In light of his emphasis on the study of the individual as a factor in the total situation, Lewin devoted a great deal of effort to devising a theoretical schema for representing environmental variables as they impinge upon the psychological individual. As a result, his system leans heavily on concepts derived from *topology*, a branch of higher mathematics that deals with transformations in space, from *vector analysis*, or the mathematics of directed lines, and from the sciences of chemistry and physics, from which Lewin borrowed such concepts as "valence," "equilibrium," and "field force." Because most of the concepts of field theory can be represented in diagrammatic form by using planes, surfaces, vectors, valence signs, fields of equilibria and disequilibria, Lewin's books and research papers are filled with diagrammatic analyses of various psychological phenomena.

Because he felt that he could not adequately represent these phenomena with the conventional concepts of mathematics, physics, and chemistry, Lewin invented a new system of geometry, called *hodological space*, which consists of a qualitative geometry emphasizing locomotion along psychological paths, the dynamic interaction of individuals in their environments, and their behavior at borders and barriers. Indeed, it has been said that Lewin's system grew out of his blackboard drawings. In the preface to his *Principles of Topological Psychology*, Lewin admits that "it occurred to me that the figures on the blackboard which were to illustrate some problems for a group in psychology might after all be not merely illustrations but representations of real concepts" (1936, p. vii).

The concept of the person in the total life space, which we discussed in Chapter 7 on developmental psychology, represents the *descriptive* or *structural* aspects of field theory to which we may now relate Lewin's dynamic concepts. In doing so we shall be dealing with the motivational aspects of the system. The fundamental concepts in the motivational system are as follows: *need, tension, valence, vector, barrier,* and *equilibrium*. Each of these will be defined and illustrated in the following paragraphs.

Need is Lewin's concept for any motivated state that can be brought about by a physiological condition, the desire for an environmental object, or the intention to achieve a goal (see Figure 12-2).

Tensions are emotional states that accompany needs. When the infant needs food, he or she is in a state of tension, which is reduced by food. Tensions may also be induced by environmental objects that have potential need significance for the individual. Thus, the child who is apparently playing contentedly may experience need arousal and the accompanying state of tension by the sight of an apple that is brought into the room (see Figure 12-2).

Objects may have either positive or negative *valence*. Objects that satisfy needs or are attractive have positive valence, whereas objects that threaten the individual or are repellent have negative valence. It is important to recognize that objects do not *literally* possess "valence" in the sense that the concept is used in chemistry. Valence, as Lewin uses the term, is a *conceptual* property of objects. Thus, to a hungry child an apple has positive valence. To a child who is experiencing the ill effects of having eaten a half-dozen green apples, the apple has a negative valence (see Figure 12-2).

Mathematically, a *vector* is a directed line. Lewin utilized the concept to represent the direction and strength of attraction of objects. If only one vector impinges upon the individual, he or she will move in the direction indicated by the vector (see Figure 12-2). If two or more vectors impel the individual in different directions, the effective movement will be the resultant of all these forces. If two equally balanced vectors are operating, the result is a conflict (see Figure 12-3).

Lewin's analysis of conflict situations is one of his best-known conceptual schemes. Consequently, we shall discuss each of these basic types in turn. The *approach-approach conflict* exists between two positive goal objects of approximately equal attractiveness. Such a situation might be illustrated by an individual who receives two equally attractive job offers simultaneously. The choice of one goal object clearly implies the rejection of the other. As a consequence, the individual remains in a state of indecision. The equilibrium is, however, an unstable one. As the individual moves toward one of the goals, a goal-gradient effect occurs in which the attractiveness of the nearer goal increases, while the attractiveness of the goal moved away from decreases. Because the individual is now in a state of imbalance, he or she will be drawn rapidly to the nearer of the two goals.

More serious is the *avoidance-avoidance conflict*, in which the individual is compelled to choose between two negative alternatives. Such a situation might be illustrated by the case of a soldier who is suffering from combat fatigue and who wishes to escape from the battlefield but is compelled to remain by social and military pressure. In this case the equilibrium tends to be a stable one, and the victim remains torn by indecision. If the soldier moves toward one alternative, the negative repelling force grows stronger and he is thrown back toward the other. But as he approaches the other alternative, its negative force increases; and so he tends to vacillate close to the middle. The solutions of such conflicts may require a choice of the lesser of two evils; or the individual may "leave the field," as the soldier does when he experiences an incapacitating psychological breakdown.

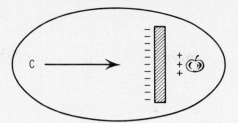

FIGURE 12-2.   The large ellipse represents the child's life space at the moment. C represents the child. The vector indicates that he is motivated to get the apple which is shown with positive valence. The crosshatched barrier is shown with negative valence. The barrier in this case might be the mother who has forbidden the child to eat the apple.

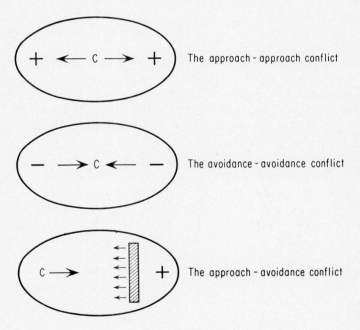

FIGURE 12-3.   The three basic types of conflict according to Lewin.

The *approach-avoidance conflict* is likely to be extremely disruptive, since the individual is both drawn to and repelled by the same situation at the same time. Thus, the drug addict may be strongly drawn toward a cure but dreads undergoing the process of withdrawal symptoms and the return to a lonely, meaningless life. The approach-avoidance conflict is characterized by a stable equilibrium, since at a certain distance from the goal the positive and negative forces are balanced. If the individual attempts to move toward the positive goal, negative factors in the situation repel him or her; consequently, movement tends to be minimal.

Lewin's analysis of conflict also admits the possibility of more complex types of situations, with two or more goals and several alternative courses of action. Moreover, individuals do not remain forever balanced between two poles; events going on in life are great resolvers of conflicts. The value of Lewin's analysis does not lie in the inclusiveness with which all possible situations are treated but in the provision of a model of basic patterns of conflict that have led to experimental analyses of approach and avoidance gradients. Figure 12-4 shows in graphic form an analysis of an approach-avoidance gradient developed by Neal Miller (1944), who trained rats to run along an alley to a food box and then gave them an electric shock as they were eating. On the next trial the animals ran to the goal more slowly and stopped short of the goal itself. Where the rats stopped was defined as the point of balance at which approach tendencies were equal to avoidance tendencies and an equilibrium was reached. The degree of hunger and the strength of shock could, of course, modify the steepness of the gradient and point of equilibrium. (At this point the reader may wish to refer back to a more detailed analysis of Miller's research on conflicts in Chapter 9.)

Barriers may be objects, people, social codes—anything that thwarts the motivated individual as he or she is moving toward a goal. As the barrier is approached, it takes on negative valence. Barriers typically give rise to exploratory behavior in which the individual tests the strength of the barrier. Exploration may also lead the individual to get around the barrier. Or, if it is impassable, the individual may launch an "attack" on the barrier.

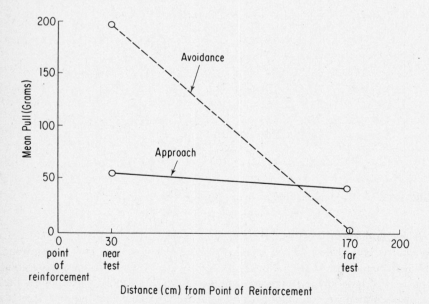

FIGURE 12-4.   Approach-avoidance gradients. For explanation see text. (From Neal E. Miller, "Experimental Studies of Conflict" in Personality and the Behavior Disorders, edited by J. McV. Hunt. Copyright 1944, Renewed © 1972 The Ronald Press Company, New York.)

In Lewin's system, the arousal of needs is accompanied by a state of *disequilibrium*. Generally speaking, disequilibrium may be defined as a state of unequal tension throughout the individual. The ultimate goal of all motivated behavior is to return the individual to a state of equilibrium in which relief from tension is obtained. For example, needs such as hunger, sexual desire, and the wish to be recognized by others create states of disequilibrium accompanied by strong tensions. When the needs are satisfied, the tension disappears and equilibrium is once again restored.

To avoid giving the impression that Lewin's system is based on nothing more substantial than strange terms and rather complex diagrammatic representations of psychological phenomena, we shall summarize several characteristic experiments carried out by Lewin and his associates. It will also be possible by this means to reinforce some of the more important concepts that we have introduced in preceding pages.

Lewin's Experimental Programs

The first of our illustrative experiments was conducted at the University of Berlin by one of Lewin's pupils, Bluma Zeigarnik (1938). The purpose of the experiment was to compare the ability to recall finished versus unfinished tasks. According to field theory, interrupting a subject in the middle of a task should have the effect of leaving him or her in a state of tension and disequilibrium. Moreover, the interruption should serve as a "barrier" to the goal of completing the task; and this should increase the subject's desire to finish the task. If the foregoing hypothetical analysis is correct, then the subjects should recall more unfinished than finished tasks under the conditions of Zeigarnik's experiment.

Zeigarnik assigned her subjects eighteen to twenty-two simple problems such as completing jigsaw puzzles, working out arithmetic problems, and making clay models. Each subject was allowed to finish half the tasks, the remainder being arbitrarily interrupted by the experimenter, who requested the subject to go on to another task. The interrupted tasks were randomly scattered throughout the entire series.

When all tasks had been either completed or experimentally interrupted, Zeigarnik requested the subjects to recall *all* tasks. Approximately 50 percent of the tasks could be recalled. However, 68 percent of the unfinished tasks were recalled as against 43 percent of the finished tasks. Moreover, tasks in which the subjects were strongly engrossed were more often recalled than those in which the subject showed only a moderate degree of interest. The experiment demonstrates the influence of experimentally aroused tensions on the persistence of needs. Tensions aroused by the task remain undischarged until the task is completed. If the task is uncompleted, the persistent tension is revealed by selective recall. However, subsequent experiments have demonstrated that the "Zeigarnik effect" depends to a large degree on the subject's ego involvement (Lewis & Franklin, 1944). Tasks in which the subject is ego-involved are more likely to be recalled—*whether completed or not*. In this case personal failure or success is the important factor; and subjects tend to recall selectively the tasks in which they experienced success.[9]

Our second illustrative experiment is particularly interesting, since it is an application of the techniques and theoretical interpretations of field theory to one of Freud's concepts. More specifically, Barker, Dembo, and Lewin (1941) studied the effects of experimentally induced frustration on the constructiveness of children's play. If, as Freud held, one reaction to frustration is regression, or returning to more primitive levels of behavior, then children's play should show some degree of deterioration as a result of frustration. The subjects were thirty children between 2 and 5 years of age. They were first allowed to play with a set of toys, some of which had parts missing (for example, an ironing board without an iron, a scoop shovel with no scoop, floatable toys but no water). However, most of the children supplied in their imagination what they lacked in reality and played happily. Observers rated the children in terms of the constructiveness of their play. Since there was a close correlation between the mental age of the child and the constructiveness of play, it was possible to rate constructiveness of play in mental-age units.

Following the pretest session, the children were permitted to play with highly attractive and complete toys in a part of the experimental room that was normally inaccessible. They were then returned to the less desirable toys but could still see the more fascinating toys through a wire screen. Again the constructiveness of play was rated by the observers. On the average, the children's play regressed 17.3 months of mental age. In terms of the number of children, twenty-five out of thirty showed some degree of destructiveness in their play. It was also possible to study "behavior at barriers," since the wire screen interposed between the children and the highly desirable toys functioned as a barrier. Some children approached the screen and attempted to reach through it to the toys beyond; some even tried to escape from the room altogether ("leave the field"). Typically, children who demonstrated greater evidence of disturbance at the barrier also showed a higher degree of "regression" in their play.

This experiment with children's toys represents a later phase of Lewin's work. In the early years his chief concern was with theoretical problems and issues, but as time went on he became more and more interested in social psychology. Nevertheless, the experiment is an excellent illustration of the holistic approach that is characteristic of field theory. The analysis of the results in terms of barrier behavior and reduction of the degree of differentiation in the constructiveness of play are also typical of field theory analyses.

Finally, we shall briefly summarize the studies made by Lewin, Lippitt, and White on authoritarian and democratic atmospheres (Lewin, Lippitt, and White, 1939; Lippitt, 1939; Lippitt & White, 1943). The objective of this series of experiments was to determine the effects of "democratic" and "authoritarian" atmospheres on the productiveness and general behavior of small groups of boys.

During the course of meetings held over an extended period, groups of boys

---

[9]The literature on conditions affecting the Zeigarnik effect is complex and contradictory. See Osgood (1953) for a discussion of the empirical findings and various theoretical interpretations.

engaged in small crafts work under the direction of group leaders. All groups were exposed to all leaders, and both types of atmosphere were induced for each group.[10] While the experiment was in progress the life space of each child was under intensive investigation. Parents, teachers, and group leaders were questioned at length about the children's behavior during various phases of the experimental program. Personality tests were also administered during the course of the experiment to determine whether the child's personality was undergoing modification as a result of his group experiences.

The following techniques were utilized by the adult leaders to create an authoritarian atmosphere. To begin with, the autocratic leader made all decisions. The final objectives of the work projects were not revealed to the children in advance. Rewards and punishments were directed at individual children. Finally, the authoritarian leader remained aloof from the children unless actively engaged in directing a project.

The democratic leader made all decisions a matter for group discussion. Alternative solutions were suggested whenever problems arose. Goals were announced in advance, and whenever it was necessary to administer praise or reproof, this was done objectively.

In general, the democratic groups were more productive, less demanding of the leader's time, more friendly in their approach to the leader, and less driven by internal dissension within the group. The democratic groups' productiveness remained relatively high, even when the leader came in late or left during the course of a session. The authoritarian groups tended to be either more aggressive or apathetic than the democratic groups. However, the apathetic groups frequently broke out in aggressive behavior when the leader was "called out" of the clubhouse. This suggests that their "apathy" was the result of suppressive measures on the part of the leader more than of a true absence of aggression in the boys themselves. During the course of an experimentally arranged "attack" on the groups, the authoritarian groups showed poor morale and a tendency to break up, while the democratic groups became more closely knit than before the attack. Finally, one of the most interesting (and disturbing) findings was that the children were able to move from a democratic to an authoritarian atmosphere more readily than they were able to shift from an authoritarian to a democratic atmosphere.

This experiment in social psychology has obvious implications for those concerned with morale, leadership, and political theory. For our purposes (along with the other experiments summarized earlier) it illustrates the novel and ingenious experimental programs developed under Lewin's inspiration.

By way of conclusion, it should be pointed out that Lewin's experimental programs have proved more acceptable to psychologists than have his theoretical views. This must not be taken to mean that his theoretical influence has not been considerable. His writings and concepts have influenced the fields of social, child,

---

[10]A laissez-faire atmosphere was also studied, partly for reasons of control. We are summarizing only the results of the main experimental variables.

and experimental psychology. In testimony to his strong personal influence many prominent contemporary social psychologists were among Lewin's circle during his professional career at Iowa and MIT. But Lewin failed to convince psychologists that his special topological and vectorial representations of psychological phenomena were superior to those derived from more conventional mathematical and verbal analyses. In the last analysis, it is premature to attempt any serious evaluation of Lewin's motivational or topological theories, since his students and associates continue to push forward the program of research in the broad area of social psychology that came into fruition under his leadership.

RECENT AND CONTEMPORARY TRENDS IN MOTIVATIONAL THEORY

As is true in the fields of perception and learning, recent motivational theorists align themselves according to the traditional systematic orientations. Behaviorists continue to emphasize the study of the animal drives; the humanistic orientation is represented in the work of several contemporary theorists; and there are still others who seek to establish miniature theories around the intensive study of a certain motive or class of motives. We cannot, of course, undertake a summary of the entire field of contemporary motivation. Those who wish to explore the diverse theoretical and research literature in this fascinating area are referred to the following sources: Cofer and Appley (1964), Bolles (1967), Goble (1971), Maslow (1954), McClelland (1971), Young (1961), Ferguson (1976), and the *Nebraska Symposium* (1953 to present).

In the remaining pages of this chapter we shall once again invoke the sampling technique and present a summary of what appear to be the most significant and active developments within the broad area of contemporary motivational theory. For this purpose we have chosen four contemporary systematic approaches: (1) the study of animal drives by the ethologists; (2) the humanistic point of view, as represented by the hierarchical theory of A. H. Maslow; (3) a specialized, or miniature, theoretical approach to social motivation, as represented by the studies of the achievement motive by D. C. McClelland and his associates; and (4) H. F. Harlow's studies of intrinsic drives. Physiological theories of motivation will be considered in Chapter 14.

Ethology and Animal Drives

Ethology (*Ethos* = custom, habit, character; *ology* = the study of) is the scientific study of animal behavior, particularly in reference to environment or habitat. The *ethogram* is any unit of behavior under investigation. This branch of zoology developed largely as a result of the work of Karl von Frisch and Konrad Lorenz in Germany and Niko Tinbergen in England. These European zoologists began their field studies of animals in the late 1930s, and by the end of World War II had attracted an impressive group of students and research workers from both Europe and America. Tinbergen's *The Study of Instinct* (1951) received worldwide attention, as did Lorenz's *King Solomon's Ring* (1952), greatly stimulating interest in ethology. Von Frisch's *Bees, Their Vision, Chemical Senses and Language* (1950), provided a key to the mystery of how bees discover honey and communicate with their hive mates. For their work Tinbergen, von Frisch and Lorenz shared the Nobel Prize in Biology in 1973. The concept of instinct, which had largely disappeared from psychology under the attacks of the behaviorists, became respectable again. As a result of these studies, American comparative and developmental psychologists joined their European colleagues in experiments directed toward the understanding of what has come to be called *species-specific behavior*. These joint efforts have resulted in an extensive literature, which we shall make no attempt to review here.[11] Instead, we shall present a summary of the fundamental concepts of ethology as they are related to our present topic, motivation.

Releasers and Imprinting

Early studies of birds and fishes by Lorenz and Tinbergen led to the formulation of the concepts of *releasers* and *imprinting*. A releaser is a highly specific stimulus that "triggers" or initiates species-specific behavior. The sight of the mother duck, for example, releases a following reaction in the ducklings approximately 13 hours after hatching. Because the behavioral response of following is acquired early in life and is irreversible, it is said to be imprinted.

The mechanism of releasers as developed in Tinbergen's studies of such ethograms as fighting reactions in the stickleback fish, begging responses in the herring gull, and escape reactions among the chicks of precocial birds (Figure 12-5) reveals an important range of behaviors under the control of external triggers. This does not mean that internal factors are without significance in these behavior patterns. On the contrary, imprinting and other released behavior depend on maturational readiness in the organism, may involve some degree of learning, and in some cases occur most readily during a *critical period* of development. For these reasons, ethologists use the term "instinct" circumspectly to characterize limited forms of behavior.

More complex behavior, such as that displayed by a young lion in capturing prey, may involve long periods of training (up to two years) and, though characteristic of the species and obviously dependent upon maturation, cannot in any sense be called instinctive. Indeed, the phylogenetic level of a species is closely related to the relative importance of instinct and learning in the genesis of behavior. The insects, whose life span is short and who receive little or no parental care, must necessarily rely on instincts for capturing prey, mating, and nest-building activity. These species display highly stereotyped patterns of adaptive behavior known as

---

[11]For short introductions to animal behavior, see Klopfer and Hailman (1967) or Manning (1967). Both volumes, designed for beginners, have excellent bibliographies. A more advanced recent text is Eibl-Eibesfeldt's *Ethology: The Biology of Behavior* (1975), which emphasizes the ethological point of view. Lorenz's (1952, 1954, 1963) and Tinbergen's (1951, 1953) popular books are invaluable for conveying the spirit of the early naturalistic studies of animals by these leaders.

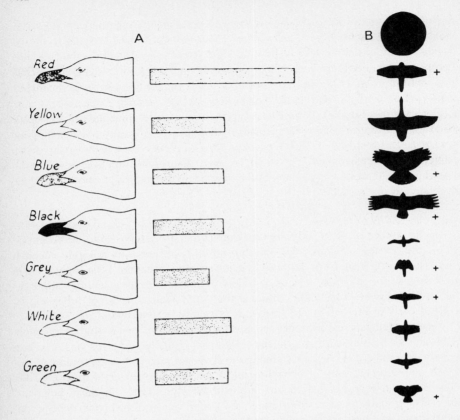

FIGURE 12-5. External triggers for species specific behavior. (a) The releasing value of herring gull models with uniform bills of varying colors. (b) Bird models for testing reactions of various birds to birds of prey. Those marked + released escape responses. (From Tinbergen, N. The Study of Instinct, Fig. 24, p. 31, and Fig. 26, p. 32, 1951. Reprinted by permission of The Clarendon Press, Oxford.)

fixed action patterns, in contrast to the higher forms whose behavior in similar activities may show considerable variation depending upon a number of factors currently under investigation.

First, sensory coding or input is important in species-specific as well as other forms of behavior. Stimulus energy from the environment must be transduced into nervous impulses, which upon arriving at appropriate brain centers release motor reactions. Thus the gull chick's color preference (Figure 12-5) is dependent upon retinal receptors bearing oil-droplet pigments (Hailman, 1964). However, the presence of appropriate sensory capability does not tell us why color spots elicit begging in the chick; it only reveals the anatomical and physiological preconditions in the herring gull's retina necessary for detecting the spots. Sensory capacity, then, is only the first step in a hierarchy of processes involved in ethograms.

Second, background information may be important in determining responses.

Hailman (1966) reports that the gull chick's pecking is not uniquely determined by stimulus-objects alone. The background color appears to be equally important, with complementary background hues eliciting the greatest frequency of pecking. Similarly, it has been known for centuries that the degree to which the protective coloration of a preyed-upon species fits that of its background (camouflage) controls the success of predatory behavior on the part of the predator.

Third, maturational readiness has been recognized as an important factor in behavior for many decades before ethology became popular. The pioneer experiments of Carmichael (1926, 1927) and Coghill (1929) on *Amblystoma* described in Chapter 7 demonstrated that swimming in this species appears at a certain critical stage in development dependent upon the maturation of proprioceptive reflex arcs in the spinal cord.

Studies of imprinting in chicks and ducklings reveal a critical period for the appearance of following reactions (Figure 12-6). The period is a relatively short one, and in instances where the natural mother is not present, the chicks will imprint on an artificial stimulus-object or on each other. Imprinting may fail to occur if the critical period is bypassed, since chicks of precocial birds will then show fear reactions to strange stimuli.

The factors responsible for maturation are complex and involve the development of sensorimotor mechanisms, hormones (particularly in sexual and migratory behavior), and, of course, the appropriate central nervous processes. Underlying all these factors is genetic endowment.

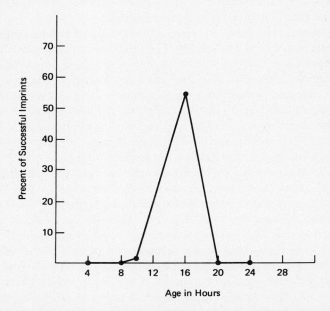

FIGURE 12-6.   The critical period for the following reaction in mallard ducklings. (After Hess, E. Effects of meprobamate on imprinting in waterfowl. Annals of the New York Academy of Sciences 1956–57, p. 728.)

The fourth factor in adaptive behavior is learning. We have already pointed out that its importance varies with the degree of complexity of the behavior involved and with the phylogenetic level of the species. However, the contribution of learning to even relatively simple forms of behavior, such as pecking in birds or swimming in salamanders, must not be overlooked, since *some* degree of experience is necessary before behavior becomes skilled. The relative contribution of learning and maturation has been and continues to be the focus of an enormous research effort.

The fifth major factor in the determination of adaptive behavior is drive. In ethology, drives are "postulated internal states of activity which interact with exterosensory input to bring about behavioral responses" (Klopfer & Hailman, 1967, p. 209).

"Why," asks ethologist Manning (1967), "postulate drive?" As he indicates, the term has taken on many conflicting meanings. Moreover, from a purely behavioral point of view it would seem ideal to account for all responses as dependent strictly upon stimulus or environmental factors operating in conjunction with maturationally ready organismic structures. The answer lies in the fact that variations in physiological states, as well as in stimulus and general environmental conditions, are important in the determination of behavior. Feeding, drinking, and sexual behavior clearly show cyclic variability that cannot be accounted for by environmental factors alone. In fact, some animals display what has been described by Tinbergen as *vacuum activities,* wherein a response—such as a bird going through the behavior of catching prey—occurs in the absence of an appropriate stimulus. Such "spontaneous" behavior clearly implies an internal drive state.

Another form of behavior that may be offered in support of the concept of drive is *displacement activities,* a term used by Tinbergen for certain apparently irrelevant forms of behavior observed in situations of danger, thwarting, or conflicting drives. Rats, for example, engage in excessive grooming when first placed in a strange environment. Another similar fixed action pattern is known as *redirection,* where the drive appears behaviorally but has been directed toward another object. For example, a cock fighting with another cock may stop suddenly and peck at grains on the ground. A herring gull engaged in a territorial dispute may stop to gather tufts of grass as if nest building during a lull in the conflict.

Cyclic behavior rhythms, spontaneous behavior, vacuum behavior , and displaced activities have been integrated into a motivation model by Lorenz (1950) in an attempt to account for the internal energizing of ethograms (Figure 12-7).

The model assumes that "action-specific energy" accumulates in animals. This energy is specifically directed at one form of behavior, such as feeding. In Figure 12-7 this is represented by the accumulation of fluid in the reservoir (R). Outflow is normally directed by a valve (V) held tightly shut by a spring (S). There are two ways that the valve can be opened. First, if the weight builds up on the balance pan (Sp), representing the presence of a specific stimulus, the valve is pulled open. Or, second, the accumulation of fluid in the reservoir itself may eventually push the valve open. Obviously, the greater the accumulation of fluid, the weaker the pull exerted by Sp need be; this situation accounts analogously for a

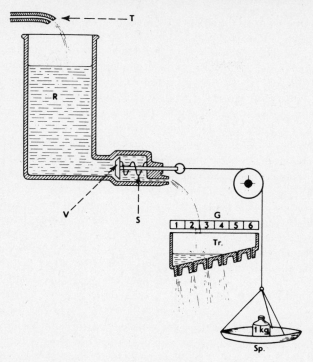

FIGURE 12-7. Lorenz's hydraulic model of motivation. (From Lorenz, Symposium of the Society for Experimental Biology and Medicine, 4, 1950.)

lowering of the threshold of behavior during increasingly long periods of deprivation. If drive pressure alone releases behavior under these conditions, we have an instance of "vacuum activity."

The graded trough (G, Tr) in Figure 12-7 represents various types of motor output. Depending upon how far the valve opens and how rapidly the fluid consequently flows, the level in the trough will build up more or less to flow out through openings 1, 2, 3, and so on.

The hydraulic model has no value in describing what actually occurs in the nervous system of the living animal—nor did Lorenz intend it to have such a use. It is best thought of as an analogy useful in stimulating research and in interpreting behavioral patterns that cannot be accounted for solely in terms of stimulus → response mechanisms.

Lorenz's motivational theory has been criticized on the grounds that it necessitates a large number of assumptions about indirect or displaced activities in order to account for exceptions to fixed action patterns. In this respect it is similar to Freud's theory, which also necessitated such concepts as displaced aggression, sublimation, and repression to account for variations in motivated behavior. Lorenz has also been criticized for his semipopular book, *On Aggression* (1963), which we shall be considering in the section to follow.

In concluding this brief discussion of ethology, we should like to emphasize that current research is directed toward the discovery of hierarchies of factors that control behavior. No longer does the unqualified term "instinct" suffice as a global explanation of behavior. Contemporary students of animal behavior are investigating mechanisms of sensory input; specific-stimulus factors; general environmental factors, such as effects of length of day on migration; the role of learning; and central nervous mechanisms in the control of behavior. Even a casual glance at the impressive record of discoveries during the past two decades serves to indicate the enormous interest in this very old, yet revitalized, field. Moreover, ethology is an excellent example of an interdisciplinary approach to the study of behavior. Developing along separate lines, the comparative psychologists concentrated on the study of learning—typically under highly restrictive laboratory conditions—while the ethologists studied a wide range of behavior under natural or seminatural conditions. At first highly critical of each other's methods and results, ethologists and psychologists discovered that they had much to learn from each other. We may confidently expect a continued evolution of this now united effort to unravel the mysteries of animal behavior.

Aggression

During the past several decades the problem of the sources of aggressive behavior has stimulated a large body of both theoretical and experimental literature. Beginning with Freud's theory of thanatos or the death instinct, one point of view holds that aggression is instinctive and therefore inevitable in both the lower animals and in man. Freud's position received virtually no support among academic psychologists during the half-century following its announcement; and it was not until the early 1960s that the instinct view of aggression gained adherents, again not so much among psychologists as among professional and popular students of animal behavior. Konrad Lorenz is the most prominent professional biologist associated with the instinctive point of view. His book, *On Aggression* (1963), whose English edition was published in 1966, generated widespread controversy. Robert Ardrey's *African Genesis* (1961) and *Territorial Imperative* (1966), both popular books by a playwright and amateur ethologist, and Desmond Morris' *The Naked Ape* (1967) had already created popular interest in aggressive behavior as an instinct in both animals and man.

Moreover, during the same decade that witnessed the publication of these books, dramatic national events—including the assassinations of President John F. Kennedy, his brother Robert, and Martin Luther King; the urban riots; increased dominance of television by violence-oriented programs; and the rising national crime rate—focused the attention of psychologists on aggression and led to the development of a strong environmentalist point of view. Environmentalists in contrast with instinct theorists hold that it is unnecessary to assume an instinct of aggression. Rather, they marshal experimental evidence to show that environmental violence reinforces imitative behavior, particularly among children, perpetuating a vicious circle of violence—but fortunately for social policies, a circle that is not inevitable, given improved social conditions. We shall summarize the evidence in favor of both the instinctive and environmental points of view.

In his book *On Aggression* Lorenz reviews a large number of studies of aggressive behavior among coral fish, greylag geese, and timber wolves, carried out both in the laboratory and in the animals' natural habitats. He finds that aggression serves three primary and biologically useful functions (1966, pp. 23–43). These are: (1) territorial balance of the distribution of animals of the same species in the available environment; (2) selection of the fittest or strongest animals by rival fighting during mating seasons; (3) defense of the young. Predation in animals involves the killing of other species, but only for food or in self-defense. But man, Lorenz argues, is unique in the animal kingdom in killing members of his own species. Why, he asks, does this species difference exist? The answer, he finds, lies first of all in fixed action patterns of behavior that inhibit aggression in the lower forms. For example, two rival male timber wolves engaged in what would appear to be mortal combat suddenly break off fighting when one turns its head and neck upward, presenting the jugular region in what from a human point of view would appear to be a suicidal gesture. On the contrary, Lorenz points out, the defeated animal's behavior acts as a stimulus sign or releaser to inhibit the fighting behavior of the aggressor. Both go their separate ways perchance to fight or mate another day. Similarly, coral fish, greylag geese, and other animals have characteristic gestures or vocalizations that signal submission and so break off aggressive behavior before it leads to the death of one member of the pair.

Lorenz argues (1966, pp. 236–274) that through some kind of evolutionary process, man has lost the ritualistic behavior necessary for the inhibition of intraspecies aggression. Moreover, the human species has developed a complex brain capable of fashioning instruments of destruction that make killing impersonal and therefore easier. Eons ago the culture of weaponry outstripped whatever vestiges of instinctive inhibition remained in human biology:

> Obviously, instinctive behavior mechanisms failed to cope with the new circumstances which culture unavoidably produced even at its very dawn. There is evidence that the first inventors of pebble tools, the African Australopithecines, promptly used their new weapon to kill not only game, but fellow members of their species as well. Pekin Man, the Prometheus who learned to preserve fire, used it to roast his brothers; beside the first traces of the regular use of fire lie the mutilated and roasted bones of *Sinanthropus pekinensis* himself. (1966, p. 239)

Thus far Lorenz's argument rests on analogy and generalization from animal studies to man. No direct evidence has been presented to show that man has a species-specific and uninhibited instinct for aggression. However, some support for the biological basis for aggression comes from experiments and clinical studies of the neural mechanisms in aggression and other emotional responses. To anticipate a more extensive discussion to be presented in Chapter 14, we may note here that electrodes implanted in the hypothalamus in cats can elicit strong aggressive responses, including attack and kill patterns directed toward rats that prior to delivery of the stimulation had been unmolested even though sharing a cage with the cats. This does not prove that similar reactions could be obtained in human subjects, but a number of clinical reports show that psychosurgical operations involving removal of the amygdala nuclei (cell masses in the frontotemporal subcortical region of the brain) can turn violent criminals into placid individuals. Incidentally, these operations were suggested by similar results obtained in monkeys where an extremely dominant male in a social hierarchy can be rendered docile by amygdalectomy.

The contrary view that aggressive behavior in man is primarily the product of environmental conditioning has been supported in the past decade by the work of social psychologists. We have already reviewed the research of Albert Bandura on the social learning of aggressive behavior (Chapter 7). It will be recalled that the substance of these studies shows that children who witness rewarded aggression are prone to show increased levels of aggression during subsequent test observations.

Leonard Berkowitz (1962, 1964, 1969a, 1969b, 1974), who has experimented and written widely in the area of aggressive behavior, believes that studies such as Bandura's support a learned interpretation of aggression. This does not mean that Berkowitz fails to recognize that there are biological mechanisms in the nervous system that make aggressive behavior possible—only that such behavior is not inevitable. He contends instead that environmental stimulation acting on neural centers may trigger aggressive behavior (Figure 12-8). Berkowitz denies that there

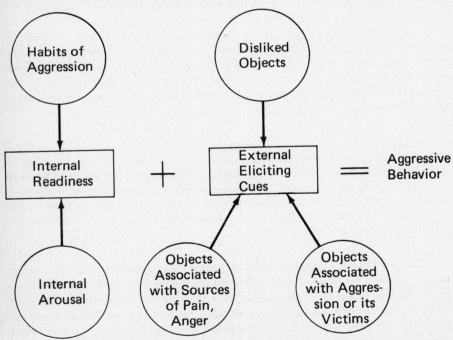

FIGURE 12-8.   Berkowitz's model of aggression. Note that both internal and external cues contribute to aggressive behavior. From Berkowitz. A Survey of Social Psychology. Dryden Press. Copyright, 1975.

is any kind of reservoir of aggression, as Lorenz's motivational model implies. Nor does he believe that humans have a need to satisfy aggression in order to obtain relief from gradually increasing tensions that would damage them psychologically if no outlet were found. Instead, aggression is environmentally controlled. Environments in which aggression is rewarded reinforce and promote further aggression. Even the mere presence of weapons in the environment may stimulate stronger aggressive behavior than would otherwise be demonstrated (Berkowitz & LePage, 1967).

Agreeing in principle with Dollard and Miller's frustration-aggression hypothesis (Chapter 7), Berkowitz suggests that frustration is one important source of human aggressive behavior. The behavior of ghetto residents of large cities during the urban riots of the 1960s exemplifies frustration as a source of aggression. Unable to cope in constructive ways with poverty, lack of vocational skills, and other disadvantages, the blacks directed their frustration at the cities. However, aggression is not an inevitable reaction to frustration. As the psychoanalytic and related schools pointed out years ago, mechanisms of sublimation and compensation can provide alternative outlets. But in a subculture of violence, in a society in which aggression is often rewarded, and in a culture in which violence is stressed as a solution to human problems, aggression is a low-threshold reaction to frustration.[12]

Most psychologists would agree that an issue such as this cannot be resolved merely by taking extreme positions on the instinctive-learning ends of the spectrum of causation. Rather, most would admit that there is a biological capacity for aggression but that this is controlled by a variety of environmental factors that make it noninevitable and therefore not a true instinct in the Lorenzian sense of the term.

Maslow's Hierarchical Theory of Motivation[13]

A. H. Maslow's (1916–1970) hierarchical theory of human motivation is a contemporary humanistic theory. There are two characteristic aspects of the theory, in which he attempts to extend the organismic point of view into relatively unexplored aspects of motivational psychology. These are (1) his hierarchical conception of motivation and (2) his efforts to develop a more valid and comprehensive psychology of motivation through the study of "self-actualizers."

The Hierarchy of Human Needs

Maslow assumes that human motives are arranged in a hierarchy of potency. The needs that have the greatest potency at any given time dominate behavior and

---

[12]For those who wish to pursue the question of the relative contribution of biological and environmental factors in aggressive behavior the following are recommended: Bandura (1972); Berkowitz (1962, 1975); Eibl-Eibesfeldt (1975); Lorenz (1966); Montagu (1968). For more technical articles the *Nebraska Symposium on Motivation* may be consulted, particularly the 1972 issue, which is devoted entirely to the subject of aggressive behavior.

[13]The exposition follows Maslow's *Motivation and Personality* (1954); see especially chaps. 5 and 12.

demand satisfaction. The individual feels "driven" by a high-priority need. When the need is satisfied, a higher-order motive (or class of motives) makes its appearance and demands satisfaction, and so on to the top of the hierarchy. Figure 12-9 is a schematic representation of the hierarchy of human motives. This formulation has as its foundation the physiological needs. If one of these needs is unsatisfied, the individual is dominated by that need. Thus the hungry individual is dominated by hunger. His or her emotions, perceptions, thought processes, and behavior in general are preoccupied solely with getting food and satisfying hunger. Similarly, the sexually deprived individual is driven by sexual desire, and other considerations become unimportant in the light of this overwhelming need.

FIGURE 12-9.   A schematic representation of Maslow's hierarchy of motivation.

Let us, however, assume that the basic physiological needs are satisfied. The next higher order of needs emerges and dominates the individual. He or she seeks safety or security. Maslow believes that safety needs are most readily observable in the child because of children's relative helplessness and dependence on adults. The child prefers a predictable, orderly routine; and reacts with feelings of fear and insecurity if confronted with novel, threatening, or terrifying stimuli. Parental quarrels and threats of separation are particularly harmful to a child's sense of well-being. On the adult level, the individual seeks security by establishing bank accounts, building a home, and finding a job with an assured future.

Maslow considers the physiological and safety needs truly lower-order needs. The good society provides for the basic needs of its members; and few healthy, normal people are dominated by hunger, thirst, sex, or other animal needs. The neurotic adult is more likely to be driven by such lower-order motives. Excessive eating or sexual promiscuity are engaged in as a means of winning love and affection. Or lack of security and consequent preoccupation with safety measures may, in reality, be in the service of frustrated higher needs for love or prestige. As these examples illustrate, Maslow allows for the possibility of one need substituting for another in cases of severe deprivation and lack of opportunity for satisfaction.

Maslow refers to the next higher order of motives as the "belongingness and love needs." These emerge if the two lower orders are reasonably well satisfied. The individual seeks friends, longs for affectionate relationships, and strives to find a place in some group, however small. Again, in our society such needs are generally well satisfied, and it is only in the neurotic or more severely pathological cases that serious deprivation occurs.

The fourth order of needs is esteem needs.[14] These include the desire for a firmly based high evaluation of the self. There is in all of us a desire for strength, for mastery and competence, leading to a feeling of independence and freedom. In addition, individuals in our society seek prestige, dominance, and recognition from others. Satisfaction of the esteem needs generates feelings of worth, self-confidence, and adequacy. Lack of satisfaction of these needs results in discouragement, feelings of inferiority, and inadequacy.

Finally, if all the foregoing needs are satisfied, the need for self-actualization impels the individual to activity. In Maslow's own words, "A musician must make music, an artist must paint, a poet must write if he is ultimately to be at peace with himself. What a man *can* be he *must be*. This need we may call self-actualization" (1954, p. 91).

Self-actualization is not, however, restricted to the creative activity characteristic of genius. A fine mother, an athlete, a good workman, may be actualizing their potential abilities in doing well what they can do best. It is nevertheless true that self-actualizers are comparatively rare and disproportionately represented among the gifted. Most of us, apparently, are seeking the satisfaction of lower-order needs.

In later papers and lectures, Maslow (Goble, 1971) added two additional classes of needs to his basic theory of motivation. These were the needs for knowing and understanding and the esthetic needs. The needs for knowing and understanding may be subsumed under the broad heading of curiosity. Maslow believes that studies of animals, children, great creative people, explorers, and ordinary mature individuals reveal that curiosity—or the desire to learn and discover, to explore the mysterious and unknown—is a fundamental aspect of human nature.

The esthetic needs are revealed in the deep-seated need for beauty expressed by some individuals. In early investigations of students' reactions to beauty and ugliness in their environments, Maslow found that ugliness was experienced as stultifying and beauty as promoting a feeling of well-being and enhancement of the self-image.

Growth and Deficiency Motivation

Maslow has distinguished between *growth motivation* and *deficiency motivation*. The self-actualizing tendency is growth motivation. In Maslow's own words,

> I could describe self-actualization as a development of personality which frees the person from the deficiency problems of growth, and from the neurotic (or infantile, or

---

[14]Maslow makes the interesting point that these are the needs stressed by Adler and the neo-Adlerians and relatively neglected by Freud and his followers.

fantasy, or unnecessary, or "unreal") problems of life so that he is able to face, endure and grapple with the "real" problems of life (the intrinsically and ultimately human problems, the unavoidable, the "existential" problems to which there is no perfect solution). (1959, p. 24)

More specifically, deficiency motivation, or D-motivation, involves *avoidance*—feelings of insecurity, inferiority, and failure; avoidance of hunger, thirst, pain, and conflict with others. Thus, the physiological needs, the safety needs, the needs for belongingness and esteem, may all be considered survival needs whose deficiency must be satisfied before self-actualization is possible.

Associated with deficiency needs is a state of *D-cognition,* which is self-centered cognition that demands decisions and action designed to remove deficiencies and therefore to ensure survival. In contrast, *B-cognition,* or being cognition, is associated with a conscious state of contemplative acceptance. It is nonjudgmental; it does not evaluate or condemn. B-cognition is the fulfillment of the need for understanding that is associated with self-actualization.

The Characteristics of Self-Actualizers

In his theoretical papers, Maslow argued for a number of years that psychologists have been overly preoccupied with neurotics, delinquents, and other psychologically underdeveloped individuals. The result, he believes, is a one-sided psychology lacking in comprehensiveness and based on the abnormal. In a unique study he attempted to correct this deficiency by investigating the personalities of self-actualizers (Maslow, 1954). Among the individuals studied were both outstanding historical figures such as Whitman, Thoreau, Beethoven, Lincoln, Einstein, and Spinoza, and people who were living at the time the study was carried out, such as Eleanor Roosevelt, Albert Schweitzer, and Fritz Kreisler. A holistic analysis of the personalities and achievements of such individuals revealed that self-actualizers show the following characteristics:

1. They demonstrate an efficient perception of reality and acceptance of it.
2. They accept themselves and others.
3. They show a high degree of spontaneity.
4. They have a problem-centered orientation to life rather than a self-centered orientation.
5. They have a need for privacy and detachment.
6. They are autonomous or relatively independent of their environments.
7. They appreciate the "basic goods of life" with continued freshness and pleasure.
8. They show, at times, profound mysticism.
9. They are able to identify with mankind.
10. They develop deep interpersonal relations with others.
11. They are democratic.
12. They keep means and ends distinguishable.
13. They possess a well-developed and unhostile sense of humor.
14. They are creative.
15. They tend to be nonconformists.

In his later years, Maslow has made a special study of the discovery that outstanding or creative individuals have mystical experiences, "moments of great awe, moments of most intense happiness, or even rapture, ecstasy, or bliss" (1965, p. 45). During these "peak experiences," as Maslow describes them, the individual tends to lose his or her self-consciousness and becomes one with the world. The veil of mystery that ordinarily keeps the person from the meaning of life is ripped aside, and he or she experiences the essence of truth and seems to grasp the secret of life, if only for a short time. This individual's cognition may be described as B-cognition—"a god-like, compassionate, non-active, non-interfering, non-doing" awareness (Maslow, 1959, p. 25).

Maslow hastens to point out that peak experiences are not supernatural; nor are they limited to highly creative people or to those who practice Zen Buddhism or Taoism. They occur in ordinary people, although they may not be recognized for what they are. A musician may have a peak experience during an especially good performance when all goes well. It is as if he or she goes far beyond the mere rendition of music to become a creator in his or her own right. A mother may experience a peak when she sees her children playing happily with their father. The sexual experience, the experience of great love or of joy, may also be peak experiences.

Maslow believes that peak experiences may be therapeutic, that they may have "ennobling and beautifying effects on the character, on the life outlook, on the way the world looks, on the way that the husband looks, or the baby" (1965, p. 47). The problem or puzzle of so many individuals is why they refuse to allow peak experiences to counteract the fear, hostility, and misery of life. Indeed, many people who have such experiences actually suppress or reject them because of the rationalistic or mechanistic attitudes characteristic of our century.

Maslow recognizes that many issues remain to be resolved before psychologists in general become willing to accept the validity of a concept traditionally associated with religious and mystical writings. We shall make no attempt at a final evaluation of Maslow's theory except to point out that it is entirely congruent with the positions advocated by Adler (1929), Fromm (1941, 1955), May (1969), and Rogers (1965a), which emphasize that healthy development depends on openness to new experience and a willingness to be spontaneous, creative, and free from deterministic attitudes about one's own future.

It is not easy to assess the validity of a theory such as Maslow's. His motivational constructs, as well as his characteristics of self-actualizers, are broad and impossible to subject to a conventional operational-experimental analysis. However, most psychologists would agree that he called attention to a range of human behavior that had been neglected, if not ignored, by traditional psychologists. It is also interesting to note that in his emphasis on self-actualization, B-cognition, and growth motivation, he antedated the popular human potential movement, which has become something of a recent fad. However, Maslow's pioneer studies are rooted in a deeper, more scholarly tradition which parallels and complements the work of the experimentalists.

McClelland and the Achievement Motive[15]

In their long-range research program, D. C. McClelland and his associates have primarily investigated human motivation through the intensive study of a single motive, the achievement motive. The general technique employed in early measurements of the achievement motive was as follows: College students were shown pictures on a screen and asked to write brief stories about the pictures. The pictures employed were taken either from Murray's Thematic Apperception Test (TAT) or were similar in design. Sometimes a combination of original TAT and specially developed pictures was employed.

In one series of experiments the investigators attempted to manipulate the achievement motive by inducing varying degrees of need for achievement in their subjects through appropriate instructions at the beginning of the experiment. Three general levels of achievement motivation were studied: (1) a relaxed condition, (2) a neutral condition, and (3) an achievement-oriented condition. In addition, various success-failure conditions were superimposed on the three basic conditions to test the effects of success and failure on the achievement motive. The relaxed condition was induced largely by the examiner's lighthearted attitude as he told the student-subjects that he was trying out "some new ideas." The subjects were given to understand that various tests—anagrams, paper-and-pencil tests, and the like—they were asked to do, were "in the developmental stage." Following completion of the tests, the subjects were given the group TAT as "a test of the creative imagination."

For the neutral condition the examiner attempted neither to increase nor decrease the level of motivation. Instructions for the tests were presented seriously, but no attempt was made to ego-involve the subjects in the tasks. In the achievement-oriented condition, a serious effort was made to get the subjects personally involved by presenting the cue tests as "intelligence tests" and indices of potential leadership. The TAT in this case was referred to as a test of "creative intelligence."

McClelland and his associates carried out both qualitative and quantitative studies of the TAT stories written by their subjects. In general, the results were positive in the sense that the higher the level of the achievement motive, the greater were the number of achievement responses in the TAT situation. There were, of course, instances of failure and of mixed types of imagery revealed in the stories. These do not necessarily indicate that the method is a bad one or that the hypothesis is invalid. As the investigators themselves point out, the project was in the nature of exploratory research; and subsequent work along the same lines has resulted in many refinements.

We cannot present the extensive quantitative data from the original study. However, we shall include several examples of the TAT stories written by the

---

[15]The primary source for this summary is *The Achievement Motive* by McClelland, Atkinson, Clark, and Lowell (1953). For further applications of the techniques, see J. Atkinson (1958). The theory as elaborated in *The Achievement Motive* is far too extensive to permit more than a bare outline in the present volume.

subjects. The picture upon which the following stories are based shows a workshop with a workbench about which are suspended various tools. A machine stands on the floor, activated from below by a large flywheel, which is half sunk in a pit. Two men are in the picture. One is shown in profile; he is working at the machine. The other man is shown in rear view, watching the first.

The first subject's story shows a high level of achievement motivation. Note particularly the words and phrases the original investigators italicized to indicate the level of motivation.

> Something is being heated in a type of furnace which appears to be of metal. The men are blacksmiths. The men have been doing *research* on an alloy of some type, and *this is the crucial test* that spells success or failure of the experiment. They want a specific type of metal. They are working for government interests. They may be successful this time. They have *invented* a metal that is very light, strong, durable, heat resistant, and so on. A *real step in scientific progress*. (McClelland et al., 1953, p. 117)

A much lower degree of motivation is revealed by the subject in the following example. Note the absence of affective terms. Some achievement motivation, however, is indicated by the goal of making a bolt and the indication of a probably successful outcome:

> There are two men working in some sort of machine shop. They are making some sort of a bolt or something. One of the men's car broke down, and he has discovered that a bolt is broken. So, being a fairly good forger, he is making a new bolt. He is discussing with the other man just how he is making this bolt and telling him about all of the details in making this bolt. When he is finished, he will take the bolt and replace the broken bolt in the car with it. He will then be able to get his car going. (McClelland et al., 1953, p. 119)

The following subject's protocol illustrates unsuccessful achievement. Again, the terms italicized by the investigators should be noted.

> The scene is a workshop. Two men are doing a very important job. They are grinding an important cog for a new jet engine which will attempt a flight to the moon. The inventor who doesn't want to let his secret out has hired these two men to work secretly for him. They are not very well known, but if the job is a success, they will be famous. They are both very tense, each knowing that one little mistake will mean *months of hard work* lost and wasted. When they are finished, they find that the piece is too small for the engine, and they have *failed* and must start again. (McClelland et al., 1953, p. 127)

McClelland (1961) later extended his theory of achievement motivation into the area of society as a whole. The achieving society, he suggests, is not especially favored by population growth, economic conditions, or natural resources, but is high in achievement motivation. The entrepreneurial spirit, the presence of executives with high levels of drive, and a social orientation that emphasizes achievement in the training of children are the factors necessary for high levels of social achievement.

McClelland has utilized such indices of economic development as general trade, the consumption of electric power, and the importation of coal, as objective measures of the extent to which a society is achieving. Because it is not practical or, in the case of past societies, possible to obtain the achievement indices of executives and other leaders by means of fantasy, McClelland has utilized the nation's popular literature—poems, songs, plays, funeral orations, and books for the education of children—as indices of achievement motivation. By means of a coding system, the level of achievement can be rated with reasonable objectivity and correlated with the indices of economic achievement.

Figure 12-10 shows how achievement motivation is correlated with rate of industrial growth in a modern nation. Change in industrial growth lags about a generation behind changes in achievement motivation, again suggesting a causal relationship. As nonachieving children grow up, economic growth declines. If subsequent adult generations begin to emphasize achievement, then, as their children reach maturity, the economic index rises.

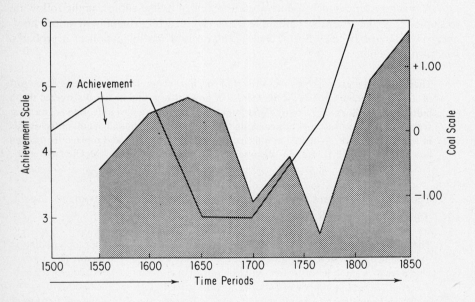

FIGURE 12-10.   A comparison of the level of *n* Achievement and utilization of coal from 1550 to 1850. (From McClelland, D. C. The roots of consciousness. Copyright 1964, D. Van Nostrand Company, Inc., Princeton, N. J.)

McClelland (1961, 1964) has made a number of interesting comparisons between modern European nations and Communist nations. In each case he presents evidence to show that it is not the economic system, political considerations, or geographical factors that are responsible for economic success, but the presence or absence of achievement motivation.

McClelland (1961, 1971) believes that the relationship among needs for achievement, affiliation, and power are important in both individuals and social groups. Studies of the needs for affiliation and power are carried out by utilizing fantasy in the form of stories developed by the subject about individuals shown in pictures. The need for affiliation is revealed by evidence of the subject's concern for establishing and maintaining positive affective relationships among the characters portrayed in the test pictures. Power needs, in contrast, are revealed by the subject's projecting expressions of control, influence, and dominance onto individuals portrayed in test stimuli.

As illustrative of how power needs influence behavior, the results of studies by McClelland, Davis, Alin, and Wanner (1971) may be summarized as follows. Men with strong power drives tend to use more alcohol, to take risks (as in gambling), to own prestige cars, and to harbor aggressive impulses. When strong power motivation is checked by a sense of social responsibility, one commits oneself to socially and politically constructive action.

On the broad group level, high power needs combined with low affiliation needs indicate a tendency for a nation to embrace a totalitarian form of government (McClelland, 1961, p. 168). Studies of police states past and present show patterns of high power needs associated with low needs for affiliation.

McClelland's assumption that fantasy techniques are valid and reliable measures of motivation is not easily assessed. In *The Achievement Motive* (1953), McClelland and his associates report that the reliability of fantasy techniques as measured by independent interscoring is high, $+0.90$ or above. That is, two or more scorers using the same protocols are in high agreement as to what the subject has revealed about his or her need for achievement by the responses to the test stimuli. Internal consistency measures of reliability and measures obtained by repeated testing are not as high, yielding correlations of $+0.65$ on the average.

One possible approach to measuring the validity of fantasy techniques is to make longitudinal studies of individuals to see if predicted achievement is realized. In a study of fifty-five college students, McClelland (1965) related test results taken 14 years earlier in college to performance in occupations. Those who had entered the business world were divided into enterpreneurial and nonentrepreneurial categories. The entrepreneurial categories were defined as involving decision-making responsibility and risk and challenge. Examples are operating one's own business or managing a large company. Nonentrepreneurial occupations included personnel management, credit management, data processing, and the like—jobs involving a minimum of risk and only low-level decisions.

When the occupational information was related to the need for achievement as measured by the tests carried out fourteen years earlier, it was found that 83 percent of individuals in entrepreneurial occupations scored high on achievement measures, as compared to only 21 percent of those in nonentrepreneurial occupations.

This type of longitudinal study of individuals lends support to the predictive value of fantasy measures for individuals. However, the studies of economic development as correlated with achievement motivation as measured by analyses of literature, speeches, and so on have yet to be validated by similar longitudinal studies of the predictive power of the psychological measures. Obviously, extremely long-term studies of nations would have to be carried out in order to realize such a goal. Consequently, it is likely that we shall have to depend on historical studies correlating achievement needs as measured in one generation against economic growth as measured in another. Whatever the future holds for such studies, McClelland and his associates have provided challenging and provocative techniques for relating individual motivation to broad social processes.

A Note on Motivation in the Behaviorist View

Behavioristic psychologists have traditionally placed great emphasis on animal drives. The term "drive," as we noted in connection with theories of learning, is used to refer to changes in physiological states that sensitize the animal to certain stimuli and are associated with behavior that is goal-directed. We also found that some behaviorists, such as Guthrie and Skinner, minimize the role of drive or make no attempt to delineate the nature of drives. Others, such as Thorndike and Hull, consider drives central to learning. An enormous body of research has been devoted to analyzing the relationship between drive and habit strength, the nature of reinforcement, and how derived drives originate from primary or inherent drives (Hilgard & Bower, 1966). The limited success and diversity of interpretations of studies of drive in relation to learning led to a diminished interest among psychologists, many of whom felt that either the wrong questions were being asked or the answers were being sought in the wrong way. The result has been a redirection of interest into other areas, or in some cases a shift in emphasis has occurred such as is typified by the work of psychologists who believe that drive reinforcement theory is inadequate to explain curiosity and manipulatory behavior.

Harlow's Studies of Intrinsic Drives

Traditionally, behaviorists explained motivated activities in terms of certain inherent and derived drives. Hunger, thirst, sex, maternal behavior, and other basic physiological drives are considered to be inherent and referable to tissue needs. The more complex motives, such as affection, gregariousness, safety, and prestige, are assumed to be derived from physiological drives through a process of learning. Thus the infant is born with a hunger drive which is satisfied by the mother. But because her presence is associated with the pleasantness of drive reduction, she comes to be demanded for her own sake. We may now speak of the presence of a motive for affection or gregariousness.

The merits of the derived drive theory have been debated, particularly by organismic psychologists. They point out that drive reduction implies that the animal or individual is seeking to reduce some kind of stimulation. The irritations associated with sex, hunger, thirst, pain, and extremes of environmental stimulation act as goads impelling the organism to take such action as will reduce or eliminate the stimuli. However, as we have already pointed out in Chapter 6, studies of sensory deprivation show that people seek stimulation and, indeed, find its absence intolerable. We also know from everyday experience that man is a curious, restless animal who enjoys activity for its own sake without any extrinsic rewards.

Psychologist Harry Harlow (Harlow, 1950; Harlow, Blazek, & McClearn, 1956; Harlow, Harlow, & Meyer, 1950; Harlow & McClearn, 1954) has brought the study of intrinsically motivated behavior into the animal laboratory and has shown that monkeys will solve complicated puzzles without being offered extrinsic rewards; indeed, introducing an extrinsic reward made learning less efficient.

Figure 12-11 shows the type of mechanical puzzle confronting the monkeys in Harlow's experiment. For 12 days they were presented with an assembled puzzle without any association between the puzzle and food or water. A control group was presented with an already disassembled puzzle during the same period. On test days the experimental animals proved to be more efficient in disassembling the puzzles than the control animals. The monkeys had learned to work the puzzle for the intrinsic reward of manipulation. When food rewards were subsequently introduced for solving the problem, the nature of the animals' behavior was markedly altered. They now worked at the puzzle only to get at the food and showed little further interest in manipulation for the sake of manipulation.

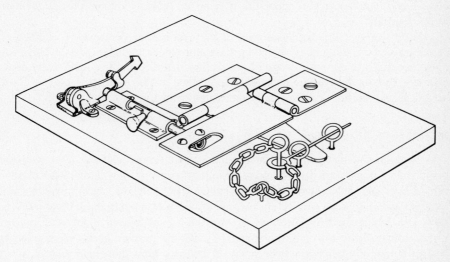

FIGURE 12-11.   A six-device mechanical puzzle for monkeys. (From Harlow, H. Learning and satiation of response in intrinsically motivated puzzle performance by monkeys. Journal of Comparative and Physiological Psychology, 1950, 43, p. 290. Copyright 1950 by the American Psychological Association. Reprinted by permission.)

Harlow has also shown that monkeys can be trained to make discriminations by utilizing the curiosity drive as a motive (Harlow & McClearn, 1954). In this type of experiment the animals are confined in a closed box that has two opaque doors with different stimulus cards attached to the inside. One door was selected by the experimenter as positive; and when the monkey pushed, it opened and the animal was allowed to look out. The other door was locked. The animals showed high rates of response to the positive door and low rates to the negative door. Moreover, studies have shown that the more interesting the scene which the animal saw (such as a toy train moving) the more rapid was the learning.

Curiosity motivation has also been observed in young children. Caron and Caron (1968) studied the reactions of infants too young to play with toys by recording where the subjects looked when presented with novel stimuli. More complex figures elicited more durable interest (as measured by the length of looking) than did simple geometric forms.

A number of studies utilizing both animal and human subjects have involved other types of exploratory, manipulatory, and curiosity motives. These have been reviewed by Cofer and Appley (1964, Chapter 6). As these authors point out, research with exploratory, manipulatory, and curiosity drives is still in its infancy; and much more work is needed before we can be sure that these are true drives under the primary control of a stimulus as opposed to external conditions. Cofer and Appley do not deny that external stimulation conditions have the capacity to arouse behavior. However, it is possible that emotional arousal brought about by placing the animal in a dark room or a novel situation may be partially responsible for the observed activity. These authors also suggest that deviations from a state of complete internal homeostasis or adaptation may be rewarding and therefore sought after by the animals.

Whatever the ultimate resolution of these points of controversy, studies of exploratory and manipulatory behavior have introduced a challenging problem for those interested in the psychology of motivation. Until it can be conclusively demonstrated that such drives are dependent upon some hidden extrinsic factor we must accept the possibility of intrinsically motivated behavior.

Summary and Evaluation

Motivational psychology is at once the most central and the least well-developed area in psychology. The great variety of points of view and diverse experimental approaches summarized in this chapter leaves one wondering whether any progress is being made toward an integrated theory of animal and human motivation. The fundamental dichotomies of atomism versus holism, hard determinism versus soft determinism, and the somatic versus the psychic basis for motivation sharply divide the behaviorist-comparative theorists from those whose concern is primarily with the human species.

The gulf between these conflicting points of view seems too wide for any early or easy resolution.[16] Perhaps as a result of disillusionment with attempts to formulate broad theoretical points of view in motivation, recent theorists have tended to explore limited areas of behavior, closely correlating more restricted theoretical points of view with empirical research. This trend, it might be noted, parallels a similar tendency in other areas of psychology we have been examining, such as learning, thinking, or perception. We shall return to the problem of motivation in Chapter 14, which deals with physiological theories of behavior. There we shall see

---

[16]Such, certainly, is the impression gleaned from the yearly symposia at the University of Nebraska. See especially the 1975 volume.

that one of the more limited approaches, the physiological foundations of motivation, has resulted in impressive gains in our knowledge of these fundamental processes in behavior.

Feeling and Emotion

13

In some respects the systematic psychology of emotional processes is in an even more unsatisfactory state than that of motivation. One of the difficulties that has stood in the way of an acceptable theory of the emotions has been disagreement over definitions. Some psychologists have held that the emotions are disruptive states of the organism resulting from a loss of cortical dominance. Others assert that the opposite is nearer the truth, namely, that the emotions are organizing states that ready the individual for action in emergency situations. Still others take a middle-of-the-road position, treating emotional states as "activating" or "energizing" processes. We shall discuss representatives of some of these divergent viewpoints later in this chapter.

Another factor that has hindered the development of a valid psychology of the emotions is the lack of reliable experimental data upon which to erect a system. Emotions are not easy to isolate for investigation in the artificial atmosphere of the laboratory. Ethical or human considerations preclude experimental induction of certain of the more violent emotions, such as hate, grief, or rage. There are equally cogent reasons why the more tender and complex emotions, such as love, are unsuitable for laboratory study. Moreover, even where it is possible to create reasonable facsimiles of genuine emotions in the laboratory, the techniques of investigation are likely to interfere with the emotions under study. For example, if the subject is asked to give a verbal report of an emotional process, the calm "intellectual" attitude that he or she must assume tends to destroy the emotion.

However, despite the difficulties of definition and experimentation just enumerated, the emotional processes have by no means been neglected by the systematists and theorists. Indeed, in the prescientific era of psychology we find a rich literature bearing on the emotions. Some of this we have touched upon in preceding chapters. We found that classical Grecian speculation on the dynamics of human behavior took the form of postulating humoral, or bodily, factors that serve to arouse motivational and emotional states. The classical ethical philosophers and the Christian theologians, such as Thomas Aquinas and Saint Augustine, were also concerned with the dynamics of human behavior; and both advocated the control of undesirable "passions," while encouraging the emotions of love for God and man.

As we move down the centuries to the modern period in philosophy, we are again confronted with interest in the emotions from the orientation of ethical and practical problems. Indeed, it has been said the underlying philosophical attitude toward the emotions that is characteristic of Western civilization has been one of suppression. In the older philosophical and moral literature the emotions are frequently characterized as "base" or as constituting man's "animal" nature. Such expressions are, of course, tinged with prejudice growing out of a particular point of view. It is interesting to note that one result of the recent scientific study of the emotions and the ascendance of the scientific point of view has been a more tolerant attitude toward the irrational and emotional side of humans. However, little would be gained by dwelling on these traditional ethical issues and controversies. What we wish to emphasize is this: The study of psychological processes from moral or ethical points of view, though legitimate within these special orientations, has little interest within the scientific frame of reference. The experimental psychologist seeks primarily to make lawful predictions about behavior. The consequences of behavior from a moral or ethical standpoint are outside his or her purview.

In accordance with the preceding argument, we shall begin our study of the emotions with the systematic view of Titchener.[1] After presenting a summary of the structuralistic point of view, we shall examine the doctrines of representatives of the other schools of psychology and conclude with a note on contemporary studies of emotion.

AFFECTION AND EMOTION IN STRUCTURAL PSYCHOLOGY

Titchener's Views[2]

Titchener (1910) introduces his systematic view of affection and emotion by considering certain problems of definition. *Affection* is defined as the elementary mental process characteristic of feeling and of the emotions, such as love, hate, joy, and sorrow. The term *feeling*[3] is used to denote a simple connection of sensation and affection in which the affective process dominates consciousness. For example, hunger is a sensation—a sensation that is linked with an affective state of feeling. It may be a gnawing hunger or a pleasant, anticipatory hunger. In either case the affective element is added to the bare sensation. Similarly, pain, a sensation, arouses concomitant feelings of unpleasantness.

Feeling may also be used in a narrow sense to denote sensations of touch, roughness, solidity, and the like. Such experiences, Titchener believes, are more properly termed "perceptions" or "touch blends" and, as such, do not enter into the psychology of feeling and emotion.

Titchener next raises the question of how affection differs as an element from sensation. He reiterates his definition of sensation as an elementary process describ-

---

[1]Those interested in the prescientific psychology of the emotions will find an exhaustive treatment in *Feeling and Emotion* by Gardiner, Metcalf, and Beebe-Center (1937).

[2]The exposition follows Titchener (1910).

[3]In practice, Titchener falls into the habit of using feeling and affection synonymously.

able in terms of the four attributes of quality, intensity, clearness, and duration. Affection, however, has but three attributes: quality, intensity, and duration. Consequently, sensations and affections are processes of the same general type inasmuch as they have three attributes in common. They differ in that affections lack clearness.

Affection has two qualities, *pleasantness* and *unpleasantness*. In other words, *any* affective state is introspectively either pleasant or unpleasant. Intensity is the dimension along which affection is described as "mildly pleasant," "disagreeable," "unbearable," and so on. Finally, an affective state may be of short or long duration. A mild pinprick gives rise to a momentarily unpleasant state, whereas a bad mood may persist for days.

Titchener next considers the laboratory techniques for investigating the affective processes. Basically, there are two: (1) the method of impression and (2) the method of expression. The method of impression is illustrated by the psychophysical method of paired comparisons. If, for example, the problem is to arrange fifty mixed color samples along a scale ranging from most pleasant to least pleasant, the observer begins by comparing the first color with every other, meanwhile recording his or her impressions as the stimuli are compared. Color number 2 is then compared with every other one, and so forth. At the end of the experiment the preferences are summarized or averaged for each color. The introspective task, Titchener adds, is simple; the lengthy comparisons, "laborious."

The method of expression involves the measurement of bodily changes that accompany the affective processes. The measures Titchener describes are the familiar techniques for recording the respiratory, circulatory, and muscular changes that occur during emotional states. Interestingly enough, he points out that the psychogalvanic response (now called the galvanic skin response, or GSR) has within "a year or two been brought into the psychological laboratory." Since the method had not yet been extensively used, Titchener prefers not to "judge of its merit."

Wundt's Tridimensional Theory

Titchener next discusses Wundt's tridimensional theory published in 1896. In essence, Wundt argued that feelings cannot be described solely in terms of their pleasantness and unpleasantness, but require three dimensions for a valid description: (1) pleasantness-unpleasantness, (2) tension-relaxation, and (3) excitement-depression (see Figure 13-1). Each feeling moves first between the poles of P-U, then between E-D, and finally between T-R (Titchener, 1910, pp. 250–251). For example, the feeling associated with mirth would move rapidly along the dimension of pleasantness, while at the same time excitement and tension would be added. The feeling, in this case, would then drop back to relaxation—tinged, perhaps, with depression and slight unpleasantness. Other feelings, depending on their nature, would take different courses.

Wundt's theory gained many adherents, but Titchener believes that it is incorrect and maintains that feelings can vary only along the dimensions already dis-

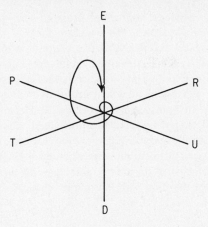

FIGURE 13-1. Diagram to represent Wundt's tridimensional theory of feeling. For explanation see text.

cussed in the preceding paragraphs. More specifically, he denies that the dimensions of tension-relaxation and excitement-depression are simple, elementary mental processes as Wundt believed, but claims instead that they are ''muscular attitudes.'' Moreover, tension and relaxation are not true opposites. Relaxation, Titchener insists, is the zero point of tension—not its opposite. Similarly, excitement and depression are not true opposites. Is not calm, he asks, a more logical opposite for excitement than depression?

With these and similar objections, Titchener attempts to show that Wundt's theory is not logically constructed and cannot meet certain experimental tests, which we need not go into here. This controversy is no longer an issue in the psychology of emotions, but this much can be said for Titchener's side of the argument: The weight of the introspective evidence suggests that pleasantness-unpleasantness is the best established of the possible affective dimensions.

Titchener and the Emotions

Turning to Titchener's treatment of the emotions, we have already pointed out that he considers the affective states or feelings to be the characteristic element in the emotional process. Because the organic, or visceral, reactions and the expressive, or bodily, aspects of the affective states are equally characteristic of the emotions, Titchener addressed himself to the problem of how the several aspects of emotional behavior are integrated. He examines and rejects the James-Lange theory,[4] then outlines his own views.

The organic or visceral responses, Titchener holds, are intensified and extended forms of the affective reaction. That is, increased heart rate, respiratory

---

[4]See the following section.

changes, glandular disturbances, and other organic reactions are, in mild form, characteristic of the affective states. More intense forms of these visceral changes occur in emotional states because the affective element is intensified as a result of the more primitive nature of the adjustment involved. Titchener believes that the organic reactions in ordinary emotions are carry-overs or vestigial processes from a period of evolutionary development when strong overt emotional reactions were invariably associated with adjustments to critical situations. In civilized society people tend to suppress their emotional reactions, and thus organic responses are primarily covert or visceral except in emergency situations. However, it should be emphasized that Titchener considers the core of emotional states to be the affective reaction. The organic processes are merely associated or parallel processes, which are exaggerated forms of the more subtle organic reactions typical of the affective states.

The Dimensional Analysis of Emotional Reactions

In discussing the expression of the emotions in behavioral and facial reactions, Titchener believes that we must look to biology for the explanation of these processes, and he invokes Darwin's theory of emotional expression in support of his position.

Darwin not only believed in the morphological evolution of species but also attempted to demonstrate a continuity of psychological functions in his classic *Expression of the Emotions in Man and Animals* (1872). In this volume he announced his famous three principles of emotional expression: (1) the principle of "serviceable associated habits," (2) the principle of "antithesis," and (3) the principle of the "direct action of the excited nervous system on the body, independently of the will and in part of habit."

The first principle assumes that many expressive behavioral and facial reactions are vestigial remnants of once practical or serviceable movements. The bared fangs of primitive jungle combat become the grimace of rage in civilized society. The expression of grief is a toned-down version of the wild sobbing of primitive people or of the infant. Presumably, as evolution proceeds, there is decreasing need for the strongly overt reactions and, as a consequence, they become more and more reduced in intensity.

Darwin's second principle, that of antithesis, is the hypothesis that opposite emotional processes tend to give rise to opposite reactions:

> Certain states of mind lead to certain habitual actions, which are of service, as under our first principle. Now when a directly opposite state of mind is induced, there is a strong and involuntary tendency to the performance of movements of a directly opposite nature, though these are of no use; and such movements are in some cases highly expressive. (Darwin, 1872, p. 28)

The principle of antithesis is exemplified in laughter, the opposite of sobbing. The former is explained as spasmodically interrupted *expiration,* the opposite as interrupted *inspiration*.

Finally, the principle of "the direct action of the excited nervous system" explains violent trembling, the paralysis characteristic of panic, and other extreme emotional reactions in which there is an overflow or spillover of the nervous processes because of the extremity of the reaction.

Darwin's interest in the expression of the emotions generated a line of research on the problem that has lasted over a century. Most of the studies have involved the judgment of facial expressions in photographs of either posed or real emotional reactions. Early studies were disappointing inasmuch as the judges confused many emotional expressions, such as contempt with disgust or surprise with happiness. However, a later series of studies by Schlosberg and his associates (Engen, Levy, & Schlosberg, 1957, 1958; Schlosberg, 1941, 1952, 1954) has shown that three dimensions of emotional expression can be judged from photographs with a satisfactory degree of reliability. These are: *pleasantness-unpleasantness, attention-rejection,* and *sleep-tension*. These investigators found in reviewing the early experiments that opposite emotions such as mirth and anger or surprise and disgust were unlikely to be confused. Only emotions close to each other such as love and mirth or happiness were likely to be confused. It was found that subjects—by employing three polar opposite scales rather than an absolute overall judgment—could make much better discriminations than had originally been considered possible (Figure 13-2).[5]

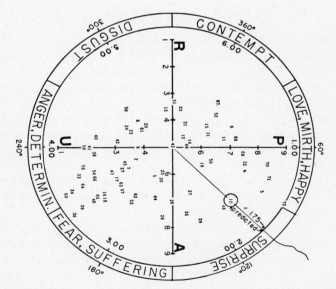

FIGURE 13-2. The dimensions of emotional expression according to Schlosberg. (From Schlosberg, H. The description of facial expressions in terms of two dimensions. Journal of Experimental Psychology, 1952, 44, 229–237. Copyright 1952 by the American Psychological Association. Reprinted by permission.)

---

[5]The reader may find it interesting to compare the Schlosberg dimensions with those of Wundt.

An interesting extension of research on judging emotions from facial expressions was carried out by Ekman (1971), who tested the hypothesis that there are unlearned and universal facial expressions for certain emotions that are the same in all cultures. Working with both photographs and videotapes, Ekman tested subjects in the United States, Brazil, Chile, Argentina, and Japan, and in two preliterate tribes in New Guinea. Photographs were shown one at a time to the subject, who stated which of six emotional categories—happiness, fear, anger, sadness, disgust, or surprise—best fit the facial expression. The results confirmed the hypothesis that subjects from different cultures were able to judge emotional expression in photographs and films. That this ability was not the result of cultural contamination through social contact was demonstrated by the fact that preliterate and isolated New Guinea subjects could make such discriminations. Ekman suggests that species-specific neuromuscular processes underlie these universal facial reaction patterns.

With this summary of the evolution of the structuralist and related studies of feeling and emotion into contemporary psychology, we bring to a conclusion our study of the structuralist treatment of affection and emotion. We shall next turn to the functionalistic school and, in doing so, will become acquainted with one of the most famous of all theories of the emotions, that formulated by William James.

FUNCTIONALISM AND EMOTION[6]

Carr treats the emotions as part of the "background of mental life." They are defined as *organic readjustments* that occur automatically in the face of appropriate behavioral situations. Thus, the emotion of anger arises when the organism is confronted with a serious obstacle to freedom of movement. In this instance the organic readjustment mobilizes energy to aid the individual in his or her efforts to overcome the obstacle. The quickened pulse, the withdrawal of blood from the viscera, the more rapid respiration, and other bodily changes enable the organism to react more energetically and vigorously. Clearly, in the case of anger and fear, Carr's definition is in keeping with his overall viewpoint. However, it would be a mistake to assume that he holds all emotions to be biologically useful. On the contrary, as Carr himself points out, such emotions as grief and joy may have no biological utility in some situations.

Driving to the heart of the problem, Carr states that "the various emotions can be readily identified and defined only in terms of the behavioral situation in which they occur" (1925, p. 278). Moreover, he points out that the reaction in emotional states is highly similar to that found in any kind of vigorous exercise or activity. The distinguishing feature of emotional states arises from the fact that they occur in cases where there is a *lack of adequate motor outlets*. Once the individual begins to react to the situation, the emotional response dies down. Carr summarizes his point of view on the basic nature of the emotional processes as follows:

---

[6]The exposition follows Carr's *Psychology* (1925).

In support of this conception, we may call attention to the well-known fact that the emotions tend to disappear with action. Our anger soon cools and wanes when we begin to fight, and terror no longer holds us in its grip when we indulge in strenuous flight. The difference between these two conditions does not consist of the presence and absence of an organic disturbance, for both fighting and flight obviously involve a very pronounced readjustment on the part of the vital activities. Evidently the disappearance of the emotions with overt action is due to a change in the character of the organic reaction. Given an adequate motor outlet, these organic activities gradually become adapted to the exigencies of the act, and hence they lose their initial tumultuous and impulsive character and the experience is no longer labelled an emotion. (1925, pp. 282–283)

He then summarizes the James-Lange[7] theory of emotions and shows how his own conceptions differ from those postulated by James and Lange. The James-Lange theory identifies the emotion with the perception of the organic changes. In James' own words:

Common-sense says, we lose our fortune, are sorry and weep; we meet a bear, are frightened and run; we are insulted by a rival, are angry and strike. The hypothesis here to be defended says that this order of sequence is incorrect, that the one mental state is not immediately induced by the other, that the bodily manifestations must first be interposed between, and that the more rational statement is that we feel sorry because we cry, angry because we strike, afraid because we tremble, and not that we cry, strike, or tremble because we are sorry, angry, or fearful, as the case may be. Without the bodily states following on the perception, the latter would be purely cognitive in form, pale, colorless, destitute of emotional warmth. We might then see the bear and judge it best to run, receive the insult and deem it right to strike, but we should not actually *feel* afraid or angry. (1892, pp. 375–376)

Further on in his famous chapter on the emotions, James attempts to support his theory by an appeal to the reader's sense of logic:

If we fancy some strong emotion, and then try to abstract from our consciousness of it all the feelings of its bodily symptoms, we find we have nothing left behind, no "mind-stuff" out of which the emotion can be constituted, and that a cold and neutral state of intellectual perception is all that remains. (1892, p. 379)

Finally, we might note that in support of his position, James asked Broadway actors and actresses whether they experienced emotions while going through the motions involved in acting out emotional scenes. Theoretically, a stage fight or love scene ought to create organic changes, and these, in turn, should arouse the appropriate emotion. James was told that such, indeed, was frequently the case. However, the evidence he was able to marshal in support of this theory is not very convincing, and

---

[7]Lange was a Danish physiologist who postulated a theory of the emotions similar to James'. Consequently, the two names are linked.

as will be brought out later in this chapter, the Cannon-Bard theory accounts for the facts of emotional experience more satisfactorily than does the James-Lange theory.

Carr differs from James and Lange in two respects. First, Carr insists on the psychophysical nature of the emotions and, as a consequence, is unable to accept the view that emotions are explicable solely as the perception of the organic processes. In other words, Carr believes there is a conscious aspect to the emotions, which is independent of the organic processes. Second, he argues that the emotion is partly responsible for the behavioral act. To relate his argument to James' example of fleeing from a bear, Carr believes the emotion of fear is partly the cause of running. James, on the other hand, made fear contingent upon the behavioral act of running.

In summary, Carr treats emotions as psychophysical events that are organic readjustments occurring in certain behavioral situations. The name given to the emotion depends upon the situation in which it occurs. Although emotions are organic readjustments, not all emotions are biologically useful. Again, the utility value of an emotion must be defined in terms of the behavioral situation in which that emotion occurs. In general, we might note that Carr's treatment of the emotions offers nothing unique or even highly characteristic of the functional point of view. As we have noted earlier, Carr is particularly interested in perception and learning. Emotions are treated somewhat incidentally as part of the "background" of mental life.

EMOTION IN GESTALT PSYCHOLOGY

As has been emphasized throughout this survey of systematic psychology, the Gestalt school's primary interest was in the fields of cognition, thinking, problem solving, and perception. Consequently, none of the original leaders of the movement developed a point of view on the emotions that attracted widespread interest or support. Even Lewin, with his strong interest in dynamic psychology, did not formulate a characteristic theory of emotion. Moreover, in contemporary Gestalt-oriented treatments of the subject, the emotions are typically viewed as inevitable concomitants of motivated behavior that have little significance if abstracted out of the motivational context. Because the Gestalt school failed to elaborate a special systematic point of view on the emotions, we shall go on to the more fertile ground of behaviorism.

FEELING AND EMOTION FROM THE BEHAVIORIST POINT OF VIEW[8]

Behaviorism and Feeling

In his *Behavior: An Introduction to Comparative Psychology* (1914) Watson admits that affection is one of two serious "stumbling blocks" standing in the way of a strictly objective psychology. The other is thinking. If the thought processes

---

[8]Our exposition of J. B. Watson's views on feeling follows his *Behavior: An Introduction to Comparative Psychology* (1914). The discussion of emotion follows *Psychology from the Standpoint of a Behaviorist* (1919).

and affective states cannot be reduced to behavioristically observable phenomena, the whole behaviorist program is in grave danger of collapse.

We have already found that Watson solved the problem of the thought processes by reducing thinking to "laryngeal habits" or "implicit" speech (see Chapter 11). In dealing with the affective states he followed the same line of reasoning, arguing that pleasantness-unpleasantness is reducible to implicit muscular and glandular reactions. More specifically, he assumed that the reproductive organs and associated erogenous zones function in affection in much the same manner that laryngeal habits function in the thought processes. The erogenous areas he believed capable of initiating two fundamental kinds of impulses: (1) a group of impulses associated with tumescence and rhythmical contractions of muscular tissues and increased glandular secretions; (2) a group connected with the detumescence of the sex organs, relaxation of associated muscular tissues, and inhibition of secretions.

The complete, overt functioning of the structures described in the first group occurs during sexual excitement and the progress of the reproductive act. As gross sexual excitement dies down, the processes described in the second group are in the ascendance. Watson goes on to contend that *the afferent impulses associated with the phenomena in the first group are the bodily substrata of pleasantness, and the afferent impulses associated with the second group of processes are the substrata of unpleasantness*. Originally, then, pleasantness and unpleasantness are aroused by sexual stimulation. If the organism is sexually receptive, the consequence is an approach reaction accompanied by tumescence, muscular tension, and increased glandular secretions. These reactions are pleasant. If, on the other hand, the organism is sexually unreceptive, the result is an avoidance reaction accompanied by inhibition of the sexual process and arousal of the affective state of unpleasantness.

Watson next deals with the problem of how objects or stimuli not originally connected with the sexual processes come to arouse feelings of pleasantness or unpleasantness. The answer to this difficulty is to be found in the ordinary mechanisms of habit or conditioning. Stimuli not originally associated with sexual behavior (and therefore not capable of arousing the pattern of reactions associated with either pleasantness or unpleasantness) can, through conditioning, arouse such reactions to a faint degree (implicit behavior). Watson presents no direct evidence for his assertions other than to note that phallic symbols, fetishes, and other phenomena from the area of sexual pathology support his contentions.

Finally, Watson suggests several avenues for assessing the validity of his theory and, at the same time, carrying out behaviorist studies of the affective processes. First, the behaviorist will attempt to determine whether the muscular and glandular processes presumed to be associated with affective reactions do indeed set up afferent impulses. He or she will also be able to carry out plethysmographic and galvanometric studies of the sex organs themselves. Finally, by eliminating the sensory tracts leading from the glands, the behaviorist can determine the effects of the absence of afferent impulses on associated feelings. Watson is convinced that the sexual impulses play "an enormous role" in artistic, esthetic, and religious behavior. He believes that the more liberal views toward the study of sex are rapidly making people lose their prejudice against acknowledging the possibility of the sexual reference of all behavior.

It is interesting to note that contemporary behavior therapists may utilize plethysmographic records of genital activity as an objective index of emotional arousal in connection with attempts to change homosexual patterns of behavior (see Chapter 17).

In summary, Watson treats the affective consciousness as an epiphenomenon unworthy of serious study. By identifying the affective states of pleasantness and unpleasantness with their bodily substrata in the erogenous zones, he believed that he had opened an avenue of approach to the behaviorist investigation of these processes. Although admitting that no such studies had been carried out successfully, Watson was satisfied that he had succeeded in bringing the difficult problem of affective psychology into his behaviorist program.

Behaviorism and Emotion

As is evident in his definition, Watson's view of the emotions is highly similar to his earlier position on feeling or affection. He defined an emotion as a *"heredi-tary 'pattern-reaction' involving profound changes of the bodily mechanism as a whole, but particularly of the visceral and glandular systems''* (1919, p. 195). By "pattern-reaction" Watson refers to the various response components that appear with some degree of regularity each time the appropriate stimulus situation arises. He believes that there are three such fundamental patterns in the human infant: *fear, rage,* and *love.* The appropriate stimulus situation for the evocation of fear is either a sudden loss of support or a loud sound. For rage, the stimulus is hampering the infant's movements; and for love, stroking or manipulating one of the erogenous zones.

The hereditary reaction-pattern characteristic of fear consists of a sudden catching of the breath, closing of the eyes, puckering of the lips, and random clutching movements of the hands and arms. For rage, the responses are stiffening of the body, screaming, and slashing or striking out with the arms and legs. For love, the responses consist of smiling, cooing, and extension of the arms as if to embrace the experimenter.

We have already noted (Chapter 7) how Watson believed that the entire range of adult emotions develops out of the basic three by a process of conditioning. It will be recalled that a child was conditioned to fear a white rat by associating the animal with a loud sound. Thus, by utilizing the principles of conditioning, Watson believed that he could account for the rich variety of human feelings and emotions. Characteristically, no importance was given to cognitive factors in emotional arousal and control.

THE CANNON-BARD THEORY OF THE EMOTIONS

One significant outcome of the broad research program directed toward the investigation of the physiological substrata of the emotions first suggested by the academic schools was the development of the famous Cannon-Bard theory of the emotions. The theory belongs to no particular school of psychology; but because it is essentially behaviorist in orientation, we have chosen to include it in this section. The theory emphasizes the fact that strong emotions ready the individual for emergency reactions. For this reason, it is frequently called the "emergency" theory of the emotions.

Basically, the theory postulates that the sympathetic division of the autonomic nervous system is dominant during emotional states. The effects of massive sympathetic stimulation are well known. The heart is speeded; digestion is inhibited; respiration is deeper and more rapid; blood is shunted to the periphery from the viscera. However, of all the visceral changes that occur, the most significant is the release of large quantities of epinephrine (adrenalin) into the bloodstream. In general, epinephrine mimics a massive sympathetic discharge. Consequently, all of the sympathetic effects already described are reinforced by this hormone's action on the various internal organs. In addition, epinephrine causes the blood to clot faster in the event that the individual is injured during the emergency, and it also acts on the muscles to lessen fatigue.

Cannon and Bard identified the hypothalamus as the main integrating center in the brain for the control of behavioral reactions in emotions. They found that when the hypothalamus is removed from animals, emotional responses become fragmentary and disintegrated. Approaching the problem from another direction, they demonstrated that electrical stimulation of certain centers in the hypothalamus results in a full-fledged rage and attack pattern. Removal of the cerebral cortex lowers the threshold for rage responses in animals, indicating that the cortex normally exerts an inhibiting influence over the hypothalamus. It has also been demonstrated that rage responses in decorticate animals are short-lived and disappear almost as soon as the stimulus is withdrawn. Moreover, the responses of such animals are lacking in direction. It is as if the animal fails to appreciate the source of the irritating stimulus. Such a hypothesis seems entirely justified, since decorticate animals lack the neurological mechanisms for perceiving, judging, and directing their behavior toward a goal.

As a result of their classic researches on the hypothalamus, Cannon and Bard postulated a "thalamic theory" of the emotions in opposition to the James-Lange theory. The thalamic theory states that nervous impulses coming into the thalamus from the receptors stimulate that center to send impulses to the cortex and viscera simultaneously (see Figure 13-3). The arrival of the thalamic impulses in the cortex gives rise to the conscious experience of an emotion. The motor impulses sent to the viscera by way of the hypothalamus and sympathetic nervous system result in the emergency state described earlier. Thus, while James and Lange made the emotional experience dependent on afferent impulses from the viscera and, consequently, a *result* of emotional behavior, Cannon and Bard hold that the emotional experience and the expressive responses both occur *at the same time* as a result of thalamic and hypothalamic activity. In diagrammatic terms the two theories can be contrasted as follows:

James-Lange: Perception → Motor reaction → Visceral arousal → Emotion

Cannon-Bard: Perception → Thalamic and hypothalamic arousal → Emotion / → Visceral arousal

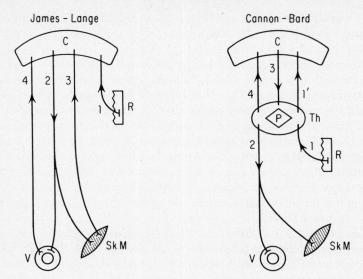

FIGURE 13-3. Diagrams of the nerve connections in the James-Lange and Cannon-Bard theories. C, cortex; R, a receptor; Th, thalamus; V, viscera; SkM, skeletal muscle; p, pattern of simultaneous thalamic impulses. Lines 1-4 represent nervous pathways. (From Walter B. Cannon, Again the James-Lange and the Thalamic Theories of Emotion. Psychological Review, 38, 1931, p. 282.)

Although the Cannon-Bard theory "explains" more of the phenomena associated with emotional behavior than the James-Lange theory and is more thoroughly supported by experimental evidence, the latter theory has not been "disproved." Despite the fact that the majority of psychologists have come to accept the Cannon-Bard theory as the better of the two, there remains a grain of truth in the contention that visceral and behavioral responses do, in part, determine how we feel. In those who are experiencing fear or anxiety, sensations arising from the shaking limbs, the dry mouth, the quivering stomach, and reactions in the other organs reinforce the feeling of fear. When it is possible to alleviate these sensations, as by the administration of drugs, fear is decreased to a considerable extent. To this extent the James-Lange theory remains good phenomenological psychology and, as such, cannot be summarily dismissed.

In concluding our survey of the contributions from within the behavioristic orientation to the psychology of feeling and emotion, the following generalizations appear to be justified. First, of all the contributions to the area of feeling and emotion within the *academic* schools, the behaviorists have done more to further our understanding *of the emotions* than any other group. It should be noted that we are careful to specify that this contribution lies within the restricted area of the *emotions*—not in feeling or affective psychology. Watson's assumptions that affective psychology could be reduced to its objective manifestations in the sex organs and glands has never been substantiated.

In the case of the emotions, however, the behaviorists may be credited with two significant contributions. First, Watson's own research on the emotional reactions of children, though erroneous in its conclusions, led to widespread studies in this area that have cast considerable illumination on the development of the emotions during childhood. Second, studies of the physiological concomitants of emotional behavior, though not exclusively of behaviorist origin, have either stemmed largely from that orientation or have been stimulated by it. In this same connection, we might point to the close parallel in the direction of research now taking place on the identification of the central brain mechanisms in both the emotional and motivational processes (see Chapter 14). It is too early to predict a merger between these two areas, but the past several decades have witnessed a growing rapprochement between these rapidly developing fields.

THE PSYCHOANALYTIC VIEW OF THE EMOTIONS[9]

Freud, it will be recalled, postulated that the sexual instinct, or libido, was the fundamental motive or driving force in the infant. Because of the urgency of the instinct, the child seeks pleasure by reduction of tension in the sexual organs and erogenous zones. For this reason, Freud spoke of the child's behavior as governed by the pleasure principle. In his own words: "It seems that our entire physical activity is bent upon *procuring pleasure and avoiding pain,* that it is automatically regulated by the pleasure-principle" (1920, p. 365).

Opposed to the sexual, or libido, instincts are the "ego instincts." The ego is Freud's equivalent for the "I," or self. One of the functions of the ego is to serve as a mediator between the libido and the environment. The ego, in other words, strives to give the libido satisfaction within the limits set by the demands of the environment. For this reason, Freud spoke of the "reality principle" as the guiding force behind the ego. Consequently, the child is operating according to the demands of two sets of instincts—the sexual, or libido, instincts governed by the pleasure principle, and the ego instincts operating according to the reality principle.

Freud believed that the pleasure principle is dominant in the early years, whereas the reality principle gains ascendance in the adult. Obviously, in the normal course of development such a transition would be necessary if the individual were to meet the demands of society successfully.

Within this theoretical framework, Freud developed his doctrines of the emotions. However, he did not attempt to formulate a systematic view of all the emotions but concentrated on the problem of anxiety, the emotion that has the greatest relevance for psychoanalytic theory.

Freud distinguishes three main types of anxiety: *objective anxiety, neurotic anxiety,* and *moral anxiety.* All three types represent reactions of weakness on the part of the ego to demands made on the individual by reality, the id, and the superego (Freud's equivalent for conscience). Objective anxiety is the consequence

---

[9]The pertinent references are Freud (1920, 1933, 1938a) and Munroe (1955).

of weakness toward the external world. Neurotic anxiety stems from weakness toward the id, and moral anxiety from weakness toward the superego.

The individual confronted by heavy demands arising from the environment becomes anxious. This first occurs at birth when the infant is suddenly overwhelmed by massive stimulation from the environment. The "birth trauma," as Freud referred to primary objective anxiety, is the prototype for the recurrence of secondary anxiety reactions later in the individual's life. Thus, whenever the individual is confronted by the likelihood of a traumatic experience, there is a reinstatement of the feelings associated with the original trauma of birth. It should be noted that anxiety is a reaction to an *anticipated* danger. Hence it is correct to speak of anxiety only when the individual expects trouble. If the danger or trauma actually occurs, the consequent reaction is *fear,* not anxiety.

By relating primary and secondary anxiety, Freud sought to explain the symptoms characteristic of adult anxiety. The tense, restricted breathing, the trembling resulting from massive motor nerve discharge, the rapid heartbeat, and so on, which are found in a typical anxiety attack, mimic the emotional conditions exhibited by the infant shortly after birth.

Neurotic anxiety is, in the last analysis, reducible to the objective anxiety from which it is derived. In neurotic anxiety, the individual fears the possible consequences of giving in to the demands of the libido. The real basis of the fear, however, is apprehension about the objective consequences of his or her own behavior. Specifically, he or she is afraid of the social consequences of engaging in forbidden sexual behavior. Thus, it is proper to consider neurotic anxiety a special form of objective anxiety.

Neurotic anxiety may take one of two forms. The first is "free-floating" anxiety, in which the individual continually anticipates the worst possible outcomes, is inclined to misinterpret chance happenings as evil omens, and is especially fearful of ambiguous situations, from which the worst consequences are foreseen. The second is a more circumscribed form in which the anxiety is aroused by specific objects and situations. The second type is most clearly exemplified in the various phobias, wherein the individual may be afraid of such objects or situations as snakes, open spaces, thunder, and diseases. Indeed, almost any stimulus-object or situation can become the condition for a phobic reaction.

However, the particular form that neurotic anxiety takes is not the fundamental problem for psychotherapy. Whether the individual is suffering from free-floating anxiety or specific phobias, the basic cause is an unconscious fear of the libidinal impulses, which must be resolved.

The third form of anxiety, moral anxiety, is also based on objective anxiety. Because the superego is developed as a result of introjected moral prohibitions and restrictions from the parents, the original source of all moral anxiety or guilt is environmental and, consequently, objective. More particularly, moral anxiety may be understood as a derivative of the original childhood fear of losing the love and goodwill of the parents, and possibly of being punished. Obviously, in the adult the whole mechanism is no longer mediated through a conscious fear of parental loss or retaliation for immoral behavior. It is, however, a secondary or derived consequence of such early fears, just as secondary objective anxiety is historically related to the primary birth trauma.

Finally, we should like to point out that Freud attributed a motivational function to both neurotic and moral anxiety, in the sense that either may lead to repression. As the ego becomes aware of danger, it takes steps to reduce the attendant anxiety by repressing the impulse that gave rise to the emotion in the first place. Looked at from this point of view, repression becomes a mechanism for dealing with anxiety.

In concluding our discussion of Freud's theory of anxiety, we should emphasize that his conception of this emotion is congruent with the behavioristic-physiological view of the emotions. More particularly, Freud looked upon primary anxiety as an instinctive reflex (birth trauma) that becomes attached to all sorts of stimuli through a process of conditioning. This formulation closely follows both Watson's and the neobehaviorist view, in which hereditary emotional responses become attached through conditioning to a variety of originally neutral or untraumatic stimuli. We may also note that Freud's organic-dynamic view of the emotions has been broadened into an entirely new branch of medicine, "psychosomatic medicine," which recognizes the close relationship between emotional (psychic) disorders and bodily (somatic) disorders.

EMOTION IN POST-FREUDIAN PSYCHIATRIC PRACTICE

The Post-Freudians and Emotions

Among adherents of the post-Freudian psychoanalytic group, the problem of anxiety continues to be of central importance in accounting for the structure of the neuroses. Karen Horney, our representative of that school, considers anxiety to be "the dynamic center of the neuroses" (1937, p. 41). According to her interpretation, the main source of neurotic anxiety is unconscious hostile impulses. These hostile impulses, in turn, arise from conflict. According to Horney, the individual in a conflict situation is caught between two incompatible motives, as we brought out more fully in Chapter 12. For example, the individual who is attempting to move toward and against people at one and the same time becomes anxious because of the repressed hostility underlying this conflicting attitude toward others. Because the neurotic is aware that others meet his or her excessive demands with rebuffs, more anxiety is generated. Therefore, the very means employed to reduce anxiety lead to its increase. The end result is the development of what Horney calls "vicious circles." She believes that such circular reactions account, in part, for the tendency of the neurotic to grow worse unless the root of the problem is unearthed through appropriate therapeutic procedures.

While placing considerably more emphasis on the contemporaneous nature of neurotic conflicts than does the traditional Freudian school, adherents of Horney nevertheless agree that every neurosis is a disturbance of the individual's character structure in childhood. In a particularly characteristic passage, Horney puts the problem as follows:

The basic evil is invariably a lack of genuine warmth and affection. A child can stand a great deal of what is often regarded as traumatic—such as sudden weaning, occasional beating, sex experiences—as long as inwardly he feels wanted and loved. Needless to say, a child feels keenly whether love is genuine, and cannot be fooled by any faked demonstrations. The main reason why a child does not receive enough warmth and affection lies in the parents' incapacity to give it on account of their own neuroses. More frequently than not, in my experience, the essential lack of warmth is camouflaged, and the parents claim to have in mind the child's best interest. Educational theories, over-solicitude or the self-sacrificing attitude of an "ideal" mother are the basic factors contributing to an atmosphere that more than anything else lays the cornerstone for future feelings of immense insecurity. (1937, p. 80)

Although the theoretical significance attributed to anxiety differs in various post-Freudian systems, there is general agreement that the emotion is generated by a lack of security or personal adequacy in stress situations. Because of the post-Freudian emphasis on the importance of security in childhood, the concept has loomed large in recent years in pediatric and educational literature. Similarly, as a result of the close causal relationship between anxiety and security, our time, with its succession of hot and cold wars, has been characterized as the "age of anxiety."

Existentialism and Anxiety

The post-Freudian emphasis on anxiety as a driving force in behavior disorders was reinforced by the *existential* movement in European philosophy. This philosophical school, which has its roots in the writings of Descartes, became one of the dominant forces in continental thinking with the rising popularity of the views of Kierkegaard, Nietzsche, Heidegger, Sartre, and others following World War II. Its fundamental themes—which we shall elaborate upon in Chapter 16—deal with being, man's place in the universe, freedom versus determinism, man's difficulties in coping with the impersonal organizations and institutions of modern society, and his relationship to God and to his fellow man.

Central to existential thinking is the concept of anxiety, which was first emphasized by Soren Kierkegaard, whose works influenced Karen Horney. Anxiety is also a central concept in the works of Sartre, Heidegger, and the literary existentialists such as Albert Camus. Existential anxiety is fundamentally a dread of nothingness or nonbeing in an alien, indifferent universe. It is the recognition that man is endowed with freedom to choose and that the price of freedom is fear or dread, which in Kierkegaard's words is the "sickness unto death." Choice, freedom, and anxiety are inseparable, since there is no longer any outside system of values to which the chooser can turn for help. In Barrett's words:

Thus with the modern period, man . . . has entered upon a secular phase of his history. He entered it with exuberance over the prospect of increased power he would have over the world around him. But in this world, in which his dreams of power were often more than fulfilled, he found himself for the first time *homeless*. Science stripped nature of its human forms and presented man with a universe that was neutral, alien, in its vastness and force, to his human purposes. Religion, before this phase set in, had been a structure that encompassed man's life, provided him with a system of images and symbols by which he could express his own aspirations toward psychic wholeness. With the loss of this containing framework man became not only a dispossessed but a fragmentary being. (1958, p. 35)

The consequence of anxiety is flight into an inauthentic mode of existence, which varies depending on the individual. It may take the form of detachment, of escaping into Don Juanism, of seeking domination over others, or of conformity—in other words, giving up freedom in order to avoid anxiety. The only authentic mode of existence—and, consequently, the only authentic method of coping with anxiety—is commitment. Commitment may be religious, social (in the true sense of deep involvement in the human condition), or creative, depending on one's philosophical and religious perspectives. But whatever the choice, commitment is fundamentally what Adler emphasized in his system of individual psychology—the discovery of a style of life authentic in respect to vocational, social, and affectional relationships with other human beings.

We shall return to the existential view of the human personality in Chapter 16, which deals with that topic. Here we need only emphasize by way of conclusion that philosophical existentialism expressed many viewpoints in common with the post-Freudians and humanistic psychologists and so became part of the *Zeitgeist* of a "third force" in psychology—the humanistic, as opposed to the behavioristic and psychoanalytic.

CURRENT DEVELOPMENTS IN EMOTIONAL THEORY

A Note on Subcortical Centers and Emotional Behavior

The most important breakthrough in the study of emotional behavior during the past half-century has been the discovery of electrically stimulable areas in the subcortical regions of the cerebrum. Because an understanding of research in this area presupposes a fairly detailed knowledge of the anatomical structures concerned, we have chosen to defer discussion of theories of emotional processes as related to brain centers to the next chapter, on the physiological basis of behavior. Meanwhile we shall consider two programs of research that have excited considerable interest in recent years among psychologists. First, we shall summarize recent research on cognitive and situational factors in emotion. Second, we shall discuss Harlow's work on affectional systems in monkeys.

Cognitive and Situational Determinants of Emotion

James, it will be recalled, stressed the perception of an emotional situation as leading to a behavioral act, such as running or fighting, with conscious awareness of the resulting bodily changes as the emotion. Clearly, this is a two-component theory.

First, there is the cognitive aspect, which involves perception of a situation leading to an appropriate response followed by awareness of the visceral concomitants of that response. Second, there is the complex of visceral changes that result from the activities of the autonomic nervous system. Early tests of James' theory involved the administration of epinephrine or adrenalin to experimental subjects in an attempt to induce widespread visceral changes, with the subjects reporting their emotional experiences, if any (Cantril & Hunt, 1932). Most subjects reported only physiological arousal, with no emotional overtones. Such a state is often referred to in the literature as a "sham" or "cold" emotion. However, what is missing in this type of experiment is any kind of cognitive or perceptual component, and for this reason such experiments are not true tests of the James-Lange theory.

In an ingenious experiment designed to evaluate the cognitive factors in emotional arousal, Schachter and Singer (1962) manipulated both their subjects' physiological state and cognitive determinants. Physiological arousal was induced by the administration of a subcutaneous injection of epinephrine. Controls received a placebo consisting of a saline solution. None of the subjects was aware of which substance was being injected. The subjects' cognitive states were manipulated by informing them that the purpose of the experiment was to test the effects of a new vitamin (called by the experimenters "Supertoxin") on vision. This, of course, disguised the real purpose of the experiment. In further manipulation of the subjects' cognitions, some were correctly informed about the physiological reactions that they could expect as a result of the injection of epinephrine. These were said by the experimenter to be "side effects" of Supertoxin. A second group was misinformed, whereas a third group was given no additional information.

The critical phase of the experiment began immediately following the injections when the subjects were individually placed in a room to "allow 20 minutes for the Supertoxin to get from the injection site into the bloodstream." In the waiting room was a confederate of the experimenters, supposedly also a subject who had just received an injection. For one-half the subjects in each experimental group the confederate behaved in a euphoric manner, playing basketball with rolled-up paper and a wastebasket, using a hula hoop, flying paper airplanes, and talking excitedly all the while. For the other subjects the confederate appeared angry at having to fill out a highly personal questionnaire, eventually tearing up the instrument and storming out of the room in a rage.

If cognitive factors are important determinates of the kind and intensity of emotional experience, then several differences among the experimental subjects should be apparent. First, those correctly informed about the effects of epinephrine—palpitations, tremor, flushing, and so on—would not be as strongly influenced by the confederate's behavior as those who were ignorant or misinformed about the effects of the injection. These latter subjects, it was assumed, would look to the situation for an explanation of their bodily states and so tend to take on whatever emotion was being acted out by the confederate.

In general, the results confirmed the hypothesis. The subjects who had no adequate explanation for their arousal state tended to label it according to the confederate's behavior. Thus, for behavioral indices of the anger condition, the epinephrine informed group showed an index of -0.18, while the epinephrine ignorant group's index was $+2.28$ and the placebo group's $+0.79$. In the euphoria condition the epinephrine informed group showed an activity index derived from the subject's imitation of the confederate of 12.72, while the epinephrine ignorant group's index was 18.28 and the misinformed group's 22.56. The placebo group's index was 16.00. Results from self-reports of their emotional experiences filled out by the subjects supported the behavioral indices.

Other studies by Schachter and his associates have demonstrated that subjects in a drug-induced condition of general arousal can be made to experience humor or anxiety (Schachter & Latané, 1964; Schachter & Wheeler, 1962). Other, independent investigators (Ross, Rodin, & Zimbardo, 1969; Wrightsman, 1960) have shown that situational factors can strongly influence emotional behavior supporting the Schachter-Singer theory of the cognitive determination of the emotions. However, additional replications of these experiments are needed before extensive generalizations about the relative contribution of physiological states and cognitive determinants can be formulated.

Affectional Responses in Monkeys

Harry Harlow, with whose studies of manipulatory motivation we are already familiar, has carried out extensive investigations with infant monkeys in an attempt to clarify the nature of affectional responses between young animals and the mother.

It will be recalled that drive reduction theory assumes that the attachment of the young to the mother is a derived, or secondary, motive based on satisfactions associated with the primary drive of hunger (see Chapter 9). Harlow has expressed strong reservations about this position in a series of theoretical and experimental papers published during the past twenty years (Harlow, 1958; Harlow & Harlow, 1962, 1965; Harlow & Zimmerman, 1959). Harlow's fundamental position is that young animals (and, by extension, human infants) demonstrate affectional responses independent of the drives and satisfactions associated with hunger and feeding.

To test this hypothesis experimentally, Harlow and his associates have utilized surrogate or substitute "mothers." Some of these mothers are made of wire; others are fabricated from wooden frames covered by sponge rubber and terry cloth (Figure 13-4). The "mothers" can be heated by means of electric light bulbs, and baby bottles can be installed in the substitutes for feeding.

In a fundamental experiment, newborn monkeys were placed in cages containing one wire mother and one cloth mother. Half of the group was fed only through the wire mother and the other half through the cloth mother. The animals were free to spend as much time as they pleased on either mother. Regardless of which mother provided the milk, the animals spent nearly all their time clinging to the cloth mother, leaving her only long enough to feed (Figure 13-5). The animals who were fed through the cloth mother formed attachments to it faster than those fed on the wire mother, but after a few weeks the strength of the attachment for the cloth mother was identical for both groups.

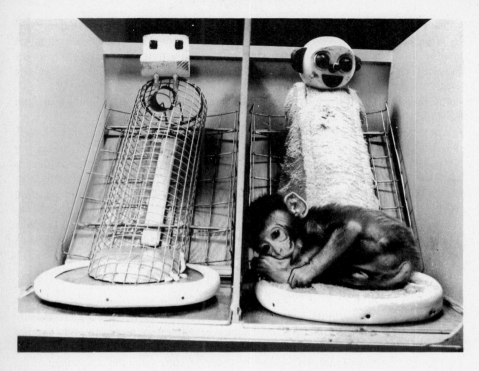

FIGURE 13-4.　　Wire and terry cloth mothers. Infant monkeys spend most of the time on cloth mothers regardless of which mother provides milk. (Photograph courtesy of Dr. Harry Harlow.)

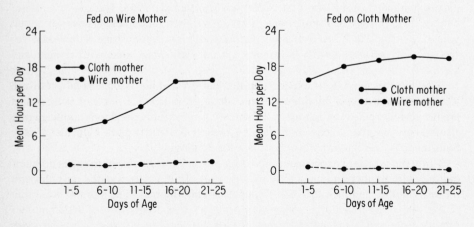

FIGURE 13-5.　　The mean hours per day spent on cloth and wire mothers by monkeys fed on both types of mother. Note that regardless of whether the animals were fed on wire or cloth mothers nearly all free time was spent on the cloth mother. (From Harlow, H. The nature of love. American Psychologist, 1958, 13, p. 676, Fig. 5. Copyright 1958 by the American Psychological Association. Reprinted by permission.)

In order to test whether or not the baby monkeys obtained a sense of security from their substitute mothers as human infants appear to from their mothers, various tests were run in which the animals were subjected to stress. For example, in open field tests they were placed in a strange, empty room in the company of a large mechanical bug. When released the monkeys would run in fear to the cloth mother—often surmounting obstacles to do so—and cling to it while gradually relaxing. In a few minutes they would begin tentative exploratory behavior, quickly returning if frightened. The wire mother provided no such creature comfort or security.

Subsequent tests have revealed that the early experiences of the experimental animals had far-reaching and durable influences on their subsequent development. Monkeys reared on either cloth or wire mothers show abnormal social responses, including uncooperativeness, aggression, and lack of sexual reactions. Other forms of aberrant behavior include stereotyped or ritualistic acts, self-mutilation, and aggressive responses to sexual advances from normally reared animals. Although the monkeys reared on cloth mothers did not show as extreme forms of aberrant behavior as those reared on wire mothers, the results nevertheless demonstrate that the cloth mother is not a substitute for the real mother. Moreover, animals who showed such abnormalities of behavior do not develop into normal animals if subsequently given opportunities to interact with other animals. As is so often true in behavioral development, there is a "critical" period during which behavioral patterns must be allowed to develop; otherwise they will be permanently retarded or perhaps fail to appear altogether.

Research by Harlow and Harlow (1962) has shown that to some degree social contact with other young monkeys may make up for lack of a real mother. Animals reared on cloth surrogates and also allowed daily periods of interaction with other young animals appear to develop normally in terms of social and sexual behavioral patterns.

Thus, Harlow's work, while demonstrating that warm contact is a partially rewarding experience independent of physical drive reinforcement, also shows contact is not a sufficient substitute for live social interaction as far as normal social development is concerned. The question of precisely what is established in the young monkeys by real mothers or peer contacts cannot be decided on the basis of present evidence. Perhaps social skills and habits of adjustment can be developed only through creature contacts. We do not know. We do know that Harlow's results show striking parallels to studies of deprived children whose inadequate contact with, or absence from, the mother leads to severe behavioral disorders (see Chapter 4).

In a symposium on the behavior of nonhuman primates, Harlow and Harlow (1965) have provided a theoretical organization for the empirical studies on affection emanating from their laboratory. The Harlows point out that five affectional systems occur in a hierarchical order of development: (1) the infant-mother affectional system, which develops the strong ties of the infant to the mother; (2) the mother-infant relationship, which is the reciprocal of the infant-mother system; (3) the infant-infant, or peer affectional, system, which develops between agemates; (4)

the sexual affectional systems, which lead to adult reproductive patterns; and (5) the paternal affectional system, in which the adult males exhibit positive responses toward infants, juveniles, and other animals in their particular social group.

From the point of view of a better understanding of Harlow's work with monkeys, the infant-mother affectional system is the most important. Moreover, Harlow and Harlow characterize it as "enormously powerful and probably less variable than any of the other systems" (1965, p. 288). This, they point out, is undoubtedly a natural adaptation for survival, since strong infant ties to the mother are essential in the animals' natural environment.

Harlow and Harlow (1965) subdivide the infant-mother affectional system into four stages: (1) a reflex stage, (2) a comfort and attachment stage, (3) a security stage, and (4) a separation stage.

The reflex stage persists from birth to the second or third week of the infant's life and consists of two groups of reflexes, those associated with nursing and those associated with grasping. The nursing reflex consists of orienting and "rooting" movements of the head to bring the mouth into contact with the nipple, whereupon sucking begins. The grasping reflex consists of strong clinging responses, which ensure that the infant can maintain contact with the mother as she travels from place to place during the day.

Harlow and Harlow identify the second stage, the period of comfort and attachment, as one in which "the infant receives little from the mother, other than the satisfaction of its basic bodily needs, nursing, contact, warmth, and probably proprioceptive stimulation and protection from danger" (1965, p. 291). Even though the mother displays strong protective behavior during this period, which ends after 60 to 80 days, the infant appears to derive only a moderate sense of security from contact with the mother.

By contrast, when the infant is tested with fear-producing stimuli during the stage of security, it runs quickly to the mother and clings to her fearfully, only gradually relaxing, as we pointed out in connection with tests of infants' reactions to surrogate mothers. Here we need only add that in the absence of the mother, infants show "freezing" behavior, crouching and clutching with their arms as if to protect or comfort themselves.

Finally, in the normal course of development, the separation stage begins to gradually terminate the infant-mother affectional relationship. In the normal environment the lure of objects, the increasing tendency to explore farther and farther away from the mother, and the development of extrafamilial social contacts weaken the bonds between mother and child.

As a result of criticisms of Harlow's early work with surrogate mothers that varied only in respect of the presence or absence of terry cloth, Harlow and Suomi (1970) developed surrogate mothers whose facial characteristics, covering, temperature, and mobility could be varied. In the experiment, monkeys were given a choice between surrogate mothers with faces that were decorative or resembled a dog's face. Facial characteristics, however, were not significantly related to time spent clinging to the mother. The infant monkeys did show a definite preference for mothers covered with terry cloth as opposed to the alternatives of rayon, vinyl, or a rough grade of sandpaper. When given a choice of a warm mother as opposed to a cold mother, the animals chose the warm surrogate. In fact, infants reared on cold mothers failed to run to them in field tests of fear, but crouched against the walls of the cage instead. And, finally, given a choice between a rocking mother and one which was still, the infants chose the rocking surrogate as evidenced by their spending more time, between 20 and 180 days of age, clinging to it. Harlow and Suomi conclude that the nature of the affectional response is determined by a complex of interrelated factors involving sensory contact, temperature, and motility.

Those familiar with the literature of development and child psychology will recognize many interesting parallels between the behavior of the infant monkey and that of the human infant. Harlow's empirical research and theoretical organization of affectional systems constitute important comparative and developmental contributions on the frontiers of the psychology of motivation and emotion.

SUMMARY AND EVALUATION

In the past three-quarters of a century the psychology of feeling and emotion has undergone a gradual evolution in the direction of becoming more ''somatically'' oriented. In the older, prescientific literature and in the structuralistic psychologies of Wundt and Titchener, the emphasis was primarily on the affective states as conscious phenomena, and only secondarily on the emotions. Moreover, in their treatment of the emotions, nineteenth-century and early twentieth-century psychologists stressed the conscious or introspective aspect of the emotional states. Beginning with the functionalistic-behavioristic studies of the behavioral expressions of the emotions, the latter came to be emphasized more and more in both experimental research and the theoretical literature.

The trend in research on the emotions has, in a sense, been from the periphery inward. The early behavioral studies emphasized either the facial expressions characteristic of the various emotions or the associated visceral changes. More recently, beginning with the researches and theoretical interpretations of Cannon and Bard, the emphasis has shifted toward the central or cerebral mechanisms in emotional behavior. In very recent years the discovery of the subcortical centers associated with animal drives (which we touched upon toward the end of Chapter 12) has reinforced interest in formulating an empirically grounded central theory of the dynamic states. Although a comprehensive account of feeling and emotion lags behind the wealth of recent experimental discoveries, the twentieth-century trend toward a behavioral science of the emotions appears to be a distinct improvement.

Physiological Theories of Behavior
14

In discussing the emergence of psychology as a natural science (Chapter 1), we emphasized the close relationship that existed between the new discipline and experimental physiology. Weber, Fechner, and Wundt—the men who were responsible for applying the methods of the natural sciences to psychological problems—brought those methods to psychology from physiology. The early psychology of the latter half of the nineteenth century not only emerged from physiology but also was often indistinguishable from it. And it is a testimony to cyclical trends in history that a large segment of contemporary psychology is scarcely distinguishable from neurophysiology.

Indeed, as we hope to demonstrate in this chapter, the explosive developments in the physiology of the nervous system in recent years have resulted in an increasing rapprochement between the two sciences. The psychologist's long quest for a better understanding of mental and behavioral activities inevitably leads to the brain as the seat of all behavior. However, the early hopes of the physiological psychologists—who looked to the nervous system for the biological basis of the cognitive, conative, and affective processes—are only now being realized, thanks to the development of precise electronic and biochemical tools that have made possible revolutionary discoveries in this oldest psychological field.

In attempting to trace the development of physiological theories of behavior, we shall have to abandon our customary approach of examining the position of the leaders of the older schools and then tracing the fate of their systematic positions as they evolved into contemporary psychology. Despite the fact that the men who founded psychology were physiologists by training, they did not have well-formulated theories of brain function and behavior—with the possible exception of the Gestalt school, whose physiological orientation in treating certain aspects of perception we examined in Chapter 6. In general, the systematists of the schools were not strong physiological theorists; and, traditionally, the physiological psychologists have not been strong systematists in the sense of developing schools or broad positions encompassing the whole of psychology. With some exceptions, their theorizing has been confined to hypothetical explanations of specific functions rather than to attempts to integrate the entire field within the structure of a physiological theory. We now begin with just such an attempt as we consider the development of theories of cortical localization in learning, which remains one of the broadest and most central problems of physiological psychology, as it was throughout the nineteenth century.

EARLY THEORIES OF CORTICAL LOCALIZATION OF FUNCTION

Phrenology

By one of the strange accidents that occur from time to time in the history of science, the study of cortical localization of function was stimulated by the pseudoscience of phrenology under the vigorous leadership of Franz Joseph Gall (1758–1828) and his pupil J. G. Spurzheim (1776–1832). Gall and Spurzheim took the position that mind is made up of a number of faculties. Some faculties are *affective,* consisting of instincts and propensities such as the will to live, aggressiveness, acquisitiveness, self-esteem, and benevolence; others are *intellective,* such as the linguistic, spatial, temporal, numerical, and musical faculties. Figure 14-1 shows a phrenological map of the brain, with some of the more important faculties as localized by the phrenologists.

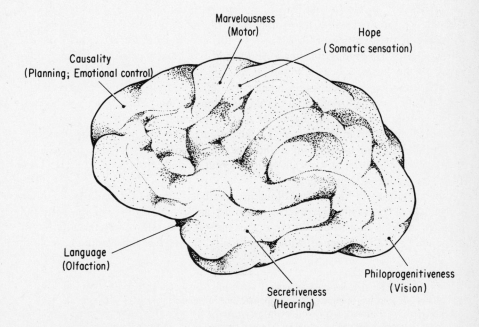

FIGURE 14-1.   A lateral view of the cerebrum showing areas of localization according to the phrenologists. The actual functions of the areas are shown in parentheses.

Gall and Spurzheim also believed that the possession of a highly developed faculty indicated a correspondingly well-developed area in the cerebral cortex and, most important, that the configuration of the overlying skull reflected this cerebral development. Thus to assess the individual's mental faculties, one would need only to make measurements of the corresponding degree of development of the localized "bumps" on the skull.

Although phrenology had enormous popular appeal, it never won widespread scientific support. Indeed, Gall and Spurzheim were ridiculed by most anatomists and neurologists, who found their assumptions about the correlation between the brain and skull untenable. However, their opponents had no specific alternative evidence to show how cortical function is localized or, if not localized, how the brain functions as a whole. Indeed, historians (Boring, 1929; Krech, 1962) credit opposition to the doctrines of Gall and Spurzheim with stimulating research that led to a better understanding of cerebral localization.

Hall and Flourens and the Method of Extirpation

We have already briefly described the work of Marshall Hall (1790–1857) and Pierre Flourens (1794–1867), who were responsible for carrying out the first scientific studies of the functions of the brain. Hall, it will be recalled, performed simple experiments showing that decapitated animals could make motor responses if appropriately stimulated.

Although he confirmed Hall's concept of broad levels of functioning (see Chapter 2), Flourens—the more important of the two men—denied the precise localization of faculties or functions[1] in the cerebral cortex as claimed by the phrenologists. He espoused instead the doctrine of a unitary principle of functioning in which the cortex acts as a whole.

Flourens was a model experimenter. He relied entirely on direct observation in formulating his conclusions about brain functions. In his extirpative work he carefully isolated a part of the brain for study, removed it, and then observed the subsequent reaction in the animal. He investigated the functions of the cerebrum, cerebellum, corpora quadrigemina (the superior and inferior colliculi), medulla, and spinal cord by removing these parts in different animals, primarily in birds. Table 14-1 summarizes his findings.

On the basis of his results, Flourens concluded that (1) the brain is a multiple organ whose functions are diverse and exist at several levels; (2) the cerebrum proper functions as a whole for the higher mental processes of cognition, volition, association, and intelligence. More specifically, he showed that although the brain

---

[1]The distinction between "faculty" and "function," though not made by the early anatomists and physiologists, is an important one. Faculties were assumed to be inherent "powers" of the mind such as will, memory, and calculational ability. These powers were held to be responsible for mental activities. The now favored term "function" refers to a process or activity characteristic of a given organ without the implication that "powers" lie behind such activities.

TABLE 14-1.   Functional Levels of the Brain According to Flourens

Anatomical Center	Results of Destruction	Function
Cerebrum	Loss of judgment, inability to initiate voluntary movement, inability to remember	Perceiving, willing, memory, intelligence
Cerebellum	Loss of coordination	Coordination of voluntary movement
Corpora quadrigemina	Disturbances in visual and auditory processes	Mediation of visual and auditory reflexes
Medulla	Death of animal	Vital functions—respiration and heartbeat

behaves as if it were several distinct organs, it functions in a unitary manner. Thus he could point to the cerebellum as the organ of coordination, the corpora quadrigemina as centers for vision, and the medulla as the center for vital functions; but he could not *localize* volition, intelligence, and perceptual processes in the cerebrum. All were coextensive functions existing inseparably from each other.

Paul Broca and the Clinical Method

Flourens' conclusions set back the cause of cortical localization for nearly a quarter of a century. His generalization that the cerebrum functions as a unity at first failed to generate serious opposition from those who championed some form of localization. Not until Paul Broca (1824–1880), a professor of surgery at the Bicêtre, announced the discovery of the speech center that bears his name (see Figure 14-2) did the issue of cortical localization come once more to the fore. Boring tells of the discovery in the following account.

> Broca's observation was in itself very simple. There had in 1831 been admitted at the Bicêtre, an insane hospital near Paris, a man whose sole defect seemed to be that he could not talk. He communicated intelligently by signs and was otherwise mentally normal. He remained at the Bicêtre for thirty years with this defect and on April 12, 1861, was put under the care of Broca, the surgeon, because of a gangrenous infection. Broca for five days subjected him to a careful examination, in which he satisfied himself that the musculature of the larynx and articulatory organs was not hindered in normal movements, that there was no other paralysis that could interfere with speech, and that the man was intelligent enough to speak. On April 17 the patient—fortunately, it would seem, for science—died; and within a day Broca had performed an autopsy, discovered a lesion in the third frontal convolution of the left cerebral hemisphere, and had presented the brain in alcohol to the Société d' Anthropologie. (1929, p. 69)

Broca had not only made an important anatomical discovery, he had also introduced a new technique—the clinical method. Other physicians had, of course, been using the clinical method as a diagnostic tool in the treatment of disease since it

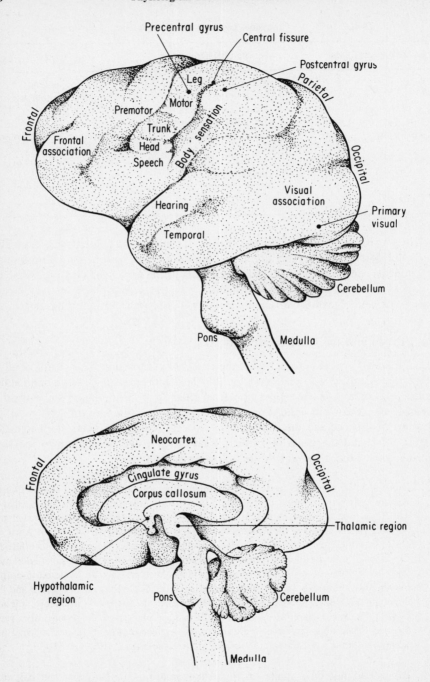

FIGURE 14-2.   Lateral views of the exterior and interior structures of the cerebrum showing the principal parts and areas of functional localization.

was described by the Greek physician Hippocrates. But Broca was the first to utilize it successfully to demonstrate localization of function in the cerebral cortex.

Broca had also chanced upon another discovery: One side of the brain is dominant over the other. His patient, Leborgne, showed no defect on the right side of the brain. The finding that speech functions are localized on the dominant side of the brain—usually the left—was quickly confirmed on other patients with similar behavioral difficulties. Incidentally, the phenomenon of laterality of function in the brain has been a puzzle whose solution has accounted for a large share of research among neurophysiologists and physiological psychologists.

Electrical Stimulation

The first experimental discovery of a localized area in the brain using the method of electrical stimulation was made by G. Fritsch (1838–1927) and E. Hitzig (1838–1907), who in 1870 applied a weak electric current to the surface of a dog's brain and showed that the animal made movements on the opposite side of the body. Together they had, in effect, discovered the motor area of the cortex, which lies along the precentral gyrus, and at the same time had inaugurated the use of what was to become a fundamental method in experimental neurophysiology—the method of electrical stimulation.

Subsequent experiments on dogs and monkeys, and isolated reports on the stimulation of the human cortex, confirmed Fritsch and Hitzig's observations and established not only that the cortex contains a highly localized motor center for the control of the limbs and body but also that several other centers concerned with eye movements, sensory processes, the ears, and the mouth could be localized in the brain.

By the end of the nineteenth century there was general agreement that localization of both motor and sensory functions had been established as a fact of cortical functioning.

To summarize the contributions of the nineteenth century to the problem of cortical localization, we may say that there were two principal discoveries: First was the development of three important methods of investigation—extirpative, clinical, and electrical. Second, the principle of cortical localization of function was well established by the turn of the century. However, localization was neither as precise nor as widespread as had been asserted by Gall and Spurzheim. What had been shown was that motor and sensory functions could be localized with considerable precision; but no one had yet demonstrated that the so-called higher mental processes were localized in specific areas of the cortex in the same manner as electrically excitable points on the motor cortex. Moreover, in the case of sensory localization, only very guarded generalizations could be made. There was no way for investigators to communicate with an animal whose sensory cortex was being stimulated in order to determine what the subject was experiencing. By contrast, upon stimulation of the motor cortex, it was easy to observe motor movements on the periphery. The method of ablation (surgical removal) did, of course, reveal gross sensory deficiencies such as blindness; but experimenters had to await the development of reliable psychological tests of sensory processes before more precise generalizations could be formulated about the role of the cortex in sensory discrimination.

THE ROLE OF THE CEREBRAL CORTEX IN MAZE LEARNING

Whereas Pavlov's research was concerned with cortical mechanisms in conditioning (Chapter 8), it was Karl Lashley (1890–1959) who first systematically utilized the psychological methods of studying learning in animals in order to investigate the role of the cerebral cortex in learning and retention.

We may begin with Lashley's classical studies of maze learning in rats, which were conducted for the purpose of testing (1) the relationship between the complexity of the problem and cerebral lesions and (2) the effects of destruction of various sizes and locations on the maze habit. Diagrams of Lashley's three mazes, known as Mazes I, II, and III, are reproduced from his *Brain Mechanisms and Intelligence* (1929) in Figure 14-3. Maze I, it will be noted, is a simple discrimination problem

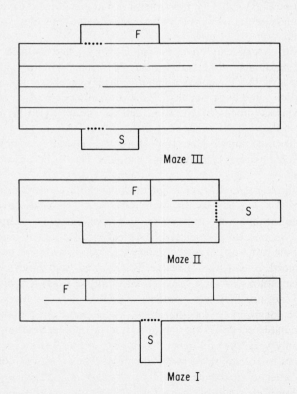

FIGURE 14-3.   Floor diagrams of Lashley's three mazes. (From Lashley, K. S. Brain mechanisms and intelligence. University of Chicago Press, 1929.)

involving only a single choice. Maze II is much more difficult, since it is a three-blind maze; and Maze III, the most difficult, has eight blinds.

The results left no doubt that there is a close relationship between the difficulty of the problem and the effect of cerebral lesions. Figure 14-4 shows this relationship in a three-dimensional surface. A careful study of the diagram reveals that small destructions of 10 percent or less have little effect on learning in any of the mazes. However, for Maze III the number of errors increases very rapidly with increasing magnitude of cortical destructions. For Mazes I and II destructions of over half of the cortex do not have a serious effect on the acquisition of the habit.[2]

The purely quantitative effects of cerebral lesions in learning might well have been predicted on logical grounds. We would expect a close relationship to exist between the magnitude of a cerebral injury and the ability to learn in situations of varying difficulty. However, not so readily predictable was Lashley's discovery that the locus, or site, of the lesion was not an important factor in retardation. Rather, the *mass* of the lesion was the crucial factor. This finding led Lashley to formulate his well-known principles of equipotentiality and mass action as follows:

> *Equipotentiality*. The term "equipotentiality" I have used to designate the apparent capacity of any intact part of a functional area to carry out, with or without reduction in efficiency, the functions which are lost by destruction of the whole. This capacity varies from one area to another and with the character of the functions involved. It probably holds only for the association areas and for functions more complex than simple sensitivity or motor co-ordination.
>
> *Mass action*. I have already given evidence which is augmented in the present study, that the equipotentiality is not absolute but is subject to a law of mass action whereby the efficiency of performance of an entire complex function may be reduced in proportion to the extent of brain injury within an area whose parts are not more specialized for one component of the function than for another. (Lashley, 1929, p. 25)

In effect, the principle of equipotentiality states that a 50 percent destruction in the anterior half of the brain would cause the same retardation as a 50 percent destruction of the posterior half *in maze learning*. We emphasize that the generalization applies to maze learning, since there are many cases of cerebral functioning where locus is important—for example, in speech.

We may now pause and ask: What is the meaning of mass action and equipotentiality? Are we to assume that in the maze problem the brain acts as a whole, exhibiting the operation of a general learning factor dispersed over the entire cortex? Such a possibility would be entirely consistent with both the principle of mass action and that of equipotentiality. However, there is another possibility, namely, that maze learning depends upon the total sensory input coming to the cortex from the

---

[2]Another way of showing the relationship between the difficulty of the problem and the magnitude of the lesion is to compare the correlations between the extent of cerebral destruction and errors for the three mazes. As reported by Lashley (1929, p. 67), these are Maze I, 0.20; Maze II, 0.58; and Maze III, 0.75.

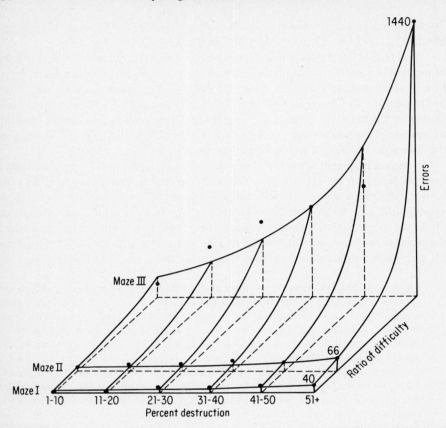

FIGURE 14-4.   Lashley's three-dimensional surface showing the relationships among the percent of destruction, ratio of difficulty, and errors in the mazes. (From Lashley, K. S. Brain mechanisms and intelligence. University of Chicago Press, 1929.)

various receptors—the eyes, ears, nose, the pads of the feet, the vibrissae, and so forth. If so, then Lashley's increasingly massive destructions would involve more and more of the localized cortical centers for these senses, until eventually all input would be affected and the animal would be unable to show a significant degree of learning.

   In the latter case we would be dealing with localized factors, which in combination destructions would give the appearance of a mass action effect. That this hypothesis may be true is strongly suggested by an experiment (1936) of Honzik's, in which the sense organs of animals were systematically destroyed, both singly and in combination. As Figure 14-5 shows, the destruction of even one important sense organ, such as vision or smell, has a severe retarding effect on maze learning. But combinations of destructions are much more serious in their effects, indicating that in the absence of one sense the animal falls back on another—just as blind people will utilize the sense of audition in place of vision. Clearly, then, as more sense organs are destroyed, the animal has fewer and fewer alternatives; consequently, retardation becomes more and more severe—and we have a mass action effect.

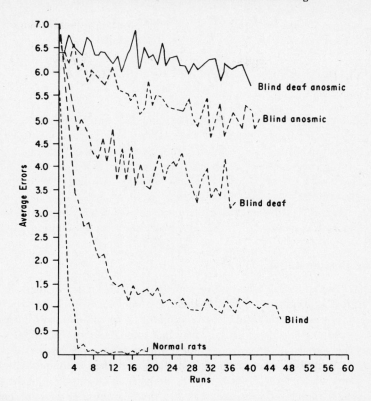

FIGURE 14-5.   Errors in the maze as a function of single and multiple destructions. (After Honzik, C. H. The sensory basis of maze learning in rats. Comparative Psychological Monograph, 1936, 13, No. 4. Originally published by the University of California Press; reprinted by permission of The Regents of the University of California.

Honzik carried out peripheral ablations of sense organs while Lashley employed central lesions. However, each receptor on the periphery is represented by a cortical projection center and its surrounding association area; and to destroy the visual cortex, for example, is to blind the animal just as if its eyes had been removed.

It is still possible that each of the projection-association areas for the various senses may have two functions: (1) a specific or localized function, called by Flourens *action propre,* and (2) a generalized function, called by Flourens *action commune.* To test this hypothesis it would be necessary to destroy the sense peripherally, measure the amount of retardation, and then destroy the appropriate cortical center. This procedure would determine whether a further retardation occurs because of loss of a general factor in the cortex associated with that sensory function. Lashley (1943) carried out such an experiment by blinding rats and then having them learn a maze. Destruction of the visual cortex resulted in a severe deficit in the animals' retention of the maze. A similar result utilizing monkeys as subjects has been reported by Orbach (1959). It appears, then, that in addition to its specific sensory function, the striate cortex also contributes a general factor in maze learning, the precise nature of which has not been discovered.

CORTICAL LOCALIZATION IN DISCRIMINATION LEARNING

Broadly speaking, there are two kinds of discrimination, one involving the subject's ability to differentiate between two intensities or brightnesses and the other requiring a discrimination between two qualities, such as two forms or two tonal patterns. Intensity discriminations are much easier for the animal subject than are form discriminations; and, not surprisingly, it turns out that the role of the cortex differs in the two situations. We shall discuss each problem separately, indicating the general experimental results and using data from visual intensity and form-discrimination problems that are typical of studies of other sensory modalities as well.

Brightness Discrimination

Again, it was Lashley who carried out the pioneer studies of the role of the cerebral cortex in brightness discrimination. Figure 14-6 shows the type of apparatus used for training the animals in his brightness discrimination problems. The unexpected result of Lashley's studies was that animals whose occipital cortices were destroyed showed no decrement in the ability to learn a brightness discrimination habit (1929, p. 47). However, if the animal was trained in the problem before cerebral lesions were imposed, the habit was abolished by destruction of the occipital cortex (1929, p. 86). If the animal was then given retraining, the habit could be relearned; and, unless the conditions of learning were modified, the course of relearning in operated animals did not appear different from that in normals. Thus, we may conclude that the occipital cortex, though normally involved in the acquisition of a brightness discrimination habit, is not essential to its formation. This further suggests that we may have to distinguish between cortical mechanisms in the *acquisition* phase of learned behavior and mechanisms of *retention*. It is possible that different neurological processes are involved; and, as will be brought out in a later section of this chapter, there is empirical evidence to show that this is the case—at least in some forms of learning.

If, however, the problem is made more difficult, say, by requiring the animal to distinguish between two lights of different intensities rather than between a light and a dark area, the postoperative animals have more difficulty in relearning the habit. This result is not inconsistent with the first if we assume that subcortical centers are capable of mediating relatively simple brightness discriminations but that increasingly more difficult discriminations involve the striate cortex. As we shall see, when discriminations become very difficult (form discrimination), the integrity of the cortex is essential to the learning of the problem.

At this point we may ask why animals trained in brightness discrimination fail to retain the habit after extirpation of the striate cortex, even though they can learn the habit without the cortex. An experiment by R. Thompson (1960) indicates that

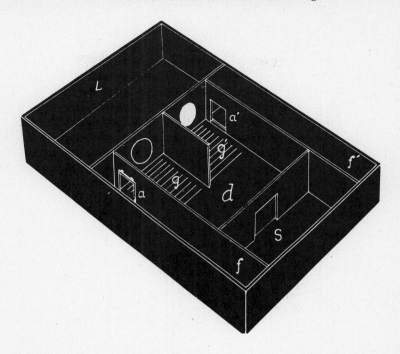

FIGURE 14-6.   A brightness discrimination box. The starting compartment is at S. Food may be obtained at f or f' depending on the discrimination required. The areas labeled g and g' are grids that may be used to apply shock; a and a' are openings leading to the food compartments. (From Lashley, K. S. Brain mechanisms and intelligence. University of Chicago Press, 1929.)

there is a lack of transfer between the pre- and postoperative situations. He trained animals in the discrimination problem and then operated in two stages. First, one side of the striate cortex was removed, and the animals were allowed to recover for several days during which training went on. Then, the other half of the cortex was removed. There was no loss of the habit. Apparently, the cortex remaining after the first operation serves as a ''bridge'' that allows the subcortical nuclei to ''acquire'' the habit.

Form Discrimination

As noted in the preceding discussion, the integrity of the striate area is necessary for visual form discrimination. Figure 14-7 shows the apparatus Lashley used in his extensive experiments on visual form discrimination problems. He found that animals lacking the striate cortex could not learn a form discrimination. Moreover, animals that had learned the problem before the lesion was imposed suffered complete and permanent postoperative amnesia. Furthermore no amount of retraining could reinstate the habit (Lashley, 1938, 1939). However, if the animals suffered only partial lesions, the habit was not abolished—even though only remnants of the

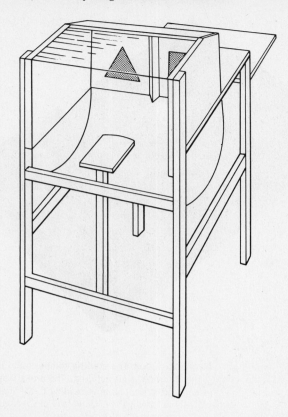

FIGURE 14-7.   Lashley's form discrimination apparatus. One of the doors (triangle or square) is left unfastened. If the animal jumps to this door he obtains food on the rear platform. If he jumps to the incorrect side, he falls into the net below. (After Lashley, K. S. The mechanism of vision: XV. Preliminary studies of the rat's capacity for detail vision. Journal of General Psychology, 1938, 18, p. 126, Fig. 1.)

cortex remained. Apparently animals with partial lesions are able to overcome the resultant scotomata, or gaps in their visual fields.

If we compare Lashley's results on form discrimination with those he obtained in the maze situation, we find that equipotentiality applies to the latter but not to the former. In other words, when learning involves a specific sensory input, such as through the eye, and no alternative path is present, another part of the brain cannot take over and function vicariously. The concept of equipotentiality, then, is limited in scope and indicates that the brain, like other organ systems in the body, possesses flexibility—but not unlimited flexibility. There is localization of function as well as mass action and equipotentiality. As is true when dealing with other concepts in psychology, we must be careful to be operationistic and to specify precisely what experimental tests we have in mind before we attempt to generalize or to assess the validity of mass action and equipotentiality.

PROBLEM SOLVING AND THE CEREBRAL CORTEX[3]

The most complex form of learning involves solutions where both the stimulus factors and the response pattern are highly complex and, as many psychologists believe, depend upon representative or cognitive factors for the mediation of the response. Returning once more to Lashley's classic studies (1929), we may begin by examining his results with the double alternation box, a relatively simple form of problem in which the animal is required to press down successively two platforms mounted on opposite sides of an enclosure containing food (see Figure 14-8). Animals suffering lesions involving 14 to 50 percent of the cortex, with an average destruction of 28.4 percent, required on the average no more trials to master the problem than normals. Similarly, animals who had learned the problem and then suffered injuries were found to be somewhat retarded in their performance but could easily relearn. There was evidence that the frontal lobes were more important in the successful solution of the problem than other portions of the brain. This finding is not surprising in view of the fact that the problem involves the use of the forelimbs, whose motor innervation is localized in the frontal regions.

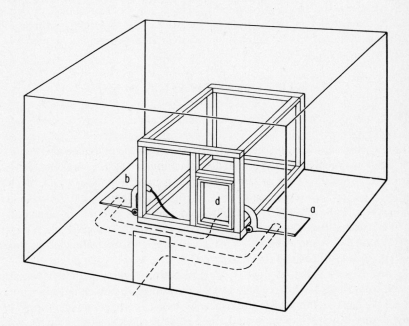

FIGURE 14-8. A double alternation problem. The animal must shuttle between levers *a* and *b*, pressing them in turn before being allowed in door *d* where a reward is obtained. (From Lashley, K. S. Brain mechanisms and intelligence. University of Chicago Press, 1929.)

---

[3]The reader should review the studies of Jacobsen and Kurt Goldstein on the role of the cerebral cortex in delayed-reaction problems and concept formation in Chapter 11.

The double alternation problem is a relatively simple one. In more difficult latch boxes involving a hard-to-reach lever that must be manipulated by one paw (the preferred paw), a high degree of localization involving only 1 to 2 percent of the cortex in the frontal region has been found to abolish the performance, although the habit can be relearned (G. M. Peterson, 1934; G. M. Peterson & Fracarol, 1938). Again, we are dealing with a specialized motor function that is dependent upon a restricted area of the cortex. However, Maier (1932) showed that small lesions involving 10 to 15 percent of the cortex could seriously disturb a reasoning problem in which the animal (rat) was required to put two previous experiences together, in order to solve a present problem (Figure 14-9).

Finally, we may briefly outline an interesting pair of experiments by Krechevsky (1933, 1935), in which he found that animals given alternate paths involving visual and spatial cues in a discrimination maze utilize both alternatives—some favoring spatial cues, some visual, and others using both. In the "spatial" rats, lesions in the frontal region disrupted the habit; whereas the "visual" animals suffered a loss of ability if the lesions were in the striate area. Once again we see that the issue of cortical localization is contingent upon the type of problem employed. If the problem requires the use of specialized cues or demands skilled manipulation, then we find cortical localization. If the problem can be solved by utilizing various cues or does not require skilled manipulation, then we are unlikely to find a high degree of cortical localization.

CORTICAL LOCALIZATION IN MAN

We have been emphasizing studies of cortical localization carried out on animals under conditions of precise experimental control. From the point of view of the experimental psychologist this situation gives the best type of evidence. Lesions can be localized in animals. The experimenter has complete control over the genetic and environmental history of his or her subjects and, most important of all, is able to devise precise pre- and postoperative tests of the psychological function under investigation. However, the typical physiological psychologist is ultimately interested in cortical localization in humans—the one species unavailable for experimental research. The psychologist must, therefore, go to the clinician in order to obtain knowledge of cortical localization.

In recent years it has become possible to perform brain operations on patients suffering from surgically correctable neurological disorders, such as focal epilepsy, while the patient is under local anesthesia and can therefore remain conscious. Local anesthetics are injected into the scalp, which is then reflected along with the bone of the skull in order to expose the brain. Paradoxically, although the brain is the seat of all pain, it does not respond with sensations of pain when stimulated directly. Thus the neurosurgeon can stimulate the cortex with a weak electric current and "map" the motor, sensory, and association areas according to the subject's reports or movements.

An impressive collection of such clinical investigations has been provided by

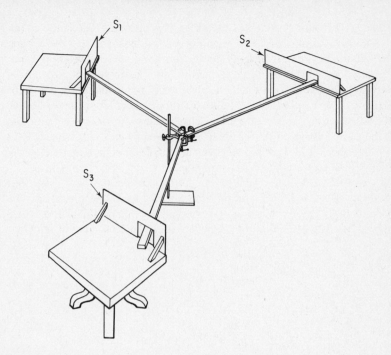

FIGURE 14-9.   Maier's reasoning problem. The animal is first allowed to explore thoroughly all runways and tables (Experience I). Food is then placed on one of the tables and the animal is permitted to eat (Experience II). The reasoning test consists of placing the animal on one of the other two tables and seeing if he will go directly to the table with food, thus showing he has put together two previous experiences. (From Maier, N. R. F. Cortical destruction in the posterior part of the brain and its effects on reasoning in rats. Journal of Comparative Neurology, 56, 1932.)

the famous Canadian neurosurgeon Wilder Penfield (1958; Penfield & Rasmussen, 1950) and by Roger Sperry (1968), both of whom worked on the alleviation of severe epileptic seizures.

In order to localize precisely the site of origin of focal epileptic seizures in his patients' brains, Penfield carefully explored the cortex with an electrode, placing sterile tags on areas that generated responses upon being stimulated. He found that sensory and motor responses could readily be elicited as well as dreamlike states, musical, and other complex memories. For example, a 26-year-old woman reported the following memory upon being stimulated near the temporal region.

> Yes, I hear voices. It is late at night, around the carnival somewhere—some sort of travelling circus—I just saw lots of big wagons that they use to haul animals in. (Penfield, 1958)

When the area causing epileptic seizures had been identified, it was removed, the cerebral covering sewn up, and the bone of the skull replaced.

Figure 14-10 shows Penfield's conception of cortical localization of function in man based on his studies of the living brain.[4] It will be noted that the old anatomical division of the brain into primary projection areas and association areas (called "interpretive areas" by Penfield) is confirmed. The Fissure of Rolando separates the pre- and postcentral gyri, which govern the motor and somesthetic processes respectively. There are also visual and auditory centers associated with the projection fibers arising from the appropriate sense organs. An interesting area is revealed along the border between the occipital and parietal lobes and labeled "visual and auditory recollection." Penfield has been able to elicit elaborate memory sequences in patients in whom this area was stimulated.

Roger W. Sperry's investigations of split-brain subjects, like Penfield's clinical observations of cortical localization, came about as a by-product of attempts to control epileptic seizures. In some cases of epilepsy that originate in one hemisphere and spread across the brain to the other, severe, even fatal, convulsions may occur.

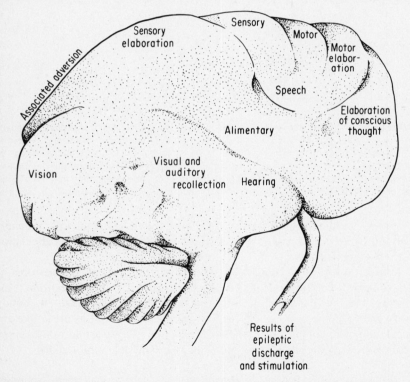

FIGURE 14-10.   The functional areas of the cerebral cortex as revealed by Penfield's clinical studies of the living cortex in conscious man. (After Penfield, W., and Rasmussen, T. The cerebral cortex of man. The Macmillan Company, 1950.)

---

[4]Figure 14-10 is a composite of Penfield and Rasmussen's figures 110 and 120 from *The Cerebral Cortex of Man* (1950).

Individuals suffering from this disabling disorder are often considerably improved by an operation in which the corpus callosum connecting the two hemispheres is severed. As an aftermath of the operation the two sides of the brain function independently. Sperry and others (Gazzaniga, 1970) have provided a series of landmark reports on the separate functions of the two hemispheres on the basis of experimental investigations of split-brain subjects.

It has long been recognized that one side of the brain is dominant over the other. In most cases involving complex motor skills, such as writing, this is the left hemisphere. It will also be recalled that Broca's speech area is localized in the left frontal cortex. However, the split-brain experiments reveal that a more complex relationship exists between the two hemispheres than was hitherto suspected.

In a typical test situation (Figure 14-11), the split-brain subject is seated in front of a table with a screen upon which words can be flashed for a fraction of a second. The subject's gaze is fixated on a spot near the center of the screen in order to prevent movements in which case information would get to both hemispheres over the optic chiasma (Figure 14-12). By keeping the eyes fixated near the center of the screen a word can be flashed to the right or left of center with information going to only one hemisphere. Let us suppose, for example, that the name of a common object, such as SPOON, is presented on the left side of the screen. The visual image

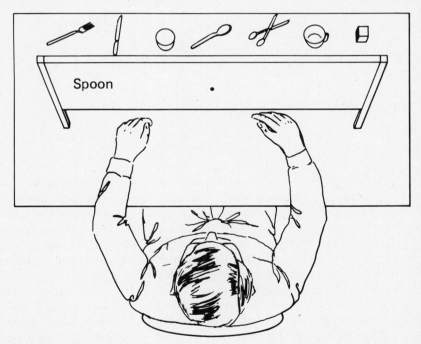

FIGURE 14-11. A typical test situation for the split-brain experiment. The subject fixates on the small dot in the center of the screen. A word is flashed to the right or left of the dot. In this case the subject can correctly select the spoon by touch, reaching under the screen, but because the word stimulates the right hemisphere he cannot articulate it.

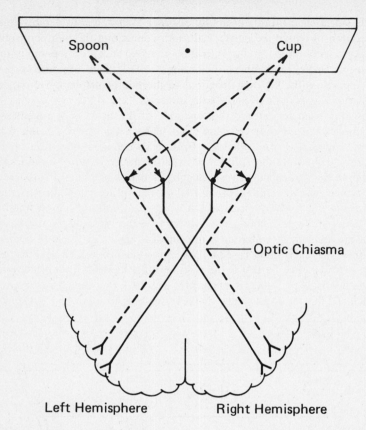

FIGURE 14-12.   A diagram showing the paths of stimulation in the split-brain experiment through the optic chiasma to the left and right cerebral hemispheres.

will be transmitted to the right side of the brain, which controls the left side of the body. With his or her left hand the subject can readily pick out the hidden spoon by touch from the objects on the table behind the screen. Surprisingly, the subject cannot tell the experimenter what word appeared on the screen. This is because language functions are localized in the left hemisphere, which in this case received no information about what appeared on the screen. For the same reason, the subject would be unable to pick out the test object with his or her right hand.

Further tests of split-brain subjects show that when blindfolded they can recognize familiar objects placed in the left hand by demonstrating that they know how to use the object—combing the hair with a comb, locking a door with a key. But they cannot verbalize their knowledge unless the right hand is involved, allowing sensory information to be transmitted to the left or language hemisphere.

In summary, the left hemisphere is the main language center and is also involved in mathematical and other types of analytic thinking. The right hemisphere is primarily involved in spatial and pattern relationships, music, and art appreciation. For left-handed individuals the pattern of functioning is reversed or the differences may be less well-defined. In his *Psychology of Consciousness* (1972), Ornstein has suggested that humans may possess dualistic modes of consciousness rather than a single or unitary mode. One mode, a function of the left hemisphere, is analytic, intellectual, highly verbal, and active. The other, dependent upon the right hemisphere, is more passive, intuitive, spatial, and Gestalt-like in perceiving. These as yet speculative generalizations about the dualistic nature of consciousness must, of course, remain highly tentative.

Summary and Recapitulation

We have come a long way in our understanding of the role of localization in the cerebral cortex. The history of the problem shows that theorists have oscillated between the extreme localization first promulgated by the phrenologists and Flourens' position that extreme unity of function or complete nonlocalization exists with respect to the higher mental processes. Our present knowledge indicates that the truth lies somewhere between these extremes. There is localization, and its precision depends upon the specificity of the function under consideration. Simple sensory and motor problems may show a fairly high degree of localization. Problems involving more general functions show less localization, sometimes involving an entire cerebral hemisphere. It may be that recent research will necessitate a reevaluation of the old concept of the unity of consciousness.

THE MEMORY TRACE

In the preceding sections we have been primarily concerned with *where* learned functions are localized in the cerebral cortex. We must now turn our attention to *how* learning occurs. That is, we shall examine theories of what events are presumed to take place in the nervous system during the course of learning. Among the earliest of such theories is some form of engram principle.

Common sense tells us that the fact that we can remember past events means that experience leaves some kind of modification in the nervous system. This popular assumption is also good psychology. From the point of view of the experimental psychologist, memories do not exist in a vacuum but are presumed to be a reflection of the functions of neural traces, or engrams. The concept of the neural trace is a very old one in psychology, which first found implicit expression in Locke's doctrine of the *tabula rasa*. If experience "writes" on the blank tablet of mind, the traces of that experience must be somewhere in the mind or, more properly, in the functions of its parallel physiological organ, the brain.

Locke did not give explicit physiological status to memory traces. His successor in the British empirical school of philosophy and the founder of associationism, David Hartley (see Chapter 1), supplied this deficiency. He accepted Newton's concept that the vibratory action of infinitely small "medullary particles" results in either sensation (if over afferent nerves) or movements of the limbs (if over efferent nerves). These minute disturbances of the inner substratum of the nerves Hartley held responsible for ideas as well as sensations and motor movement. The vibrations for ideas are simply fainter and more diminutive (Hartley called them "vibratiuncles") than those for sensation. Hartley accounted for associations, or the bonds between ideas, on the basis of a law of contiguity, arguing that if two sets of vibratiuncles occur in temporal proximity, one develops the power to excite the other.

Although Hartley's doctrine is stated in a very general way and in terms of physiological processes that are no longer acceptable, the doctrine *in essence* states both the problem and the solution that every subsequent theory of the memory trace has invoked in some manner. The heart of the problem is that of accounting for the linkage of two or more neuronal systems, which were unrelated before being modified by a new learning experience. Moreover, any theory of memory has to explain the nature of the persistence of the connection during intervals of no practice or rehearsal.

No responsible modern theory of memory holds that neural activity persists as long as memories last. Such a theory would demand that the nervous impulses for all memories from the beginning of earliest childhood persist in many instances throughout life—a physiological impossibility. However, assuming that a new linkage or network of neurons is formed as a result of a new experience, contemporary theory does postulate that the network, once formed, persists. All that is required to reinstate a memory is the reactivation of the network. For example, let us assume that a piano player learned "Yankee Doodle" years ago and shows that he or she remembers it by sitting down and playing. We may assume that the sight of the piano, and the pattern of keys in particular, serves to reactivate the motor circuits mediating the responses by way of neural impulses arriving over afferent neurons.

Widely influential in stimulating research on cortical changes as a result of learning, is Hebb's (1949) theory. The most fundamental postulate in his theory is that of the "cell assembly." A cell assembly is a group of cortical neurons that bear a functional relationship to each other, or more simply, are circuits in the cerebral cortex that are made up of interconnected neurons. Now the most interesting and challenging of Hebb's postulates is the further assumption that such assemblies can be developed through practice. In fact, the very foundation of Hebb's theory is the assumption that neurons can become functionally associated with each other through learning. More specifically, he suggests that learned neuronal associations may come about through the development of synaptic knobs on neuronal endings which are in close proximity to active cell bodies or to the dendrites of other neurons.

Cell assemblies, in turn, make up "phase sequences" which are collections or groups of simple cell assemblies. For example, in the perceptual learning of a triangle, each side and each angle activates a cell assembly as the child's eyes sweep around the figure. The totality of the three angle assemblies joined with the assemblies for the sides makes up the phase sequence which yields the sense of triangularity. Thus even the simplest act of perceptual learning, the learning of triangularity, involves not only a simple fixation on a triangle, but a complex process that is dependent upon the formation of a number of complex cortical circuits.

Evidence in support of Hebb's theory when it originally appeared came from the work of psychologists who collected records on individuals who had been blind from birth and whose vision was restored at maturity by surgical operations. Such people were found to have extreme difficulty in distinguishing simple geometric figures such as triangles and squares from each other. Even more incredible, such patients have difficulty learning to associate the concept "triangle" with visually presented triangles—this in spite of the fact they they do recognize solid triangular figures by touch. When at last they do learn the name for a visual figure that has been presented many times, they still fail to recognize it if it is presented in a slightly altered form.

In attempting to provide a theoretical account of the exact mechanism by which one neuron can be functionally linked to another by practice or experience, physiological psychologists have invoked a number of models and hypotheses. We shall examine several of the more influential of these in turn.

Consolidation Theory

Reverberatory circuits were first discovered in the autonomic nervous system. There they consist of linkages of neurons arranged in such a manner that once a nervous impulse gets into the chain it may persist for some time without further external stimulation. In the autonomic nervous system these circuits can, in part, account for the persistent effects of autonomic arousal. We have also seen (Chapter 6) how they may serve as the neural substrate for perceptual learning. More generally, some physiological psychologists interested in accounting for (1) the problems involved in distinguishing short-term from long-term memory and (2) the neurological mechanism of consolidation of the memory trace—particularly its vulnerability to disruption immediately following learning—believe that reverberatory circuits offer an attractive explanation of these phenomena.

The reverberatory circuit seems a logical mechanism for mediating short-term memory. Presumably when one looks up a telephone number and remembers it long enough to complete dialing, some electrical activity persists in cortical or subcortical circuits at least long enough to mediate the memory. If conditions are such that the memory must become long-term, then it is further assumed that a more permanent trace—some anatomical or neurohumoral change—is left in the nervous system as a result of consolidation effects, making possible the retrieval of information days, weeks, or even years later.

Consolidation theory can also account for the vulnerability of retention during the period immediately following learning. We pointed out how retrograde amnesia occurs following a blow to the head (Chapter 10). We also noted in the same connection that electroconvulsive shock disrupts retention for events immediately preceding the shock, presumably because the consolidation process is disrupted. As a result of this discovery—first made on certain psychotics whose behavior is often improved by shock treatments—a considerable body of research has been conducted on the effect of shock on recent memory.

However, as R. Thompson (1975) and Carlson (1977) point out in attempting to summarize and synthesize the experimental findings on shock and recent memory, the effects vary with the experimental paradigms employed. Moreover, shock becomes aversive to subjects, inhibiting their performance not because of memory loss but because of fear or anxiety.

The variable nature of the effects of shock is revealed in the differences obtained in simple avoidance learning and in conditioned emotional reactions. In simple avoidance learning, electroconvulsive shocks given immediately after learning significantly disrupt memory for the task, while shock administered an hour or more after learning has no effect. However, when a conditioned emotional response is developed in the animal by pairing a bar-pressing-for-food response with a painful shock to the foot, electroconvulsive shock disrupts the tendency to avoid bar pressing that normally develops during the course of the experiment. But the disruption occurs, even though the shock treatment is given for up to 30 days after initial training (J. V. Brady, 1952). Evidently what is being disrupted in such cases cannot be traces undergoing consolidation, but access to established memories of aversive events.

However, to complicate the picture still further, electroconvulsive treatments themselves become aversive upon repetition for both human and animal subjects. And so it may be difficult to tell whether a decrement in performance is due to the failure of trace consolidation after shock or to a conditioned avoidance reaction to shock itself. Control experiments involving *memory for punished responses* indicate that shock-treated animals perform the punished response more often than control animals. Presumably, if the memory for punished responses was intact it would block performance. Since performance is not blocked, the effects of shock on recent memory appear to outweigh its aversive properties (see McGaugh & Madsen, 1964).

The electroconvulsive shock studies discussed thus far involve delivering shock to the entire brain, as is the case when the technique is employed in treating psychotic patients. However, by means of microelectrodes, shock can be delivered to restricted regions of the cerebral cortex or to subcortical centers. Among the structures that have been implicated directly in the memory process are portions of the limbic system, whose detailed anatomy and functions we shall be considering later in this chapter. Here we may note that the hippocampal region, a forebrain structure of the temporal area, appears to be critical for the formation of long-term memory. Persons whose hippocampus is injured may be unable to remember events a few minutes after they are experienced even though their previous memories are intact. Such persons, for example, cannot remember street names or the names of new acquaintances. Although an old telephone number is easily called to mind, a new one cannot be remembered more than a few minutes even after dozens of repetitions. These observations suggest that the consolidation process is absent in such cases preventing short-term memory from becoming long-term. This interpretation is supported by studies of animals in which electric shock is delivered to the hippocampus (McDonough & Kesner, 1971). In avoidance training situations, shocked animals experience amnesia after training trials.

Further support for the consolidation hypothesis comes from studies on the improvement of learning by the use of stimulating drugs. Strychninelike substances, by blocking synaptic inhibition, might be expected to allow facilitation of consolidation. McGaugh and Krivanek (1970) utilized strychnine sulfate in discrimination learning situations comparing the drug group to control groups who were injected with saline solutions. Figure 14-13 shows that with increasing doses (up to an optimal level), the facilitating drug gives improved performance whether utilized in the pre- or post-trial period. However, note that the closer the time of injection to the actual trial run the more noticeable the effect.

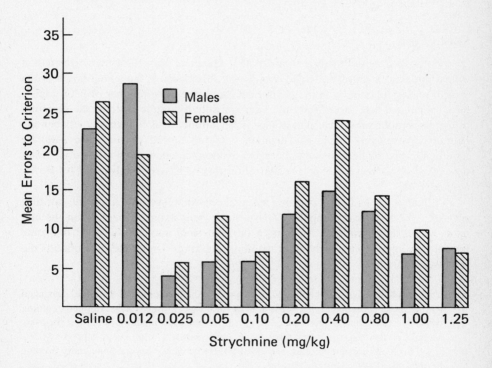

FIGURE 14-13. The effects of strychnine sulphate on discrimination learning. The beneficial effects of the drug are apparent in this case for doses of .025 mg/kg to 1.25 mg/kg. The saline group serves as a control group. Reprinted with permission from Physiology and Behavior, 5, 1970, McGaugh and Krivanek, Strychnine effects on discrimination learning in mice. Effects of dose and time administration. Copyright, Pergamon Press, 1970.

On the negative side of the question, it has been known for some years that depressant drugs inhibit the consolidation process. The drug scopolamine, which is sometimes administered to women during childbirth, does not render the individual unconscious but does leave her amnesic for the birth process and its attendant discomfort.

In summary, then, experiments with electroconvulsive shock have not proved as clear-cut in resolving the problems of the vulnerability of traces undergoing consolidation as early investigators had hoped. The facts that such treatments operate differentially in different types of learning and that they become aversive complicate the issue. Despite these difficulties, the effects of shock treatments (particularly where given only once and therefore not aversive) on memory for recent events is taken as positive evidence for the consolidation process as the first stage in the formation of long-term memory and for the operation of reverberatory circuits, particularly in short-term memory. What this research does *not* reveal is the precise neurological changes that occur during consolidation. Similarly, the use of stimulating drugs has been found to facilitate learning, presumably through enhancing the consolidation process.

Sensitization

Because it has long been known that chemical substances are secreted at synaptic junctions (adrenergic and cholinergic substances in the autonomic nervous system and acetylcholine in the central nervous system), a number of neurologists have speculated that during learning, neuronal activity might facilitate the secretion of the transmitter substance, which establishes a functional connection between the neurons. Presumably, once sensitization occurred during practice, the resultant modification in the neurons would persist, making the connection relatively permanent. A general version of the sensitization theory has been advanced by P. M. Milner (1961).

Milner assumes that in forming associations some synaptic knobs do not fire, regardless of how many impulses arrive along their axons, *except* when the cell upon which they terminate happens to be fired from another source at the same instant that impulses are arriving at the nonfiring knob. Under these conditions the impulse is able to

> . . . invade that synaptic knob, and in the process the membrane of the knob is changed so that it can subsequently be fired, at least for a time, by any further impulses coming down its axon. This sensitization of the synaptic knob to its input may only last for a few seconds on the first occasion it takes place, but if the same thing keeps happening (i.e., if the two cells concerned often fire together), the sensitization may eventually become permanent. (P. M. Milner, 1961, p. 122)

Milner makes it clear that his theory does not imply a neurobiotaxic process in which new knobs develop. Rather, he assumes that nonfunctional knobs already present become functional by a process of sensitization. In this way complex networks of neurons can develop through learning or experience. The reader will note that the theory is very similar to Hebb's in all essential respects except in the manner in which synaptic linkage is achieved.

A more specific theory utilizing recent research on neurochemical transmitters has been proposed by J. A. Deutsch (1969). Essentially, Deutsch and his associates propose that a cholinergic neurohumoral transmitter is responsible for synaptic transmission. However, the precise manner in which learning results in increased production of cholinergic compounds, which, in turn, are presumed to facilitate learning, is not yet known. Within the past ten years an enormous amount of research has been devoted to the study of cholinergic and other neurohumoral facilitators (and inhibitors) in an attempt to clarify the nature of synaptic facilitation. Because of the highly technical nature of this work we shall make no attempt to summarize it here. The interested reader may consult the Deutsch review (1969).

DNA and RNA

The discovery of deoxyribonucleic acid (DNA) and ribonucleic acid (RNA) made possible a highly sophisticated theory of learning that has excited considerable attention among neurophysiologists in recent years. Essentially, the theory, as proposed by Hydén (1961), assumes that learning causes changes in RNA, and these altered RNA substances govern the metabolic activities of the cell and obtain "instructions" from DNA, the macromolecular substance that forms the genetic information complement in the cell nucleus. Since it involves a relatively permanent change in behavior, learning is presumably related to a relatively permanent change in cellular structure—in this case, in the neuron. Possibly such changes are reflected as changes in the cell's ribonucleic acid components. Most other nonprotein cellular substances are too transitory to account for the durability of modifications due to learning. More specifically, the proponents of the RNA theory argue that practice excites metabolic changes in the cell, which cause changes in RNA, which then manufactures new proteins; and these presumably become the permanent end products of learning and are capable of facilitating neural transmission.

A number of experiments too extensive to review here have been carried out in support of the RNA hypothesis. These are summarized by Carlson (1977, pp. 590–607), with references to appropriate primary sources. Here we may briefly outline two typical experiments in order to illustrate the technique and design of research in this area.

Hydén (1961) trained rats to climb a rope. An analysis was then made of the composition of RNA in the nuclei of cells in the first vestibular relay nucleus and in the nuclei of the surrounding glial cells. Changes in the composition of RNA were found. Control animals were subject to rotation to induce vestibular stimulation, but these animals did not show significant changes in RNA. Critics have pointed out that the vestibular relay nucleus is a peripheral nucleus and that, despite Hydén's controls, we cannot be sure the changes in the nuclei of the cells comprising the relay nucleus might be due to vestibular disturbances rather than to learned modifications. However, if confirmed for higher centers, the results would be highly significant, showing as they do that fundamental cellular changes can occur as a result of experience.

In a widely quoted experiment by R. Thompson and J. McConnell (1955), planaria (flatworms which have the ability to regenerate amputated parts) were conditioned to contract to a light when the experimenters repeatedly paired a light with a shock. The worms were then cut in two, and both halves were allowed to regenerate. The regenerated worms were again tested in the conditioning situation, and they showed significant retention of the response. Presumably this experiment indicates that the memory trace was transferred to the new halves by means of RNA transfer.

These experiments on planaria stimulated a wave of investigations on transfer of training in which extracts were taken from the brains of trained donors and administered to untrained experimental animals. Experimental paradigms have involved conditioning, brightness discrimination, avoidance training, and habituation of the startle response. Unfortunately, results of such experiments are contradictory, some yielding positive, and some, negative results. Moreover, it is not clear what fraction of the extracts employed is responsible for transfer when it is found. As Grossman (1973) points out:

> All extracts contain RNA, proteins, peptides, and some sugars in varying concentrations. Most of the experimenters in this field initially believed, in accordance with the then dominant biochemical explanation of learning, that the active ingredient might be RNA. However, it has been shown that the large RNA molecules probably do not cross the blood-brain barrier in significant quantities and that procedures which tend to inactivate RNA or eliminate it from the extract do not interfere with the transfer effect. Most contemporary investigators consequently hold that the active substance must be a small molecule which is most probably a peptide. (1973, p. 448)

Therefore, despite over a decade of intensive research, we cannot be sure that RNA transfer[5] is the biological basis of memory. A vast amount of research[5] is in progress on the psychochemistry of learning—research on animals in which experimenters are testing the effects of RNA injections in the bloodstream and brain, and in which various pharmacological substances are administered either orally or by injections to test whether RNA transfer is inhibited or facilitated. Careful assays of the brain are being made before and after experiences to determine whether changes in the level of various substances believed to be associated with neural transmission and memory, such as acetylcholine, are increased. We shall now turn our attention to research representative of this line of investigation.

Brain Changes and Enriched Experience

In addition to studies of differences in the level of DNA and RNA as a result of learning, a number of investigators have been evaluating other biochemical and anatomical changes in the brain that result from experience. At the University of California at Berkeley a series of experiments (Rosenzweig, Bennett, & Diamond, 1972a, 1972b) (Rosenzweig, Krech, & Bennett, 1958), extending over nearly two

---

[5]See Carlson (1977) or Thompson (1975) for introductions to the literature on psychochemistry. Both sources contain references to original papers and advanced surveys.

decades has been directed at the investigation of such relationships. In general, the design of the Berkeley experiments involves rearing rats in both enriched and impoverished environments and comparing their brain chemistry and microanatomy. For purposes of control, littermates of the experimental animals are reared in standard laboratory cages.

An enriched environment consists of a colony-type cage in which a dozen or so animals have a number of playthings—swings, slides, shelves for climbing, scrub brushes—to investigate; these are changed daily. An impoverished environment consists of a single-unit cage housing one animal with no playthings. Since the amount of locomotor activity, stress, and handling might affect cortical development, control experiments have been carried out to ensure that these factors are not responsible for the observed differences.

Rosenzweig et al. (1972a, 1972b, 1976) report consistent and significant differences in the cerebral cortices of experimental animals maintained from four to ten weeks in their respective environments (Figure 14-14). Several of these differences

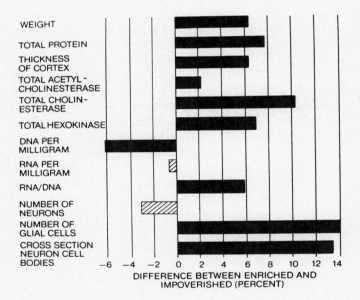

FIGURE 14-14. Differences in brain weight, anatomy, and chemistry of rats reared in complex versus restricted environments. (From "Brain changes in response to experience" by M. R. Rosenzweig, E. L. Bennett, and M. C. Diamond. Copyright © 1972 by Scientific American, Inc. All rights reserved.)

merit discussion. First, total brain weight, cortical thickness, the number of glial cells, and the size of cortical cell bodies and nuclei all showed positive differences ranging between 6 and 14 percent in favor of the animals in the enriched environment.

Most significantly, animals reared in more complex environments show more branching of dendrites in the cortical neurons, indicating a larger number of synaptic connections. These anatomical differences—which, of course, are interrelated—are considered to be a direct result of the animals' experiences, since control experiments have ruled out such changes as being correlated with increased handling or stress. Particularly interesting is the very large difference in the number of glial cells. These cells—long believed to be largely supportive in function—are now thought to have a variety of functions involving transportation and metabolism of materials between the bloodstream and nerve cells and may possibly be involved in learning if Rosenzweig's and similar experimental findings are confirmed.

Several differences in brain chemistry were also reported for the experimental animals by Rosenzweig and his colleagues. Total acetylcholinesterase, cholinesterase, and hexokinase showed increases as a result of enriched environments. Acetylcholine, it will be recalled, is a chemical transmitter in the nervous system; and acetylcholinesterase is an enzyme that neutralizes acetylcholine. Hexokinase is an enzyme associated with carbohydrate metabolism, the chief source of energy for neural functions.

DNA and RNA changes per milligram of tissue were also noted. The large decremental DNA change presumably was due to the increased bulk of the cortex, since the amount of DNA in the nuclei remained constant. The increased ratio of RNA to DNA suggests a higher metabolic activity in the nervous systems of the enriched experienced animals.

We must be cautious in generalizing from these results, tempting as it would be to do so. The anatomical and biochemical differences between enriched- and impoverished-environment animals, while reliable and statistically significant, are very small. Until further research is carried out we cannot assume that these same differences would be found among subjects chosen from higher phylogenetic forms, whose brains are far more complex than those of rodents. However, we may conclude that this and allied research has provided a significant and penetrating method for investigating the biochemical and neuroanatomical substrates of learning and experience.

In concluding this brief survey of the physiological psychology of memory it seems reasonable to say that the old theory of the engram has survived for more than a century. However, its vitality has depended more upon logic than upon hard fact. The seemingly straightforward task of showing that changes occur in the brain directly as a result of learning has proved extremely difficult of accomplishment. Indirectly the engram theory has found correlative support in the consolidation hypothesis for which, in turn, there is evidence in studies of retrograde amnesia, retroactive inhibition, sleep, electroshock, and the administration of stimulating or inhibiting drugs. To date the best *direct* evidence in support of the engram theory is the work of Rosenzweig and his associates. What is needed is a refinement of the technique of microscopic study of synapses to show that specific learning rather than generally enriched environments produce changes in the cortical synapses. The technical difficulties in the way of such a demonstration are formidable.

DYNAMIC PROCESSES AND THE SUBCORTEX

By dynamic processes we refer to motivational and emotional activities, or those behavioral and physiological functions that come under the old classification of conative (motivational) and affective (emotional) processes as opposed to cognitive (sensory and perceptual) processes. Traditionally, the cognitive processes have been identified with the functions of the cerebral cortex. Sensing, perceiving, intellectual activities, and associational or learned process have all been ascribed to the "higher" centers in the cortex. It has also long been assumed that the "lower," or subcortical, centers mediate the dynamic aspects of behavior. As we shall see, this distinction has considerable merit. We have already found that the cortex is highly specialized for sensory and associational functions. However, there are also centers in the cortex that are concerned with visceral processes; and, as will be brought out, the subcortex and cortex are by no means isolated in their respective activities but work as a team.

We cannot undertake a detailed anatomical and physiological account of the nuclei that make up the subcortical centers, many of which are primarily concerned with motor processes. Rather, we shall study the centers that recent research has linked with motivational and emotional behavior. Even in this limited area, research activities and the flood of new knowledge have been phenomenal. Neurologists have taken a new look at the older portions of the brain, which humans inherited from their animal forebears, and found hitherto unsuspected functional correlations between these centers and dynamic processes. Much of this work has been made possible through the recently discovered use of electrode implantation into areas that were virtually inaccessible using older techniques.

For convenience we shall divide these centers into three major categories: the reticular, the hypothalamic, and the limbic. We hasten to admit that these divisions are inevitably arbitrary to some degree, following as they do the old anatomical considerations that prevailed before physiological techniques revealed a surprising degree of integration among the so-called lower centers. However, the *primary* functions of these three centers are identifiable; and we shall point out their interrelations from time to time, thus minimizing the risk of separating the inseparable.

The Reticular Formation and Activation[6]

Psychologists and physiologists have always associated consciousness with the activities of the cerebral cortex. And in a sense this position has never been challenged. An infant whose cortex is nonfunctional shows signs of consciousness only

---

[6]Our account has been taken from a variety of sources. For good general treatments with references to primary sources, see Grossman (1973, chaps. 8 and 14), R. Thompson (1975, chap. 10), and Carlson (1977, chaps. 14 and 15). Horace Magoun's *The Waking Brain* (1963) is the "classic" in the field, written by the man who did most of the research establishing the importance of the formation.

for brief periods. Those with the congenital defect of anencephaly (absence of the cortex) never achieve any real appreciation of their surroundings. They remain vegetative idiots. However, a complex system of fibers in the medulla and brain stem has been shown to make an important contribution to consciousness, alertness, and sleep. When this region is seriously damaged, the individual becomes comatose and cannot be aroused.

Mechanisms of arousal

The reticular formation—or, as it is commonly known, the ascending reticular activating system (ARAS)—is a loosely organized network (reticulum = network) of fibers that runs up from the spinal cord through the medulla to the brain stem and beyond. It was first described by the famous Spanish neurologist, Rámon y Cajal, over half a century ago. As Figure 14-15 shows, sensory impulses coming in from the periphery over the afferent neurons must go through the ARAS, where they are either inhibited or facilitated. Inhibited impulses never reach the cortex and therefore cannot generate a conscious awareness of stimulation. Impulses whose passage is facilitated spread out upon the appropriate projection areas in the cortex, arousing functional activity and awareness of stimulation. Facilitation takes the form of

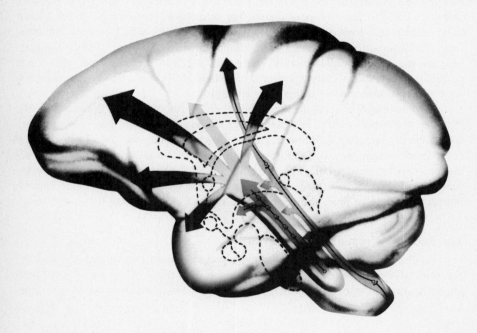

FIGURE 14-15.   A diagrammatic representation of the principal pathways of the reticular activating system. (From Magoun, H. W. Nonspecific brain mechanisms. In Harlow, H. F., and Wollsey, C. N. (eds.), Biological and biochemical bases of behavior. University of Wisconsin Press, 1958.)

collateral impulses generated by the ARAS, which "alert" the cortex for the reception of peripheral impulses. The effect, called the arousal reaction, may be measured by impulses recorded from the cerebral cortex. If large segments of the reticular formation are destroyed, the experimental animal becomes comatose and cannot be aroused. In human subjects the barbiturate drugs and some anesthetics have a similar effect through depressing the reticular network.

It would be a mistake, however, to assume that all ARAS functions are peripherally controlled. Impulses from parts of the cortex itself play upon the ARAS and can stimulate it into action. For example, stimulation of certain areas in a monkey's cortex will awaken the sleeping animal. If the stimulation is delivered to a monkey that is already awake, the animal stops its ongoing activity, looks around intently, and appears puzzled—as if taken unawares by a stimulus (French, 1957). In addition to cortical influences on the ARAS, cerebellar and subcortical areas play a role in the activation of the ARAS. It should also be noted that a descending reticular system is intimately concerned with regulation of peripheral reflexes and muscle tone.

Relating the ascending and intracranial channels of ARAS activity to everyday life, we may take the example of a sleeping person who is bombarded during the night by all sorts of exteroceptive and proprioceptive stimuli.[7] Only important stimuli get through—the smell of smoke, the distress cries of the baby, the growling of the family dog. Clearly, if all stimuli got through, sleep would be impossible. Yet, as our examples show, parts of the cortex are sufficiently alert to "direct traffic," instantly commanding a flood of alerting stimuli to pass the reticular formation if necessity demands. The close interplay between cortex and ARAS is even more dramatically revealed by the ability of most people to awaken at or near a certain hour if necessity demands. They tell themselves that they wish to awaken; and, at the appropriate time, signals go out from the cortex to the ARAS and back again alerting the cortical centers.

In order to complete the picture of cerebral activation, we need to point out that extrinsic cortical activation originates from two sources. First, there are the ascending sensory tracts in the spinal cord and the sensory components of the cranial nerves. Because these tracts mediate specific sensory information and since they are all routed through the nuclei of the lateral thalamus, they make up what is known as the *specific cortical projection system*. The second source of activation comes from the *nonspecific thalamocortical system,* whose nuclei lie in the middle of the thalamus and are not as discretely localized as the lateral nuclei. Stimulation of these nuclei generates large, long-lasting changes in the cortex over widely scattered areas. By contrast, stimulation of the lateral nuclei generates rapid-acting waves of short duration that are localized in the sensory areas of the cortex. These experimental findings suggest that the nonspecific thalamic system, in conjunction with the reticular system, controls the overall level of activation of the cerebral cortex.

---

[7]It has been estimated that over 4 million impulses *per second* reach the ARAS. Obviously, only a small fraction of these ever get through to the cortex.

Brain Mechanisms and Sleep

Michel Jouvet, in collaboration with his associates at the University of Lyons in France, has developed a widely discussed theory of the neural mechanisms of sleep (Jouvet, 1967, 1969). He distinguishes among three states of arousal: wakefulness, light sleep, and what he calls "paradoxical sleep." The latter is a deep sleep characterized by brain waves, eye movements, muscle movements of the neck, and other physiological indices that are *strikingly similar to those recorded in wakefulness,* hence the designation "paradoxical."

Jouvet and others have tentatively identified the *nuclei of raphe,* a collection of nerve cells at the midline of the brain stem, as a possible sleep center. Neurons from the raphe nuclei project to the reticular formation, hypothalamus, and limbic system of the forebrain. When these nuclei are destroyed in cats (excellent subjects for sleep research, since they sleep 80 percent of the time), the animals become sleepless, sleeping less than 10 percent of the time. Jouvet believes that the nuclei of raphe—as the chief sources of serotonin, a neurohumor believed to be a transmitter in the nervous system—function as a humoral regulator of sleep. He found that injections of drugs that interfere with production of serotonin (or suppress its effect) cause long periods of insomnia, while direct injections of serotonin into the brain stem can induce light sleep in cats (Jouvet, 1969).

On the basis of these results, Jouvet believes serotonin is involved in the induction of light sleep. However, noradrenalin appears to be the regulator in paradoxical sleep, since drugs that selectively block its production result in a marked depression in paradoxical sleep. The site at which paradoxical sleep is produced by noradrenalin is tentatively identified by Jouvet as the *locus coeruleus,* a center in the brain stem. Jouvet concludes:

> We can put together a tentative working hypothesis about the brain mechanisms that control sleep. It seems that the raphe system is the seat responsible for the onset of light sleep, and that it operates through the secretion of serotonin. Similarly, the locus coeruleus harbors the system responsible for producing deep sleep, and this uses nor-adrenalin as its agent. In cyclic fashion these two systems apply brakes to the reticular activating system responsible for wakefulness and also influence all the other nerve systems in the brain, notably those involved in dreaming. (Jouvet, 1967, p. 36)

Not all investigators are in agreement with Jouvet. Certain inconsistencies have been reported in the literature[8] on the use of serotonin and noradrenalin in stimulating sleep centers. The regulation of sleep appears to be more complex than Jouvet's research has indicated. We do not mean to imply that all the phenomena of sleep and wakefulness can be accounted for by the activities of the ARAS. There are other centers in the midbrain, hypothalamus, and thalamus that are closely connected to the ARAS and contribute to cycles of sleep and wakefulness. However, neurologists generally concede that the ARAS is one of the primary mechanisms that control

---

[8]For references to this literature, see Carlson (1977).

alertness and somnolence, and Jouvet's brilliant series of investigations has stimulated extensive research on the age-old mystery of sleep.

Paradoxical sleep is also called REM (rapid eye movement) sleep, since rapid eye movements have been observed during this type of sleep and have been correlated with dreaming. Research carried out over the past two decades has shown that sleep is a series of stages of EEG changes, which may be grouped into a slow-wave sleep area (including Stages 1–4), and an active REM sleep, which is characterized by fast, low-amplitude alpha waves, muscular relaxation, and conjugate movements of the eyes. If awakened during this stage of sleep, the subject is likely to report a dream (Dement & Kleitman, 1957). More recent work has indicated that the REM state appears to be a necessary part of sleep, since prolonged REM deprivation has been shown to lead to behavioral changes, including anxiety, increased irritability, and difficulty in concentrating. These psychological changes disappear when subjects are allowed to sleep an entire night and to "recover" their lost REM sleep (Dement, 1960).

Freud, it will be recalled, attached considerable significance to dreaming and believed dreams to be wish-fulfilling in nature. That subjects deprived of sleep during which dreaming takes place show behavioral disturbances appears to support Freud's theory. However, the evidence is inconclusive. Dreams may be indicative of a state of primitive vigilance or are simply the result of an endogenous rhythmic period of a more primitive, aroused sleep. For a detailed discussion of theories of dreaming in relation to REM sleep, the reader is referred to E. J. Murray (1965) or Webb (1968, 1973).

Although we have been emphasizing the role of the ARAS in sleep and alertness, we should also like to suggest that in this diffuse network of cells, psychologists may have the key to the old problems of set, attention, and selectivity of perception. It had always been assumed that these processes have their neurological counterparts; but until the ARAS was identified, no useful working model had been suggested. We now know that the ARAS adapts to repeated sensory stimulation by a tonal pattern (loss of attention), but if the sound pattern is changed the animal is once again alert. In this connection, one investigator has concluded that the reticular formation is, indeed, an "integrating machine," which functions in the manner that we have suggested:

> The ARAS seems to be such a machine. It awakens the brain to consciousness and keeps it alert; it directs the traffic of messages in the nervous system; it monitors the myriads of stimuli that beat upon our senses, accepting what we need to perceive and rejecting what is irrelevant; it tempers and refines our muscular activity and bodily movements. We can go even further and say that it contributes in an important way to the highest mental processes—the focusing of attention, introspection, and doubtless all forms of reasoning. (French, 1957, p. 60)

Much more research remains to be done before our knowledge of these complex mechanisms is complete. But in the course of a generation we have gained the equivalent of centuries of knowledge on the fundamental problems of the neurological basis of cognition.

THE HYPOTHALAMUS, THE REGULATION OF BODILY
NEEDS, AND EMOTION

Although the hypothalamic area was described by the medieval anatomists, our knowledge of its functions is relatively recent. Not until the early part of this century did neurophysiologists first attempt experimental investigations of the region. In 1909 two German investigators, J. P. Karplus and A. Kreidl (cited by Fulton, 1949), showed that stimulation of the hypothalamus causes changes in autonomic functions—specifically in heart rate, blood pressure, sweating, and vasoconstriction. In the 1920s Bard began his classic studies of hypothalamic functions showing that the caudal or posterior portion is involved in the expression of rage. It was on the basis of this work and his own investigations that Cannon postulated the hypothalamic theory of the emotions that we discussed in Chapter 13.

Between the early electrical and extirpative investigations of the 1920s and the present time, a vast amount of research on the hypothalamic region has identified it not only as an area concerned in the expression of emotional behavior but also as an area for the control of hunger and thirst, sexual behavior, body temperature, and the regulation of visceral processes through the autonomic nervous system. Moreover, a number of investigators have pointed to the close anatomical and functional relationships between the ARAS and hypothalamus, and between the limbic system (see the following section) and the hypothalamic nuclei. Here we shall be primarily concerned with the role of the hypothalamus in the regulation of hunger and thirst, and of general emotional expression.

The Hypothalamus and Hunger[9]

There are two areas of the hypothalamus for the regulation of hunger which work in opposite ways. The ventromedial nuclei exert a restraint or control over eating, and the lateral nuclei stimulate eating (see Figure 14-16). As far back as 1939 a number of investigators began producing lesions in the ventromedial nucleus with the consistent result that the animals become hypothalamic hyperphagics, or excessive eaters. Immediately after the operation such animals eat several times as much as normal; and as a consequence of their excessive appetites, they become extremely obese. After several weeks their intake tends to level off; nevertheless, they remain obese. Animals whose ventromedial nuclei are stimulated while they are eating stop—a result to be expected, since this area is responsible for regulating feeding behavior. Lesions in the lateral thalamic nuclei, on the contrary, produce aphagic (without appetite) animals who refuse to eat to the point of starvation, and special methods must be employed to keep them alive.

Because numerous investigators have confirmed the role played by the ven-

----

[9]The literature of the regulation of hunger has exploded in volume in the past two decades. We can only touch on the highlights of hypothalamic mechanisms in hunger regulation. For analytic summaries of the older literature, see Rosenzweig (1962). More recently, Thompson (1975) and Carlson (1977) have assessed the current status of the field.

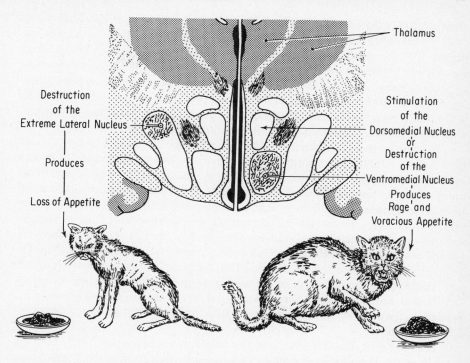

FIGURE 14-16.   A diagrammatic representation of the principal nuclei of the hypothalamus. (From Krech, D., and Crutchfield, R. S. Elements of psychology. Alfred A. Knopf, 1958.)

tromedial and lateral nuclei, these have come to be known as *satiety* and *feeding* centers, respectively. In other words, if the ventromedial nuclei are intact, they serve as "stop" centers in the regulation of eating, whereas the lateral nuclei are "go" centers. We should also note that *stimulation* of the lateral nucleus (Delgado & Anand, 1953) produces increased intake—an interesting fact that corroborates the go function of the lateral nuclei. In normal animals, then, the balance between the two centers serves to regulate intake of food.

Investigators have also found that emotional and appetitive behavior are correlated. Ingram (1956) showed that cats with lesions in the ventromedial nuclei become savage as well as hyperphagic. Animals with lesions in the lateral system of nuclei tend to become placid, possibly as a result of increasing weight loss and general debility.

Unfortunately for the elegant simplicity of the theory of discrete satiety and feeding centers in the ventromedial and lateral nuclei, more recent investigations have shown that destruction of *tracts* that run along the ventromedial nuclei can produce hyperphagia and obesity (Gold, 1973; Kapatos & Gold, 1973). Similarly, interrupting a tract that runs lateral to the hypothalamus will produce hypophagia in animals just as effectively as destroying the lateral nuclei. These findings suggest that control of intake is much more widespread in the hypothalamus and related brain structures than was formerly believed. Moreover, a number of related limbic system sites when stimulated with adrenergic substances will elicit feeding behavior. It is also interesting to note the relationship between feeding and drinking brought out by these experiments—a not surprising finding, since eating, particularly of dry foods, elicits drinking and partially controls water intake. Indeed, in one stage of the aphagia characteristic of the lateral hypothalamic syndrome, the animals will eat only wet, highly palatable food; and only in an advanced state of recovery will they take water and dry food (Teitelbaum & Epstein, 1962).

Because of their acceptance of only palatable foods, aphagic animals are said to be finicky eaters and are much more sensitive to sensory aspects of food than to caloric considerations. Finally, it is interesting to note that initial body weight at the onset of the lateral hypothalamic syndrome is important in determining rate of recovery. Animals that have been reduced to 80 percent of their normal weight by prelesion starvation survive the initial anorexia, or food rejection phase, of aphagia and show markedly accelerated recovery (Powley & Keesey, 1970). This discovery has led to the concept of the *central set point* for body weight regulation, which is lowered by lateral hypothalamic lesions. Thus, if the animal is of normal weight, it must undergo considerable loss before feeding begins—with consequent danger of dehydration and starvation if forced feeding is not initiated. The weight-reduced animal, on the other hand, does not have to wait for a new set point and so begins to eat more rapidly.

It would be misleading to assume that eating and appetite are solely under the control of the hypothalamic nuclei. These centers and tracts are of undoubted importance in the regulation of the *amount* of food eaten. Other subcortical centers are also known to be important (Grossman, 1973). We do not know what central nervous factors play upon the centers to initiate eating—possibly impulses from the cortex generated by the sight and smell of food. We know from extensive researches that biochemical and endocrine factors are important in protein, fat, carbohydrate, mineral, and vitamin appetites. Indeed, there are a number of theories of hunger developed around the role of amino acids, blood glucose level, and liver glycogens. As yet we are forced to conclude that the control of food intake is extremely complex, involving the head receptors, gastric, duodenal, and blood factors, the liver, endocrine system, and the hypothalamus. Last but not least, appetite is profoundly influenced by habit, cultural, and social factors.

The Hypothalamus and Thirst

The early accounts of the regulation of water intake tended to emphasize local stimulus factors in the mouth and throat. Thus, Cannon's local theory (1929) explained the thirst motive as dependent upon the dryness and stickiness in the oral cavity, which results from decreased salivary functioning caused by a general depletion of water in the blood. There is no question that such local factors play some part in the initiation of drinking and its cessation, but a variety of experiments

(Rosenzweig, 1962; Grossman, 1973) have shown that total water intake—the primary factor in maintaining proper water metabolism—is not dependent upon these local factors. In addition to oral factors, the condition of the blood, the hydration of body cells, secretions from the posterior pituitary gland, and hypothalamic factors are also involved in the regulation of water intake. Here we are primarily concerned with the role of the hypothalamus, and the evidence seems conclusive that, as in the case of eating, special centers regulate water intake.

Three general approaches have been utilized in establishing the precise location of nuclei concerned with water intake: extirpative, electrical, and chemical. We shall consider each, briefly, in turn.

Extirpation of the region near the supraoptic nucleus causes excessive drinking, or polydipsia (Ralph, 1960). The high intake of water is accompanied by a high output of urine (polyuria); however, the latter does not develop until the animal has already become waterlogged. Moreover, excessive drinking may be demonstrated in animals with esophageal fistulas (Bellows & Van Wagenen, 1938). Taken together, these results show that the polydipsia is a primary consequence of the lesion, not a secondary result of polyuria.

Lesions in the medial and anterior hypothalamus can cause cessation of drinking in animals to the point of severe dehydration and death (Andersson & McCann, 1956). This finding suggests that for thirst, as for hunger, there may be stop and go centers in the hypothalamus which regulate water intake.

That such regulatory mechanisms exist in the normal animal is supported by studies involving electrical stimulation (Andersson & McCann, 1955). Weak currents applied to the midregion of the hypothalamus evoke almost immediate drinking, which continues to the point of water intoxication.

Finally, the results of chemical injections directly into the hypothalamic nuclei further strengthen the position that precise regulatory mechanisms exist in this part of the brain. In a widely cited investigation, Andersson (1953) injected both hypotonic and hypertonic saline solutions directly into the hypothalamus of goats. Hypertonic injections initiated drinking even in animals that had all the water they needed. Hypotonic solutions, on the other hand, caused a cessation of drinking even in animals suffering from water deprivation who were drinking at the time of injection.

It has been suggested by Verney (1947) and others that the cells of the hypothalamus concerned with water intake may be osmoreceptors that are sensitive to the level of saline and other minerals in solution in the blood and body fluids. As the saline level becomes higher (greater than normal osmotic pressure) because of water loss from perspiration, respiration, urination, and the like, the cells stimulate drinking behavior. Then, as the surrounding fluids become hypotonic (less than normal osmotic pressure), the cells inhibit drinking.

In addition to regulation by osmoreceptors, water intake is controlled by volumetric receptors believed to be located in the walls of blood vessels. These receptors are sensitive to the volume of extracellular fluids in the circulatory system. Dramatic evidence for the existence of such receptors is seen in severely injured people who have lost a considerable volume of blood through hemorrhage. They are intensely thirsty even though the *concentration* of water in the remaining blood has not changed, leaving the osmoreceptors in the hypothalamus unaffected.

Under normal conditions volumetric control of water intake is believed to operate as follows. As the blood gives up water to the tissues, volume falls, triggering the secretion of renin, a hormone, by the kidney. Renin has two effects. First, it causes constriction of the blood vessels in an effort to maintain constancy of volume and pressure. Second, it releases another hormone, angiotensin, which is synthesized from blood factors by the kidney tubules. Angiotensin is believed to act on cells in the hypothalamus initiating drinking. Evidence for this mechanism comes from studies in which angiotensin is injected into the hypothalamus in animals, a procedure that immediately initiates drinking.

Finally, we might note that the hypothalamus is intimately connected with the pituitary gland. Cellular dehydration that stimulates the osmoreceptors in the hypothalamus to initiate drinking also stimulates the posterior part of the pituitary gland to release an antidiuretic hormone (ADH) that directs the kidneys to shut down urine formation thus conserving blood water.

In summary, there are two major mechanisms for control of water intake. One is associated with osmoreceptors in the hypothalamus. When these are stimulated by cellular dehydration, impulses are sent to the cerebral cortex and pituitary gland initiating both drinking and the reabsorption of water in the kidney. The other mechanism is volumetric and depends upon decreased blood volume in the kidney, which triggers the release of angiotensin. This hormone stimulates volume receptors in the hypothalamus to initiate drinking and simultaneously causes constriction of blood vessels to conserve volume and pressure. The mechanisms for the regulation of fluid intake are shown in diagrammatic form in Figure 14-17.

The Hypothalamus and Emotion

We have already pointed out how the Cannon-Bard theory of the emotions developed out of Bard's discovery that destruction of the posterior hypothalamus leaves the animal unable to initiate a complete rage reaction. We also indicated that in the absence of the cerebral cortex the animal can still manifest a complete rage response, but the threshold for rage is lower and the response lacks directionality.

The fact that complete rage responses are possible only with an intact hypothalamus led Cannon and Bard to identify that division of the brain as the center of the emotions. Today we know this to be an oversimplified view. It is true that rage responses appear to be mediated by the lateral hypothalamus. Delgado (1966) has shown that a full-fledged integrated and meaningful attack pattern in cats can be initiated by stimulation of the lateral hypothalamus (Figure 14-18). But this same investigator has also shown that centers for fear may be located more anteriorly in the posteroventral nucleus of the thalamus. However, other investigators have obtained a variety of emotional responses by stimulation of the hypo-

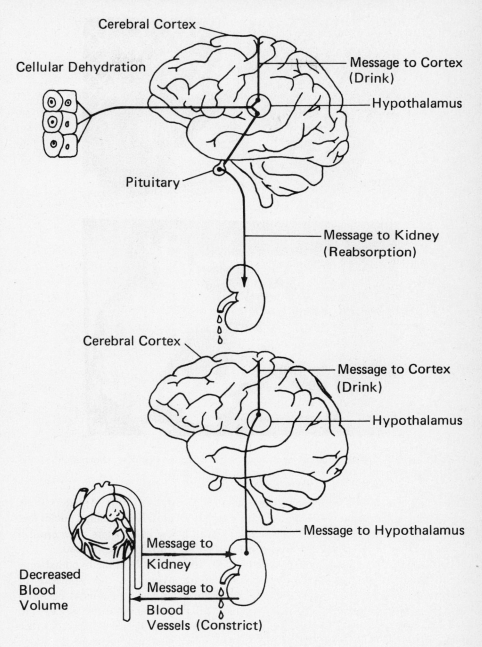

FIGURE 14-17. A diagrammatic representation of the mechanisms of water regulation.

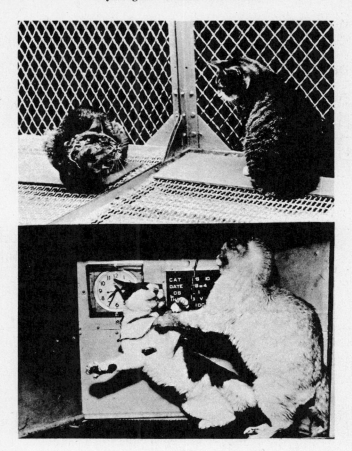

FIGURE 14-18.   Cats showing aggressive patterns upon electrical stimulation to the hypothalamic region. (Photographs courtesy of Dr. José Delgado.)

thalamus—not always with consistent results (J. V. Brady, 1960). Apparently the typography of the region is complex, with a variety of closely associated nuclei that mediate emotional or emotionlike reactions. Even a few millimeters difference in the placement of an electrode can result in an entirely different response.

The safest generalizations that can be made about the role of the hypothalamus in the emotions are that (1) the posterior nuclei are involved in the expression of rage and attack patterns, since if these nuclei are destroyed, the animal becomes placid and unemotional; (2) the ventromedial nuclei are centers for the suppression or control of rage, since if these are destroyed, the animal becomes ferocious (see Figure 14-16); (3) stimulation of the medial hypothalamus results in an attack pattern of emotional arousal. If the more lateral nuclei are stimulated, stalking and actual predation can be elicited; and (4) the hypothalamus in conjunction with the limbic system is involved in other aspects of emotional behavior in an as yet poorly understood manner.

The Limbic System[10]

Theoretical accounts of the role played by the limbic system in the emotions date from a classic paper by James W. Papez which appeared in 1937. Entitled "A Proposed Mechanism of Emotion," the report described the limbic system anatomically, tracing its known connections with higher centers and summarizing the meager clinical evidence in support of the hypothesis that the system is an emotional center rather than part of the olfactory brain, a commonly held opinion of its function that had prevailed for over a century. In his revolutionary account, Papez concluded that "the hypothalamus, the anterior thalamic nuclei, the gyrus cinguli, the hippocampus and their interconnections constitute a harmonious mechanism which may elaborate the functions of central emotion, as well as participate in emotional expression" (1937, p. 743).

Because of the dominance of the Cannon-Bard theory and its emphasis on hypothalamic mechanisms, Papez's theory received little attention from neurophysiologists or psychologists at the time of its publication. Not until the introduction of microelectrode stimulating techniques after World War II did his remarkable chain of reasoning begin to obtain sound experimental support.

Considerable credit is due Paul D. MacLean (1949, 1954, 1957, 1958), who called the attention of neurophysiologists to Papez's original statement and at the same time extended its theoretical implications. MacLean also cited considerable experimental evidence in its support. In the intervening years the limbic system has attracted a legion of experimenters seeking to delimit its functional connections and to relate them to emotional behavior.

Figure 14-19 shows the various parts of the limbic system. It will be noted that the system consists basically of two divisions, cortical and subcortical. The largest of the cortical areas is the *cingulate gyrus,* which lies deep within the longitudinal fissure above the corpus callosum. The *hippocampal gyrus* also lies deep within the longitudinal fissure but posterior to the corpus callosum. Finally, the *pyriform lobe* near the olfactory bulbs is the third cortical center commonly associated with the limbic system.

The subcortical portions of the limbic system are the *fornix,* lying under the corpus callosum; the *hippocampus,* a sea-horse-shaped structure, lying below the fornix; the *septum,* in the anterior of the frontal region; the *amygdala,* a nuclear mass in the lower part of the brain; and the *mammillary bodies,* in the front and central regions of the subcortex. There is general agreement about the inclusion of the foregoing cortical and subcortical areas in the limbic system. However, some authorities would also include the hypothalamic nuclei, the nonspecific nuclei of the thalamus, the olfactory bulbs, and other and less familiar subcortical structures.

---

[10]The volume of research on the limbic system has become so large as to virtually defy summarizing. Moreover, much of it is highly technical and only poorly related to theoretical interpretations of behavior. We have followed our usual practice of sampling and have based our discussion primarily on the work of Paul D. MacLean, whose research has centered on a particular theoretical position and to whose theory the work of other investigators can readily be related. References to MacLean's research are made at appropriate places in the text.

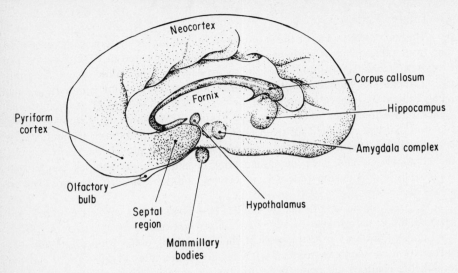

FIGURE 14-19.   A diagrammatic view of the principal structures of the limbic system.

Because of its close connections with the amygdaloid complex, the temporal lobe is often included in a discussion of the limbic system.

Figure 14-20 shows Papez's circuit in simplified form. The various sensory systems stream into the region from the special sense organs in the head and up through the reticular formation from the lower parts of the body. Upon reaching the limbic system, they are channeled into the hippocampus and from there radiate out to the amygdaloid complex, the cingulate gyrus, hippocampal gyrus, pyriform cortex, and other structures.[11]

The Frontotemporal Cortex

One of the earliest indications that the limbic system is involved in motivational and emotional behavior comes from surgical operations in the frontotemporal cortex that produce the well-known Klüver-Bucy syndrome (1939). The syndrome, named for its discoverers, consists of dramatic changes in feeding behavior and sexuality. Animals become indiscriminate in their feeding behavior, attempting to eat nuts and bolts, bits of wood, feces, and foods that are ordinarily rejected. They also show extreme sexuality and attempt to copulate with cage mates regardless of sex or even species. Frequent masturbation and oral eroticism are also evident in the behavior of such animals. Thus, we may assume that in the normal animal, sexual restraint is exerted by the frontotemporal cortex and its associated subcortical centers; and, as MacLean suggests, oral behavior—licking, chewing, eating and the

---

[11]For a more detailed account of the connections of the limbic system, see J. V. Brady (1958) or Noback (1967).

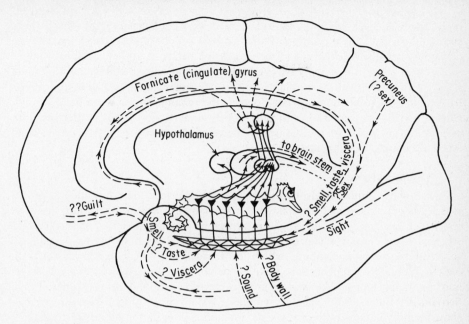

FIGURE 14-20.   The circuits of the limbic system as conceived by MacLean on the basis of his own work and Papez' theory of the functions of the system. (From MacLean, P. D. Psychosomatic disease and the "visceral brain." Recent developments bearing on the Papez theory of emotion. Psychosomatic Medicine, 11, 1949.)

like—also appear to be under the control of that region. Evidently the lesions produced by Klüver and Bucy involved the underlying nuclei of the amygdala complex since lesions in certain parts of the amygdala can produce the Klüver and Bucy syndrome.

The amygdala

As we have indicated, lesions of the nuclei of the amygdaloid complex produce tameness and docility in animals (Pribram, 1969). Conversely, stimulation of the amygdala elicits rage and ferocity. The amygdala also interacts with the ventromedial hypothalamus and septal regions in the intact animal. Lesions in either of the latter areas will produce ferocity, which can then be reversed by amygdalectomy. Thus, it appears that the amygdaloid complex is intimately concerned in limbic reaction patterns of fear, rage, placidity, and ferocity, although the various neurological relationships of the region to the rest of the system and to other parts of the brain have not been fully worked out.

Clinical support for the amygdala as a center for the control of rage has been offered by surgical attempts to control violent behavior in individuals by performing amygdalectomies. This highly controversial form of psychosurgery has been performed on a number of criminals whose consent had been obtained for the procedure. In addition, a limited number of noncriminal persons suffering from episodic periods of violent behavior—often associated with epileptic seizures—have been subjected to the same operation. Proponents of psychosurgery claim that amygdalectomy greatly reduces violent or aggressive behavior without seriously interfering with other functions. However, many ethical and scientific questions are involved in this as well as in other forms of psychosurgery. As Valenstein (1973) has pointed out in his book, *Brain Control,* the relationship between behavior dynamics and limbic centers is still only poorly understood, and it is premature to assume cause-and-effect relationships between the destruction of certain centers and changes in behavior.

The hippocampus

The hippocampus is also involved in emotional reactions. Stimulation of the region may elicit fear and rage patterns in animals. Lesions of the area do not give consistent results; some investigators report no change in emotional behavior, whereas others report enhancement of both fear and rage. However, somewhat surprisingly, the hippocampus—which for decades was considered to be a part of the "smell brain"—appears to be involved in memory. As we pointed out earlier, in humans, hippocampal lesions often produce severe memory deficits (Milner, 1959; Scoville & Milner, 1957). Patients with large lesions of the hippocampus invariably show memory deficits for recent events, including amnesia for periods up to several months before the lesion. Earlier memories are, however, intact. That the hippocampus is involved in memory is confirmed by animal studies showing that a variety of learned reactions are affected adversely by hippocampal lesions. Interestingly enough, a number of investigators are in agreement that a major reason for learning deficits following hippocampal lesions appears to be the inability of the animals to show flexibility in novel situations (see, for example, D. P. Kimble & Kimble, 1965).

The septal area

Evidence from animal studies demonstrates that the septal region is involved in the inhibition of autonomic and behavioral emotional arousal. Its removal in rats results in exaggerated emotionality. Such animals become feral and difficult to handle. Moreover, animals with septal lesions perform poorly in *conditioned emotional response* (CER) situations. These situations involve an unavoidable shock to which the animal normally responds by "freezing" and crouching when given a signal that the shock is approaching. Animals with septal lesions fail to freeze and crouch in such situations and continue whatever behavior is ongoing. However, in a *conditional avoidance response* (CAR) situation involving the animal's running from one side of a shuttle box to another to avoid a shock, animals with septal lesions are not impaired. But in *passive avoidance* situations in which the animal must stop ongoing behavior (for example, stop eating) in order to avoid a shock, animals with septal lesions are again inferior. Generalizing these results has led McCleary (1966), an investigator who has carried out extensive research utilizing these techniques, to conclude that septal-lesioned animals are *unable to suppress ongoing behavior,* an ability clearly needed in CAR and passive avoidance situations. Apparently, the high level of arousal and aggressiveness of animals with septal lesions makes it difficult for them to halt activities in progress. However, in studies utilizing mice, cats, or monkeys, removal of the septum does not necessarily produce an increase in aggressiveness. The results are contradictory depending upon the species. We are once again reminded of the dangers of generalizing about brain functions from studies carried out on a single species.

The cingulate gyrus

In mediating affective functions the septal nuclei are complemented by the cingulate gyrus, which appears to serve as a center for stimulating emotional reactions. Animals with cingulate lesions show little or no emotional behavior. Cingulectomy has been used to relieve the excessive emotionality of human patients suffering from anxiety or obsessive reactions. It is interesting to note that animals with cingulate lesions have difficulty with active avoidance response (AAR) situations. However, in passive avoidance situations such animals are actually improved in performance. These results, it should be noted, are opposite to those found in animals with septal lesions.

The hypothalamus

We have already noted that ventromedial lesions of the hypothalamus produce ferocity in animals, whereas lesions of the lateral region result in placidity. We may also point out here that the anterior portion of the hypothalamus is the most important site for producing positive reactions in self-stimulation situations and that stimulation of the posterior portion results in aversive reactions. In order to integrate these findings it will be necessary to consider intracranial brain stimulation in reward and punishment centers in more detail.

Brain Stimulation and Mechanisms of Reward and Punishment

The chance discovery by Olds and Milner (1954) that rats appear to like stimulation in a region near the septum has led to considerable research effort to investigate the nature of intracranial stimulation and its relation to reward and punishment. In the original experiment Olds and Milner observed that the animals (rats) were attracted to the specific place in an open field where the stimulation had been administered. They sniffed the area and could be drawn to any spot where appropriate stimulation was given. Following this lead, Olds and Milner demonstrated that rats would self-stimulate themselves by bar pressing in a Skinner box. Indeed, animals under these conditions appeared to be insatiable, sometimes responding at the rate of 2000 responses an hour for 15 or 20 hours until exhausted (Olds, 1958a). Moreover, animals can be trained to traverse mazes by rewarding them with brain stimulation for entering the correct segments (Olds, 1956). Olds and other investigators (Delgado, 1955; N. E. Miller, 1958) have also demonstrated that certain sites in the brain are aversive, and the animal will avoid bar pressing or manipulating a bar to turn off stimulation.

The research effort that has resulted from these early findings in recent decades has sought the answers to three fundamental questions: (1) What sites are rewarding or punishing? (2) What is the relationship between behavior elicited by ordinary drives and reinforcers and intracranial stimulation? (3) What is the nature of reward and punishment in intracranial stimulation?

Broadly speaking, the reward sites lie in the limbic system or are closely associated with it. Positive reward effects in the animal's behavior can be elicited by stimulation of the posterior and lateral hypothalamus, the region of the caudate nucleus, the septal region, and the dorsal portion of the thalamus. The most reliable or consistently rewarding sites are the septum and medial forebrain bundle, a diffuse system of fibers near the base of the brain that communicates with the hippocampus, septum, and hypothalamus. It might be noted that the sensory and motor structures of the brain are not rewarding areas. We may also note that rate of responding in bar-pressing experiments varies with the reward site—the hypothalamic sites eliciting the highest rate (Olds, 1958a, 1958b, 1960, 1961, 1969).

The anatomical locus of aversive behavior has been discovered by Delgado (1955), N. E. Miller (1958), and others. In general, aversive behavior can be elicited by stimulation of areas in the tegmentum, amygdala, and hippocampus. Surprisingly, these do not correspond to the classic pathways for pain.

The relationship of intracranial stimulation and ordinary drives and reinforcements is complex and not yet fully understood. There is no doubt that the two are related (J. V. Brady, 1961; Kling & Matsumiya, 1962; Olds, 1958a; Wilkinson & Peele, 1963). In general, under conditions of food, water, or sexual deprivation, animals show higher rates of bar pressing for self-stimulation than they show under conditions of satiation. Moreover, stimulation of lateral or posterior hypothalamic nuclei may elicit eating or drinking or sexual behavior; this finding demonstrates the intimate relationship between behavior elicited by intracranial stimulation and the primary drives.

The remaining question of the nature of the rewards and punishments in intracranial stimulation is the most interesting one from a theoretical or systematic point of view. Unfortunately, there is no definitive answer to the question. It is possible that rewards and punishments resulting from intracranial stimulation are only laboratory artifacts and are unrelated to ordinary drives and reinforcers. Some support for this viewpoint may be found in the fact that the self-stimulation drives appear to be mechanical in nature (the animal working until exhaustion), unlike the primary drives, which satiate relatively quickly. Moreover, self-stimulation behavior, unlike primary drive behavior, is difficult to maintain on ratio schedules of reinforcement or to associate with neutral stimuli by conditioning (Brodie, Malid, Moreno, & Boren, 1960). Intracranial stimulation conditioning is therefore easily extinguished, unlike ordinary conditioning under conditions of primary drive.

One theoretician (J. A. Deutsch, 1963) has postulated that reward stimulation not only may reinforce the response that produces it but also may provide a rapidly decaying drive to obtain additional stimulation. Thus, the difficulty in explaining the rapid extinction under large ratio reinforcements would be at least partially accounted for. Another investigation (Kent & Grossman, 1969) has provided evidence that in some instances intracranial stimulation may result in a kind of approach-avoidance conflict for the animal. This view assumes that stimulation has both positive and negative effects, with the positive effects having a somewhat shorter temporal decay period than the negative component. This difference would account for the rapid decay of the reinforcement effects under ratio schedules and in certain other anomalous situations. It could theoretically account for the nonsatiating effects of intracranial self-stimulation in situations where the reinforcement is continuous. It is possible that the animal is pressing the bar rapidly *in order to avoid the negative component.*

Clearly, the nature of rewards and punishments in intracranial stimulation has not yet been established. The entire research area is in a state of rapid development and change, and a more definitive theory of the relationship between primary drive effects and those associated with intracranial stimulation may be expected in the near future.

In concluding, we may note that extensive research in recent years devoted to a better understanding of the limbic system demonstrates the validity of Lewin's dictum that "there is nothing more practical than a good theory." Thus, once Papez and MacLean had provided a theoretical framework for understanding the subcortical areas of the brain, extensive research was generated, leading to a rich harvest of empirical data. These efforts were, of course, made possible partly by the development of microelectrode techniques following World War II. But before the development of the necessary theory and technology, there was too little theory and too few facts many of which are contradictory. At the present time there are too many facts for any theory to encompass, and it is likely to be some time before theory again catches up with the mass of empirical data now available. All that investigators in the area are now agreed upon is that intracranial stimulation is not identical with reinforcement as traditionally defined by learning theorists.

SUMMARY AND CONCLUSIONS

Most of our knowledge of the neurological foundations of behavior is less than a century old. The vast bulk of what we know has been learned in the twentieth century. Progress in neurophysiology has been slower than in other fields because of the forbidding complexity of the structures involved and because discovery in this area had to await the development of techniques in other fields, particularly in electronics. Nevertheless, great progress has been made. We have seen how cortical localization for sensory, motor, and associative functions has been established with the help of experimental and clinical techniques. In the functions of the reticular system we now have a sound theoretical explanation of sleep, arousal, and attention. The recent breakthrough in the study of the limbic system has provided a major stride forward in understanding the neurological basis of motivational and emotional behavior, although many of the relationships remain to be worked out.

Quantitative Psychology

15

In this and the following chapter we shall be concerned primarily with theories within the broad division of the field known as *differential psychology*. The differential psychologist approaches human behavior through the investigation of individual differences, largely in the areas of intelligence and personality. On the other hand, psychologists in the field of *general psychology* are primarily concerned with establishing broad general laws of behavior within such traditional areas as motivation, learning, thinking, and perception.

From a somewhat different point of view, general psychology studies people in terms of how they are alike, whereas differential psychology looks at people in terms of how they differ. In reality, the two fields are complementary, since if we could know all the ways in which people are alike, it follows that we would know the ways in which they differ, and vice versa. The distinction between the two fields is, in part, historical and, in part, a matter of convenience. Traditionally, psychologists whose primary interest was the development of aptitude and personality tests came to be associated with differential psychology, while those whose interests remained within the areas of greatest concern to the schools were considered general experimental psychologists.

Because the investigation of individual differences has relied heavily on quantitative techniques, particularly the use of correlational and normative statistics, psychologists working in the area of differential psychology are sometimes known as "quantitative" psychologists. The distinction is merely a question of emphasis, since to some degree, all contemporary psychologists rely on quantitative methods in designing experiments and interpreting the results. Furthermore, psychologists in the area of sensation, such as Hecht and Stevens, have developed mathematical theories of sensory processes. Similarly, in learning (traditionally a "general" area), psychologists have developed mathematical models of the learning process and are more "quantitative" in their orientation and methodology than many differential psychologists. Another recent development within the field is the utilization of information processing theory in model making. Again, because information processing theory relies heavily on quantitative techniques, we have chosen to include it here.

ORIGINS AND DEVELOPMENT OF QUANTITATIVE METHODS

The first application of statistical methods and the theory of the normal probability curve to the interpretation of biological and social data was made by Adolph Quetelet (1796–1874), a Belgian astronomer. The normal curve had been discovered earlier by mathematicians who applied it to the distribution of measurements and errors in scientific observations. However, until Quetelet demonstrated that anthropometric measurements carried out on unselected samples of people typically yield a normal curve, the law had never been applied to human variability. Quetelet employed the phrase, *l'homme moyen,* "the average man," to express the fact that most individuals tend toward the average or center of the normal curve on measured traits and characteristics, with fewer and fewer cases represented near the extremes.

Sir Francis Galton (1822–1911), famous for his studies of hereditary genius, became interested in Quetelet's applications of the normal curve and greatly extended the latter's work. Galton also established a laboratory for the large-scale testing of individual differences. For these investigations, he designed a number of pieces of equipment, among which was a whistle for determining the upper limit for pitch, a bar for measuring the individual's ability to judge visual extents, and a pendulumlike reaction-time device for measuring simple reactions. For decades, during the "brass instrument" phase of psychology, the Galton whistle and Galton bar were standard equipment in laboratories throughout the world.

However, of even greater importance was Galton's development of various statistical tools for interpreting the results of his experiments—the median, the standard score, and the method of correlation. The last-named constitutes his single greatest contribution to quantitative psychology. The modern techniques for establishing the validity and reliability of tests, as well as the various factor analytic methods, are direct outgrowths of Galton's discovery. Working with Charles Darwin, Galton found in 1876 that inherited characteristics tend to "regress" toward the mean of a distribution of those characteristics. Specifically, in the case of human stature, the sons of very tall men are, on the average, not as tall as their fathers. Conversely, the sons of very short men are, on the average, taller than their fathers.

More generally, the unusual combinations of genes that make for extreme deviations in any human characteristic occur only rarely, while the most probable combinations result in average characteristics. The symbol for the coefficient of correlation, r, is taken from the first letter of *regression* in recognition of its origin in Galton's discovery of the tendency toward mediocrity in the inheritance of human traits.

Finally, among the originators of the basic tools of descriptive statistics was Karl Pearson (1857–1936), who developed a large number of formulas for the treatment of psychological data. Pearson was also responsible for the present form of the product-moment coefficient of correlation, which frequently bears his name. Galton's measure of correlation was a crude one since it was based on the median and the interquartile range. Pearson modified it by utilizing the mean and standard deviation. Pearson also founded a journal, *Biometrika,* for the publication of the results of quantitative researches in biology and psychology.

While the basic measures of descriptive statistics were undergoing development in the hands of Quetelet, Galton, Pearson, and others, the psychophysical tradition was already well under way in the work of Weber and Fechner. As we pointed out in Chapter 3, the evolution of the psychophysical methods went hand in hand with the growth of experimental psychology. For this reason, some historians distinguish between the "mental test tradition," embracing the work of the "statisticians" and test developers, and the "psychophysical tradition," which evolved out of the researches of Weber and Fechner. Despite the fact that both traditions utilize the same fundamental statistical approaches, each has developed relatively independently of the other. The mental test tradition has attracted psychologists whose main interest lies in the area of individual differences, while the psychophysical tradition has remained closely allied to the general-experimental area.

However, as is so often true with broad generalizations and dichotomies, there have been exceptions—psychologists who, though trained in the experimental-psychophysical tradition, have made some of their most significant contributions in the area of individual differences. Such was the case of James McKeen Cattell (1860–1944), one of America's greatest psychologists and one who in many ways best epitomizes the spirit of American psychology. Cattell's postgraduate education in psychology was primarily German—but German with Cattell's highly individualistic stamp impressed upon it. Indeed, one of the most famous anecdotes in the history of psychology concerns Cattell's introduction to Wundt. As reported by Boring (1929), Cattell became Wundt's first assistant—self-appointed, it might be noted. He appeared at Wundt's laboratory and said, "Herr Professor, you need an assistant, and I will be your assistant!" Cattell, moreover, made it clear that he would choose his own research problem—the psychology of individual differences. Wundt, according to Boring, is said to have characterized Cattell and his project as *ganz amerikanisch* ("totally or altogether American").

Cattell's investigations of individual differences centered largely on the reaction-time experiment, which at that time was enjoying tremendous popularity. In fact, the whole field of differential psychology may be said to have originated out of the discovery that individuals differ in respect to the speed with which they react to a stimulus. The discovery occurred in 1796, when Maskelyne, the royal astronomer at Greenwich Observatory, dismissed his assistant, Kinnebrook, because the latter observed stellar transits approximately a half-second later than he did. This "error," as it was originally supposed to be, eventually became known as the "personal equation" in astronomy. Years later, in Wundt's laboratory, the investigation of reaction time under various conditions appeared to provide an avenue for the precise measurement of the mental processes. In general, the early investigators set themselves the problem of attempting to measure "conduction time" over the sensory and motor nerves. Once this had been accomplished, it was hoped that conduction time could be "subtracted out," thus yielding accurate temporal measures of such mental processes as sensory and motor sets, discriminations of various types, will, and association.[1]

Many of the classic experiments in the area of reaction time were carried out by Cattell. He investigated the speed of reaction as a function of the sense modality stimulated and compared simple reaction time to discrimination and association reaction times. In addition to his investigations of reaction time, he also contributed to psychophysics by developing the order-of-merit method, in which stimuli ranked by a number of judges can be placed in a final rank order by calculating the average rating given to each item. For example, as Cattell applied the method to eminent American scientists, he asked ten scientists to rank a number of their outstanding colleagues and averaged the results by assigning an order of merit to the scientists on the basis of the pooled results. He also went to England where he familiarized himself with Galton's tests which he introduced to the United States at the University of Pennsylvania in 1888–1889. Finally, Cattell and an associate devised a number of simple mental tests, which they administered to Columbia freshmen, marking the first large-scale testing of human subjects for the purpose of determining the range of individual differences.

In general, Cattell is credited with having influenced the overall development of American psychology in the direction of an eminently practical, test-oriented approach to the study of the mental processes. His was a psychology of human abilities as opposed to a psychology of conscious content. In this sense he comes close to being a functionalist, though he was never formally associated with that school. Thus he represents a transition between the Germanic psychophysical tradition and the American functionalistic spirit, which has always emphasized the study of mental processes in terms of their utility to the organism.

THE MENTAL TESTING MOVEMENT AND THEORIES OF INTELLIGENCE

The mental testing movement began with the development of the first intelligence test by Binet and Simon in 1905. The test sprang from the purely practical goal of discovering an objective method of assessing the intellectual level of French schoolchildren. The Minister of Public Education had become concerned with the problem of how to identify and eliminate retarded children who were unable to profit from public school education. He commissioned Binet and Simon to devise a scale that would select such children and, at the same time, indicate the nature of special instruction from which they could profit. A secondary objective was the improved diagnosis of severely retarded institutionalized children.

Binet and Simon rejected the tests utilized by Galton and Cattell as being too narrowly sensory and physiological and developed a scale around a theoretical framework involving three conceptions of the nature of intelligence: (1) the goal or

---

[1]For a detailed history of reaction-time experiments, see Woodworth (1938).

direction of the mental processes involved, (2) the ability to show adaptable solutions, and (3) the capacity to show selectivity of judgment and self-criticism of choices. In attempting to measure these processes, Binet and Simon constructed their test from items of common information, word definitions, reasoning items, ingenuity tests, and the like. By giving the test to a large sample of children, they were able to arrange the items according to an age scale by placing them at a point where 50 to 75 percent of the children passed. For example, if a given item was passed by 50 percent of 4-year-olds, it was considered appropriate for that level.

Generalizing this reasoning to the test as a whole, Binet and Simon were obviously assuming that intelligence grows or develops in parallel with the child's chronological age. By comparing the child's rate of intellectual growth to the average rate of growth of the standardization group, they were then able to measure any given child's intellectual level. Thus, as the Binet and other mental-age scales are now used, the child who passes all the items at the 7-year level *is mentally 7 years of age irrespective of his or her chronological age.* In other words, the child is able to do test items that 50 to 75 percent of 7-year-old children can pass. This concept of *mental age* as measured by a graded scale was Binet and Simon's great contribution.[2]

Such, briefly, was the reasoning behind the Binet-Simon test. The critics, however, quickly began to voice their objections to the theoretical assumptions underlying the scale. First, is intelligence goal direction, adaptability, and critical judgment? If so, did the hodgepodge of test items employed by Binet and Simon measure the abilities they were designed to measure? Moreover, is intelligence a unitary or general ability as implied by the practice of lumping scores on a variety of items into a single mental-age score? The answers to these seemingly straightforward questions are still being sought some three-fourths of a century after the publication of the Binet scales.

Broadly speaking, psychologists have taken two avenues of approach in attempting to formulate a definition of intelligence and to solve the problems involved in its measurement. The first is the ''armchair'' or deductive, method, wherein the psychologist seeks to define intelligence on the basis of his or her expert opinion and then proceeds to construct a test he or she believes will measure the processes identified in the definition. Hopefully, the results of testing will yield empirical evidence to support that definition. Clearly, this technique was the one employed by Binet and Simon. The second approach involves the analysis of already existing tests in an attempt to discover just what the tests are measuring. Obviously, the second technique involves the a priori assumption that existing tests are *generally valid.* That is to say, it is assumed that already existing tests do measure intelligence, not perfectly perhaps, but with sufficient precision to make the proposed analyses meaningful.

Because the deductive technique is not quantitative, we shall not attempt to

---

[2]The almost universally employed IQ, which is calculated by dividing mental age (MA) by chronological age (CA) was suggested by a German psychologist, William Stern.

review the definitions offered by those in the field, many of which have never been supported by empirical data. Rather, the present discussion will be limited to theories of intelligence that depend upon mathematical analyses for the identification of intellectual functions. Following our usual "sampling technique," we shall explore two contrasting views that have been highly influential: Charles Spearman's two-factor theory and L. L. Thurstone's weighted group-factor theory.

Spearman's Two-Factor Theory[3]

Charles Spearman (1863–1945) announced his two-factor theory of intellectual ability in 1904, thus antedating the Binet test by one year. However, his theory did not come into prominence until the mental testing movement had been given impetus by the development of intelligence tests. Once it had come into its own, the theory became the center of international discussion and controversy, as well as the starting point for rival theories of intelligence formulated on the basis of mathematical analyses of tests.

Spearman's basic assumption is that all mental tasks require two kinds of ability, a general ability, G, and a specific ability, s. G, or general ability, as the term implies, is common to all intellectual tasks, whereas s is always specific to a given task. Consequently, there is one G but as many s's as there are different intellectual tasks. For the sake of simplicity, let us assume that we are dealing with two tests, a vocabulary test and an arithmetic test. Both tests draw upon the common general ability, G; yet, in addition, each requires specialized abilities, which are independent of each other. In this case we may assume that the vocabulary test draws upon a specific verbal ability, s_1, and the arithmetic test a specialized numerical ability, s_2. Moreover, it follows that because the two tests require a common ability, they will be positively correlated. The correlation will not be perfect, however, because of the fact that s_1 and s_2 are independent or specialized abilities that have nothing in common. The situation which we have been describing is represented graphically in Figure 15-1.

Let ellipses V and A represent the vocabulary and arithmetic tests, respectively. Because the tests are correlated, the ellipses overlap. The area of overlap represents G. The areas of independence represent s_1 and s_2 as indicated. Applying the same reasoning more generally, *all* intellectual tests, according to Spearman, "center" on G, since all are positively correlated. Indeed, the basic evidence for the two-factor theory was derived from Spearman's finding that various intellectual tests are positively correlated and to a moderately high degree. By a complex process involving the use of tetrad equations,[4] Spearman was able to show mathematically that his two-factor theory could account for the empirical interrelationships existing among tests.

---

[3]For primary sources, see Spearman (1924, 1927).

[4]The tetrad difference method of establishing factors is now considered obsolete. For the mathematical processes involved, the reader may consult Spearman (1927).

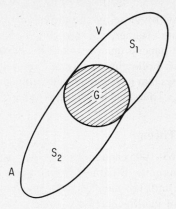

FIGURE 15-1.   A diagram to represent Spearman's G and s theory of intellectual abilities. For explanation see text.

Spearman's theory is able to explain the observed fact that children who show ability in one intellectual area also show ability along other lines. In short, the theory supports the Binet-Simon concept of an all-around general intellectual ability. However, because specific abilities are held to be independent of *G* and of each other, the theory also allows for the observed fact that individuals do show differences in their more specialized aptitudes. For example, an individual of average ability as measured by a general intelligence test may, if given appropriate special tests, demonstrate more verbal than numerical ability. On the general test, the two more specialized abilities "balance out," and the overall average rating is the result. Such fluctuations in abilities are most marked in the case of highly specific aptitudes, such as musical or mechanical ability. Being relatively independent of *G*, highly specific aptitudes may be well developed in persons of generally low overall ability or may be poorly developed in individuals of relatively high general intelligence.

Spearman's theory as originally formulated subsequently underwent revision in the light of further studies. He discovered that tests of mental abilities that are highly similar correlate to a greater extent than can be accounted for on the basis of their common overlap with *G*. As a result, he acknowledged the possibility of group factors such as verbal ability and spatial ability. He did not, however, abandon his original position with regard to *G* and *s*. The new group factors are conceived to be intermediate in scope, while *G* remains the overall factor of greatest importance. Finally, he proposed the existence of additional *general* factors, *p, o,* and *w*, which stand for perseveration, oscillation, and will, respectively. Perseveration and oscillation are additional intellective factors, which Spearman describes as follows: Perseveration represents the inertia of the individual's supply of mental energy, and oscillation the extent to which it fluctuates from time to time. Finally, *w* represents will, a motivational-personality factor that enters into the taking of intelligence tests.

Before leaving Spearman's two-factor theory, some mention ought to be made of his assumptions as to the nature of G. He believes that G is basically the ability to grasp relationships quickly and to use them effectively. Because his definition of G is so broad, he is able to account for the ability required to solve virtually any kind of intellectual problem. Thus the child who knows word definitions understands relationships between concepts and their definitions. Similarly, the ability to solve arithmetic reasoning problems, such as occur in the Binet test, requires a knowledge of relationships between the elements of the problem. Even the duck hunter must have the ability to take into account such factors as distance, speed of flight, wind direction, and force, as well as the power of his or her shotgun in order to solve the "problem" of shooting the duck. Although Spearman's views as to the nature of G are relatively unknown compared with his operationally formulated G and s theory, he devoted an entire volume (1924) to the elaboration of his conceptions of the nature of the cognitive processes with special reference to intellective factors. We shall return to Spearman's two-factor theory near the end of this section. Meanwhile, let us examine Thurstone's group-factor theory.

Thurstone's Weighted Group-Factor Theory[5]

L. L. Thurstone (1887–1955), our second representative of the factor theorists, has been identified since the early 1930s with a weighted group-factor theory of primary mental abilities. Thurstone is equally well known for his development of the method of *factor analysis,* which he used in isolating group factors. Both Thurstone's theory of primary mental abilities and his factor analytic methods have gained international recognition not only in the area of intelligence testing but also in other areas where factor analysis can be used as a tool for identifying the variables responsible for observed relationships.

Thurstone denies the existence of G and s. Rather, he conceives of mental organization in terms of group factors of intermediate scope. However, his group factors are not believed to be the result of the overlapping of highly specific abilities of narrow range. Rather, such factors are revealed by correlation clusters occurring among similar tests, which in turn are drawing upon certain primary mental abilities. For example, let us assume that a group of individuals are given a large variety of tests, among which are included tests of verbal, spatial, arithmetic, and perceptual ability. Let each of these tests be represented by small ellipses with appropriate subscripts v_1, v_2, v_3, s_1, s_2, s_3, and so on. If all tests are intercorrelated, the result will be the appearance of clusters of tests that are highly correlated among themselves but show only a low correlation *between* clusters (see Figure 15-2).

As indicated in Figure 15-2, the area of common overlap in each cluster defines a primary mental ability. In one large-scale investigation, Thurstone (1935) found evidence for seven primary mental abilities. Briefly, these are

---

[5]For sources, see Thurstone (1935, 1947).

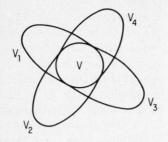 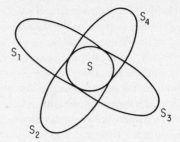

FIGURE 15-2.   A diagrammatic representation of Thurstone's group-factor theory. The ellipses v_1, v_2, v_3, and v_4 represent four tests of verbal ability; the ellipses s_1, s_2, s_3, and s_4, spatial tests. The verbal tests correlate highly with each other as indicated by the area of common overlap. Similarly, the spatial test show relatively high correlations. V and S represent Verbal and Spatial ability, respectively, and are defined by the correlation clusters found among tests of verbal and spatial ability. Note that the group factors are independent and do not correlate with each other.

1. Verbal. The ability to understand and utilize verbal ideas effectively.
2. Number. The ability to carry out the fundamental arithmetic operations of addition, subtraction, multiplication, and division.
3. Spatial. The ability to deal with objects in space and spatial relationships, as demanded in geometric problems.
4. Perceptual. The ability to identify objects quickly and accurately, as required in reading, map work, and the like.
5. Memory. The ability to learn and retain information.
6. Reasoning. The ability to perceive and utilize abstract relationships; to put together past experiences in the solution of new problems.
7. Word fluency. The ability to think of words rapidly. Word fluency may be related to personality variables as well as to intellective factors.

On the basis of his findings, Thurstone undertook a program of test construction for the purpose of developing more refined measures of the primary mental abilities. He believed that the traditional method of rating the individual's intellectual ability by means of a single, overall score was wrong. Instead, the testee's standing on each of the primary mental abilities is reported in terms of percentiles. In this way a psychogram of the individual's pattern of abilities can be reported. Thurstone believes that this method gives a more valid and useful appraisal of the abilities than the traditional IQ score, which, he feels, obscures the underlying pattern of mental aptitudes.

Finally, it should be noted that Thurstone's analytic techniques reveal that various tests show different "factor loadings" or varying degrees of relationship with the several correlation clusters. For example, Test A might correlate 0.76 with a verbal factor, 0.10 with a numerical factor, and 0.06 with a perceptual factor. In this case we are obviously dealing with a test of verbal ability. In the same factor analysis, Test B correlates 0.16 with the verbal factor, 0.80 with the number factor, and 0.28 with the perceptual factor. In this instance the test is drawing primarily upon number ability and to a lesser extent upon perceptual ability. More generally, the degree of refinement of a battery of tests determines, in part, how closely each test will correlate with each of the underlying factors. Theoretically, if we had perfectly reliable tests that measured one and only one mental ability with complete accuracy, the relation of each test to its underlying factor would be perfect.

The last statement also presumes that there is no general ability G or, to put it another way, that there is no intercorrelation among the various abilities. Such is not the case. Thurstone discovered low positive correlations among the various primary abilities, indicating the existence of a low order of general ability. Moreover, he found that for adults the correlations among primary abilities are low, while for children the correlations are higher.

Independent confirmation of this finding has been provided by H. E. Garrett (1946) and his associates, who, in a series of investigations reaching down to the third and fourth grades, found that the intercorrelations among various tests *increase* with samples of younger children and decrease markedly with high school and college students. On the basis of these findings, Garrett has postulated a developmental theory of intelligence to the effect that, with increasing age, abilities differentiate out of general abstract intelligence into relatively independent factors. He believes that the differentiation occurs as a result of both maturation and increasing specialization of interests on the young adult level.

Thurstone's and Garrett's findings with respect to intellective factors suggest that the general factor and group-factor theories may not be as far apart as they appeared to be when originally postulated. The present evidence indicates that both points of view are partially correct and practically useful when appropriately applied. The concept of a unitary intelligence measured by a general intelligence test appears to be valid for young children, while the concept of more specialized aptitudes or group factors measured by appropriate tests seems to be more valid for older children and adults.

Recent Developments

The leading American exponent of the factor analytic approach to the study of individual differences in intelligence and personality is Raymond B. Cattell. In the following chapter we shall discuss his application of factor analysis to personality. Here we may briefly indicate his extension of the Thurstone technique to the analysis of intelligence. Cattell believes that his modification of the Spearman-Thurstone techniques provides evidence for two fundamental types of intelligence, both of which are underlying general-order factors. These are *crystallized intelligence* and *fluid intelligence* (Cattell, 1941, 1963, 1971).

Fluid intelligence is the capacity for insight into complex relationships. In other words, it is the capacity for acquiring new concepts and demonstrating general "brightness" and adaptability in novel situations. Consequently, fluid intelligence is relatively independent of education, and tests that measure it minimize scholastic training and cultural factors.

Crystallized intelligence is a combination of acquired knowledge and developed intellectual skills. In Cattell's own terminology it is the "investment" of fluid intelligence in the higher-level skills of the culture to which the individual is exposed. Crystallized intelligence factor loadings (correlations) are highest on the Thurstonian primary abilities tests that are influenced by educational experience. Various samples at different ages show correlations of $+0.30$ to $+0.72$ between reasoning and crystallized intelligence. For verbal tests the correlations range between $+0.50$ and $+0.74$; for numerical tests the range is $+0.35$ to $+0.74$.

At the Institute for Personality and Ability Testing at the University of Illinois, Cattell and his associates have developed a culture-fair test that shows high positive loadings ($+0.48$ to $+0.78$) on the fluid intelligence dimension in factor analytic studies and low negative loadings (-0.02 to -0.11) on the crystallized intelligence dimension. The culture-fair test makes use of perceptual relations items consisting of geometric forms in which the testee's answer must be developed as a logical eduction or correlate from given relationships (see Figure 15-3). Theoretically, tests of this type are "culture fair" in the sense that they do not draw upon educational achievement and minimize differences in performance that are the result of cultural factors.

Cattell's concept of fluid intelligence is, as the reader may have noted, comparable to G, which Spearman defined as the ability to grasp relationships quickly or, more technically, to educe correlates from given elements of a relationship.

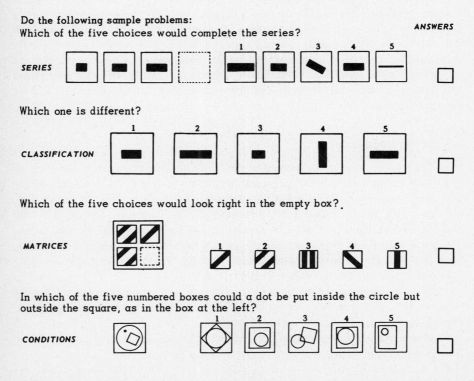

FIGURE 15-3. Sample items from Cattell's Culture Fair Intelligence Tests (© 1957 by the Institute for Personality & Ability Testing, Champaign, Illinois. Reproduced by permission.)

Cattell believes that this type of ability is primarily related to the mass of the cortical association areas in the brain and therefore finds support in studies such as Lashley's and Hebb's, which show that impairment following brain injury is proportional to the mass of cortical association tissue destroyed. Crystallized ability, on the other hand, reveals the greatest decrement in cases of injuries to specific motor or sensory areas. Verbal ability, for example, would be seriously impaired by injuries to the speech center, or Broca's area.

Cattell also presents evidence to show that fluid and crystallized intelligence undergo a different course of development over the trajectory of life. Between infancy and age 15 the two types of intelligence show identical growth curves with rapid negative acceleration. However, at age 15 the curves diverge—with that for crystallized intelligence remaining virtually unchanged or perhaps rising a little and that for fluid intelligence showing a steady and relatively steep decline. This finding can account for the well-known difficulty that older persons experience in mastering new materials or facts that are contrary to prior and well-entrenched knowledge. At the same time knowledge and judgment based on past experience (crystallized intelligence) hold up well.

Finally, the concept of a fluid intelligence that is measured independently of culture and education would seem to lend itself to helping resolve the nature-nurture controversy—that is, the degree to which intelligence is dependent upon heredity versus environment. To this issue we shall turn our attention after concluding the present section.

A radically different factor theory of intelligence has been proposed by J. P. Guilford (1967), who denies the existence of a general factor, G, or even the possibility that intelligence can be reduced to a few factors. Instead, he proposes that there are 120 unique intellectual abilities.

One of the dimensions of intelligence according to Guilford is *content,* of which there are four basic varieties: (1) *figural;* (2) *symbolic;* (3) *semantic;* and (4) *behavioral*. Figural content refers to the utilization of pictures or images; symbolic content is largely mediated through numbers and letters; semantic content, through verbal meaning; and behavioral content, by interpreting another's behavior (social intelligence).

The second broad dimension of intelligence is *operations,* or what is done with content. This involves five categories: (1) *cognition;* (2) *memory;* (3) *convergent production;* (4) *divergent production;* and (5) *evaluation*. Cognition refers to awareness of the meaning of words or concepts, memory refers to the ability to retain information; convergent production is the ability to come to a valid or logical conclusion on the basis of given pieces of information; divergent production is essentially creativity; and evaluation is judging wisely in behaving.

The third broad dimension of intelligence is *products,* or the result of operations on content. There are six kinds of products: (1) *units;* (2) *classes;* (3) *relations;* (4) *systems;* (5) *transformations;* and (6) *implications*. Units are single products such as a word or number; classes refers to a class of units such as a noun, a species; relations are relationships between units such as similarities or differences; systems refers to plans or systems for action; transformation involves a change; and implications involves making a prediction.

Since there are 4 contents, 6 products and 5 operations, the resulting combinations involve a total of 120 (4 × 5 × 6 = 120).

A task such as giving the definition of a word in a vocabulary test would involve cognition of units with semantic content. Doing the famous ball-and-field problem on the Binet test (the child is asked to plan a search for a lost ball in a large field) draws on abilities for figural content, systems, and evaluation.

Guilford's theory has the advantage of breadth and can better account for creativity than traditional theories. However, from a practical point of view it would appear difficult to measure so many different combinations of mental contents and functions.

Conclusions

In concluding our survey of factor theories of intelligence, we can make several generalizations regarding the significance of the developments within this area of psychological investigation. First, it must be emphasized that factor analytic methods are purely descriptive techniques. The mathematical manipulation of tables of intercorrelations by factorial methods reveals the smallest number of factors that can account for the correlations. The psychologist must then make assumptions about the nature of the psychological processes involved. He or she names the factors discovered on the basis of these assumptions. If a number of verbal tests correlate highly among themselves, he or she assumes that the relationship is logically and validly explained by hypothesizing that all of the tests draw upon the same underlying ability. When the smallest number of factors that can account for the correlations has been discovered and when the factors have been identified with their corresponding psychological processes, the psychologist is in possession of a *theoretical description of the system he or she is seeking to establish*. The validity of the system, however, is contingent upon the validity of (1) the operations from which it was derived and (2) the psychologist's judgment upon which the assumptions are based.

Second, as has been previously noted, factor analytic methods must begin with already existing tests that are assumed to have overall validity. Since most of the widely used tests of intelligence are heavily loaded with verbal and numerical items, it is natural that these factors—especially the verbal—should show heavy weightings on the factor loadings. In the last analysis, one gets out of a factorial study only what has been put into the correlation matrix in the first place. This does not mean that the method itself is invalid but only that we must not jump to the conclusion that because certain factors show up strongly in the final correlation clusters, they *are* the essence of intelligence. Given a different set of initial assumptions, a different set of factors would emerge from the analysis. However, in fairness to those engaged in research on the nature of intelligence through the factorial approach, it should be pointed out that their programs are not static but dynamic. The factor analysts not only are active in analyzing already existing tests but are striving to develop better measures of the intellectual functions their techniques have revealed.

Finally, we should like to note that factor analytic techniques have proved useful in a variety of applications outside the area of intelligence. They have been successfully applied to the isolation of personality traits (see Chapter 16), to problems in human engineering, to the measurements of interests, and, to a limited extent, to the field of experimental psychology.[6] We have been able to do no more than summarize the usefulness of this interesting and powerful statistical method in the limited area of intelligence. There can be little doubt that as time goes on factor analysis will continue to find increasingly wider ranges of application in other areas of psychology.

CONTROVERSIAL ISSUES IN TESTING

Just as there are differences of opinion among psychologists over the definition of intelligence and the type of quantitative analysis that ought to be employed in seeking a valid basis for a definition, so there are differences among experts about the interpretation of test results. From the onset of testing in the United States in the early part of this century, questions have been asked about such issues as the (1) constancy of the IQ from test to retest, (2) sexual differences in intelligence, (3) rural and urban differences, (4) occupational group differences, and (5) racial differences.[7]

In all of these cases differences have been found, which are greater or lesser depending upon the test employed and the particular sample under investigation. Controversy arises only over the significance and interpretation of the observed differences. It is beyond the scope of a volume such as this to enter into all of these complex and as yet unresolved controversies. The interested reader may consult any of the standard texts on aptitude and personality testing for an in-depth discussion of the literature. Invoking once again our sampling technique, we have chosen to comment on the issue that has generated the greatest degree of controversy because of its profound social and educational implications, and that is the issue of racial differences in intelligence. This issue has, moreover, the advantage of allowing us to reexamine once again a question that we first introduced in connection with classical perception (Chapter 5): Are individual differences innate or determined by experience? In perception, it will be recalled, this is the nativism-empiricism issue. In intelligence it is the nature-nurture issue, or more simply, heredity versus environment.

Stated in its simplest form the issue is this: Are differences in intelligence due to heredity or to environment? In order to answer the question two basic experiments are necessary: (1) Heredity must be held constant while environment is varied. (2) Environment must be held constant while heredity varies. In the first case

---

[6]For a more extensive treatment of factor analysis and its potential applications, see Cattell (1965, 1971), Guilford (1954, 1967).

[7]In recent years an extensive popular attack on testing and counseling has arisen among various segments of the population (Herrnstein, 1973).

all individual differences in measured intelligence will be due to environment and in the second to heredity.

Nature provides psychologists with the first "experiment" in instances where identical twins are reared apart. Because the heredity of identical twins *is* identical, all differences must be environmentally determined. The second basic experiment must be carried out on animals whose environments can be kept constant while they are selectively bred—bright with bright and dull with dull. A classic example of such an experiment was carried out by Tryon (1940).

On the average, identical twins reared apart show close relationships in IQ despite their different environmental backgrounds. As measured by the correlation coefficient, the relationship is between 0.80 and 0.90, a very high relationship. In terms of *average* group differences where each member of a pair of identical twins is put into a separate group and the two groups are then averaged, the magnitude of the difference is 8 to 10 IQ points (see Table 15-1). Some of the differences, it will be noted, are smaller than the average difference, and some are considerably larger. However, the average difference is not considered significant, since an individual who is tested on several occasions will differ from himself or herself by this magnitude.

TABLE 15-1.   Differences in the IQ Scores of Identical Twins Reared Apart[a]

Case Number	Sex	Age at Separation	Age at Testing (months)	Twin Difference in IQ
11	F	18 months	35	24
18	M	1 year	27	19
4	F	5 months	29	17
8	F	3 months	15	15
1	F	18 months	19	12
2	F	18 months	27	12
17	M	2 years	14	10
19	F	6 years	41	9
6	F	3 years	59	8
12	F	18 months	29	7
9	M	1 months	19	6
10	F	1 year	12	5
5	F	14 months	38	4
3	M	2 months	23	2
16	F	2 years	11	2
14	F	6 months	39	1
13	M	1 month	19	1
15	M	1 year	26	1
7	M	1 month	13	1

Mean difference = 8.3

[a]Adapted from A. Anastasi, *Differential Psychology* (3rd ed.). New York: Macmillan, 1958, p. 299. From data assembled in H. H. Newman, F. N. Freeman, and K. J. Holzinger, *Twins: A Heredity and Environment.* Chicago: University of Chicago Press, 1937.

When animals are selectively bred for learning ability (the psychologist's test of animal intelligence), there is no doubt that in as few as seven generations a "race" of bright and a race of dull animals can be developed (see Figure 15-4). However, there is some doubt about whether or not such breeding experiments are selecting intelligence or activity and emotionality which lead to superior maze learning.

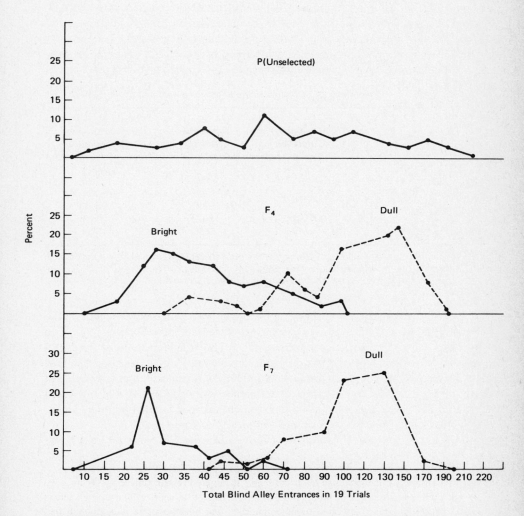

FIGURE 15-4. Inheritance and maze learning ability in rats. The parental group (P) is unselected genetically. Note that F_4, the fourth generation, is showing distinct distributions of bright (B) and dull (D) groups. By F_7 the distributions are almost completely separate. (After Tryon, R. C. Reprinted, with permission, from Intelligence: Its Nature and Nurture. Comparative and Critical exposition. Thirty-ninth Yearbook of the National Society for the Study of Education, Part I. Bloomington, Ill.: Public School Publishing Co., 1940, p. 113.)

Utilizing results on these basic experiments—along with a wealth of other data on (1) how much IQ can be changed under varying environmental conditions (in foster homes, special schools, Head Start, and so on) or (2) how IQ varies as dependent upon different degrees of consanguinity or relationship (Table 15-2)—some psychologists have attempted to estimate the proportion of IQ due to heredity and that due to environment. One such well-known estimate by Burks (1928) attributed 80 percent of the variance in IQ among the population to heredity and 20 percent to environment. Because Burks' estimate was an *estimate* based on *her* interpretation of the available data bearing on the question, it started a controversy that has persisted to the present day, with many psychologists believing that the original estimate of environmental influence was too conservative.

TABLE 15-2.   **Theoretical and Obtained Correlations for Intelligence Test Scores[a]**

	Obtained Correlation	Theoretical Correlation	Difference between Obtained and Theoretical
Identical twins together	.92	.9274	−.0074
Identical twins apart	.87	.8376	+.0324
Fraternal twins together	.54	.5326	+.0074
Siblings together	.53	.5326	−.0026
Siblings apart	.44	.4428	−.0028
Unrelated together	.27	.0897	+.1803

[a]J. L. Jinks and D. W. Fulker "Comparison of the Biometrical Genetical, MAVA, and Classical Approaches to the Analysis of Human Behavior" *Psychological Bulletin*, 73, 1970, pp. 311–349. Copyright 1970 by the American Psychological Association. Reprinted by permission.

In 1969 the controversy reached an historical high with the publication in the *Harvard Educational Review* of a paper by Arthur Jensen entitled "How Much Can We Boost IQ and Scholastic Achievement?" The article is a long one—123 pages—and is a searching analysis of a considerable body of data in respect to how much IQ can be changed by environmental influences. Because Jensen chose to cast much of the argument in the matrix of differences between the IQ's of black and white children, an intense and often emotionally charged controversy developed, which is still raging in the popular and technical literature.

Jensen's article opens with a provocative discussion of what he calls "The Failure of Compensatory Education."

Compensatory education has been tried and it apparently has failed. Compensatory education has been practiced on a massive scale for several years in many cities across the nation. It began with auspicious enthusiasm and high hopes of educators. It had unprecedented support from Federal funds. It had theoretical sanction from social scientists espousing the major underpinning of its rationale: the "deprivation hypothesis" according to which academic lag is mainly the result of social, economic and educational deprivation and discrimination—an hypothesis that has met with wide, uncritical acceptance in the atmosphere of society's growing concern about the plight of minority groups and the economically disadvantaged. (1969, p. 2)

Because black children are the largest single group of disadvantaged in the United States, most special programs of compensatory education have centered on them, particularly since the inception of the civil rights movement. If, as Jensen suggests, such programs have failed, does this mean that the American black is substandard in achievement because of an inferior IQ, which, in turn, is the result of inferior heredity?

Jensen first reviews (1969, pp. 1–80) twin studies, studies of foster children, selective breeding experiments in animals, and other data that bear upon the definition of IQ and what proportion of IQ is due to heredity and what proportion to environment. He concludes, as did Burks nearly half a century earlier, that 0.80 is determined hereditarily and 0.20 environmentally. He then raises the question of the significance of differential black-white scholastic achievement and the IQ differences found among samples of the two groups. On the average, there is a consistent difference of 15 IQ points in favor of whites.

These differences were known to psychologists long before Jensen's article was published. However, all but a few believed that they reflect not so much a hereditarily determined difference as one attributable to the disadvantaged environment of the black. Jensen believes in the possibility of a different interpretation—namely, a hereditary explanation. Citing evidence from the Coleman report (1966), Jensen first points out (pp. 85–86) that American Indian children are far more environmentally disadvantaged than black children yet score about half a standard deviation higher than the blacks.

Jensen next dismisses the "matriarchal theory" of black inferiority first suggested in the famous Moynihan report. This is the argument that in many black homes the father is absent, and therefore the children are deprived of half of the normal parental influence and stimulation enjoyed by the great majority of white children. Again citing studies by Coleman, Jensen concludes that parental presence or absence is not correlated in any systematic way with the differences found between blacks and whites on IQ tests. Nor is Jensen impressed by the IQ gains of disadvantaged children (pp. 97–101). When such children are given special preschool programs, the IQ gain is on the order of only two or three points.

In concluding his analysis of IQ gains in such situations Jensen writes:

> The evidence so far suggests the tentative conclusion that the pay-off of preschool and compensatory programs in terms of IQ gains is small. Greater gains are possible in scholastic performance when instruction techniques are intensive and highly focused, as in the Bereiter-Engelmann program. Educators would probably do better to concern themselves with teaching basic skills directly than with attempting to boost overall cognitive development. By the same token, they should deemphasize IQ tests as a means of assessing gains, and use mainly direct tests of the skills the instructional program is intended to inculcate. The techniques for raising intelligence per se, in the sense of G, probably lie more in the province of the biological sciences than in psychology and education. (1969, p. 108)

In fairness to Jensen, nowhere does he state directly that blacks' IQs are inferior on the average to those of whites because whites have hereditary superiority. Yet, he appears to be suggesting such hereditary inferiority and superiority by discounting environmental influences as of little importance.

More recently Jensen has extended his analysis of the genetic factor in intelligence and educability in a volume entitled, *Educability and Group Differences* (1973). In this book he reaffirms his position that those intellectual qualities most closely related to educability cannot be accounted for by the environmentalists' deprivation hypothesis. In a final recapitulation chapter he clearly states that the differences between whites and blacks are best explained genetically:

> In view of all the most relevant evidence which I have examined, the most tenable hypothesis, in my judgment, is that genetic, as well as environmental, differences are involved in the average disparity between American Negroes and whites in intelligence and educability, as here defined. All the major facts would seem to be comprehended quite well by the hypothesis that something between one-half and three-fourths of the average IQ difference between American Negroes and whites is attributable to genetic factors, and the remainder to environmental factors and their interaction with genetic differences. (1973, p. 363)

Although he does not associate himself with Jensen's position on the genetic basis of white-black differences, Herrenstein (1973) has also engendered a storm of controversy by arguing that socioeconomic class differences are closely associated with genetic factors and that if all children from all socioeconomic classes were given equal opportunity in our educational system *hereditary differences would be accentuated* and we would end up with a hereditary "meritocracy." Herrnstein's argument is based on essentially the same pool of empirical data as Jensen's.

In an attempt to develop an objective analysis of the relative contribution of genetic and environmental factors to racial differences in intelligence, a study by Loehlin, Lindzey, and Spuhler (1975) has been prepared under the auspices of the Social Science Research Council. Once again it is an analysis of the concepts, the issues, and the supporting studies in the heredity-environment controversy. After a thorough review of the literature, the authors conclude:

1. Observed average differences in the scores of members of different U.S. racial-ethnic groups on intellectual ability tests probably reflect in part inadequacies and biases in the tests themselves, in part differences in environmental conditions among the groups, and in part genetic differences among the groups. It should be emphasized that these three factors are not necessarily independent, and may interact.
2. A rather wide range of positions concerning the relative weight to be given these three factors can reasonably be taken on the basis of current evidence, and a sensible person's position might well differ for different abilities, for different groups, and for different tests.
3. Regardless of the position taken on the relative importance of these three factors, it seems clear that the differences among individuals *within* racial-ethnic and socio-economic groups greatly exceed in magnitude the average difference between such groups. (1975, pp. 238–239)

These and other psychologists who are critical of the genetic position believe that (1) environmental differences have not been given sufficient weight by Jensen and others who take the genetic position; (2) not enough is known about the hereditary mechanisms in intelligence to conclude that blacks are genetically inferior; (3) special programs for the disadvantaged have either been inadequate in scope or incorrectly assessed; (4) nature of intelligence itself is not sufficiently well understood to permit valid racial comparisons on the basis of existing tests (Cancro, 1971; Kamin, 1974).

QUANTITATIVE THEORIES AND MODELS IN LEARNING

Immediately after World War II psychologists began to show increasing interest in mathematical models of learning. This development was partly the result of stimulation from the new sciences of cybernetics and information theory, along with related technological advances in computer processing. But it was also due in part to disenchantment with currently existing theories of learning, particularly in respect to their lack of precision and the disagreements among theorists over the nature of learning and reinforcement. The new quantitative psychologists are less concerned with understanding the nature of the learning process (or why reinforcers reinforce) and are more concerned with formulating models that will accurately predict performance. These investigators argue that if a phenomenon can be predicted with precision, the fact that it may not be completely understood is not important. The astronomer is able to make extremely accurate predictions about the placement of heavenly bodies at any time but has only an incomplete understanding of celestial mechanics. Gravity, his major "intervening variable," remains undefined and, in reality, explains nothing. Similarly, the mathematical model maker has sidestepped the explanatory issues that divide his theoretical-minded colleagues and has concentrated on prediction.

However, the developers of mathematical models must make *some* assumptions about the nature of learning. In general, mathematical model theorists assume that learning can be treated essentially as a stimulus → response process—a modest assumption, but an assumption nonetheless.

Two publications that appeared a year apart marked the beginning of the postwar interest in mathematical models of learning. William K. Estes' initial formulation of his statistical sampling model was published in 1950. The first published report of the linear operator model by R. R. Bush and F. Mosteller appeared in 1951.[8] Estes' theory has been modified and revised in a number of subsequent publications and has become the leading mathematical model in the literature of learning. For this reason we have chosen to include a summary of it here as representative of contemporary mathematical models of learning.

-----

[8]A book-length treatment of the Bush-Mosteller model by its originators appeared in 1955; and a summary of this model appeared in the first edition of our text (Chaplin & Krawiec, 1960).

Estes' model, like other contemporary mathematical models, utilizes the probabilities of responses as its dependent variables. From these the model attempts to derive various interrelationships among the experimental measures, such as response rate, time, frequency, latency, and the effects of schedules of reinforcement. Estes' model is not a theory of learning in the sense that Hull's theory is, since it makes no claim to be a complete representation of the learning process. Indeed, it does not matter whether Estes' theory is true in a conventional sense as long as it enables the psychologist to make accurate predictions about the course of learning under various conditions. Therefore, assumptions are not necessary about the learning process per se but only about its outcome. Put somewhat differently, the statistical model of learning treats learned performances as processes or sequences of events in terms of the probability of their occurrence or nonoccurrence. Assumptions are made about how the course of performance may change from trial to trial depending upon changes in both subject and environmental conditions.

Estes begins by assuming that all possible responses can be grouped into two categories: those that result in a given outcome and those that do not (Estes, 1959a). The rat either presses the bar or it does not; the human learner reports a nonsense syllable correctly or does not. Similarly, any learned response—a conditioned response, a turn in a discrimination box, a chess move—can be treated in terms of its probability of occurrence.

On the stimulus side, Estes assumes that any situation is made up of many stimulus elements, which are further assumed to be independently variable. Moreover, only a sample of elements is operative in any given experimental trial. If the experimental situation is rigidly defined, we may assume that the stimulus elements will vary less from trial to trial than in situations that are highly complex.

Since only a sample of elements is operative for any given trial, a particular sample has only a certain probability of occurring. The situation is analogous to the classic probability problem of drawing balls from a jar and then replacing them and intermixing the population before the next sample is taken. Under these conditions, any given sample of balls will have only a certain probability, p, of being sampled on subsequent trials independent of how many other balls are sampled. Estes assumes that the same set of conditions holds for stimulus elements and represents this as probability θ.

It was pointed out above that Estes assumes all responses may be divided into two classes: those that produce a given outcome and those that do not. Following Estes, we may designate these classes as A_1 and A_2, respectively. Now it is further assumed that each stimulus element is conditioned (connected or attached) to one of the responses, A_1 or A_2. In a bar-pressing experiment, for example, some elements would be conditioned to pressing (A_1) and others to not pressing (A_2). Naturally, at the beginning of the experiment all elements are conditioned to not pressing. Learning, then, means that more and more elements become conditioned to A_1 as time goes on.

It is not necessary to know which of the stimulus elements are conditioned to which response in order to be able to predict response probability. All that needs to be known is what proportion of the stimulus elements are conditioned to each response. We may, in fact, assume that all elements have the same probability of being sampled in any given trial. This is the probability represented by θ. Under these conditions the probability of obtaining A_1 is equivalent or equal to the proportion of stimulus elements connected to A_2. Clearly, under conditions of reinforcement, this probability keeps changing. On any given trial, n, the probability that an element is conditioned to A_1 on the next trial, or $n + 1$, is given by the formula (Estes, 1959a, p. 398):

$$Pn + 1 = Pn + \theta(1 - Pn)$$

The equation states that the probability of a response on the next trial ($Pn + 1$) is equal to the probability on the given trial, or Pn, plus a fraction of the probability required to reach $p = 1.00$—or, in other words $(1 - Pn)$.

This equation is called a difference equation, since it expresses the change in probability that occurs from one trial to the next. If the equation is written over and over beginning with the first trial and ending on any given trial, n, it may be given the form (Estes, 1959a, p. 401):

$$Pn = 1 - (1 - p_1)(1 - \theta)n - 1$$

We now have a generalized equation for a learning curve expressing the increments (or decrements) in response probability on a trial-by-trial basis.

Figure 15-5 shows the Estes equations transformed to apply to four learning situations in order to test their goodness of fit. It will be noted that curves A and B are plotted from data from bar-pressing experiments; and curves C and D from T-maze data. All are excellent fits.

Estes' model must, of course, do more than provide a generalized curve for predicting acquisition of response. It must also be able to handle situations involving stimulus generalization, discrimination, extinction, drive, and reinforcement.

Stimulus generalization can be accounted for by assuming that generalization will occur only when similar situations actually contain several identical elements. Aside from the fact that Estes deals with acts rather than movements, the assumption is the same as Guthrie's or Thorndike's.

In simple discrimination learning situations, it must be assumed that the subject learns a response (A_1) to one set of stimulus elements and another response (A_2) to another set. If the stimulus elements occur in nonoverlapping sets, then the extension of the model to cover the situation involves only the additional assumption that A_1 is reinforced in the presence of one set of stimuli and A_2 in the presence of the other, with consequent independent curves developing over time. If, however, the two stimulus situations have some elements in common, the situation is much more complicated; nevertheless, the model has proved successful in predicting the outcome in some situations. However, Estes (1959a, p. 432) reports instances of failure and difficulties in developing tests of the model with highly complex discrimination problems, such as the Lashley jumping stand. For a more detailed discussion of current problems in probability models of discrimination learning

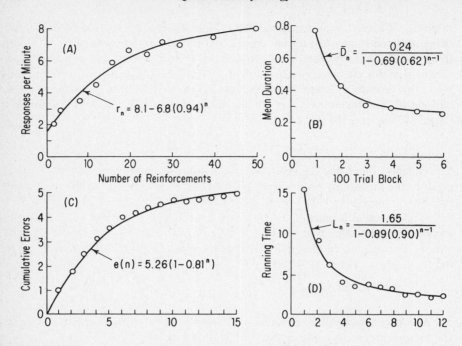

FIGURE 15-5.   Estes' model applied to four learning situations. Curves A and B are from a bar-pressing experiment. C and D are from a T-maze experiment. Clearly, the curves are an excellent fit. (From Psychology: A Study of a Science, Vol. 2, by S. Koch (ed.). Copyright © 1959, McGraw-Hill Book Company. Used by permission of McGraw-Hill Book Company.)

being worked out by Estes and his associates and others, see R. C. Atkinson and Estes (1963), Kintsch (1970a, 1970b), and Millward (1971).

Extinction, retroactive inhibition, forgetting, and spontaneous recovery provide no formidable difficulties for the theory. It is assumed that during extinction, stimulus elements originally conditioned to A_1 are reconditioned to A_2.

Figure 15-6 shows a schematic representation of how Estes accounts for retroactive inhibition by assuming that new stimulus elements become associated with original material during interpolated learning and persist into the retention tests.

Forgetting is accounted for by assuming that during learning a certain set of stimulus elements is sampled, but after an interval of time some of these elements are no longer available for sampling. For example, we may assume that the characteristics of the learner and the conditions in the environment during learning vary from time to time, thus producing varying stimulus complexes. If such variations occur between the learning and retention situations, then stimulus elements conditioned to A_1 will no longer be available to A_1 and will be connected to A_2.

Spontaneous recovery is accounted for by postulating the forgetting of extinction. More specifically, stimulus elements reconditioned to A_2 during extinction may, after an interval, be reconnected to A_1 because of changes in the learning situation or the learner.

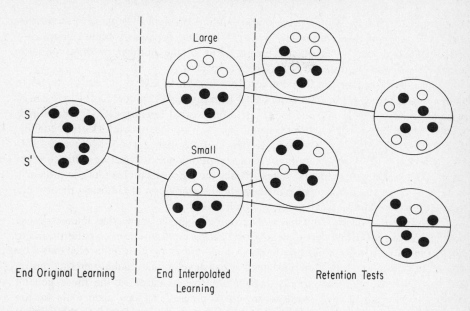

End Original Learning   End Interpolated   Retention Tests
                         Learning

FIGURE 15-6. Retroactive inhibition according to Estes' theory. New stimulus elements (open circles) become associated with original learning (black dots) during interpolated learning. "Large" and "small" denote relative amounts of interpolated learning. (From Psychology: A Study of a Science, Vol. 2, by S. Koch (ed.). Copyright © 1959 by McGraw-Hill Book Company. Used by permission of McGraw-Hill Book Company.)

Reinforcement is handled by Estes in much the same manner as it is by Skinner. That is, a reinforcer is a set of conditions that determines the response category to which a given set of stimulus elements will be conditioned. It is not necessary to specify "explanatory" principles of reinforcement—as Hull attempted to do in relating reinforcement to drive reduction or drive-stimulus reduction. In Estes' own words:

> Upon reviewing the many attempts to formulate simple, closed explanatory principles of reinforcement and the still more numerous attempts to test the formulations, I have been led strongly to suspect that no hypothesis as simple or unitary as those envisaged by contemporary contiguity or drive-reduction theorists is going to prove adequate. It appears, rather, than associative learning depends upon a complex of causal factors or conditions. The experimental operation we refer to as a reinforcement for a given response in a given situation is one which supplies the factor or factors missing from the complex needed for acquisition in that situation. (1959a, p. 460)

Drive is a set of stimulus elements. It need not be regarded as "energizing," as Hull regarded it. Instead, the level of energy may be accounted for in terms of the number of stimulus elements operative under various degrees of drive. If we assume that under conditions of low drive only a few stimulus elements are present, then clearly the probability of sampling them is small. If, on the other hand, we assume that under conditions of high drive many stimulus elements are present, the probability of sampling them becomes greater. Thus the apparently higher energizing effect of drive can be accounted for in terms of the number of drive-stimulus elements that are conditioned to different responses.

We have summarized the simplest formulation of Estes' statistical model in order to illustrate a mathematical model of learning. Estes' model has been tested in a wide variety of learning situations—including verbal learning (R. C. Atkinson & Estes, 1963; Estes, 1959a, 1959b; Estes, Koch, MacCorquodale, Meehl, Mueller, Schoenfeld, & Verplanck, 1954; L. Keller, Cole, & Estes, 1965; Millward, 1971; Weinstock, 1970). In its simplicity of assumptions and its dealing with contiguously connected S-R elements, Estes' theory strongly resembles Guthrie's theory; indeed, it is, in a sense, a precise mathematical formulation of Guthrie's theory, but one with a potentially wider range of applicability.

More recently Estes and his associates have shown increasing interest in extending mathematical models to deal with stimulus configurations or patterns and to make predictions in situations that involve small numbers of stimulus elements—on the order of one to three. Particular interest has developed in making predictions on the basis of one-element models, which are special cases of the more general stimulus-sampling theory. These recent developments in Estes' theory are far too extensive and technical to include here, and the reader is referred to the original reports by Estes and others, cited in this section; they provide numerous examples of mathematical models of learning with their mathematical derivations.[9]

By way of summary and evaluation we may point out that mathematical models of learning provide information in a form suitable both for making predictions and testing their validity. Because mathematics is a rigorous discipline, the psychologist must define his or her position carefully and with greater precision than is possible in ordinary language. Moreover, he or she is able to manipulate and test the soundness of the mathematical system before it is applied to experimental data. This, of course, does not guarantee that the assumptions themselves are correct. One can set up irrational mathematical systems that are internally logical but have no relationship to the world of reality. The moral is this: the psychologist must choose his or her mathematics wisely; but if a mathematical system is chosen, the logical thinking required tends to ensure rigor and precision in the definitions, predictions, and applications of the system.

However, as Hilgard (1956) points out, there are certain additional dangers and cautions that must be taken into consideration by those working with mathematical theories and models. First, he emphasizes that most great scientific discoveries in the physical sciences that involved mathematics came about through the use of simple mathematical relationships such as Mendel's 3:1 ratio in genetics or Mendeleev's Periodic Table of the Elements. Hilgard further suggests that the complex mathematical procedures employed by learning theorists may be more appropriate

---

[9]For additional analyses of probability theory in learning, see Estes (1959a, 1959b, 1961), Estes and Burke (1955), Estes and Hopkins (1961), Estes and Straughan (1954), and current issues of the *Journal of Mathematical Psychology*.

for a later stage of theory development, while the more fundamental (and simpler) mathematical interpretations are perhaps being missed.

Hilgard also points out that the proponents and critics of models often overlook the fact that all models thus far developed in the area of learning are limited in their scope and, consequently, should neither be overgeneralized in terms of their applicability nor criticized for failing to fit situations for which they were never intended.

Finally, he suggests that despite their usefulness, models will not make other types of theorizing obsolete. "Verbal" theories may suggest new types of mathematical models, which in turn may supplement or complement already existing models and theories.

In a similar vein, Hilgard and Bower (1966) suggest that although mathematical models of learning have demonstrated their usefulness and have shown that it is possible to make very accurate predictions, model making appears to lack an integrating frame of reference. One result of this has been a proliferation of small-scale models of limited usefulness. However, Hilgard and Bower further suggest that this state of affairs is most likely attributable to the essential newness of the field. Model making, they conclude, will remain a strong current in the literature of learning.

INFORMATION PROCESSING THEORY[10]

Information processing theory is an aspect of mathematical models that has attracted increased attention among psychologists in recent years and therefore requires special comment. Information processing theorists assume that psychological processes can best be understood if analyzed as though they were physical communications systems. The organism is treated as if it were a "black box" that receives, processes, and acts upon messages in the same way that electronic devices detect and encode information in the form of signals, store it or modify it in some way, and reproduce it upon demand in decoded form.

The home television receiver provides a handy example of an information processor that has certain broad parallels to human behavior (see Figure 15-7). Sensors in the form of the elements of the antenna system detect and pick up "messages," or electric signals from the transmitter, encode and amplify them within the internal circuits of the receiver, and then decode them to produce electrical impulses that excite the phosphor screen of the picture tube. In this communication system we have an *S-O-R* mechanism capable of sensing, modifying, and responding—just as living organisms respond to cues in the environment on the basis of their sense organs, the contribution of *O* factors, and central processes.

With the development of digital computers we have an even more striking analogy to organismic systems. The computer is "instructed" by means of a special symbolic language that can be punched into tapes or cards. Special sensors detect the information and convey it to the "memory" banks, where it is stored until

---

[10]For additional information on this complex field, see Haber (1968, 1969), Neisser (1967), Newell (1973), and Norman (1969).

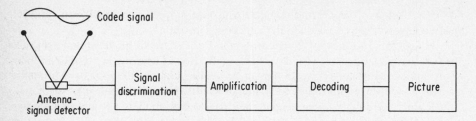

FIGURE 15-7.   A schema of the functional parts of a television receiver.

required for the solution of a problem. The machine solves a problem presented to it by drawing on its memory bank in order to apply the appropriate variables and transformations. Answers are given in printed form, either in mathematical symbols or in ordinary language. By proper programming, computers can play games with their human operators, "sing" Christmas carols, do in a few seconds work that would take several hand calculators a period of months, decide on the compatibility of two matrimonial candidates, or detect and accurately plot the course and target area of an enemy missile seconds after it leaves the launching pad.

These fantastic technological developments of the postwar years were of immediate interest to psychologists, who saw in them the possibility of developing information processing models of human behavior. If a machine capable of reading or translating a foreign language can be built, the engineer who builds it gives a convincing demonstration that he or she has a considerable understanding of the processes involved. Psychologists, however, who specialize in information processing theory are careful to point out that analogies and simulations are not explanations and do not provide psychological or physiological interpretations of behavior. Information processing theory (or digital computers) can be used by individuals regardless of their knowledge of behavioral processes or their systematic or theoretical biases. Moreover, the machine can make and carry out decisions, but not policy. Computers that tell us that an enemy missile is on the way do not say what should be done about it. Nevertheless, psychologists interested in information processing theory believe that the design and analysis of such models can lead to fruitful ideas about the nature of perception, memory, and thinking. We shall provide an illustration of how information processing theory deals with each of these areas after introducing a few basic concepts.

The information processing theorist uses the term *information* in approximately the same way it is employed in everyday life. It is the opposite of uncertainty. Thus, as Attneave (1959) has suggested, the parlor game of "Twenty Questions" illustrates how informative statements about the animal, vegetable, and mineral nature of the substance to be identified can reduce uncertainty until the precise answer is obtained. In order to be able to quantify information, the *bit* (from binary digit) has been chosen as the unit of information. More precisely, the bit is defined as the unit of information gained when the number of alternatives is reduced by half. Thus, if we ask about the toss of a coin (whether it came up heads or tails), the answer reduces the alternatives by half and, incidentally, in this case, removes all further uncertainty. Of course, it is necessary to formulate questions in advance in such a manner that the uncertainty is reduced by half; otherwise some other measure will have to be employed.

The concepts of *chunk* and *chunking* refer to items of information that have been combined into larger units. Thus a date, such as 1776, is a chunk of information consisting of four items. As G. A. Miller (1956) pointed out in a classic paper on information processing theory, the average person can remember about seven items of information—the immediate memory span. Some individuals can remember a few more, some less, and in recognition of this Miller entitled his paper "The Magical Number Seven, Plus or Minus Two." If items are chunked, however, the individual can remember large amounts of information. Thus, the person who can remember only five random digits may have no difficulty with a sequence of dates, such as 1776, 1940, 1960, 1984. With the aid of chunking, the same individual can process and remember sixteen items of information instead of five.

In dealing with bits and chunks of information, the theorist usually must apply stochastic or probability processes to the problem. The difficulty here is similar to that found in learning situations. The theorist can only make assumptions about what the learner will do on the next trial. He or she cannot be certain. In information processing theory the concept of *redundancy* defines the message property that reduces the error of prediction to less than chance probability by virtue of the fact that the message contains information about what will probably happen next. For example, the message that an infantry position is soon to be under attack by either Able or Charley artillery companies is not redundant insofar as it provides information at no better than chance accuracy about which unit will attack. If the message adds "You may expect an attack by Able company," it will become redundant.

Information processing systems may be subject to *noise,* or interference. In the television receiver this often takes the form of "snow" or "tearing" or other distortions of the picture. Noise, therefore, reduces the amount of useful information that can get through. Technically, noise is said to raise the level of *entropy,* or uncertainty. The term *entropy* has been borrowed by information processing theorists from physical systems, in which it represents the amount of heat generated or energy wasted—thus the energy unavailable for work.

The concept of *sensory gating* is used in information processing theory, as well as in the literature of physiological psychology, to refer to the inhibition of one sensory channel by another. Thus when the subject is visually attending to a stimulus, information coming through other sensory avenues is reduced or attenuated. This mechanism provides for selectivity of attention and is believed to be, in part, a function of the ascending reticular activating system. It has been suggested that the Chinese technique of acupuncture for the blocking of pain may work according to this principle.

Finally, two additional basic concepts may be mentioned: *input* and *output*. These terms refer to the signals entering a communications system and the decoded message coming out of the system. They are often used as broadly analogous to sensory data and responses in organisms.

ILLUSTRATIVE APPLICATIONS OF INFORMATION
PROCESSING THEORY

By way of illustrating the complexity and range of problems studied by means of information processing theory, we may begin with the most fundamental of all perceptual problems: How do we recognize or discriminate a pattern? Can a machine be built that will model the human organism's ability to recognize and classify printed material?

If the problem is the relatively simple one of recognizing standard and invariable patterns, such machines are not difficult to build. Indeed, banks all over the world have been employing them for years to "recognize" checks for the purpose of charging and crediting accounts. The numbers printed in special characters on the face of the check are scanned by a photosensitive machine, which matches each digit of the number to a programmed pattern or template stored in the memory bank. However, if the input signals are variable (as they are, for example, in reading books set in different type or in handwriting), the problem is vastly more complicated. As Figure 15-8 shows, the machine might make a better match between an incorrect template and an unknown letter than a correct one. One solution to the problem is shown in Figure 15-9, where *sequential processing analysis*[11] reveals how a machine might discriminate among several letters on the basis of their characteristics (Selfridge & Neisser, 1960).

Machines have been built that can solve the problem of recognizing cursive writing or Morse code signals. However, these machines do not show perceptual learning in the sense that they can build their own storehouse of future information on the basis of the past experience. Rather, they are only able to apply information already put into the memory banks.

Machines have also been shown to be capable of solving reasoning problems, such as proving geometric theorems. Indeed, the first important computer system to show the ability to "think" was the Logic Theorist developed by Newell and Simon (1956). The Logic Theorist utilized heuristic methods. It demonstrated its remarkable capabilities by proving 38 of the first 52 theorems of Whitehead and Russell's *Principia Mathematica*, some of the proofs being more sophisticated than previously offered by mathematicians. That machines are able to solve such problems is more than a mere tour de force of technological wizardry. It is a rigorous demonstration of the fundamental processes involved. Moreover, once the machine solves such a problem, it can often specify additional problems or solutions not recognized by the programmers.

There are basically two approaches to problem solving using information processing models: *algorithmic* and *heuristic*. In algorithmic solutions the problem is solved by specifying and trying out all possible sequences or solutions. Thus, the

---

[11]*Parallel processing* refers to the ability of a processor to keep track of several parallel streams of information at the same time. In this case, humans, who can use parallel processing, are masters of the machine, which must use sequential processing.

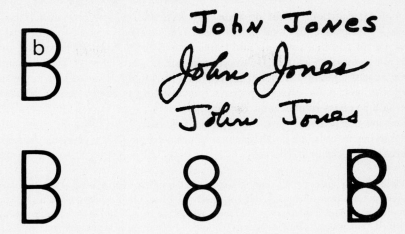

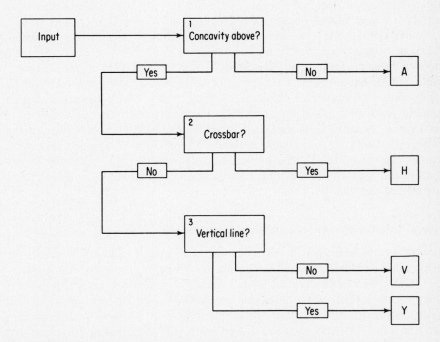

FIGURE 15-8.   Template matching. If the unknown figure (small b) is in a different type face than the template (large B), the match may be impossible. Cursive writing presents difficulties because of its variability. If the template is too close in size and shape to an incorrect figure (the 8) an incorrect match may occur.

FIGURE 15-9.   A sequential-processing solution to the problem of distinguishing four letters. (From "Pattern recognition by machine" by Oliver G. Selfridge and Ulric Neisser. Copyright © 1960 by Scientific American, Inc. All rights reserved.)

combination to a vault might be found by trying all possible combinations of numbers—an astronomical total in this case. The heuristic method specifies a limited number of possible solutions and further specifies that certain successful, even though not necessarily perfect, solutions will be allowed. Clearly, for most problems the heuristic method is more practical than the algorithmic and is the approach used by the human information processor in thinking out the possible moves in games such as chess or checkers, for example.

Perhaps the problem with the greatest fascination for those who are using model making in order to understand the mental processes involved is chess. As Feigenbaum and Feldman put it:

> Game playing has many fascinating aspects to the researcher. Affectively, it provides a direct contest between man's wit and machine's wit. On a more serious level, game situations provide problem environments which are relatively highly regular and well defined, but which afford sufficient complexity in solution generation so that intelligence and symbolic reasoning skill play a crucial role. In short, game environments are very useful task environments for studying the nature and structure of complex problem solving processes. (1963, p. 39)

The authors go on to point out that a number of programs have been written for computers, some of which have been developed with sufficient sophistication to be able to beat a weak human player. Early programs are reviewed by Newell, Shaw, and Simon (1963). More recently Zobrist and Carlson (1973) have reviewed sophisticated chess programs that are capable of defeating fairly advanced players. Moreover, these programs can "take advice" from masters. One of these authors, Newell (1963), has provided a flowchart of the essential operations involved in programming a computer for chess (see Figure 15-10). The complexity of programming for such a game is a formidable task. For each move there are, in a normal game, about 30 legal alternatives, and for the machine to look ahead even two moves involves 30^4, or 810,000 decisions. Clearly, it will be some time before machines can enter master chess tournaments. However, it is a testimony to the versatility and ingenuity of the computer processing model that so much has been accomplished thus far.

Artificial Intelligence and the General Problem Solver

A major breakthrough in the evolution of computer processing models of thinking came with the formulation of Simon and Newell's (1964) General Problem Solver (GPS). Previous individual programs had one major deficiency: They were unable to solve a wide variety of human problems. Some, like the Logic Theorist (Newell & Simon, 1956), specialized in the solution of mathematical theorems. Others, like EPAM, the Elementary Perceiver and Memorizer, developed by Feigenbaum (1963), could learn paired associates, and, as we noted, some programs could solve game problems, such as those occurring in chess or checkers.

The General Problem Solver simulates a wide variety of the kinds of concep-

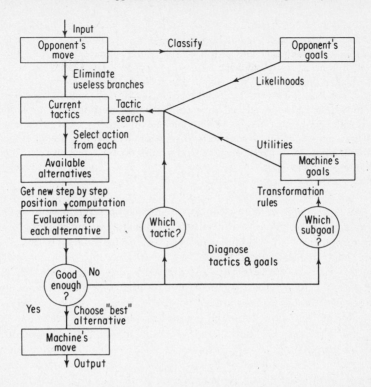

FIGURE 15-10.   A diagrammatic representation of a programmed sequence for chess. (From Newell, A. The chess machine, from Proceedings of the Western Joint Computer Conference, 1963.)

tual and heuristic strategies that are believed to underlie human problem solving capability whether in chess, mathematics, musical composition, or verbal reasoning. Basically, the program is capable of attacking a problem in terms of a series of operations which test the validity of solutions to subgoals leading to the eventual total solution. If an operation proves valid for the solution of a subgoal, the program can explore its appropriateness for further work on the problem as a whole. If it is not found appropriate, it is discarded.

Clearly, the technique is analogous to the way the human thinker works. Assumptions are made about how to organize and attack a problem. Tentative attempts may be carried out and discarded if they prove unfruitful until one is found that leads to the final general solution. In fact, Newell (1973) has pointed out that one test of the validity of any computer program that demonstrates artificial intelligence is that it generates outputs during the solving process that are comparable to the verbal reports of the human thinker as he or she evaluates his or her progress.

Basically, Newell and others who favor information processing models of thinking take the view that man's

. . . behavior can be seen as the result of a system consisting of memories containing discrete symbols and symbolic expressions (i.e., occurrences of symbols), and processes that manipulate these symbols. The central notion is that of the symbol, which is taken to mean essentially what it does in computer science, an entity with a certain functional property, to wit: that when a process has a token of a symbol it has access to information about what that symbol designates (encoded in symbolic expressions). The processes that can be performed on symbols are their creation (and, possibly, destruction), the obtaining of designated information, the creation of symbolic expressions, and the manipulation of these symbolic expressions by insertion, deletion, replacement, and reordering. A symbolic expression is a collection of symbol tokens connected by relations of access—e.g., the tokens S, Y, M, B, O, L connected by the relation *next*, which provides a token of the word SYMBOL. (Newell, 1973, p. 27)

If this analysis is correct, then information-processing programs should be capable of simulating human cognitive processes in all areas of thinking: immediate and long-term memory, reasoning or problem solving, attitudinal or belief systems, linguistic analysis, neurotic thinking and psychotherapy, and creativity. It is eloquent testimony to the versatility and ingenuity of psychologists specializing in the field of information processing theory that programs for most of these areas have been developed, including a computer "psychotherapist" (Colby, 1965).

By way of limitation, although computers can solve problems by processes simulating human insight, they do not work creatively but only according to a carefully prepared program of instructions. If the human programmer makes a mistake or feeds in inappropriate information, the computer has no way of rectifying such errors. In this sense man remains master of the machine—and the terrifying events portrayed in *2001: A Space Odyssey* when Hal, the computer in charge of the flight, became creatively deranged cannot occur.[12]

It seems appropriate to note here, as we did in Chapters 6, 10, and 11, that in recent years there has been increasing emphasis on cognitive interpretations in mathematical models and information processing theories of learning, perception, and thinking. In other words, the learning theory dominant in formal models of the higher mental processes during the first half of the present century is giving way to descriptions and interpretations in terms used to describe perception, thinking, and linguistic processes. In general, then, a significant rapprochement has occurred among psychologists working in the once diverse fields of sensation, perception, learning, memory, and thinking, borrowing freely from each other and finding common ground in moving toward more cognitive interpretations of these processes.

At this writing no psychologist is in a position to evaluate the probable outcome of mathematical and information processing models of behavior. The pioneers in this new movement are still carrying forward their programs, most of which are either incomplete or have to undergo thorough testing. It is to these investigators'

----

[12]See Newell (1973) for a thought-provoking general review of computer processing views of the nature of human intelligence and the concept of mind.

credit that they have already been able to synthesize or reconstruct complex mental processes with considerable precision—an accomplishment considered impossible not many years ago because of the complexity of the processes involved. To what extent these models will lead to improved theories with greater truth value than those we possess at the present time is for the research of the future to decide.

CONCLUDING REMARKS

Our survey of quantitative systems in psychology has emphasized three main subdivisions within the general area: (1) the evolution of quantitative systems of intelligence, (2) the development of mathematical models of learning, and (3) the information processing models of thinking. We have deliberately omitted any attempts to trace the evolution of descriptive and inferential statistical methods in psychology. Statistics per se does not belong to psychology; nor does this branch of mathematics constitute a psychological system. Instead, statistical methods are tools belonging to all sciences and employed by psychologists in summarizing data and drawing inferences from their research. However, as we have shown, the emergence of sophisticated mathematical approaches to psychological processes has in recent decades led to the formulation of theories and models in many areas—especially in intelligence, learning, and physiological psychology.

Most specialists in these fields are quite cautious in assessing the significance of this strong trend in contemporary psychology. All new developments that promise interesting leads tend to be exploited rapidly. In the long history of science some apparently significant approaches have led nowhere, whereas others have resulted in gigantic strides forward. We have no intention of dismissing the recent developments in quantitative psychology as a temporary fad. Indeed, the whole history of science shows that as each science matures, it tends to become more and more quantitative in its approach.

The ultimate test of the values of mathematical laws and constructs is their power to predict the phenomena with which they are concerned. As our brief survey of the recent work in this area of psychology suggests, it is at the stage of developing and testing *limited* quantitative systems valid only over a restricted range of phenomena. At the present time it appears that in psychology, at least, the development of general quantitative laws with the universality and predictive value of laws in the physical sciences lies far in the future.

Personality

16

Theories of personality, like systematic theories of intelligence, evolved largely outside of the traditional academic schools. As we pointed out in the introduction to Chapter 15, the differential psychologist approaches human behavior through the study of individual differences rather than by seeking general laws that apply to all mankind. In the case of personality, as is true of intelligence, the differential psychologist's program of investigation is most readily accomplished through the psychometric analysis of personality and individual clinical studies.

There is, however, another reason why personality theory has never been closely identified with the traditional schools. The concept of personality implies the study of the individual as a whole; and, as we have emphasized throughout this volume, the schools were reductionistic in their approach to behavior. The chief exception was, of course, the Gestalt school, and it is significant that of the traditional schools only Lewin in his Gestalt-like field theory attempted to encompass personality. Finally, as C. Hall and G. Lindzey (1978) have pointed out, personality theorists have typically been ''rebels''; consequently they have been reluctant to remain within the framework of a conventional school.

The study of personality, however, has never wanted for adherents. The challenge and interest inherent to the field is reflected by the fact that the third edition of Hall and Lindzey's *Theories of Personality* (1978) deals with twelve major contemporary theories. Even this relatively large number represents a small selection from the many existing theories. In fact, the great diversity of viewpoints in the area creates considerable difficulty for anyone who attempts to survey the field. However, as is true of all psychological theories, it is possible to group the various systems of personality according to such dimensions as the relative weight given to biological as opposed to social factors, the emphasis on learning as opposed to perception, the relative importance of the self in the system, and so forth.

Because of space limitations, our usual sampling approach will be invoked; consequently we shall limit our discussion to theories representative of the following general orientations: (1) the psychoanalytic, as represented by Freud; (2) the factorial, as represented by R. B. Cattell; (3) the individual, as represented by Gordon W. Allport; (4) the personalistic, as represented by H. A. Murray; (5) the self, or ego-integrative, as represented by Carl Rogers; and (6) the behavioristic. We believe that the six theories discussed in the present chapter provide a fair sample of the chief orientations to personality in contemporary psychology.

FREUD'S PSYCHOANALYTIC THEORY[1]

In discussing Freud's system of motivation and emotion (Chapters 12 and 13), we found it necessary to introduce a number of concepts that bear on personality. In view of this, there will obviously be a certain amount of overlap with the present chapter. Such a situation is virtually unavoidable in dealing with a highly integrated and deterministic theory such as Freud's. However, in the last analysis, this partial duplication can be looked upon as an advantage from the student's point of view, since it will serve to bring together these interrelated aspects of Freudian theory.

Freud's anatomy of personality is built around the concepts of the *id, ego,* and *superego*. Each of these aspects of personality is related to the other two both genetically and functionally. The id is the primary aspect of personality, of which little is known. It is, in Freud's own words, "a chaos, a cauldron of seething excitement" (1933, p. 104). Freud believed that the id is "somewhere" in direct contact with the somatic or bodily processes from which it accepts the instinctual needs and converts them into wishes. Because the id is a mass of blind instincts, it has no logical organization. Indeed, contradictory impulses may exist in it side by side. There is, moreover, no sense of time; thus, impulses either originally in the id or forced into it by repression can remain unaltered for an indefinite period. In this way Freud is able to account for the persistence of repressed traumatic experiences from childhood into adulthood. Finally, the id is amoral. It possesses no sense of values and, therefore, cannot distinguish between good and evil. It is dominated by the pleasure principle.

For the very good reason that id processes are unconscious, Freud's evidence for the structure of the id is entirely indirect. He deduced its characteristics from the study of dreams and neurotic symptom formation. Because dreams represent wishes and since symptoms are essentially compromises between the direct impulses of the id and the demands of the ego and superego, the id is best characterized as the conative, unconscious aspect of personality. Thus Freud conceived of a confluence of instincts as the driving force that constitutes the substratum of personality. These instincts originate in tissue needs and are expressed in the form of wishes or desires to get rid of the accompanying bodily excitation. Of these instincts, the most important from the Freudian point of view is, of course, the sexual, or libidinal, instinct (see Chapter 12).

The ego is "that part of the id which has been modified by its proximity to the external world and the influences the latter has on it, and which serves the purpose of receiving stimuli and protecting the organism from them, like the cortical layer with which a particle of living substance surrounds itself" (Freud, 1933, p. 106). Freud further characterizes the ego-id relationship as one in which the ego represents external reality to the id and, at the same time, arbitrates the blind, chaotic striving of the id and the superior forces and demands of the environment. If the id

---

[1]The primary source from which our exposition is taken is *New Introductory Lectures on Psychoanalysis* (1933, chap. 3).

were not so protected, it would be destroyed. The essential mechanism by which the ego accomplishes its protective function is the "reality test." Specifically, after observing the external world, the ego searches its own perceptions in order to determine whether traces of internal impulses have crept in and distorted the picture. In this way the ego "dethrones" the pleasure principle in favor of the reality principle, which in the long run "promises greater security and greater success" (Freud, 1933, p. 106).

The ego, as previously pointed out, is the logical, ordered aspect of personality—as it must be if it is to deal effectively with reality. This latter aspect is what Freud believes chiefly distinguishes the ego from the id. The organizational, critical, and synthesizing abilities of the ego make possible a life of reason, despite the fundamentally animalistic nature of man. However, it must be emphasized that the ego's power is derived entirely from the id and that the ego's ultimate goal is to meet the demands of the id as far as possible by compromising with reality. Consequently the ego is in the position of an executive whose powers have been delegated from below. He or she must try to run the organization in a way to maximize both owner and customer satisfaction.

The superego is the aspect of the ego that makes possible the process of self-observation commonly called "conscience." Although Freud believes that the superego is an aspect or function of the ego, he views the superego at the same time as more or less autonomous in function; he therefore deals with it as if it were a separate entity. The self-observation function of the ego is a necessary prerequisite to the critical and judicial aspects of the superego. In other words, one must be able to stand apart from oneself before being able to serve as one's own critic. The moral and judicial aspects of the superego come largely from internalization of parental restrictions, prohibitions, customs, and the like through the process of *identification* (Freud, 1933, p. 90). The child wishes to be like the parents; therefore, he or she unconsciously acquires the parents' moral point of view. Freud further points out that the child's superego is not modeled on the parents' behavior, but on the parents' superego. The superego therefore becomes the vehicle of tradition, for, in a sense, it is handed down from generation to generation. Freud believes that this helps to explain why racial traditions tend to remain relatively fixed and yield but slowly to new developments. Finally, the superego is the source of human idealism. All striving for perfection arises out of the superego.

Because of their antithetical nature, the id, ego, and superego cannot exist side by side as a harmonious triumvirate. Instead, the id and superego are in constant conflict with the ego. The id, of course, demands satisfaction that the superego cannot countenance. Consequently, the ego is at the mercy of the other two aspects of personality. Moreover, as indicated previously, the ego must meet the demands of reality if the individual is to function in society. As Freud puts it, "the poor ego . . . has to serve three harsh masters, and has to do its best to reconcile the demands of all three" (1933, p. 108). Because of the imminent danger inherent in allowing the id the satisfaction of its demands, the ego, when hard pressed, experiences anxiety. But if it rids itself of intolerable anxiety by giving in to the demands of the id, the superego punishes the ego by generating a sense of guilt and inferiority.

In its attempts to mediate between the pressures of the environment, on the one hand, and the demands of the superego and id, on the other hand, the ego develops *defense mechanisms,* which are modes of behavior that serve to relieve ego tensions. Generally speaking, the defense mechanisms function unconsciously in that the ego is unaware of what is taking place. Because of this, the mechanisms are able to fulfill their primary function of distorting the ego's perception of reality in such a way as to take the pressure off the ego. We shall discuss each of the principal defense mechanisms in turn.

First, and of greatest significance for both the individual and Freudian theory, is the mechanism of *repression.* In modern psychoanalytic theory, repression has two related meanings. First, it refers to the forceful ejection from consciousness of painful or shameful experiences. Second, repression refers to the process of preventing unacceptable impulses or desires from reaching consciousness. A soldier's inability to remember fleeing the battlefield exemplifies the first type of repression, and the child's unconscious sexual attraction to the parent of the opposite sex exemplifies the second. In either case, the purpose is essentially the same, namely, to protect the ego from experiences and impulses incompatible with the individual's high evaluation of the self.

When repressions occur, they are maintained by an expenditure of libidinal energy. Consequently the individual's limited store of energy is partly used up and is therefore unavailable to the ego. Moreover, because of their dynamic nature, repressions are exceedingly difficult to resolve. Thus the individual who suffers from too many repressions becomes weakened and eventually experiences a neurosis or psychosis. The tenacity with which such individuals maintain repressions is revealed in a general way by the length of a typical Freudian psychoanalysis and more specifically by resistance during analysis. Therefore, the chief goal of psychoanalysis is the resolution of repressions.

Reaction formation is a mechanism that functions to replace repressed wishes by their opposites. The husband whose wife is a hopeless invalid may unconsciously wish to be rid of her, but because any direct wish that she die would be abhorrent, the negative wish is expressed through reaction formation as excessive concern for her welfare and attentiveness to her needs. If the process were conscious, we would say that the husband "leans over backwards" to show love and concern in a trying situation.

Regression occurs when the individual reverts to satisfactions more appropriate to an earlier level of development. The older child who begins to wet the bed when a new baby arrives may be seeking the mother's attention yet be unable to demand it consciously because the need arises out of jealousy and is therefore unacceptable. Similarly, but far more serious in its nature, is the adult psychotic's playing with dolls. Here regression has progressed to a truly remarkable degree.[2]

Rationalization is a defense mechanism commonly observed in daily life. We all rationalize whenever we give "good" or socially acceptable reasons for our conduct in place of real reasons.

---

[2]See Chapter 12 for an experimental demonstration of regression.

Less common, and more undesirable from the point of view of adjustment, is the related mechanism of *projection,* which means attributing to others one's own undesirable impulses or behavior patterns. The classic example of projection occurs in paranoia, where the psychotic's delusions of persecution take the form of attributing destructive impulses to other people or social groups.

Fantasy is another commonly observed variety of behavior, which as an ego-defense mechanism takes the form of seeking imaginary satisfactions in place of real ones.

In addition to these defense mechanisms, we have already encountered *identification,* wherein the individual satisfies directly unattainable desires by putting himself or herself in another's place (Chapter 12). Similarly, we found *sublimation,* or the transformation of libidinal urges into socially acceptable interests and activities, to be one of the normal mechanisms of psychosexual development (Chapter 12). Finally, *conversion* is the changing of mental conflicts into physical symptoms.

In concluding our discussion of id, superego, and ego functions, we must emphasize that Freud did not conceive of these aspects of personality as real entities or little spiritlike creatures that inhabit the mind and control the individual as if he or she were a puppet worked by a system of strings. Rather, Freud utilized the concepts as symbolic of processes or systems of thought. As Hall and Lindzey (1978) have pointed out, the id may be considered the *biological component* of personality, the ego the *psychological,* and the superego the *social.* Thinking of the three interacting processes in this way makes them seem less mysterious and, at the same time, avoids the danger of personification.

The dynamics underlying the development of personality have already been discussed in Chapter 7. It will be recalled that the child moves through three basic stages of psychosexual development—the *oral, anal,* and *genital*—and that differences in the adult personality are related to the manner in which the individual resolves the various conflicts associated with his or her early development. The student should also review Freud's theory of anxiety discussed in Chapter 13, on emotion, since the various types of anxiety are closely related to the functions of the ego and superego.

Freud's system has been the most widely influential of all theories of personality. His views have had a profound influence not only in the fields of psychology and psychiatry but also in art, literature, ethics, philosophy, and related disciplines. Although psychologists acknowledge psychology's debt to Freud, not all agree on the validity of his basic assumptions and the emphasis he placed on the various aspects of psychological development. Perhaps the chief target of academic psychologists' criticism is Freud's methodological procedures (Hall & Lindzey, 1978; Heidbreder, 1933; Hilgard, 1956). Freud's biased samples, uncritical acceptance of his patients' statements, and his instinct-oriented approach to personality have come under heavy fire in the past half-century. On the other hand, his concept of the unconscious determination of much of our behavior, his causal determinism, and his emphasis on childhood as the critical period for personality development have been well received by many academic psychologists, especially the behaviorists.

In recent years Freudian theory has undergone considerable evolution in the hands of his followers; and some years ago academic psychologists made a serious attempt to subject many of his basic concepts to experimental verification (Hilgard, 1956; R. Sears, 1943, 1944). Although the psychoanalysts and academicians have not yet discovered enough broad areas of agreement to effect a rapprochement between the two disciplines, the once bitter antagonisms have largely disappeared.

R. B. CATTELL'S FACTORIAL SYSTEM[3]

Since we are already familiar with the factor analytic method in the investigation of psychological processes, we may begin our study of R. B. Cattell's (b. 1905) factorial theory with a definition. Personality is defined as *"that which permits a prediction of what a person will do in a given situation"* (Cattell, 1950, p. 2). More recently Cattell (1965) has formulated his definition as $R = f(S \cdot P)$ which reads, R, the nature and magnitude of a response, is a function, f, of both environmental situations in which the individual finds himself, S, and his personality, P. However, Cattell makes it clear that this definition is more denotative (or restrictive) than connotative (or broad). Because personality connotes all of the behavior of the individual, precise description and measurement, which are the first stages of the scientific study of personality, must begin with a relatively restricted definition. When adequate descriptions and measurements have been carried out, the more restricted units of behavior must be integrated into the larger whole—which, in the last analysis, is the true picture of the functioning personality as it exists in its natural environment.

After discussing both types and traits as possible units of description and measurement, Cattell makes it clear that he favors the trait approach as the more fruitful. Traits are defined as a "characterological or relatively permanent feature of personality" (Cattell & Scheirer, 1961, p. 500). Traits are inferred from the individual's behavior and are of two fundamental kinds: *surface traits* and *source traits*. Surface traits are revealed by correlating "trait-elements" or "trait-indicators," which are essentially behavior samples that "go together." For example, tests or ratings of independence, boldness, alertness, enthusiasm, and energy level tend, when correlated, to form a cluster revealing the existence of a surface trait of "energy, boldness, spiritedness" (Cattell, 1945, p. 147).

By means of such correlation techniques, Cattell found that the hundreds of traits used to describe and measure personality could be reduced to between fifty and sixty "nuclear clusters." Obviously, if two trait tests correlate positively to a relatively high degree, they are describing or measuring essentially the same behavior. One might expect, for example, that tests of "dominance" and "ascendance" would show high positive correlations. In this case both tests are evidently measures of the same trait, and, even more important, are related to the same underlying functional unity.

---

[3]The exposition is primarily based on Cattell (1950, 1965) and on Cattell and Scheirer (1961), except as otherwise indicated.

In order to exemplify Cattell's general approach, we have reproduced a sample list of ten rating traits in Table 16-1. As Cattell suggests (1965, p. 62), such traits might be used by raters in assessing the personality traits of young men or women with whom they are well acquainted. When fifty to sixty such traits are rated and correlated, they form the clusters of related traits referred to above.

TABLE 16-1.   List of Ten Rating Traits[a]

1. *Adaptable:* flexible; accepts changes of plan easily.	vs.	*Rigid:* insists that things be done the way he or she has always done them.
2. *Emotional:* excitable; cries a lot (children), laughs a lot, shows affection, anger, all emotions to excess.	vs.	*Calm:* stable, shows few signs of emotional excitement of any kind.
3. *Conscientious:* honest; knows what is right and generally does it.	vs.	*Unconscientious:* somewhat unscrupulous; not too careful about standards of right and wrong where personal desires are concerned.
4. *Conventional:* conforms to accepted standards, ways of acting, thinking, dressing, and the like.	vs.	*Unconventional, eccentric:* acts differently from others.
5. *Prone to Jealousy:* begrudges the achievement of others.	vs.	*Not jealous:* likes people even if they do better than he or she does.
6. *Considerate, polite:* deferential to needs of others.	vs.	*Inconsiderate, rude:* insolent, defiant, and "saucy" to elders (in children); ignores feelings of others.
7. *Quitting:* gives up before thoroughly finishing a job.	vs.	*Determined, persevering:* sees a job through in spite of difficulties or temptations.
8. *Tender:* governed by sentiment; intuitive, emphathetic, sympathetic.	vs.	*Tough, hard:* governed by fact and necessity rather than sentiment.
9. *Self-effacing:* blames himself or herself (or nobody) if things go wrong.	vs.	*Egotistical:* blames others whenever there is conflict or things go wrong.
10. *Languid, fatigued, slow:* lacks vigor; vague and slow in speech.	vs.	*Energetic, alert, active:* quick, forceful, active, decisive, full of pep, vigorous, spirited.

[a]Adapted from R. B. Cattell. *The Scientific Analysis of Personality,* pp. 62–64. Copyright © Raymond B. Cattell, 1965. Reprinted by permission of Penguin Books Ltd.

It will be observed that traits are described as bipolar opposites. This convention is typical of personality systems that depend upon statistical methods of description and measurement. The assumption is that traits are normally distributed in a continuous manner, with a few individuals showing extreme degrees of the trait and with most people falling in the middle or median range (see Figure 16-1).

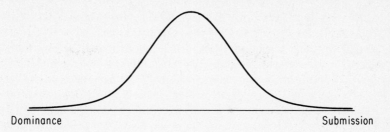

Dominance   Submission

FIGURE 16-1.   The theoretical distribution of the personality trait dominance-submission in the population at large. Few individuals are extremely dominant or submissive; most individuals fall in the median range.

Source traits are revealed by factor analysis and represent deeper, less variable, and more significant aspects of personality. Whereas surface traits are merely *descriptive* units, the source traits upon which they depend are partly *explanatory* and, therefore, represent causes of the correlations observed among surface traits. Cattell believes that with further research source traits will be found to correspond to the most fundamental influences—physiological, temperamental, and social—that give rise to personality.

In repeated factorial studies of surface trait correlation clusters, Cattell has found evidence for the existence of as many as twenty source traits. Table 16-2 shows a list of Cattell's personality factors, with both their technical and popular names.

TABLE 16-2.   Technical and Popular Labels for Personality Factors A to Q_4[a]

Low-Score Descriptions[b]	Factor		Factor	High-Score Descriptions[b]
Reserved (sizothymia)	A−	vs.	A+	Outgoing (affectothymia)
Less intelligent (low "g")	B−	vs.	B+	More intelligent (high "g")
Emotional (low ego strength)	C−	vs.	C+	Stable (high ego strength)
Humble (submissive)	E−	vs.	E+	Assertive (dominance)
Sober (desurgency)	F−	vs.	F+	Happy-go-lucky (surgency)
Expedient (low superego)	G−	vs.	G+	Conscientious (high superego)
Shy (threctia)	H−	vs.	H+	Venturesome (parmia)
Tough-minded (harria)	I−	vs.	I+	Tender-minded (premsia)
Trusting (alaxia)	L−	vs.	L+	Suspicious (protension)
Practical (praxernia)	M−	vs.	M+	Imaginative (autia)
Forthright (artlessness)	N−	vs.	N+	Shrewd (shrewdness)
Placid (assurance)	O−	vs.	O+	Apprehensive (guilt-proneness)
Conservative (conservatism)	Q_1−	vs.	Q_1+	Experimenting (radicalism)
Group-tied (group adherence)	Q_2−	vs.	Q_2+	Self-sufficient (self-sufficiency)
Casual (low integration)	Q_3−	vs.	Q_3+	Controlled (high self-concept)
Relaxed (low ergic tension)	Q_4−	vs.	Q_4+	Tense (ergic tension)

[a]Adapted from R. B. Cattell. *The Scientific Analysis of Personality*, pp. 62–64. Copyright © Raymond B. Cattell, 1965. Reprinted by permission of Penguin Books Ltd.
[b]The technical labels appear in parentheses.

It will be noted that Factor A is the familiar trait of being reserved, withdrawn, and lacking in affective or emotional reactivity toward others as opposed to outgoingness, sociability, and warmth in emotional reactions toward others. Cattell formerly referred to this trait as cyclothymia-schizothymia, but modified the name because it was derived from schizophrenia and manic-depressive psychoses and had connotations of mental disorders. Other neologisms such as *harria, alaxia, threctia,* and *praxernia* have been coined by Cattell to avoid the connotations which have accrued to the more popular descriptions of the corresponding personality traits or to such shopworn technical terms as *extroversion* and *introversion*.

Not all of this extensive list of traits has been repeatedly confirmed by studies. The list of Cattell's traits is constantly undergoing revision on the basis of empirical research and clinical data, as is to be expected in the case of a viable theory.

Source traits, such as those shown in Table 16-2, may be further categorized according to whether they arise out of the operation of environmental or hereditary influences. Those which result from environmental forces are *environmental-mold traits,* and those which are hereditarily determined are called *constitutional traits*. Factor A (sizothymia versus affectothymia) exemplifies a constitutional trait, whereas Q_1 (conservatism versus radicalism) is probably an environmental-mold trait. Surface traits, on the other hand, reflect the operation of more than one source trait and therefore cannot be divided into environmentally versus constitutionally determined classes.

Finally, in regard to the descriptive phase of Cattell's system, traits may be categorized as *dynamic, ability,* or *temperamental*. This threefold category refers to the manner in which the trait is expressed. Dynamic traits are concerned with goal-directed behavior; ability traits, with how well or effectively the individual works toward a goal; and temperamental traits, with the emotional reactivity, speed, or energy with which he or she responds. Cattell believes there is a practical advantage in identifying traits according to their manner or modality of expression. If, for example, one is concerned with the measurement of intelligence, the testee's dynamic and temperamental traits should be at an optimum level. If not, the results of the test will reflect combinations of traits rather than single traits. Similarly, in clinical investigations, abilities may be ignored in favor of dynamic and temperamental traits.

Thus far we might summarize Cattell's personality theory as follows. From the psychological point of view human personality may be considered as an integration of traits. The individual's behavior as he or she interacts with the environment reflects a relatively large number of *surface traits*. In any given culture such traits are common to most individuals and can, therefore, be measured by objective tests and ratings. Surface traits are dependent upon underlying *source traits,* which may be identified by factor analytic studies of surface trait correlation clusters. Such studies have thus far revealed a limited number of such traits, some of which are related to basic constitutional factors and others to environmental influences. Traits may also be described in terms of how they are expressed—as abilities, as dynamic (or goal-directed) traits, or as reactive-temperamental traits.

In the further development of his system, Cattell is primarily concerned with (1) the dynamics of the functioning personality and (2) its development. Central to the problem of dynamics are his concepts of *ergs* and *metaergs*. Equally crucial to the problem of development are his principles of personality formation. We shall consider each of these aspects of the theory in turn.

In essence, an *erg* is a dynamic, constitutional source trait. In terms of a formal definition, an erg is

> . . . an innate psychophysical disposition which permits its possessor to acquire reactivity (attention, recognition) to certain classes of objects more readily than others, to experience a specific emotion in regard to them, and to start on a course of action which ceases more completely at a certain specific goal activity than at any other. The pattern includes also preferred behavior subsidiation paths to the preferred goal. (Cattell, 1950, p. 199)

Cattell points out that the definition emphasizes four main points. First, the goal-directed individual is selectively tuned toward certain environmental objects. Second, an ergic pattern carries with it a certain characteristic emotion. Third, the pattern results in a specific type of goal satisfaction. Fourth, there is an innate preference for certain paths leading to the goal.

Cattell is not yet ready to present a complete list of human ergs; but on the basis of preliminary research he indicates that sex, self-assertion, fear, gregariousness, parental protectiveness, appeal or self-abasement, play, curiosity, and narcissism are fundamental (1950, p. 198).[4] More recently Cattell (1965, pp. 185–186) has emphasized the essentially instinctive nature of fundamental motives or ergs. Referring to his *dynamic lattice* (see Figure 16-2), Cattell notes that various attitudes, sentiments, and motives eventually reduce to basic, instinctive goals.

A *metaerg* is like an erg in all respects except that it is an environmental-mold source trait rather than a constitutional source trait. In short, metaergs are learned, whereas ergs are innate. Cattell considers sentiments as the most important of the various metaergs. By definition, sentiments are "major acquired dynamic trait structures which cause their possessors to pay attention to certain objects or classes of objects, and to feel and react in a certain way with regard to them" (Cattell, 1950, p. 161).

Following Cattell's own example, we can conveniently illustrate the concept of sentiment by an individual's feelings toward his or her home. Home means first of all the partial satisfaction of the basic ergs such as sex, gregariousness, and parental protection. Furthermore, one's sentiment toward home is compounded of attitudes and opinions about insurance, marriage, gardening, children, education, and so forth. Such an interrelated complex of processes Cattell describes as a "dynamic lattice." Attitudes are evolved out of sentiments, and these, in turn, arise out of the

---

[4]See also Cattell (1950, pp. 180–181) for a more extensive "preliminary" list of possible ergs.

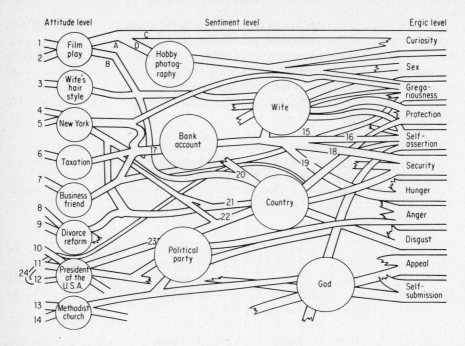

Attitude level   Sentiment level   Ergic level

FIGURE 16-2.   A dynamic lattice showing subsidiation of attitudes, sentiments, and ergic levels. (From Personality by R. B. Cattell. Copyright © 1950 by the McGraw-Hill Book Company.)

fundamental ergs. For example, the sentiment toward one's country is developed on the basis of security, protection, and disgust (presumably one is not always satisfied with one's country!). The sentiment toward country, in turn, governs attitudes toward the movies, New York, divorce, the President of the United States, and so on. Cattell's general term for the interdependence of attitudes, sentiments, and ergs is *subsidiation.*

Finally, one of the most important sentiments is the *self-sentiment,* or the ability to contemplate one's self. The self-sentiment is, of course, founded on the concept of the *self,* which Cattell considers to be an integration of the ego and superego. Cattell admittedly favors the Freudian conception of self, but believes that he has discovered independent evidence in factor analytic studies to support Freud's clinically derived concepts of the ego and superego as aspects of the self. In any case, Cattell argues that the "ultimate integration (of sentiment structures) is to be accounted for only by a conscious sentiment centered in the self and including ego and superego" (1950, p. 267).

Cattell views the development of the human personality as the unfolding of maturational processes and their modification through learning and experience. Generally speaking, maturation contributes the basic perceptual and motor abilities, whereas learning is responsible for the modification of innate ergs, the elaboration of metaergs, and the organization of the self. The course of personality development and the "principles of personality formation" are contained in chapters 19–21 of

Cattell's *Personality* (1950) and are far too extensive to summarize here. Instead, we shall attempt to present only a broad outline of his views.

During the period from conception to puberty the child's personality undergoes its most significant developmental phases. The years from 1 to 5 are critical for the development of both normal and abnormal traits. Either type of trait remains remarkably constant from 5 until puberty. About the ages of 7 to 8 the child begins to be weaned from parental influence. He or she acquires the social code of the culture, the dominant trends in interests, and characteristic emotional patterns; finally, leader-follower characteristics also begin to appear. Around the age of 10 or 11, secondary groups, such as the gang and school, begin to exert as much influence on the developing personality as does the home. Depending upon the rate of development, some children at this age begin to experience the cleavage between home- and peer-group-approved forms of behavior. At the end of the period, adolescent interests start to emerge.

Adolescence is a period that makes great demands on the child. At one and the same time he or she is confronted with the many biological and intellectual changes typical of the period. He or she must adjust to the demands of sex, accompanied as they are by increasing self-assertion, and at the same time is under pressure to postpone the satisfaction of sexual needs. He or she must also strive to maintain parental approval in the face of growing independence. In short, the child must attempt to satisfy four different sets of demands, which arise from the following sources: (1) parents, (2) adolescent peers, (3) adult culture patterns, and (4) the internal "residues" of childhood (superego).

The period of maturity is one of a gradual but steady decline of most of the biologically based mental processes. During this period the average individual tends to substitute familial for social interests, grows more philosophical, and becomes increasingly more stable emotionally. With the onset of old age, new adjustments are demanded as a result of both loss of occupation and the decreased social value of the aged in our culture.

In later years Cattell's highly active research program has led him to apply his theoretical findings to practical situations. In *The Meaning and Measurement of Neuroticism and Anxiety* (1961), written with I. H. Scheirer, Cattell has returned to his early clinical interests to offer techniques for the assessment of neuroticism and anxiety. In a more recent semipopular book, *The Scientific Analysis of Personality* (1965), he shows how his factor analytic approach may be applied to problems in vocational, educational, and clinical psychology. Special attention is given to personality testing of schoolchildren and to the relationship of personality theory to the broad social problems involved in psychotherapy and mental health, and to culture-fair tests of intelligence (1971).

In attempting to evaluate Cattell's factorial theory of personality we are confronted with many of the problems that arise in attempts to assess factor theories of intelligence (see Chapter 15). That the method itself is precise and highly quantitative, if correctly applied, cannot be doubted. Moreover, as Hall and Lindzey (1978) point out, the entrance of factor theories into the area of personality has provided a refreshingly empirical emphasis in a field otherwise weighted with subjective theories. However, as is true in the study of intelligence, the factor analyst must at some stage in the research name the factors revealed by empirical manipulations of the correlational matrices. It is at this point that subjectivity is likely to creep into the picture. However, as Cattell and others who employ factorial techniques have pointed out, refinement of the tests upon which the studies depend will, to a great extent, eliminate this particular criticism.

The whole question of whether the highly objective, trait-dominated approach to personality is to be preferred to the clinically oriented, idiographic approach is, of course, a long-standing controversy in the field. The objective method has the advantage of providing general principles of personality development and operation, whereas the clinical, individual approach has the advantage of dealing with real individuals instead of statistical abstractions. In the long run the two orientations are not antagonistic, but complementary. The clinician needs tests—tests that must be standardized by means of large-scale testing programs. The quantitative psychologist, on the other hand, cannot afford to lose sight of the individual personality. Consequently, he or she needs the clinician's insights and observations to provide points of departure for the construction of tests and the design of research programs.

GORDON W. ALLPORT'S PSYCHOLOGY OF INDIVIDUALITY[5]

Gordon W. Allport's (1897–1968) systematic views on personality were developed over a period of 30 years, during which time he was guided by two basic principles: (1) to do justice to the *complexity* of personality, compounded as it is of hereditary, temperamental, social, and "psychological" factors, and (2) to recognize the *uniqueness* of each individual personality despite the many commonalities that exist among different people. To put it another way, Allport attempted to develop a psychology of personality that recognized the value of the nomothetic approach—especially in regard to the foundations of personality and its quantitative measurement—and at the same time recognized the value of the idiographic method.

Let us begin with his well-known definition of personality: "Personality is the dynamic organization within the individual of those psychophysical systems that determine his characteristic behavior and thought" (1961, p. 28).[6] Allport characterizes his definition as a "synthesis" of contemporary definitions and goes on to point out the denotation of the more important elements within the definition.

By "dynamic organization" he means that personality is a developing, changing organization that reflects motivational conditions. By stressing an active organization Allport avoids what he terms the "sterile enumerations of the omnibus definitions."

---

[5]Except as noted, the exposition follows G. W. Allport (1937, 1950, 1955, 1961).

[6]In the 1937 edition of *Personality* the definition reads: "Personality is the dynamic organization within the individual of those psychophysical systems that determine his unique adjustments to his environment" (p. 48). Thus, the later definition is only slightly modified from the original.

"Psychophysical," as Allport uses the phrase, refers to habits, attitudes, and traits. Obviously, the choice of the term "psychophysical" is a recognition of the fact that both bodily *and* mental factors must be considered in the description and study of personality.

"Systems" refers to complexes of more elemental processes. Habits, traits, and concepts exemplify such systems.

"Characteristic" refers to the uniqueness of each individual's behavior.

"Behavior and thought . . . are a blanket to designate anything whatsoever an individual may do" (G. W. Allport, 1961, pp. 28–29). In general, they make for survival and growth in the environment.

The inclusion of the term "determine" is a natural consequence of Allport's psychophysical point of view. Personality is *not* synonymous with mere activity or behavior, but is that which *underlies* behavior. The psychophysical systems that constitute personality are "determining tendencies," which when set into motion by appropriate stimuli give rise to behavioral acts through which we come to know personality.

Basic to Allport's definition is the underlying idea of personality as a *dynamic* (motivated), *growing* system. The concept of the functional autonomy of motives provides the necessary foundation for the system. We must now examine the concept at some length, for in many ways it constitutes the core of Allport's system.

Functional autonomy *"refers to any acquired system of motivation in which the tensions involved are not of the same kind as the antecedent tensions from which the acquired system developed"* (G. W. Allport, 1961, p. 229). Thus, a child originally may be motivated to practice the piano because of tensions associated with fear of parental retaliation if he or she fails to put in the daily stint. Indeed, he or she might prefer to be out playing baseball. However, after five or six years of training, the child may practice for the sole reason that playing is enjoyed for its own sake. The activity of piano playing, which once served to reduce the fear of punishment, has now become self-motivating. Moreover, we may assume in this case that the original motive has long since subsided.

Allport cites as examples of functionally autonomous behavior such everyday instances as the good workman continuing to do an excellent job, even though his income no longer depends on it; the urban citizen's longing for the hills of home; the "unwilling" mother's eventual acquisition of love for her child; and the businessman's amassing of more wealth than he can ever spend.

Allport distinguishes between two types of functionally autonomous systems: the *perseverative* and the *propriate*. Perserverative functional autonomy refers to physiologically based motivational systems that, once activated, can continue to function for a time without further environmental stimulation. Thus, the animal or man who becomes habituated to cycles of feeding or to drugs becomes restless and active at regular intervals corresponding to the usual time of ingestion of the food or drug. Allport also cites task perseveration, such as occurs in the Zeigarnik effect (see Chapter 10), as an example of perseverative striving.

Propriate functional autonomy involves higher-order processes such as interests, attitudes, and life-style. Allport suggests that interests tend to follow abilities, and people tend to do what they can do best. Such interests are functionally autonomous when the present reason for exercising the ability is no longer related to the original reason except in a historical sense. Thus the college student who is required to take a course and does so only reluctantly may develop an interest in it and perhaps even major in the subject area. Similarly, one may acquire values and an entire life-style through training programs in childhood, which—though accepted reluctantly—later become functionally autonomous of the original fear or coercion that compelled their original acceptance. It is these latter processes that are central to the major trends of life and become the organizing core of personality. In discussing propriate motivation Allport also stresses the close relationship between motives and cognitive processes. All motives are a blend of both motives and cognitive processes. Because of these blends the individual develops a "cognitive style," which is dependent upon how the culture and the self are perceived.

The principle of functional autonomy of motivation—as the examples indicate—stresses both the *contemporaneity* and *variety* of adult human motives. Clearly, Allport is in direct opposition to the psychoanalytic view of personality dynamics, in which all present behavior must be traced to its genetic origins. Present motives, Allport asserts, are *continuous* with original motives, just as a modern city is historically related to its origins. But neither the adult human being nor the modern city *depends* on its origins for its present "drive." Similarly, Allport divorces his system from the earlier instinct psychologies, such as McDougall's. Instincts may appear in the course of development, but having appeared they are transformed under the influence of learning.

The principle of functional autonomy is also in opposition to the behaviorists' theory of acquired drives. It will be recalled from Chapter 12 that the behaviorist accounts for acquired drives by invoking the principle of generalization of conditioned stimuli. That is, if a fear is originally acquired by conditioning it to an arbitrary stimulus, theoretically it can become attached to a multitude of additional stimuli by further conditioning. But in such cases the determining factor in arousing and maintaining behavior is the continuing reinforcement provided by the various conditioned stimuli, not the activity itself.

Finally, Allport's concept of functional autonomy is in opposition to the principle of homeostasis, since once a motive becomes functionally autonomous it is self-sustaining. Homeostasis, on the other hand, implies the cyclic appearance of motivation dependent upon changes in physiological rhythms.

On the positive side, the principle of functional autonomy explains the transformation of the selfish child into the socialized adult. It can account for phobias, delusions, and other forms of compulsive behavior. Further, the driving force behind such complex activities as craftsmanship, artistic endeavor, and genius is explained as love of the activity for its own sake. Allport argues that all these cases require a strained and illogical interpretation of human nature to account for adult motivation in terms of its genetic origins. Functional autonomy is, in Allport's words, "a declaration of independence" for personality theory (1937, p. 207). Although the concept of functional autonomy is a central principle in Allport's system, it cannot account for all complexities of personality. Rather, the principle is concerned with how the dynamics underlying the "psychophysical systems" that constitute personality develop and serve the adult. Allport is perfectly willing to admit the importance of the role of learning in personality development. However, he makes it clear that learning as he defines it is not the quasi-mechanical learning of the behaviorists (1961, p. 108).

Allport makes it obvious that he favors the trait as the most valid concept for the description of personality. By definition, a trait is *"a neuropsychic structure having the capacity to render many stimuli functionally equivalent, and to initiate and guide equivalent (meaningfully consistent) forms of adaptive and expressive behavior"* (G. W. Allport, 1961, p. 347).

The definition further implies that traits are *consistent* modes of behavior, which are similar to habits but are more generalized. In principle, traits are more like attitudes than habits, since they are determining tendencies rather than specific modes of behavior. Consistency is revealed by the Uriah Heep who is always sycophantic in all situations and who always puts himself in an obsequious position. Similarly, the honest man is presumably consistent in his behavior. We must, however, be careful to recognize that traits are not necessarily generalized from situation to situation. A child may be *consistently* honest in a given situation, say, in handling money in a grocery store, but occasionally dishonest in school. Thus, the consistency of traits is, in part, dependent upon the consistency of the situation in which they are aroused. Obviously, such considerations are important for the practical measurement and prediction of traits.

Allport next distinguishes *individual* traits and *common* traits. In a sense every trait is an individual trait, since each personality is different from every other. However, this view of traits, if taken literally, would make cross-comparisons between individuals impossible. Indeed, if such conditions prevailed, there could be no science of personality. However, because members of a given culture are subject to common evolutionary and social influences, there are many aspects of behavior on which members of a given culture can be compared. These are common traits. In terms of a more formal definition:

> *A common trait is a category for classifying functionally equivalent forms of behavior in a general population of people. Though influenced by nominal and artificial considerations, a common trait to some extent reflects veridical and comparable dispositions in many personalities who, because of a common human nature and common culture, develop similar modes of adjusting to their environments, though to varying degrees.* (G. W. Allport, 1961, p. 349)

In research programs employing tests, rating scales, and the like, the psychologist is making use of the common-trait (nomothetic) approach. Allport, himself, has provided such a technique in the Allport-Vernon-Lindzey Scale. The scale allows for a cross-comparison of the individual with a standardization group on the relative strength of common values—theoretical, economic, esthetic, social, political, and religious.

Allport further distinguishes between *cardinal traits, central traits,* and *secondary traits.* A trait that is outstanding, all-pervasive, and dominant in the individual's life is a cardinal trait. It is, so to speak, a "ruling passion." For this reason cardinal traits are relatively rare. Central traits, on the other hand, are the foci of personality. They are the traits ordinarily measured by rating scales, mentioned in conversation, and described in letters of recommendation. Secondary traits are the less important or minor traits, which usually escape notice except by the careful observer or close acquaintance.

To summarize thus far, Allport's theory of personality revolves around the central concepts of *traits* and *the functional autonomy of motives*. Relating the two, *traits are functionally autonomous reaction tendencies aroused by certain classes of stimulus situations*. Such reaction tendencies are, in a sense, unique for each individual personality; but because of common biological and environmental influences, many traits may be considered as *common traits,* thus allowing for the measurement and prediction of behavior. In some individuals a trait may be of such central importance as to be the dominant factor in life. These rare traits are *cardinal traits*. For the most part the psychology of personality is concerned with *central traits,* which are the building blocks of personality, and to a minor extent with *secondary traits*.

No psychologist—least of all Allport—believes that a human personality is a mere congeries of unrelated traits. Personality demonstrates a unity and integration of traits. Such terms as the "ego" or the "self" reflect the traditional psychological view that there is an overall unifying principle to which traits, motives, experiences, and so on are related. In his later publications Allport has shown an increasing concern with the problem of identifying and describing the inner essence of personality. We shall now consider his position on this aspect of the psychology of personality.

The pivotal problem for the psychology of growth, as well as the question around which the integration and uniqueness of personality revolve, is the concept of the self. As Allport points out, the self lost out in the dominant psychological systems of the late nineteenth century and the early twentieth century. But more recently the concept has regained favor, at least in systems which have been characteristically subjective in their approach. However, while Allport is wholeheartedly in favor of a self-psychology, or ego-psychology, he warns of the danger of personifying the ego or self, thus making these concepts a *deus ex machina* to account for all behavior (G. W. Allport, 1950, p. 139; 1955, p. 39; 1961, p. 38).

Allport adopts the concept of the *proprium* to represent what psychology has traditionally included under the terms *self, ego, style of life,* and so on. As he employs it, the proprium includes the bodily sense (coenesthesis); self-identity, or the awareness of the continuity of self; ego enhancement and ego extension, or the identification of external objects with the self; rational and cognitive functions; the self-image; and propriate striving. The last concept—propriate striving—is of first importance in Allport's system.

Propriate striving refers to motivated behavior that is of central importance to the self, as opposed to behavior peripheral to the self. Examples of propriate striving include all forms of behavior that serve self-realization. The scientist, the explorer, the craftsman, the parent, the artist—all strive for goals that are in a sense forever unattainable but which confer unity to motivation and which make life meaningful. In Allport's words:

> Here seems to be the central characteristic of propriate striving: its goals are, strictly speaking unattainable. Propriate striving confers unity upon personality, but it is never the unity of fulfillment, of repose, or of reduced tension. The devoted parent never loses concern for his child; the devotee of democracy adopts a lifelong assignment in his human relationships. The scientist, by the very nature of his commitment, creates more and more questions, never fewer. Indeed the measure of our intellectual maturity, one philosopher suggests, is our capacity to feel less and less satisfied with our answers to better and better problems. (G. W. Allport, 1955, p. 67)

Propriate striving represents *growth,* or abundancy motivation, as opposed to deficiency motivation. In Allport's opinion, too much emphasis has been placed by contemporary psychologists on such concepts as tension reduction, homeostasis, and drive reduction. These are fragmentary, peripheral aspects of personality, which—while important for survival—represent but one side of human motivation. Man seeks variety, new horizons, and the freedom to explore, as well as relief from the irritations attendant upon deficiencies. The essence of personality is the individual's *way of living.* The ego or self, then, becomes the integration of the propriate functions that constitute the unified style of life.[7] In the last analysis, the style of life for the normal, healthy individual is, to use the title of G. W. Allport's 1955 volume, "becoming."

By way of concluding our summary of Allport's personalistic theory we should like to make several evaluative comments. First, the theory has been widely influential among psychologists whose major concern is the area of personality. Perhaps one reason for its success in this respect has been Allport's insistence (from the very beginning) on the individuality of personality and his allowance, at the same time, for the possibility of the quantitative, nomothetic approach through his principle of functional autonomy and his trait theory orientation.

Second, Allport's insistence on a psychology that recognizes the self as a central concept—though launched in a period when subjective concepts were still unpopular—has been vindicated. As he himself points out, the self has crept back into psychology in recent years. However, it is to Allport's credit that he has never accepted a personified self; and in his later publications he has emphasized his concern with this danger by developing the concept of the proprium to represent ways of behaving traditionally subsumed under self-functions. Because of his emphasis on the self and ego functions, Allport's is an academic theory that has been acceptable to clinically oriented psychologists.

Third, Allport's system as a whole may be characterized as on the more phenomenological, subjective side of psychological theorizing. In terms of the

---

[7]It should be noted that Allport's psychology of the proprium is closely related to Adlerian theory (Chapter 11) and to Maslow's system of motivation (Chapter 11).

systems reviewed in this volume, its closest affiliations are with the systems advocated by Adler, Maslow, the functionalists, and the Gestalt psychologists. This must not be taken to mean that Allport has simply borrowed from other systems. Rather, the influences of these systems "show through" Allport's original contributions.

Finally, in the concluding chapter of his *Pattern and Growth in Personality* (1961), Allport demonstrates his individualism and humanism in maintaining that psychology cannot sever all links with philosophy. He believes that a purely psychological conception of the individual neglects the broader problem of human nature and man's place in the cosmos. By thus accepting the validity of a broader philosophical point of view, Allport aligns himself with the humanistic psychologists who oppose the dominant *S-R* approach of contemporary American psychology. In his own words, he pleads that "Ancient wisdom, both philosophical and theological, should be consulted and incorporated lest we find ourselves dealing with elaborate trivialities" (G. W. Allport, 1961, p. 566).

H. A. MURRAY'S PERSONOLOGY[8]

Like Allport, H. A. Murray (b. 1893) developed his system over several decades. Moreover, Murray's theory also resembles Allport's in its humanistic, holistic, and eclectic orientation to the problems involved in developing a science of personality. Unlike Allport's, Murray's theory has been strongly influenced by psychoanalytic conceptions of personality and has also placed greater stress on the importance of environmental influences on the individual. Finally, by way of introduction, it should be noted that Murray has consistently stressed the fundamental significance of the physiological processes that underlie behavior; the latter, perhaps, is a reflection of its author's medical training (H. A. Murray, 1959, pp. 9–12).

As a point of departure for examining Murray's theory, let us begin with a definition: "Personality is the continuity of functional forms and forces manifested through sequences of organized regnant processes and overt behaviors from birth to death" (Murray & Kluckhohn, 1953, p. 49). There are several principal components within this definition. First, personality exhibits *continuity*. In other words, it evolves as a continuous process over the entire lifetime of the individual. Second, "regnant processes" refer to dynamically organized brain activities. Murray has always emphasized the functional dependence of personality and mental events in general on brain processes. In Murray's own words:

> Since in the higher forms of life the impressions from the external world and from the body that are responsible for conditioning and memory are received, integrated, and conserved in the brain, and since all complex adaptive behavior is evidently coordinated

---

[8]The exposition is based on the following primary sources: H. A. Murray (1938, 1951, 1959); H. A. Murray and Kluckhohn (1953). For the best summary of Murray's theory, see his 1951 article. However, the need-press theory is not elaborated in this article, which is intended only to outline certain basic considerations for personality theory.

by excitations in the brain, the unity of the organism's development and behavior can be explained only by referring to organizations occurring in this region. (1938, p. 45)

Elsewhere Murray has said that "Personality may be biologically defined as the governing organ, or superordinate institution, of the body. As such, it is located in the brain. No brain, no personality" (1951, p. 267). Thus, personality as the reflection of regnant processes is the organizing and integrating agency in the individual's life, and governs all the organismic processes.

Third, the definition emphasizes the "functional forms," or more simply the activities of personality as it contributes to the individual's adaptation to his or her environment. It is with this latter aspect of Murray's definition that we shall begin our detailed study of his system, since the most characteristic aspect of the theory is the dynamic or functional nature of personality as it mediates between the individual's needs and the demands of the environment.

It will be convenient to begin with Murray's definition of need, followed by a list of the more important needs as revealed in the elaborate studies of human personality carried out by Murray and his associates. Needs are defined as follows:

A need is a construct (a convenient fiction or hypothetical concept) which stands for force (the physicochemical nature of which is unknown) in the brain region, a force which organizes perception, apperception, intellection, conation, and action in such a way as to transform in a certain direction an existing, unsatisfying situation. (H. A. Murray, 1938, pp. 123–124)

The fundamental needs are shown in Table 16-3.[9]

TABLE 16-3. A Selected List of Murray's Latent and Manifest Needs[a]

Need	Behavioral Characteristics
Abasement	To be subservient; to surrender
Achievement	To master, manipulate, overcome; to excel; to rival
Affiliation	Friendliness, loyalty, respect for others; to be cooperative
Aggression	To attack; to overcome opposition by force; to injure or hurt others
Autonomy	To be independent or free; to be unattached or irresponsible
Deference	Compliance, comformity; to praise, support, or yield to others
Dominance	To control others; to direct or lead; to persuade; to restrain
Exhibition	To impress, to excite, to amaze others; to shock, fascinate, entertain
Harmavoidance	To avoid pain or danger; to take precautions
Infavoidance	To avoid humiliation; to avoid possible failure
Nurturance	To give sympathy or kindness; to feed, help, or support others
Rejection	To abandon, to snub; to be indifferent to another
Sex	To seek erotic relationships; to have sexual outlets
Succorance	To be nursed, supported, advised, or consoled

[a]From Murray, H. A., *Explorations in personality,* New York: Oxford, 1938, pp. 144–145.

---

[9]For more extended definitions of these and other needs listed see H. A. Murray (1938, pp. 146–227).

In general, it should be noted that Murray's needs lean heavily on Freudian and other psychoanalytic conceptions of childhood and developmental patterns. Moreover, with other psychologists, Murray recognizes the interrelatedness of needs. Needs may fuse so that behaviorally they have the same outcome. Needs may also be in conflict. The child may experience feelings of love and hate for the same person. In addition, needs may be interrelated by *subsidiation*. This concept refers to instances in which one need is placed in the service of another. Thus, an individual who is anxious and who feels inferior in social situations may nevertheless desire close personal attachments (affiliation). But, because of anxiety and inferiority, he or she can approach others only with extreme deference and so conforms strictly to custom. Excessive praise is showered on those he or she admires. He or she yields eagerly to their wishes. This pattern (deference) is, therefore, in subsidiation to the need for affiliation.

Needs may be either *latent* or *overt*. Needs that are latent are repressed or restrained. Those that are overt are expressed freely and are consciously recognized by the individual. In thus distinguishing between latent and overt needs, Murray again reveals the influence of the psychoanalytic systems of Freud and Jung.

Needs are also defined in terms of whether they are *proactive* or *reactive*. Proactive needs arise from within the individual without the necessity for environmental stimulation. The strong need for the creative individual to produce artistic or intellectual works exemplifies proactive needs in operation. Reactive needs are aroused by stimulation from the environment. Thus the sight of an attractive member of the opposite sex may arouse strong reactive needs in a young adult. However, in the final analysis all needs are processes within the individual whether aroused centrally or environmentally.

Finally, we may distinguish between Murray's concept of *process activities, modal needs,* and *effect needs*. Process activities are actions performed for their own sake without regard to some definite goal or the reduction of tensions associated with physiological needs. Thus the musician will make music on many occasions when alone, because he or she enjoys playing for its own sake. The concept of process activities is obviously closely related to G. W. Allport's functional autonomy.

Modal needs refer to the individual's desire for excellence. The musician not only plays; he or she strives to play well, to achieve a high degree of facility or excellence in rendition.

An effect need is one that leads to a goal. Playing a piano concerto in order to compete in a contest is an effect need. Many additional examples of effect needs could be found in the direct reduction of viscerogenic drives, such as hunger, thirst, and sex.

Finally, in commenting on needs, we may note that Murray accepts the widely used concept of tension reduction or the search for homeostasis, or equilibrium, as a fundamental class of needs. However, humans also have needs to generate tension; to seek excitement, novelty, and experiences that temporarily disturb their equilibrium. Thus, in Murray's system, a human is not a creature entirely at the mercy of tensions or viscerogenic irritations but partly governs his or her own need states.

At this point we should like to pause for the purpose of interpolating a brief outline of the method employed by Murray and his collaborators in identifying the needs discussed above and the perceptual press to be considered subsequently. Briefly, the need-press findings grew out of an elaborate series of investigations of fifty normal adults by Murray and a team of experts associated with the Harvard Psychological Clinic (Murray, 1938). All told, twenty-eight specialists worked together for two-and-a-half years in planning, carrying out, and evaluating the results of the project. So that the study would have scope and penetrating quality, twenty-five different procedures were employed for assessing the subject's personality. Among these were conferences, questionnaires, the Rorschach test, various experimental tests, hypnotic and analytic sessions, and the Thematic Apperception Test. The last named, familiarly known as the TAT, was especially designed by H. A. Murray and C. D. Morgan for the investigation of fantasy and is now a classic projective technique. As should be evident from even this brief outline of the procedures employed in need-press studies, Murray's conceptions are well grounded in empirical evidence. With this in mind we may go on to examine his theory of perceptual press.

A perceptual press of an object or person is "what it can do *to the subject* or *for the subject*—the power that it has to affect the well-being of the subject in one way or another" (H. A. Murray, 1938, p. 121). The common press of childhood, as revealed by the study by Murray and his Harvard co-workers, are shown in Table 16-4.

It must be emphasized that press are perceptual processes and do not represent objects or persons in the environment in a literal sense. The distinction between press and environment in Murray's theory parallels the distinction between the

TABLE 16-4. A Selected List of Murray's Perceptual Press[a]

Press	Environmental Events
Affiliation	Presence of friends or an affiliated group
Aggression	Maltreatment by others
Birth of sibling	Advent of a brother or sister
Danger of misfortune	Loss of support; being alone; storms, accidents; dangerous animals
Deception or betrayal	Fraud; artifice; lying on the part of others
Dominance, coercion, prohibition	Presence of domineering persons; administration of discipline; religious training
Family insupport	Absence, illness, or death of parent; family discord
Inferiority	A superior physical, social, or intellectual environment
Lack or loss	Deprivation of food, possessions, or companions
Nurturance, indulgence	Presence of others who are tolerant and sympathetic
Rejection	Unconcern or scorn on the part of others
Retention	Withholding of objects by others
Rival	Presence of a competing contemporary
Sex	Exposure, seduction, or parental intercourse

[a]From Murray, H. A., *Explorations in personality,* New York: Oxford, 1938, pp. 291–292.

situation and the field of Gestalt theory. Moreover, it should be noted that needs and press are interrelated in the sense that needs are fundamental to press. Invoking once more the example of a boy and an apple, if the boy is satiated the apple has little or no interest for him. If he is hungry, or at least not satiated, the apple is perceived as a desirable object. Murray, in relating needs and press, refers to the interaction of the individual and his or her needs and perceptual press with the environment in a behavior episode as a *thema*. Thus, in using the Thematic Apperception Test, or one of the other projective techniques, the psychologist *infers* the individual's needs from the themas revealed as the subject "interacts" with the test stimuli.

The discussion of the interrelation of needs and press leads us to what Murray considers the basic data of psychological observation—*proceedings*. Proceedings are the concrete activities of an individual during a specific period of time. *Internal proceedings* are the individual's consciousness of memories, fantasies, plans for the future, bodily events, and so forth. *External proceedings*, on the other hand, refer to the individual's active coping with the environment during a given temporal period. The external proceeding is "the psychologist's *real entity,* the thing he should observe, analyze, try to reconstruct, and represent if possible with a model, and thus explain it" (1953, p. 9).[10]

It has already been emphasized that the individual personality possesses continuity. The concept of proceedings does not contradict the principle of continuity. Proceedings leave traces behind them. In some little way each experience makes the individual different from what he or she was before that event occurred. Moreover, Murray employs the concept of *serials* to represent the functional interrelatedness of proceedings, which are dynamically related, although they occur discretely in time. Perhaps one of the best examples of serials is the long-term striving necessary to reach an important goal. Many proceedings stretched into programs of serials are involved in reaching an important objective such as a degree in medicine.

So much for the building blocks of Murray's conception of personality. In terms of the *development* of personality, Murray leans heavily on Freudian concepts. The concepts of the id, ego, and superego are accepted by Murray with modifications. Specifically, the id, from Murray's point of view, is not entirely constituted of unacceptable impulses, especially during the infancy period. There is, at this stage of the individual's development, nothing unacceptable about the various spontaneous and natural emotions and impulses that make possible the child's continued existence.

The ego's functions are complex, but in the main they involve perception, intellection, and conation (or will).[11] In general, Murray's view of the ego is consistent with Freud's. However, in Murray's system the ego is less of an authoritarian principle or the personification of a police force whose primary function is id suppression. Murray believes that the ego can achieve important and socially

---

[10]See also H. A. Murray (1951, pp. 268–269).

[11]The best source for Murray's view of personality organization is his article in Murray and Kluckhohn (1953).

acceptable satisfactions and that the individual is not necessarily torn by unresolved conflicts. Similarly, the superego is viewed as a product of cultural internalization, as is the case in Freudian theory. Murray also distinguishes a fourth aspect of mind, the ego ideal, which, while intimately related to the superego, is distinguishable from it. The ego ideal is the individual's guiding image; it is his or her view of the self at some future date. The ego ideal may correspond approximately to the superego—as it does in the normal, average individual. In other cases—such as the criminal or psychotic—it may be far removed from the superego's essentially social conceptions of morality.

Murray also accepts the psychoanalytic concept of infantile complexes and fixations, which lead to certain recognizable modes of adult behavior. Specifically, he recognizes the anal, oral, and castration complexes of classical Freudian theory; in addition, he emphasizes several varieties of *claustral complexes,* which are related to the individual's prenatal existence. Some people wish to reinstate the comforts of their prenatal life. In others, the complex may revolve around the anxiety attendant upon separation from the mother (birth trauma); and in still others it may take the form of anxiety over the possibility of confinement (claustrophobia). Finally, Murray recognizes the existence of a *urethral complex.* In childhood this complex involves enuresis and urethral eroticism. In the adult it takes the form of an interest in fires (spraying fires with water is presumably symbolic of urination), a tendency toward narcissism, and ambition that dissolves (becomes fluid) when the individual is faced with frustration.

In emphasizing Murray's use of the psychoanalytic complexes we must not lose sight of the fact that he also strongly emphasizes the role of environmental determinants in the ontogenesis of behavior. It will be recalled that in his concepts of thema, proceedings, and press he shows his strong interest in constantly relating the individual and the environment. Moreover, in a statement of the background of his theory Murray (1959) specifically acknowledges the influences of cultural anthropology and sociology in the formulation of his principles.

It has been possible to present only the barest summary of what appear to be the main outlines of Murray's complex theory. Despite this limitation, the more salient features and emphases should be apparent. First, the theory is eclectic in that Murray recognizes contributions from many other points of view. Moreover, his interest in anthropology, medicine, literature, and their allied disciplines has contributed both richness and diversity to his system. Second, the theory ranks high in its emphasis on dynamic and perceptual factors; on the other hand, it does not put a premium on self and individuality. It is difficult, therefore, to classify the theory with any degree of ease or precision.[12] However, its emphasis on genetic factors in personality development and on unconscious determinants in behavior, its free use of Freudian concepts, and its essentially analytic methodology place it in the psychoanalytic camp, broadly speaking. Third, Murray's theory is detailed and

---

[12]This difficulty is related to the richness of the background influences which have gone into Murray's system (1959).

complex, reflecting his broad interests and his eclecticism. But more basically, the complexity of the theory reflects Murray the man—a theorist who is highly imaginative, complex in personality, and very much the rebel in his orientation to psychology.

ROGERS' SELF THEORY[13]

Carl R. Rogers' (b. 1902) self theory is unique among the academic theories of personality that we have examined in that it grew directly out of clinical practice—a world-famous practice that began more than a half-century ago and continues in its service of maladjusted people. Client-centered therapy, or, as some prefer to call it, nondirective counseling, has attracted a group of loyal followers from both the United States and Europe. But regardless of whether a contemporary therapist practices nondirective therapy, he or she must take cognizance of Rogers' challenging and novel conception of the therapeutic process.

The Personality Theory

Table 16-5 presents the essence of Rogers' view of the normal, fully functioning person. Using the propositions in the table as points of departure, we may summarize Rogers' theory of personality.

Actualization of the self is Rogers' single dynamic construct. All other motives—whether viscerogenic or socially conditioned—are aspects of this fundamental motive. From Rogers' point of view, growth and development involve a constant tendency toward autonomy and away from control by external forces. The concept of actualizing as he employs it is very similar to the concepts of self-actualization and self-realization postulated by Maslow (Chapter 12). By adopting this point of view, Rogers aligns himself with the humanistic theorists.

We have already commented on the importance of symbolization of experiences in connection with the therapeutic process. Here we might add that the normal individual may ignore such experiences; he or she may symbolize them and make them a part of the self, or he or she may distort them and deny them symbolization. This proposition is central to Rogers' theory of the neuroses and is broadly analogous to Freud's theory of repression and the unconscious. Therapy consists in bringing distorted experiences to the patient's full awareness, so that they may be made congruent with the self. Clearly, the fully functioning and healthy person cannot have large segments of noncongruent or distorted experiences.

Positive regard and positive self-regard refer to (1) attitudes of warmth, respect, liking, and acceptance on the part of others toward the self and (2) similar attitudes with regard to one's own experiences independent of social transactions

---

[13]The primary sources for this account are C. R. Rogers (1942, 1951, 1959, 1961a, 1961b, 1963, 1965a, 1965b) and C. R. Rogers and Dymond (1954).

TABLE 16-5.   Essence of Rogers' View of the Normal, Fully Functioning Person[a]

A. The individual has an inherent tendency toward *actualizing* his organism.

B. The individual has the capacity and tendency to *symbolize experiences* accurately in *awareness.*

    1. A corollary statement is that he has the capacity and tendency to keep his *self-concept* congruent with his *experience.*

C. The individual has a *need for positive regard.*

D. The individual has a *need for positive self-regard.*

E. Tendencies A and B are most fully realized when Needs C and D are met. More specifically, Tendencies A and B tend to be most fully realized when

    1. The individual *experiences unconditional positive regard* from significant others.

    2. The pervasiveness of this *unconditional positive regard* is made evident through relationships marked by a complete and communicated *empathic* understanding of the individual's *frame of reference.*

F. If the conditions under E are met to a maximum degree, the individual who experiences these conditions will be a fully functioning person. The fully functioning person will have at least these characteristics:

    1. He will be *open to his experience.*

    (a) The corollary statement is that he will exhibit no *defensiveness.*

    2. Hence, all *experiences* will be *available to awareness.*

    3. All *symbolizations* will be as accurate as the experiental data permit.

    4. His *self-structure* will be congruent with his *experience.*

    5. His *self-structure* will be a fluid gestalt, changing flexibly in the process of assimilation of new *experience.*

    6. He will *experience* himself as the *locus of evaluation.*

    (a) The *valuing process* will be a continuing *organismic* one.

    7. He will have no *conditions of worth.*

    (a) The corollary statement is that he will *experience unconditional positive self-regard.*

    8. He will meet each situation with behavior that is a unique and creative adaptation to the newness of that moment.

    9. He will find his *organismic valuing* a trustworthy guide to the most satisfying behaviors, because

    (a) All available experiential data will be available to *awareness* and used.

    (b) No datum of *experience* will be *distorted in,* or *denied to,* awareness.

    (c) The outcomes of behavior in *experience* will be *available to awareness.*

    (d) Hence, any failure to achieve the maximum possible satisfaction because of lack of data will be corrected by this effective reality testing.

    10. He will live with others in the maximum possible harmony, because of the rewarding character of reciprocal *positive regard.*

---

[a]From S. Koch (Ed.), *Psychology: A Study of a Science,* Copyright 1959 by McGraw-Hill Book Company. Used with permission of McGraw-Hill Book Company.

---

with others. What Rogers is saying is that every healthy individual needs both types of regard—social and personal—and that the individual cannot be normal and function adequately if he or she does not experience regard for others as well as a realistically based sense of his or her own worth. And, as indicated in E in Table 16.5, self-actualizing tendencies and the congruent symbolization of experience are most fully realized under conditions of social and self-regard. It might also be noted that in therapeutic situations, regard must be unconditional and be communicated empathically by the therapist (Items 1 and 2 under E in Table 16-5).

Rogers' characteristics of the fully functioning person are listed under F in Table 16-5. Openness to experience (Characteristics 1 and 2) means that all stimuli—whether external or internal in origin—are freely transmitted through the individual's nervous system without undergoing distortion by defense mechanisms. Obviously such experiences are fully available to awareness and are also available to symbolization and self-congruency. Situations of threat, as has been suggested earlier, preclude the possibility of openness to experience. It is for this reason that children in threatening situations or individuals in therapy who feel threatened cannot adequately symbolize experiences and bring them to full awareness.

Here we must give the concept of symbolization more explicit meaning. It is essentially synonymous with awareness or consciousness. Consequently, accuracy of symbolization (Characteristic 3) means that in his or her transactions with the environment the individual will form hypotheses about reality that can be tested or validated by acting upon them. Thus the individual who makes an estimate of his or her ability based upon experiences of success or failure will neither seriously underestimate nor overestimate future potential, whereas the psychotic's estimates are likely to bear little relationship to reality.

In Rogers' own words, the self-structure (Characteristics 4 to 6) refers "to the organized, consistent conceptual Gestalt composed of perceptions of the characteristics of the I or me and the perception of the relationships of the I or me to others and to various aspects of life, together with the value attached to these perceptions" (1959, p. 200).

The self is the central concept in Rogers' theory. He confesses that the concept evolved very slowly out of his clinical experience and in opposition to his own early skepticism that such a concept could be defined in a meaningful and accurate manner. He found, however, that individuals undergoing therapy experience violent fluctuations in how they evaluate themselves, how they perceive the world about them, and how they are perceived by others. Even minor incidents can, in some cases, change the entire configuration (gestalt) of the individual's self-perception. However, regardless of how real the self may appear to the client or to the therapist, the problem of discovering an operational definition remains. Such a definition was realized, Rogers believes, in the development of the Q technique. As he and his associates use it, the technique consists of having the individual sort a pack of cards containing statements applicable to the self along a continuum or distribution. For example, seven or nine categories or reference points might be placed before the subject expressing varying degrees of self-evaluative statements, ranging from "most like" to "least like" the self. These could be taken directly from clinical protocols. When the subject has sorted the pack of statements according to the way he or she believes they describe his or her present condition, a median or average rating for the various categories can be calculated, thus giving a specific rating to each card. In this manner a quantitative estimate of the individual's self-picture can be obtained before and after therapy. Subjects who make initial sorts but who do not undergo therapy for a significant interval of time can be used as members of a control group in order to assess the effect of therapy. Clearly, if therapy changes the subject in a positive direction, we have an operational characterization not only of the self but also of the results of therapy.[14]

As a result of the flux of environmental events the self undergoes changes, which also affect its self-evaluation. The healthy individual refers to his or her own self-structure for evaluation; the neurotic or the submissive child perceives the locus of evaluation in others. Thus, Rogers offers the tragicomic example of the little girl who when asked her name replied, "Mary Ann Don't." Such a child would have only the weakest sense of self-evaluation and a strong sense of value judgments localized in others.

The seventh characteristic of the fully functioning person is that "He will have no *conditions of worth*." Conditions of worth refer to self-experiences that are sought or avoided because they are perceived as being more or less worthy of self-regard. Thus, a mother may stress the importance of eating a certain food, and the child may accept her value judgment, even though it is incongruent with his or her self, because of the risk of incurring her displeasure is not acceptable. A fully functioning creative artist, on the other hand, will reject praise or criticism that he or she knows to be invalid. Beethoven's last quartets, for example, were dismissed by his contemporaries as the meanderings of a failing mind. Beethoven judged them quite differently and, as it turned out, more accurately. Today they are regarded as examples of the most profound music ever composed. To put this in the corollary phase of Characteristic 7, Beethoven, the master composer, experienced unconditional self-regard.

Characteristic 8 needs little interpretive comment. It refers to the essentially creative and adaptive adjustment of the healthy, mature personality. The neurotic, on the contrary, reacts obsessively and with rigidity to new experiences.

Characteristic 9 and its corollaries summarize concepts that we have already considered in outlining Rogers' theory of therapy. These characteristics are the opposite of those in the neurotic, who fails to bring significant experiences to awareness and denies or distorts them. The healthy, fully functioning person accepts and utilizes all experiences. He or she grows with each novel experience, utilizing it fully and relating it to the self-construct.

Finally, Rogers describes the tendency of the fully functioning individual to live in harmony because of "the rewarding character of reciprocal *positive regard*." The fully functioning person is, in other words, one who has achieved an optimal adjustment in his or her interpersonal relations. More specifically, positive regard is used here in the same way that it is employed in Characteristics C and D—that is, as attitudes of warmth, liking, and respect.

---

[14]For research reports utilizing the Q technique see C. R. Rogers (1959); C. R. Rogers and Dymond (1954).

Even this casual reading of Rogers' theory reveals his deep optimism about the possibility of human growth, in contrast to Freud's essential pessimism. Moreover, Rogers places himself in an antithetical position to Freud in his willingness to accept what the individual says about himself or herself at face value. It is in this latter respect that client-centered therapy has been severely criticized as "superficial." The psychoanalysts—whether of the Freudian persuasion or not—believe that there is overwhelming evidence for the unconscious determination of behavior. Moreover, Rogers has been challenged on the grounds that self-deception and the unreliability of subjective reports cast doubt on the validity of the subject's statements. However, Rogers does accept the possibility that the subject distorts experiences, and, as we pointed out above, so practices self-deception. Nevertheless, Rogers' profound optimism leads him to conclude that given the proper environment, the individual will arrive at an undistorted, undefensive view of the self.

Rogers' theory is a still-evolving conception of human personality that has an enthusiastic group of followers. For this reason to attempt to evaluate it at this time would be premature. We can only agree with Hall and Lindzey (1970) that Rogers' theory has been highly influential in bringing the self back into psychology and making it a valid object of empirical investigation. In this respect Rogers must share credit with G. W. Allport, the post-Freudians, and the small group of humanistic motivational theorists who have returned the person to a rightful place in personality theory.

A NOTE ON EXISTENTIALISM AND PERSONALITY THEORY

Existentialism is neither a theory of personality nor a unified system of psychotherapy. It is a philosophical movement European in origin and spirit, made up of diverse points of view, but with a number of common themes. Yet, as Maddi (1972) observes in his comparative study of personality theory, it is a movement having implications for personality theory and psychotherapy that cannot be ignored. Existentialism has already had a significant impact on psychology, psychiatry, and religion in Europe and in the United States. It has been allied with the third force of humanistic systems of psychology; and there are parallels—sometimes striking—between its central concepts and those developed by the humanistic systematists such as Adler, Kurt Goldstein, Maslow, G. W. Allport, and C. R. Rogers. Some clinicians, psychoanalysts, and philosophers, such as May, Ellenberger, Frankl, Boss, and Binswanger, have attempted to develop systems of psychotherapy based on the fundamental concepts of existential psychology and philosophy.

Because of the diversity of viewpoints among existential philosophers and the derivative systems in psychology and psychiatry, we shall abandon our usual policy of sampling one theorist's point of view as representative of all and summarize instead those core concepts that appear to us to have had the greatest influence on psychological theory and practice at the present writing. In doing so we shall be drawing on several primary and secondary sources.[15]

The most basic of all existential concepts is that of *being*. This ancient concept is strongly emphasized in the writings of Heidegger and Sartre and the existential psychotherapists. In German, as Heidegger introduced it, it is *Dasein,* composed of *sein* (to be) and *da* (there). Being, then, as the existentialist defines it, is *being-in-the-world.* It is living among things, animals, institutions, people, and their concerns. It is living with one's self. The world in being-in-the-world takes several forms. These are: *Umwelt, Mitwelt,* and *Eigenwelt. Umwelt* (literally, the world around) means the physical and biological environment—the ecology. *Mitwelt* (with the world) connotes the world of people or other human beings. *Eigenwelt* (own world) refers to the internal world of one's own consciousness. However, it is important to note that all three forms of being-in-the-world involve consciousness, for all we really know is our perception of the biological, physical, and social worlds around us. And so we are inescapably a part of the world, and the world is a part of us. In traditional philosophy and psychology, the existentialists argue, being has been treated as an abstraction, as a "thing," and they wish to emphasize that this is not the meaning of being-in-the-world. Being, the abstract noun of tradition, has become a participle or verb form in existential literature. It is becoming rather than being.

Looked at somewhat differently, being is conscious *existence* while nonbeing is *essence*. A rock, an inert mass of chemicals, a mathematical concept such as pi, are fixed essences and givens without consciousness and without the freedom to direct their future. Existence, on the other hand, is not fixed and is always becoming. It directs its own future by acting on the *Umwelt, Mitwelt,* and *Eigenwelt.* In May's phrase, being is a *potentia* (May et al., 1958, p. 41) capable of further development, never fixed until death.

As we have emphasized, being—in contrast to nonbeing—is free. That is, the human personality possesses freedom of choice as an integral part of being. One may, therefore, commit himself or herself to whatever project is desired. As Adler put it, "Everybody can do everything." Freedom is, of course, not as complete as a literal interpretation of Adler's remark would imply—and Adler himself surely never intended his remark to be taken literally. And so even existentialists who

---

[15]Primary sources in existential philosophy are directed at professionals and are often extremely technical. These include Heidegger's *Being and Time* (1962; originally published in 1927) and Sartre's *Being and Nothingness* (1956), both of which have directly influenced clinical psychology. Neitzsche's works are readable, but the beginner is advised to start out with Kaufmann's *Nietzsche* (1950). Kierkegaard's *Fear and Trembling* . . . (1954), a treatise on anxiety and alienation, is not technical but is difficult to relate directly to contemporary existential psychology. Good secondary sources are Barrett (1958), May (1969), and May, Angel, and Ellenberger (1958). May's introductory chapters to *Existence: A New Dimension in Psychiatry and Psychology*—the last reference cited—remains the best introduction to existential thinking as applied to psychology.

strongly emphasize freedom admit that there are contingencies or limitations to freedom. One cannot flap one's arms and fly because of the inherent physical limitations of the human body. However, one can choose freely within the limitations or contingencies that are part of the human condition.

Existential emphasis on freedom stands in sharp contrast to Freudian and behavioristic determinism. Existentialism emphasizes the future and becomingness as opposed to the past and fixedness. Existentialism is also opposed to "essences" in personality theory, such as the id, ego, and superego of Freud or the traits, factors, and types of the academicians. Each individual is held to be unique and so cannot be forced into a categorical mold. We can understand the individual only as a *being* in the world and not as a *kind* of being. In this respect existential thinking is reminiscent of the individual case or idiographic psychology as opposed to a nomothetic psychology of processes (essences).

Because freedom is inherent in being, so is anxiety. To choose is necessarily to take risks, possibly to lose all or to make a disastrous choice that could ruin future prospects for happiness. Moreover, being is aware of its own finitude. Therefore, added to anxiety (inherent in choice) is dread of nonbeing. The powerful emotion of existential anxiety is not, as Freud claimed, a symptom or something that the patient *has* but *is* a part of everyone's being. Anxiety lies coiled like a worm in the heart of being, and man, in Sartre's language, is "condemned to be free."

As we pointed out in Chapter 13, anxiety may impel a flight into an inauthentic mode of existence—detachment, hedonistic pursuits, or loss of individuality in comformity. However, anxiety can be overcome, if not eliminated, by authentic living through commitment. To paraphrase Sartre, the individual *is* his or her projects. Authentic projects develop an authentic being or personality. The authentic man or woman must make honest choices with full awareness of the consequences, even if these involve an increase in anxiety. He or she must, moreover, act not in self-interest alone, but as if he or she were acting for all mankind. Thus, existential choice, like Adler's choice of life-style, must be based on social interest—in other words, a commitment to the *Mitwelt*.

As Maddi (1972, p. 143) suggests, existential psychology exemplifies a *fulfillment model* of personality theory. Existentialism emphasizes as a core concept freedom of choice and commitment in contrast to classical psychoanalytic systems, which are *conflict models*. In this respect existential psychology may be placed in the same category as the systems developed by Adler, Maslow, C. R. Rogers, and G. W. Allport—all of whom stress self-fulfillment as the superordinate motive in the development of personality.

The existential psychologist must, of course, answer why some individuals make painful, maladaptive choices, such as the neurotic or psychotic is prone to do. Sartre's answer to this dilemma is that as children when fundamental choices are made and when the life-style is developing, such individuals lack sufficient experience to choose wisely in an unfavorable environment. Existential analysis, or *Daseinanalyse,* provides an opportunity for exploring the foundation of being and for reexamining choices in the light of mature perspectives. Hence, the existential therapists reject the unconscious determinism of maladaptive behavior, just as they reject the genetic determinism of classical psychoanalysis. The dynamics of behavior must be examined in terms of how the individual functions in the world of the present, not the past. If he or she functions poorly because of unfortunate choices in the past, he or she is free to choose anew for the future. To do so, however, requires a thorough exploration of being, with the analyst serving as the *Mitwelt* for the patient.

Existential philosophers beginning with Kierkegaard and Nietzsche have also emphasized the plight of the modern individual as having lost the sense of being-in-the-world. He or she is alienated from the factory and from impersonal educational, social, and religious institutions. Many individuals are alienated from the traditional church, whose forms and dogmas became empty and irrelevant to life in the real world and separated man from God. And, finally, in his attempts to escape from anxiety, man is alienated from himself.

The loss of God, the evil of global war and the death camps, the incredible destructiveness of the atomic age, and institutional and personal alienation are productive not only of anxiety but of despair. The existential psychologist believes that no individual personality or being can be completely understood unless it is granted that the individual is a being in a world that is dehumanizing and indifferent to his or her interests.

Existentialism has been criticized as failing to offer an empirical psychology of personality and psychotherapy. In fact, it does not even offer a unified body of theory. As Maddi observes, "much of existential thought really constitutes a set of attitudes for living, a manifesto more than a systematic theory of personality" (1972, p. 129). Although an evaluation of existentialism's permanent place in personality theory and psychotherapy would be premature, humanistic psychologists believe that it offers positive as well as negative attitudes. Specifically, they find its insistence on the exploration of being, its emphasis on the study of existence as opposed to abstractions or essences, and its reaffirmation of individual freedom refreshing developments that support a trend toward a more humanistic view of the human personality.

BEHAVIORISM AND PERSONALITY

Personality, as the behaviorist views it, is a symbolic construct without explanatory value. Therefore, as traditionally defined there can be no behavioristic theory of personality. The concept of traits is equally objectionable to the behaviorist, since trait theory assumes broad predispositions that generate behavior with a high degree of stability in a wide variety of situations over long periods of time—a supposition that is denied by behaviorists. In place of these hypothetical inner controls, the behaviorist postulates environmental variables as the antecedent conditions for behavior. That some behavior appears to be stable from situation to situation is accounted for by assuming that the situations in question may be identical or nearly so. Because the behaviorist takes the position that all behavior is learned, reinforcement has played a major role in traditional behavioristic accounts of habit formation. For these reasons behavioral psychologists assume that the history of environmental stimulus conditions and reinforcement are the critical determiners of individual differences among people.

It is also important to note that the behaviorist seeks the laws of behavior in carefully controlled experiments in which changes in environmental stimulus conditions and schedules of reinforcement are manipulated and quantitatively related to changes in behavior. In this kind of program there is no room for the traditional methods of the personologist—tests, questionnaires, rating scales, projective techniques, or clinical interviews. The behaviorist believes that these techniques of assessment are of dubious reliability and validity and are therefore too imprecise for serious scientific use. In their place he or she utilizes the functional analysis of behavior through direct observation and experimental manipulation.

It must also be emphasized that the behaviorist's program is nomothetic, not idiographic. Individual differences are considered troublesome artifacts or weaknesses in design that leave variables uncontrolled. This, of course, is in sharp contrast with traditional personality theory which holds individual differences to be the focus of study while situational variables are the artifacts. In commenting on this problem Skinner has observed:

> But our experience with practical controls suggests that we may reduce the troublesome variability by changing the conditions of the experiment. By discovering, elaborating, and fully exploring every relevant variable, we may eliminate *in advance of* measurement the individual differences which obscure the differences under analysis. (1959, p. 372)

Finally, in contrasting behavioristic with traditional approaches, we should note that in treating personality disorders traditionalists emphasize verbal therapy. A premium is placed on achieving insight into the origin of the problem in childhood, exploring its ramifications in the adult personality, discovering how it may be related to disabling repressions and finally to seeking its resolution. An important by-product of this kind of therapy is some degree of restructuring of the personality, particularly in those individuals who have undergone psychoanalytic and related therapies.

By contrast, behavior therapists minimize verbal techniques while maximizing the direct application of some form of conditioning procedure in order to modify behavior. To put it another way, the attack is directed at the troublesome symptoms so scorned by the Freudians as mere symbols of underlying pathology. Moreover, the behavior therapist places no emphasis whatsoever on insight or personality restructuring. The patient's elaboration of symptoms is accepted as the crux of the problem, and since symptoms are assumed to be learned habits, the goal is to eliminate them through relearning. By way of example, sexual dysfunctions, such as impotence in a married male, is treated by showing the couple techniques that will enhance and maintain erection to the point of orgasm. No attempt is made to explore the individual's childhood sexuality, his oedipal problems, or any traumatic experiences that may have resulted in repressions that interfere with sexual capability.

With these general principles in mind we are now in a position to examine several representative behavioristic points of view on personality.

Watson and Hull

As we discovered in our examination of systems and theories of psychology, all positions undergo modification with the passage of time. The once radical and inflexible position advocated by the founder of a school or system is modified and liberalized by associates and followers. This has been no less true in the behavioristic account of personality than in other areas.

In the beginning, Watson held up Pavlovian conditioning as the model technique for the study of all forms of behavior. To show how it could serve to explain complex behavioral patterns traditionally classified under personality, he carried out his famous experiment on Albert, conditioning the child to fear a white rat, and, through generalization, a variety of similar objects. By extension, phobias and anxiety reactions that personality theorists accounted for by assuming complex intervening variables are in reality simple conditioned responses dependent on environmental variables.

The Hullians modified Watson's position to emphasize instrumental learning, drive, habit strength, and other intervening variables. We have already seen how Miller (Chapter 9) utilized instrumental learning to show how conflicts influence behavior and how anxiety can serve as a drive in learning.

Spence, another of Hull's students and associates, went even further. He and his associates employed a traditional type of personality assessment in measuring anxiety to show that its influence can be objectively measured in verbal learning situations. Figure 16-3 presents the results of a representative experiment. In this situation the Taylor Manifest Anxiety Scale was used to select two groups of subjects, a high-anxiety group and a low-anxiety group. The learning task was a paired-associates list. It will be noted that under the relatively simple conditions of the experiment, anxiety served as a drive and the high-anxiety group's performance was superior. However, Spence and his associates agree that anxiety, like other drives, may be disruptive if at too high a level and present data to show that under difficult learning conditions high-anxiety subjects do poorly.

Social Learning Theory[16]

In discussing the process of development (Chapter 7) we found that Dollard and Miller employed an early form of social learning theory to account for imitation and matched-dependent behavior. It will be recalled that—according to their analysis—drives, cues, and reinforcement all have crucial roles in the establishment of behavior patterns involving imitation and modeling.

---

[16]See Bandura (1969), and Bandura and Walters (1963) for comprehensive discussions of social learning theory as an alternative to traditional personality theory.

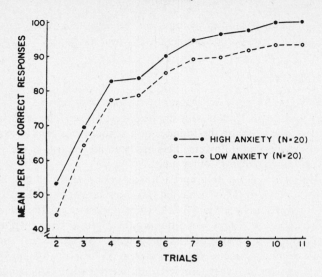

FIGURE 16-3.   Paired associates learning as function of anxiety level under conditions of minimal interpair competition and high initial stimulus-response associative strength. (From Spence, K. W., Farber, I. E., and McFann, H. The relation of anxiety (drive) level to performance in competitional and non-competitional paired associates learning. Journal of Experimental Psychology, 1956, 52, p. 300, Fig. 1. Copyright 1956 by the American Psychological Association. Reprinted by permission.)

More recently social learning theory has evolved to where it is assumed that new and highly complex forms of behavior can be acquired independently of reinforcement, and, further, that cognitive factors and self-direction may be important in the subsequent control of learned behavior.

One basic assumption of contemporary social learning theory is that most human learning is observational or vicarious. That is, a great deal of the skills that we acquire both as children and adults are developed through observing models. The golfer observes how the pro gets out of a sand trap; the adolescent boy watches the mechanic tuning up an engine. Both can learn the skills involved observationally and without immediate reinforcement. It may be months before either the boy mechanic or the golfer needs to apply what has been learned.

If reinforcement is not necessary for learning, then what is its role? The answer is that it controls performance. The reader will recall the experiments by Bandura and his associates discussed in Chapter 7 where children who watched adults carry out aggressive acts against a BoBo doll subsequently showed an increased level of aggression, particularly if the model was rewarded. But most important, conditions could be arranged so that children not immediately reinforced by allowing them to engage in aggressive behavior showed that they had nevertheless learned such behavior when reinforcement was subsequently introduced.

Several learning theorists recognize that the social environment puts limitations on the learning of complex skills by modeling. No one can learn to play the violin vicariously. The processes involved are far too complex to be mastered even in a series of observations. Similarly, even though acts may easily be learned by observation, social reinforcement may control their appearance. Most people know how to throw a brick through a window or shout "Fire!" in a crowded theater. However, these behaviors are not likely to be reinforced in a manner satisfactory to the performer and so appear relatively infrequently.

Social learning theory also makes use of expectancy and self-regulation in accounting for what the individual will do in a given situation (Bandura, 1969). Expectancy or cognitive control of responsiveness depends upon prior response consequences that the subject has experienced in conjunction with various temporal and social cues. Given similar circumstances in the future, the individual tends to infer the probability with which a given response will be rewarded or punished.

Self-control of behavior from the point of view of social learning theory implies that individuals can regulate their own behavior by arranging contingencies of reinforcement for themselves. However, as Bandura (1969, pp. 225–257) cautions, the objectives must be well-defined and goals clearly specified. Vague promises of aims that have no direct behavioral consequences are no more likely to succeed than the average individual's New Year's resolutions.

In applying the technique of self-regulation to those desiring to stop smoking, some kind of "contractual arrangements" must be made whereby the number of cigarettes smoked is gradually decreased, with records kept of the time and place in which smoking is tolerated. If the individual obtains satisfaction in keeping the no-smoking bargain, this serves to reinforce contracts, further reducing smoking. A similar program might be undertaken in the case of obesity, with graphic records of decreased intake being maintained.[17]

Because contingencies of reinforcement that involve reduction of highly desired activities are unpleasant, positive reinforcers may be selected to be contingent upon the performance of the desired behavior. Thus, a candy reward, food treats, or drinking coffee might be made contingent upon not smoking. The obese individual who undereats his budget for the day might "reward" himself or herself with a cocktail. In all such cases the decrease in the undesirable activity is made gradual so as to minimize the unpleasant consequences of change in habits.

The Therapeutic Program and Behavior Modification

Traditionally, personality theories have shown interest in psychopathology and psychotherapy. In fact, as we have seen, a number of personality theories have developed out of or were closely allied with therapy. The behaviorists have not been reluctant to meet the challenge of developing behavioral techniques for modifying undesirable behavior patterns.

---

[17]For a lengthy analysis of the behavior modification approach to the control of eating see Krasner and Ullman (1973, pp. 316–325).

Behavior Modification

Much of the current interest in the new therapy may be attributed to the relatively recent work of Joseph Wolpe, who, utilizing a classical conditioning model, developed a system called *reciprocal inhibition therapy* (Wolpe, 1958). Wolpe reasoned that since neurotic disorders, such as phobias or anxiety reactions, are learned patterns of behavior, they can be effectively eliminated only through unlearning.

Basic to his treatment of neurotic disorders is the concept of reciprocal inhibition, after which the system is named. In reciprocal inhibition the stimuli for fear or anxiety are presented during a controlled period when the patient is making responses incompatible with those of fear or anxiety. For example, if a patient is thoroughly relaxed, stimuli associated with fears or anxieties are gradually introduced without arousing the usual anxiety reaction, since the responses involved in relaxation and anxiety are incompatible. Thus a fear of snakes might be overcome by gradually introducing a snake from some distance after the patient is thoroughly relaxed. In such cases several sessions are typically required; and if any signs of fear are exhibited during a learning session, the stimulus for fear arousal is temporarily withdrawn or lessened. Eventually the patient is said to be systematically desensitized. The technique is most useful with phobic or anxiety reactions.

While reciprocal inhibition therapy was being developed in South Africa, Skinner and his associates were simultaneously formulating procedures for shaping behavior by utilizing appropriate schedules of reinforcement. A number of behaviorally oriented psychologists immediately recognized the potential significance of shaping in therapeutic situations. We shall summarize several representative techniques utilizing operant conditioning methods of behavior therapy.

By means of a technique called the "token economy" the behavior of patients in institutions for the mentally retarded or for those with behavior disorders can be shaped in ways considered desirable by the staff. The tokens employed may be traded in for food rewards, privacy, leaves, television-watching time, and so on. By such methods schizophrenics can be trained to do useful work as waitresses, janitors, or secretarial or recreational assistants; and retarded children can be trained in personal hygiene or social behavior (Ayllon, 1963; Ayllon & Azrin, 1965).

J. P. Brady and Lind (1965) report success in the treatment of an individual who was suffering from hysterical blindness of over two years' duration. Conventional psychiatric treatment had not improved his vision. The behavioral treatment consisted of placing the patient in a small room in front of a desk with his hand on a button. He was instructed to space his responses of button pressing between 18 and 21 seconds apart, whereupon a buzzer sounded (the reinforcement). Incorrect responses over or under the 18- to 21-second interval merely reset the apparatus for the next trial. Following some initial practice trials, visual stimuli of varying intensities were introduced in the room. During the initial phase of the treatment a light bulb in back of the patient was illuminated after 18 seconds and went off after 21 seconds. Thus, the correct interval was illuminated for the patient, who could improve his performance if he responded appropriately to the stimulus. After the intensity of the illumination was varied, more complex visual cues in the form of changing patterns of lights on a panel in front of the patient signaled the proper time interval.

Figure 16-4 shows the results of the procedure. The black bars represent the correct interval; the white bars, the subject's range of responses. However, responses between 3 and 12 seconds are eliminated, since they occurred only rarely. The patient's performance improved gradually, and he was eventually able to read fine print outside the experimental situation. In evaluating the results of this experiment, it must be remembered that persons who are hysterically blind are just as truly unable to function visually as those with organic defects.

Behavioral methods have also been widely used in the outpatient treatment of alcoholism and homosexuality. In these cases aversive conditioning procedures are employed. The homosexual may receive a shock upon seeing nude pictures of members of the same sex flashed on a screen and receive no shock when the picture is of a member of the opposite sex. Alcoholics may be given an injection of a

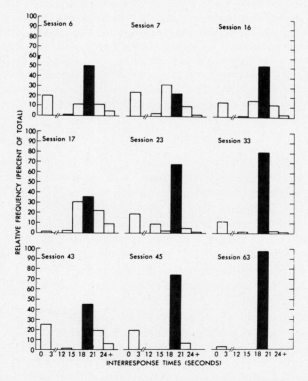

FIGURE 16-4. Relative frequency of interresponse time grouped into class intervals of 3 seconds each. Those responses falling within the 18 to 21 second interval are reinforced. Responses falling between 3 to 12 second intervals have been omitted. (From Experimental analysis of hysterical blindness, by Brady and Lind, Archives of General Psychiatry, 1961, 4, 331–339. Copyright 1961, American Medical Association.)

nausea-producing drug while being allowed to drink. The feelings of nausea come to be associated with alcohol, which itself becomes aversive. Theoretically, aversion therapy is based on respondent conditioning, in which the conditioned stimulus (CS) is paired with a naturally aversive unconditioned stimulus (US), such as electric shock or nausea-producing drugs.

We have already seen how modeling can be utilized in reinforcing aggressive behavior in children. The same basic technique can be employed therapeutically for overcoming phobias. Here is a description of how Bandura and his associates applied the method to overcoming a phobia of snakes.

> In the application of this method to the elimination of snake phobia, at each step the experimenter himself performed fearless behavior and gradually led subjects into touching, stroking, and then holding the snake's body with first gloved and then bare hands while he held the snake securely by the head and tail. If a subject was unable to touch the snake after ample demonstration, she was asked to place her hand on the experimenter's and to move her hand down gradually until it touched the snake's body. After subjects no longer felt any apprehension about touching the snake under these secure conditions, anxieties about contact with the snake's head area and entwining tail were extinguished. The experimenter again performed the tasks fearlessly, and then he and the subject performed the responses jointly; as subjects became less fearful the experimenter gradually reduced his participation and control over the snake until subjects were able to hold the snake in their laps without assistance, to let the snake loose in the room and retrieve it, and to let it crawl freely over their bodies. Progress through the graded approach tasks was paced according to the subjects' apprehensiveness. When they reported being able to perform one activity with little or no fear, they were eased into a more difficult interaction. (Bandura, 1969, p. 185)

Figure 16-5 shows the number of snake approach responses in a posttraining test involving the handling of a large snake. Note that the densitization procedure and symbolic modeling (largely seeing films in which children handled snakes fearlessly) were less effective than live modeling.

Research on both normal and abnormal individuals is under way or has been successfully applied in the analysis and control of psychotic behavior, neurotic symptoms, sexual deviations, drug abuse, weight control, and classroom behavior—as well as in the elimination or reduction of anxiety. For more complete reports the reader may consult Bandura (1969), Krasner and Ullmann (1973), and Lundin (1969, pp. 337–430).

Many therapists remain cautious about the long-range effectiveness of behavior therapy in the treatment of complex disorders such as alcoholism, homosexuality, or neurotic and psychotic reactions. Nevertheless, there is widespread interest among therapists in exploring such techniques as substitutes for the more complex, expensive, and often unsatisfactory verbal methods. However, the already demonstrated effectiveness of classical and operant conditioning procedures in many therapeutic situations is testimony to their practical utility in the treatment of behavior disorders.

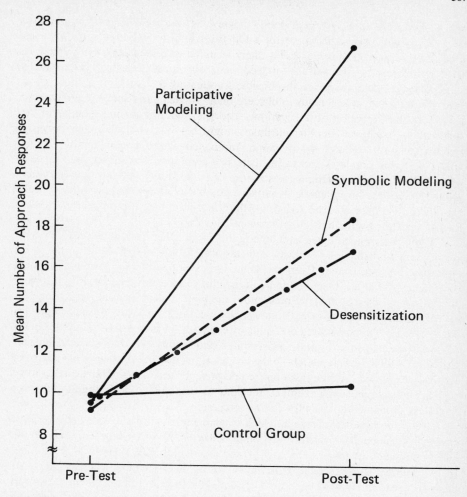

FIGURE 16-5. Mean number of snake-approach responses before and after thee types of treatment. Modified from Bandura, Principles of Behavior Modification. New York, Holt, Rinehart and Winston. Copyright, 1969.

SUMMARY AND EVALUATION

In reflecting on the theories of personality that we have examined, one cannot help but be impressed by the diversity of theoretical and methodological orientations represented. In part, this may be attributed to the fact that the subject matter of personality is so broad that the field has attracted psychologists with widely divergent points of view. Indeed, it is difficult to conceive of *any* orientation that cannot encompass the study of the human personality. As we have seen, personality may be approached from such divergent points of view as the factor analytic, humanistic, behavioral, and psychoanalytic. But aside from this diversity in orientation and despite disputes over specific issues, there is more agreement among the theorists than is apparent on the surface. Indeed, it is our contention that differences in *methodological* orientation are responsible for creating a significant portion of surface disagreement, which tends to obscure many fundamental areas of agreement.

With the exception of the learning theorists, there is general agreement that personality—whatever its other attributes might be—is characterized by *purpose*. Purpose, in turn, reflects the dynamic, motivated nature of personality. Again, noting the same previous exception, there is a common, ever-increasing emphasis upon the self, or ego functions, as the core of personality. The self that is gaining ground is not the mechanistic Freudian ego, but a more "psychological" self, perhaps best represented by Gordon Allport's concept of the proprium, by Carl Rogers' self, or by the existential concept of being.

There is also good agreement among the various theories on the continuity and consistency of behavior—both as a theoretical aspect of personality and as an important practical issue. Even the behaviorists are willing to admit situational consistency. After all, there would be little value in measuring personality if it were discontinuous, thereby making prediction, the final goal of measurement, impossible. The enduring quality of personality, along with the necessity for measurement, has resulted in the postulating of "units of behavior"—traits (R. B. Cattell, G. W. Allport), mechanisms (Freud), proceedings and serials (H. A. Murray), characteristics (C. R. Rogers)—which, in the last analysis, are different ways of looking at aspects of *behavior*. Although no one would pretend that such similar modal units of analysis indicate present agreement, it cannot be denied that these similar units may provide a fundamental basis for future agreement.

The more important areas in which disagreement is the rule are (1) the relative emphasis on unconscious determination of behavior, (2) the role of learning, (3) the contemporaneity of motivation, and (4) the use of symbolic constructs. Freud and H. A. Murray strongly emphasize unconscious determinants, whereas the other theorists give a moderate role to such determinants or de-emphasize them in favor of conscious ego determinants. Obviously, the critical factor here is the degree of influence of psychoanalytic concepts on personality theory. The psychoanalysts and those who favor psychoanalytic formulations have traditionally emphasized unconscious motives and mechanisms; those from other backgrounds have tended more toward conscious, modifiable determinants.

Similarly, the less psychoanalytically inclined tend to emphasize contemporaneity in motivation and, at the same time, to maximize the role of learning and cultural determinants in the development of personality.

All traditional theories of personality have freely used symbolic constructs such as the ego, self, trait, or complex. Here the behaviorists are sharply in disagreement. As we noted, they reject such constructs in favor of situational determinants and reinforcement history.

Once more, it is apparent how heavily contemporary theories have been influenced by the background systems from which they evolved. At the same time, the mutual interaction between method and theory is once again apparent. All systems and theories are compounded of the individual, the background, and the method. Yet each, like the human personality from which it springs, maintains its uniqueness.

Systems and Theories in Social Psychology[1]

17

Social psychology is the branch of psychology that studies how the behavior of individuals is influenced by others. As G. W. Allport (1968) has pointed out, others need not be physically present in order to exert an influence on the individual. Their presence may be implied or imagined, which accounts for the fact that social products and institutions as well as other people may be important determiners of behavior. Indeed, it is often emphasized that *all* behavior is social in the sense that no one, even when alone, can escape the influences exerted by society. However, in practice the field has traditionally limited itself to the study of more direct social influences, such as may be observed in the socialization of the child; the influence of social classes on behavior; problems of leadership; the study of conformity, attitudes, interpersonal, and group relations; and language.

The definition of social psychology as the study of social influences on the individual implies a corresponding body of *theory, methodology,* and *data*. That is, the social psychologist, like the general experimental psychologist, develops a body of theory to help explain social phenomena; and in this sense he or she is a systematist. He or she also employs a varying set of research tools—experiments, attitude scales, surveys, and so on—for collecting information and testing hypotheses. And, finally, the social psychologist contributes data. Out of this collection of factual information he or she attempts to formulate the broad principles and laws governing social influences and processes.

The social psychologist, like his or her colleagues in other areas, has never been reluctant to borrow from other disciplines. He or she may employ concepts and data from sociology, social or cultural anthropology, economics, and other be-

---

[1]This chapter was prepared under the joint authorship of James P. Chaplin and James G. Ferguson.

havioral sciences as appropriate. However, the distinctive feature of social psychology is its emphasis on the *psychological analysis* of the individual in society. The two most closely related disciplines are sociology, which focuses on institutions, and social or cultural anthropology, which is primarily concerned with culture—particularly nonliterate cultures. Although both of these other disciplines are allies, their methods and concepts are distinct from those employed in social psychology.

In this final survey of systems and theories in psychology we shall be primarily concerned with the theoretical aspects of social psychology rather than with its research methodology or its body of data as such. Naturally, the various aspects of the field are inseparably interrelated, and we shall necessarily utilize data and methodology to illustrate how theory is developed—just as we shall be concerned with the impact of theory on research design and data collection.

The critical reader may have wondered: Are not the same fundamental systematic and theoretical points of view available to the social psychologist as to those in other areas of psychology? The answer is yes, and we shall see examples of how $S \rightarrow R$, Gestalt, and psychoanalytic theories have been utilized by social psychologists and made direct contributions to the field.[2] However, the social psychologist has developed distinctive theoretical positions closely related to his or her particular methodology, and it is these in which we shall be primarily interested. Following our evolutionary sampling approach, we shall first examine the historical roots of modern social psychology and then present representative examples of the work of contemporary theorists. We shall begin with a brief summary of points of view that evolved out of the fountainhead of all modern knowledge, *philosophy*. We shall then consider *social empiricism* as a transition phase in the development of contemporary social psychology, before concluding with an examination of contemporary *social analysis*.[3]

SOCIAL PHILOSOPHY

Throughout recorded history scholars have sought the answer to the question: What is the nature of man? The answer is of great practical importance for organizing social institutions, developing systems of ethics and law, and for engineering rational social change. That the question has never been answered satisfactorily is clear from the continuing emergence of new points of view on the subject after 2000 years.

Fundamentally, the social philosopher may take one of two possible views of human nature. With Plato and Socrates he may hold that human nature, while not completely free of its biological heritage, is profoundly amenable to environmental influences. From this point of view society is the cause of human nature, and for this

---

[2]For book-length examples of how traditional theories have been applied in social psychology see M. Deutsch and Krauss (1965), Lindzey and Aronson's *Handbook of Social Psychology* (1968), and Shaw and Costanzo (1970).

[3]We are following Hollander (1976, pp. 32–34) in enumerating three stages of development of social psychology.

reason Plato argued for a designed society in which each child's role would be determined by appropriate education. Utopianists throughout history—including Skinner in our own time—have made a similar assumption about the perfectibility of man. The second point of view, held by Aristotle, is that human nature is primarily determined by biological or instinctive forces and cannot be significantly modified. Therefore, Utopias are not possible.

Plato's and the rationalists' position that man and society can be improved through reasoned design is *idealism,* as opposed to the *realism* of Aristotle and the instinct school. Platonic idealism can be found in the doctrines of Kant, Goethe, and Rousseau. They believed that humans are inherently good or at least potentially good. It is an imperfect society which turns people toward evil. The key, then, to changing human nature is social change.

Machiavelli, author of *The Prince* (1513), and Thomas Hobbes, the British empiricist known for the *Leviathan* (1651), held that man is inherently evil—the victim of his own cruel instincts—and must be forced by law to behave in a civilized manner in order to make society possible. To achieve this end, Hobbes and his followers advocated the application of *hedonism,* the principle that people seek pleasure and avoid pain, which (as we have seen in Chapter 12) became the dominant philosophical justification for British common law. The assumption of the power of reward and punishment in the control of human behavior remained a strong trend in subsequent social thinking and continues to be strong to the present day.

However, one fundamental dimension of social philosophy separates it from social psychology, and that is its failure to verify its assumptions and programs through empirical methods. There is no limit to how many views of human nature can be postulated in social philosophy, nor is there any restriction on the type of utopian society that can be designed on paper. Although the social psychologist may find such speculation provocative, it is not the stuff of science; and he or she demands empirical tests of assumptions about human nature and social influences on the individual.

SOCIAL EMPIRICISM

When the psychologist begins to describe group processes objectively, social philosophy evolves gradually into empiricism and suggests the profitability of categorizations and crude analysis. Theorizing is no longer an end in itself but becomes an adjunct to objective techniques. Social empiricism is relatively recent, beginning in the latter half of the nineteenth century with early European sociology and social psychology.

Tarde and Durkheim: Early French Sociology

Gabriel Tarde (1843–1904) deserves brief mention in any account of the development of social psychology for the *theory of imitation* developed in his well-known *The Laws of Imitation* (1903, originally published in 1890). Tarde was a jurist and a student of criminal behavior who became impressed with the power of suggestion in the genesis and spread of delinquent behavior. Indeed, imitation—which he held to be the behavioral consequence of suggestion—was posited as a fundamental law of criminality and invoked to explain all social phenomena. What one man invents, ninety-nine others imitate. Customs, Tarde wrote, are the imitation of things of the past; fashions are the imitation of things of the present. The universal tendency of human beings to imitate each other is the cause of the diffusion of behavior through large stable social institutions as well as through small collectives or groups.

For Tarde the law of imitation was an explanation *sui generis*. In his view neither imitation, suggestion, nor invention demanded further explanation, since they were irreducible individual processes. Consequently, his account of group behavior was individualistic or psychological, not sociological. Group psychology, he held, can be reduced to individual psychology. Because he ran counter to developing trends, Tarde failed to attract a school of sociologists whose members could champion and develop his viewpoint further. However, as we will see, the principle of suggestion loomed large in other early accounts of group behavior.

Tarde's theoretical position was in opposition to that developed by Émile Durkheim (1858–1917), one of the founders of modern sociology and one of the first European thinkers to stress the significance of the group in the determination of human conduct. In methodology Durkheim was an empiricist; in spirit he was a moralist. His empiricism led him to sponsor the use of factual information and statistics in the analysis of social phenomena, such as in his famous analysis of suicide in various social groups—a study in which he was a pioneer. His moralism is reflected in his position that society is moral. The maxims embodied in public morality, religious observances, and the rules of professional conduct are, for Durkheim, social facts with true objective reality, since they exert an observable restraining influence on individuals. Indeed, society is dependent for its very existence on a high degree of conformity to social norms on the part of individuals. And because most individuals do conform to social codes most of the time, society is relatively stable and durable.

For the student of social psychology, one of Durkheim's most important theoretical formulations is that social facts are not reducible to individual facts. In his concept of the *collective conscience,* described in the *Rules of Sociological Method* (1895), Durkheim emphasizes the principle that the fusion of individuals into a social aggregate generates a psychic unity that is not the mere sum of its parts. The group is a gestalt, a whole that thinks, feels, and acts in a manner different from that of the individuals who compose it. Thus, social psychology and sociology begin and end with the group. Social psychology cannot be reduced to the psychology of individuals or to their generic propensities or mechanisms.

Durkheim's rather extreme sociological realism has not been widely accepted by social psychologists. However, his emphasis on empirical observation and his principles of the psychic unity of crowds became dominant themes in the social psychology of the later nineteenth century.

Gustave LeBon: The Psychology of the Crowd

With the concepts of Gustave LeBon (1841–1931) we arrive at a pivotal point in the development of early theories of social behavior. His book, *The Crowd* (1960; originally published in 1895), is the outstanding classic in the field of group psychology and the first serious attempt to formulate a comprehensive and dynamic viewpoint about the nature of collective behavior. LeBon, a French physician whose spirit was thoroughly aristocratic, had a profound distrust of the masses and hence of democracy as a political institution. But at the same time he harbored an equally well-developed contempt for autocratic leaders, whom he saw as corrupt men all too willing to pander to the base instincts of the masses in order to reinforce their own power. And so LeBon was a pessimist, convinced that government by the masses is the beginning of the end of civilization, and equally disenchanted with autocratic forms of government. Moreover, LeBon held that the rise of modern science and its attendant social changes are responsible for two fundamental processes that jointly create an atmosphere of anarchy in the modern age.

> The first is the destruction of those religious, political, and social beliefs in which all elements of our civilization are rooted. The second is the creation of entirely new conditions of existence and thought as the result of modern scientific and industrial discoveries. (LeBon, 1960, p. 14)

His strong conservatism and pessimism are combined with a highly developed determinism. He viewed man as a creature of instincts on whom the crown of reason rests uneasily. Mass man reverts to primitive man, the victim of drives over which he has no real control. LeBon was never precise as to the nature of these instincts—it remained for Freud to specify their basis in the sexual and aggressive drives—but there is no question of their baseness or of the manner in which they are diffused in groups.

First, and this is LeBon's primary law of the crowd, any group presents characteristics entirely different from those of the individuals who make up the group. This he called the "law of the mental unity of crowds" (LeBon , 1960, p. 24). In a characteristic paragraph LeBon defines the law of mental unity as follows:

> The most striking peculiarity presented by a psychological crowd is the following: Whoever be the individuals that compose it, however like or unlike be their mode of life, their occupation, their character, or their intelligence, the fact they have been transformed into a crowd puts them in possession of a sort of collective mind which makes them feel, think, and act in a manner quite different from that in which each individual of them would feel, think, and act were he in a state of isolation. (1960, p. 27)

Although LeBon does not specify what motives are responsible for the manner in which crowds feel, think, and act, he does believe that a glimpse of the truth can be discerned by recognizing that unconscious processes play a preponderant role in governing the intellective side of life. This unconscious substratum he considers to be hereditary in nature. It is the common body of characteristics of the race handed down from generation to generation. Therefore, even though the shoeshine boy and the great mathematician are worlds apart from the point of view of abstract intelligence, they are inexorably bound together in terms of their primitive human impulses. And in a crowd, the bootblack and the scientist are reduced to a common denominator; consequently, their unconscious racial characteristics gain the upper hand.

LeBon is careful to point out that his law of mental unity does not imply that a crowd is a mere average or aggregate of its members. Rather, as is true in the creation of a chemical compound, something new emerges. Just as water bears no resemblance to the hydrogen and oxygen that compose it, the behavior of individuals in crowds bears no resemblance to their behavior as individuals. The emergent characteristics of behavior in crowds are compounded of the primitive animalistic, unconscious characteristics of the race.

Why, LeBon asks, do such characteristics emerge in a crowd when they do not appear in isolated individuals? The answer, he believes, lies in three primary causal processes (LeBon, 1960, pp. 30–31). First, because of his or her embeddedness in numbers of people, the individual in a group acquires a conviction of invincible power that allows him or her to yield to instincts which would have been kept under control had he or she been alone.

Second, contagion intervenes both to determine the special characteristics of crowds and to establish the trend that such characteristics take. Contagion refers to the spread of impulses and behavior patterns through a crowd much as an infection spreads through a mass of people.

Third, contagion is related to suggestibility, a hypnoticlike phenomenon that allows base and unconscious instincts to surface, with the result that the individual in a crowd loses his or her civilized identity and becomes a barbarian.

Because the exciting causes that generate them are varied, crowds are extremely mobile, impulsive, and irritable. From one moment to the next they may pass from ferocity to heroism. The crowd may sacrifice itself for a revolutionary cause, thus acting the martyr's role; but it may also turn with savage vindictiveness on its own kind, taking the role of executioner. Moreover, because crowds are impulsive, they cannot engage in premeditation but are creatures of the moment and easily diverted. An impassioned plea by a demagogue will turn a harmless crowd into a bloodthirsty mob.

Crowds are also intolerant. They see issues in black and white and refuse to accept contradictions. Consequently, their heroes have the characteristics of the autocrat. Crowds are conservative. Although they may appear to destroy tradition, sometimes in a violent and revolutionary manner, the change is superficial and transitory. They quickly fall back on tradition and become once more its slaves and the enemies of change.

In the closing chapter of the first part of *The Crowd,* LeBon compares the sentiments exhibited by crowds to religious convictions. The crowd, like the extremely religious individual, is intolerant, fanatic, and blindly submissive to the commands of dogma and authority. Moreover, both the worshiper and the crowd member seek to convince others of the righteousness of their cause.

The violence of the Revolution, its massacres, its need of propaganda, its declarations of war upon all things, are only to be properly explained by reflecting that the Revolution was merely the establishment of a new religious belief in the mind of the masses. (LeBon, 1960, p. 77)

The greater part of *The Crowd* deals with what we now would call social movements in which the role of the leader is paramount in the dynamics of the group's behavior. The principal techniques utilized by the leader are identified by LeBon as *affirmation, repetition,* and *contagion.* Affirmation is the appeal to faith, and is, therefore, the antithesis of the appeal to reason. The latter implies discussion, understanding, and intelligent conviction; the former, blind acceptance on the basis of the prestige and authority of a leader. Critical thinking in the masses is lulled by appeals to illusions; reality is brushed aside, and action in the direction desired by the leader is assured. Repetition means driving home an appeal by reiteration rather than reason, and contagion is the hypnoticlike process already referred to by which ideas and impulses are spread through a group. Today we would say that the degree to which the leader can ensure contagion for his or her ideas depends upon his or her charisma.

In concluding this summary of LeBon's primary concepts, we may agree with Robert K. Merton, who in his introduction to a reissue of *The Crowd* (1960), observed that LeBon was a problem finder rather than a problem solver. His was not the empirical method of the contemporary social psychologist, who collects and analyzes data in an attempt to confirm or reject a hypothesis. Instead, LeBon depended on the validity of his own insights and observations, which were based on the behavior of crowds he observed while traveling in India and on his reading of the history of the French Revolution. LeBon's aristocratic bias distorted his view of mass man and led him to make unacceptable categorizations. Nevertheless, he must be credited with stimulating a generation of followers to seek a more definitive explanation of group phenomena. One of his admirers was Sigmund Freud, whose group psychology we shall now examine.

Freud and the Libido Theory

Freud and LeBon were both products of their age and had much in common intellectually. Both moved from their strict medical training to wider interests in group psychology. Both were determinists who believed that the individual is a victim of forces over which he or she has at best only incomplete control. These vital forces were attributed to the unconscious, primitive mind by both Freud and LeBon. Finally, as a natural consequence of their medical backgrounds, both tended toward a somatic explanation of mental phenomena. However, LeBon attributed the unconscious drives to unidentified hereditary mechanisms, whereas Freud extended the concept of the libido to serve as the foundation of all social phenomena.

It is the concept of the libido that Freud employs in his *Group Psychology and the Analysis of the Ego* (1921) to keynote his theoretical differences with LeBon. The latter explains the cohesion of individuals in groups as a result of the hypnoticlike process of suggestion. But Freud argues that suggestion, or more properly suggestibility, is neither an explanatory concept nor a primitive, irreducible phenomenon; it is a complex process that demands analysis and explanation. Freud offers in its place the concept of the libido, or sexuality, and all its derivations in the form of love and affection to account for both the hypnotic relationship between subject and operator (or among group members) and the group ties that bind the leader to the group and the individual members to each other.

Freud (1921) devotes a chapter to the exposition of his libido theory of group formation, utilizing the army and the church as exemplary prototypes of highly organized groups. Both, he points out, depend upon strong leader-follower ties; and the vitality of both necessitates strong ties among the individual members. These ties, Freud believes, are libidinal in nature. He admits that even though the followers are bound to the leader libidinally, they may have powerful feelings of ambivalence, or contradictory attitudes, toward their leader. A familiar example is the soldier who may respect and admire his commander yet harbor strong feelings of hostility toward him. Similarly, the priest may be both loved and feared by his penitents. Rather than contradicting the libido theory, feelings of ambivalence in groups offer further proof of its essential validity. The same ambivalence can be found in the most primitive group of all, the family, and this familial ambivalence is the prototype for ambivalence in larger collectives. Freud (1938b) reminds us in ''Totem and Taboo'' that the family originated in the primal horde when the lusty young sons banded together to kill the father, who kept them from the women, only to elevate him to the status of a supernatural father (god) because of the feelings of guilt and fear consequent upon their terrible deed.

In support of his libido theory of group formation, Freud cites the phenomenon of panic among military groups as a negative instance of the importance of libidinal ties. The dissolution of an army marks the sudden collapse of such ties. Thus, panic is not caused by fear but by the loss of libidinal ties, which generates the same anxiety the child experiences when separated from the parents.

The heightened suggestibility of crowds is explained by Freud in terms of identification. Just as the subject in the hypnotic trance abrogates his or her own will for that of the hypnotist, in the group the individuals renounce their wills for that of the leader. The leader's ideals become their ideals, his or her goals their goals. This same process of identification of the individual with the leader accounts for what LeBon called the *mental unity of the crowd*. As identification takes place, the individual's reactions are reinforced in the crowd; thus the collective reaction surpasses what would be predicted from the totality of individual reactions. Freud, like LeBon, holds a low opinion of the mass mind.

We are reminded of how many of these phenomena of dependence are part of the normal constitution of human society, of how little originality and personal courage are to be found in it, of how every individual is ruled by those attitudes of the group mind which exhibit themselves in such forms as racial characteristics, class prejudices, public opinion, etc. The influence of suggestion becomes a greater riddle for us when we admit that it is not exercised only by the leader, but by every individual upon every other individual; and we must reproach ourselves with having unfairly emphasized the relation to the leader and with having kept the other factor of mutual suggestion too much in the background. (Freud, 1921, pp. 117–118)

In a later volume, *Civilization and Its Discontents* (1930), Freud returns to the problems of society less as an empirical psychoanalyst attempting to establish his libido theory and more as a philosopher dealing with existential problems. In this work he deals with the broad question of man's place in the world, which he regards as an unresolvable conflict between the demands of society and the individual's claim to freedom. Civilization is made possible only through renouncement of individual instincts of aggression and sexual satisfaction. Through sublimation and repression the instincts are either suppressed altogether or are changed into the processes of social living. The transformation, however, is never complete; hence civilization always carries with it discontent.

Freud's contribution to social psychology was a limited one. His *Group Psychology* borrowed heavily from LeBon. Indeed, it was essentially Freud's attempt to meld LeBon's descriptive theory of crowd behavior with his own explanatory libido theory. Even those disposed to view Freud's effort favorably must agree that his theory is chiefly applicable to collectives or groups with distinct leadership, such as military or church groups. Nevertheless, the theory lent support to McDougall's parallel attempt to formulate a social psychology around instinct theory.

McDougall and Instincts in Social Psychology

William McDougall (1871–1938) formulated his social psychology around instinct theory; and his formulation was treated too kindly by his contemporaries, and too harshly by history. His *Introduction to Social Psychology* (1921; first published in 1908) was received enthusiastically. *The Group Mind* (1920)—the book he considered his greatest—was coldly received and marked the end of his preeminence in United States social psychology. However, between 1908 and 1921 his textbook of social psychology had gone through fourteen editions and had carried his instinct theory all over the world.

Simply stated, the theory holds that individual and group behavior springs from instincts. These are

. . . innate or inherited tendencies which are the essential springs or motive powers of all thought and action, whether individual or collective, and are the bases from which the character and will of individuals and nations are gradually developed under the guidance of the intellectual faculties. (McDougall, 1921, p. 20)

Among the more important basic instincts are flight, curiosity, pugnacity, the reproductive drive, gregariousness, and acquisition. Each of these instincts has its accompanying emotion—flight is accompanied by fear, curiosity by wonder, pugnacity by anger, parental instincts by tender emotions, and so on. The basic instincts can be combined into sentiments. Love, although it has a sexual component, also includes other tendencies, such as care of the young and fear if the young are threatened. Consequently, sentiments are more complex than the simple instincts. They are also more enduring. Instincts are quickly aroused and quickly satisfied; sentiments may endure for years. But because instincts can be modified through learning or experience, McDougall allows for an almost infinite latitude in a system that at first glance appears to be severely limited.

The Group Mind (1920) builds upon McDougall's basic instinct theory. McDougall had been criticized for calling his theory a social psychology when he failed to show precisely how instincts issue forth in the crowd. His new book was to answer such criticism. The general theme is stated in the opening paragraph of the second chapter, "The Mental Life of the Crowd."

> It is a notorious fact that, when a number of men think and feel and act together, the mental operations and the actions of each member of the group are apt to be very different from those he would achieve if he faced the situation as an isolated individual. (McDougall, 1920, p. 31)

The group mind he had already defined earlier:

> It consists of the same stuff as individual minds, its threads and parts lie within these minds; but the parts in the several individual minds reciprocally imply and complement one another and make up the system which consists wholly of them. (McDougall, 1920, p. 15)

In short, any group of people—a crowd, a church, a trade union, a nation—possesses a group mind, which is greater than the sum of the individual minds that compose it because of the interactive effects of individuals upon individuals.

The cement that binds the group together is *intensification of emotion:*

> By participation in the mental life of a crowd, one's emotions are stirred to a pitch that they seldom or never attain under other conditions. This is for most men an intensely pleasurable experience; they are as they say carried out of themselves, they feel themselves caught up in a great wave of emotion, and cease to be aware of their individuality and all its limitations; . . . this is probably the principal cause of the greater excitability of urban populations as compared with dwellers in the country, and of the well-known violence and fickleness of the mobs of great cities. (McDougall, 1920, p. 35)

McDougall obviously agrees with LeBon that the excesses observed in crowds are the result of the operation of the primary instincts and emotions. Using panic as an example, McDougall compares crowds of human beings in a panic situation to a herd of mindless animals reacting instinctively as they trample each other to death in a blind attempt to escape danger. He attributes such reactions to *primitive sympathy.*

The greater part of McDougall's *The Group Mind* deals with group processes in primitive societies and in modern industrialized nations in an attempt to show

how the extension of the instinct theory is capable of explaining mass movements, national characteristics, and the structure of permanent social institutions. And yet for all his effort, his lasting contribution must be evaluated as minimal. His concepts of the intensification of emotion and primitive sympathy, though offered as explanatory concepts, do not go beyond the level of description. The system had appeal in the early twentieth century because it rode the crest of a wave of Darwinism, which was popular at that time and sought to link humans and animals through instincts. McDougall's theory was unable to survive the strong behaviorist reaction set in motion with the ascendance of J. B. Watson and his school. Although they looked kindly on animal psychology, these behaviorists sought to rid it (and human psychology) of instincts, propensities, and other nonobservables.

SOCIAL ANALYSIS

Social analysis goes beyond description to bring the tools of the experimental method into social psychology. Although Wundt and his associates had established the utility and validity of quantitative and experimental methods for sensory and perceptual research, they failed to apply them to the investigation of social variables. This task remained for a number of pioneers whose work during the opening decades of the twentieth century not only demonstrated the validity of the experimental and quantitative methods for social psychology but also left a heritage of fundamental discoveries that have become part of the body of social psychology. To several of these pivotal individuals we shall now turn our attention.

F. H. Allport and Social Facilitation

Two experimenters working almost a generation apart—Triplett in 1897 and Moede in 1920—carried out the first true experiments in social psychology and at the same time provided the foundation for F. H. Allport's principle of social facilitation. Triplett investigated the influence of competition on a simple motor task—speed in winding a fishing reel. On half the trials each subject performed alone; on the other half each competed with another child. Even though the instructions were "to go as rapidly as possible so as to make a record," the competitive situation led to faster performance for many subjects.

Moede's experiment tested the willingness of boys 12 to 14 years of age to withstand "intolerable" pain when alone as compared to their willingness to do so in the presence of others. Again, the results favored the social situation.

Integrating these pioneer studies into his own systematic research during the years 1916–1919 at Harvard, F. H. Allport (1924, pp. 260–291) developed the concept of *social facilitation* to characterize the facilitating effect of others on the individual's performance. Utilizing tests of cancellation, multiplication, reversible perspective, speed of association, and psychophysical comparisons, Allport found that the presence of others facilitated performance on most of the tasks. However, he was careful to point out that there were individual differences in the degree of susceptibility to group influences and that the presence of others had a detrimental effect on the performance of some tasks.

Allport distinguishes between *coacting* and *face-to-face* groups. The former work side by side, deriving social facilitation from watching others, listening to their reactions, and other such peripheral cues. In face-to-face interaction, conversation, exchange of opinions, ascendant and submissive behavior, and other interactive processes greatly complicate the results. Although he formulated the distinction and recognized the different degree of complexity of the two situations, Allport worked only with coacting groups. He believed that the problems of control were too complex to permit valid research on face-to-face interactions.

In summarizing the results of his research, Allport concluded:

The social stimulations present in the co-acting group bring about an increase in the speed and quantity of work produced by the individuals. This increase is more pronounced in work involving overt, physical movements than in purely intellectual tasks. In adults the group produced no improvements in the constancy of attention or in the quality of the work performed. Some individuals in fact do inferior work in the presence of co-workers. There is a lowering of the logical value of reasoning carried out in the group; but an increase in the number of words by which such reasoning is expressed. . . . The social increment is subject to individual differences in respect to age, ability, and personality traits. It is greatest for the least able workers and least for the most able. (1924, p. 284)

More recently, Zajonc (1965, 1966) had suggested that the influence of coaction can be bivalent (acting in opposite directions), in that the performance of previously learned behavior tends to be enhanced, whereas the learning of novel material tends to be impaired. Zajonc further proposes that this is as true of a passive audience watching the behavior as it is of the coactors.

The pioneer studies conducted by Allport led to diverging lines of research on the effects of social interaction on many variables—attitudes, social norms, conformity, and so on. Indeed, the potential effects of groups on individuals' and other groups' reactions offer unlimited opportunities for research even today. For a recent comprehensive review of the literature on group processes, group problem solving, individual versus group performance, and group information exchange processes, see Kelley and Thibaut (1969).

Sherif and the Study of Social Norms

A little over a decade after F. H. Allport published his theory of social facilitation, Muzafer Sherif (1936) conducted his classic study on the formation of social norms. Social norms are patterns of behavior typical of a particular group and sanctioned by that group. In effect, they become standards of reference by which the behavior of individuals or of a subgroup can be judged. Utilizing the autokinetic effect, or the apparent movement of a pinpoint of light in a dark room, Sherif showed that individual judgments could be made to converge to a group norm in the microsociety of the laboratory.

In the first phase of the experiment the subjects were tested alone on a number of trials, reporting the amount and direction of observed movement of the light. On the experimental trials the subjects were tested in the presence of others, all of whom reported their observations aloud. Convergence in the average judgment of the light's apparent movement was shown to increase with each succeeding judgment in the social situation (see Figure 17-1). Thus, a standard had been established for an arbitrary norm. Most significant was the fact that subsequent tests showed that the subjects retained the group standard as a basis for judgment rather than reverting to their own preexperimental standards.

Sherif's experiment became a model for a number of similar experiments in which the presence of others—often confederates of the experimenter—was shown to influence judgments. For example, Jacobs and Campbell (1961) utilized essentially the same technique to demonstrate not only that normative judgments can be established in the laboratory but that they may be transmitted across generations of subjects' judgments. In their experiment, naive subjects made judgments of the autokinetic effect in the presence of the experimenter's confederates, who gave prearranged sets of judgments aloud. As the trials went on, confederates were removed and new naive subjects were brought into the laboratory. These subjects were also serially removed in order of their seniority as the judgments went on. A generation consisted of thirty trials, each involving one discrete judgment by each

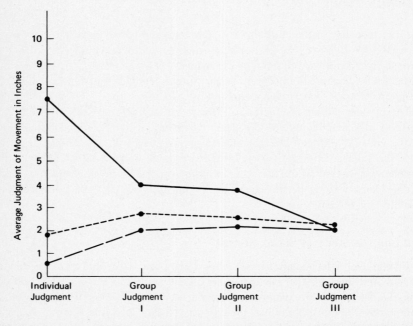

FIGURE 17-1. Convergence in average judgments of autokinetic movement for three subjects, beginning with individual judgments. (From Figure 6, p. 103 from The Psychology of Social Norms by Muzafer Sherif. Copyright 1936 by Harper & Row, Publishers, Inc.; renewed 1964 by Muzafer Sherif. Reprinted by permission of Harper & Row, Publishers, Inc.)

person. Control subjects, meanwhile, made judgments alone. The results clearly showed that the initial judgments of the naive subjects were strongly influenced by the presence of the experimenter's confederates and that these influences were transmitted to a new generation of subjects, the effects persisting over ten generations of trials.

In social psychology today considerable interest has developed around the variables of conformity and nonconformity and risk taking in social situations. Many of these experiments (Hollander, 1976, Chapter 13) utilize the basic technique of measuring the effect of confederate influence on naive subjects, which evolved from the work of Sherif and his successors.

Thurstone and Attitude Measurement

G. W. Allport has emphasized that the concept of attitude is "the most distinctive and indispensable" in American social psychology (1968, pp. 59–60). Defined as relatively stable and enduring predispostions to act in a certain way toward persons, objects, or events, attitudes are characterized by *cognitive, affective,* and *action* components. That is, attitudes are beliefs that are emotionally held and embody a set or readiness to respond in a certain way. Because attitudes vary in intensity, social psychologists have undertaken the development of scales for their measurement. Among the most prominent pioneers in this effort was L. L. Thurstone, with whose factor analytic theories of intelligence we are already familiar.

Thurstone and his collaborator E. J. Chave (1929) developed a scaling procedure that allows people to endorse items reflecting their own attitudes on an anti-pro dimension. Suppose, for example, the question on which the psychologist wishes to measure attitudes is compulsory military service. First a pool of items containing as many as 100 to 150 statements concerning military service is generated. Following Thurstone's instructions, it is important that the items be unambiguous in meaning and that they cover all ranges of the issue from strongly anti to strongly pro. These items are then presented to a large number of judges whose task is to sort them into a number of piles (typically seven, nine, or eleven), with one end pile representing the anti extreme and the other end pile representing the pro extreme. When all of the judges have completed the sorting task, the scale values for each statement can be calculated. Assuming, for example, that seven categories or piles were used (see Figure 17-2), any statement falling into Pile 1 would, for that judgment, be given a scale value of 1. Similarly, all other statements are given the appropriate value as determined by their placement in the piles.

The final goal of the process is the development of a set of about twenty unambiguous statements, which are distributed along the anti-pro continuum. The subject whose attitude we are interested in measuring is asked to endorse any of the twenty items with which he or she agrees. The mean or median of the items selected is the subject's attitudinal score on the issue.

In addition to his caution concerning the construction of unambiguous and representative items, Thurstone provides additional computational procedures for

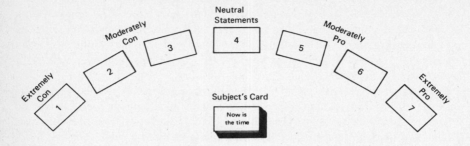

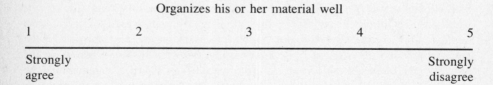

FIGURE 17-2.   The Thurstone-Chave technique for scaling attitudes. The subject sorts the statements according to how he or she believes they match or approach the seven representative categories.

eliminating high-variance items as well as the judgments of judges who appear to have been careless in their execution of the sorting task. Considerable research has been directed toward Thurstone's fundamental assumption that the judges' ratings of the original items are independent of the judges' own position on the issue, with the general conclusion being that the assumption is valid (Hovland & Sherif, 1952; Upshaw, 1962, 1964, 1965).

Thurstone's procedure is complex and certain assumptions behind the scaling procedure have been called into question. In an effort to avoid some of the difficulties associated with Thurstone's category scaling, R. A. Likert (1932) developed a scaling technique now in wide use, which involves simply collecting positive and negative statements and allowing the subject to indicate his or her degree of agreement or disagreement by rating the item on a scale of 1 to 5 or 1 to 7. Thus, if the scale involves the measurement of attitudes toward teachers, an item might appear as follows:

Organizes his or her material well

1	2	3	4	5

Strongly   Strongly
agree   disagree

Each subject sampled would check a point along the line corresponding to the extent of his or her agreement with the statement. The overall score for the scale would be obtained by summing the individual values for each of the responses. While the ease of using the Likert technique is a compelling consideration, it has two limitations. First, the technique tends to be more satisfactory for items describing the extremes of a continuum; and, second, it tends to be more specific to a given group of respondents (Upshaw, 1968).

The pioneer work of Thurstone and Likert provided social psychologists with a powerful technique for investigating the strength of attitudes. Psychologists interested in attitude measurement also put these quantitative techniques to work in the practical problems involved in public opinion surveying. Although these techniques do not involve scaling, they do employ specialized methods of construction and representative sampling. So familiar is their use in assessing voter preferences on various issues that further commentary is unnecessary.

Lewin and Group Dynamics

Kurt Lewin (1890–1947) has had a greater impact on the field of social psychology than any other individual. We are already familiar with the fundamental concepts of his field theory (Chapter 12). We have also illustrated the application of field theory to experiments in group atmospheres, behavior at barriers, and the Zeigarnik effect.

Group dynamics is the investigation of the interrelationships among individuals in a group, how the group was formed, and how it reacts with other groups. Group dynamics also includes studies of group cohesiveness, leadership, decision making, and the formation of subgroups.

Group dynamics first became prominent in Lewin's writings in the late 1930s (see Lewin, 1939a, 1939b). After the early 1940s he contributed very little to his already considerable body of theory and data on individual psychology. From that point until his death, Lewin's energies were directed toward the study of group processes. During this brief period of half a dozen years Lewin and his associates not only launched group dynamics but also founded action research and laid the foundation for the sensitivity training movement.

Lewin characterized the group as a dynamic whole. This does not mean that he accepted the group mind theory. Rather, it means that the group must be studied as a whole, or gestalt. In other words, a group cannot be analyzed by analyzing the individuals in it. The group has properties that are different from the sum of its parts. And just as the individual cannot be understood apart from the life space and the environment, so neither can a group be understood apart from the social environment. Moreover, groups must be understood in terms of their contemporaneous dynamics. Present behavior depends upon the causal interrelationships among members of the group and subgroups, and not upon historical events.

One of Lewin's essential, key concepts in describing and analyzing groups is *cohesiveness*. This refers to all forces that bind the parts of the group together and resist disruption. Cohesiveness depends upon the positive valence or attractive force between members of the group, the strength of barriers against leaving the group, and the degree of individual motivations for membership. M. Deutsch (1968), himself a student of Lewin's, summarizes a number of studies by former students and associates of Lewin's bearing on group cohesiveness. Typical of such research is Back's experiment (1951) in which subjects worked together in pairs interpreting a set of pictures. Groups were formed on one of three bases: (1) liking the other group members; (2) liking the group because membership conferred prestige on its members; (3) liking the group because it is a means to achieving personal goals. Regardless of the reason for attractiveness among pairs of members, the more cohesive pairs made greater efforts to reach agreement and were more influenced by group discussion.

We have already discussed in Chapter 12 how leadership influences group cohesiveness. It will be recalled that a democratic atmosphere in which group decisions and goals are the rule leads to a more cohesive and productive group. In a related line of research Schachter (1951), another of Lewin's associates, found that clubs with high cohesiveness can be formed by grouping participants with moderate to high interest in the group's activities.

Group dynamics research has also revealed that conformity and communication are important variables affecting cohesiveness. As might be expected, conformity is highest among more cohesive groups (Berkowitz, 1954). Similarly, a high degree of communication based on similarity of interest and attitudes stimulates cohesiveness. In a basic study at the Massachusetts Institute of Technology carried out by Festinger, Schachter, and Back (1950), it was found that friendship ties among married students living in apartments developed most strongly among those nearest each other. Couples living in the same wing of a building tended to form close friendships, to develop similar attitudes, and to communicate more frequently and effectively with each other. Obviously cohesiveness, communication, and conformity are interrelated factors, each of which contributes to the other.

Group dynamics, as indicated earlier, also studies change within the group. In an early experiment, Lewin (1947) found that group decisions have a more lasting effect on individuals in a group than do commitments made when alone. In the experiment some mothers of infants were given individual instruction about the desirability of using orange juice in the baby's diet. Others were placed in groups of six and allowed to discuss the advantages of varying their infants' diets with the goal of reaching a common decision about the use of orange juice. The mothers who participated in the group decision were more strongly committed to giving orange juice than those who modified their infants' diets because of individual instruction. Group discussion, therefore, facilitates decision making and reinforces the decision once it is made. Obviously, the more important the group to its members, the more influential the group will be in bringing about change.

Lewin's interest in group change led him to develop *action research* (1948), a practical application of group dynamics. Noting that various community agencies concerned with eliminating social problems are often unsuccessful no matter how well-intentioned they may be, Lewin's program for action research called for discovering techniques for transforming goodwill into efficient action by careful analysis of the problem, development of data, and feedback into the organization, so that better strategies might be developed.

From Lewin's point of view, several critical areas must be taken into account to promote effective action in such situations:

1. The conditions which improve the effectiveness of community leaders who are attempting to better intergroup relations. For example, what are the most effective and practical methods of training such leaders? What are the principles governing the choice of trainees? What can be done to promote the maintenance of the operating efficiency to which such leaders are brought as a result of training?

2. The effect of the conditions under which contact between persons from different groups takes place. For example, what conditions result in an improvement of

attitude and in harmonious relations and what conditions bring about the converse? What conditions of contact result only in the formation of particular friendships as against the formation of friendly feelings toward other cultural groups taken as a whole? What conditions result in the formation of lasting favorable attitudes as against those susceptible to easy reversal in a prejudiced environment?

3. The influences which are most effective in producing in minority-group members an increased sense of belongingness, an improved personal adjustment, and better relations with individuals of other groups. (Marrow, 1969, p. 192)

In applying his theories to real life social groups, Lewin and his associates attacked the problems of gang warfare in New York City, admissions discrimination in colleges, integration of black sales personnel in department stores, and integrated housing among New York City's racial groups. These pioneer efforts were planned and put into operation before civil rights programs became commonplace.

Finally, as representative of Lewin's multifaceted genius for pioneering significant new developments in social psychology, we will briefly describe his initiation of the *sensitivity training group,* or *T-group* movement in 1946. The Connecticut State Interracial Commission had requested Lewin's assistance in training leaders and conducting research programs on the best means for combating racial prejudice. A two-week training workshop held in June 1946 and attended by forty-one participants marked the beginning of the sensitivity group movement. In the Connecticut groups, participants hoped to gain insight into themselves and others and to develop techniques for effecting attitude change. So successful was the program that the National Training Laboratories at Bethel, Maine, were established shortly afterwards. In the decades following Lewin's pioneer work, the sensitivity training movement has become one of the most rapidly growing social phenomena of the twentieth century.

Lewin's enduring influence is to be found not only in the body of theory and data which he left behind as a direct result of his productive career but also in the large and still active number of students and associates who are carrying forward his innovative ideas. He was one of the few truly practical theorists.

CONTEMPORARY TRENDS

Perhaps the most marked change in the field of social psychology characteristic of the past 30 years has been the emphasis on laboratory experimentation. Social psychology has become almost without exception "experimental" social psychology, so that even contemporary European social psychologists think of themselves as experimentalists. This clearly is a break with tradition—a break inspired and encouraged by the teaching of Kurt Lewin. In a sense this explosion of experimentation complicates the task of the systematist in his attempt to bring some theoretical unity to the array of accumulated findings; this difficulty has been noted elsewhere (McGuire, 1968). We shall treat it by merging summaries of contemporary empirical findings with the theoretical streams developed earlier in the chapter—particularly in conformity behavior, dissonance theory, attitude change theory, and social perception and judgment (attribution theory).

Conformity Behavior and Social Influence

Conformity behavior is illustrative of the strong trend toward experimentalism discussed above, since the research of the last quarter-century on conformity has been marked by the increasing tendency to bring observations into the laboratory. In contrast to the collective phenomena discussed by Tarde, Freud, McDougall, and LeBon, we find small-group studies conducted under controlled laboratory conditions, as typified in the work of Asch (1951), Crutchfield (1955), M. Deutsch and Gerard (1955), and Gerard and Rotter (1961).

In contrast to the earlier work, however, the laboratory examination of conformity behavior has been aimed at the empirical validation of the principles implicit in the theory of social influence or the extent to which the individual is subject to group pressure, especially in the everyday areas in which he or she is ordinarily thought to have the most autonomy. Specifically, although the collective-behavior theorists were concerned with phenomena that arose from the interaction of crowd-induced pressures and individual behavioral tendencies, the conformity behavior investigators have typically dealt with a context in which some basic skill, such as visual identification, is pitted against the "judgment" of a small group. Let us consider the paradigm developed by S. E. Asch that became the starting point for a great deal of subsequent research.

The subject is introduced to a setting in which he and seven other "subjects" (actually the experimenter's confederates) are seated in a semicircle in front of a blackboard. The task has been described to the subject as an exercise in visual perception. He is therefore not surprised to find that each time the experimenter calls on him he is to indicate which of three black lines of different lengths on a comparison card matches the single black line on the standard card. Furthermore, this matching appears to be a reasonable task, since each pair of standard and comparison cards has a line in common (see Figure 17-3). However, recall the setting for a moment. The subject is seated in the seventh position in a semicircle of eight "subjects," and his judgment on each trial follows that of six other people. In the basic experiment (Asch, 1951) the trials proceed as follows: During the first two trials, the seven other "subjects" (the experimenter's confederates) give the correct judgments; for the remaining sixteen trials, however, the confederates give twelve unanimous false judgments and four unanimous correct judgments. Clearly, the

 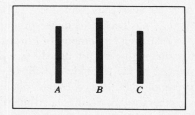

FIGURE 17-3.   A typical line judgment situation. S is the standard; A, B, and C are the comparison stimuli. (From Jones, E. E., and Gerard, H. Foundations of Social Psychology, 1967, p. 388, Fig. 11.1. By permission of John Wiley & Sons.)

subject is faced with a crisis of confidence in which he must choose between the evidence seen by his own eyes and the apparent social consensus marshaled against that evidence. This crisis, of course, is precisely the point of concern to the theory of social influence. To what extent is the individual capable of being influenced by an apparent consensus of his or her peers?

The data from the first set of experiments are quite convincing in that Asch presents ample evidence for conformity to the false majority. For the original 123 subjects, the average rate of yielding to the false majority was 7.08 yields on a total of 24 critical trials (control groups showed no errors). That this was not simple acquiescence on the part of subjects who found themselves in an artificial setting is documented by the extracts from the subject's postexperimental protocols (Asch, 1956). Subjects found the dilemma an agonizing one.

The implications of the findings from the original experiment become even more interesting as one traces the experimental extensions of the phenomenon. In the original group setting, for example, Asch varied the size of the "majority" from one to sixteen members and found that beyond a majority of three there was little increase in conformity. In other words, the phenomenon does not depend upon large numbers. In this same vein other investigators (Crutchfield, 1955; M. Deutsch & Gerard, 1955) were concerned with the effect on the subject of a "public" versus a "private" majority; that is: To what extent was the observed finding a function of an implicit public commitment by the subject to a majority judgment that he or she did not totally endorse? Would deviating from the "public" majority cause the subject to appear inconsistent and, therefore, to lose esteem in the group?

In order to remove the public pressure from the conformity context, subjects were isolated from each other through the use of cubicles. In this case there were four subjects, each of whom thought he was "Subject 3." By a manipulation of the apparatus, the subjects responded with their judgments simultaneously when the experimenter called for the response from Subject 3. As in the earlier Asch studies, the subjects were making judgments of line length; however, in this instance, the "judgments" of Subjects 1, 2, and 4 were supplied by the experimenter through the use of colored light panels in each subject's cubicle. Similarly, the true subjects indicated their judgments by throwing a switch on this panel instead of making verbal statements. Recalling that the essential point of both of these later studies was to remove any influence that may have been attributable to the public presence of other subjects, it is interesting to examine the actual conformity data. In contrast to the rate of 7.08/24 yields/critical trials, we find a rate of 5.92/24 yields/critical trials (M. Deutsch & Gerard, 1955). There was a reduction in yields, but conformity behavior under "private" conditions is still significant.

Research with the basic experimental paradigm during the ensuing years has extended the generality of the conformity phenomenon in a number of ways. For example, conformity (errors in the judgment task) was found to increase when stimulus ambiguity increased (Asch, 1951), when subjects anticipated future encounters with other subjects (Raven, 1959), and when other subjects were from the same membership group (Thibaut & Strickland, 1956). Additional research revealed that conformity behavior decreased when the subject is made to feel more "expert" (A. Snyder, Mischel, & Lott, 1960), when a partner from the "majority" appears to join forces with the subject during the series of judgments (Gerard & Greenbaum, 1962), and when individual goals of judgment accuracy are substituted for group goals (M. Deutsch & Gerard, 1955; E. E. Jones, Wells, & Torrey, 1958). At this point it is appropriate to question the extent to which these various findings might be artifacts of an unreal laboratory setting. Thus, before leaving conformity, we shall discuss briefly two more real-life applications of this research in the forms of risk-taking and obedience studies.

Conventional wisdom states that groups are inherently conservative as decision-making bodies, and this wisdom was essentially unchallenged until the appearance of a master's thesis by Stoner at MIT in 1961. Stoner had subjects read a series of twelve brief narrative descriptions of rather serious personal or professional conflicts. These "life dilemmas" were stated so as to place the subject in the position of advising the central person in the narrative on which of two courses of action he should take. For example, should the person contemplate a new position at a higher salary in an unknown firm or should he remain in his present position? In the first part of the experiment, subjects were individually asked to indicate the level of risk they would accept before advising each of the twelve hypothetical figures to embark on the more risky alternative in each dilemma. Specifically, they were asked to indicate what probability level of success they would have to have before advising the person to select the risk alternative. After completing this section of the experiment, subjects were brought together in small groups and asked to discuss and evaluate the same twelve situations—now in the context of making group decisions about the degree of risk to be advised. Contrary to previous expectations, the group decisions revealed a significant shift toward risk—a result that has received considerable support from other investigators (Teger & Pruitt, 1967; Wallach & Kogan, 1965b; Wallach, Kogan, & Bem, 1962, 1964).

Some recent research has indicated that the risky-shift phenomenon is, in part, a function of the situation. Depending upon the nature of the instructions given by the experimenter (Willems & Clark, 1969) or on the nature of the risk, whether hypothetical or real, the shift may or may not occur (Clement & Sullivan, 1970).

When the risky shift does take place, there are several alternative theoretical explanations for the effect. One is that a diffusion of responsibility occurs in the group judgment situation. Clearly, if others share a risk, the individual feels less personal risk (Wallach & Kogan, 1965b). The second alternative is that group discussion enhances the value of risk taking, making it more acceptable to each individual (R. Brown, 1965). Finally, the third possibility is that by sharing information in the group situation the individual's judgment may be altered. For example, the individual may find that others are more risky than he or she thinks they are and so modifies his or her response in the direction of more liberal risk taking (Pruitt, 1969).

It is not certain which of these alternatives accounts for the risky shift where it does occur. Perhaps all factors are simultaneously operating to some degree. However, a more clear-cut case for diffusion of responsibility comes from experiments on obedience and altruism.

The now classic studies on obedience by Milgram (1963, 1965) utilized an experimental paradigm in which a subject was deceived into thinking he or she was in an experiment investigating the effects of punishment on learning and that he or she would be the "teacher," while the other subject (a well-trained experimental confederate) would be the "learner." The apparatus includes a genuine electric chair in which the "learner" sat and a very realistic panel of stepped shocking levers whose voltages range from 30 to 450 volts. The "learning" trials followed a pattern arranged by the experimenter, in which the subject was required to give more and more intense "shocks" to the "learner" as a function of failure to learn the material. All this was accompanied by increasingly fervent pleas to stop and extremely convincing displays of intense pain and discomfort on the part of the "learner." In the meantime the experimenter encouraged the subject with certain set phrases appealing to the scientific merit of the study and attempted to get the subject to continue in spite of the apparent agony shown by the "learner." The dependent measure was the voltage level at which the subject refused to administer any more "shocks." It is rather disconcerting to read that the number of subjects who actually complete the sequence through the "450-volt" level is quite high (66 percent in the first experiment). Milgram uses this high rate of conformity to the wishes of an authority figure as evidence for the pervasiveness of what might be called the "Eichmann phenomenon," after the Nazi officer who was "just following orders" as he directed the execution of millions of Jews in concentration camps during World War II.

Studies of altruism also reflect, in part, diffusion of responsibility, although other factors are admittedly involved. Experimental work in altruistic or helping behavior received enormous impetus from the tragic case of Kitty Genovese, a young Queens, New York, woman who was stabbed to death one night in 1964 while an estimated 38 people stood silently by in their apartments refusing to go to her assistance or even call the police.

In laboratory or field studies of altruism a variety of situations has been employed to test the willingness of bystanders to aid those who appear to be in need of assistance (Darley & Batson, 1973; Latané & Darley, 1970). Typical of such experimental situations, subjects hear someone in an adjoining room fall and injure themselves, or sound as if they are having a seizure. The experimental measure is what percentage of bystanders is willing to help. The answer is a high percentage—up to 70 percent—*if the bystander is alone or thinks he or she is alone*. But if others are present as few as 5 to 7 percent intervene or go for assistance. Clearly, as in the case of Kitty Genovese, people are inhibited from intervening by the presence of others. Some of the failure to act is no doubt due to the diffusion of responsibility when a group is present. However, if an apparent victim of an accident or medical crisis is helped by a model (confederate of the experimenter's), then strangers will be more willing to help. And so conformity to the social value of the Good Samaritan takes precedence over the sense of diffuse responsibility.

Cognitive Dissonance

The first systematic exposition of cognitive dissonance theory appeared in 1957 in Leon Festinger's *A Theory of Cognitive Dissonance*. A student of Kurt Lewin's, Festinger developed the dynamics of cognitive dissonance from field theory emphasizing the tendency for cognitive processes to seek equilibrium.

In its simplest form, the theory reduces the relationships between two cognitive elements to the following possibilities: *consonance, dissonance,* or *irrelevance.* Consonance results if the implication of the two cognitions are consistent with each other, do not contradict each other, or do not imply the reverse of each other. Irrelevance occurs when the cognitions have no implications for each other, as is the case for "The coffee is warm" and "May follows April." Dissonance is created when the two cognitions contradict each other or imply inconsistent conclusions. It is not simple inconsistency that produces dissonance; instead, the two cognitions must have confounded behavioral implications. As E. E. Jones and Gerard note, "The cognitions may be inconsistent or incompatible and not produce dissonance if they do not have mutually incompatible behavioral implications" (1967, p. 190).

The notion of "behavioral implication" underscores another crucial aspect of the original formulation: the status of dissonance as a drive or motivational state. Although we shall have more to say of this later, it is important to note here that according to Festinger a dissonant relation between two cognitions generates an unpleasant drivelike state that initiates a process designed to reduce the dissonance and restore the individual to a balanced or consonant state. This process has been the subject of a continuing research effort since 1957 and has attracted some important criticism (Bem, 1965, 1968; Chapanis & Chapanis, 1965). Before discussing current developments and elaborations, let us consider the classic Festinger and Carlsmith (1959) experiment.

Subjects were recruited for an experiment involving an hour's performance of an exceedingly dull and repetitive motor task. At the conclusion of this boring experience, the subject is informed that the experimenter's assistant has failed to show up and that the experimenter needs an assistant to interact with the next subject and other subjects in the future. Specifically, the experimenter wants someone to describe the experiment to the next subject as a fascinating and worthwhile experience. Furthermore, depending on the experimental condition (high or low dissonance, respectively), the subject is offered one dollar or twenty dollars for this assistance. The crucial dependent measure is taken later when the subject fills out a "departmental" questionnaire, which among other things asks him or her to indicate how interesting the experiment was. In accordance with the theoretical prediction, the low-dissonance subjects showed higher liking for the experimental task. Why?

Let us recall the two essential facts of the experimental setting: The subject has just engaged in an hour of exceedingly dull and monotonous labor, and he or she has just agreed to lie about this experience to the next subject or other future subjects. Thus, according to the rudiments of the theory, we have the necessary elements for dissonance production and the corresponding attempt to reduce it. That is, there are two discrepant cognitions—"The task was dull" and "I have agreed to tell someone that the task was very interesting"—and they presumably are generating an unpleasant pressure that must be reduced by modifying the relation between the two cognitions. If we now consider the two incentive levels, we have the answer. We would expect the subject who was offered twenty dollars to see that sum as sufficient justification for lying about the experimental task. However, we would expect the subject who was offered one dollar to see that amount as an insufficient reward for telling a lie about the task.

On this basis, there are grounds for differential predictions on how the subjects would rate the experimental task. The one-dollar subjects should rate the task as more enjoyable than do the twenty-dollar subjects, and the data confirm this expectation. According to Festinger, the results provide confirmation for the theory because the one-dollar subject has now brought the cognition of "agreeing to tell someone that the task was interesting" into consonance by evaluating the task as more interesting. The twenty-dollar subject, on the other hand, feels no such pressure and rates the task as exceedingly dull.

It must be noted that the dissonance effect is not always in the direction of the greatest change for the least reward. In an experiment similar in design to the original Festinger and Carlsmith experiment, Carlsmith, Collins, and Helmreich (1966) found that subjects who had to make a public statement or commitment contrary to their beliefs experience more dissonance than if the statement is made privately in an essay to be seen only by the experimenter. Another important condition is that the subject must have a sense of freedom of choice. If an individual is forced by higher authority to take a stance against his or her convictions, less dissonance will be aroused than if he or she freely makes such a choice. And so the soldier forced to kill on the battlefield may find no inconsistence or dissonance with his civilian attitudes that killing is wrong.

In addition to experiments concerned with the phenomenon of insufficient reward, numerous other studies have been conducted in the area of postdecisional selective exposure to information. The theory of cognitive dissonance assumes that decision making is a dissonance-producing activity and predicts that postdecisional searching for information in support of the decision will be directed toward reducing the dissonance aroused by the decision. A person making a choice among several automobiles, for example, would be expected to ignore information about the models not selected, while maximizing his or her exposure to information favorable to the model he or she did select. A derived expectation is that previously unimportant negative features of the unchosen alternatives will be magnified. A complementary process is expected to occur with respect to the chosen alternative. We shall now summarize the data that bear on this point.

A number of experiments (Adams, 1961; Brock, 1965; Ehrlich, Guttman, Schonbach, & Mills, 1957; Feather, 1962; Mills, Aronson, & Robinson, 1959; Rosen, 1961) have been conducted in an attempt to demonstrate the subject's active avoidance of information that does not support his or her decision choice. Typically, it has been found that subjects may choose to expose themselves to information supporting their choice. But they may also choose to examine information opposed to their choice, as the cigarette smoker may read articles concerning the hazards of smoking. Thus, as in so many cases in psychology, the complexity of human behavior turns out to be greater than can be accounted for by simplistic theory. Mills (1965) cites evidence in support of his contention that the failure to produce experimental avoidance of dissonant information is a partial function of not controlling for the inherent interest of the information; but it is more generally the case that many dissonance theorists do not agree that the validity of cognitive dissonance theory is dependent upon the results of postdecisional information avoidance, and the issue remains in doubt (Brehm & Cohen, 1962).

Turning to another aspect of the problem, a vigorous attack has been launched on one of the basic (and presently untestable by objective means) tenets of dissonance theory—the assumption that dissonance produces a quasi-physiological aversive state that does not abate until the dissonance is reduced. In fact, Festinger holds that this individually felt aversive state is absolutely essential to cognitive dissonance. Arguing from a behaviorist orientation, Bem (1965, 1967, 1968) has suggested that it is superfluous to require the assumption of an internal aversive state, since we typically infer our attitudes from our behavior (for example, "I must like carrots, since I am always eating them"). To support his contention, Bem has conducted a series of ingenious experiments based on what he calls "interpersonal replication."

In essence, this procedure exposes subjects to the written or verbal description of one of the dissonance experiments (Brehm & Cohen, 1962) and asks them to supply the rating or dependent variable measure supplied by the subjects in the "real" experiment. The fact that Bem's interpersonal replication subjects closely reproduce the results gathered from the earlier experiments is taken as evidence by him that it is not essential that an internal aversive state accompany the dissonance-producing situation. This finding seriously calls into question the logical status of dissonance theory by demonstrating that its supposedly unique empirical findings can be replicated without the assumption of an internal aversive state.

In a spirited experimental exchange (Bem, 1968; E. E. Jones, Linder, Kiesler, Zanna, & Brehm, 1968) the issue came into sharp focus through a careful duplication of Bem's interpersonal replication experiments. From these replications it became clear that certain experimental artifacts in Bem's designs may have caused his subjects to infer special properties or idiosyncratic attitudinal positions on the part of the subjects in the *original* experiments and that this inference may have allowed them to replicate the results so closely. In fact, when these artifacts are eliminated in the Jones et al. experiments, the interpersonal replication subjects are unable to reproduce the original findings. In a subsequent experiment, Arrowood, Wood, and Ross (1970) give evidence for the assumption of individually felt aversive states by showing that a subject who has undergone the induction of dissonance through laborious preparation for a difficult examination can estimate his or her own probability of taking the examination. However, he or she cannot infer a neighboring subject's expectations about taking the examination, even though there is no objective basis on which to infer a state different from his or her own. Arrowood, Wood, and Ross interpret this finding as a requirement that dissonance must be individually perceived by "involved" subjects and that its effects cannot be estimated by uninvolved individuals.

The debate between self-perception theory and dissonance theory continues, and in a 1972 article, M. Snyder and Ebbesen note that some of the difficulties attending the controversy may have resulted from "simplistic conceptions" of the phenomena as well as methodological problems. That is to say, people do not always hide their heads in sand like the mythical ostrich when they experience dissonance. As Aronson has pointed out, an individual who has paid a great deal of money for a new home *will* see water in the basement after the first rain. Similarly, the smoker who begins to cough up blood no longer ignores the evidence on the danger of smoking. As these everyday examples suggest, dissonance and the consequent selectivity of perception are limited phenomena dependent on the issues involved and the situational context—a conclusion that is generally valid for all psychological processes. In a way, this suggestion seems a fitting conclusion for our section on dissonance theory, inasmuch as the theory holds great promise if it becomes empirically testable. Berkowitz puts it this way:

> The proponents of dissonance theory can also help their cause by concentrating less on obtaining "nonobvious" findings and selecting at least some of their problems on the basis of systematic and even parametric considerations. Among the most important features of this research should be the utilization of independent measures of dissonance arousal and reduction. As it is now, some theoretical generalizations are logically circular; behavior x is said to be the result of dissonance, and we are assured that dissonance existed because behavior x occurred. Having these independent measures, furthermore, we would be able to tell whether exceptions to the dissonance (and cognitive balance) formulations are due to the ability to tolerate tension under certain conditions or to the non-existence of tension in those situations. (1969a, p. 102)

Attitude Change

Before discussing the various models of attitude change, we should point out that attitude change is one of the oldest and most persistent areas of investigation in social psychology. In fact, as noted by E. E. Jones and Gerard (1967), many of the variables manipulated or examined in attitude-change experiments (such as types of appeals, medium used, prestige of the speaker) are derived directly from Aristotle's *Rhetoric*. Furthermore, although the majority of the empirical investigations in the past 30 years have been directed toward many of the points suggested by Aristotle, very few researchers have concerned themselves with attempting to validate the definition of an attitude (as given earlier in the chapter) or the assumed interrelationship between behavior, cognition, and affect (Ostrom, 1969). However, a change is in the wind, and more recent work has been directed toward "theories of attitudes" (Greenwald, Brock, & Ostrom, 1968).

In the previous section we spent some time discussing Festinger's dissonance theory. One could argue that his theory deals with attitude change because it is based on the premise of cognitive balance. It is therefore appropriate to keep

Festinger's theory in mind as we describe the cognitive consistency approaches to attitude change.

For the purpose of this section, we shall divide attitude-change theories into two rather crude categories: reinforcement theories and cognitive consistency theories. In each case the key concept is assumed to provide the motivational base for attitude change.

The reinforcement theory approach to attitude change is primarily associated with Carl Hovland and the Yale Communication Research Program (Hovland, Janis, & Kelley, 1953). Working mainly with the principles derived from Hull's learning theory, the Yale group developed an attitude-change theory around the premise that attitude change was a function of reinforced learning. In other words, a person accepts a new position on an attitudinal issue because he or she is reinforced for doing so. In general, three types of experiments fall under the reinforcement rubric: classical conditioning studies, verbal conditioning studies, and fear-arousing communication studies. Let us consider each briefly.

The classical conditioning attitude-change experiment (Blandford & Sampson, 1964; Insko & Oakes, 1966; A. Staats and Staats, 1958; A. Staats, Staats, & Heard, 1960; C. Staats & Staats, 1957) typically requires the pairing of some previously neutral word or nonsense syllable with a second evaluative stimulus for a fixed number of presentations, after which the neutral words are tested for an evaluative response by the subject. For example, A. Staats and Staats (1958) conducted experiments using either first names such as *Harry, Tom,* and *Bill* or names of nationalities such as *Dutch, Swedish,* and *German* as relatively neutral stimuli, which were paired with positive, negative, or nonevaluative adjectives. At the conclusion of the learning trial period, subjects were asked to reevaluate the previously neutral names or nationalities. The results typically show a change in evaluation in the predicted direction.

Studies of instrumental conditioning involving verbal reinforcement (Hildum & Brown, 1956; Insko, 1965; Insko & Cialdini, 1971; Krasner, Knowles, & Ullmann, 1965; Singer, 1961) are based upon an effect first noticed in a study by Greenspoon (1955). In this investigation subjects who were instructed to say words could be led to increase their emission of plural nouns by the use of "Mhmmm" by the experimenter. In similar fashion, the subject in the verbal conditioning experiment is reinforced for making a particular response. As an example, Insko (1965) reports a study in which students at the University of Hawaii were contacted by telephone concerning the creation of a spring festival called "Aloha Week." During the course of the conversation, the subjects were reinforced with "Good" by the interviewer if they agreed or disagreed with the statements concerning the new festival. A questionnaire was passed out a week later to all members of the class from which the subjects had been drawn. In contrast to the other students in the class, the students who had taken part in the telephone "survey" were expected to respond differentially to an item dealing with the establishment of Aloha Week. They did so, and Insko (1967) takes this as evidence for the enduring nature of the reinforcement.

A note of caution should be sounded before we leave our discussion of the verbal reinforcement and classical conditioning attitude-change studies. There has been considerable controversy over the issue of the subject's awareness of the reinforcement contingency in verbal reinforcement experiments. Speilberger (1962) cites evidence that shows a correlation between awareness and conditioning in the verbal reinforcement literature and contends that the verbal conditioning results are artifacts. However, since degree of awareness is determined through postexperimental interviews with subjects, it is also possible that the experimenter's probing sensitizes the subjects to the appropriate response. The issue is an important one, which has yet to be resolved.

Experiments involving fear-arousing communications (Berkowitz & Cottingham, 1960; Janis & Feshbach, 1953; Leventhal & Niles, 1964; Leventhal & Singer, 1966; Leventhal, Singer, & Jones, 1965) form the last group of the reinforcement-based studies in attitude change. In this case, a subject is generally exposed to a fear-producing message, from which he or she can theoretically escape by the ability to change his or her attitude on the appropriate dimension.

In the Janis and Feshbach (1953) study, for example, different groups of high school subjects were presented with one of three fear-arousing communications concerning tooth decay. Presumably, the three communications differed in the intensity of the fear produced in the subjects, so that there were "high," "medium," and "low" levels of fear arousal. To assess the effect of the manipulation, subjects were given a questionnaire concerning their dental hygiene practices a week before the experimental sessions. In the week following the experiment a second questionnaire was administered to determine the amount of change produced by the various fear levels. Contrary to what one might expect (and to most of the literature), the high-fear communication produced the least change with respect to the increase in tooth brushing claimed by the subject, and the low-fear communication produced the most change. Why?

The interpretation offered by Janis and Feshbach maintains that the high-fear communication may have overwhelmed any perceived benefit from modifying a tooth-brushing practice, so that subjects were actually less inclined to pay attention to the suggestions made by the dental hygiene message. While higher fear levels have generally produced more observed attitude change in other studies, Janis (1967) points out that the overall relationship between emotional arousal and attitude change may be a complicated one and that perhaps researchers should be looking for sophisticated interaction effects between manipulations and indicators of change. Furthermore, it should be noted that much of the research in this area deals with *assumed* fear levels; and only recently has there been an interest in measuring *both* the fear level produced by the communication and the a priori vulnerability of the subject to this communication (Steinberg, 1971).

Some mention must also be made of factors that were discovered to be important in attitude change resulting from classical or instrumental learning situations. Among these are variables associated with the source of the communication. In general, it has been found that the greater the credibility, expertise, attractiveness, and status of the communicator, the more likely he or she is to succeed in bringing about attitude change in the audience. Insofar as the communication itself is concerned, such factors as repetition, novelty, and discrepancy are important variables, with repetition and novelty generally favoring change. Discrepancy must not be too great or audience resistance is likely to be increased rather than decreased.

We turn now to a consideration of the other main category of attitude-change theories, which can be grouped according to Insko (1967) as "equilibrium" theories. Although all these formulations operate around the general notion that attitude change occurs through pressures to reduce cognitive imbalance, a further distinction can be made between the more mathematically based "congruity" theory of Osgood and Tannenbaum (1955) and the "balance" or "consistency" theories of Heider (1958), Newcomb (1959), and Rosenberg and Abelson (1960).

Fundamental to all of the equilibrium formulations (including dissonance theory) is the assumption that a balanced cognitive state produces a satisfied state. Put differently, it is assumed that cognitive imbalance—in the form of disagreement among related ideas or beliefs—contains the seeds of cognitive balance through the application of the appropriate attitude-change mechanism. Most often this mechanism takes the form of changing one of the existing cognitions or adding a new cognition to rectify the imbalance.

Figure 17-4 shows Heider's (1958) theoretical analysis of balanced and imbalanced states. In the diagram P stands for Perceiver, O for other, and X for an object

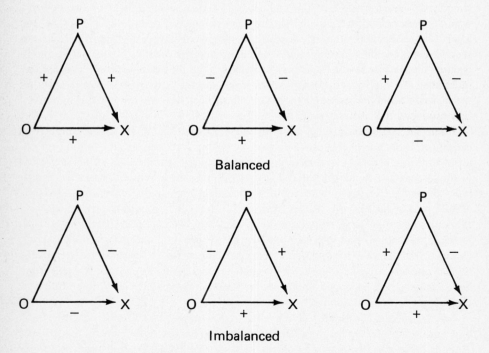

Balanced

Imbalanced

FIGURE 17-4.   A representation of Heider's balance theory. P = person; O = other; X = an object, idea, or event. Balance results if there are no negatives or two negatives. Imbalance results from one or three negatives.

toward which either P or O may have an attitude. Thus, in (1) a balanced state, P and O—who have a positive attitude toward each other—also have a positive attitude toward X. However, in (2) P and O have a positive attitude toward X but a negative attitude toward each other. For a balanced cognitive state to occur, P and O must change their attitude toward each other or both must change their attitude toward X. A situation such as this might arise between two acquaintances who do not like each other initially but subsequently discover that each has a strong positive interest in the Republican party. We might predict that their attitudes would be modified in the direction of greater liking for each other. It is obviously unlikely that their mutual attraction toward the Republican party would change.

More generally, as Figure 17-4 shows, balance occurs where the product of the signs is positive. This can take place if there are no negative signs, or if there are two negative signs. To take one more example, this time a negative one, if as in (3) P dislikes O and P also dislikes X, then it does not matter to P that O likes X.

A large number of studies have been directed to the examination of this process, and for the present purpose we have selected one of the more representative experiments—the ''Fenwick'' study of Rosenberg and Abelson (1960).

Subjects were asked to play the part of a department store owner who was concerned with three things: a rug salesman named Fenwick, the volume of rug sales, and the effect of modern art displays on rug sales. In addition, all subjects shared common information relating the various concepts—that is, Fenwick plans a display of modern art in the rug department; displays of modern art reduce sales; and Fenwick has increased sales volume in the past. Experimental manipulations varied subjects' perceptions of the three initial concepts in the following ways: one-third of the subjects were told to have positive feelings toward Fenwick, modern art, and sales; one-third were told to have positive feelings toward Fenwick and sales, and negative feelings toward modern art; and one-third were told to have positive feelings toward sales and negative feelings toward Fenwick and modern art (see Figure 17-5).

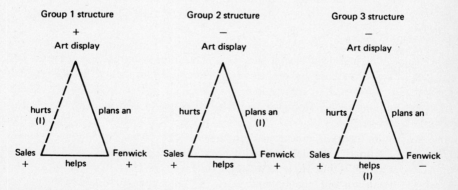

FIGURE 17-5.   Three cognitive structures. (I) denotes the locus of imbalance; dashed lines indicate negative relations; and solid lines, positive relations. (After Rosenberg, M., et al. Attitude Organization and Change. Fig. 128. Copyright © 1960 by Yale University Press.)

After receiving these various inductions, the subjects were given three communications from some of the "store officers." The communications stated that (1) Fenwick has not maintained sales, (2) Fenwick does not plan to have a modern art display, and (3) sales are increased by modern art displays. Subjects were then asked to evaluate each of these three messages in terms of its "pleasantness," its "accuracy," and its "persuasiveness." According to expectations derived from consistency theory, subjects should have evaluated most highly the communications that restore balance to the structure with the least amount of rearrangement. Thus, in Figure 17-5, Group 1 should have rated number 3 most highly, Group 2 should have rated number 2 most highly, and Group 3 should have rated number 1 most highly. Furthermore, the communications requiring two structural changes to achieve cognitive balance were expected to be preferred to those requiring three changes. In both cases the data gave unequivocal support to the predictions.

It is interesting to note in connection with the consistency model that Rosenberg and Abelson carried out additional replications of this experiment in which the strength of the various communications was varied; and they reported instances in which inconsistency would be tolerated if it implied realization of another dominant value, such as increased sales. Perhaps, as Rosenberg (1965) points out, the toleration of inconsistency is a function of the implied hedonic tone of the imbalance in that we are bothered by inequity more quickly if it has negative implications for us.

Not all social psychologists are in agreement with a simple balance or consistency theory of attitude change. Some have emphasized that the degree of balance or imbalance is an important factor (Osgood & Tannenbaum, 1955), while others have emphasized that agreement about significant behaviors is more important than feelings of liking or disliking (Newcomb, 1953). The fact that people may share the same attitudes toward peace and so avoid conflict is more important than their personal likes or dislikes toward each other. We must therefore conclude that balance and consistency of attitudes is one important element generating attitude change but not the only one. As we turn to attribution theory in the following section we shall learn more about the complexities of perceiver-object relationships.

Attribution Theory

Social perception and social judgment have burgeoned during the past two decades as areas of theoretical and experimental concern to include a wide range of phenomena, but we shall narrow our discussion to one particularly active subarea—attribution theory. However, we shall also briefly consider impression formation in this section.

Attribution theory is concerned with an ancient problem, in which interest was reawakened primarily through the writings of Fritz Heider (1944). In its simplest terms, the problem is this: How do we come to make stable assumptions of causality about the events in our phenomenal world? A disarmingly simple question, its answer is infinitely complicated by the fact that data that might be marshaled to supply the answer depend upon perceptual processes that are far from veridical or "truthful"; and it is precisely this difficulty that has attracted the attention of the attribution theorists. Let us make clear at the outset that the attribution process assumes a relatively normal observer. In the words of E. E. Jones, Kanouse, Kelley, Nisbett, Valins, and Weiner, "Attribution theory deals with the rules the average individual uses in attempting to infer the causes of observed behavior" (1972, p. x).

Whereas the writings of Heider were germinal, the chief responsibility for the theoretical development of the attribution process belongs to E. E. Jones and Davis (1965) and Kelley (1967). Interestingly enough, while both theories draw heavily upon the basic work of Heider, they are oriented toward rather different perspectives of the attribution process. Kelley tends to concentrate more on the self and its attempts to achieve stable attributions; Jones and Davis are more concerned with attributions made by the observer about another's behavior, "the *actor*." Let us look at each position briefly.

Jones and Davis (1965) assume the perspective of an observer who is watching the actions of an actor and whose attribution task is the discernment of underlying dispositions from the manifested behavior. In order to achieve this goal, the observer is required to work his or her way back from the observable (the perceived event) to the inferred (the actor's disposition). According to Jones and Davis this process (see Figure 17-6) requires observation of the effects produced by a given act, followed by the perceiver's decision about whether the actor himself or herself was aware that the effects would follow from *that* action. Clearly, if we cannot infer an actor's awareness of an action, we cannot infer his or her intent. However, assuming that the actor has been credited with advance knowledge of the effects of the act, there remains the additional test of the actor's ability to carry out an act before the perceiver can proceed with the analysis. It is certainly the case that we often possess the knowledge for doing something without possessing the ability to do it. The example comes to mind of lifting a 500-pound weight. It should be apparent that both the test for ability to perform and the test for knowledge must be positive for an intention to be inferred.

This brief outline of the process suggested by Figure 17-6 suffices to illustrate the skeleton of the Jones and Davis model, but we must now bring in additional concepts in order to indicate more clearly the process from the perceiver's point of

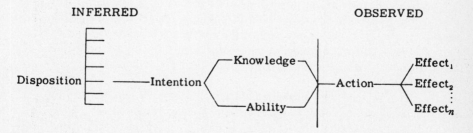

FIGURE 17-6. The effect-disposition model. (From Jones, E. E., and Davis, K. E. From acts to dispositions, in L. Berkowitz (Ed.), Advances in experimental social psychology, Vol. 2, 1965. Academic Press, Inc.)

view. The model assumes that behavior is more useful for the inference of dispositions to the extent to which it departs from cultural or societal norms. Thus, the fact
that a man eats his meals with chopsticks is presumably more informative than the
fact that he eats. This assumption becomes central to the formulation with the
introduction of the concept of *correspondence*.

Since the perceiver is concerned with achieving stability in his or her attributions, he or she is by definition most interested in inferences that achieve an accurate
"mapping" of the connection between the observed effect and the underlying
disposition or attribute of the actor—the so-called attribute-effect linkage. Jones and
Davis contend that the perceiver achieves a highly correspondent inference to the
extent that he or she is convinced an observed effect was produced by an actor
whose standing on a particular attribute differs from the standing of the "average"
person on that attribute. Furthermore, the more the given effect departs from norms
of social desirability, the higher the correspondence of the inference. It is for these
reasons that we tend to attribute full intention to act with corresponding underlying
disposition to persons who deviate markedly in sexual behavior, such as rapists and
child molesters.

In addition to correspondence, we must introduce two final concepts in order to
comprehend Jones and Davis' view of the attribution process. These are *hedonic
relevance* and *personalism,* both of which are involved in the perceiver's conclusions about the actor. In hedonic relevance it is assumed that acts and their effects
vary in the degree to which they promote or impede a perceiver's welfare, and that
to the extent that the effects of a given act are seen to impinge on the perceiver, they
will be hedonically relevant. That is, they will affect the perceiver's well-being.
Jones and Davis argue that increasing the hedonic relevance of an act will tend also
to increase the correspondence of the attribution inference.

Looking now at personalism, we encounter another test the perceiver must
consider to assure a degree of correspondence in making inferences. An act perceived to be hedonically relevant may or may not have been aimed at the perceiver.
As Jones and Davis note, it is up to the perceiver "to decide whether the act was
uniquely conditioned by the fact that he was its target" (1965, p. 247). This is the
meaning of personalism. Clearly, in those cases in which acts are perceived to
impinge upon the self, personality variables could have wide implications. At one
extreme paranoia would lead to excessive inferences of personalism, and at the
other extreme insensitivity would lead to failure to perceive actual personalistic
intent by the actor. However, we can see the emergence of additional questions for
the perceiver who has concluded a personalistic intention by an actor: Am I the
target because of who I am? Am I the target because of what I can do for this
person? And so on.

We have sketched the attribution framework from the perspective of the observer and an actor. Let us now combine the two and consider Kelley's approach to
the attribution problem (Kelley, 1967).

In this instance we are dealing (in the simplest case) with a person who has a
reaction to an event and who is attempting to determine whether to attribute the
reaction to himself or herself, to the event, or to a combination of the two. If we
examine Figure 17-7, the method implied by Kelley's model becomes quite clear.

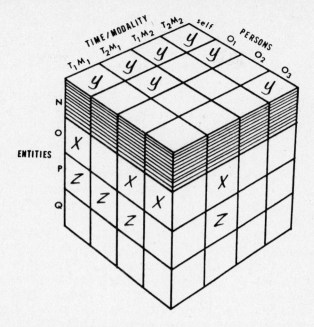

FIGURE 17-7. Data pattern indicating attribution of effect Y to entity N. (Reprinted from "Attribution Theory in Social Psychology," by H. H. Kelley, in Nebraska Symposium on Motivation, 1967, by David Levine, Ed. by permission of University of Nebraska Press.)

Let us assume that a person has had a reaction to a given event—a lecture, for example. Keeping in mind the emphasis on achieving stability of attributions, it follows that the person (in this case the "self") is interested in determining the source of his or her perceived reaction to the event. The model provides us with several information sources that can be consulted in the attribution process.

Assuming that we are confining our interest to a single event (the lecture), we might derive evidence from friends (persons) who attended the same lecture. Additionally, we could inquire of people who heard the lecture at a different hour (time) or on closed-circuit television (modality). As we sample these various information sources, we start to become aware of the degree to which we share a common reaction (Y) with our friends across varying times and modalities. Furthermore, if this reaction is unique to the particular happening (the lecture as opposed to grocery shopping), we have assembled the requisite information for the attribution test.

According to Kelley, the person must meet the following criteria in order to achieve "external validity": distinctiveness, consistency over time, consistency over modality, and consensus. To illustrate these tests we might imagine that we have just met a person who at first impression seems highly intelligent. The test of distinctiveness is met, since our new acquaintance appears to be able to solve all kinds of problems in school with ease and stands out at the top of the class. The test of time is met when we discover that he or she has had a history of outstanding academic work starting in the grades. Our impression is further strengthened when we find upon further acquaintance that our new friend performs consistently from situation to situation in different modalities—not only in the classroom, but in everyday life, in playing amateur chess, and so forth. Finally, our impression is further validated when we discover that others who know our friend agree that he or she is a highly intelligent person. When we have fulfilled these criteria, we have met the essential conditions for attributional consistency; however, as Kelley notes, this may not be equivalent to veridicality. In fact, as we saw in the section on conformity, social consensus may oppose veridicality.

The last few pages have been devoted to a discussion of two theoretical models to the exclusion of empirical studies, and the reader may wonder whether this treatment reflects the true state of affairs in attribution theory. To deal with this question, let us turn to a brief consideration of *impression formation* literature.

The early work in impression formation (Asch, 1946; Luchins, 1948) was concerned with the process subjects use in combining attributes to form impressions of hypothetical persons. In such experiments the subject is given a list of hypothetical traits such as "cheerful," "outgoing," and "honest," from which to describe a personality. Despite the seemingly fragmented nature of the information, subjects do not find the task difficult. A particular concern was whether there were certain organizing traits, such as "warm-cold," that would tend to alter the meaning of other attributes in the personality composite (Kelley, 1950).

It was found that there are, indeed, central traits. For example, the term "warm" or "cold" when used in describing a hypothetical person makes a great deal of difference. When Asch presented the same list of traits (such as intelligent, industrious, determined, for example), except that half of the judges also heard the individual described as "cold" and the other half as "warm," there was a dramatic difference in the impressions. The individual characterized as "warm" was described by the judges in highly positive terms, whereas the individual characterized as "cold" was described in negative terms by the judges.

Becoming interested in the information processing aspect of the problem, Anderson (1962, 1968) extended the research domain to include an investigation of the mathematical model used by perceivers in combining the information to generate an impression. Convinced at first of the validity of a simple additive model for combining information, Anderson has come increasingly to favor a more interactive model in which the value of each new piece of information is seen to be a partial function of the value of the preceding pieces of information. In other words, some sort of order effect was found to be operative here.

Order effects have certainly been observed in impression formation (Aronson & Linder, 1965; Luchins, 1957; Sigall & Aronson, 1967; Thibaut, Walker, & Lind, 1972), but it is necessary to consider additional variables in the attribution context, and this has been recently accomplished (E. E. Jones & Goethals, 1971; E. E. Jones, Kanouse, et al., 1972). In essence, the implication of the order effects associated with the impression formation findings is that although we typically process information about some person according to a sequence (which may or may not be prearranged), the effect of that sequence is dependent upon other factors. For example, an advance expectation concerning the ability of a given person may totally offset the effect of a behavior sequence we might observe—or it might not.

E. E. Jones, Rock, Shaver, Goethals, and Ward (1968) report an instance in which a person with high attributed ability performs below expectation and one in which a person with low attributed ability performs above expectation. In the first instance subjects perceive the performance as due to temporary "motivational variations" or "outside distractions," whereas in the second case, the good performance is attributed to luck. When something more transient than an ability (such as a mood) is seen to change over time, however, subjects seem more willing to change their attribution in the direction of the change suggested in the behavior sequence (E. E. Jones & Goethals, 1971).

This brief glimpse of impression formation does little justice to the area but serves to give some insight into potential applications of attribution theory. Perhaps, as Kelley suggests, in time we may discover that "many social psychologists have been using attribution theory all their lives without knowing it" (1967, p. 192).

CONCLUSION

Obviously, we have been eclectic in our coverage of the field of social psychology. However, we have attempted to suggest the significant directions that theory and research have taken in the past half-century. Even though the areas we have covered have been substantive ones in terms of theories or collections of empirical data, a few broader issues have encompassed the field in recent years—issues that are more or less independent of content and whose resolution (or lack of it) will have great impact on the future of social psychology.

Of immediate concern for experimenters are the issues raised in an article by Orne (1962) entitled, "On the Social Psychology of the Psychological Experiment: With Particular Reference to Demand Characteristics and Their Implications," and a book by R. Rosenthal (1966), *Experimenter Effects in Behavioral Research*. Briefly, it is the message of these and many subsequent publications that research designs running the gamut from rudimentary animal learning studies to complicated social psychological deception experiments were laboring under a common difficulty—the experimenter's expectations of the experimental outcome. Ample data (R. Rosenthal, 1963) have been cited to show that the experimenter's hypothesis about the outcome can, for example, cause previously undifferentiated rats to appear "dull" or "bright"—depending upon the expectation for that particular group. Needless to say, far more dramatic effects have been observed in human experimentation. Perhaps most alarming is the reported extension of this effect into the classroom, where the teacher's expectation of a student's performance has been seen to be causally related to the student's performance (R. Rosenthal, 1968). The effect is often called the self-fulfilling prophecy.

The immediate concern of the social psychologist, however, should be an effort to minimize this influence when it is a nuisance in experimental designs. In addition, he or she should be directing considerable attention toward replicating many studies now considered classic in the field. Obviously, this replication throws a greater burden on the experimenter, since it doubtless will require more sophisticated measures of behavior taken over longer periods of time at greater expense.

Furthermore, certain areas of social psychology will feel the impact more than others. For example, attitude-change experiments—in which the manipulation and the dependent measure are separated by an hour or less—may have to be abandoned. But the argument that these changes will produce a more relevant body of social psychological research is compelling indeed.

A second issue, in some ways inseparable from the first, concerns the ethics of experimentation, particularly with respect to deception and potential emotional and psychological damage to the subject. In the earlier days of experimental social psychology it was common practice to give subjects electric shocks or to tell them elaborate lies to enhance the "social realism" of the laboratory setting. More recently, however, psychologists have become concerned about possible enduring effects from experiments involving shock or deception. For example, one must ask whether the apparent intense discomfort encountered by subjects in the Milgram studies of obedience summarized earlier in this chapter was offset by the knowledge gained from the experiments—particularly when many of the field events in the war in Vietnam seem to have reconfirmed the Eichmann phenomenon. Moreover, Kelman (1967) raises the issue that the very extremity of the deception in such studies may elicit a feeling of complete incredulity in the subject, which would make doubtful the validity of the findings produced under such circumstances.

The area that should, perhaps, provoke the most thought with respect to social psychology is at the heart of an exchange between Ring (1967) and McGuire (1967) on current experimental practices and the future of social psychology. The substance of the debate is whether social psychological experimentation exists for the edification of other social psychologists or is directed toward more useful ends. In addition, much discussion is devoted to the role of theoretical investigations in social psychology as well as to the relative merits of the field and laboratory settings for research.[4]

Since experimental social psychology today is still grappling with heeding the exhortations of Kurt Lewin, its founding father, it seems appropriate to note that Rohrer and Sherif's book title, *Social Psychology at the Crossroads,* is as apt today as it was in 1951.

---

[4]The reader is directed to this exchange as well as to J. Jung's *The Experimenter's Dilemma* (1971) for a more thorough treatment of those questions as well as those concerning experimenter effects, deception, and ethics in experimentation.

Epilogue

18

Our survey of systems of psychology has covered more than twenty centuries and perhaps as many different theoretical points of view. But psychology is truly a child of the nineteenth and twentieth centuries, for only a little over 100 years ago did it emerge from philosophy and physiology as an independent discipline. It is also true that psychology is a product of the age of analysis—an age that has witnessed an ever-increasing proliferation of scientific disciplines as the analytic method of the natural sciences rolls back the frontiers of knowledge. Thus within the brief period of a single century, psychologists have sought to define their subject and to establish its broad foundations as a science.

As we have seen, the problem of definition has proved to be a knotty one. Each emergent leader sought to establish psychology in the image of his or her own preconceptions—with the result that psychology's infancy was characterized by a diversity of opinions as to the nature of the new science. As an inevitable consequence of the multiplicity of definitions, there was disagreement over methodology. Because controversies attract supporters to either side, divergent viewpoints came to be organized into schools of psychology. Although schools as such no longer exist in academic psychology, the old viewpoints are still evident, as we have tried to show in tracing the emergence of contemporary trends and theoretical orientations.

Although so many divergent points of view have had their day in court, no generally acceptable definition of psychology has emerged. Rather, the disharmony engendered by the schools gave rise to distrust of all systematic orientations that pretended to be sufficiently comprehensive to encompass the whole of psychology. As a result, "miniature systems" began to emerge around the end of the 1930s and became the dominant trends in psychology prior to World War II. Since the war, miniature systems have given way to more limited theories and models. In retrospect, the collapse of the schools appears to have been a salutary development. Theory and systematizing had far outrun their empirical foundations. However, the miniature systems still show the dominant characteristics of their ancestry in the parent schools. A study of Table 18-1, which summarizes the major systems and their derivatives, will help to bring out these genetic relationships.

THE ENDURING ISSUES

There are two enduring fundamental issues in psychology as it has evolved over the centuries. The first is definitional, the second methodological. Cast in the form of

TABLE 18-1. The Major Systems of Psychology and Their Derivatives

Major Systems	Founder(s) or Chief Exponents	Chief Method of Original School	Subject Matter or Object of Study	Chief Areas of Concern of Original School	Representative Derivatives or Related Systems and Exponents
Associationism	Hartley and the British empiricists	Philosophical analysis	Cognitive processes	Laws of memory, nature of learning	Experimental associationism—Ebbinghaus, Thorndike, Robinson
Psychophysics and quantitative psychology	Weber, Fechner, Galton, Binet	Quantitative measurement	Sensory processes and individual differences	Sensory processes and individual differences	Factor analysis—Thurstone, model making; cybernetics; scaling—S. S. Stevens
Structuralism	Wundt, Titchener	Introspection	Consciousness	Sensation, attention, images, affective processes	None
Functionalism	James, Dewey, Angell, Carr	Objective experimental studies, introspection	Mind viewed in terms of its adaptive significance for the organism	Perception, learning, mental testing	Würzburg School Dynamic psychology—Robert S. Woodworth; functionalistic perceptual theorists—E. Brunswik, the Ames group; functionalistic learning theorists—McGeoch, Melton, Piaget

Behaviorism	J. B. Watson	Objective experimentation, especially conditioning	Behavior	Sensation, animal learning, Physiological processes	Purposive behaviorism—Tolman; conditioning theorists—Guthrie, Hull, Skinner "Physiological" theorists[a] Lashley, Hebb, Behavior therapy
Gestalt	Wertheimer, Köhler, Koffka	Phenomenological experimentation	Mental and behavioral processes as wholes	Perception, thinking	Field theory—Lewin; organismic and holistic psychology—K. Goldstein; most contemporary cognitive theories
Psychoanalysis	Freud	Free association and dream analysis	Analysis of unconscious dynamic processes	Psychotherapeutic treatment of the neurotic	Individual psychology—Adler; analytic psychology—Jung; post-Freudian psychoanalysis—Horney, Fromm, Gardiner, Sullivan, Thompson
Humanistic and existential psychology	Maslow, Rogers, May, and European existentialists	Phenomenological analysis	Modes and problems of existence	Being and personality	Daseinanalyse

[a]Not all behaviorists are physiologically oriented. There is, however, a tendency for the two to go together.

questions, these issues are: First, what is psychology? Second, how should psychologists go about investigating psychological phenomena?

The hope of the pioneer experimentalists was to see psychology quickly evolve into a science of the mental processes comparable in precision of definition and methodology to chemistry, physics, or physiology. By adopting the experimental method of the natural sciences, they believed that mental processes could be categorized and analyzed and their interaction reduced to fundamental laws that would enable psychologists to make the kind of quantitative, exact predictions characteristic of the other sciences. However, soon after its founding the science of psychology began to undergo revisions in definition. Some leaders, such as Watson, defined it as the study of behavior. Some emphasized the study of phenomenal experience. Others, such as Freud, believed that psychology should be primarily concerned with unconscious processes. But whatever the definition, all agreed that it should seek to be a science modeled after the natural sciences with the aim of establishing the laws of its phenomena.

At the end of a half-century of experimentation and vigorous theorizing, Edna Heidbreder in concluding a survey of the seven major systems of psychology that had evolved out of definitional differences arrived at the following assessment:

> Psychology is, in fact, interesting, if for no other reason, because it affords a spectacle of a science still in the making. Scientific curiosity, which has penetrated so many of the ways of nature, is here discovered in the very act of feeling its way through a region it has only begun to explore, battering at barriers, groping through confusions, and working sometimes fumblingly, sometimes craftily, sometimes excitedly, sometimes wearily, at a problem that is still largely unsolved. For psychology is a science that has not yet made its great discovery. It has found nothing that does for it what the atomic theory has done for chemistry, the principle of organic evolution for biology, the laws of motion for physics. Nothing that gives it a unifying principle has yet been discovered or recognized. As a rule, a science is presented, from the standpoint of both subject-matter and development, in the light of its great successes. Its verified hypotheses form the established lines about which it sets its facts in order, and about which it organizes its research. But psychology has not yet won its great unifying victory. It has had flashes of perception, it holds a handful of clues, but it has not yet achieved a synthesis or an insight that is compelling as well as plausible. (Heidbreder, 1933, p. 425)

Since the time Heidbreder wrote this pessimistic analysis about the adolescent science, approximately another half-century has passed. What progress, we may ask, has been made toward agreement on definition and methodology and in establishing psychology as a science during these intervening years?

In a major examination of psychology's conceptual and methodological foundations at the Nebraska Symposium on Motivation in 1975 (Arnold, 1976), leaders in theoretical psychology and the philosophy of science agreed that definitional and methodological issues remain sharply divided. The unifying principle has not yet been found nor have laws of human behavior been established that are comparable to those in the physical sciences.

Koch (1975, pp. 477–577), one of the participants in the symposium and editor of the series, *Psychology: The Study of a Science,* believes that psychology is hopelessly multidimensional, multimethdological, and is rooted in erroneous and simplistic conceptions of what science is. He would prefer the designation "psychological studies" in place of "the science of psychology" as a more realistic reflection of the state of psychology today. Koch makes it clear that he believes no progress has been made in reducing the fractionation among psychologists and in discovering a valid methodology. Instead, diversity is increasing.

Other participants, such as Royce (1975, pp. 1–58) and Rychalk (1975, pp. 205–280), while agreeing that psychology is multidimensional, multitheoretical, and multidisciplinarian, believe that by its very nature it must remain so. Royce argues persuasively that, in their rush to gather empirical facts, psychologists of the twentieth century have neglected theory. For too many years the empiricists guided their research by a philosophy of logical positivism that is no longer viable and in its original form has long since been rejected by contemporary physicists. In essence, Royce suggests that psychology needs to recognize the fact that no one theory or paradigm can encompass the broad range and complexity of human behavior.

Similarly, Rychalk, a humanistic psychologist, believes that to its disadvantage psychology has been dominated by the empirical, mechanistic, and deterministic model of man inherited from Aristotle and fostered by succeeding generations of empiricists. What has been neglected is the Kantian model, which admits the validity of human reasoning independent of simple empirical facts or experience. What distinguishes humans as opposed to material objects is our ability to make choices, to reason, and to go against the probabilities. Therefore psychology, like modern physical science, needs to broaden its aim and to encourage the development of alternative theories that can account for the same empirical data just as the big-bang and continuous-creation theories in astronomy provide alternative accounts of the energy transformations that take place in the evolution of the stars. The search for a single unifying explanation in any science can only prove to be a delusion.

Clearly then, one enduring issue is the old issue of psychology as a strongly empirical science emphasizing precision, quantitative formulation, precise experimental procedures, and data collecting versus psychology as a broader, multidimensional, and multimethodological discipline that makes no pretense of modeling itself after elementary conceptions of physics and chemistry. The humanists in particular believe that the behaviorism that has dominated psychology for the past half-century has restricted psychological studies to artificial situations involving simple stimulus-response units modeled largely on animal behavior. Meanwhile the richness and complexity of behavior involved in creativity and in motivational, emotional, and more cognitive processes has been neglected.

Aside from these fundamental problems of definition and basic methodology are several other important issues, which have proved enduring and difficult of solution. We shall discuss these briefly.

Mind versus Body

The oldest psychological issue going back to Plato is the mind-body problem. Plato, we found, resolved it through dualism, declaring that mind and body are separate noninteracting entities. Each of the systematists of succeeding generations has grappled with the problem; and each has had to come to terms with it in his or her own way, whether through a modified kind of dualism, such as psychophysical parallelism or, as the behaviorists would have it, by excluding mental events from the domain of psychology altogether.

As the issue presents itself in contemporary psychology, it is concerned with the validity of studying behavioral or mental events independently of their underlying nervous mechanisms. Some psychologists believe that until we can translate mental events into nervous phenomena, and vice versa, we have failed to explain the total organism. It is important to note that this same issue divides even the behaviorists. Some, like Skinner, believe that we need not concern ourselves with the neural mechanisms of behavior but only with the analysis of behavior itself.

The physiological psychologists, as representative of those whose special field of interest brings them head on with the problem, strive to relate the two without necessarily assuming that we can bridge that final chasm between consciousness and the events going on in the nervous system. This point of view has led to the rich research in the area of brain mechanisms in learning and the motivational and emotional processes that we described in Chapter 14.

Nature versus Nurture

The old issue of nature versus nurture, or heredity versus environment, in the causation of behavior is alive and well. First clearly formulated in the *tabula rasa* doctrine of Locke, it continues to underlie a great deal of the research in developmental psychology, studies of individual differences in intelligence and personality, and in certain aspects of the field of motivation. We saw how it engendered early research on the relative contribution of maturation and learning to the development of locomotor behavior, linguistic behavior, and emotional development. Nature is assumed to provide the basic framework for the stages in cognitive development postulated by Piaget's theory, whereas environment presumably contributes the more specific social skills. The controversy has flared up again sharply in recent years in the area of minority differences in intelligence and in psychologists' and ethologists' concern with aggression—the debate centering around the issue of whether it is innate or learned. However, the issue in nature versus nurture is no longer stated in the language of either/or but in terms of the relative contribution of each to any given mode of behavior. Unfortunately, in recent years the answer to the question has been clouded by emotionalism because of its implications for assessing the basis for minority group differences in intelligence. However, so long as we are not certain of the relative weight to be assigned to genetic and environmental factors in the determination of behavior or abilities, the issue will remain a vital and legitimate one.

Analysis versus Synthesis

First clearly formulated by the Gestalt psychologists, the issue is one of whether we can best understand behavior by analyzing it into components and then reassembling those components much as the chemist analyzes and synthesizes compounds; or whether the whole is different from the parts and, even more important, whether the whole *determines* the nature of the parts.

Without in any way belittling the contribution of the Gestalt psychologists, the dominance of behaviorism tipped the balance toward analysis and reductionism. This was especially true up through the 1950s in the areas of learning, sensation, and physiological psychology. In the past two decades the reemphasis on cognitive processes has shifted the balance somewhat toward a more Gestalt-like point of view. As examples we cited the work on concept formation, where overall strategies determine the course of concept development, and how in perception and memory, central processes impose configurational properties on parts, and how in psycholinguistics, language acquisition processes appear to generate sentences independently of whether or not the elements of those sentences have been previously experienced and synthesized. We should also note that the phenomenological approach favored by the Gestalt psychologists has also met a favorable reception among certain humanists and existentialists who, as we have seen, strongly oppose analysis and reductionism.

It appears that by its very nature the whole versus part issue can never be resolved. Just as the chemist studies matter both in terms of elements and compounds, so will psychologists continue to study mental processes in both analytic and synthetic terms.

Subjectivity versus Objectivity

Should psychologists admit the validity of subjective phenomena or should they concern themselves exclusively with objective data? Or is it even possible that from the broadest point of view all data are subjective or conceptualizations in the mind of man?

On the side of admitting subjective data are personality theorists such as Rogers, Maslow, and the existentialists and, in the field of perception, phenomenologists who readily admit the validity of subjective data. The radical behaviorists traditionally represent the opposite point of view, namely, that subjective methods and subjective constructs or mentalisms do not belong within the domain of science.

The issue is a difficult one. The human being, who is the subject matter of psychology, possesses consciousness and can observe his or her own feelings, thoughts, and sensations and attributes to these a kind of intuitive, direct validity. This elemental awareness is what James meant by the "stubborn fact of consciousness," which even though dismissed by the behaviorists refuses to go away but instead remains a vivid reality in the individual's awareness. The Cartesian who cries *cogito, ergo sum,* the patient who is hallucinating, the man or woman experiencing love, hate, or terror, the existentialist who puts existence ahead of essence, all agree on the priority of directly experienced consciousness. The objectivists following in the tradition of empiricism, logical positivism, and behaviorism, while admitting that people have such private experiences, still deny that they are the stuff of science. The data of science, they maintain, must be open to public observation and scientific laws founded upon—indeed must be restricted to—such data. And so the issue remains unresolved.

CONCLUSION

When the first edition of this book was published nearly 20 years ago, we expressed the opinion that the task for psychologists of the future was ultimately to discover a unifying principle that would integrate all points of view into one. We added the further thought that perhaps future empirical findings would gradually lead the way to such a principle; or, alternatively, that one day a genius of the stature of Newton or Einstein would bring to psychology a comprehensive theoretical structure with the integrating force of atomic theory in physics and chemistry. Two decades later in the perspective of hindsight, this hope seems both simplistic and naive. It appears simplistic in the sense that it is unlikely that any one point of view or theory can encompass the richness and complexity of human behavior. It seems naive in that, aside from elementary accounts of physics and chemistry, the physical sciences are characterized by uncertainties and diversities of opinion and by research where each new discovery generates as many questions as it answers. This is not to say that the "laws" of psychology work as well as the laws of physics or chemistry, only that given the complexity of the human organism we cannot expect the simple certainties characteristic of elementary experimentation in the college laboratory of chemistry or physics.

What the long-term future holds for psychology no one knows. In the near term it appears that the field will continue to be richly diverse, with shifting emphases and a multiplicity of definitional viewpoints, methods, and theories. As such we can only conclude that in remaining so it will mirror human nature.

References

Aborn, M. The influence of experimentally induced failure on the retention of material acquired through set and incidental learning. *Journal of Experimental Psychology,* 1953, 45, 225–231.

Adams, J. S. Reduction of cognitive dissonance by seeking consonant information. *Journal of Abnormal and Social Psychology,* 1961, 62, 74–78.

Ades, H., F. Mettler, and E. Culler. Effects of lesions in the medial geniculate bodies in the cat. *American Journal of Physiology,* 1939, 125, 15–23.

Adler, A. *Understanding human nature.* New York: Greenberg Publishers, Inc., 1927.

Adler, A. *The practice and theory of individual psychology.* New York: Harcourt Brace Jovanovich, 1929.

Allport, F. H. *Social psychology.* Boston: Houghton Mifflin, 1924.

Allport, F. H. *Theories of perception and the concept of structure.* New York: Wiley, 1955.

Allport, G. W. *Personality: A psychological interpretation.* New York: Holt, Rinehart and Winston, Inc., 1937.

Allport, G. W. *The nature of personality: Selected papers.* Reading, Mass.: Addison-Wesley, 1950.

Allport, G. W. *Becoming: Basic considerations for a psychology of personality.* New Haven, Conn.: Yale University Press, 1955.

Allport, G. W. *Pattern and growth in personality.* New York: Holt, Rinehart and Winston, Inc., 1961.

Allport, G. W. The historical background of modern social psychology. In G. Lindzey and E. Aronson (Eds.), *The handbook of social psychology* (2nd ed.). Vol. 1. Reading, Mass.: Addison-Wesley, 1968.

Allport, G. W., and L. Postman. *The psychology of rumor.* New York: Holt, Rinehart and Winston, Inc., 1947.

Ames, A., Jr. Reconsideration of the origin and nature of perception. In S. Ratner (Ed.), *Vision and action.* New Brunswick, N.J.: Rutgers University Press, 1953.

Amoore, J. E. Current status of the steric theory of odor. *Annals of the New York Academy of Science,* 1964, 116, 457–476.

Anastasi, A. *Differential psychology* (3rd ed.). New York: Crowell-Collier-Macmillan, 1958.

Anderson, N. H. Application of an additive model to impression formation. *Science,* 1962, 138, 817–818.

Anderson, N. H. Application of a linear-serial model to a personality-impression task using serial presentation. *Journal of Personality and Social Psychology,* 1968, 10, 354–362.

Andersson, B. The effect of injection of hypertonic NaCl solutions into different parts of the hypothalamus of goats. *Acta Physiologica Scandinavica,* 1953, 28, 188–201.

Andersson, B., and S. M. McCann. A further study of polydypsia evoked by hypothalamic stimulation in the goat. *Acta Physiologica Scandinavica,* 1955, 33, 333–346.

Andersson, B., and S. M. McCann. The effect of hypothalamic lesions on water intake on the dog. *Acta Physiologica Scandinavica,* 1956, 35, 312–320.

Ansbacher, H. L., and R. Ansbacher. *The individual psychology of Alfred Adler.* New York: Basic Books, 1956.

Arkes, H. R., and J. P. Garske. *Psychological theories of motivation.* Belmont, Calif.: Brooks/Cole, 1977.

Arnold, W. J. (Ed.). *Nebraska Symposium on Motivation.* Lincoln: University of Nebraska Press, 1976.

Aronfreed, J. M., S. A. Messik, and J. C. Diggory. Reexamining emotionality and perceptual defense. *Journal of Personality,* 1953, 21, 517–528.

Aronson, E. The theory of cognitive dissonance: A current perspective. In L. Berkowitz (Ed.), *Advances in experimental social psychology.* Vol. 4. New York: Academic Press, Inc., 1969.

Aronson, E., and D. Linder. Gain and loss of esteem as determinants of interpersonal attractiveness. *Journal of Experimental Social Psychology,* 1965, 1, 156–172.

Arrowood, A. J., L. Wood, and L. Ross. Dissonance, self-perception, and the perception of others: A study in *cognitive* cognitive dissonance. *Journal of Experimental Social Psychology,* 1970, 6, 304–315.

Asch, S. E. Forming impressions of personality. *Journal of Abnormal and Social Psychology,* 1946, 41, 258–290.

Asch, S. E. Effects of group pressure on the modification and distortion of judgments. In H. Geutzkow (Ed.), *Groups, leadership, and men.* Pittsburgh: Carnegie Press, 1951.

Asch, S. E. Studies of independence and conformity: A minority of one against a unanimous majority. *Psychological Monographs,* 1956, 70 (9, Whole No. 416).

Atkinson, J. (Ed.). *Motives in fantasy, action, and society.* Princeton, N.J.: Van Nostrand, 1958.

Atkinson, J. W., *Introduction to motivation.* New York: Van Nostrand, 1978.

Atkinson, R. C., and W. K. Estes. Stimulus sampling theory. In R. D. Luce, R. R. Bush, and E. Galanter (Eds.), *Handbook of mathematical psychology.* New York: Wiley, 1963.

Atkinson, R. C., and R. M. Shiffrin. The control of short-term memory. *Scientific American,* 1971, 224, 82–90.

Attneave, F. *Applications of information theory to psychology: A summary of basic concepts, methods, and results.* New York: Holt, Rinehart and Winston, Inc., 1959.

Averbach, E. The span of apprehension as a function of exposure duration. *Journal of Verbal Learning and Verbal Behavior,* 1963, 2, 60–64.

Averbach, E., and A. S. Coriell. Short term memory in vision. *The Bell System Technical Journal,* 1961, No. 3756, 309–328.

Ayllon, T. Intensive treatment of psychotic behaviour by stimulus satiation and food reinforcement. *Behaviour Research and Therapy,* 1963, 1, 53–61.

Ayllon, T., and N. H. Azrin. The measurement and reinforcement of behavior of psychotics. *Journal of the Experimental Analysis of Behavior,* 1965, 8, 357–383.

Back, K. W. Influence through social communication. *Journal of Abnormal and Social Psychology,* 1951, 46, 9–23.

Baldwin, A. Theories of child development. New York: Wiley, 1967.

Bandura, A. A case of no-trial learning. In L. Berkowitz (Ed.), *Advances in experimental social psychology.* Vol. 2. New York: Academic Press, 1965. (a)

Bandura, A. Behavioral modifications through modeling procedures. In L. Krasner and L. P. Ullman (Eds.), *Research in behavior modification.* New York: Holt, Rinehart, and Winston, Inc., 1965. (b)

Bandura, A. Influence of models' reinforcement contingencies on the acquisition of imitative responses. *Journal of Personality and Social Psychology,* 1965, 1, 589–595. (c)

Bandura, A. *Principles of behavior modification.* New York: Holt, Rinehart and Winston, Inc., 1969.

Bandura, A. *Aggression: A social learning analysis.* Englewood Cliffs, N.J.: Prentice-Hall, 1972.

Bandura, A., and W. Mischel. Modification of self-imposed delay of reward through exposure to live and symbolic models. *Journal of Personality and Social Psychology,* 1965, 2, 698–705.

Bandura, A., D. Ross, and S. Ross. Transmission of aggression through imitation of aggressive models. *Journal of Abnormal and Social Psychology,* 1961, 63, 575–582.

Bandura, A., and R. Walters. *Social learning and personality development.* New York: Holt, Rinehart and Winston, Inc., 1963.

Barclay, J. R. *Controversial issues in testing.* Boston: Houghton Mifflin, 1968.

Barker, R., T. Dembo, and K. Lewin. Frustration and regression: An experiment with young children. *University of Iowa Studies in Child Welfare,* 1941, 18, No. 386.

Barrett, W. *Irrational man.* New York: Doubleday, 1958.

Barron, F. The psychology of creativity. In F. Barron, W. C. Dement, W. Edwards, H. Lindman, L. D. Phillips, and J. and M. Olds (Eds.), *New directions in psychology.* Vol. 2. New York: Holt, Rinehart and Winston, Inc., 1965.

Bartlett, F. C. *Remembering: An experimental and social study.* New York: Cambridge, 1932.

Bartley, S. H. *Vision.* Princeton, N.J.: Van Nostrand, 1941.

Bartley, S. H. *Principles of perception.* New York: Harper & Row, 1958.

Barton, R. F. *A primer on simulation and gaming.* Englewood Cliffs, N.J.: Prentice-Hall, 1970.

Bartz, W. H. Repetition and the memory stores. *Journal of Experimental Psychology,* 1969, 80, 33–38.

Békésy, G. Von. Experimental models of the cochlea with and without nerve supply. In G. L. Rasmussen and W. F. Windle (Eds.), *Neural mechanisms of the auditory and vestibular system.* Springfield, Ill.: Charles C. Thomas, 1960.

Bellows, R. T., and W. P. Van Wagenen. The relationship of polydypsia and polyuria in diabetes insipidus. *Journal of Nervous and Mental Diseases,* 1938, 88, 417–473.

Bem, D. J. An experimental analysis of self-persuasion. *Journal of Experimental Social Psychology,* 1965, 1, 199–218.

Bem, D. J. Self-perception: An alternative interpretation of cognitive dissonance phenomena. *Psychological Review,* 1967, 74, 183–200.

Bem, D. J. The epistemological status of interpersonal simulations: A reply to Jones, Linder, Kiesler, Zanna, and Brehm. *Journal of Experimental and Social Psychology,* 1968, 4, 270–274.

Berkowitz, L. Group standards, cohesiveness, and productivity. *Human Relations,* 1954, 7, 509–519.

Berkowitz, L. *Aggression: A social-psychological analysis.* New York: McGraw-Hill, 1962.

Berkowitz, L. Aggressive cues in aggressive behavior and hostility catharsis. *Psychological Review,* 1964, 71, 104–122.

Berkowitz, L. Social motivation. In G. Lindzey and E. Aronson (Eds.), *The handbook of social psychology* (2nd ed.). Vol. 3. Reading, Mass.: Addison-Wesley, 1969. (a)

Berkowitz, L. *The frustration-aggression hypothesis revisited.* In L. Berkowitz (Ed.), *Roots of aggression.* New York: Atherton Press, 1969. (b)

Berkowitz, L. Some determinants of impulsive aggression: The role of mediated associations with reinforcements for aggression. *Psychological Review,* 1974, 81, 165–176.

Berkowitz, L. *A survey of social psychology.* Hinsdale, Ill.: The Dryden Press, 1975.

Berkowitz, L., and D. R. Cottingham. The interest value and relevance of fear arousing communications. *Journal of Abnormal and Social Psychology,* 1960, 60, 37–43.

Berkowitz, L., and A. LePage. Weapons as aggression-eliciting stimuli. *Journal of Personality and Social Psychology,* 1967, 7, 202–207.

Berlyne, D. E. *Conflict, arousal and curiosity*. New York: McGraw-Hill, 1960.

Berlyne, D. E. Recent developments in Piaget's work. In R. C. Anderson and D. Ausubel (Eds.), *Readings in the psychology of cognition*. New York: Holt, Rinehart and Winston, Inc., 1965.

Bijou, S. W., and E. Ribes-Inesta. *Behavior modification: Issues and extensions*. New York: Academic Press, 1972.

Birch, H. G. The relation of previous experience to insightful problem-solving. *Journal of Comparative Psychology*, 1945, 38, 367–383.

Blake, R. R., and G. V. Ramsey (Eds.). *Perception: An approach to personality*. New York: Ronald, 1951.

Blanford, D. D., and E. Sampson. Induction of prestige suggestion through classical conditioning. *Journal of Abnormal and Social Psychology*, 1964, 69, 332–337.

Bolles, R. C. *Theory of motivation*. New York: Harper & Row, 1967.

Boring, E. G. *A history of experimental psychology* (1st ed.). New York: Appleton, 1929.

Boring, E. G. *Sensation and perception in the history of experimental psychology*. New York: Appleton, 1942.

Boring, E. G. *A history of experimental psychology* (2nd ed.). New York: Appleton, 1950.

Boring, E. G., H. S. Langfeld, and H. P. Weld. *Foundations of psychology*. New York: Wiley, 1948.

Bourne, L. E., Jr. Learning and utilization of conceptual rules. In B. Kleinmuntz (Ed.), *Concepts and the structure of memory*. New York: Wiley, 1967.

Bourne, L. E., B. R. Ekstrand, and R. L. Dominowski. *The psychology of thinking*. Englewood Cliffs, N.J.: Prentice-Hall, 1971.

Bower, T. G. R. Discrimination of depth in premotor infants. *Psychonomic Science*, 1964, 1, 368.

Bower, T. G. R. Stimulus variables determining space perception in infants. *Science*, 1965, 149, 88–89.

Bower, T. G. R. Slant perception and shape constancy in infants. *Science*, 1966, 151, 832–834.

Brady, J. P., and D. L. Lind. Experimental analysis of hysterical blindness. In L. P. Ullmann and L. Krasner (Eds.), *Case studies in behavior modification*. New York: Holt, Rinehart and Winston, Inc., 1965.

Brady, J. V. The effect of electro-convulsive shock on a conditioned emotional response: the significance of the interval between the emotional conditioning and the electro-convulsive shock. *Journal of Comparative and Physiological Psychology*, 1952, 45, 9–13.

Brady, J. V. The paleocortex and behavioral motivation. In H. F. Harlow and C. N. Woolsey (Eds.), *Biological and biochemical bases of behavior*. Madison: University of Wisconsin Press, 1958.

Brady, J. V. Emotional behavior. In J. Field, H. W. Magoun, and V. E. Hall (Eds.), *Handbook of Physiology*. Vol. 3. Washington, D.C.: American Physiological Society, 1960.

Brady, J. V. Motivational-emotional factors and intracranial self-stimulation. In D. E. Sheer (Ed.), *Electrical stimulation of the brain*. Austin: University of Texas Press, 1961.

Brehm, J. W., and A. R. Cohen. *Explorations in cognitive dissonance*. New York: Wiley, 1962.

Brett, G. S. *History of psychology*. (Abridged and edited by R. S. Peters). London: G. Allen, 1953.

Bricker, P. D., and H. Chapanis. Do incorrectly perceived stimuli convey some information? *Psychological Review*, 1953, 60, 181–188.

Bridges, K. M. B. Emotional development in early infancy. *Child Development,* 1932, 3, 324–341.

Bridgman, P. W. *The logic of modern physics.* New York: Crowell-Collier-Macmillan, 1927.

Bridgman, P. W. Remarks on the present state of operationalism. *The Scientific Monthly,* 1954, 79, 224–226.

Briggs, C. E. Retroactive inhibition as a function of degree of original and interpolated learning. *Journal of Experimental Psychology,* 1957, 53, 60–67.

Brock, T. C. Commitment to exposure as a determinant of information receptivity. *Journal of Personality and Social Psychology,* 1965, 2, 10–19.

Brodie, D. A., J. L. Malid, O. M. Moreno, and J. Boren. Nonreversibility of the appetitive characteristics of intracranial stimulation. *American Journal of Physiology,* 1960, 199, 707–709.

Brown, P. K., and G. Wald. Visual pigments in single rods and cones of the human retina. *Science,* 1964, 144, 45–52.

Brown, R. *Social psychology.* New York: Free Press, 1965.

Brown, R. *Psycholinguistics.* New York: Free Press, 1970.

Brown, R. *A first language: The early stages.* Cambridge, Mass.: Harvard University Press, 1973.

Brown, R., C. Cazden, and U. Bellugi. The child's grammar from 1 to 11. In A. Bar-Adon and W. F. Leopold (Eds.), *Child language: A book of readings.* Englewood Cliffs, N.J.: Prentice-Hall, 1970.

Brown, W. Growth of memory images. *American Journal of Psychology,* 1935, 47, 90–102.

Brownfield, C. A. *Isolation.* New York: Random House, 1965.

Bruner, J. S., and C. C. Goodman. Value and need as organizing factors in perception. *Journal of Abnormal and Social Psychology,* 1947, 42, 33–44.

Bruner, J. S., J. J. Goodnow, and G. A. Austin. *A study of thinking.* New York: Wiley, 1956.

Bruner, J. S., and D. Krech (Eds), *Perception and personality: A symposium.* Durham, N. C.: Duke University Press, 1950.

Brunswik, E. Organismic achievement and environmental probability. *Psychological Review,* 1943, 50, 255–272.

Bryan, W. L., and N. Harter. Studies in the physiology and psychology of telegraphic language. *Psychological Review,* 1897, 4, 27–53.

Bryan, W. L., and N. Harter. Studies on the telegraphic language. *Psychological Review,* 1899, 6, 345–375.

Bugelski, B. R. *The psychology of learning.* New York: Holt, Rinehart and Winston, Inc., 1956.

Burks, B. S. The relative influence of nature and nurture upon mental development: A comparative study of foster parent-foster child resemblance and true parent-true child resemblance. *27th Yearbook of the National Society for the Study of Education.* Bloomington, Ill.: Public School, 1928. Part I, pp. 219–316.

Burtt, H. E. An experimental study of early childhood memory. *Journal of Genetic Psychology,* 1941, 58, 435–439.

Bush, R. R., and F. Mosteller. *Stochastic models for learning.* New York: Wiley, 1955.

Buss, A. H. *Psychology: Man in perspective.* New York: Wiley, 1973.

Cancro, R. *Intelligence: Genetic and environmental influences.* New York: Grune & Stratton, 1971.

Cannon, W. B. *Bodily changes in pain, hunger, fear, and rage.* New York: Appleton, 1929.

Cantril, H. *The "why" of man's experience*. New York: Crowell-Collier-Macmillan, 1950.

Cantril, H. *The pattern of human concerns*. New Brunswick, N.J.: Rutgers University Press, 1965.

Cantril, H., and W. A. Hunt. Emotional effects produced by the injection of adrenalin. *American Journal of Psychology*, 1932, 44, 300–307.

Carlsmith, J. M., B. E. Collins, and R. L. Helmreich. Studies in forced compliance: 1. The effect of pressure for compliance on attitude change produced by face-to-face role playing and anonymous essay writing. *Journal of Personality and Social Psychology*, 1966, 4, 1–13.

Carlson, N. R. *Physiology of behavior*. Boston: Allyn and Bacon, 1977.

Carmichael, L. The development of behavior in vertebrates experimentally removed from the influences of stimulation. *Psychological Review*, 1926, 33, 51–58.

Carmichael, L. A further study of development of behavior in vertebrates experimentally removed from the influence of stimulation. *Psychological Review*, 1927, 34, 34–47.

Carmichael, L. (Ed.). *Manual of child psychology*. New York: Wiley, 1946.

Carmichael, L., H. P. Hogan, and A. A. Walter. An experimental study of the effect of language on the reproduction of visually perceived form. *Journal of Experimental Psychology*, 1932, 15, 73–86.

Caron, R. F., and A. J. Caron. The effects of repeated exposure and stimulus complexity on visual fixation in infants. *Psychonomic Science*, 1968, 10, 207–208.

Carr, H. A. *Psychology: A study of mental activity*. New York: McKay, 1925.

Carr, H. A. The laws of association. *Psychological Review*, 1931, 38, 212–228.

Carr, H. A. *An introduction to space perception*. New York: McKay, 1935.

Carterette, E. C. and M. P. Friedman (Eds.). *Handbook of perception*. Vol. V. New York: Academic Press, 1975.

Cattell, R. B. Some theoretical issues in adult intelligence testing. *Psychological Bulletin*, 1941, 38, 592.

Cattell, R. B. The principal trait clusters for describing personality. *Psychological Bulletin*, 1945, 42, 129–161.

Cattell, R. B. *Personality*. New York: McGraw-Hill, 1950.

Cattell, R. B. Theory of fluid and crystallized intelligence: A critical experiment. *Journal of Educational Psychology*, 1963, 54, 1–22.

Cattell, R. B. *The scientific analysis of personality*. Baltimore: Penguin Books, 1965.

Cattell, R. B. *Abilities: Their structure, growth, and action*. Boston: Houghton Mifflin, 1971.

Cattell, R. B., and I. H. Scheirer. *The meaning and measurement of neuroticism and anxiety*. New York: Ronald, 1961.

Chapanis, N. P., and A. Chapanis. A critical evaluation of the theory of cognitive dissonance. In E. A. Southwell and M. Merbaum (Eds.), *Personality: Readings in theory and research*. Belmont, Calif.: Wadsworth, 1965.

Chaplin, J. P. *Dictionary of the occult and paranormal*. New York: Dell, 1976.

Chaplin, J. P., and T. S. Krawiec. *Systems and theories of psychology*. New York: Holt, Rinehart and Winston, Inc., 1960.

Chaplin, J. P., and T. S. Krawiec. *Systems and theories of psychology*. (2nd ed.). New York: Holt, Rinehart and Winston, Inc., 1968.

Chomsky, N. *Syntactic structures*. The Hague: Mouton and Co., 1957.

Chomsky, N. Review of B. F. Skinner, *Verbal behavior*. *Language*, 1959, 35, 26–58.

Chomsky, N. *Aspects of the theory of syntax*. Cambridge, Mass.: MIT Press, 1965.

Chomsky, N. The formal nature of language. In E. H. Lenneberg (Ed.), *Biological foundations of language*. New York: Wiley, 1967.

Chomsky, N. *Language and the mind*. New York: Harcourt Brace Jovanovich, 1968.

Chown, S. M. (Ed.). *Human ageing*. Middlesex, England: Penguin Books, 1972.

Cieutat, V. J., F. E. Stockwell, and C. E. Noble. The interaction of ability and the amount of practice with stimulus and response meaningfulness (*m* and *m'*) in paired-associate learning. *Journal of Experimental Psychology*, 1958, 56, 193–202.

Clement, D., and D. Sullivan. No risky shift effect without real groups and real risks. *Psychonomic Science*, 1970, 18, 243–245.

Cofer, C. N. Properties of verbal materials and verbal learning. In J. W. Kling and L. Riggs (Eds.), *Woodworth and Schlosberg's experimental psychology* (3rd ed.). New York: Holt, Rinehart and Winston, Inc., 1971.

Cofer, C. N., and M. Appley. *Motivation: Theory and research*. New York: Wiley, 1964.

Coghill, G. *Anatomy and the problem of behavior*. New York: Macmillan, 1929.

Colby, K. M. Computer simulation of neurotic processes. In R. W. Stacey and B. D. Waxman (Eds.), *Computers in biomedical research*. New York: Academic Press, 1965.

Coleman, J., E. Campell, C. Hobson, J. McPartland, A. Mood, F. Weinfield, and R. York. *Equality of educational opportunity*. Washington, D.C.: U.S. Government Printing Office, 1966.

Cornsweet, T. N. *Visual perception*. New York: Academic Press, 1970.

Cotton, J. W. On making predictions from Hull's theory. *Psychological Review*, 1955, 62, 303–314.

Craik, R. I. M. The fate of primary memory items in free recall. *Journal of Verbal Learning and Verbal Behavior*, 1970, 9, 143–148.

Cramer, P., and C. N. Cofer. The role of forward and reverse association in transfer of training. *American Psychologist*, 1960, 15, 463.

Cronbach, L. J. The two disciplines of scientific psychology. *American Psychologist*, 1957, 12, 671–684.

Crutchfield, R. S. Conformity and character. *American Psychologist*, 1955, 10, 191–198.

Culler, E. A. An experimental study of tonal localization in the cochlea of the guinea pig. *Annals of Otology, Rhinology, and Laryngology*, 1935, 44, 307–313.

Cuming, E., and W. E. Henry. *Growing old, the process of disengagement*. New York: Basic Books, 1961.

Darley, J. M., and C. D. Batson. ". . . From Jerusalem to Jericho." A study of situational and dispositional variables in helping behavior. *Journal of Personality and Social Psychology*, 1973, 27, 100–108.

Darwin, C. R. *Expression of the emotions in man and animals*. London: Murray, 1872. (American edition D. Appleton Co., 1873.)

Deese, J. *The psychology of learning* (2nd ed.). New York: McGraw-Hill, 1958.

Deese, J. *Psycholinguistics*. Boston: Allyn and Bacon, 1970.

Deese, J., and S. H. Hulse. *The psychology of learning* (3rd ed.). New York: McGraw-Hill, 1967.

Delgado, J. M. R. Study of some cerebral structures related to transmission and elaboration of noxious stimulation. *Journal of Neurophysiology*, 1955, 18, 261–275.

Delgado, J. M. R. Emotions. In J. A. Vernon (Ed.), *Introduction to general psychology: A self-selection textbook*. Dubuque, Iowa: William C. Brown Company, Publishers, 1966.

Delgado, J. M. R., and B. K. Anand. Increased food intake induced by electrical stimulation of the lateral hypothalamus. *American Journal of Physiology*, 1953, 172, 162–168.

Delgado, J. M. R., W. W. Roberts, and N. E. Miller. Learning motivated by electrical stimulation of the brain. *American Journal of Physiology,* 1954, 179, 587–593.

Dement, W. The effect of dream deprivation. *Science,* 1960, 131, 1705–1707.

Dement, W., and N. Kleitman. The relation of eye movements during sleep to dream activity: An objective method for the study of dreaming. *Journal of Experimental Psychology,* 1957, 53, 339–346.

Dement, W., and E. Wolpert. The relation of eye movements, body motility, and external stimuli to dream content. *Journal of Experimental Psychology,* 1958, 55, 543–553.

Dennis, W. Historical beginnings of child psychology. *Psychological Bulletin,* 1949, 46, 224–235.

Dennis, W. Causes of retardation among institutional children. *Journal of Genetic Psychology,* 1960, 96, 47–59.

Dennis, W. Creative productivity between the ages of 20 and 80 years. *Journal of Gerontology,* 1966, 21, 1–8.

Dennis, W., and M. Dennis. The effects of cradling practices upon the onset of walking in Hopi children. *Journal of Genetic Psychology,* 1940, 56, 77–86.

Deutsch, J. A. Learning and electrical self-stimulation of the brain. *Journal of Theoretical Biology,* 1963, 4, 193–214.

Deutsch, J. A. The physiology basis of memory. *Annual Review of Psychology,* 1969, 20, 85–104.

Deutsch, J. A., and D. Deutsch. *Physiological psychology.* Homewood, Ill.: The Dorsey Press, 1966.

Deutsch, M. Field theory in social psychology. In G. Lindzey and E. Aronson (Eds.), *Handbook of social psychology* (2nd ed.). Vol. 1. Reading, Mass.: Addison-Wesley, 1968.

Deutsch, M., and H. G. Gerard. A study of normative and informational social influence upon individual judgment. *Journal of Abnormal and Social Psychology,* 1955, 51, 629–636.

Deutsch, M., and R. Krauss. *Theories in social psychology.* New York: Basic Books, 1965.

DeValois, R. L., and G. H. Jacobs. Primate color vision. *Science,* 1968, 162, 533–540.

Dewey, J. The reflex arc concept in psychology. *Psychological Review,* 1896, 3, 357–370.

Dixon, N. F. *Subliminal perception: The nature of a controversy.* New York: McGraw-Hill, 1971.

Dollard, J., and N. E. Miller. *Personality and psychotherapy.* New York: McGraw-Hill, 1950.

Dunbar, F. *Emotions and bodily changes* (4th ed.). New York: Columbia University Press, 1954.

Duncker, K. On problem solving. *Psychological Monographs,* 1945, 53 (Whole No. 270).

Durant, W. *The story of philosophy* (Rev. ed.). New York: Simon & Schuster, 1933.

Durkheim, E. *Rules of sociological method.* Glencoe, Ill.: Free Press, 1950 (First published in 1895).

Ebbinghaus, H. *Memory: A contribution to experimental psychology* (Translated by H. A. Ruger and C. E. Bussenius). New York: Teachers College, 1913.

Ehrlich, D., J. Guttman, P. Schonbach, and J. Mills. Postdecision exposure to relevant information. *Journal of Abnormal and Social Psychology,* 1957, 54, 98–102.

Eibl-Eibesfeldt, I. *Ethology: The biology of behavior* (2nd ed.). New York: Holt, Rinehart, and Winston, Inc., 1975.

Ekman, P. Universals and cultural differences in facial expressions of the emotions. In J. Cole (Ed.), *Nebraska Symposium on Motivation.* Lincoln: University of Nebraska Press, 1971.

Ekstrand, B. R. Effect of sleep on memory. *Journal of Experimental Psychology,* 1967, 75, 64–72.

Ellenberger, H. F. *The discovery of the unconscious.* New York: Basic Books, 1970.

Elliott, M. H. The effect of change of reward on the maze performance of rats. *University of California Publications in Psychology,* 1928, 4, 19–30.

Ellis, W. *A source book of Gestalt psychology.* London: Routledge, 1938.

Emmons, W. H., and C. W. Simon. The nonrecall of material presented during sleep. *American Journal of Psychology,* 1956, 69, 76–81.

Engen, T., N. Levy, and H. Schlosberg. A new series of facial expressions. *American Psychologist,* 1957, 12, 264–266.

Engen, T., N. Levy, and H. Schlosberg. The dimensional analysis of a new series of facial expressions. *Journal of Experimental Psychology,* 55, 1958, 455–458.

Enoch, J. M. Physical properties of the retinal receptor and response of retinal receptors. *Psychological Bulletin,* 1964, 61, 242–251.

Epstein, A. N. The lateral hypothalamic syndrome: Its implications for the physiological psychology of hunger and thirst. In E. Stellar and J. M. Sprague (Eds.), *Progress in physiological psychology.* Vol. 4. New York: Academic Press, Inc., 1971.

Erdelyi, M. H. A new look at the new look. *Psychological Review,* 1974, 81, 1–25.

Eriksen, C. W. An experimental analysis of subception. *American Journal of Psychology,* 1956, 69, 625–634. (a)

Eriksen, C. W. Subception: Fact or artifact? *Psychological Review,* 1956, 63, 74–80. (b)

Eriksen, C. W. Discrimination and learning without awareness: a methodological survey and evaluation. *Psychological Review,* 1960, 67, 279–300.

Eriksen, C. W., and C. T. Brown. An experimental and theoretical analysis of perceptual defense. *Journal of Abnormal and Social Psychology,* 1956, 52, 224–230.

Erikson, E. H. *Young man Luther: A study in psychoanalysis and history.* New York: Norton, 1958.

Erikson, E. H. *Childhood and society.* New York: Norton, 1950, (2nd ed.) 1963.

Erikson, E. H. *Insight and responsibility.* New York: Norton, 1964.

Erikson, E. H. *Identity: Youth and crisis.* New York: Norton, 1968.

Estes, W. K. Toward a statistical theory of learning. *Psychological Review.* 1950, 57, 94–107.

Estes, W. K. The statistical approach to learning theory. In S. Koch (Ed.), *Psychology: A study of a science.* Vol. 2. New York: McGraw-Hill, 1959. (a)

Estes, W. K. Component and pattern models with Markovian interpretations. In R. R. Bush and W. K. Estes (Eds.), *Studies in mathematical learning theory.* Stanford, Calif.: Stanford University Press, 1959. (b)

Estes, W. K. New developments in statistical behavior theory: Differential tests of axioms for associative learning. *Psychometrika,* 1961, 26, 73–84.

Estes, W. K. (Ed.). *Handbook of learning and cognitive processes.* Vol. 1. Hillsdale, N.J.: Lawrence Erlbaum Associates, 1975.

Estes, W. K., and C. J. Burke, Application of a statistical model to simple discrimination learning in human subjects. *Journal of Experimental Psychology,* 1955, 50, 81–88.

Estes, W. K., and B. L. Hopkins. Acquisition and transfer in pattern-vs-component discrimination learning. *Journal of Experimental Psychology,* 1961, 61, 322–328.

Estes, W. K., S. Koch, K. MacCorquodale, P. E. Meehl, G. G. Mueller, Jr., W. N. Schoenfeld, and W. S. Verplanck. *Modern learning theory.* New York: Appleton, 1954.

Estes, W. K., and J. H. Straughan. Analysis of a verbal conditioning situation in terms of statistical learning theory. *Journal of Experimental Psychology,* 1954, 47, 225–234.

Evans, B. *The natural history of nonsense*. New York: Vintage Books, 1958.

Feather, N. T. Cigarette smoking and lung cancer: A study of cognitive dissonance. *Australian Journal of Psychology*, 1962, 14, 55–64.

Feigenbaum, E. A. The stimulation of verbal learning behavior. In E. A. Feigenbaum, and J. Feldman (Eds.), *Computers and thought*. New York: McGraw-Hill, 1963.

Feigenbaum, E. A. Information processing and memory. In D. A. Norman (Ed.), *Models of human memory*. New York: Academic Press, 1970.

Feigenbaum, E. A., and J. Feldman (Eds.). *Computers and thought*. New York: McGraw-Hill, 1963.

Ferguson, E. D. *Motivation: An experimental approach*. New York: Holt, Rinehart and Winston, Inc., 1976.

Festinger, L. *A theory of cognitive dissonance*. New York: Harper & Row, 1957.

Festinger, L., and J. M. Carlsmith. Cognitive consequences of forced compliance. *Journal of Abnormal and Social Psychology*, 1959, 58, 203–211.

Festinger, L., S. Schachter, and L. Back. *Social pressures in informal groups: A study of human factors in housing*. New York: Harper & Row, 1950.

Finan, J. L. Delayed responses with pre-delay reinforcement in monkeys after removal of the frontal lobes. *American Journal of Psychology*, 1942, 55, 201–214.

Flaherty, C. F., L. W. Hamilton, R. J. Gandelman, and N. Spear. *Learning and memory*. Chicago: Rand McNally, 1977.

Foder, J. A., T. G. Beven, and M. F. Garrett. *The psychology of language*. New York: McGraw-Hill, 1974.

Fogel, L. J. *Human information processing*. Englewood Cliffs, N.J.: Prentice-Hall, 1967.

Ford, D. H., and H. B. Urban. *Systems of psychotherapy*. New York: Wiley, 1963.

Forgays, D. G., and J. Forgays. The nature of the effect of free-environmental experience in the rat. *Journal of Comparative and Physiological Psychology*, 1952, 45, 322–328.

Forgus, R. H. The effect of different kinds of form pre-exposure on form discrimination learning. *Journal of Comparative and Physiological Psychology*, 1958, 51, 75–78.

Forgus, R. H. *Perception*. New York: McGraw-Hill, 1966.

French, J. D. The reticular formation. *Scientific American*, 1957, 196, 54–60.

Frenkel-Brunswik, E. Personality theory and perception. In R. R. Blake and G. V. Ramsey (Eds.), *Perception: An approach to personality*. New York: Ronald, 1951.

Freud, S. *A general introduction to psychoanalysis*. New York: Liveright, 1920.

Freud, S. *Group psychology and the analysis of the ego*. London: Hogarth, 1921.

Freud, S. *Collected papers*. London: Hogarth, 1924–1950. 5 Vols.

Freud, S. *Civilization and its discontents*. New York: Norton, 1930.

Freud, S. *New introductory lectures on psychoanalysis*. New York: Norton, 1933.

Freud, S. The psychopathology of everyday life. In A. A. Brill (Ed.), *The basic writings of Sigmund Freud*. New York: Random House, 1938. (a)

Freud, S. Totem and taboo. In A. A. Brill (Ed.), *The basic writings of Sigmund Freud*. New York: Random House, 1938. (b)

Fromm, E. *Escape from freedom*. New York: Holt, Rinehart and Winston, Inc., 1941.

Fromm, E. *The sane society*. New York: Holt, Rinehart and Winston, Inc., 1955.

Fulton, J. F. (Ed.), *Howell's textbook of physiology* (15th ed.). Philadelphia: Saunders, 1946.

Fulton, J. F. *The physiology of the nervous system* (3rd ed.). New York: Oxford, 1949.

Galambos, R., and H. Davis: The response of single auditory-nerve fibers to acoustic stimulation. *Journal of Neurophysiology*, 1943, 6, 39–57.

Ganz, L. Is the figural aftereffect an *after*effect? A review of its intensity, onset, decay, and transfer characteristics. *Psychological Bulletin*, 1966, 66, 151–165.

Gardiner H. M., R. C., Metcalf, and J. G. Beebe-Center (1937). *Feelings and emotion: A history of theories.* New York: American Book, 1937.

Gardner, M. *Fads and fallacies in the name of science.* New York: Dover, 1957.

Gardner, R. A., and B. T. Gardner. Teaching sign language to a chimpanzee. *Science,* 1969, 165, 664–672.

Garrett, H. E. A developmental theory of intelligence. *American Psychologist,* 1946, 1, 327–377.

Gazzaniga, M. S. *The bisected brain.* New York: Appleton, 1970.

Gelb, A., and K. Goldstein. Über Farbennamenamensie. *Psychologische Forschung,* 1924, 6, 127–186.

Geldard, F. A. *The human senses.* New York: Wiley, 1973.

Gerard, H. B., and C. W. Greenbaum. Attitudes toward an agent of uncertainty reduction. *Journal of Personality,* 1962, 30, 485–495.

Gerard, H. B., and G. S. Rotter. Time perspective, consistency of attitude, and social influence. *Journal of Abnormal and Social Psychology,* 1961, 62, 565–572.

Gesell, A., and H. Thompson. Learning and growth in identical twins: An experimental study by the method of co-twin control. *Genetic Psychology Monographs,* 1929, 6, 1–124.

Gibson, E. J. Perceptual learning. *Annual Review of Psychology,* 1963, 14, 29–56.

Gibson, E. J. *Principles of perceptual learning and development.* New York: Appleton, 1969.

Gibson, E. J., R. D. Walk, H. L. Pick, Jr., and T. J. Tighe. The effect of prolonged exposure to visual patterns on learning to discriminate similar and different patterns. *Journal of Comparative and Physiological Psychology,* 1956, 49, 239–242.

Gibson, J. J. Reproduction of visually perceived forms. *Journal of Experimental Psychology,* 1929, 12, 1–39.

Gibson, J. J. Adaptation, after-effect, and contrast in the perception of curved lines. *Journal of Experimental Psychology,* 1933, 16, 1–31.

Gibson, J. J. *The perception of the visual world.* Boston: Houghton Mifflin, 1950.

Gibson, J. J. Theories of perception. In W. Dennis (Ed.), *Current trends in psychological theory.* Pittsburgh, University of Pittsburgh Press, 1951.

Gibson, J. J. Perception as a function of stimulation. In S. Koch (Ed.), *Psychology: The study of a science.* Vol. 3. New York: McGraw-Hill, 1959.

Gibson, J. J. *The senses considered as a perceptual system.* Boston: Houghton Mifflin, 1966.

Glanzer, M., and A. R. Cunitz. Two storage mechanisms in free recall. *Journal of Verbal Learning and Verbal Behavior,* 1966, 5, 351–360.

Goble, F. G. *The third force.* New York: Grossman, 1971.

Gold, R. M. Hypothalamic obesity: The myth of the ventromedial nucleus. *Science,* 1973, 182, 488–490.

Goldfarb, W. The effects of early institutional care on adolescent personality. *Journal of Experimental Education,* 1943, 12, 107–129.

Goldfarb, W. Effects of psychological deprivation in infancy and subsequent stimulation. *American Journal of Psychiatry,* 1945, 102, 18–33.

Goldstein, H., D. L. Kranz, and J. Rains. *Controversial issues in learning.* New York: Appleton, 1965.

Goldstein, K. *The organism.* New York: American Book, 1939.

Goldstein, K. Organismic approach to the problem of motivation. *Transactions of the New York Academy of Sciences,* 1947, 9, 218–230.

Goldstein, K., and M. Scheerer. Abstract and concrete behavior. An experimental study with special tests. *Psychological Monographs,* 1941, 53 (Whole No. 239).

Granit, R. *Receptors and sensory perception*. New Haven, Conn.: Yale University Press, 1955.

Greenspoon, J. The reinforcing effect of two spoken sounds on the frequency of two responses. *American Journal of Psychology,* 1955, 68, 409–416.

Greenwald, A. G., T. C. Brock, and T. M. Ostrom. *Psychological foundations of attitudes*. New York: Academic Press, 1968.

Grossman, S. P. *Textbook of physiological psychology*. New York: Wiley, 1967.

Grossman, S. P. *Essentials of physiological psychology*. New York: Wiley, 1973.

Guilford, J. P. *Psychometric methods*. (1st ed.) New York: McGraw-Hill, 1936.

Guilford, J. P. *General psychology,* Princeton, N.J.: Van Nostrand, 1939.

Guilford, J. P. *Psychometric methods*. (2nd ed.) New York: McGraw-Hill, 1954.

Guilford, J. P. *The nature of human intelligence*. New York: McGraw-Hill, 1967.

Gulick, W. L. *Hearing*. New York: Oxford, 1971.

Guthrie, E. R. *The psychology of human conflict*. New York: Harper & Row, 1938.

Guthrie, E. R. *The psychology of learning* (Rev. ed.). New York: Harper & Row, 1952.

Guthrie, E. R. Association by contiguity. In S. Koch (Ed.), *Psychology: A study of a science*. Vol. 2. New York: McGraw-Hill, 1959.

Guthrie, E. R., and G. P. Horton. *Cats in a puzzle box*. New York: Holt, Rinehart and Winston, Inc., 1946.

Guthrie, G., and M. Wiener, Subliminal perception or perception of partial cues with pictorial stimuli. *Journal of Personality and Social Psychology,* 1966, 3, 619–628.

Haber, R. N. Effect of prior knowledge of the stimulus on word-recognition processes. *Journal of Experimental Psychology,* 1965, 69, 282–286.

Haber, R. N. (Ed.). *Contemporary theory and research in visual perception*. New York: Holt, Rinehart and Winston, Inc., 1968.

Haber, R. N. (Ed.). *Information-processing approaches to visual perception*. New York: Holt, Rinehart and Winston, Inc., 1969.

Haber, R. N. and M. Hershenson. *The psychology of visual perception*. New York: Holt, Rinehart and Winston, Inc., 1973.

Hailman, J. P. Coding of the colour preference of the gull chick. *Nature,* 1964, 204, 710.

Hailman, J. P. Mirror image color-preferences for background and stimulus-object in the gull chick. *Experientia,* 1966, 22, 257.

Hall, C., and G. Lindzey. *Theories of personality* (1st ed.). New York: Wiley, 1957.

Hall, C. and G. Lindzey. *Theories of personality* (3rd ed.). New York: Wiley, 1978.

Hall, J. F. *The psychology of learning*. Philadelphia: Lippincott, 1966.

Hansel, C. E. M. *ESP: A scientific evaluation*. New York: Scribner, 1966.

Harden, L. M. A quantitative study of the similarity factor in retroactive inhibition. *Journal of General Psychology,* 1929, 2, 421–430.

Harlow, H. F. The formation of learning sets. *Psychological Review,* 1949, 56, 51–65.

Harlow, H. F. Learning and satiation of response in intrinsically motivated complex puzzle performance by monkeys. *Journal of Comparative and Physiological Psychology,* 1950, 43, 289–294.

Harlow, H. F. The nature of love. *American Psychologist,* 1958, 13, 673–685.

Harlow, H. F. The heterosexual affectional system in monkeys. *American Psychologist,* 1962, 17, 1–9.

Harlow, H. F., N. Blazek, and G. McClearn. Manipulatory motivation in the infant rhesus monkey. *Journal of Comparative and Physiological Psychology,* 1956, 49, 444–448.

Harlow, H. F., and M. K. Harlow. Social deprivation in monkeys. *Scientific American,* 1962, 207, 136–146.

Harlow, H. F., and M. K. Harlow. The affectional systems. In A. M. Schrier, H. F. Harlow, and F. Stollnitz (Eds.), *Behavior of nonhuman primates*. Vol. 2. New York: Academic Press, 1965.

Harlow, H. F., M. K. Harlow, and D. Meyer. Learning motivated by a manipulation drive. *Journal of Experimental Psychology,* 1950, 40, 228–234.

Harlow, H. F., and G. McClearn. Object discrimination learned by monkeys on the basis of manipulation motives. *Journal of Comparative and Physiological Psychology,* 1954, 47, 73–76.

Harlow, H. F., and S. J. Soumi. Nature of love—simplified. *American Psychologist,* 1970, 25, 111–168.

Harlow, H. F., and R. R. Zimmerman. Affectional responses in the infant monkey. *Science,* 1959, 130, 421–432.

Harris, C. S. Perceptual adaptation to inverted reversed and displaced vision. *Psychological Review,* 1965, 72, 419–444.

Hartshorne, H., and A. May. *Studies in deceit*. New York: Macmillan, 1928.

Hastorf, A. H., and A. L. Knutson. Motivation, perception and attitude change. *Psychological Review,* 1949, 56, 88–97.

Hebb, D. O. *The organization of behavior*. New York: Wiley, 1949.

Hebb, D. O. The semi-autonomous process: Its nature and nurture. *American Psychologist,* 1963, 18, 16–27.

Hecht, S. The nature of the photoreceptor processes. In C. Murchinson (Ed.), *Foundations of experimental psychology*. Worcester, Mass.: Clark University Press, 1929.

Hecht, S. The photochemical basis of vision. *Journal of Applied Psychology,* 1938, 9, 156–164.

Heidbreder, E. *Seven psychologies*. New York: Appleton, 1933.

Heidbreder, E. The attainment of concepts. I. Terminology and methodology. *Journal of General Psychology,* 1946, 35, 173–189. (a)

Heidbreder, E. The attainment of concepts. II. The problem. *Journal of General Psychology,* 1946, 35, 191–223. (b)

Heidbreder. E. The attainment of concepts. III. The process. *Journal of Psychology,* 1947, 24, 93–138.

Heidbreder, E. The attainment of concepts. VI. Exploratory experiments on conceptualization at perceptual levels. *Journal of Psychology,* 1948, 26, 193–216.

Heidegger, M. *Being and time*. New York: Harper & Row, 1962.

Heider, F. Social perception and phenomenal causality. *Psychological Review,* 1944, 51, 358–374.

Heider, F. *The psychology of interpersonal relations*. New York: Wiley, 1958.

Held, R., and A. V. Hein. Adaptation of disarranged hand-eye coordination contingent upon re-afferent stimulation. *Perceptual and Motor Skills,* 1958, 8, 87–90.

Helson, H. Adaptation-level as a basis for a quantitative theory of frames of reference. *Psychological Review,* 1948, 55, 297–313.

Helson, H. Adaptation level theory. In S. Koch (Ed.), *Psychology: A study of a science*. New York: McGraw-Hill, 1959.

Helson, H. *Adaptation level theory*. New York: Harper & Row, 1964. (a)

Helson, H. Current trends and issues in adaptation level theory. *American Psychologist,* 1964, 19, 26–38. (b)

Hempel, C. G. *Philosophy of natural science*. Englewood Cliffs, N.J.: Prentice-Hall, 1966.

Henle, M., J. Janes, and J. Sullivan. *Historical conceptions of psychology*. New York: Springer, 1973.

Herrnstein, R. J. *I.Q. in the meritocracy*. Boston: Little, Brown, 1973.

Hertz, M. *Zeitschrift für vergleichende Physiologie*. Vol. 7, 1928. Summarized in considerable detail by W. Köhler. *Gestalt psychology*. New York: Liveright, 1929.

Hildum, D., and R. Brown. Verbal reinforcement and interview bias. *Journal of Abnormal and Social Psychology*, 1956, 53, 108–111.

Hilgard, E. *Contemporary theories of learning*. (2nd ed.) New York: Appleton, 1956.

Hilgard, E., and G. H. Bower. *Theories of learning*. (3rd ed.) New York: Appleton, 1966.

Hobhouse, L. T. *Mind in evolution*. New York: Macmillan, 1901.

Hochberg, J. Perception: II, Space and Movement. In J. W. Kling and L. A. Riggs (Eds.), *Woodworth and Schlosberg's experimental psychology*. New York: Holt, Rinehart and Winston, Inc., 1971.

Hollander, E. P. *Principles and methods of social psychology*. (3rd ed.) New York: Oxford, 1976.

Holt, R. R. Individuality and generalization in the psychology of personality. *Journal of Personality*, 1962, 30, 377–404.

Honzik, C. H. The sensory basis of maze learning in rats. *Comparative Psychology Monographs*, 1936, 13 (Whole No. 64).

Horney, K. *The neurotic personality of our time*. New York: Norton, 1937.

Horney, K. *New Ways in psychoanalysis*. New York: Norton, 1939.

Horney, K. *Our inner conflicts*. New York: Norton, 1945.

Horton, D. L., and R. R. Hartman. Verbal mediation as a function of associative directionality and exposure frequency. *Journal of Verbal Learning and Verbal Behavior*, 1963, 1, 361–364.

Horton, D. L., and P. M. Kjeldegaard. An experimental analysis of associative factors in mediated generalization. *Psychological Monographs*, 1961, 75 (Whole No. 11).

Horton, D. L., and T. W. Turnage. *Human learning*. Englewood Cliffs, N.J.: Prentice-Hall, 1976.

Houston, S. A. A reexamination of some assumptions about the language of the disadvantaged child. *Child Development*, 1970, 41, 464–497.

Houston, S. H. The study of language: trends and position. In John Eliot (Ed.), *Human development and cognitive processes*. New York: Holt, Rinehart and Winston, Inc., 1971.

Hovland, C. I. Experimental studies in rote-learning theory. III. Distribution of practice with varying speeds of syllable presentation. *Journal of Experimental Psychology*, 1938, 23, 172–190.

Hovland, C. I., I. Janis, and H. Kelley. *Communication and persuasion*. New Haven, Conn.: Yale University Press, 1953.

Hovland, C. I., and M. Sherif. Judgmental phenomena and scales of attitude measurement: Item displacement in Thurstone scales. *Journal of Abnormal and Social Psychology*, 1952, 47, 822–832.

Howie, D. Perceptual defense. *Psychological Review*, 1952, 59, 308–315.

Hubel, D. H. Integrative processes in ventral visual pathways of the cat. *Journal of the Optical Society of America*, 1963, 53, 58–66. (a)

Hubel, D. H. The visual cortex of the brain. *Scientific American*, 1963, 209, 54–62. (b)

Hubel, D. H., and T. N. Wiesel. Receptive fields of single neurons in the cat's striate cortex. *Journal of Physiology* (London), 1959, 148, 574–591.

Hubel, D. H., and T. N. Wiesel. Receptive fields, binocular interaction and functional architecture in the cat's visual cortex. *Journal of Physiology* (London), 1962, 160, 106–154.

Hubel, D. H., and T. N. Wiesel. Receptive fields and functional architecture in two nonstriate visual areas (18 and 19) of the cat. *Journal of Neurophysiology,* 1965, 28, 229–289.

Hubel, D. H., and T. N. Wiesel. Abberant visual projections in the siamese cat. *Journal of Physiology* (London), 1971, 218, 33–62.

Hull, C. L. Quantitative aspects of the evolution of concepts. *Psychological Monographs,* 1920, 28 (Whole No. 123).

Hull, C. L. The goal gradient hypothesis and maze learning. *Psychological Review,* 1932, 39, 25–43.

Hull, C. L. The conflicting psychologies of learning—a way out. *Psychological Review,* 1935, 42, 491–516.

Hull, C. L. *Principles of behavior.* New York: Appleton, 1943.

Hull, C. L. *Essentials of behavior.* New Haven, Conn.: Yale University Press, 1951.

Hull, C. L. *A behavior system.* New Haven, Conn.: Yale University Press, 1952.

Hull, C. L., C. I. Hovland, R. T. Ross, M. Hall, D. T. Perkins, and F. B. Fitch. *Mathematico-deductive theory of rote learning.* New Haven, Conn.: Yale University Press, 1940.

Hulse, S. H., J. Deese, and H. Egeth. *The psychology of learning.* New York: McGraw-Hill, 1975.

Humphrey, G. *Directed thinking.* New York: Dodd, Mead, 1948.

Hunt, E. B. *Concept learning: An information processing problem.* New York: Wiley, 1962.

Hurvich, L. M., and D. Jameson. An opponent-process theory of color vision. *Psychological Review,* 1957, 64, 384–404.

Hydén, H. Satellite cells in the nervous system. *Scientific American,* 1961, 205, 62–70.

Ingram, W. R. The hypothalamus. *Clinical Symposia,* 1956, 8 (Whole No. 4). Ciba Pharmaceutical Products, Inc.

Insko, C. A. Verbal reinforcement of attitude. *Journal of Personality and Social Psychology,* 1965, 2, 621–623.

Insko, C. A. *Theories of attitude change.* New York: Appleton, 1967.

Insko, C. A., and R. B. Cialdini. *Interpersonal influence in a controlled setting: The verbal reinforcement of attitude.* New York: General Learning Press, 1971.

Insko, C. A., and W. Oakes. Awareness and the "conditioning" of attitudes. *Journal of Personality and Social Psychology,* 1966, 4, 487–496.

Iscoe, I., and J. A. Carden. Field dependence, manifest anxiety and sociometric status in children. *Journal of Consulting Psychology,* 1961, 25, 184.

Ittelson, W. H. *The Ames demonstrations in perception.* Princeton, N.J.: Princeton University Press, 1952.

Ittelson, W. H., and H. Cantril. *Perception: A transactional approach.* New York: Doubleday, 1954.

Jacobs, G. H. Color vision. In M. R. Rosenzweig and L. W. Porter (Eds.), *Annual Review of Psychology.* Palo Alto, Calif.: Annual Reviews, 1967.

Jacobs, R. C., and D. T. Campbell. The perpetuation of an arbitrary tradition through several generations of a laboratory microculture. *Journal of Abnormal and Social Psychology,* 1961, 62, 649–658.

Jacobsen, C. F. Influence of motor and pre-motor lesions upon the retention of skilled movements in monkeys and chimpanzees. *Journal of Nervous and Mental Diseases,* 1934, 13, 225–247.

Jacobsen, C. F. Functions of the frontal association areas in primates. *Archives of Neurology and Psychiatry,* 1935, 33, 558–569.

Jacobsen, C. F. Studies of cerebral functions in primates: I. The functions of the frontal association areas in monkeys. *Comparative Psychology Monographs,* 1936, 13 (Whole No. 63).

Jacobsen, C. F. The effects of extirpations on higher brain processes. *Physiological Review,* 1939, 19, 303–322.

Jacobsen, C. F., and G. M. Haslerud. Studies of cerebral functions in primates: III. A note on the effect of motor and premotor area lesions on delay responses in monkeys. *Comparative Psychology Monographs,* 1936, 13 (Whole No. 63).

Jacobson, E. *Progressive relaxation.* Chicago: University of Chicago Press, 1929.

Jacobson, E. Electrophysiology of mental activities. *American Journal of Psychology,* 1932, 44, 677–694.

James, W. *The principles of psychology.* Vol. 1. New York: Henry Holt and Company, Inc., 1890.

James, W. *Psychology, briefer course.* New York: Henry Holt and Company, Inc., 1892.

Janis, I. L. Effects of fear arousal on attitude change: Recent developments in theory and experimental research. In L. Berkowitz (Ed.), *Experimental social psychology.* Vol. 3. New York: Academic Press, 1967.

Janis, I. L., and S. Feshbach. Effects of fear-arousing communications. *Journal of Abnormal and Social Psychology,* 1953, 48, 78–92.

Jasper, H. Reticular-cortical systems and theories of the integrative action of the brain. In H. F. Harlow and C. N. Woolsey (Eds.), *Biological and biochemical bases of behavior.* Madison: University of Wisconsin Press, 1958.

Jenkins, J. G. Instruction as a factor in "incidental" learning. *American Journal of Psychology,* 1933, 45, 471–477.

Jenkins, J. G., and K. M. Dallenbach. Obliviscence during sleep and waking. *American Journal of Psychology,* 1924, 35, 605–612.

Jenkins, J. J. Mediated associations: Paradigms and situations. In C. N. Confer and B. S. Musgrave (Eds.), *Verbal behavior and learning: Problems and processes.* New York: McGraw-Hill, 1963.

Jensen, A. R. How much can we boost IQ and scholastic achievement? *Harvard Educational Review,* 1969, 39, 1–123.

Jensen, A. R. *Educability and group differences.* New York: Harper & Row, 1973.

Jersild, A. *Child psychology.* Englewood Cliffs, N.J.: Prentice-Hall, 1954.

Jones, E. *The life and work of Sigmund Freud.* New York: Basic Books, 1953. 3 vols.

Jones, E. E., and K. E. Davis. From acts to dispositions: The attribution process in person perception. In L. Berkowitz (Ed.), *Advances in experimental social psychology.* Vol. 2. New York: Academic Press, 1965.

Jones, E. E., and H. B. Gerard. *Foundations of social psychology.* New York: Wiley, 1967.

Jones, E. E., and G. R. Goethals. *Order effects in impression formation: Attribution context and the nature of the entity.* New York: General Learning Press, 1971.

Jones, E. E., D. E. Kanouse, H. H. Kelley, R. E. Nisbett, S. Valins, and B. Weiner. *Attribution: Perceiving the causes of behavior.* New York: General Learning Press, 1972.

Jones, E. E., L. Rock, K. G. Shaver, G. R. Goethals, and L. M. Ward. Pattern of performance and ability attribution: An unexpected primacy effect. *Journal of Personality and Social Psychology,* 1968, 10, 317–340.

Jones, E. E., H. H. Wells, and R. Torrey. Some effects of feedback from the experimenter on conformity behavior. *Journal of Abnormal and Social Psychology,* 1958, 58, 207–213.

Jones, R. A., D. E. Linder, C. A. Kiesler, M. Zanna, and J. W. Brehm. Internal states or external stimuli: Observer's attitude judgments and the dissonance-theory—self-persuasion controversy. *Journal of Experimental Social Psychology,* 1968, 4, 247–269.

Jost, A. Die Assoziationsfestigkeit in ihrer Abhängigheit von der Verteilung der Widerholungen. *Zeitschrift für Psychologie,* 1897, 14, 436–472.

Jouvet, M. The states of sleep. *Scientific American,* 1967, 216, 62–72.

Jouvet, M. Biogenic amines and the states of sleep. *Science,* 1969, 163, 32–41.

Judd, C. H. The relation of special training to general intelligence. *Educational Review,* 1908, 36, 28–42.

Jung, C. *Psychological types.* New York: Harcourt Brace Jovanovich, 1923.

Jung, C. *Psychology of the unconscious.* New York: Dodd, Mead, 1931.

Jung, C. *Modern man in search of a soul.* New York: Harcourt Brace Jovanovich, 1933.

Jung, J. Transfer of training as a function of degree of first-list learning. *Journal of Verbal Learning and Verbal Behavior,* 1962, 1, 197–199.

Jung, J. Effects of response meaningfulness *(m)* on transfer of training under two different paradigms. *Journal of Experimental Psychology,* 1963, 65, 377–384.

Jung, J. *The experimenter's dilemma.* New York: Harper & Row, 1971.

Kagan, J. S. Differential reward value of incomplete and complete sexual behavior. *Journal of Comparative and Physiological Psychology,* 1955, 48, 59–64.

Kagan, J. S. Inadequate evidence and illogical conclusions. *Harvard Educational Review,* 1969, 39, 274–277.

Kallmann, F. J. Psychogenetic studies of twins. In S. Koch (Ed.), *Psychology: A study of a science.* Vol. 3. New York: McGraw-Hill, 1959.

Kamin, L. *The science and politics of IQ.* Potomac, Md.: L. Erlbaum Associates, 1974.

Kamiya, J. Conscious control of brain waves. *Psychology Today,* 1968, 1, 57–60.

Kapatos, G., and R. M. Gold. Evidence for ascending noradrenergic mediation of hypothalamic hyperphagia. *Pharmacology, Biochemistry, and Behavior,* 1973, 1, 81–87.

Kaplan, A. *The new world of philosophy.* New York: Vintage, 1963.

Kappers, C. U. A. On the structural laws in the nervous system. The principles of neurobiotaxis. *Brain,* 1921, 44, 125.

Katona, G. *Organization and memorizing.* New York: Columbia University Press, 1940.

Kaufman, L. *Sight and mind: An introduction to visual perception.* New York: Oxford, 1974.

Kaufmann, W. *Nietzsche.* Cleveland: World Publishing, 1950.

Keller, F. S. *The definition of psychology.* New York: Appleton, 1937.

Keller, L., M. Cole, and W. K. Estes. Reward information values of trial outcomes in paired associate learning. *Psychological Monographs,* 1965, 79 (Whole No. 12).

Kelley, H. H. The warm-cold variable in first impressions of persons. *Journal of Personality,* 1950, 18, 431–439.

Kelley, H. H. Attribution theory in social psychology: In D. Levine (Ed.), *Nebraska Symposium on Motivation.* Lincoln: University of Nebraska Press, 1967.

Kelley, H. H., and J. W. Thibaut. Group problem solving. In G. Lindzey and E. Aronson (Eds.), *The Handbook of social psychology* (2nd ed.). Vol. 4. Reading, Mass.: Addison-Wesley, 1969.

Kelman, H. C. Human use of human subjects: The problem of deception in social psychological experiments. *Psychological Bulletin,* 1967, 67, 1–11.

Kendler, H. H. "What is learned?"—A theoretical blind alley. *Psychological Review,* 1952, 59, 269–277.

Kendler, H. H., and T. S. Kendler. Vertical and horizontal processes in problem solving. *Psychological Review,* 1962, 69, 1–16.

Kendler, H. H., and T. S. Kendler. *Form discrimination learning to cognitive development:*

a neobehavioristic odyssey. In W. K. Estes (Ed.), *Handbook of learning and cognitive processes*. Hillsdale, N.J.: Lawrence Erlbaum Associates, 1975.

Kendler, T. S., and H. H. Kendler. *Experimental analysis of inferential behavior in children*. In L. P. Lipsett and C. C. Spiker (Eds.), *Advances in child development and behavior*. Vol. 3. New York: Academic Press, 1967.

Kenshalo, D. R. The cutaneous senses. In J. W. Kling and L. A. Riggs (Eds.), *Woodworth and Schlosberg's experimental psychology* (3rd ed.). New York: Holt, Rinehart and Winston, Inc., 1971.

Kent, E., and S. P. Grossman. Evidence for a conflicting interpretation of anomalous effects of rewarding brain stimulation. *Journal of Comparative and Physiological Psychology*, 1969, 69, 381–390.

Kierkegaard, S. *Fear and trembling and the sickness unto death*. New York: Doubleday, 1954.

Kilpatrick, F. P. *Human behavior from the transactional point of view*. Hanover, N.H.: Institute for Associated Research, 1952.

Kilpatrick, F. P. Two processes in perceptual learning. *Journal of Experimental Psychology*, 1954, 47, 362–370.

Kilpatrick, F. P. (Ed.), *Explorations in transactional psychology*. New York: New York University Press, 1961.

Kimble, D. P., and R. J. Kimble. Hippocampectomy and response perseveration. *Journal of Comparative and Physiological Psychology*, 1965, 60, 474–476.

Kimble, G. A. *Hilgard and Marquis' conditioning and learning* (2nd ed.). New York: Appleton, 1961.

Kintsch, W. Models for recall and recognition. In D. A. Norman (Ed.), *Models of human memory*. New York: Academic Press, 1970. (a)

Kintsch, W. Stochastic learning theory. In M. H. Marx (Ed.), *Learning: Theories*. New York: Crowell-Collier-Macmillan, 1970. (b)

Kintsch, W., and H. Buschke. Homophones and synonyms in short-term memory. *Journal of Experimental Psychology*, 1969, 80, 403–407.

Kling, J. W., and Y. Matsumiya. Relative reinforcement values of food and intracranial stimulation. *Science*, 1962, 135, 668–670.

Kling, J. W., and L. A. Riggs. *Woodworth and Schlosberg's experimental psychology* (3rd ed.). New York: Holt, Rinehart and Winston, Inc., 1971.

Klopfer, P., and J. Hailman. *An introduction to animal behavior*. Englewood Cliffs, N.J.: Prentice-Hall, 1967.

Klüver, H., and P. C. Bucy. Preliminary analysis of functions of the temporal lobes in monkeys. *Archives of Neurology and Psychiatry*, 1939, 42, 979–1000.

Koch, S., and Clark Hull. In W. K. Estes, K. MacCorquodale, P. E. Meehl, C. G. Mueller, Jr., W. N. Schoenfeld, and W. S. Verplanck (Eds.), *Modern learning theory*. New York: Appleton, 1954.

Koch, S. (Ed.), *Psychology: A study of a science*. Vol. 1. New York: McGraw-Hill, 1959.

Koch, S. *Language communities, search cells, and the psychological studies*. In W. J. Arnold (Ed.), *Nebraska Symposium on Motivation*. Lincoln: University of Nebraska Press, 1975.

Koffka, K. *Principles of Gestalt Psychology*. New York: Harcourt Brace Jovanovich, 1935.

Kohlberg, L. *Moral and religious education and the public schools: A developmental view*. In T. Sizer (Ed.), *Religion and public education*. Boston: Houghton Mifflin, 1967.

Kohlberg, L. *Stage and sequence: The cognitive-developmental approach to socialization*. In D. Goslin (Ed.), *Handbook of socialization theory and research*. Chicago: Rand McNally, 1969.

Kohler, I. The formation and transformation of the visual world. *Psychological Issues,* 1964, 3, 28–46.

Köhler, W. *The mentality of apes.* Translated by E. Winter. New York: Humanities Press, 1927.

Köhler, W. *Gestalt psychology.* New York: Liveright, 1929.

Köhler, W. *Dynamics in psychology.* New York: Liveright, 1940.

Köhler, W., and J. Fishback. The destruction of the Muller-Lyer illusion in repeated trials: I. An examination of two theories. *Journal of Experimental Psychology,* 1950, 40, 267–281.

Köhler, W., and R. Held. The cortical correlate of pattern vision. *Science,* 1949, 110, 414–419.

Köhler, W., and H. Wallach. Figural after-effects: An investigation of visual processes. *Proceedings of the American Philosophical Society,* 1944, 88, 269–357.

Kohn, M. Satiation of hunger from food injected directly into the stomach versus food ingested by mouth. *Journal of Comparative and Physiological Psychology,* 1951, 44, 412–422.

Kraeling, D. Analysis of amount of reward as a variable in learning. *Journal of Comparative and Physiological Psychology,* 1961, 54, 560–565.

Krasner, L., J. Knowles, and L. Ullmann. Effects of verbal conditioning of attitudes on subsequent motor performance. *Journal of Personality and Social Psychology,* 1965, 1, 407–412.

Krasner, L., and L. P. Ullmann. *Research in behavior modification.* New York: Holt, Rinehart and Winston, Inc., 1965.

Krasner, L., and L. P. Ullmann. *Behavior influence and personality: The social matrix of human action.* New York: Holt, Rinehart and Winston, Inc., 1973.

Krawiec, T. S. (Ed.), *The psychologists.* New York: Oxford, Vol. 1, 1972; Vol. 2, 1974.

Krech, D. Cortical localization of function. In L. Postman (Ed.), *Psychology in the making,* New York: Knopf, 1962.

Krech, D., and R. S. Crutchfield. *Theory and problems of social psychology.* New York: McGraw-Hill, 1948.

Krech, D., and R. S. Crutchfield. *Elements of psychology.* New York: Knopf, 1958.

Krechevsky, I. Hereditary nature of "hypotheses." *Journal of Comparative Psychology,* 1933, 16, 99–116.

Krechevsky, I. Brain mechanisms and "hypotheses." *Journal of Comparative Psychology,* 1935, 19, 425–468.

Krueger, W. C. The effect of overlearning on retention. *Journal of Experimental Psychology,* 1929, 41, 432–441.

Kübler-Ross, E. *On death and dying.* New York: Macmillan, 1969.

Kuffler, S. W. Discharge patterns and functional organization of mammalian retina. *Journal of Neurophysiology,* 1953, 16, 37–68.

Kuhn, T. *The structure of scientific revolutions* (2nd ed.). Chicago: University of Chicago Press, 1970.

Landis, C., and W. Hunt. *The startle pattern.* New York: Holt, Rinehart and Winston, Inc., 1939.

Larsen, K. S. *Aggression myths and models.* Chicago: Nelson-Hall, 1978.

Lashley, K. S. *Brain mechanisms and intelligence.* Chicago: University of Chicago Press, 1929.

Lashley, K. S. The mechanism of vision: XV. Preliminary studies of the rat's capacity for detailed vision. *Journal of General Psychology,* 1938, 18, 123–193.

Lashley, K. S. The mechanism of vision: XVII. The functioning of small remnants of the visual cortex. *Journal of Comparative Neurology,* 1939, 70, 45–67.

Lashley, K. S. Studies of cerebral function in learning: XII. Loss of the maze habit after occipital lesions in blind rats. *Journal of Comparative Neurology,* 1943, 79, 431–462.

Lashley, K. S. The problem of serial order in behavior. In L. A. Jeffress (Ed.), *Cerebral mechanisms in behavior: The Hixon symposium.* New York: Wiley, 1951.

Latané, B., and J. M. Darley. *The unresponsive bystander: Why doesn't he help?* New York: Appleton, 1970.

LeBon, G. *The crowd.* New York: Viking, 1960.

Lefcourt, H. M. Internal versus external control of reinforcement: A review. *Psychological Bulletin,* 1966, 65, 206–220. (a)

Lefcourt, H. M. Belief in personal control: Research and implications. *Journal of Individual Psychology,* 1966, 22, 185–195. (b)

Lenneberg, E. *The biological foundations of language.* New York: Wiley, 1967.

Lettvin, J. Y., H. R. Maturana, W. S. McCulloch, and W. H. Pitts. What the frog's eye tells the frog's brain. *Proceedings of the Institute of Radio Engineers,* 1959, 47, 1940–1951.

Leuba, C., and C. Lucas. The effects of attitudes on descriptions of pictures. *Journal of Experimental Psychology,* 1945, 35, 517–524.

Leventhal, H., and P. Niles. A field experiment on fear arousal with data on the validity of questionnaire measures. *Journal of Personality,* 1964, 32, 459–479.

Leventhal, H., and R. P. Singer. Affect arousal and positioning of recommendations in persuasive communication. *Journal of Personality and Social Psychology,* 1966, 4, 137–146.

Leventhal, H., R. Singer, and S. Jones. Effects of fear and specificity of recommendation upon attitudes and behavior. *Journal of Personality and Social Psychology,* 1965, 2, 20–29.

Levine, R., I. Chein, and G. Murphy. The relation of intensity of a need to the amount of perceptual distortion. *Journal of Psychology,* 1942, 13, 283–293.

Lewin, K. *A dynamic theory of personality.* New York: McGraw-Hill, 1935.

Lewin, K. *Principles of topological psychology.* New York: McGraw-Hill, 1936.

Lewin, K. *Contributions to psychological theory.* Durham, N.C.: Duke University Press, 1938.

Lewin, K. Experiments in social space. *Harvard Educational Review,* 1939, 9, 1–32. (a)

Lewin, K. Field theory and experiments in social psychology: Concepts and methods. *American Journal of Sociology,* 1939, 44, 868–879. (b)

Lewin, K. Behavior and development as a function of the total situation. In L. Carmichael (Ed.), *Manual of child psychology.* New York: Wiley, 1946.

Lewin, K. Group decisions and social change. In T. M. Newcomb and E. L. Hartley (Eds.), *Readings in social psychology.* New York: Holt, Rinehart and Winston, Inc., 1947.

Lewin, K. *Resolving social conflicts.* New York: Harper & Row, 1948.

Lewin, K., R. Lippitt, and R. White. Patterns of aggressive behavior in experimentally created "social climates." *Journal of Social Psychology,* 1939, 10, 271–299.

Lewis, H. B., and M. Franklin. An experimental study of the role of the ego in work. II. The significance of task-orientation in work. *Journal of Experimental Psychology,* 1944, 34, 195–215.

Likert, R. A. A technique for the measurement of attitudes. *Archives of Psychology,* 1932, No. 4.

Lindzey, G., and E. Aronson. (Eds.) *The handbook of social psychology* (2nd ed.). Vol. 1. Reading, Mass.: Addison-Wesley, 1968.

Lindzey, G., and E. Aronson. (Eds.) *The handbook of social psychology* (2nd ed.). Vol. 3. Reading, Mass.: Addison-Wesley, 1969.

Lippitt, R. Field theory and experiment in social psychology: Autocratic and democratic group atmospheres. *American Journal of Sociology,* 1939, 45, 26–49.

Lippitt, R., and R. White. The "social climate" of children's groups. In R. Barker, J. S. Kounin, and H. F. Wright (Eds.), *Child behavior and development.* New York: McGraw-Hill, 1943.

Loehlin, J. C., G. Lindzey, and J. N. Spuhler. *Race differences in intelligence.* San Francisco: W. H. Freeman, 1975.

Lorenz, K. The comparative method in studying innate behavior. *Symposium of the Society for Experimental Biology and Medicine,* 1950, 4, 221–268.

Lorenz, K. *King Solomon's ring.* New York: Crowell, 1952.

Lorenz, K. *Man meets dog.* London: Methuen, 1954.

Lorenz, K. *On aggression.* New York: Harcourt Brace Jovanovich, 1966.

Luchins, A. S. Forming impressions of personality: A critique. *Journal of Abnormal and Social Psychology,* 1948, 43, 318–325.

Luchins, A. S. Experimental attempts to minimize the impact of first impressions. In C. Hovland (Ed.), *The order of presentation in persuasion.* New Haven, Conn.: Yale University Press, 1957.

Luh, C. W. The conditions of retention. *Psychological Monographs,* 1922, 31, (Whole No. 142).

Lundin, R. W. *Personality: A behavioral analysis.* New York: Macmillan, 1969.

MacCorquodale, K., and P. E. Meehl. Edward C. Tolman. In W. K. Estes, S. Koch, K. MacCorquodale, P. E. Meehl, C. G. Mueller, Jr., W. N. Schoenfeld, and W. S. Verplanck (Eds.), *Modern learning theory.* New York: Appleton, 1954.

MacLean, P. D. Psychosomatic disease and the "visceral brain": Recent developments bearing on the Papez theory of emotion. *Psychosomatic Medicine,* 1949, 11, 353–383.

MacLean, P. D. Some psychiatric implications of physiological studies on fronto-temporal portions of the limbic system (visceral brain). *Neurosurgery,* 1954, 11, 29–44.

MacLean, P. D. Chemical and electrical stimulation of the hippocampus in unrestrained animals, II. Behavioral findings. *Archives of Neurology and Psychiatry,* 1957, 78, 128–142.

MacLean, P. D. The limbic system with respect to self-preservation and the preservation of the species. *Journal of Nervous and Mental Diseases,* 1958, 127, 1–11.

MacNichol, E. F., Jr. Retinal mechanisms of color vision. *Vision Research,* 1964, 4, 119–133. (a)

MacNichol, E. F., Jr. Three-pigment color vision. *Scientific American,* 1964, 211, 48–56. (b)

Maddi, S. R. *Personality theories: A comparative analysis* (Rev. ed.). Homewood, Ill.: The Dorsey Press, 1972.

Magoun, H. W. Nonspecific brain mechanisms. In H. F. Harlow and C. N. Woolsey (Eds.), *Biological and biochemical bases of behavior.* Madison: University of Wisconsin Press, 1958.

Magoun, H. W. *The waking brain* (2nd ed.). Springfield, Ill.: Charles C. Thomas, 1963.

Maier, N. R. F. Cortical destruction in the posterior part of the brain and its effects on reasoning in rats. *Journal of Comparative Neurology,* 1932, 56, 179–214.

Malmo, R. B. Interference factors in delayed response in monkeys after removal of frontal lobes. *Journal of Neurophysiology,* 1942, 5, 295–308.

Manning, A. *An introduction to animal behavior.* Reading, Mass.: Addison-Wesley, 1967.

Marrow, A. *The practical theorist.* New York: Basic Books, 1969.

Marx, M. H. *Theories in contemporary psychology.* New York: Crowell-Collier-Macmillan, 1963.

Marx, M. H. (Ed.). *Learning: Theories*. New York: Crowell-Collier-Macmillan, 1970.

Marx, M. H., and W. Hillix. *Systems and theories in psychology* (2nd ed.). New York: McGraw-Hill, 1973.

Maslow, A. H. *Motivation and personality*. New York: Harper & Row, 1954.

Maslow, A. H. Deficiency motivation and growth motivation. In M. R. Jones (Ed.), *Nebraska Symposium on Motivation*. Lincoln: University of Nebraska Press, 1955.

Maslow, A. H. Critique of self-actualization. I. Some dangers of Being-cognition. *Journal of Individual Psychology*, 1959, 15, 24–32.

Maslow, A. H. Lessons from the peak experiences. In R. E. Farson (Ed.), *Science and human affairs*. Palo Alto, Calif.: Science and Behavior Books, 1965.

May, R. *Existential psychology*. New York: Random House, 1969.

May, R., E. Angel, and H. F. Ellenberger. (Eds.) *Existence: A new dimension in psychiatry and psychology*. New York: Basic Books, 1958.

McCleary, R. A. Response-modulating functions of the limbic system: Initiation and suppression. In E. Stellar and J. M. Sprague (Eds.), *Progress in physiological psychology*. Vol. 1. New York: Academic Press, 1966.

McCleary, R. A., and R. S. Lazarus. Autonomic discrimination without awareness. *Journal of Personality*, 1949, 18, 171–179.

McClelland, D. C. *The achieving society*. Princeton, N.J.: Van Nostrand, 1961.

McClelland, D. C. *The roots of consciousness*. Princeton, N.J.: Van Nostrand, 1964.

McClelland, D. C. Need achievement and entrepreneurship: A longitudinal study. *Journal of Personality and Social Psychology*, 1965, 1, 389–392.

McClelland, D. C. *Assessing human motivation*. New York: General Learning Press, 1971.

McClelland, D. C., J. Atkinson, R. Clark, and E. Lowell. *The achievement motive*. New York: Appleton, 1953.

McClelland, D. C., W. N. Davis, R. Alin, and H. E. Wanner. *Alcohol and human motivation*. New York: Free Press, 1971.

McConnell, D. G. Chemical theories. *Psychological Bulletin*, 1964, 61, 252–261.

McConnell, R. A. ESP and credibility in science. *American Psychologist*, 1969, 24, 531–538.

McDonough, J. H., and R. P. Kesner. Amnesia produced by brief electrical stimulation of the amygdala or dorsal hippocampus in cats. *Journal of Comparative and Physiological Psychology*, 1971, 77, 171–178.

McDougall, W. *The group mind*. New York: Putnam, 1920.

McDougall, W. *An introduction to social psychology*. (14th ed.) Boston: Luce, 1921.

McGaugh, J. L., and J. Krivenek. Strychnine effects on discrimination learning in mice. Effects of dose and time administration. *Physiology and Behavior*, 1970, 5, 1437–1442.

McGaugh, J. L., and M. C. Madsen. Amnesic and punishing effects of electro-convulsive shock. *Science*, 1964, 144, 182–183.

McGeoch, J. A. The influence of degree of learning upon retroactive inhibition. *American Journal of Psychology*, 1929, 41, 252–262.

McGeoch, J. A. The influence of associative value upon the difficulty of nonsense-syllable lists. *Journal of Genetic Psychology*, 1930, 37, 421–426.

McGeoch, J. A. *The psychology of human learning*. New York: Longmans, 1942.

McGeoch, J. A., and A. L. Irion. *The psychology of human learning* (Rev. ed.). New York: McKay, 1952.

McGinnies, E. Emotionality and perceptual defense. *Psychological Review*, 1949, 56, 244–251.

McGuire, W. J. Some impending reorientations in social psychology: Some thoughts provoked by Kenneth Ring. *Journal of Experimental Social Psychology*, 1967, 3, 124–139.

McGuire, W. J. Personality and attitude change: An information-processing theory. In A. G. Greenwald, T. C. Brock, and T. M. Ostrom (Eds.), *Psychological foundations of attitudes*. New York: Academic Press, 1968.

McNeill, D. Developmental psycholinguistics. In G. A. Miller and F. Smith (Eds.), *The genesis of language*. Cambridge, Mass.: MIT Press, 1967.

McNeill, D. On theories of language acquisition. In T. R. Dixon and D. L. Horton (Eds.), *Verbal behavior and general behavior theory*. Englewood Cliffs, N.J.: Prentice-Hall, 1968.

Melton, A. W. Learning. In W. S. Monroe (Ed.), *Encyclopedia of educational research* (Rev. ed.). New York: Crowell-Collier-Macmillan, 1950.

Melton, A. W., and J. M. Irwin. The influence of degree of interpolated learning on retroactive inhibition and the overt transfer of specific responses. *American Journal of Psychology*, 1940, 53, 173–203.

Melzack, R. The perception of pain. *Scientific American* 1961, 204, 41–49.

Melzack, R., and P. D. Wall. Pain mechanisms: A new theory. *Science*, 1965, 150, 971–979.

Milgram, S. Behavioral study of obedience. *Journal of Abnormal and Social Psychology*, 1963, 67, 371–378.

Milgram, S. Some conditions of obedience and disobedience to authority. *Human Relations*, 1965, 18, 57–76.

Mill, J. *Analysis of the phenomena of the human mind*. London: Longmans and Dyer, 1829.

Miller, G. A. The magical number seven, plus or minus two: Some limits on our capacity for processing information. *Psychological Review*, 1956, 63, 81–97.

Miller, G. A. The psycholinguists. *Encounter*, 1964, 23, 29–37.

Miller, G. A. Some preliminaries to psycholinguistics. *American Psychologist*, 1965, 20, 15–20.

Miller, N. E. Experimental studies of conflict. In J. McV. Hunt (Ed.), *Personality and the behavior disorders*. Vol. 1. New York: Ronald, 1944.

Miller, N. E. Studies of fear as an acquired drive. I. Fear as motivation and fear-reduction as reinforcement in the learning of new responses. *Journal of Experimental Psychology*, 1948, 38, 89–101.

Miller, N. E. Comments on multiple-process conceptions of learning. *Psychological Review*, 1951, 58, 375–381.

Miller, N. E. Central stimulation and other new approaches to motivation and reward. *American Psychologist*, 1958, 13, 100–108.

Miller, N. E. Liberalization of basic *S-R* concepts: Extensions to conflict behavior, motivation, and social learning. In S. Koch (Ed.), *Psychology: A study of a science*. Vol. 2. New York: McGraw-Hill, 1959.

Miller, N. E., and L. V. DiCara. Instrumental learning of heart rate changes in curarized rats. *Journal of Comparative and Physiological Psychology*, 1967, 63, 12–19.

Miller, N. E., and L. V. DiCara. Instrumental learning of vasomotor responses by rats: Learning to respond differentially in the two ears. *Science*, 1968, 159, 1485–1486.

Miller, N. E., and J. Dollard. *Social learning and imitation*. New Haven, Conn.: Yale University Press, 1941.

Miller, N. E., and M. L. Kessen. Reward effects of food via stomach fistula compared with those of food via mouth. *Journal of Comparative and Physiological Psychology*, 1952, 45, 555–564.

Mills, J. Avoidance of dissonant information. *Journal of Personality and Social Psychology*, 1965, 2, 589–592.

Mills, J., E. Aronson, and H. Robinson. Selectivity in exposure to information. *Journal of*

Abnormal and Social Psychology, 1959, 59, 250–253.

Millward, R. B. Theoretical and experimental approaches to human learning. In J. W. Kling and L. A. Riggs (Eds.), *Woodworth and Schlosberg's experimental psychology* (3rd ed.). New York: Holt, Rinehart and Winston, Inc., 1971.

Milner, B. The memory deficit in bilateral hippocampal lesions. *NLM Psychiatric Research Reports,* 1959, 11, 43–52.

Milner, P. M. The application of physiology to learning theory. In R. Patton (Ed.), *Current trends in psychological theory.* Pittsburgh: University of Pittsburgh Press, 1961.

Minami, H., and K. M. Dallenbach. The effect of activity upon learning and retention in the cockroach. *American Journal of Psychology,* 59, 1946, 1–58.

Mishkin, M., and K. H. Pribram. Analysis of the effects of frontal lesions in the monkey: II. Variations of delayed response. *Journal of Comparative and Physiological Psychology,* 1956, 49, 36–40.

Moede, W. Einzel und Gruppenarbeit. *Praktische Psychologie,* 1920, 2, 71–78, 108–115.

Montagu, M. F. A. *Man and aggression.* New York: Oxford, 1968.

Morgan, C. T. *Physiological psychology* (1st ed.). New York: McGraw-Hill, 1943.

Morgan, C. T. Physiological mechanisms in motivation. In M. R. Jones (Ed.), *Nebraska Symposium on Motivation.* Lincoln: University of Nebraska Press, 1957.

Morgan, C. T. Physiological theory of drive. In S. Koch (Ed.), *Psychology: A study of a science.* Vol. 1. New York: McGraw-Hill, 1959.

Morgan, C. T. *Physiological psychology* (3rd ed.). New York: McGraw-Hill, 1965.

Morgan, C. T., and E. Stellar. *Physiological psychology* (2nd ed.). New York: McGraw-Hill, 1953.

Morrell, F. Electroencephalographic studies of conditioned learning. In M. A. B. Brazier (Ed.), *The central nervous system and behavior.* New York: Josiah Macy, Jr., Foundation, 1959.

Morris, D. *The naked ape.* New York: McGraw-Hill, 1967.

Mowrer, O. H. *Learning theory and behavior* New York: Wiley, 1960.

Mowrer, O. H., and E. G. Aiken. Contiguity *vs.* drive-reduction in conditioned fear: Temporal variations in conditioned and unconditioned stimulus. *American Journal of Psychology,* 1954, 67, 26–38.

Munn, N. L. *The evolution and growth of human behavior* (2nd ed.). Boston: Houghton Mifflin, 1965.

Munroe, R. L. *Schools of psychoanalytic thought.* New York: Holt, Rinehart and Winston, Inc., 1955.

Murdock, B. B., Jr. Perceptual defense and threshold measurement. *Journal of Personality,* 1954, 22, 565–571.

Murdock, B. B., Jr. The retention of individual items. *Journal of Experimental Psychology,* 1961, 62, 618–625.

Murdock, B. B., Jr. Distractor and probe techniques in short-term memory. *Canadian Journal of Psychology,* 1967, 21, 25–36. (a)

Murdock, B. B., Jr. Recent developments in short-term memory. *British Journal of Psychology,* 1967, 58, 421–433. (b)

Murdock, B. B., Jr. Short-term memory for associations. In D. A. Norman (Ed.), *Models of human memory.* New York: Academic Press, 1970.

Murdock, B. B., Jr. *Human memory: theory and data.* Hillsdale, N.J.: Lawrence Erlbaum Associates, 1974.

Murphy, G. *Historical introduction to modern psychology* (Rev. ed.). New York: Harcourt Brace Jovanovich, 1949.

Murray, E. J. *Motivation and emotion.* Englewood Cliffs, N.J.: Prentice-Hall, 1964.

Murray, E. J. *Sleep, dreams, and arousal.* New York: Appleton, 1965.

Murray, H. A. *Explorations in personality.* New York: Oxford, 1938.

Murray, H. A. Some basic psychological assumptions and conceptions. *Dialectica,* 1951, 5, 266–292.

Murray, H. A. Preparations for a scaffold of a comprehensive system. In S. Koch (Ed.), *Psychology: A study of a science.* Vol. 3. New York: McGraw-Hill, 1959.

Murray, H. A., and C. Kluckhohn. Outline of a conception of personality. In C. Kluckhohn, H. Murray, and D. Schneider (Eds.), *Personality in nature, society and culture* (2nd ed.). New York: Knopf, 1953.

Mussen, P. (Ed.). *Carmichael's manual of child psychology* (3rd ed.). New York: Wiley, 1970.

Neisser, U. Decision time without reaction time: Experiments in visual scanning. *American Journal of Psychology,* 1963, 76, 376–385.

Neisser, U. Visual search. *Scientific American,* 1964, 210, 94–102.

Neisser, U. *Cognitive psychology.* New York: Appleton, 1967.

Neisser, U., and H. K. Beller. Searching through word lists. *British Journal of Psychology,* 1965, 56, 349–358.

Neisser, U., and R. Lazar. Searching for novel targets. *Perceptual and Motor Skills,* 1964, 19, 427–432.

Neisser, U., R. Novik, and R. Lazar. Searching for ten targets simultaneously. *Perceptual and Motor Skills,* 1963, 17, 955–961.

Newcomb, T. An approach to the study of communicative acts. *Psychological Review,* 1953, 60, 393–404.

Newcomb, T. Individual systems of orientation. In S. Koch (Ed.), *Psychology: A study of a science.* Vol. 3. New York: McGraw-Hill, 1959.

Newell, A. The chess machine. In K. M. Sayre and F. J. Crosson (Eds.), *The modeling of mind.* Notre Dame, Ind.: University of Notre Dame Press, 1963.

Newell, A. Artificial intelligence and the concept of mind. In R. C. Schank and K. M. Colby, (Eds.), *Computer models of thought and language.* San Francisco: W. H. Freeman, 1973.

Newell, A., J. C. Shaw, and H. A. Simon. Chess-playing programs and the problem of complexity. In E. A. Feigenbaum and J. Feldman (Eds.), *Computers and thought.* New York: McGraw-Hill, 1963.

Newell, A., and H. A. Simon. The logic theory machine: a complex information processing system. *Transactions Information Theory Institute of Radio Engineers,* 1956, 1 T, No. 3, 61–79.

Newman, H. H., F. N. Freeman, and K. J. Holzinger. *Twins: A study of heredity and environment.* Chicago: University of Chicago Press, 1937.

Noback, C. R. *The human nervous system.* New York: McGraw-Hill, 1967.

Norman, D. A. *Memory and attention: An introduction to information processing.* New York: Wiley, 1969.

Norman, D. A. *Models for human memory.* New York: Academic Press, 1970.

Norman, D. A., and D. E. Rumelhart. A system for perception and memory. In D. A. Norman (Ed.), *Models of human memory.* New York: Academic Press, 1970.

Olds, J. Run-way and maze behavior controlled by basomedial forebrain stimulation in the rat. *Journal of Comparative and Physiological Psychology,* 1956, 49, 507–512.

Olds, J. Effects of hunger and male sex hormones on self-stimulation of the brain. *Journal of Comparative and Physiological Psychology,* 1958, 51, 320–324. (a)

Olds, J. Self-stimulation of the brain. *Science,* 1958, 127, 315–324. (b)

Olds, J. Differentiation of reward systems in the brain by self-stimulation techniques. In E. R. Ramey and D. S. O'Doherty (Eds.), *Electrical studies on the unanesthetized brain.* New York: Hoeber, 1960.

Olds, J. Differential effects of drive and drugs on self-stimulation at different brain sites. In D. E. Sheer (Ed.), *Electrical stimulation of the brain.* Austin: University of Texas Press, 1961.

Olds, J. The central nervous system and the reinforcement of behavior. *American Psychologist,* 1969, 24, 114–132.

Olds, J., and P. Milner. Positive reinforcement produced by electrical stimulation of septal area and other regions of rat brain. *Journal of Comparative and Physiological Psychology,* 1954, 47, 419–427.

Orbach, J. Disturbances of the maze habit following occipital cortex removals in blind monkeys. *AMA Archives of Neurology and Psychiatry,* 1959, 81, 49–54.

Orne, M. T. On the social psychology of the psychological experiment: With particular reference to demand characteristics and their implications. *American Psychologist,* 1962, 17, 776–783.

Ornstein, R. E. *The psychology of consciousness.* San Francisco: W. H. Freeman, 1972.

Osgood, C. E. The similarity paradox in human learning: A resolution. *Psychological Review,* 1949, 56, 132–143.

Osgood, C. E. *Method and theory in experimental psychology.* New York: Oxford, 1953.

Osgood, C. E., and P. Tannenbaum. The principle of congruity in the prediction of attitude change. *Psychological Review,* 1955, 62, 42–55.

Ostrom, T. M. The relationship between the affective, behavioral, and cognitive components of attitude. *Journal of Experimental Social Psychology,* 1969, 5, 12–30.

Papez, J. W. A proposed mechanism of emotion. *Archives of Neurology and Psychiatry,* 1937, 38, 725–743.

Patrick, C. Creative thought in poets. *Archives of Psychology,* 1935, 26 (Whole No. 178).

Patrick, C. Creative thought in artists, *Journal of Psychology,* 1937, 4, 35–73.

Pavlov, I. P. *Conditioned reflexes.* New York: Oxford, 1927.

Pavlov, I. P. *Lectures on conditioned reflexes.* New York: International Publishers, 1928.

Penfield, W. *The excitable cortex of conscious man.* Liverpool: Liverpool University Press, 1958.

Penfield, W., and T. R. Rasmussen. *The cerebral cortex of man.* New York: Crowell-Collier-Macmillan, 1950.

Peterson, G. M. Mechanisms of handedness in the rat. *Journal of Comparative Psychology,* 1934, 9, 1–67.

Peterson, G. M., and L. Fracarol. The relative influence of the locus and mass of destruction upon the control of handedness by the cerebral cortex. *Journal of Comparative Neurology,* 1938, 68, 173–190.

Peterson, L. R., and M. J. Peterson. Short-term retention of individual verbal items. *Journal of Experimental Psychology,* 1959, 58, 193–198.

Pfaffmann, C. Gustatory nerve impulses in the rat, cat, and rabbit. *Journal of Neurophysiology,* 1955, 18, 429–440.

Pfaffmann, C. The sense of taste. In J. Field, H. W. Magoun, and V. E. Hall (Eds.), *Handbook of physiology.* Vol. 1. Washington, D.C.: American Physiological Society, 1959.

Pfaffmann, C., and J. K. Bare. Gustatory nerve discharges in normal and adrenalectomized rats. *Journal of Comparative and Physiological Psychology,* 1950, 43, 320–324.

Phillips, J. L., Jr. *The origins of intellect: Piaget's theory.* San Francisco: W. H. Freeman, 1969.

Piaget, J. *The language and thought of the child.* New York: Harcourt Brace Jovanovich, 1926.

Piaget, J. *Judgment and reasoning in the child.* New York: Harcourt Brace Jovanovich, 1928.

Piaget, J. *The child's conception of the world.* New York: Harcourt Brace Jovanovich, 1929.

Piaget, J. *The child's conception of physical causality.* New York: Harcourt Brace Jovanovich, 1930.

Piaget, J. *The origins of intelligence in children.* New York: Norton, 1952.

Piaget, J. *The construction of reality in the child.* New York: Basic Books, 1954.

Piaget, J. *Play, dreams, and imitation in childhood.* New York: Norton, 1962.

Piaget, J., and B. Inhelder. *The psychology of the child.* New York: Basic Books, 1969.

Piotrowski, Z. A. *Perceptanalysis.* New York: Crowell-Collier-Macmillan, 1957.

Postman, L. The history and present status of the law of effect. *Psychological Bulletin,* 1947, 44, 489–563.

Postman, L. Transfer of training as a function of experimental paradigm and degree of first-list learning. *Journal of Verbal Learning and Verbal Behavior,* 1962, 1, 109–118.

Postman, L. Studies of learning to learn. II. Changes in transfer as a function of practice. *Journal of Verbal Learning and Verbal Behavior,* 1964, 3, 437–447.

Postman, L. Transfer, interference and forgetting. In J. W. Kling and L. A. Riggs (Eds.), *Woodworth and Schlosberg's experimental psychology* (3rd ed.). New York: Holt, Rinehart and Winston, Inc., 1971.

Postman, L., and T. G. Alper. Retroactive inhibition as a function of the time of interpolation of the inhibitor between learning and recall. *American Journal of Psychology,* 1946, 59, 439–449.

Postman, L., W. C. Bronson, and G. L. Gropper. Is there a mechanism of perceptual defense? *Journal of Abnormal and Social Psychology,* 1953, 48, 215.

Postman, L., J. S. Bruner, and E. McGinnies. Personal values as selective factors in perception. *Journal of Abnormal and Social Psychology,* 1948, 43, 142–154.

Postman L., and R. S. Crutchfield. The interaction of need, set, and stimulus structure in a cognitive task. *American Journal of Psychology,* 1952, 65, 196–217.

Postman, L., and D. A. Riley. Degree of learning and interserial interference in retention. *University of California Publications in Psychology,* 1959, 8, 271–396.

Powley, T. L., and R. E. Keesey. Relationship of body weight to the lateral hypothalamic feeding syndrome. *Journal of Comparative and Physiological Psychology,* 1970, 70, 25–36.

Premack, D. A functional analysis of language. *Journal of the Experimental Analysis of Behavior,* 1970, 14, 107–125.

Pribram, K. H. Interrelation of psychology and the neurological disciplines. In S. Koch (Ed.), *Psychology: A study of a science.* Vol. 4. New York: McGraw-Hill, 1962.

Pribram, K. H. The amnesic syndromes: Disturbances in coding? In G. A. Talland and N. C. Waugh (Eds.), *The pathology of memory.* New York: Academic Press, 1969.

Pruitt, D. G. The "Walter Mitty" effect in individual and group risk taking. *Proceedings of the 77th Annual Convention of the APA,* 1969, 425–426.

Pryor, W. A. *Free radicals.* New York: McGraw-Hill, 1966.

Ralph, C. L. Polydypsia in the hen following lesions in the supraoptic hypothalamus. *American Journal of Physiology,* 1960, 198, 528–530.

Ratliff, F., and H. K. Hartline. The response of limulus optic nerve fibers to patterns of illumination on the receptor mosaic. *Journal of General Physiology*, 1959, 42, 1241–1255.

Raven, B. H. Social influence on opinions and the communication of related content. *Journal of Abnormal and Social Psychology*, 1959, 58, 119–128.

Rawcliffe, D. H. *Illusions and delusions of the supernatural and the occult*. New York: Dover, 1959.

Reitman, J. S. Computer simulation of an information-processing model of short-term memory. In D. A. Norman (Ed.), *Models of human memory*. New York: Academic Press, 1970.

Restorff, H. von. Über die Wirkung von Bereischbildungen im Spurenfeld. In W. Köhler and H. von Restorff. Analyse von Vorgängen im Spurenfeld. *Psychologische Forschung*, 1933, 18, 299–342.

Rhine, J. B. *Extrasensory perception*. (Rev. Ed.) Boston: Humphries, 1964.

Rhine, J. B. (Ed.). *Progress in parapsychology*. Durham, N.C.: Parapsychology Press, 1971.

Rhine, J. B. *Mind over matter*. New York: Macmillan, 1970.

Richards, W. Visual space perception. In E. C. Carterette and M. P. Friedman (Eds.), *Handbook of perception*. Vol. 5. New York: Academic Press, 1975.

Richter, C. P. Total self-regulatory functions in animals and human beings. *The Harvey Lecture Series*, 1942, 38, 63–103.

Riesen, A. H. The development of visual perception in man and the chimpanzee. *Science*, 1947, 106, 107–108.

Riesen, A. H., R. L. Ramsay, and P. D. Wilson. Development of visual acuity in rhesus monkeys deprived of patterned light during early infancy. *Psychonomic Science*, 1964, 1, 33–34.

Riggs, L. A. Vision. In J. W. Kling and L. A. Riggs (Eds.), *Woodworth and Schlosberg's experimental psychology* (3rd ed.). New York: Holt, Rinehart and Winston, Inc., 1971.

Ring, K. Experimental social psychology: Some sober questions about some frivolous values. *Journal of Experimental and Social Psychology*, 1967, 3, 113–123.

Robinson, E. S. Some factors determining the degree of retroactive inhibition. *Psychological Monographs*, 1920, 28 (Whole No. 128).

Robinson, E. S. The "similarity" factor in retroaction. *American Journal of Psychology*, 1927, 39, 297–312.

Robinson, E. S. *Association theory today: An essay in systematic psychology*. New York: Appleton, 1932.

Rock, I., and P. Engelstein. A study of memory for visual form. *American Journal of Psychology*, 1958, 72, 221–229.

Rogers, C. R. *Counseling and psychotherapy*. Boston: Houghton Mifflin, 1942.

Rogers, C. R. *Client-centered therapy: Its current practice, implications, and theory*. Boston: Houghton Mifflin, 1951.

Rogers, C. R. A theory of therapy, personality, and interpersonal relationships as developed in the client-centered framework. In S. Koch (Ed.), *Psychology: A study of a science*. Vol. 3. New York: McGraw-Hill, 1959.

Rogers, C. R. *On becoming a person: A therapist's view of psychotherapy*. Boston: Houghton Mifflin, 1961. (a)

Rogers, C. R. Two divergent trends. In R. May (Ed.), *Existential psychology*. New York: Random House, Inc., 1961. (b)

Rogers, C. R. Toward a science of the person. *Journal of Humanistic Psychology*, 1963, 3, 72–93.

Rogers, C. R. Some questions and challenges facing a humanistic psychology. *Journal of Humanistic Psychology,* 1965, 5, 1–5. (a)

Rogers, C. R. Some thoughts regarding the current philosophy of the behavioral sciences. *Journal of Humanistic Psychology,* 1965, 5, 182–195. (b)

Rogers, C. R. The process of the basic encounter group. In J. T. Bugental (Ed.), *Challenges in humanistic psychology.* New York: McGraw-Hill, 1967.

Rogers, C. R., and R. F. Dymond. *Psychotherapy and personality change.* Chicago: University of Chicago Press, 1954.

Rohrer, J. H., and M. Sherif. *Social psychology at the crossroads.* New York: Harper & Row, 1951.

Rosen, S. Postdecision affinity for incompatible information. *Journal of Abnormal and Social Psychology,* 1961, 63, 188–190.

Rosenberg, M. Some content determinants of intolerance for attitudinal inconsistency. In S. Tomkins and C. Izard (Eds.), *Affect, cognition, and personality.* New York: Springer, 1965.

Rosenberg, M., and R. Abelson. An analysis of cognitive balancing. In C. Hovland and M. Rosenberg (Eds.), *Attitude organization and change.* New Haven, Conn.: Yale University Press, 1960.

Rosenthal, E. Experimenter expectancy and the reassuring nature of the null hypothesis decision procedure. *Psychological Bulletin Monograph,* 1968, 70, 30–47.

Rosenthal, R. On the social psychology of the psychological experiment: The experimenter's hypothesis as unintended determinant of experimental results. *American Scientist,* 1963, 51, 262–283.

Rosenthal, R. *Experimenter effects in behavioral research.* New York: Appleton, 1966.

Rosenzweig, M. R. The mechanisms of hunger and thirst. In L. Postman (Ed.), *Psychology in the making.* New York: Knopf, 1962.

Rosenzweig, M. R., and E. L. Bennett. Enriched environments: facts, factors and fantasies. In J. L. McGaugh and L. Petrinovich (Eds.), *Knowing, thinking and believing.* New York: Plenum Press, 1976.

Rosenzweig, M. R., E. L. Bennett, and M. C. Diamond. Brain changes in response to experience. *Scientific American,* 1972, 226, 22–29. (a)

Rosenzweig, M. R., E. L. Bennett, and M. C. Diamond. Chemical and anatomical plasticity of brain: replications and extensions. In J. Gaito (Ed.), *Macromolecules and behavior.* New York: Appleton, 1972. (b)

Rosenzweig, M. R., D. Krech, and E. L. Bennett, Brain chemistry and adaptive behavior. In H. F. Harlow and C. N. Woolsey (Eds.), *Biological and biomedical bases of behavior.* Madison: University of Wisconsin Press, 1958.

Rosenzweig, M. R., D. Krech, and E. L. Bennett. Heredity, environment, brain biochemistry, and learning. In R. Patton (Ed.), *Current trends in psychological theory.* Pittsburgh: University of Pittsburgh Press, 1961.

Ross, L., J. Rodin, and P. Zimbardo. Toward an attribution therapy: The reduction of fear through induced cognitive-emotional misattribution. *Journal of Personality and Social Psychology,* 1969, 12, 279–288.

Royce, J. R. Psychology is multi-methodological, variate, epistemic, world view, systemic, paradigmatic, theoretic, and disciplinary. In W. Arnold (Ed.), *Nebraska Symposium on Motivation.* Lincoln: University of Nebraska Press, 1975.

Rubin, R. D., H. Fensterheim, J. Henderson, and L. P. Ullman. *Advances in behavior therapy.* New York: Academic Press, 1972.

Rychalk, J. Psychological science as a humanist views it. In W. Arnold (Ed.), *Nebraska*

Symposium on Motivation. Lincoln: University of Nebraska Press, 1975.

Saltz, E. *The cognitive basis of human learning*. Homewood, Ill.: The Dorsey Press, 1971.

Sanford, R. N. The effects of abstinence from food upon imaginal processes. *Journal of Psychology*, 1936, 2, 129–136. (a)

Sanford, R. N. The effects of abstinence from food upon imaginal processes: A further experiment. *Journal of Psychology*, 1936, 3, 145–159. (b)

Sarason, I. G. Effect of anxiety, motivational instructions, and failure on serial learning. *Journal of Experimental Psychology*, 1956, 51, 253–260.

Sarason, S. B., C. Mandler, and P. C. Craighill. The effect of differential instructions on anxiety and learning. *Journal of Abnormal and Social Psychology*, 1952, 47, 561–565.

Sartre, J. P. *Being and nothingness*. New York: Philosophical Library, 1956.

Schachter, S. Deviation, rejection, and communication. *Journal of Abnormal and Social Psychology*, 1951, 46, 190–207.

Schachter, S., and B. Latané. Crime, cognition and the autonomic nervous system. In D. Levine (Ed.), *Nebraska Symposium on Motivation*. Lincoln: University of Nebraska Press, 1964.

Schachter, S., and J. Singer. Cognitive, social and physiological determinants of emotional state. *Psychological Review*, 1962, 69, 379–399.

Schachter, S., and L. Wheeler. Epinephrine, chlorpromazine and amusement. *Journal of Abnormal and Social Psychology*, 1962, 65, 121–128.

Schafer, R., and G. Murphy. The role of autism in visual figureground relationship. *Journal of Experimental Psychology*, 1943, 32, 333–343.

Schank, R. C., and K. M. Colby. *Computer models of thought and language*. San Francisco: W. H. Freeman, 1973.

Schlosberg, H. A scale for judgment of facial expressions. *Journal of Experimental Psychology*, 1941, 29, 497–510.

Schlosberg, H. The description of facial expressions in terms of two dimensions. *Journal of Experimental Psychology*, 1952, 44, 229–237.

Scholsberg, H. Three dimensions of emotion. *Psychological Review*, 1954, 61, 81–88.

Schneider, A. M. and B. Tarshis. *An introduction to physiological psychology*. New York: Random House, 1975.

Scoville, W. B., and B. Milner. Loss of recent memory after bilateral hippocampal lesions. *Journal of Neurology, Neurosurgery, and Psychiatry*, 1957, 20, 11–21.

Schultz, R. *The psychology of death, dying, and bereavement*. Reading, Mass.: Addison-Wesley, 1978.

Sears, P. S. Levels of aspiration in academically successful and unsuccesful children. *Journal of Abnormal and Social Psychology*, 1940, 35, 498–536.

Sears, R. Survey of objective studies of psychoanalytic concepts. *Social Science Research Council Bulletin*, 1943, No. 51.

Sears, R. Experimental analyses of psychoanalytic phenomena. In J. McV. Hunt, (Ed.), *Personality and the behavior disorders*. New York; Ronald, 1944.

Selfridge, O., and U. Neisser. Pattern recognition by machine. *Scientific American*, 1960, 203, 60–80.

Selye, H. *The stress of life*. New York: McGraw-Hill, 1956.

Seward, J. P. An experimental study of Guthrie's theory of reinforcement. *Journal of Experimental Psychology*, 1949, 39, 177–186.

Shapere, D. *Philosophical problems of natural science*. Chicago: University of Chicago Press, 1965.

Shaw, M. E., and P. R. Costanzo. *Theories in social psychology*. New York: McGraw-Hill, 1970.

Sheffield, F. D., and T. B. Roby. Reward value of a nonnutritive sweet taste. *Journal of Comparative and Physiological Psychology*, 1950, 43, 471–481.

Sherif, M. *The psychology of social norms*. New York: Harper & Row, 1936.

Sherman, M. The differentiation of emotional responses in infants. I. Judgments of emotional responses from motion picture views and from actual observation. *Journal of Comparative Psychology*, 1927, 7, 265–284. (a)

Sherman, M. The differentiation of emotional responses in infants, II. The ability of observers to judge the emotional characteristics of the crying of infants, and of the voice of an adult. *Journal of Comparative Psychology*, 1927, 7, 335–351. (b)

Siegman, A. W. Some factors associated with the visual threshold for taboo words. *Journal of Clinical Psychology*, 1956, 12, 282.

Sigall, H., and E. Aronson. Opinion change and the gain-loss model of interpersonal attraction. *Journal of Experimental and Social Psychology*, 1967, 3, 178–188.

Siipola, E. M. A study of some effects of preparatory set. *Psychological Monographs*, 1935, 46 (Whole No. 210).

Simon, H. A., and A. Newell. Information processing in computer and man. *American Scientist*, 52, 281–300, 1964.

Singer, R. Verbal conditioning and generalization of prodemocratic responses. *Journal of Abnormal and Social Psychology*, 1961, 63, 43–46.

Skinner, B. F. *The behavior of organisms*. New York: Appleton, 1938.

Skinner, B. F. ''Superstition'' in the pigeon. *Journal of Experimental Psychology*, 1948, 38, 168–172. (a)

Skinner, B. F. *Walden II*. New York: Crowell-Collier-Macmillan, 1948. (b)

Skinner, B. F. Are theories of learning necessary? *Psychological Review*, 1950, 57, 193–216.

Skinner, B. F. How to teach animals. *Scientific American*, 1951, 185, 26–29.

Skinner, B. F. *Science and human behavior*. New York: Crowell-Collier-Macmillan, 1953.

Skinner, B. F. *Verbal behavior*. New York: Appleton, 1957.

Skinner, B. F. *Cumulative record*. New York: Appleton-Century-Crofts, 1959.

Skinner, B. F. Behaviorism at fifty. In T. W. Wann (Ed.), *Behaviorism and phenomenology*. Chicago: University of Chicago Press, 1964.

Skinner, B. F. *Contingencies of reinforcement: A theoretical analysis*. New York: Appleton, 1969.

Skinner, B. F. *Beyond freedom and dignity*. New York: Knopf, 1971.

Skinner, B. F. *About behaviorism*. New York: Knopf, 1974.

Skinner, B. F., and C. B. Ferster. *Schedules of reinforcement*. New York: Appleton, 1957.

Slobin, D. I. Universals of grammatical development in children. In F. D'Arcais and J. M. Levelt (Eds.), *Advances in psycholinguistics*. Amsterdam: North-Holland, 1970.

Slobin, D. I. *Psycholinguistics*. Glenview, Ill.: Scott, Foresman, 1971.

Snyder, A., W. Mischel, and B. E. Lott. Value, information, and conformity behavior. *Journal of Personality*, 1960, 28, 333–341.

Snyder, M., and E. B. Ebbesen. Dissonance awareness. A test of dissonance theory versus self-perception theory. *Journal of Experimental Social Psychology*, 1972, 8, 502–517.

Solomon, R. L., and D. Howes. Word frequency, personal values, and visual duration thresholds, *Psychological Review*, 1951, 58, 256–270.

Spaet, T., and H. F. Harlow. Problem solution by monkeys following bilateral removal of the prefrontal areas. II. Delayed-reaction problems involving the use of the matching-from-sample method. *Journal of Experimental Psychology*, 1943, 32, 423–434.

Spearman, C. *The principles of cognition and the nature of intelligence*. New York: Crowell-Collier-Macmillan, 1924.

Spearman, C. *The abilities of man*. New York: Crowell-Collier-Macmillan, 1927.

Spence. K. W. *Behavior theory and conditioning*. New Haven, Conn.: Yale University Press, 1956.

Spence, K. W. *Behavior theory and learning*. Englewood Cliffs, N.J.: Prentice-Hall, 1960.

Spence, K. W., G. Bergmann, and R. Lippitt. A study of simple learning under irrelevant motivation-reward conditions. *Journal of Experimental Psychology,* 1950, 40, 539–551.

Spence, K. W., I. E. Farber, and H. McFann. The relation of anxiety (drive) level to performance in competitional and non-competitional paired associates learning. *Journal of Experimental Psychology,* 1956, 52, 296–305.

Sperling, G. The information available in brief visual presentations. *Psychological Monographs,* 1960, 74 (Whole No. 498).

Sperry, R. W. Hemispheric deconnection and unity in conscious awareness. *American Psychologist,* 1968, 23, 723–733.

Sperry, R. W., M. S. Gazzaniga, and J. E. Bogen. Function of neocortical commissure: syndrome of hemispheric deconnection. In P. J. Vinken and G. W. Bewyn (Eds.), *Handbook of clinical neurology*. Amsterdam: North-Holland, 1968.

Spielberger, C. The role of awareness in verbal conditioning. *Journal of Personality* (Supplement), 1962, 30, 73–101.

Spitz, H. H. The present status of the Köhler-Wallach theory of satiation. *Psychological Bulletin,* 1958, 55, 1–29.

Staats, A., and C. Staats. Attitudes established by classical conditioning. *Journal of Abnormal and Social Psychology,* 1958, 57, 37–40.

Staats, A., C. Staats, and W. Heard. Attitude development and ratio of reinforcement. *Sociometry,* 1960, 23, 338–350.

Staats, C., and A. Staats. Meaning established by classical conditioning. *Journal of Experimental Psychology,* 1957, 54, 74–80.

Stacey, R. W. and B. D. Waxman (Eds.). *Computers in biomedical research*. New York: Academic Press, 1965.

Stagner, R., and R. T. Karwoski. *Psychology*. New York: McGraw-Hill, 1952.

Steinberg, J. J. Fear reactions, attitude change, sex differences, and objective vulnerability in fear-arousing communications. Unpublished master's thesis, University of Vermont, 1971.

Stellar, E. The physiology of motivation. *Psychological Review,* 1954, 61, 5–22.

Stevens, S. S. Psychology and the science of science. *Psychological Bulletin,* 1939, 36, 221–263.

Stevens, S. S. (Ed.). *Handbook of experimental psychology*. New York: Wiley, 1951.

Stevens, S. S., and H. Davis. *Hearing*. New York: Wiley, 1938.

Stoddard. G. *The meaning of intelligence*. New York: Crowell-Collier-Macmillan, 1943.

Stoner, J. A. F. A comparison of individual and group decisions including risk. Unpublished master's thesis, School of Industrial Management, Massachusetts Institute of Technology, 1961.

Sullivan, H. S. *The interpersonal theory of psychiatry*. New York: Norton, 1953.

Tarde, G. *The laws of imitation*. New York: Henry Holt and Company, Inc., 1903.

Taylor, J. A. A personality scale of manifest anxiety. *Journal of Abnormal and Social Psychology,* 1953, 44, 61–64.

Teger, A. I., and D. G. Pruitt. Components of group risk taking. *Journal of Experimental Social Psychology,* 1967, 3, 189–205.

Teitelbaum, P., and A. N. Epstein. The lateral hypothalamic syndrome: Recovery of feeding and drinking after lateral hypothalamic lesions. *Psychological Review,* 1962, 69, 74–90.

Teuber, H. L., W. S. Battersby, and M. B. Bender. *Visual field defects after penetrating missile wounds of the brain.* Cambridge, Mass.: Harvard University Press, 1960.

Teuber, H. L., and S. Weinstein. Ability to discover hidden figures after cerebral lesions. *Archives of Neurology and Psychiatry,* 1956, 76, 369–379.

Thibaut, J. W., and L. H. Strickland. Psychological set and social conformity. *Journal of Personality,* 1956, 25, 115–129.

Thibaut, J., W. L. Walker, and E. A. Lind. Adversary presentation and bias in legal decision making. *Harvard Law Review,* Dec. 1972, Vol. 86, No. 2, 386–401.

Thistlewaite, D. L. A critical review of latent learning and related experiments. *Psychological Bulletin,* 1951, 48, 97–129.

Thompson, G. G. *Child psychology.* Boston: Houghton Mifflin, 1952.

Thompson, R. Retention of a brightness discrimination following neocortical damage in the rat. *Journal of Comparative and Physiological Psychology,* 1960, 53, 212–215.

Thompson, R. *Introduction to physiological psychology.* New York: Harper & Row, 1975.

Thompson, R., and J. V. McConnell. Classical conditioning in the planarian, Dugesia dorotocephala. *Journal of Comparative and Physiological Psychology,* 1955, 48, 65–68.

Thomson, G. H. *The factorial analysis of human ability* (3rd ed.). Boston: Houghton Mifflin, 1948.

Thorndike, E. L. *Animal intelligence.* New York: Macmillan, 1911.

Thorndike, E. L. *Educational psychology.* Vol. 1. *The original nature of man.* New York: Teachers College, 1913. (a)

Thorndike, E. L. *Educational psychology.* Vol. 2. *The psychology of learning.* New York: Teachers College, 1913. (b)

Thorndike, E. L. *Human learning.* New York: Appleton, 1931.

Thorndike, E. L. *The fundamentals of learning.* New York: Teachers College, 1932.

Thorndike, E. L. A proof of the law of effect, *Science,* 1933, 77, 173–175.

Thorndike, E. L., and I. Lorge. The influence of relevance and belonging. *Journal of Experimental Psychology,* 1935, 18, 574–584.

Thorpe, L. P., and A. M. Schmuller. *Contemporary theories of learning.* New York: Ronald, 1954.

Thurstone, L. L. *Vectors of mind.* Chicago: University of Chicago Press, 1935.

Thurstone, L. L. *Multiple factor analysis.* Chicago: University of Chicago Press, 1947.

Thurstone, L. L., and E. J. Chave. *The measurement of attitude.* Chicago: University of Chicago Press, 1929.

Tinbergen, N. *The study of instinct.* New York: Oxford, 1951.

Tinbergen, N. *The herring gull's world.* London: Collins, 1953.

Titchener, E. B. *A textbook of psychology.* New York: Macmillan, 1910.

Tolman, E. C. *Purposive behavior in animals and man.* New York: Appleton, 1932.

Tolman, E. C. *Drives toward war.* New York: Appleton, 1942.

Tolman, E. C. There is more than one kind of learning. *Psychological Review,* 1949, 56, 144–155.

Tolman, E. C. *Collected papers in psychology.* Berkeley: University of California Press, 1951.

Tolman, E. C. Principles of purposive behaviorism. In S. Koch (Ed.), *Psychology: A study of a science.* Vol. 2. New York: McGraw-Hill, 1959.

Tolman, E. C., and C. H. Honzik. Degrees of hunger, reward and non-reward, and maze learning in rats. *University of California Publications in Psychology,* 1930, 4, 241–256. (a)

Tolman, E. C., and C. H. Honzik. Introduction and removal of reward and maze performance in rats. *University of California Publications in Psychology,* 1930, 4, 257–275. (b)

Toulmin, S. *The philosophy of science.* New York: Harper & Row, 1960.

Triplett, N. The dynamogenic factors in pace-making and competition. *American Journal of Psychology,* 1897, 9, 507–532.

Tryon, R. C. Genetic differences in maze-learning in rats. *39th Yearbook of the National Society for the Study of Education.* Bloomington, Ill.: Public School, 1940, pp. 111–119.

Twedt, H. M., and B. J. Underwood. Mixed versus unmixed lists in transfer studies. *Journal of Experimental Psychology,* 1959, 58, 111–116.

Underwood, B. J. The effect of successive interpolation on retroactive and proactive inhibition. *Psychological Monographs,* 1945, 59 (Whole No. 273).

Underwood, B. J. Interference and forgetting. *Psychological Review,* 1957, 64, 49–60.

Underwood, B. J. *Experimental psychology* (2nd ed.). New York: Appleton, 1966.

Underwood, B. J., and R. W. Schultz. *Meaningfulness and verbal learning.* Philadelphia: Lippincott, 1960.

Upshaw, H. S. Own attitude as an anchor in equal-appearing intervals. *Journal of Abnormal and Social Psychology,* 1962, 64, 85–96.

Upshaw, H. S. A linear alternative to assimilation and contrast: A reply to Manis. *Journal of Abnormal and Social Psychology,* 1964, 68, 691–693.

Upshaw, H. S. The effect of variable perspectives on judgments of opinion statement for Thurstone scales: Equal-appearing intervals. *Journal of Personality and Social Psychology,* 1965, 2, 60–69.

Upshaw, H. S. Attitude measurement. In H. M. Blalock and A. B. Blalock (Eds.), *Methodology in social research.* New York: McGraw-Hill, 1968.

Utall, W. R. *The psychobiology of sensory coding.* New York: Harper & Row, 1973.

Vaihinger, H. *The philosophy of 'as if': A system of theoretical, practical and religious fictions of mankind.* New York: Harcourt Brace Jovanovich, 1924.

Valenstein, E. S. *Brain control.* New York: Wiley, 1973.

Van Buskirk, W. L. An experimental study of vividness in learning and retention. *Journal of Experimental Psychology,* 1932, 15, 563–573.

Van de Castle, R. L. The facilitation of ESP through hypnosis. *American Journal of Clinical Hypnosis,* 12, 37–56, 1969.

Vandenberg, S. G. The hereditary abilities study: Hereditary components in a psychological test battery. *American Journal of Human Genetics,* 1962, 14, 220–237.

van Ormer, E. B. Sleep and retention. *Psychological Bulletin,* 1932, 30, 415–439.

Verney, E. B. The antidiuretic hormone and the factors which determine its release. *Proceedings of the Royal Society,* 1947, 135, 25–106.

Vernon, M. D. *Perception through experience.* New York: Barnes & Noble, 1970.

Vinacke, W. E. *The psychology of thinking.* New York: McGraw-Hill, 1974.

Voeks, V. W. Postremity, recency, and frequency as bases for prediction in the maze situation. *Journal of Experimental Psychology,* 1948, 38, 495–510.

Voeks, V. W. Formalization and clarification of a theory of learning. *Journal of Psychology,* 1950, 30, 341–362.

Voeks, V. W. Acquisition of S-R connections: A test of Hull's and Guthrie's theories. *Journal of Experimental Psychology,* 1954, 47, 137–147.

von Frisch, K. *Bees, their vision, chemical sense, and language.* Ithaca, N.Y.: Cornell University Press, 1950.

Vygotsky, L. V. *Thought and language.* Cambridge, Mass.: MIT Press, 1962.

Wade, M. The effect of sedatives upon delayed responses in monkeys following removal of the prefrontal lobes. *Journal of Neurophysiology,* 1947, 10, 57–61.

Wald, G. The chemistry of rod vision. *Science,* 1951, 113, 287–291.

Wald, G. The photoreceptor process in vision. In J. Field, H. W. Magoun, and V. E. Hall (Eds.), *Handbook of physiology.* Vol. 1. Washington, D.C.: American Physiological Society, 1959.

Wallach, M. A., and N. Kogan. A new look at the creativity-intelligence distinction. *Journal of Personality,* 1965, 33, 348–369. (a)

Wallach, M. A., and N. Kogan. The roles of information, discussion and consensus in group risk taking. *Journal of Experimental Social Psychology,* 1965, 1, 1–19. (b)

Wallach, M. A., N. Kogan, and D. J. Bem. Group influence on individual risk-taking. *Journal of Abnormal and Social Psychology,* 1962, 65, 75–86.

Wallach, M. A., N. Kogan, and D. J. Bem. Diffusion of responsibility and level of risk-taking in groups. *Journal of Abnormal and Social Psychology,* 1964, 68, 263–274.

Wallas, G. *The art of thought.* New York: Harcourt Brace Jovanovich, 1926.

Wann, T. W. (Ed.). *Behaviorism and phenomenology.* Chicago: University of Chicago Press, 1964.

Ward, B. Reminiscence and rote learning. *Psychological Monographs,* 1937, 49 (Whole No. 220).

Warren, H. C. *A history of the association psychology.* New York: Scribner, 1921.

Watson, J. B. Psychology as the behaviorist views it. *Psychological Review,* 1913, 20, 158–177.

Watson, J. B. *Behavior: An introduction to comparative psychology.* New York: Henry Holt and Company, Inc., 1914.

Watson, J. B. *Psychology from the standpoint of a behaviorist.* Philadelphia: Lippincott, 1919; 2nd ed., 1924.

Watson, J. B. *Behaviorism.* New York: Norton, 1925.

Watson, J. B. *The psychological care of the infant and child.* New York: Norton, 1928.

Watson, J. B. *Behaviorism.* (2nd ed.). New York: Norton, 1930.

Watson, R. I. *Psychology of the child* (2nd ed.). New York: Wiley, 1965.

Watson, R. I. *The great psychologists* (4th ed.). Philadelphia: Lippincott, 1978.

Webb, W. B. *Sleep: An experimental approach.* New York: Crowell-Collier-Macmillan, 1968.

Wechsler, D. Mental health in later maturity., Supplement No. 168 to *Public health report,* Federal Security Agency, U.S. Public Health Service, Washington, U.S. Government Printing Office, 1942.

Weinstock, S. Estes' statistical learning theory. In Marx, M. H. (Ed.), *Learning: Theories.* New York: Macmillan, 1970.

Werner, H. *Comparative psychology of mental development* (Rev. ed.). Chicago: Follet, 1948.

Werner, H., and S. Wapner. Sensory-tonic field theory of perception. *Journal of Personality,* 1949, 18, 88–107.

Werner, H., and S. Wapner. Toward a general theory of perception. *Psychological Review,* 1956, 50, 315–337.

Werner, H., and S. Wapner (Eds.). *The body percept.* New York: Random House, 1965.

Wertheimer, Max. *Productive thinking.* New York: Harper & Row, 1945.

Wertheimer, Max. *Productive thinking.* (Enlarged and edited by Michael Wertheimer). New

York: Harper & Row, 1959.

Wertheimer, Michael. *A brief history of psychology*. New York: Holt, Rinehart and Winston, Inc., 1970.

Wertheimer, Michael. *Fundamental issues in psychology*. New York: Holt, Rinehart and Winston, Inc., 1972.

Wever, E. G., and C. W. Bray. Action currents in the auditory nerve in response to acoustical stimulation. *Proceedings of the National Academy of Science,* 1930, 16, 344–350. (a)

Wever, E. G., and C. W. Bray. The nature of the acoustic response: The relation between sound frequency and frequency of impulses in the auditory nerve. *Journal of Experimental Psychology,* 1930, 13, 373–387. (b)

White, R. W. Competence and the psychosexual stages of development. In M. R. Jones (Ed.), *Nebraska Symposium on Motivation*. Lincoln: University of Nebraska Press, 1960.

White, S. The learning theory tradition and child psychology. In *Carmichael's manual of child psychology*. Revised by P. H. Mussen. New York: Wiley, 1970.

Whorf, B. L. *Language, thought, and reality*. New York: Wiley, 1956.

Wilkinson, H. A., and T. L. Peele. Intracranial self-stimulation in cats. *Journal of Comparative Neurology,* 1963, 121, 425–440.

Willems, E., and R. Clark. Dependency of risky shift on instructions: a replication. *Psychological Reports,* 1969, 25, 811–814.

Witkin, H. A. The role of cognitive style in academic performance and in teacher-student relations. *Educational Testing Service Research Bulletin*. Princeton, N.J.: ETS, 1973.

Witkin, H. A., R. B. Dyk, H. F. Faterson, D. R. Goodenough, and A. Karp. *Psychological differentiation*. New York: Wiley, 1962.

Witkin, H. A., H. B. Lewis, M. Hertzman, K. Mackover, P. B. Meissner, and S. Wapner, *Personality through perception*. New York: Harper & Row, 1954.

Wohlwill, J. F. Perceptual learning. *Annual Review of Psychology,* 1966, 17, 201.

Wohlwill, J. F. The concept of experience: S or R? *Human Development,* 16, 90–107, 1973.

Wollberg, A., and J. D. Newman. The auditory cortex of the squirrel monkey: Response patterns of single cells to species-specific vocalizations. *Science,* 1971, 175, 212–214.

Wolman, B. B. *Contemporary theories and systems in psychology*. New York: Harper & Row, 1960.

Wolpe, J. *Psychotherapy by reciprocal inhibition*. Stanford, Calif.: Stanford University Press, 1958.

Woodworth, R. S. *Experimental psychology* (1st ed.). New York: Holt, Rinehart and Winston, Inc., 1938.

Woodworth, R. S. *Contemporary schools of psychology* (Rev. ed.). New York: Ronald, 1948.

Woodworth, R. S., and H. Schlosberg. *Experimental psychology* (2nd ed.). New York: Holt, Rinehart and Winston, Inc., 1954.

Woodworth, R. S., and M. R. Sheehan. *Contemporary schools of psychology,* (3rd ed.). New York: Ronald, 1964.

Woolsey, C. N. Organization of somatic sensory and motor areas of the cerebral cortex. In H. F. Harlow and C. N. Woolsey (Eds.), *Biological and biochemical bases of behavior*. Madison: University of Wisconsin Press, 1958.

Woolsey, C. N. Organization of cortical auditory system. In W. A. Rosenblith (Ed.), *Sensory communication*. Cambridge, Mass.: MIT Press, 1961.

Wrightsman, L. S. Effects of waiting with others on changes in level of felt anxiety. *Journal of Abnormal and Social Psychology,* 1960, 61, 216–222.

Wrightsman, L. S. *Social psychology in the seventies*. Monterey, Calif.: Brooks/Cole, 1972.

Wulf, F. Über die Veränderung von Vorstellungen. *Psychologische Forschung,* 1972, 1, 333–373.

Wundt, W. *Grundriss der Psychologie*. Leipzig: W. Englemann, 1896.

Yates, A. *Behavior therapy*. New York: Wiley, 1970.

Young, P. T. *Emotion in man and animal*. New York: Wiley, 1943.

Young, P. T. Psychologic factors regulating the feeding process. In *Symposium on Nutrition and Behavior*. New York: National Vitamin Foundation, 1957, pp. 51–59.

Young, P. T. *Motivation and emotion*. New York: Wiley, 1961.

Young, P. T. *Emotion in man and animal* (2nd ed.). New York: Robert E. Krieger, 1973.

Zajonc, R. B. Social facilitation. *Science,* 1965, 149, 269–274.

Zajonc, R. B. *Social psychology: An experimental approach*. Belmont, Calif.: Wadsworth, 1966.

Ziegarnik, B. Über das Behalten von erledigten and unerledigten Handlungen. *Psychologische Forschung,* 1927, 9, 1–85.

Ziegarnik, B. On finished and unfinished tasks. In W. Ellis (Ed.), *A source book of Gestalt psychology*. London: Routledge, 1938.

Zeller, A. F. An experimental analogue of repression. I. Historical summary. *Psychological Bulletin,* 1950, 47, 39–51. (a)

Zeller, A. F. An experimental analogue of repression. II. The effect of individual failure and success on memory measured by relearning. *Journal of Experimental Psychology,* 1950, 40, 411–422. (b)

Zeller, A. F. An experimental analogue of repression. III. The effect of induced failure and success on memory measured by recall. *Journal of Experimental Psychology,* 1951, 42, 32–38.

Zobrist, A. L., and F. R. Carlson. An advice-taking chess computer. *Scientific American,* 1973, 228, 92–105.

Zubek, J. P. *Sensory deprivation: Fifteen years of research*. New York: Appleton, 1969.

Zubin, J. Memory functioning in patients treated with electric shock therapy. *Journal of Personality,* 1948, 17, 33–41.

Name Index

Subject Index